Populism, Memory and Minority Rights

Populism, Memory and Minority Rights

Central and Eastern European Issues in Global Perspective

Edited by

Anna-Mária Bíró

Managing Editor

Evelin Verhás

BRILL
NIJHOFF

LEIDEN | BOSTON

Library of Congress Cataloging-in-Publication Data

Names: Bíró, Anna-Mária, editor. | Tom Lantos Institute, issuing body.
Title: Populism, memory, and minority rights : Central and Eastern European issues in global perspective / edited by Anna-Mária Bíró ; managing editor, Evelin Verhás.
Description: Leiden ; Boston : Brill Nijhoff, [2018] | Includes bibliographical references.
Identifiers: LCCN 2018045185 (print) | LCCN 2018045232 (ebook) | ISBN 9789004386426 (ebook) | ISBN 9789004386419 (hardback : alk. paper)
Subjects: LCSH: Minorities--Civil rights--Europe, Central. | Minorities--Civil rights--Europe, Eastern. | Minorities--Legal status, laws, etc.--Europe, Central. | Minorities--Legal status, laws, etc.--Europe, Eastern. | Populism--Europe, Central. | Populism--Europe, Eastern. | Europe, Central--Ethnic relations. | Europe, Eastern--Ethnic relations.
Classification: LCC KJC5144.M56 (ebook) | LCC KJC5144.M56 P67 2018 (print) | DDC 323.143--dc23
LC record available at https://lccn.loc.gov/2018045185

Typeface for the Latin, Greek, and Cyrillic scripts: "Brill". See and download: brill.com/brill-typeface.

ISBN 978-90-04-38641-9 (hardback)
ISBN 978-90-04-38642-6 (e-book)

Contents

PART 5
Report

Preface

Anna-Mária Bíró

An international human and minority rights organization based in Budapest (Hungary), the Tom Lantos Institute (TLI) is honoured to launch the first volume of the series *International Studies in Human Rights and Identity*. The initial idea for the series emerged from the desire to share TLI's research on minority issues and to situate our regional activities and thinking in a global perspective through a collection of invited contributions. In our research and educational activities, we filter the analysis of local minority politics through the normative prism of international human and minority rights, most often in the context of comparable, sometimes counterintuitive, global cases. This practice prompted recurring questions and dilemmas about the problem-solving capacity of the current international minority protection regime and, more generally, about just, peaceful and sustainable ways of accommodating ethno-cultural diversity in our age. The purpose of this series is to explore systematically some of the critical issues of local, regional and global scope that we have encountered and identified in our work. Combined with our educational activities, we see our research as a tool for social transformation that gives voice to denigrated, disadvantaged and excluded minorities.[1]

The first volume of the series aims to introduce TLI's work in terms of its mandated issue areas of research and the methodologies it employs and to cast light on some of the distinctive characteristics of its approach to the study of minority issues and related normative frameworks. As an institution established in Hungary, TLI focuses on minority issues of historical importance in Hungary and Central and Eastern Europe, including Roma rights and citizenship, Jewish life and antisemitism, and Hungarian and other national minorities.

An integral part of European society for centuries, Roma are the largest ethnic minority group in Europe and here suffered slavery, expulsions and genocide. Today, the discrimination of the Roma continues in the form of geographical and educational segregation, racial hostility, cultural subordination,

1 For ongoing debates on the potential of social transformation in mixed methods research, see Teresa Sorde Marti and Donna Mertens, "Mixed Methods Research with Groups at Risk: New Developments and Key Debates," *Journal of Mixed Methods and Research* 8, no. 3 (2014): 207–211. See also Donna Mertens, "Mixed Methods as Tools for Social Change," *Journal of Mixed Methods Research* 5, no. 3 (2011): 195–197; and Linda T. Smith, *Decolonizing Methodologies: Research and Indigenous Peoples* (London: Zed Books, 1999).

extreme poverty and exclusion from public and political affairs.[2] There are around 10–12 million Roma living in the 28 member states of the European Union, with the highest numbers in Bulgaria, the Czech Republic, Hungary, Romania and Slovakia, where they account for more than 5–10% of the population. According to a 2011 census, Roma amounted to 3.16% of Hungary's population, making them the largest minority group. However, various estimates put their number as high as 5–10% of the total population.[3] Despite marginal improvements, rampant discrimination and racial abuse, as well as severe poverty, including segregated housing and education and poor health standards, continue to plague the everyday lives of Roma.[4] This deeply-rooted and widespread discriminatory pattern permeates knowledge-production about the Roma in Europe, where for decades the vast majority of research on them was conducted without their input, inadvertently silencing, missing or misrepresenting some of their issues, memories and values.[5] For instance, the history of the Roma Holocaust has only recently and partially been recognized as a field of study in its own right by leading academic journals and publishing houses, and the involvement of Roma academics and researchers in its study has only been sporadic.[6] TLI is committed to the inclusion of Roma

2 For an overview of the situation of the Roma in the European Union, see FRA and UNDP, *The Situation of Roma in 11 EU Member States: Survey Results at a Glance* (Luxembourg: Publications Office of the European Union, 2012); FRA, *Roma Survey – Data in Focus: Poverty and Employment: The Situation of Roma in 11 EU Member States* (Luxembourg: Publications Office of the European Union, 2014); FRA, *Second European Union Minorities and Discrimination Survey: Roma – Selected Finding* (Luxembourg: Publications Office of the European Union, 2018); Galina Kostadinova, "Minority Rights as a Normative Framework for Addressing the Situation of Roma in Europe," *Oxford Development Studies* 39, no. 2 (2011): 163–183.

3 For estimates on the Roma population in European countries, see "Roma and Travellers Team", Council of Europe website, accessed March 30, 2018, https://www.coe.int/en/web/portal/roma. In this preface, I use numbers presented in Christine O'Hanlon, "The European Struggle to Educate and Include Roma People: A Critique of Differences in Policy and Practice in Western and Eastern EU Countries," *Social Inclusion* 4, no. 1 (2016): 1–10, accessed March 30, 2018, https://www.cogitatiopress.com/socialinclusion/article/viewFile/363/363.

4 For the situation of Roma in Hungary, see European Commission against Racism and Intolerance, *ECRI Report on Hungary* (Council of Europe, 2015), accessed March 30, 2018, https://www.coe.int/t/dghl/monitoring/ecri/Country-by-country/Hungary/HUN-CbC-V-2015-19-ENG.pdf.

5 Ramon Flecha, "Using Mixed Methods from a Communicative Orientation: Researching with Grassroots Roma," *Journal of Mixed Methods Research* 8, no. 3 (2014): 245–254.

6 A critical summary and history of academic research on the genocide of the Roma is available in Ilsen About and Anna Abakunova, *The Genocide and Persecution of Roma and Sinti. Bibliography and Historiographical Review* (Berlin: International Holocaust Remembrance Alliance, 2016), 139. The overdue involvement of Roma in the research of the Holocaust is exemplified by the belated appointment of Romani scholar Ethel Brooks to the US Holocaust

in the generation of knowledge about their own history and issues that affect them. The section on *Roma Rights and Citizenship* in this volume reflects this approach, since it was written by Roma authors who have defined and explored themes of critical importance for achieving social justice for the Roma in Hungary and beyond.[7] Their contributions include a critical review of the nature and effectiveness of the integration of Roma in Europe; an essay on (breaking) the silence on the history of Roma in mainstream historiography in Hungary and Europe; the life story of Ágnes Daróczi, a prominent Hungarian Roma activist and scholar; and an empirical study on (the lack of) local public participation of Roma women in Hungary.

The history of the Holocaust in Hungary is relatively well-established.[8] Out of a Jewish population of around 780,000 in the interwar years, approximately half a million were exterminated during the Shoah, with the eager assistance of the Hungarian state under German occupation. Hungarian Jewry outside the capital was annihilated almost completely, while a relatively large group survived in Budapest, where the majority of the Jewish population was ultimately not deported. Given their historic aversion to being counted and listed, today the number of those who formally identify their religion as Judaism is rather small, amounting to around 11,000.[9] However, informal estimates suggest a considerably larger number, ranging from 80,000 to 150,000, representing 0.8–1.5% of the Hungarian population.[10] This would make the Hungarian Jewish community the largest Jewish group in Central and Eastern Europe. By some estimates, it is the third largest Jewish population in Europe, after France and the

---

Memorial Council, the governing body of the Washington-based US Holocaust Memorial Museum, by President Obama in 2016. On a political level, for the first time ever, it was only in January 2018 that the European Parliament's annual event to commemorate International Holocaust Remembrance Day marked both the Holocaust of the Jews and the genocide of the Roma and Sinti populations.

7 A further example is TLI's collection of working papers on Roma resistance during the Holocaust and in its aftermath, which was conceptualized, researched and published in cooperation with Roma organizations and scholars. See Angéla Kóczé and Anna Lujza Szász, eds., *Roma Resistance during the Holocaust and in its Aftermath* (Budapest: Tom Lantos Institute, 2018).

8 See Randolph L. Braham, *The Politics of Genocide: The Holocaust in Hungary*, vol. 2 (New York: Columbia University Press, 1981). See also Randolph L. Braham and András Kovács, *The Holocaust in Hungary – Seventy Years Later* (Budapest: Central University Press, 2016); and Zoltán Vági, László Csősz and Gábor Kádár, *The Holocaust in Hungary: Evolution of a Genocide* (Lanham: AltaMira Press, 2013), 510.

9 According to a census conducted in 2011, 10,965 people in Hungary identified their religion as Judaism.

10 András Kovács, ed., *Zsidók és zsidóság a mai Magyarországon* [Jews and Jewry in contemporary Hungary] (Budapest: Múlt és Jövő Kiadó, 2002), 23–24.

United Kingdom. As elsewhere in Central and Eastern Europe, Jews have been an integral part of Hungarian society, contributing significantly to its cultural, economic and political advancement. However, even in times of reasonably harmonious coexistence, antisemitism in Hungary has been considerable.[11] In this volume, besides a review essay by György Csepeli on home-grown antisemitism (and philosemitism), the dominant thematic focus is on the politics of memory, collective remembrance and memory construction in the region and in contemporary Hungary.[12] Public debates and disputes induced by the present politics of memory direct attention to the difficulties surrounding the unambiguous admission of responsibility for past wrongs by both states and societies. Arie Nadler's study on the conditions for intergroup reconciliation maps out some of these difficulties from a social-psychological perspective, highlighting the destructive role of competitive victimhood in intergroup conflict and possible ways to alleviate its impact. Situating his analysis in the theoretical framework outlined by Nadler, Gergely Romsics assesses Hungary's present potential for intergroup reconciliation against the background of the historical trajectories taken by Hungary's wartime allies, Germany and Austria. With this choice of themes in the section on *Jewish Life and Antisemitism*, TLI intends to connect studies of reconciliation and transitional justice to the normative framework of minority rights, raising questions about its effectiveness when intergroup tensions and mistrust persist due to a lack of reconciliation.[13]

From the perspective of competitive victimhood, Hungary's role in intergroup reconciliation is further complicated by the fact that, in much of mainstream Hungarian historiography and collective memory, the country is portrayed as a victim of the 1920 Trianon Peace Treaty that formally concluded

11 For the history of antisemitism in Hungary, see Krisztián Ungváry, *A Horthy-rendszer mérlege: Diszkrimináció, szociálpolitika és antiszemitizmus Magyarországon* [The balance of the Horthy-regime: discrimination, social policy and antisemitism in Hungary] (Pécs: Jelenkor Kiado, 2012); and, more recently, Ildikó Barna, "Hungary," in *Modern Antisemitism in the Visegrád Countries*, ed. Ildikó Barna and Anikó Félix (Budapest: Tom Lantos Institute, 2017), 47–77.

12 These issues are further explored in Andrea Pető and Helga Thorson, eds., *The Future of Holocaust Memorialization: Confronting Racism, Antisemitism and Homophobia through Memory Work* (Budapest: Tom Lantos Institute, 2015). This publication can be retrieved at http://tomlantosinstitute.hu/wp-content/uploads/2017/02/hm_final.pdf. See also Mónika Kovács, *Kollektív emlékezet és holokausztmúlt* [Collective memory and the past of the Holocaust] (Budapest: Corvina Kiadó, 2016).

13 For an analysis of the relationship between the "politics of reconciliation" and "politics of difference", exploring their potential convergence and divergence, see Will Kymlicka and Bashir Bashir, eds., *The Politics of Reconciliation in Multicultural Societies* (Oxford: Oxford University Press, 2008).

World War I. As a result of this treaty, Hungary lost nearly two-thirds of its territory and one-third of its Hungarian speaking population, which, with the exception of a short interlude during the interwar period, became national minorities in neighbouring countries and were subsequently exposed to policies of assimilation, marginalization and discrimination. Since the fall of the Iron Curtain in 1989, Hungary has embarked upon a kin-state policy, thereby influencing the political mobilization of Hungarian minorities to varying degrees. It is in the triadic nexus of nationalisms unfolding among the host-state, kin-state and the national minority in question that the policies of Hungarian minorities are analyzed in articles by Tamás Kiss and Gergely István Székely, two Hungarian minority scholars from Romania. Both articles point out that some of the well-established theories explaining kin- and host-state behaviour, as well as competitive minority party politics, should be revisited in the light of empirical studies. The section on *Hungarian Minorities* illustrates TLI's commitment to multidisciplinary empirical research in the field of minority protection and politics, emphasizing the need for empirically-driven research in order to test systems design in the study of international minority rights where the legal interpretation of norms has so far been preponderant. Lessons from empirical research could better inform the implementation and increase the effectiveness of the extant minority protection regime and contribute to its further development.[14]

Hungarian historian Ferenc Eiler's study on the interwar Congress of European Nationalities discusses the little-known history and operation of what was probably Europe's first transnational minority rights advocacy platform. Eiler's article provides an insight into the early history and politics of international norm-making by analyzing the mobilization, resources and tactical repertoires of minority norm-entrepreneurs who set out to use the political opportunities that had emerged as a result of the establishment of the League of Nations to their advantage – albeit with little success.[15] This study, which

14 On the importance of empirically-driven research in the field of international minority protection, see Anna-Maria Bíró and Corinne Lennox, "Global Governance on Minority Rights: Assessing the Participation of Non-State Actors (NSAs) in the UN Forum on Minority Issues" (paper presented at the Annual Convention of the International Studies Association, Baltimore, US, 2017), on file with authors.

15 Ferenc Eiler's study relies on archival research undertaken in both Hungarian and German. It is a valuable addition to John Hiden's book documenting and discussing the liberal origins of norm-making in the Congress of European Nationalities spearheaded by the Baltic German minority scholar Paul Schiemann. See John Hiden, *Defender of Minorities: Paul Schiemann, 1876–1944* (London: Hurst & Company, 2004), 326. For further analysis see also, Anna-Mária Bíró, "The internationalisation of minority protection in Europe: an INGO perspective," (PhD Thesis, Eötvös Lóránd University, 2012).

highlights some of the Central and East European origins of transnational minority rights activism, introduces the section on *General Issues*, which links regional particularities to themes of universal scope in the context of international minority protection.

In this section, in the ambivalent nexus of human rights law and group identities, Gaetano Pentassuglia addresses one of the key persisting dilemmas of international minority protection, namely the legal status of ethno-cultural groups and their associated rights. Assessing the continuities and discontinuities in relevant legal narratives on the concept of ethno-cultural group identity, he points out the hybridity of human rights practice on minority/indigenous identities and argues in favour of more coherent justifications for the legitimacy of group claims. Discussing the right to freedom of religion in Europe, Kathleen Cavanaugh's article explores another crucial contemporary theme in human rights law impacting religious minorities. She points out that due to significant demographic changes in Europe, with the exception of the United Kingdom, Muslims account for the largest religious immigration bloc and that, whenever questions of freedom of religion arise at either the national or European level, the protection of religion is relegated strictly to the private sphere. Cavanaugh argues that Europe has moved to secularize the public square in the name of an illiberal secularism that reproduces a hegemonic knowledge regime deeply rooted in Christianity.

Joshua Castellino's article and Fiona McConnell's note continue the discussion of contentious contemporary themes, this time with a focus on the global rise of exclusionary populism that adversely impacts scapegoated minorities, a political trend robustly present in Hungary.[16] Castellino points out that this trend in politics is partly due to the failure of democratically elected governments to answer legitimate questions facing their populations, including increased structural inequalities within societies. He emphasizes the need for pragmatic answers that are guided by the context rather than the approach and include all who are affected. In her note, McConnell emphasizes the importance of minority agency in countering exclusionary populism. She argues that by setting up the framework of "pure people" versus a "corrupt elite", populists deny the legitimacy of a multiplicity of different groups. McConnell shows that minorities and indigenous peoples who join transnational human and minority rights advocacy coalitions reconceptualize causes that are conventionally seen in terms of ethnic nationalism. By constructing frames that

16 András Bozóki and Zoltán Ádám, "State and Faith: Right-wing Populism and Nationalized Religion in Hungary," *Intersections: East European Journal of Society and Politics* 2, no. 1 (2016): 98–122.

transcend geographical and cultural boundaries and negotiate difference, minorities become the promoters of solidarity and internationalism from below.

The section on *General Issues* reflects TLI's interest in the nexus between the particular and the universal in human and minority rights[17] and how local political phenomena impacting minorities relate to (enabling or sanctioning) regional and global political and normative trends. In the Central and East European context, national minority issues have historically been regarded as being of a transboundary nature, thereby requiring local minority politics to navigate the tensions arising from inter-state (kin- and host-state) relations and, simultaneously, to become active agents in shaping international norms directly affecting them. Hence, the struggle for justice by ethno-cultural minorities has been strategically located at the intersection of domestic and global politics, where they seek to overcome local limitations by using regionally and globally available opportunities and gaining access to relevant international fora via transnational activism. Future volumes in this series will explore and analyze crucial themes and issues of local identity politics and minority norm-entrepreneurship at the intersection of domestic and global politics.

Reiterating TLI's commitment to engage in research oriented towards social change, the volume concludes with a report on human rights education in the Visegrád countries[18] by Louise Métrich. The report points out the significant shortcomings in the socialization of human rights as standards of behaviour in Hungary and the region, which is a central concern in TLI's work. By situating struggles for liberal multiculturalism in the broader framework of human rights[19] in our research, we highlight and address the incomplete and insufficient integration of the minority protection regime in the global governance

17 For an interesting treatment of human rights as a complex blend of the universal and the particular, see Neil Walker, "Universalism and Particularism in Human Right," in *Human Rights: The Hard Questions*, ed. Cindy Holder and David Reidy (Cambridge: Cambridge University Press, 2013), 39–58. For Walker's approach applied in the field of international minority protection, see Gaetano Pentassuglia, "Introduction: The Unpacking of Ethno-cultural Diversity," in *Ethno-Cultural Diversity and Human Rights*, ed. Gaetano Pentassuglia (Leiden/Boston: Nijhoff/Brill, 2018).

18 The Visegrád Group is an alliance of four Central European states (the Czech Republic, Hungary, Poland and Slovakia) for the purpose of advancing political, cultural and economic – as well as energy and military – cooperation.

19 The nexus between liberal multiculturalism, minority rights and human rights in the context of established democracies and post-communist societies is examined in Will Kymlicka, "Minority Rights in Political Philosophy and International Law," in *The Philosophy of International Law*, ed. Samantha Besson and John Tasioulas (Oxford: Oxford University Press, 2010), 377–383.

of human rights, including the structures of the United Nations and the work of major international human rights NGOs.[20]

The idea for this publication was first raised by Gudmundur Alfredsson, a member of TLI's Advisory Board, and was brought to fruition under the firm guidance of our publishing consultant, Alan Stephens. We are immensely grateful for their trust and cooperation. Lindy Melman and Bea Timmer of Brill/Nijhoff Publishers helped us in the planning, editorial and production process with much needed practical advice, for which we are extremely thankful. Evelin Verhás, the Managing Editor of this book, contributed greatly to the editorial process with professionalism, attention to detail and characteristic dedication. We would like to thank the contributing authors for the many interesting and inspiring conversations we had with them throughout the editorial process and for submitting their manuscripts on time. We would also like to extend our appreciation to the members of the Editorial Board, who reinforced our work with their advice and guidance and as contributing authors. We feel honoured by the trust and support shown to us by the members of the Advisory Board, who encouraged the launch of this series. Finally, we would like to thank the Hungarian Ministry of Foreign Affairs and Trade for supporting this project financially.

20 For an excellent account of the poor integration of international minority rights in the UN system and beyond, see Gay McDougall, "Introduction," in *The First United Nations Mandate on Minority Issues*, ed. Gay McDougall (Leiden/Boston: Nijhoff/Brill, 2015).

Illustrations

Figures

Tables

Notes on Contributors

János Bársony

is a researcher focusing on Roma rights, Roma history, and folk music. He was the Secretary of the Budapest Roma Coordination Committee in 1977–1990 and participated in the development of the Roma Folklore movement. János is the founder of Phralipe and Amalipe Roma organizations, and worked for the Roma Civil Rights Foundation (1996–2004). He has authored numerous articles and co-edited the following volumes with Ágnes Daróczi: *The fate of Roma during the Holocaust* (New York: IDEBATE press, 2008), *Vrana mámi mesél* (Budapest: SuliNova, 2005) [Mother Vrana's fairytales]. He was the screenwriter and editor of an educational film series about Roma history entitled *Historia romani* and, the editor of the 35-minute documentary film *Untouchables.*

Anna-Mária Bíró

PhD, is the Director of the Tom Lantos Institute, an international human and minority rights organization focusing on research and education based in Budapest, Hungary. From 2007–2011, Anna-Mária was a senior consultant to the Managing Multiethnic Communities Programme of LGI/Open Society Foundations, and was the director of the course "Incorporating Ethnocultural Diversity into the Teaching of Public Administration" organized by Central European University. Prior to this, she directed the Europe office of Minority Rights Group International for eight years. She has also worked as the Advisor on Minority Affairs at the OSCE Mission in Kosovo and as an Advisor on International Relations to the President of the Democratic Alliance of Hungarians in Romania. Anna-Mária holds an MSc in Public Administration and Public Policy from the London School of Economics and a PhD in political sciences from the Eötvös Loránd University, Faculty of Law and Political Science, Budapest, Hungary. Among others, Anna-Mária is co-editor of *Diversity in Action: Local Public Management of Multi-ethnic Communities in Central and Eastern Europe* (Budapest: LGI/OSI, 2001) and co-author of *Minority Rights Advocacy in the European Union: A Guide for NGOs in South-East Europe* (London: MRG, 2006). In 2011 she co-edited with Corinne Lennox volume 18(2) of the *International Journal on Minority and Group Rights* (Leiden: Brill Academic Publishers, 2011) on civil society contributions to the international regime of minority protection. Since 2018, she is Editor-in-Chief of the series International Studies in Human Rights and Identity published by Brill/Nijhoff Academic Publishers.

Joshua Castellino

PhD, is Professor of Law at the School of Law at Middlesex University London, and Adjunct Professor of Law at the Irish Centre for Human Rights, Galway, Ireland. He is the Executive Director of Minority Rights Group International and founder of the Annual Summer School on Minorities, first held in June 2001 in Galway, Ireland. Joshua has held visiting positions in Ireland, Spain, Hungary and Italy. He worked as a journalist in Mumbai, India, with the Indian Express Group, was awarded a Chevening Scholarship to pursue an MA in International Law and Politics in 1995 and completed his PhD in International Law in 1998. Joshua has authored seven books on international law and human rights law, on self-determination, title to territory and indigenous peoples rights, in addition to over fifty academic articles on a range of these and other legal sub-topics. Joshua was part of the EU-China Experts and Diplomatic Dialogue and Lawyers for the New Millennium: Support for the Arab Law Union. He regularly engages with multilateral organizations, law societies, the judiciary and NGOs in Europe, Asia, the Middle East and Latin America, on issues related to human rights advocacy and public international law. He sits on the Leadership Council of the United Nations Sustainable Development Solutions Network (UNSDSN) convened by Jeffrey Sachs under the auspices of the UN Secretary General, where he co-chairs the working group entitled Gender, Social Exclusion and Vulnerable Groups.

Kathleen Cavanaugh

PhD, is socio-legal scholar and currently a Lecturer in the Faculty of Law, Irish Centre for Human Rights, National University of Ireland, Galway. She holds a PhD in Comparative Politics from the London School of Economics and Political Science and an LLM from the Queen's University of Belfast, Northern Ireland. She has held several Visiting Lectureships including: Visiting Research Fellow, Minerva Centre for Human Rights, Hebrew University, Israel, and Visiting Lecturer, Department of International Relations, Boston University, Massachusetts, USA, and was awarded a Fellowship at the Centre for Socio-Legal Studies, University of Oxford. Her areas of expertise include: nationalism, ethnic conflict, political violence, states of emergency, narratives on Islamic law and rights, freedom of religion and militant democracy. She held the position of Chair of the Executive Committee of Amnesty International Ireland (2004–2010), and was a member of the International Policy Committee of Amnesty International and a Board member of Amnesty International USA (2012–2015). As a consultant, she has undertaken numerous missions on behalf of Amnesty International including to Northern Ireland, Israel/Palestine and to Iraq (where she focused on the conduct of the occupying powers in relation to detention and security). She has conducted trainings for governmental as well as non-governmental organisations throughout the Middle East (Yemen, Jordan, Egypt, Iran, Morocco, Syria, Lebanon, and Sudan), India, and the Republic of Ireland.

György Csepeli

PhD, DSc, is Professor of Social Psychology and head of the Interdisciplinary Social Research Doctoral Program at the Faculty of Social Sciences of the Eötvös Loránd University, Budapest, chair of the Interdisciplinary Social Research Doctoral Program at the Faculty of Social Sciences, ELTE, and Doctor of the Hungarian Academy of Sciences. He is the president of the Hungarian Sociological Association. His areas of expertise include social psychology of intergroup relations including national identity, antisemitism, xenophobia and anti-Roma sentiments. His research interests have recently turned toward the relationship between the internet and society. He has taught at various American universities (Oregon State, UCLA, Michigan State, New School for Social Research, Montclair State).

Ágnes Daróczi

is a Roma activist, minority researcher, and journalist. She has been actively involved in promoting Roma rights in Hungary, and has focused on empowerment and memoralization at the European level. She promoted these issues through the Human Rights Days, Roma Holocaust Remembrance Days and other public events. She organized the very first Roma Fine Arts Exhibition, founded the first Roma TV-Magazine, and was an initiator of the Roma Folklore movement. She produced several films, authored and published numerous articles, and co-edited several books with Bársony János, including *The fate of Roma during Holocaust* (New York: IDEBATE press, 2008), *Vrana mámi mesél* (Budapest: SuliNova, 2005) [Mother Vrana's fairytales]. She co-produced an educational film series entitled *Historia romani* about the history of Roma for the Romedia Foundation.

Ferenc Eiler

PhD, is a Senior Research Fellow at the Institute for Minority Studies, Centre for Social Sciences, Hungarian Academy of Sciences and is the Editor of the journal Századok. He obtained his PhD in 1998 at the Modern Universal History Department, Janus Pannonius University of Sciences, Pécs and his Master's degree in History and German at the József Attila University of Sciences Szeged in 1994. His research interests include the minority policies of the German and Hungarian governments, and the history of the German and Hungarian minorities. Ferenc authored the book *Németek, helyi társadalom és hatalom. Harta, 1920–1989* [Germans, Local Society and Power: Harta, 1920–1989]

(Budapest: Argumentum, 2011); and *Kisebbségvédelem és revízió. Magyar részvétel az Európai Nemzetiségi Kongresszuson 1925–1939*. [Minority Protection and Revisionism. Hungarian Participation at the Congress of European Nationalities between 1925 and 1939] (Budapest: Gondolat, 2007). Ferenc also co-edited the volume *Czech and Hungarian Minority Policy in Central Europe 1918–1938*. (Praha: Masaykuv Ústav-MTA-ENKI, 2009).

Tamás Kiss

PhD, is a researcher at the Romanian Institute for Research on National Minorities in Cluj, Romania. He obtained an MA in sociology at Babeș-Bolyai University and a PhD in cultural studies at the University of Pécs (Dissertation title: *The Administrative Gaze. Towards a Comparative Analysis of the Hungarian Demographic Discourses in Romania. On the Statistical Construction of the Transylvanian Hungarian Population*). His main research interests are ethnic politics, demography and ethnicity (processes of census ethnic categorization, differences of demographic and migratory behaviour), and demographic discourses (both in global and national perspective). His English language papers have been published in various journals, including *Eastern European Politics and Society*, *Problems of Post-Communism* and *Nationality Papers*. Tamás was the editor of the volume, *Unequal Accommodation of Minority Rights. Hungarians in Transylvania* (London: Palgrave Macmillan, 2018).

Angéla Kóczé

PhD, is a sociologist. She is currently a Visiting Assistant Professor at Wake Forest University. She is also a research fellow at the Hungarian Academy of Sciences, Institute of Sociology, and an affiliated research fellow at Central European University, Centre for Policy Studies. Angéla has done research focused mainly on social and legal inequalities of Roma in various European countries, as well as on the intersection of gender, ethnicity, and class with respect to minority and migrant populations in Europe. She has written extensively about the racialization and the unequal access to social, economic and political rights of Roma in Europe. Some of her work was published in various books by Palgrave and Ashgate, as well as by international organisations such as the UNDP. In addition to her academic career, Angéla also worked as a senior policy adviser in the Hungarian government (2004–2008). Previously, while working on her PhD, she worked as a funding director at the European Roma Information Office (ERIO) in Brussels (2003–2004), and as the director of the human rights education programme at the European Roma Rights Centre (1998–2003) in Budapest, Hungary. Moreover, she was the founding director of the Romaversitas programme (1996) in Budapest, which offers a scholarship and mentorship programme for underprivileged Roma minority university students.

Alex Maws
is Head of Educational Grants and Projects at the Association of Jewish Refugees (AJR), the largest dedicated funder of programmes which promote teaching and learning about the Holocaust in the United Kingdom. In this capacity, he engages with a range of organizations to promote good practice across the Holocaust education and remembrance sectors. From 2007–2017, he worked at the Holocaust Educational Trust, developing training programmes for teachers and educational resources used by thousands of British schools. He has led nearly 50 study visits to Holocaust sites for teachers and students. Alex continues to serve as Education Advisor to the Holocaust Educational Trust. He is a member and former Chair of the International Holocaust Remembrance Alliance's (IHRA) Education Working Group and served on the Board of Directors of the British Association of Holocaust Studies from 2013–2016. He earned an MA in Social Justice & Education from the University of London-Institute of Education and a BA in Political Science from the University of Michigan.

Fiona McConnell
PhD, is Associate Professor in Human Geography at the University of Oxford and Tutorial Fellow at St Catherine's College, Oxford. She holds a BA in Geography from the University of Cambridge, and a PhD from Queen Mary, University of London. As a political geographer, Fiona's research aims to develop new areas of thinking regarding governance beyond the state and different modes of political legitimacy. In particular, she is interested in how communities officially excluded from formal state politics are nevertheless engaging with aspects of statecraft, and in using such seemingly anomalous cases as a lens to critically examine the 'norms' of governance. Her doctoral and post-doctoral research focused on the political institutions and practices of the exile Tibetan government based in India, an institution which engages in state-like functions despite being legally unrecognised and lacking jurisdiction over territory. Her current research focuses on the practices and pedagogy of diplomacy in the margins and in 2017 she held a British Academy Mid-Career Fellowship for a project titled 'Representing the unrepresented: the politics and practices of subaltern diplomacy'. Fiona is author of *Rehearsing the State: the political practices of the Tibetan Government-in-Exile* (Chichester: Wiley, 2016), co-editor of *Geographies of Peace* (London: IB Tauris, 2013) and *Diplomatic Cultures and International Politics* (Abingdon: Routledge, 2016) and has published in journals

including *Progress in Human Geography, Geoforum, Transactions of the Institute of British Geographers, Annals of the Association of American Geographers, Geopolitics* and *Environment and Planning D.* Fiona is an Associate Editor at *Political Geography*, and sits on the Board of Directors of the Tibet Justice Center, an independent volunteer committee of lawyers and scholars which advocates for human rights and self-determination for Tibetans.

Louise Métrich
holds a French-German double degree in political sciences from the Institute of Political Sciences of Lille and the University of Münster, and an MA in "Identity, Culture and Power" from the School of Slavonic and East European Studies, University College London. During her studies, she focused on the political integration of Roma in Romania as well as representations of marginality. Louise interned at the Romanian Institute for Research on National Minorities in Cluj-Napoca, the Friedrich Ebert Foundation office in Bucharest and the French Democratic Confederation of Labour in Paris, before working as a human rights and civil society officer at the Embassy of France to the Czech Republic. She worked for several years as a Programme Manager at the Tom Lantos Institute, where she was in charge of Roma Rights and Citizenship and later on Human and Minority Rights Programme. She is currently deputy director of the Brussels branch of Vie Féminine, a 100-year old Belgium grassroots women's organization that works specifically with impoverished and migrant women.

Arie Nadler
PhD (Psychology, Purdue University, USA), is a Full Professor of Social Psychology at the Tel Aviv University. He served as the Head of the Psychology Department (1984–1988) and Dean of the Faculty of Social Sciences at Tel Aviv University (1993–1998). He co-founded the Tami Steinmetz Center for Peace Research and served as the first head of its academic committee (1992–2002), and established and was the first head of the Institute for Diplomacy and Regional Cooperation at Tel Aviv University (1999–2003). Since 2000, Professor Nadler holds the Argentina Chair for Research of Psychology of Conflict and Cooperation. Funds to establish the Chair were donated by the Argentinean Friends of Tel Aviv University. Since May 2006, Professor Nadler serves as the Chairperson of the board of the Israeli Trustees Foundation, which supports research in the social sciences and education in Israeli Universities and Colleges. Professor Nadler also served as the chairperson of ISEF (Israeli Sepharadic Education Foundation) and Yeladim. Professor Nadler

also has consulting experience in his areas of expertise in non-profit and business organizations

Erzsébet Anita Német

holds a graduate degree in Sociology and Social Anthropology from Central European University. Erzsébet gained professional experience at various organizations in the fields of applied research, different aspects of social integration and in human rights. She participated in the multi-sited comparative, international research of the European Roma Rights Centre that aimed at collecting ethnographic data on the access, quality and affordability of water supplies in poor neighbourhoods inhabited by Roma. As a research fellow at the Snétberger Foundation, she investigated the living conditions of talented young Roma and developed their talent management strategy. Erzsébet was the Programme Manager for Roma Rights and Citizenship at the Tom Lantos Institute. Her current research interests focus on spatial dimensions of inequalities, dynamics of sub-regional development, and the way poverty is produced, reproduced and resisted at the local level.

Szilvia Rézműves

heads the Social Inclusion Unit of the Partners Hungary Foundation and coordinates the project entitled "Together for better health, for us with us", supported by GlaxoSmithKline, a global healthcare company that aims to provide better access to health services for Roma people through mediation. She is also the coordinator of the "TOY for Inclusion" project which opened a Community Play Hub in a Hungarian village to improve the early childhood education of Roma children. She obtained her Master's degree in social policy from the Eötvös Lóránd University Faculty of Social Sciences. In 2012, she was a research fellow at the Center for Policy Studies at Central European University where her research analyzed the effect of the Public Education Act on Roma children. She is currently participating in the accredited mediation course managed by Partners Hungary Foundation. Between 2014 and 2017, she was the national project officer of the ROMED2 joint program of the Council of Europe and European Commission which promotes Roma participation and democratic governance.

Gergely Romsics

PhD, is senior research fellow at the Research Centre for the Humanities, Hungarian Academy of Sciences and teaches at the Department of Social Science at Eötvös Loránd University, Budapest. He holds graduate degrees from Eötvös Loránd University and Central European University. He submitted his doctoral dissertation in the field of modern international history in 2007 about the legacy of the Habsburg Empire and its role in political thinking and historiography during the interwar period. He has held doctoral and postdoctoral research fellowships from the Zeit Stiftung, Hamburg, Collegium Budapest, Financial Research Plc, Budapest, the Institute of European History, Mainz, as well as the Tom Lantos Institute and was a visiting scholar at the Harriman Institute, Columbia University for two academic years. From 2014 to 2017, he was director of the Hungarian Cultural Center in New York City. His primary field of research is the history of political thought and historiography. He is the author of several monographs, including *Myth and Remembrance* (Wayne: Columbia University Press, 2006) and *The Memory of the Habsburg Empire* (Wayne: Columbia University Press, 2010). His additional research interests include collective memory and mnemonic practices, as well as the traditions of international political theory.

Gaetano Pentassuglia
PhD, teaches international law and human rights at the University of Liverpool, UK, where he is also School Director of Postgraduate Research within the Faculty of Humanities and Social Sciences. He has published widely in the field, especially on human rights issues relating to minority groups, including indigenous peoples, and broader aspects of public international law. He has taught at several universities such as Munich, Lund, Toronto, Palermo, Milano-Bicocca, and the European University Institute in Florence, and was recently a Visiting Professor at the University of Deusto (Bilbao, Spain). His latest books include *Ethno-Cultural Diversity and Human Rights: Challenges and Critiques* (Leiden: Brill Academic Publishers, 2018); *Minority Groups and Judicial Discourse in International Law: A Comparative Perspective* (Leiden: Brill Academic Publishers, 2009); and *Minorities in International Law: An Introductory Study* (Flensburg: ECMI, 2002), among several other leading works. He is Co-Editor of the *International Journal on Minority and Group Rights* and serves on the Advisory Boards of *Europa Ethnica* and *Human Rights and Identity*. He has acted as consultant to a number of international and non-governmental institutions and is a former member of the International Law Association Committee on the Rights of Indigenous Peoples. He is also a frequent contributor to online magazines and discussion forums.

István Gergő Székely
PhD, is a researcher at the Romanian Institute for Research on National Minorities and a lecturer at the Faculty of Political, Administrative and

Communication Sciences of the Babeș-Bolyai University, Cluj-Napoca, Romania. He obtained a PhD in Political Science from Central European University, Budapest, in 2014. His research focuses on ethnic mobilization and the electoral behaviour of ethnic and national minorities. Recent publications include "Shifting linkages in ethnic mobilization: the case of RMDSZ and the Hungarians in Transylvania," *Nationalities Papers* 44, no. 4 (2016): 591–610 (with Tamás Kiss); "Diversity recognition and minority representation in Central and Southeast Europe: a comparative analysis," *Nationalities Papers,* 42, no. 3 (2014): 426–448 (with István Horváth); as well as the edited volume *Autonomy Arrangements around the World: A Collection of Well and Lesser Known Cases* (Cluj-Napoca: RIRNM, 2014) (with Levente Salat, Sergiu Constantin and Alexander Osipov).

Evelin Verhás
is Head of Programmes at the Tom Lantos Institute. Evelin holds a Bachelor's degree in Political Science from the University of California at Berkeley and a Master's degree in Human Rights from the London School of Economics, where her research centred on international human rights law, transitional justice and international criminal law. Evelin began her career working as an intern at Minority Rights Group Europe in Budapest and Amnesty International in London. From 2010 to September 2016, she worked in the conflict prevention team and the legal department at Minority Rights Group International (MRG) in London. She was responsible for delivering programmes aiming to promote and protect rights of minority communities in Europe, East-Africa, Middle East and North Africa, and South-East Asia through strengthening their voices at national and international level through advocacy and litigation and building their capacity at grassroots through training. From 2013 to 2016, Evelin coordinated MRG's anti-discrimination project in Bosnia and Herzegovina and worked on the implementation of the ground-breaking judgment of the European Court of Human Rights in the case of Sejdić and Finci v. BiH, addressing constitutionally entrenched discrimination against minorities. Since 2018, she is a Managing Editor of the series International Studies in Human Rights and Identity published by Brill/Nijhoff Academic Publishers.

PART 1

Roma Rights and Citizenship

CHAPTER 1

A Forbidden People Has No History

János Bársony and Ágnes Daróczi

Abstract

To this day, the world knows very little of what befell the Roma of Europe during the Holocaust. We had no Church, no intelligentsia, no institutions. Very few people committed our sufferings to paper, and no one has provided a precise account of our losses. In this modest essay, we strive both to present the essential facts of the lesser known fate of this lesser known people and to examine the development of a culture of memory.

1 Introduction: Who Has the Right to a History?

According to the generally accepted view, history is the scholarly summary of humanity's past. Historian E.H. Carr contends that "history begins with the handing down of tradition; and tradition means the carrying of the habits and lessons of the past into the future. Records of the past begin to be kept for the benefit of future generations."[1]

In the philosophical debates that took place in the nineteenth century, the viewpoint gradually emerged that the subject of history was the presentation of the decisive, relevant facts, events and processes of a given era (i.e. the presentation of the lives of rulers and the battles and fates of empires), and in this context national and religious struggles became increasingly important. In the modern critical approaches of the twentieth century (for instance in the work of Edward Said[2]), a notion began to gain traction according to which the apparent common consent among scholars rested on perceptions of the past entirely from the perspective of the European man. This revelation – the dawning realization that history had largely been defined from a single perspective – later led to a proliferation of micro-histories. Cultures and disciplines themselves became subjects of inquiry, as did the historical facts of minorities, local communities and other groups. People began to pay more attention to the

1 Edward H. Carr, *What is History* (New York: Random House, 1961), 108.
2 Edward W. Said, *Orientalism* (New York: Pantheon Books, 1978).

 | DOI:10.1163/9789004386426_002

roles of sources and the processes through which facts were allegedly revealed, as well as to the distinctive features of narrative structures.

The brief discussion above suffices to bring to the foreground the increasingly acknowledged relativity – from the perspective of both substance and theory – of the "essence of the past." It also sheds lights on the presence in the disciplines of numerous possibilities and competing narratives, existing in parallel or in opposition to one another and endeavouring to assert an exclusive claim to historical reliability. Today, we can clearly discern the increasingly palpable presence of struggles relating to "memory politics" all around us. In these struggles, each narrative strives to establish an indisputable claim to a single scholarly "truth."

We feel compelled to begin by making note of these – admittedly – relatively familiar ideas due to some questions that are constantly troubling us: Is modern scholarship still shaped by the principle of *vae victis* (woe to the vanquished)? Is it true even today that "history is written by the victors"? In order to understand the problems and issues of Roma identity today, what can we learn from the national movements of the middle of the nineteenth century, from the processes that set these movements in motion and from the processes that these movements set in motion? Finally, what can we learn from the ways in which recently liberated or independent African, Asian and Latin American peoples, nations, nationalities and religious minorities relate to earlier canons in order to address contradictions when composing historical constructs that rest on scholarly and scientific foundations?

The history of the Roma and the processes of their identity formation bear many similarities to the histories and identity-forming processes of colonized peoples. For centuries, the Roma were citizens who did not enjoy full and equal rights in their European home countries. Other communities around them tended to see them (much as they saw the native peoples of colonized lands) as underdeveloped, exotic, wild, flawed and abnormal pariahs and as a dangerous "other." This perception was arguably part of a process that culminated in the Nazi "Übermensch" ideology and the notion of a life-and-death struggle against "racial inferiors," as well as the policies of ethnic cleansing and extermination that were adopted as part of this alleged struggle.

For a long time, the history of the Roma and the questions and problems of Roma identity were subjects that met with little interest among the scholarly community in Hungary and most of the rest of Europe. Hungarians were not colonizers, and the lingering problems of racism and ideologies of racial and cultural superiority were not blatantly conspicuous, since they were veiled in the rhetoric of the party-state dictatorship, which trumpeted the virtues of egalitarianism and internationalism. Today, however, with the slow progression of Roma emancipation and the emergence of intellectual and middle-class circles in Hungary, the problems of Roma identity have come to the foreground. Debates concerning the nature of the shared Roma identity, culture, languages, scholarship and communities have emerged. Furthermore, there are debates about the need for accommodation, loyalty, respect, dignity and equality, as well as the possibilities for coexistence between Roma and non-Roma. The creation of public consensus and canons, which promote self-respect and foster knowledge of the past (which in turn promotes scholarship based on scientific fact, competitiveness and success), has proven a more serious challenge.

Regrettably, Hungarian society is hardly immune to racist, "colonial" notions of superiority. For this reason, the process of constructing Roma identity through the discipline of history is often met with a lack of understanding and even chauvinistic dismissal – sometimes despite the existence of compassion and good will. In addition, it is important to mention the fear of competition that grips scholars in the "professional guilds" when they are confronted with different narratives expounded by new arrivals to their disciplines or by individuals from outside the formal institutions of their disciplines whose approach is based on different value systems.

For example, in his assessment of our historical account of the Roma Holocaust – *Pharrajimos. Romák sorsa a Holocaust idején* (Pharrajimos: The fate of the Roma during the Holocaust)[3] – Attila Landauer criticizes us for allegedly not confronting the "historical truth." However, the "historical truth" that Landauer presents in the name of objectivity seems like an attempt to deny the plan to deprive the Roma of their rights and exterminate them – a fate suffered by many thousands of Roma who were deported to Germany and murdered, who were murdered in the so-called Komárom/Komárno Star Fort[4] and in other mass shootings, who slaved in the Roma internment camps in Hungary as forced labourers or who were dragged to the front as forced labourers and foot soldiers.[5]

In addition, some historians, such as László Karsai, contend that in general the Nazis were not concerned with the Roma living in the territories under occupation or the territories of the Axis allies. They were systematic in their

3 János Bársony and Ágnes Daróczi, eds., *Pharrajimos. Romák sorsa a nácizmus idején* (Budapest: L'Harmattan, 2004). Translated by Gábor Komáromy as *Pharrajimos: The Fate of the Roma during the Holocaust* (New York: International Debate Education Association, 2008).

4 The Star Fort is part of the system of fortifications around the Hungarian and Slovakian city of Komárom/Komárno on the southern bank of the Danube and the site of the largest mass murder of Roma.

5 Attila Landauer, "Mi is ez a könyv?" [So what is this book?], *Kritika* 45, nos. 5–6 (2016): 20–25.

persecution of the Roma in the German Reich but otherwise regarded the Roma merely as a "problem for the police and the administration."[6]

These examples are adequate to draw a picture of the darker side of memory politics.

The fundamental question, therefore, is whether or not the history of the Roma and the lessons and processes of this history can be turned into an independent subject of scholarly inquiry. Are society and the community of historians prepared to accept a historical narrative that is based on Roma and/or Roma-Hungarian perspectives? Can a distinctive or shared canon be formed through mutual consensus based on research and debate? Will the Roma of Hungary be permitted to have a past (as only then does it become possible to imagine their future)? Will future generations, Roma and non-Roma, be allowed to learn from the successes, values, sins, achievements and failures of their forebears?

2 Historical Memory

2.1 *The Hungarian Gypsy Cultural Association*

When the Hungarian Gypsy Cultural Association was formed at the initiative of Mária László after the Hungarian Revolution of 1956,[7] one of its first tasks was to go from village to village to compile lists of people who had been deported, who had survived and who had never returned. A long list of names was sent to the so-called Commission of Persecutees of Nazism (*Nácizmus Üldözöttei Bizottság*). Unfortunately, this list has never been found. However, according to Kamill Erdős,[8] an ethnographer and scholar on Roma culture who in the 1950s researched the songs, customs and tales on the peripheries of the villages in Hungary, some 55,000 Hungarian Roma were murdered by the Nazis and their henchmen.

6 László Karsai, *Holokauszt* [Holocaust] (Budapest: Pannonica, 2001), 16.

7 In 1954, newspaper reporter Mária László made an attempt, in the company of Gyula Toki Horváth, leader of a Roma band, and the Gypsies of Pánd, to prevail on the government to allow the Roma of Hungary to have an organization like other minority communities. At the time, the Central Committee of the Hungarian Communist Party rejected her request. See *Magyarországi Cigányok Kulturális Szövetsége* [Hungarian Gypsy Cultural Association] (internal publication, Institute for the People's Education, 1986).

8 Kamill Erdős, *Békés megyei cigányok, cigány dialektusok Magyarországon* [The Gypsies of Békés County and Gypsy dialects in Hungary] (Gyula: Gyulai Erkel Ferenc Múzeum, 1961).

2.2 *A Forbidden People Has No History*

Until the 1990s, hardly any research was undertaken into the fate of the Roma in Hungary during the Second World War, and virtually nothing was published on this subject. This is perhaps not surprising given that the Roma were a *forbidden people* before the regime change. The Hungarian Gypsy Cultural Association, which was allowed to form in 1957, was closed down in 1961 at the behest of the Communist Party. The notion that there was a Roma culture or a Roma language was rejected, although some scholars were able to obtain prestigious academic titles by authoring books on the syntax and lexicography of this "non-existent" language.

At the same time, the failure to examine the fate of the Roma unquestionably lead to the misappropriation of the Holocaust in Hungary. Although numerous survivors had recollections of their experiences with the Roma who suffered alongside them, these recollections only began to come to the fore in the 1990s. As early as 1974, the revived Roma emancipation movement in Hungary demanded that a monument be erected to the victims of the mass murders committed by the Arrow Cross in Várpalota, a town in western Hungary. The regime undermined the initiative by claiming that the Roma had been cooperating with the Soviet troops. Essentially, the Roma were released from their status as a forbidden people only after the regime change. However, the time had still not come for the writing of a history of the Roma or a common history from a Roma perspective.

Given this remarkable and unusual situation, which essentially continues until the present day, the so-called "Roma question" has been raised in the world of politics first and foremost as a matter of national security.[9] The Roma are vastly over-represented among the poor (by a factor of eight), racial discrimination against the Roma is common and, instead of social emancipation, the Roma can be said to be suffering oppression. Their efforts to form their own historical, linguistic and cultural identity are hindered. The main justification offered for this treatment is the fear of a shift in the proportions of the majority and minority populations. This claim is made in spite of the fact that the Roma in Hungary identify themselves as Hungarians. More precisely, the Roma of Hungary have a dual identity. They consider themselves as belonging both to the Hungarian people and to the smaller Roma family. The real reason why the "Roma question" has remained on Hungary's political and cultural agenda

9 Parliamentary Assembly of the Council of Europe, *Recent Rise in National Security Discourse in Europe: The Case of Roma*, October 5, 2010, Doc. 12386, available at: http://www.refworld.org/docid/4d8b19772.html (accessed August 14, 2017).

as a matter of national security until the present day is simply that it serves the short-term interests of political parties, which are only concerned with gains at the polls. In addition, it is linked to the failure to implement a process of lustration in Hungary.

2.3 *The First Publication*

The aforementioned historian, László Karsai, son of Elek Karsai, chose the Roma Holocaust as the subject of his doctoral dissertation. The main body of his book, which was published in 1992,[10] is based on archival information. Karsai's book was a milestone in the scholarship on the Roma in Hungary, as the subject was finally given the attention of a historian and approached from the perspective of the discipline of history. Nonetheless, Karsai's interpretation of the facts and information gathered was the spark that ignited a debate between him and us, the authors of this article.

2.4 *The Appearance of the International Roma Movement*

2.4.1 The Movement of the Sinti and Roma in Germany

In 1982, the Sinti and Roma living in the sixteen federal states of West Germany (the Federal Republic of Germany) created an umbrella organization called the Central Council of German Sinti and Roma,[11] which was meant to unite the civil movements and protest groups that had been active until then. After the defeat of the Third Reich, the Sinti and the Roma had not been given any form of compensation, and the genocide that had been committed against them was not addressed during the Nuremberg trials. Indeed, the files that the Nazis had kept on the Roma continued to be used by the police as criminal files. In the 1970s, under the leadership of Vinzenz Rose,[12] Roma survivors and their supporters began to organize protests.

Between 16 and 20 May 1981, the Third World Romani Congress[13] took place in Göttingen to discuss the fate of the Roma in the Third Reich. The

10 See László Karsai, *A cigánykérdés Magyarországon 1919–1945. Út a cigány Holocausthoz* [The Gypsy question in Hungary 1919–1945: The path to the Gypsy Holocaust] (Budapest: Cserépfalvi Kiadó, 1992).

11 Zentralrat Deutscher Sinti und Roma, http://www.minderheitensekretariat.de/en/minority-council/central-council-of-german-sinti-and-roma (accessed August 17, 2017).

12 A short biography of Vinzenz Rose is available at: http://www.gdw-berlin.de/en/recess/biographies/index_of_persons/biographie/view-bio/vinzenz-rose/?no_cache=1 (accessed August 9, 2017).

13 The World Romani Congress is a series of forums for debating issues relating to the Roma people in the world at large. The first World Romani Congress was held in 1971 in Orpington (United Kingdom).

international Roma movement was able to count on shows of solidarity from the people of the university town, as well as the financial and organizational assistance of left-wing civil movements. After thirty-five years, at the initiative of Tilmann Zülch, founder and general secretary of the Society for Threatened Peoples, the organization published a book entitled *Pogrom Sonderausgabe*.[14] The book was compiled together with Romani Rose, a prominent German Roma activist who lost many family members to the Nazis.[15]

The book turned the crimes committed by the Nazis against the Roma and the Sinti into a topic of widespread discussion and eventually led to the recognition and acknowledgement of their persecution and genocide. Naturally, a single book – or for that matter a series of books – would not have brought about such a substantial change had it not been accompanied by a series of demonstrations organized by the survivors and their descendants. The influence of the media and public discourse was also important. At the same time, we cannot ignore the importance of the process of confronting the past and admitting the crimes of the past, which by that time was already underway in Germany. Eventually, prominent public debates, awareness-raising demonstrations, church occupations and political hunger strikes led to the recognition of the crimes committed by the Nazis against the Roma.

In 1982, following the highly successful Third World Romani Congress, the German Sinti and Roma organizations joined to form the aforementioned Central Council of German Sinti and Roma. The Central Council had local organizations in every federal state of West Germany in which survivors, their children, prominent public figures and activists gathered. Romani Rose was chosen to lead the organization. Under Rose's leadership, the Central Council became increasingly politically organized and also began to develop a network of international ties. The Roma and the Sinti finally had credible ambassadors to represent their cause, which was particularly important because they had previously lacked effective political representation. Their policy focused on the Holocaust and Holocaust scholarship, but they did not overlook culture or the importance of international ties. In 1991, the Documentation and Cultural Centre of German Sinti and Roma opened in Heidelberg. The Centre carries

14 Tilmann Zülch, ed., *Pogrom Sonderausgabe* [Pogrom special issue], Society for Threatened Peoples/Association of German Sinti, March-April 1981.

15 Born in Heidelberg in 1946, Romani Rose is a leading figure in European Roma human rights activism and the struggle for civil rights of the Sinti and Roma in Germany. Since 1982, Rose has been the chairman of the Central Council of German Sinti and Roma. Since 1991, he has been the director of the Documentation and Cultural Centre of the German Sinti and Roma. For more information, see http://auschwitz.org/en/museum/auschwitz-council/iac-members/romani-rose (accessed August 9, 2017).

out research and disseminates facts concerning the Roma Holocaust. International and German visitors to the Centre are confronted – often for the first time – with the fact that the Roma, like the Jews, were targeted for extermination by the Nazis. One very important difference is that the fact that the Roma were also victims was suppressed for decades. The label "antisocial," which was applied to the Roma by the Nazis, continued to be used for administrative purposes and in criminal investigations, as it continued to be regarded as suitable.

Given the facts and circumstances outlined above, one of the crucial milestones of the Roma's struggle for recognition of their suffering was the unveiling of the Memorial to the Sinti and Roma Victims of National Socialism in 2012 near the Reichstag in Berlin. The monument was designed by Israeli sculptor Dani Karavan.

If the monument did not bear the remarkable significance that it does from the perspective of memory politics and minority politics in general, then perhaps we could merely regard the process of its erection as an example of official insolence: construction began in 2004 but only came to an end in 2012. In 2011, under the leadership of Tímea Junghaus, the European Roma Cultural Foundation invited the Romani Elders (Ceija Stojka, Rosa Taikon, Hans Caldaras, Nicolae Gheorghe, Romani Rose and Ágnes Daróczi) to a ceremony marking the struggle to gain recognition for the human rights of the Roma and the Sinti, which has been going on for decades. On the second day of the ceremony, the "celebrated" Romani Elders held a demonstration to protest the delay in the construction of the monument. As part of an event organized within the framework of the Berlin Biennale, they pledged that they would attend the unveiling ceremony in Berlin (which had already been scheduled and postponed four times), either to protest, if it were to be postponed again, or to finally welcome the monument's completion. The demonstration had important diplomatic implications and reverberations. It in no way resembled an attempt to find someone to blame or name the people responsible. The intention was not to find fault. Instead, the demonstration called on all those involved in the project to set aside the question of the reason for the conflict and form a true alliance so that the monument could finally be completed.

At the prompting of Nicolae Gheorghe,[16] who at that point was in the final stages of a serious illness, the Romani Elders took another important step.

16 Born in Romania, Nicolae Gheorhge (1946–2013) was an internationally recognized Roma human rights activist and sociologist. Following the regime change in Romania in 1989, he served in the government as an expert on Roma minority issues. In 1993, he founded the Centre for Social Intervention and Studies (Romani CRISS) in Bucharest, a leading NGO advocating for Roma rights. Gheorghe was appointed as the first Contact Point for Roma and Sinti Issues of the OSCE's Office for Democratic Institutions and Human Rights (ODIHR) in 1999, and subsequently as ODIHR's first Adviser on Roma and Sinti Issues, a

They set in motion an initiative to encourage the European Union to acknowledge that the Roma and the Sinti had been victims of Nazi racial persecution and murder and establish an official Roma Holocaust Memorial Day on August 2 that would be included as a national day of commemoration in all EU member states. They also launched an initiative to secure sources and resources for research on the Roma and Sinti victims of the Holocaust and narratives (research and publications) concerning what had befallen them. There was one other important message, namely that this was not simply a matter of acknowledging that our ancestors were the victims of Nazi policies – it was also a warning that the denial of this part of history meant that it was constantly being relived. Hate crimes committed today are directly linked to this ideology, which has never been properly exposed and extinguished. We therefore all bear a shared responsibility to ensure that it is finally stubbed out.

Lívia Járóka, a Hungarian Roma member of the European Parliament,[17] tried to garner support for the proposal. In 2012, however, the European Parliament was not yet prepared to take such a drastic step. Only later, Soraya Post – a Swedish politician, member of the Feminist Initiative and member of the European Parliament[18] – was able to secure adequate recognition of and support for the Roma goal. In a resolution passed on April 15, 2015,[19] the European Parliament established August 2 as the European Roma Holocaust Memorial Day and set in motion the process of having the day recognized as a national day of commemoration in each of the member states. On the other hand, we are still waiting for financial resources in support of research, and the Roma Holocaust is not yet part of the curriculum in schools. However, there are some positive signs.

---

position he held until 2006. In addition to his work as an activist, Gheorghe made significant academic contributions on Roma issues, authoring numerous articles and publications in this area.

17 Lívia Járóka is a former Member of the European Parliament (MEP). She was elected as part of the Hungarian centre-right Federation of Young Democrats-Civic Alliance Party (Fidesz) list in 2004 and served until 2014. She was the first Roma woman ever to be elected to the European Parliament. Járóka is a social anthropologist by profession.

18 Soraya Viola Heléna Post is a Swedish MEP on behalf of Feminist Initiative, which is part of the Progressive Alliance of Socialists and Democrats. Post became the party's first elected MEP and the first Roma woman to be selected as a candidate for a political party in Swedish history. She has a mixed ethnic background: her father was a German-born Jew and her mother was a Roma whose ancestors were Norwegian and Swedish Travellers. Post has worked on issues relating to national minorities in the Västra Götaland County Justice and Equality Committee and has also worked on issues relating to the Roma people.

19 For the text of the resolution, see http://www.europarl.europa.eu/sides/getDoc.do?type=MOTION&reference=B8-2015-0326&language=EN (accessed August 2, 2017).

2.4.2 The International Romani Union and the Gypsy World Federation

The upswing of the left-wing movements in 1968 also had a palpable effect on the Roma movement. In Paris, the International Roma Committee was formed under the leadership of Vankou Ruda. At the first congress of the Committee, which was held in Orpington (United Kingdom) in 1971, the International Romani Union (IRU) was formed.[20] The first president of the IRU was physician Jan Cibula, himself a refugee from Czechoslovakia. The vice-presidents included the Hungarian writer Menyhért Lakatos, and the secretary general was the Englishman Grattan Puxon. At the founding session, Slobodan Berberskia, who had once been a partisan alongside Tito, and the world-famous American actor Yul Brynner took part, as did H.D. Ramirez Hereida, the Spanish-Roma representative in the European Parliament, and professor Weer Rajendra Rishi, who later founded the Chandigarh Roma Museum.

In 1971, an image of a Chakra circle with sixteen spokes against a green and blue background was accepted as the Roma flag, and "Gelem, Gelem," a text written by Žarko Jovanović to the melody of a familiar Gypsy folk song, was selected as the Roma anthem. At the second congress of the IRU, working committees were established in Geneva, one of which dealt with the victims of the Holocaust and demanded recognition of the persecution and murder of the Roma and financial compensation from Germany. Although the IRU managed to gain observer status in the Economic and Social Council (ECOSOC)[21] of the United Nations in 1979, the question of compensation for Roma victims of the Holocaust never became an agenda item with the attention and urgency it deserved.

The Roma and Sinti victims of the Holocaust were only given the proper attention in the course of the 1999–2000 court cases in the United States concerning non-financial compensation for the survivors who are still alive.

2.4.3 The Fiftieth Anniversary

In early spring 1993, Andrej Mirga approached the major television stations in the countries in which Roma communities had been affected by the Holocaust and asked them to broadcast the commemoration ceremony and concert that had been organized in Auschwitz and Krakow on the occasion of the fiftieth anniversary of the Roma Holocaust. The initiative had two essential goals: to secure recognition for the suffering of the Roma under the Nazis and, by

20 Anton Weiss-Wendt, ed., *The Nazi Genocide of the Roma: Reassessment and Commemoration* (New York and Oxford: Berghahn Books, 2013).

21 Ilona Klimova-Alexander, *The Romani Voice in World Politics: The United Nations and Non-State Actors* (Aldershot, UK: Ashgate, 2005).

holding a politically significant commemoration ceremony, to compel the new regime to devote adequate attention to Roma issues.

As the director of the editorial board of the first Hungarian television programme on Roma issues, the *Patrin* magazine, I (Ágnes Daróczi) announced, immediately after the board had been formed, that on the occasion of the fiftieth anniversary of the Roma Holocaust we were proposing an independent Roma Day on Hungarian television. Hungary's second democratic election was beneficial from the perspective of the fate of this initiative. László Kasza, who at one time had served as the editor-in-chief of Radio Free Europe, was the vice-president of Hungarian television, and he supported our international effort. In May 1994, we were given permission, although we had no independent budget or organizational help at all.

The most important part of the Roma Day[22] was the film *Megöltétek ártatlan családom* (You murdered my innocent family), which was directed by Miklós Jancsó.[23] Polish television broadcast *Harfy Papuszy* (The harps of Papusza), a work by Polish composer Jan Kanty Pawluśkiewicz.[24] It was subsequently also broadcast by Hungarian television and all the state television stations of the European Broadcasting Union member states. This was the first time that a commemoration had been held for the Roma victims of the Holocaust that was international in nature and reached a wide range of large audiences.

---

22 The following year, the Hungarian television Roma Day was not allowed to be screened on August 2. Instead, the socialist-liberal government allowed films and features on the lives of Roma to be broadcast on Human Rights Day (December 10). However, the complete lack of funding was typical and revealing of the circumstances of the Roma minority.

23 Miklós Jancsó (1921–2014) was an internationally acclaimed Hungarian film director and screenwriter. He started his career in 1954 by making documentary newsreels. He received international recognition for works entitled *Szegénylegények* (The Round-Up, 1965), *Csillagosok, katonák* (The Red and the White, 1967) and *Még kér a nép* (Red Psalm, 1971). A recurring theme in his films is the abuse of power, and his films are often regarded as allegorical commentaries on Hungary under communism and the Soviet occupation. Jancsó received five nominations for the Best Director award at the Cannes film festival. He was awarded the Kossuth Prize in Hungary and received awards for his life's work in 1979 and 1990 at the Cannes and Venice film festivals.

24 Jan Kanty Pawluśkiewicz is a contemporary composer and musician born in Nowy Targ, Poland. He is also known for his compositions for stage and film. He is a founding member of the student cabaret Anawa. He has arranged and composed music for stage productions in Krakow and Warsaw. In 1977, he co-wrote the musical adaption of Stanislaw Witkiewicz's *Szalona Lokomotywa* (The Crazy Locomotive), together with K. Jasiński and Marek Grechuta. He also co-wrote the operas *Kur zapiał* (A rooster crowed) and *Opera żebracza* (The beggar's opera). He is also known for his compositions for short films and feature films by directors such as Krystztof Kieślowski, Feliks Falk, Agnieszka Holland and Márta Mészáros.

The German chancellor and the Polish head of state laid wreaths at the site of what had once been a Roma internment camp, and thousands of people from many European countries brought flowers to Birkenau to commemorate Roma victims. Eight buses arrived with participants from Hungary who represented strong civil movements.

In 1995, Miklós Jancsó directed a new film for international Roma Holocaust Memorial Day, entitled *Temetetlen holtak* (Unburied dead). The film drew attention to the massacre of the Gypsies in the Hungarian village of Lajoskomárom and the 52-year period of silence concerning the massacre. The film could only be completed with the cooperation of *Kreatív Média Műhely* (Creative Media Workshop) and only modest external funding was available. However, Jancsó's collaboration marked the beginning of an important new chapter in the history of documentary films on the Roma Holocaust. The story, which had remained untold for half a century, inspired other works. As a result, interviews conducted with Roma Holocaust survivors have become part of the series of testimonials recorded by the Spielberg Foundation, and Hungarian documentary film-maker Ágota Varga[25] reached the zenith of her creative career with her films on the Roma Holocaust.

In 1998, the Swiss government initiated and funded a search for the identification of Roma Holocaust survivors in order to provide financial support. They were helped by the local Red Cross organization. Ágota Varga joined this initiative. She not only used her camera to record group and individual confessions and testimonials made by Roma survivors but also took them to the place where they had once been compelled to assemble, the city of Komárom on the southern bank of the Danube. Szabolcs Szita, who founded the Hungarian Auschwitz Foundation, was an expert consultant for the film, which was released in 2000. Szita was the first Hungarian historian to include Roma victims in his research on the Holocaust. In his books and essays, he writes about the Holocaust – perhaps the greatest trauma in human history – in great detail. In Varga's 2005 documentary film *Leszármazottak* (Descendants), the children of war criminals speak about their parents' and grandparents' crimes. The contrast in attitudes is striking. While the children of the victims are forgiving, the children of the perpetrators seem to feel no shame and appear unable to confront the past.

---

25 Ágota Varga is a Béla Balázs award-winning documentary film director. She has also worked as a programme editor and a chief editor for television. Since 1990, Varga has made documentaries as well as investigative reports. She has received invitations to festivals and events throughout Europe and Asia, as well as North and South America. Her films have been aired on public television channels. Her films that have received the most international recognition are *Szemünk fénye* (The apple of our eyes, 2007), *Leszármazottak* (Descendants, 2005) and *Porrajmos* (Gypsy Holocaust, 2000).

3 Research, Publications and Conflicts

3.1 *Pharrajimos*

In 2004, in our book *Pharrajimos – Romák sorsa a Holocaust idején* (Pharrajimos – The fate of the Roma during the Holocaust),[26] we identified 570 Hungarian settlements that had not given any account of the fate of the Gypsies who had lived there, on the basis of the research of János Bársony. The publication caused a scandal. Many people felt that we were trying to hold members of the next generation responsible for the crimes of their fathers. Yet all we sought to do was call attention to the importance of confronting the past. We simply wanted to highlight the importance of breaking once and for all with the view – all too readily accepted in the past – that the Roma and the Jews were shiftless criminals and parasites, a view which led to a campaign of genocide against both peoples.

A collection of survivor testimonials formed one of the essential sources for our research. This database and resource would never have come into existence had the US justice system not taken several important steps in the course of a series of court cases against Swiss banks and German institutions in the 1990s. The American court could not understand why there were no Gypsies among the claimants. American troops had been present at the liberation of the concentration camps, and so the Americans knew that Roma from seventeen European countries had been held in the Auschwitz-Birkenau Gypsy camp and other Nazi camps. The court concluded, on the basis of this simple fact, that there had been two peoples whom the Nazis had persecuted and sought to exterminate: the Jews and the Gypsies.

In any attempt to understand the history of the Pharrajimos and the ways in which it was kept silent for so long, it is important to keep in mind that the vast majority of the Roma had little social prestige, almost no chance of exerting any political pressure, very limited financial resources, little to no experience with self-organization and communication and often very little formal education. For decades, these disadvantages made it virtually impossible to reveal the scale of the losses suffered by Roma communities, come to a collective recognition of these losses and inform both the Roma themselves and the societies in which they lived (including Hungarian society) of the persecution and devastation the Roma had suffered. The shock of the upheaval wore off very slowly, and the fear that lingered in its wake was only aggravated by the fact that for the most part those who returned found their homes and dwellings plundered. They were shown very little compassion for their suffering. Many of them hid for months in the forests, still gripped with fear after having been

26 Bársony and Daróczi, *Pharrajimos*.

liberated from the camps. Sometimes, if a lone survivor dared to ask about the members of his family or their belongings, he would be chased off by fellow villagers bearing mattocks and scythes.

The isolation of the communities in which they lived and the general lack of information often contributed to the fears of the Roma, as did the fact that many of the policemen and gendarmes who had carried out the deportations remained in their positions. After the end of the war, they represented the continuation of the "culpable, persecuting foreign power" and may well have used threats to silence the victims who returned. In communities that speak Roma languages, common history and shared traditions are passed on from generation to generation through oral folklore, songs and ballads. The history of the Pharrajimos has also been preserved in collective Roma memory in this form.

After the Pharrajimos, the Roma community tried using its own tools to seek justice for the devastation that had been wrought upon it. A Roma informant named Bánó had helped the gendarmes round up the Roma in the area around Csallóköz[27] and Komárom. After the war, the Roma community took revenge on him. In accordance with the decision of the local Roma leadership, a trap was set for him and he was captured in Szőny (part of the city of Komárom). In an attic, five people stabbed him to death. His body was then sewn inside the body of a dead horse and buried in a manure pit. This "people's verdict" is recorded in a ballad.

In 1946, Hungarian writer György Faludy called on the Hungarian public to recognize the Pharrajimos[28] and acknowledge its obligation to commemorate the genocide of the Roma. His call met with very little response. On January 2, 1952, barely seven years after the Pharrajimos, the Ministry of Internal Affairs issued a proposal to compile a list of Gypsy settlements and their inhabitants, send the inhabitants to internment camps and work camps under "police supervision" and place their children in state asylums. In 1953, the police began compiling a list of inhabitants of Gypsy settlements and gathered information on more than 10,000 "vagrant Gypsy-settlement dwellers." On October 11, 1955, in the seventh issue of *Rendőrségi Utasítások* (police directives) issued by the National Police Headquarters of the Ministry of Internal Affairs, Major General Tibor Pőcze issued instructions concerning the provision of identity cards for "vagrants and people shirking employment." The term "vagrant" obviously referred to the Roma. The personal identification card was valid for one year, and it was of a different colour than the identification cards issued to all other

27 A river island in southern Slovakia. The Slovak name of the island is Žitný ostrov.

28 Balázs Majtényi and György Majtényi, *A Contemporary History of Exclusion: The Roma Issue in Hungary from 1945 to 2015* (Budapest: Central European University Press, 2016).

citizens. The era of the black identification cards, as the system was known, only came to an end at the beginning of the 1960s.

In addition to the above-mentioned Bánó case, we know of only two other cases in which someone was held "responsible" for the mass murder of Roma. Both of these cases took place in the mid-1950s, after the perpetrators were recognized by Roma. In the case of the vast majority of mass murders, no one was ever held accountable, and the victims rest in unmarked mass graves in Lajoskomárom, Pocsaj, Szabadbattyán, Szabadegyháza, Kiskassa, Lenti and the aforementioned Star Fort of Komárom/Komárno.

3.2 *The First Signs of Commemoration*

The first commemorative plaque for the Roma who were deported to the concentration camps was put up by the Roma population of Ondód in 1984, on the fortieth anniversary of the Roma Holocaust, on the wall of the Torony kindergarten. The Roma were taken from this village to Ravensbrück, where many of them died.

The second statue commemorating the Roma who were deported was erected by the Amalipe Centre for Inter-Ethnic Dialogue and Tolerance and the Nagykanizsa municipal council. There had been a camp in Nagykanizsa, but Roma from the city had also been deported to Draškovec (or Ligetvár in Hungarian), Komárom and the German camps.[29]

The third monument, a sepulchral stone, was erected by the Cultural League of Hungarian Gypsies in the cemetery in Nyiregyháza on the forty-ninth anniversary of the creation of the ghettos on April 28, 1993. In 1996, a wooden headstone was erected in Babócsa in memory of the Roma who had been deported. In 1997, at the initiative of the local Roma minority self-government, a commemorative stone was erected in Szombathely on the site of the former Városmajori ghetto. One year later, a debate broke out in the media and the municipal government concerning the justification for the existence of the memorial. There were reports according to which unidentified perpetrators had desecrated the site.[30]

In 2006, at the initiative of various Roma organizations (Romaversitas, the Roma Civil Rights Foundation and Romédia) and with the unanimous support of the municipality of Budapest, the Pharrajimos memorial was unveiled in Budapest's Nehru Park on the banks of the Danube.[31] As a result, the commemorations, which had previously been held in front of the Parliament building,

29 Bársony and Daróczi, *Pharrajimos*.
30 Ibid.
31 Ibid.

acquired their own site. Over the past few years, local Roma minority self-governments and organizations have worked together with local governments to erect monuments to victims of the Roma Holocaust in several settlements, including Pécs, Pocsaj, Várpalota and Bük.

Due to the influence of commemorations held in Hungary, similar commemorations have also been held in three locations in southern Slovakia and monuments have been erected in memory of the Roma victims of mass murders committed by the Hungarian gendarmes and members of the Arrow Cross party. The central memorial event is held every year in Dunaszerdahely/Dunajská Streda, in commemoration of the massacre that took place in the nearby village of Nyárasd/Topoľníky. The Independent Gypsy Organization of Vas County was the first Roma organization in Hungary to hold commemorations in Dachau and Ravensbrück. In 1994, on the fiftieth anniversary of the Roma Holocaust, a group of several hundred Hungarians (sent as representatives of various organizations) bowed their heads in Auschwitz in memory of the victims.

Since 1995, a series of commemorative events and a non-denominational religious service and vigil have been held every year in memory of the victims of the Pharrajimos, first in front of the Hungarian Parliament and later in Nehru Park on the eastern bank of the Danube. The events are organized by the Roma Civil Rights Foundation and Romédia. Between 1,000 and 2,000 people have generally taken part in these events, in particular when it was still possible for the organizations in charge of the programme to apply for financial support.

Since 1997, the National Roma Self-Government (*Országos Cigány Önkormányzat* – OCÖ) has held commemorations every year in the city of Nagykanizsa. In 2004, a commemorative plaque was unveiled at the seat of OCÖ, and the official commemoration ceremonies were held there for the next six years. In 2010, the new OCÖ, under the leadership of Flórián Farkas, removed the plaque, and since then no official commemoration ceremony has been held. In 2015, the Roma Citizens Group, a civil society organization, created an 80-square-metre "commemoration centre" in Csepel, near Budapest. The centre welcomed visitors with an exhibition, a guided tour and a film. On January 27, 2017, the head of the organization announced in a press conference that the centre would have to close due to a lack of funds.

In 2004, the Holocaust Memorial Centre was opened on Páva Street in Budapest. The opening was accompanied by an independent Pharrajimos exhibition that remained on display for three years and was then taken down. In its place, the Memorial Centre now presents the stories of the suffering of three Roma families within the framework of a new permanent exhibition.

4 Closing Remarks

When we speak out in every possible forum in support of recognizing the persecution of the Roma during the Holocaust, many people's response is undeniably shaped at least in part by their fear of a long-term aspiration to found a "Roma country." This fear, which is based neither on facts, nor an examination of events, nor the progression of the history of the Roma, is nevertheless palpable.

It is important to note that no such aspiration has actually been expressed in Hungary or any international context. For us, the Holocaust is not a "Jewish affair" or a "Roma affair" but rather a part of our common past. It is a "Hungarian affair," because the crimes of the Holocaust were committed against (and at times unfortunately by) Hungarian citizens. Hungarians were denied membership in the Hungarian nation, and this denial led to murder and attempted genocide. For us, it is quite clear that we must confront the Holocaust together, as part of our common past, precisely for this reason. We must speak of it and know of it in order to ensure that it never takes place again.

While we are fully aware that one of the pillars of Roma identity is our history during the Holocaust, we consider it equally – if not more – important to create and teach about the positive pillars of Roma identity. It is important that we learn from the forms of cooperation and accommodation that were developed over the course of centuries of coexistence. We must make ourselves socially indispensable through our knowledge, expertise and services to ensure that we food on the table. We must pursue research and pass on knowledge about Roma heroes and the everyday stalwart people of our common past in order to ensure that we feel and live our simultaneous bonds to these two peoples as if this dual identity were as natural as breathing.

CHAPTER 2

Shouldn't We Have a History?

*Ágnes Daróczi**

I come from a Gypsy family in which four of seven adults didn't come back from the Second World War. Among them was my grandfather.

When steps were being taken to set up the National Gypsy Council within the framework of the Patriotic People's Front[1] in 1986, the Hungarian Communist Party had already adopted a resolution calling for the examination of the possibility of establishing a Gypsy association providing interest-based advocacy and promoting cultural activities. This represented significant progress, as well as an important milestone, considering that the Gypsies were previously regarded as "a forbidden people." Sometime around 1979, the Communist Party passed a resolution stipulating that it would, after all, be worthwhile to establish Gypsy organizations that could serve as motors of development, change and integration. The Communist Party luminaries decided that the Gypsies urgently needed not one but two organizations, although its intelligentsia numbered only a handful of members. They were quite aware of what they were doing and why they were doing it. They attempted to introduce interest-based advocacy within the Patriotic People's Front, modelled on consumer-protection organizations. In addition to Gypsy intellectuals who had previously come forward with demands, they invited one Gypsy leader (*cigányvajda*) from each county to participate. Csaba Vas – who at the time was the personal secretary of the leader of the Patriotic People's Front, Imre Pozsgay, and served as the party secretary of the Patriotic People's Front – said during one of the Front's meetings that the whole movement had, in fact, become distorted. He claimed that individuals rising from the lowest stratum of Gypsy society with no historical perspective and organization behind them were nevertheless trying to reach the top of the hierarchy despite the fact that they had their own Gypsy leaders to represent them. In effect, the Communist Party tried to revive a social structure going back to the Middle Ages, which

* This article is based on an interview conducted by Éva Blénesi.

1 The Patriotic People's Front functioned as a mass organization in Hungary from 1954 until 1990. Its main objective was to unite all social organizations and cultural institutions of the period.

 | DOI:10.1163/9789004386426_003

after the First World War had begun to function as a network of police informants. This was particularly true during the Horthy era.

The removal of the men from our communities resulted in the mutilation of those communities, in which women had to play the leading role and the type of security and knowledge only men could provide no longer existed. There were no big gatherings or celebrations. We didn't have any reserves. Thus, we belonged to the lowest rank of the Gypsies, its poorest group. It didn't matter that my grandfather and even his younger sister had known how to read and write since childhood. It didn't matter that they were educated and that my grandfather's generation already spoke several languages, held all the knowledge of the peasants and Gypsy traders and had seen the world. With all of these skills, they could have belonged to the cream of the crop of the Gypsies – if the war hadn't come along, if they hadn't been taken away and if they had returned home.

And how interesting and unique it was what the women did in that community. My grandfather was called up along with another villager, Imre Bukics, and my grandmother thought he had been drafted into the army. They were actually called up under SAS orders in October of 1944.[2] The corn had already been cut and stood in shocks in the field.

My grandfather didn't want to be called up because one could already hear the Russian tanks in Nagyvárad (Oradea, Romania). He knew that the war would soon be over and that he only had to hold out for a few more days. Poor fellow, he didn't want to join his unit. Then his older brother convinced him to do so because he had discovered that his sister-in-law was disappearing each night in order to take water, food and clean clothing to my grandfather. My grandfather's brother forced my grandmother to tell him where he was and then told him: "They are going to shoot us all down here in one pile before your very eyes and before the eyes of the children. Do you want that? Others have already been in the war. I was in it myself and I came back. I did my military service." Then my grandfather joined his unit. He never came back.

One time – I remember I was in high school and I was going to Debrecen by train – Imre Bukics looked at me and said: "You're Guszti's granddaughter, right?" "Yes," I answered. "Well, do you know that I was the last person to see your grandfather alive in Focşani? He was very sick; he caught typhus." But even he didn't tell me that they had been trench diggers because Bedő was a village of different nationalities in which the Romanians were regarded as

2 SAS was the Hungarian acronym for "Sürgős, Azonnal Siess" (Urgent: Hurry Immediately), an emergency call-up of reserves in Hungary during the Second World War. It was popularly known by its mocking nickname "Siess Adolfnak Segíteni" (Hurry to Help Adolf).

being just as unreliable as the Gypsies. As a result, they were not designated for armed combat but as cannon fodder of sorts.

My grandmother did not want to have my grandfather declared dead, and not one of the widowed women in the village remarried. They remained widows for their entire lives, although they were young – maybe 35 or 36 years old – when their husbands died. They formed a community, and they believed that there was another world in which we are all the same and equal. At this time, I was already attending elementary school – in the same class as the son of the president of the local council – but the "duster" was still coming to us, to the Gypsy row. He dusted our beds and even our heads with Matador (disinfectant powder) in order to make sure that we weren't infested with lice. One time, my mother decided she couldn't put up with this anymore. So she went to see the council president, opened his door and said to him: "Listen here, the reactionary world has come to an end. Only send the duster to us if he first stops at your place." She truly believed that the reactionary world was over, and she taught us this too. As a result, I began to believe in myself and became aware that others were by no means better than me!

Perhaps this is what gave me the courage to enter different competitions with the encouragement of my teachers. It also made me be bold enough, as a girl from a little village, to apply to one of the best high schools in the country: the Kossuth Training School in Debrecen. We were placed into unsegregated, unified classes. I read a lot, loved chemistry and mathematics, and wanted to become a chemical engineer. But meanwhile, my reading and my love for literature proved to be much stronger, and I strenuously endeavoured to hold my own. I studied a lot, and I am still grateful to my classmates today for having helped me in my struggles. My friends, Eszter Bornemissza and Tünde Doró, who are still my dear friends today, gave me a lot of support so that I could catch up with my classmates. I was the one and only Gypsy kid, not just in the class but in the entire school. It took at least another 30 years before I learned that I was not alone in having a persistent inferiority complex, because the commuting pupils were struggling with the same kind of problem.[3] It's really interesting that we never spoke about these things until decades later. It's also remarkable that I was a student in the E-class for only two years, yet I still regard it as the environment that shaped me as a person. It was an elite class; all my classmates became doctors, lawyers and engineers. Out of the 32 students in the class, there was only one who didn't go to university. Indeed, we were the elite class of the school. For me, it was a pathway to university. In fact, by the end of the second year, I had already made an appearance at

3 This term refers to students who commuted from the surrounding villages.

national student days, where I won first place in a poetry recital. This also had a consequence, because the headmistress, Erzsike Szilágyi, called my mother in and told her: "Listen here, your daughter is really trying to hold her own in the chemistry-physics section, but her abilities are directing her much more towards the humanities. How about if she transfers to the general class [class with no particular major] where she could perform better in accordance with her own talents?" Within a half year, I improved my GPA from 3.9 to 4.4[4] without much effort. I was also reading a lot in addition to studying, so I was able to satisfy my passions.

In my third year of high school, my teachers entered me in the *Ki Mit Tud?* (Who knows what?) competition, a multi-genre talent show broadcast on Hungarian Television from 1962 to 1996. I didn't enter myself, they just told me: "You are going to represent our school! Go!" I said: "But...." To which they responded: "There's no 'but,' you'll be great, you'll do it." So I went, I listened to their encouragement, and later I advanced to Eötvös Loránd University (ELTE) in Budapest without any problem. By this time, I already knew János Bársony, who has now been my companion for 45 years. We began our career in the Monszun Együttes (Monsoon Group). We sang political songs and folk songs. Meanwhile, I recited poetry and hosted a programme, and slowly the decision began to ripen in us that we should focus more on Gypsy folklore. In 1976, we founded the Romano Glaszo group,[5] and in 1978 the Kalyi Jag group.[6] I recited poetry and folk tales, hosted performances and managed the group. This lasted until 1984, by which time I had not only gained entry to the People's Cultural Institute (Népművelődési Intézet), at the invitation of Iván Vitányi,[7] but also organized the first international performances of Kalyi Jag, first at the *Collegium Hungaricum* in Vienna[8] and then at Strasbourg's City Hall and Cultural Centre, where I developed international contacts and brought a 28-member delegation. Invitations subsequently arrived one after another. Therefore, it was not difficult for me to write a letter to the Ministry of Culture in 1985

4 In Hungary, a five-point grading scale is used. There is one failing grade: 1 – insufficient. The passing grades are: 2 – sufficient to pass; 3 – satisfactory; 4 – good; and 5 – excellent.

5 Romano Glaszo (Human Voice in the Romani language) is a folk-music chorus and dance group.

6 Kalyi Jag (Black Fire in the Romani language) was the first musical group in Hungary and Europe that sang songs related to Gypsy folklore in the Romani language.

7 Iván Vitányi is a sociologist, ethnographer and emblematic figure of left-wing politics. Vitányi was appointed to serve as the director of the People's Cultural Institute in 1972.

8 The *Collegium Hungaricum*, like similar Hungarian cultural institutions, operates under the auspices of the Balassi Institute. The objective of the Balassi Institute is to cultivate and disseminate unified and universal Hungarian culture throughout the world, including among Hungarians living as minorities in countries surrounding Hungary.

proposing that Kalyi Jag finally be permitted to make a record, because the importance of folk music can be measured only in comparison to classical music, because this music stands the test of time and will still be of value in five, 50 or even 100 years. This is how Kalyi Jag was able to make its first record. They compiled the folk songs themselves, mostly from collections that we have continued – János Bársony and I – and which the younger generation has, of course, continued in the same spirit. The modesty that we brought to this matter is clear from the fact that not a single song bears our name, noting that we collected or composed it. There is a paradox here, because every one of these songs is part of a collection, although without stating where and when it was collected or by whom. Thus, they are at most arrangements that are being sung, although the lyrics and the composition of the instrumental accompaniment is all individual work.

In 1981, I organized the first national folklore meeting with the participation of twenty groups. A noted member of the Hungarian Academy of Sciences, György Martin, and Tibor Erdélyi, who is known as a folk dancer, provided assistance, as well as local experts such as László Felföldi, Árpád Együd and György Demarcsek, whom we caught up with at the county cultural centres.

It was at this time that József Lojkó Lakatos[9] made his first film about the Holocaust, entitled *Elfelejtett holtak* (Forgotten Dead). Poet Károly Bari[10] told us that we should also focus on this issue. Along with my husband, I declined this task at the time, on the grounds that so many books had already appeared on the Holocaust and we had so many other things to do. At the beginning of the 1990s, as a result of certain unplanned events, I realized that there were also Holocaust survivors and stories in my own family and that this somehow showed our history in another light. We thus began to deal with the issue much more. We collected material and also recorded footage.

Changes finally took place at Hungarian Television in 1992. During the presidency of Elemér Hankiss,[11] the head of TV2 invited us to work there so that Hungarian Television would finally have a Roma minority programme on which Roma served as editors and didn't just play silent roles in cutaway shots.

9 József Lojkó Lakatos is a theatre and film director, poet and writer who founded the Harlequin Children's Theatre.

10 Károly Bari is an internationally recognized poet, painter, graphic artist, translator, ethnographer, Holocaust researcher and editor. Bari is one of the most prominent and important figures among the Gypsies of Hungary.

11 Elemér Hankiss was a sociologist and cultural researcher who served as the first president of Hungarian Television following the regime change. His main objective as the head of Hungarian Television was to introduce BBC-style balanced news coverage in Hungary.

This was an open-minded period in the history of the Hungarian media, when the representatives of the press kept their finger on the pulse of genuine developments, when important things that were happening in the country received proper coverage in the press, and when multi-cultural Hungary became an everyday reality and experience for all of us. Political parties were formed and organized, and the entire world was present in our everyday lives to a much greater degree. Thus, the kind of global village facilitated by technological development – in which television played a big role at the time – suddenly became a reality.

In May 1992, while still only working part-time, I undertook to help put together a Gypsy magazine programme. On September 6, 1992, a 25-minute weekly programme was launched with the title *Patrin Magazin*. Finally, we had an independent programme, as those who produced the programme were also Roma. We had the technology at our disposal to shoot wherever we wanted, and if I asked government ministers talk to us they placed themselves at our disposal with the greatest of pleasure. This kind of openness never existed before and is certainly less evident today. There was also a very strong sense of solidarity. The concepts of liberty, equality and fraternity were very prominent at this time, although we had already organized a genuine movement during the second half of the 1980s. And by the time the political movements got to the point of organizing themselves into parties, our independent Gypsy organization, Phralipe, already existed. In fact, it is worth noting that one of the greatest: hypocrisies of socialism in Hungary, namely that it said one thing and did another, was demolished precisely in the field of Roma affairs through the Anti-Ghetto Committee.[12]

When I began to edit *Patrin Magazin*, we were in a quandary because we wanted to inform the public not only about our own values and knowledge, which provide a basis for self-respect and the respect of others, but also about certain wrongdoings that were going on at that time. Thus we went to fine arts exhibitions and other cultural events but also focused on the double murder

12 The planned relocation of Roma living in Miskolc in northeastern Hungary to 29-square-meter homes located outside the city as part of the municipal leadership's downtown renovation plan formulated in 1980 formed the initial stimulus for the foundation of the Anti-Ghetto Committee nine years later. The young Gypsy teacher Aladár Horváth was the first person to draw attention to the fact that relocating Roma to the isolated site along the Sajó river, which lacked adequate infrastructure, risked creating a ghetto. The Anti-Ghetto Committee, which was established with the support of the non-Roma opposition, was the first advocacy organization in the history of Central and Eastern Europe to effectively promote Roma interests.

in Tura and the Kétegyháza arson attack,[13] as well as instances of police abuse. Meanwhile it became clear that 25 minutes a week was hardly enough for anything. The fact that *Patrin Magazin* appeared on Hungarian Television's channel 2 at eight o'clock in the morning placed us in a time slot that occasionally attracted an exceptionally large audience – sometimes as large as that of the news. Tens of thousands of people didn't go out to the market until they had watched our programme. And when they did, it was the subject of conversation at the market. I myself experienced this on countless occasions. People talked to me about what had been on the *Magazin* and asked more questions, and I kept the conversation going.

From the very outset, we considered it important that our several-hundred-year history be a permanent theme and a recurring educational part of the programme. Since I knew by this time how little-researched and little-known the history of our suffering during the Holocaust was, we consciously and continuously conducted interviews with survivors. Of course, very little of this could be included in the time we had at our disposal, but the material accumulated and we became more and more determined. In the spring of 1993, Andrzej Mirga[14] came to visit us at Hungarian Television, as the existence of *Patrin Magazin* had by then attracted considerable attention throughout Europe. Television stations from neighbouring countries came to visit us and reported that Gypsies were working at Hungarian Television and producing their own show. The truth is that Hungary's democratic change set an example for many countries. By then, I had very broad and extensive international contacts, from Associated Press to the BBC and *Le Monde*. Thus, if they came to see us, I could incorporate them into our existing connections. In a similar way, I helped in the making of films about Greek, English and Austrian Roma.

In connection with the visit of Polish Roma activist Andrjez Mirga, the editors of *Patrin Magazin* proposed that Hungarian Television should finally organize a Roma day on the 50th anniversary of the Roma Holocaust and that a multitude of programmes connected to the Roma should determine the entire stream of programming. Since there was a parliamentary election in the spring of 1994, we didn't really get an answer to our proposal for a year. However, despite the approach of the election, the Hungarian Television leadership relented after all and embraced the idea. President Árpád Göncz made a

13 For more information regarding the Tura double murder and the Kétegyháza arson attack, see György Fehér, Holly Cartner and Lois Whitman, *Struggling for Ethnic Identity: The Gypsies in Hungary* (New York: Human Rights Watch [Helsinki Watch], 1993), 53.

14 Andrzej Mirga is a Polish anthropologist and the chair of the board of the Roma Education Fund.

congratulatory speech. Although Prime Minister Gyula Horn did not personally attend, he apologized to the Roma in a letter for what had happened. Miklós Jancsó[15] made a film about the Roma Holocaust. The basis of the film was a lengthy interview that I conducted with a survivor. The second part consisted of the portrayal of one of our ancient rites, namely the breaking of the mourning period. The custom is that after six weeks, or in the case of a close relative after one year, the mourners break the mourning period, take off their black clothing and begin to dance and play music again. This tradition lives on to this day. When we linked this ritual to the 50th anniversary of the Roma Holocaust and the testimony of the survivors in the film, we were trying to send a message to the wider world that what's done is done and a new era has begun. It is important to look forward as well as back. We must live on, and it is time to utilize what is good and beautiful within us.

We wanted to hold another Roma day in 1995, but the authorities did not permit it.[16] Moreover, no matter how well-watched we were, we noticed that *Patrin Magazin* had been moved to an almost unwatchable time slot – Friday afternoon at one o'clock. This change served to prevent the audience from getting used to us and reduced the impact of the programme. Suddenly we noticed that, no matter how much more money the minority editorial staff received, somehow they weren't spending it on our programme. We had fewer and fewer resources at out disposal. We had to ask for a camera three days in advance and had to submit a production plan indicating where we were going to be shooting features on Roma issues three weeks in advance. By 1998, the old system of oversight had essentially been restored. For months I was unable to sleep between Wednesday and Thursday because that was when the director of the editorial staff was working as a censor. Every Thursday, he found something that needed to be corrected. I had previously had a lot of conflict with Zoltán Ács, who was the director at that time, although I was confident that I could take care of things with him because he knew very well that sitting in front of him was an intellectual who had been involved in the political transformation. Moreover, we had a certain amount of creative autonomy, which he respected even if he sometimes disagreed. Suddenly, however, we felt like we were gasping for air, like we were being sucked deeper and deeper into some kind of quagmire and that this was no longer the thing that we wanted.

15 Miklós Jancsó is a Kossuth Prize- and Balázs Béla Prize-winning film director and scriptwriter and an outstanding figure in the Hungarian film industry.

16 From 1994 to 1998, Hungarian Socialist Party (HSP) Prime Minister Gyula Horn led a left-wing government coalition composed of the HSP and the Alliance of Free Democrats.

In August 1998, I sent a series of questions by fax to the Roma National Self-Government[17] in preparation for the municipal and minority elections:

– What kind of institutions have you established?
– What is the timetable for coordination with the ruling government?
– What are you most proud of?
– What do you regret the most?
– What is the Roma National Self-Government's annual budget?

These were simple, straightforward and objective questions. One week later, I was no longer the head of the editorial staff that I had founded, assembled and successfully led for five years. They dismissed me on the grounds that our reporting had not been balanced. The Gypsy issue remained an issue of national security, just as it had been before. I was considered the eternal dissident, a dangerous destabilizing force, because they wanted to preserve the mentality and status quo that we remain on the bottom, that we are despised, that we are outsiders, that we don't count, that we don't need government spending, work or quality education. My mere presence was an attack against all this, especially if I had certain means at my disposal as a journalist and a television producer. So I became unemployed. Though it seems that I was not completely lacking in talent and competence, because my old workplace eventually took me back. By this time, the institute had changed its name from the People's Culture Institute to the National Public Education Centre. In 2000, in a way that was both symbolic and peculiar, I organized the third national Roma fine arts exhibition in the same Cultural Center in Pataky Művelődési Központ where I had started in 1979. In 1989, when we still had illusions about a true political change, the exhibition was held at the Museum of Ethnography, which was located across from the Parliament. I continued to work at the National Public Education Centre until 2012. The mentality was the same as before. It was filled with the best experts in the country, who were committed to culture, education and community building, really understood their profession and were able to come up with new things and bring in new blood. While we were organizing exciting symposiums for the leaders of the community, including a major national conference on "Identity, Culture and History," we realized that connecting different disciplines with public education could really help to finally clarify some fundamental questions, for example concerning

17 The Roma National Self-Government is part of Hungary's minority self-government regime, which focuses primarily on issues pertaining to cultural autonomy. For more details on Hungary's minority self-governments, see Balázs Dobos, "The Minority Self-Governments in Hungary," January 2016, available at: http://www.world-autonomies.info/ntas/hun/Documents/Hungary_2016-01-15.pdf (accessed June 20, 2017).

the components of identity. We also realized that a cleansing process and a hierarchy of values needed to be established within the community, as it had in the surrounding society, and that we needed to inform people about our centuries-long history. The "Identity, Culture and History" initiative, in which social psychologists, historians, museologists and Roma and non-Roma were able to participate, thus turned out to be very exciting.

In fact, from this time onwards, our research on the Roma Holocaust became a purposeful pathway for us. On the one hand, this was due to the fact that in 2000 I directed the Hungarian aspect of the public relations work that a US Court had initiated in seventeen European countries in the context of a class-action compensation suit. It was at this time that the submission of non-property compensation claims against Swiss banks and institutions began.

The US Court realized in the course of the lawsuit against Swiss banks and other organizations that only people of Jewish heritage were appearing as plaintiffs, although they were well aware that Gypsies had been also persecuted in the same way on racial grounds. The US army had witnessed that there were also Gypsies among the prisoners they had liberated. Some of them were marked with a red triangle to indicate that they were politically unreliable people, some of them were marked with a brown one because of their skin colour, and some of them were marked with a black one as common criminals. The US Court concluded that the surviving Gypsy prisoners were illiterate and that the relevant information had not reached them or that, if it had reached them, they would be unable to fill out the questionnaires. The Court therefore set up advisory offices in seventeen countries. I was the director of the Hungarian advisory office. I had the extraordinary luck of being able to include historians and researchers of this period in our work, including Professor Szabolcs Szita and János Bársony. We gathered data, including names and addresses, and went to every county in the country. There was press coverage, there was an educational film, and there were questionnaires. Indeed, my students – at the time I was helping to run the Romaversitas Foundation[18] – went back to their hometowns or travelled the country, to interview the elderly survivors. From May to December 2000, we interviewed 2,573 survivors, whose data was forwarded to the offices of the International Organization for Migration in Switzerland.[19] They came forward as applicants or plaintiffs who could expect to receive

18 The Romaversitas Foundation was the first foundation in Hungary to provide talented young Roma with a complex educational structure. In its twenty years of existence, the foundation has furnished more than 300 young Roma with assistance in preparation for obtaining a diploma.

19 The International Organization for Migration (IOM) was established in 1951 to serve an intergovernmental intermediary and consultative role.

compensation. Less than a year later, I attended a meeting of the directors of the seventeen national advisory offices and the directors of the American PR office.[20] They asked me how it was possible that there were so many applications from survivors in Hungary. Instead of me, the director of the American PR office answered: "There are several reasons for this. In Hungary, the deportations started the latest. Thus they potentially had the greatest chance of survival. And don't forget that in Hungary professional logistics were available. Ágnes Daróczi led the promotion campaign with the help of Romaversitas students." For example, I made a Gypsy-language educational film using interviews we had already conducted. This helped people in other countries understand the types of cases for which it was possible to apply for compensation. Later, we used these interviews for the short film *Hej, gettó!* (Hey Ghetto!), which was broadcast by Duna Television (a prominent Hungarian satellite TV station).

I constantly encountered explicit requests to research this unspoken and unexplored history. Once the logistical work was finished, we had a lot of data and a vast number of interviews (in which we could not use names since we did not have permission to do so). At least two books have been published as a consequence of this knowledge. János Bársony did the historical research. He was originally a lawyer, but history always stood at the centre of his interests. I conducted interviews with survivors and refined and edited the books. L'Harmattan published the first book, entitled *A Pharraimos. Romák sorsa a holocaust idején* (Pharrajimos: The Fate of the Roma during the Holocaust), in 2004. This volume consisted primarily of essays, including studies by Gyula Pucsi Barna, János Ury and Szabolcs Szita and an article on the Holocaust in Gypsy folk poetry by the poet Károly Bari. I edited the second volume, which contains the kind of visual documentation that can be used to organize exhibitions in even the smallest villages and classrooms. As a consequence of our research, we gained knowledge of nearly 570 settlements where survivors were born or from which they were taken. To this day, most of them have not accounted for the fate of their Roma citizens during the Holocaust. We have thus created an archive for future generations, which will enable them to conduct detailed research into local history. In addition, it can provide material for the Gypsy exhibition of the Holocaust Museum.

English and Croatian versions of the book have also been published. We were approached by IDEBATE Press.[21] They told us that everything in the volume was interesting to them and that they would publish it in English. A modest

20 AB Data provides auxiliary PR services in class-action cases for US courts and engages in the search for plaintiffs.

21 The objective of IDEBATE Press is to assist teachers worldwide with supplementary educational materials.

volume, *Pharrajimos: The Fate of the Roma during the Holocaust,* appeared in Gábor Komáromi's translation in 2008. It was also translated into Croatian in 2013. This is particularly interesting, as Croatia also lags behind in its research on its own Gypsies. Researchers who finally began to dig into the history of the Roma told us that our volume had a very inspirational effect.

There was also interest from Romania. The truth is that we were in a very unique situation at Hungarian Television. At this time, a young college student studying film directing in Bucharest, Andrea Varga, asked us to provide her with editing facilities so that she could finish her graduation film, which focused on the history of the Romanian Jewish Holocaust. I watched the raw material and talked to Andrea about what she was doing and why she was doing it. In return for helping her with editing, we made her promise that the Romanian Roma Holocaust would be the next phase in her research. Andrea was very conscientious and thanks to her interest and research films and written documentation connected to the deportation of the Gypsies came to light. She published this material in several volumes. If we have gained a more thorough image of the sufferings of Romanian Roma during the Second World War, it is largely thanks to the work of Andrea Varga, and if we were an inspiration for her in this regard then we are very grateful. However, the truth is that the history of the Transylvanian Gypsies has still not been sufficiently researched and does not receive enough attention. Gypsy labour battalions performed forced labour in the Romanian communes of Gyergyótölgyes (Tulgheş) and Ojtoz (Oituz), but these battalions have not received much publicity and we don't have enough knowledge about them.

A heated dispute on the Romanian Roma Holocaust led to the birth of another volume, entitled *Kali Trash* (Black Fear).[22] This title originates from the archaic language of Ukrainian Roma, who used this phrase to refer to the black-uniformed SS soldiers who came to conduct punitive actions. Roma did not call them the SS or *Einsatzgruppen* but *kali trash*.

The dispute involved the historian László Karsai, who published a book on this issue in 1992. At first he placed the number of Gypsy victims at around 10,000 based on data from the archives. However, he later reduced this number to 2,000 without having conducted any further research. Karsai's research only covered the western half of the country and the period following the German occupation of Hungary in March 1944, whereas our research revealed that there were Gypsies among those murdered in Kamyanets-Podilsky.[23] This is also apparent from the correspondence of the Lord Lieutenant of Ugocsa County.

22 János Bársony and Ágnes Daróczi, *Kali Trash* (Budapest: Romano Instituto, 2015).

23 Between 15,000 and 16,000 Jewish deportees from Hungary were executed in this city located in southwestern Ukraine on August 27–28, 1941.

It is interesting that the relevant slip of paper was transferred from the Hungarian archives to the Roma and Sinti documentation centre in Heidelberg,[24] although its historical relevance was only discovered later. At a conference held at the Hungarian Academy of Sciences in 2004, László Karsai[25] himself stated that he had encountered such papers. Subsequent analysis also shows that the eastern half of the country was not untouched, but it is usually claimed that the deportation of the Gypsies of Hungary began between November 4 and 6, 1944. One can speculate as to why this might be the case. Why did the Germans conduct these raids when such persecution was already regular and systematic? However, the testimonies of the survivors reveal that there were 55 agricultural and military forced-labour camps on the territory of Hungary where Gypsies were made to work. This fact is still not generally known, but the testimonies of the survivors support it. Because of these testimonies, we were able to name the relevant settlements in *Kali Trash*. Moreover, we have done this at the very last minute, since the average life expectancy of Roma is ten to fifteen years shorter than that of the general population[26] and hardly any of the Holocaust survivors are alive anymore. That is why it is even more important to collect testimonies, analyze local documents and research the living memory passed down to the relatives of the survivors.

This is very significant and also forced me to revise my original position. I had to accept that it is not true that people today don't know very much about the Holocaust: they are simply unable to recall their memories due to cultural constraints. Animism still plays a powerful role in Gypsy life, including the belief that things that have been named come to life. That is why, in many places, Gypsies greet one another by saying "*latchoj tyo dyes*," which means "your day is good." We say it like that because we believe that it will come to life and happen if we do. There is therefore only one occasion when one is not only permitted but actively encouraged to speak about these persecutions, namely "*dur amender*" – during the vigil.

The vigil is a moment when we are immersed in sadness, when there is a place for sad stories and when survivors and their loved ones can tell these stories. This is when old wounds are opened up and personal pain is eased through collective grief. Yet this moment also presents a pitfall because the

24 The Documentation and Cultural Centre of German Sinti and Roma in Heidelberg provides a comprehensive and unparalleled memorial to the history and victims of the Roma and Sinti Holocaust in Germany and other European countries within the framework of a permanent exhibition. See http://www.sintiundroma.de/en/centre/about-us.html.

25 Historian, professor and Holocaust researcher.

26 Dena Ringold, Mitchell Alexander Orenstein and Erika Wilkens, *Roma in a Expanding Europe: Breaking the Poverty Cycle* (Washington, DC: World Bank Publications, 2005).

personal pain is nevertheless stronger and never-ending. Moreover, because only the survivors can tell their stories, each personal account also includes a miraculous escape. For this reason, the history of the Roma Holocaust is connected in a very unique way to the history of miracles, while at the same time being very much based in reality. The Roma's imprinting and preservation of memory are thus not the same as they are, for example, in the Jewish community, where the story is supported with dates, names and the names of settlements. Among the Roma, the individual is the most important element in every story. This is the difference between history based on an oral tradition and history based on a written culture and its traditions. In the case of the Gypsies, the passing down of experience takes place through living memory. That is why I was touched when, back in the day, Zsuzsa Horváth began her story by saying that "it was four o'clock in the morning of November 6." This is so precise – and that rarely happens. For example, I once met a group of survivors in which one survivor said of another survivor that he had been born in the synagogue of Ózd, but a year later than the date written in the person's identity card. It had been impossible to register the birth right way because of the way things were at that time. By this time, they had been gathered up and all the Jews were taken away. They then collected the Gypsies at the synagogue, where the person in question was born. Nobody really remembered exactly when things had happened, so they later entered what turned out to be incorrect data in the birth records. The person in question is actually one year younger than stated in his official documents.

When we were collecting survivors' testimonies, I had to give my students detailed instructions on how to collect data and what kind of questions to ask. For example: What was the weather like? What were you wearing? What was at the border? Was there snow? Had they picked the corn already? Had they harvested wheat or picked peas? What kind of work were they doing on the land? What communities were the others from? Whom do you remember? Can you name them? Have you met them since? In addition, I always asked survivors if they had spoken among themselves or told their story to their closest relatives.

It is very significant that the old and sick often said things like: "Nothing interests these young people. They don't care about what happened a long time ago. All their problems are about how they are going to earn their bread and butter." Such statements are very distressing, because they reveal not only the shaken state of the elderly but also the dreadful vulnerability of the younger generations, which have to focus all their energy on staying alive, survival and looking for work.

The Holocaust Memorial Centre in Budapest had already been preparing for the 60th anniversary of the Holocaust for five years when the Roma Press

Centre called our attention to the fact that they did not plan to say a single word about the fate of the Roma. With great difficulty, we were able to get them to invite us to the preparatory meetings and managed to state during a public discussion that silence is part of oppression. Historian Mária Ormos[27] was the one who amplified this statement by politely suggesting that it might be necessary to deal with the fate of the Gypsies as well. Finally, I had to blackmail the board of trustees by telling them that, if they didn't include an exhibition about the fate of the Roma in the memorial centre, we would hold an exhibition on their front doorstep or in the underpass across the street. We had a total of three weeks until the opening of the 60th anniversary events. During these three weeks, we established contacts with researchers and organizations from Paris to London and from Heidelberg to Washington. At the same time, we organized an exhibition in the gallery section of the synagogue. (HDKE Holocaust Documentation Center nowadays) based primarily on the testimonies of survivors and the research of János Bársony. As a result, we started to break into the official public discourse, so that others would pay attention as well. For over ten years, our non-governmental organizations had been holding memorials in front of the Parliament, evoking our vigil-keeping customs and calling for a memorial to be built for the Roma victims. These demands and initiatives dragged on and on but nothing ever happened. With the approach of the 60th anniversary, I realized that spoken words fly away, while written words remain, so I submitted a written proposal to the representative body for a memorial to the Roma victims in Budapest. The Romedia Foundation,[28] the Romaversitas Foundation and the Roma Civil Rights Foundation signed the letter as initiators. We didn't want it to be some isolated memorial on some site on the outskirts of the city. Instead, we wanted the Budapest Galéria to implement the project and put it out to tender, as in the case of other public statues. We strove to ensure that there would be ample public support and reinforcement. It was an exceptionally good feeling when the public panel agreed with the decision of the professional panel, paving the way for the establishment of a memorial designed by Munkácsy Prize-winning sculptor Tamás Szabó and environmental engineer Ákos Maurer Klimes in Budapest's Nehru Park.[29]

27 Mária Ormos is a Széchenyi Prize-winning Hungarian historian, a member of the Hungarian Academy of Sciences and a recognized researcher of twentieth-century Hungarian history.

28 The Romedia Foundation is a Roma-operated non-profit foundation and NGO that was founded in 1992. See http://en.romediafoundation.org.

29 This park, which was established in 1966, is named after the first prime minister of independent India. It was designed by Zoltán Krizsán, Vilmos Jancsó and Ferenc Mészáros. At the time of its creation, it was the second largest public park in Budapest. The park underwent renovation in 1984 (which was planned by Katalin Baraczka). Since then, there

The 50th anniversary of the Holocaust was a turning point, because from that time onwards commemorations of the Roma Holocaust have taken place in Hungary at our initiative. On the occasion of the 50th anniversary, eight buses full of young people and survivors went from Hungary to Auschwitz and held a vigil at the camp. This kind of collective ownership of the past represents an extremely important milestone. The first memorial to Roma victims of the Holocaust was built, at our initiative, in Nagykanizsa in 1994, followed by memorials in Nyíregyháza and other communities, as detailed in the book *Kali Trash*. However, there are still nearly 100 settlements in which the fate of the Gypsy community has not been acknowledged.

My activities so far have helped educate multiple generations, and this important work is being continued by my own family. My daughter, Kata Bársony, has made more than 40 documentary films in the *Mundi Romani* series,[30] which shows the fate of Roma from India to Albania and from Portugal to Germany through the eyes of the Roma. As a strong and self-respecting woman, and with the help of the Romedia Foundation, she made the campaign film "I am a European Roma Woman," which reached millions of people worldwide and was supported by Amnesty International. The Romedia Foundation has a blog that takes this idea further by introducing female characters who all conclude what they have to say with the statement: "I am a European Roma woman." This process demonstrates the changing role of Roma women, as well as the fact that women are "the face of change."

The Romedia Foundation participated in the international "Auschwitz Requiem" project in 2012. The Frankfurt Roma Philharmonic Orchestra performed Roger Morena Rathgeb's classical work, which is based on the structure of the Christian liturgical requiem, in six major European cities. A memorable musical programme was performed at Müpa Budapest, under the direction of Roma conductor Riccardo M. Sahiti, with the participation of local artists and choruses.[31] This was the first and only occasion on which George Soros has spoken publicly about his own Holocaust experiences. It is quite remarkable that it was the Gypsies who provided him with this opportunity and that all of this took place at the Müpa in the Budapest.

After the concert, everybody received a rock inscribed with the name of a victim of the Roma Holocaust, symbolizing that the past cannot be forgotten.

has been just one intervention in the structure of the park, which was carried out in 1998. This is where the Roma Holocaust memorial was later placed.

30 See http://www.mundiromani.com (accessed August 17, 2017).

31 Müpa Budapest, formerly known as the Palace of Arts, is a multi-functional cultural facility in Budapest. Müpa Budapest provides venues for the musical, visual and dramatic arts. Architect Gábor Zoboki designed the facility, which was built between 2002 and 2005.

CHAPTER 3

Roma Women's Local Initiatives in Hungary: Driving Force for Community Participation and Empowerment

Erzsébet Anita Német and Szilvia Rézműves

Abstract

In this descriptive-analytical case study, we detail the work, potential, and challenges of local initiatives led by Roma women in Hungary, and examine the social conditions necessary for achieving their full potential. We assert that these initiatives represent "subaltern counterpublics," operating parallel to the mainstream public sphere and providing opportunities for community discourse. Data was collected through focus-group discussions with representatives of these initiatives and with the use of demographic questionnaires. Fraser's normative model of the public sphere and Habermas' concept of civil society serve as the analytical framework through which the data was interpreted. The research indicates that, although these initiatives have been successful in providing fora where community members can voice their opinions and participate in a public arena, few have managed to establish meaningful dialogue with decision-makers outside of the community and with other members of the local power elite.

1 Introduction

In terms of social exclusion, Roma women living in disadvantaged regions represent one of the most vulnerable groups of all due to intersectional disadvantages arising from their gender, ethnic background and class affiliation.[1]

1 The number of Roma living in Hungary is approximately 700,000, or roughly 7 per cent of the country's total population. The gender distribution of Hungary's Roma population is equal. Around 97 per cent of Roma households live in conditions of material deprivation. In addition to poverty and social exclusion, Roma women face multiple types of discrimination vis-à-vis the majority population as well as within their own Roma communities. Underlying the frequent cases of early marriage and childbearing among Roma women are labour-market discrimination, asymmetrical power relations within the family and the traditional gender roles within Roma culture. These factors not only result in them leaving school at an early age but also serve to impede their labour-market activity and their ability to improve

 | DOI:10.1163/9789004386426_004

The needs and perspectives stemming from their unique status frequently remain invisible to decision-makers, just as Roma women themselves often remain unseen within the various fora of the public sphere. However, the initiatives of Roma women that have emerged over recent years demonstrate that they are seeking a place in public life and wish to make their voices heard in social discourses. It was precisely this contrast between their social invisibility and their active presence at the local level that aroused our research interest.[2] How, under what conditions and in the interest of attaining what objectives has one of the most marginalized groups in contemporary Hungarian society activated its resources? We attempted to find answers to these questions in the course of three focus-group discussions organized in provincial cities in Hungary, involving twenty-six representatives from eleven Roma women's initiatives. These discussions – interwoven with common, reflective thinking, lively debates and encouraging feedback – helped us uncover deeper correlations in relation to our theme and paint a more nuanced picture. The present study attempts to describe the interpretation that crystallized in our minds in the course of this process. We therefore do not wish to draw general conclusions regarding Roma women who are active in civil society or the civil activism of Roma women. The following is simply an attempt to draw a portrait inspired by the narratives of those who participated in the initiatives we examined. Besides presenting the work, potential and challenges of the Roma women's initiatives, we also try to shed light on the social conditions necessary for these initiatives to be able to achieve their full potential.

In our study, we have combined critical social-theory and interpretative sociology. The normative dimension provides an analytical perspective to

their financial circumstances. See Niall Crowley, Angela Genova and Silvia Sansonetti, *Country Report on Hungary: Empowerment of Romani Women within the European Framework of National Roma Inclusion Strategies* (European Parliament: Directorate-General for Internal Policies, 2013), http://www.europarl.europa.eu/RegData/etudes/etudes/join/2013/493021/IPOL-FEMM_ET(2013)493021_EN.pdf (accessed June 16, 2017).

The Strasbourg Declaration on Roma states the following with regard to the rights and gender equality of Roma women: "(22) Put in place effective measures to respect, protect and promote gender equality of Roma girls and women within their communities and in the society as a whole. (23) Put in place effective measures to abolish where still in use harmful practices against Roma women's reproductive rights, primarily forced sterilisation." *The Strasbourg Declaration on Roma*, Doc. CM(2010)133, adopted at the Council of Europe High Level Meeting on Roma, Strasbourg, October 20, 2010.

2 This study was prepared in the framework of the Tom Lantos Institute's Roma Rights and Citizenship Programme, whose primary objective is to promote and support the meaningful participation of Roma communities in social, economic and cultural life, as well as in public affairs.

determine the requirements and imperatives of democratic political practice, while the interpretative approach enables us to anchor these in empirical reality so that we can reconstruct the narratives of our interlocutors from our own research perspective. In other words, we examine and construe the discourses and interpretations of our interlocutors through the lens of normative democratic theory, which also serves as a basis for scrutinizing the democratic political practice in these localities.

Grassroots organizations and informal groups springing from civil society open up the possibility of participation and emancipation for Roma women and their communities. We assert that the initiatives examined in the research represent "subaltern counterpublics,"[3] alternative public spheres that operate parallel to the mainstream public sphere and provide opportunities for community-themed discourse. Through the consolidation of these narratives, communities – intentionally or unintentionally – construct and express their common identity, thereby entering the realm of the public sphere as a collective group. In the course of this process, they become capable of formulating common positions with regard to public affairs affecting them and framing counter-narratives opposing the dominant discourse, which also serves as the driving force for their activities. With the formulation of common community interests, new issues also rise to the surface, which they try to address, to the best of their abilities, in the ever-widening public sphere. Some initiatives provide an opportunity for interest mediation of varying degrees. However, while they are capable of navigating between the community and local decision-makers, they are unable to participate as an equal partner in consultative mechanisms. Indeed, as a result of their exclusion from the wider public sphere, the majority of these initiatives are unable to transmit the voice of the community to decision-makers. In this way, they can be regarded as internal, and, in a certain sense, exclusive workshops of the community that ensure participatory parity in public affairs through a parallel structure. However, they cannot ensure the equal participation of the Roma community or properly advocate for the community's interests in local decision-making processes. Moreover, their activism as Roma women is by no means devoid of struggle. Their presence and advocacy activities upset existing power relations and generate tension not only in the local power arena but also within the internal realm of the community and the intimate sphere of the household. Despite these difficulties, Roma women still undertake these struggles because they

3 Nancy Fraser, "Rethinking the Public Sphere: A Contribution to the Critique of Actually Existing Democracy," in *Habermas and the Public Sphere*, ed. Craig Calhoun (Cambridge, MA: MIT Press, 1992), 109–142.

believe that the discourses they generate, and the actions connected to them, increase their own participation and equality, as well as the participation and equality of community members affected by their initiatives, and boost the level of democracy prevailing in their locality. At the same time, their exclusion from the wider public sphere, the absence of channels of communication for genuine dialogue and the lack of participatory parity in interactions with decision-makers limit their potential to strengthen local democracy. However, this not only attests to the importance of the local initiatives but also provides a glimpse into the diagnosis of their current political and social environments.

The present study is divided into three parts. First, we describe our research methodology. We then examine the relevant literature, which provides the study's conceptual vocabulary and analytical framework, before discussing the results of our research. The study concludes with a summary of our research findings.

2 Research Methodology

Since the topic is under-researched and the transparency of Roma women's initiatives is low, we mapped the initiatives using the snowball method. We paid careful attention to ensure that both Roma women's non-governmental organizations and informal initiatives were included in our research sample. With a few exceptions, all local Roma women's initiatives we approached agreed to participate. Our interlocutors arrived from various environments, thus reflecting – or at least displaying – the heterogeneity and social and cultural layout of domestic Roma communities.[4] Our interlocutors ranged from residents of Roma settlements of economically decaying small towns to inhabitants of bustling big cities, and from public-sector employees and mediators[5]

4 The Roma population of Hungary can be divided into three main subgroups – the Oláh (Vlach), the Romungro (Hungarian-speaking Roma) and the Beás (Beash or Boyash) – that distinguish themselves from one another on the basis of language, culture and traditional occupations.

5 The mediators and community action-group members who spoke to us during our research participated in a regional project implemented in Hungary aimed at promoting the self-organization of Roma communities, increasing their participation in local public affairs and fostering local social dialogue. "Intercultural" Roma mediators and community action groups composed of local residents supported by mediators were the key players in this project. The objective of these community action groups is to assert community interests through dialogue and cooperation with the local decision-makers participating in the project.

to former local minority council representatives[6] and college-graduate association presidents. There was a prominent Beás organization leader, a Lovari-speaking foundation employee and a Romungro community activist. What they all had in common was that they were of Roma origin, that they were women and that they wanted to shape the development of their own destiny and that of their community.

We collected our data applying both qualitative and quantitative methods. In addition to using questionnaires containing demographic data, we organized three focus-group discussions in major provincial towns in Hungary. The discussions, which focused on preset topics and involved twenty-six representatives from eleven local Roma women's initiatives, were guided by the following main themes:

- the main pillars of participation in the initiatives;
- the arenas for inclusion of the Roma community and patterns of activism;
- the formation of women's roles in the participatory processes; and
- advocacy and interest-representation capacity and inhibiting factors.

Several participants had not yet met, and the focus-group discussions thus also provided them with a platform for presenting their aspirations, their strategies and their results. Beyond simply sharing experiences, this interaction provided participants of the focus-group discussions with inspiration and concrete ideas. According to many of them, it also contributed to the identification of common interests and possible areas of future cooperation. With the help of this method, we were also able to reproduce debates and contradictions connected to cultural and social affairs that would not otherwise have risen to the surface, or only with great difficulty.[7]

Participants agreed both verbally and in writing to participate in the research, to the recording of the focus-group discussions and to the anonymous use of the data provided.

---

6 Section 2 of the explanatory provisions of Article 6/A of Act LXXVII of 1993 on the Rights of National and Ethnic Minorities (amended in 2005) contains the following definition of minority self-government: "an organisation established by democratically held elections in accordance with the provisions of this Act and with the procedure set forth by a separate law, having the task of providing public services under the law, operating as a body with legal personality, being formed in order to enforce minority rights, to protect and to represent the interest of minorities, and to independently conduct minority public affairs on a local, regional (county and Budapest) or national level."

7 Here we are thinking primarily of the divergent cultural traditions, customs and gender-role concepts of the various Roma subgroups in Hungary. However, an examination of these differences is beyond the scope of this study.

3 Analytical Framework

Although there is broad agreement that civil society is an essential element of a functioning democratic society, the conceptual relationship between civil society and the democratic public has so far received little scholarly attention.[8] This is partly due to the increasing influence of social-capital and communitarian theories pertaining to civil society. As a result, solidarity-based social organizations and the community norms established by them have become the focus of attention. As Lang points out, civil society is often defined as an isolated domain at the boundary of the private and public sphere, a "semi-privatised moral school for solidarity-based citizenship."[9] Thus, by virtue of its apolitical character, civil society sharply differentiates itself from affairs requiring interest mediation.[10] While Lang regards solidarity networks and the norms they generate as indispensable subjects and analytical units of examination, she cautions that placing them in focus provides only a superficial glimpse into the empirical reality of civil society, posing a number of analytical problems. From our perspective, the most important element of Lang's criticism is that the most influential paradigms pertaining to civil society "write" the public sphere "out" of the discourse. Consequently, they ignore the potentially critical function of civil society in providing social space for expressing the opinion of the "politically engaged public."[11] Civil society itself can display, construct and, in certain cases, represent public affairs. As a result, communitarian and social-capital theories do not provide an analytical tool for the examination of the modes and conditions of these mechanisms. According to Lang's convincing argument, the functions of civil initiatives that also carry the promise of social transformation become analysable only by "writing" the public sphere "back into" the discourse.

Below we describe the complex interplay between civil society and democratic political practice through the concept of the public sphere. The concept of the public sphere does not only serve to "write" the critical role of civil society "back into" the representation of public interests but also contributes to normative democratic theory. As we demonstrate, the public sphere is an essential concept for both critical social theory and democratic political practice.

8 Sabine Lang, *NGOs, Civil Society, and the Public Sphere* (New York: Cambridge University Press, 2013).

9 Ibid., 44.

10 Lang notes on several occasions that the concepts of civil society formed in these discourses seep down to the level of practice as the state and certain donors construct civil society and the interactions that take place with it.

11 Lang, *NGOs*, 43.

3.1 *Civil Society and the Public Sphere*

Habermas produced a seminal body of work[12] on the concept of the public sphere. The enormous amount of critical literature published in connection with his work serves to verify its landmark importance. His 1998 book *Between Facts and Norms* is the most relevant in terms of discussing civil society and the public sphere within the same analytical framework. Habermas places discourse at the centre of his democratic theory – discourse that resolves differences of opinion, makes collective action possible and provides institutions with a democratic character. Furthermore, Habermas endows civil society, as a body of diverse organizations assembled to build public discourse, with a strong normative quality:

> The core of civil society comprises a network of associations that institutionalises problem-solving discourses on questions of general interest inside the framework of organised public spheres.[13]

For Habermas, civil society organizes the opinions of private individuals regarding public affairs into a discourse. In other words, it creates a public arena for the expression of opinions regarding public affairs, the generation of debate and the formation of common viewpoints. In this "weak public," horizontal communication takes place among the rationalities, and opinion is formed through deliberative practice, but no decision is made.[14] At the same time, civil society also conducts vertical communication in the course of which opinions crystallizing within the "weak public" are channelled towards the institutions of political decision-making ("strong public"), thus influencing and questioning decisions made in these institutions. The precondition for this two-step mechanism is that civil society is open to everybody and the border between the two types of public is permeable. However, if we understand discourse generated in the public sphere as the harmonization and aggregation of interests based on which the representation of community interests can take place vis-à-vis decision-makers, then, in our opinion, numerous other conditions must

12 See Jürgen Habermas, *The Structural Transformation of the Public Sphere: An Inquiry into a Category of Bourgeois Society*, trans. Thomas Burger and Frederick Lawrence (Cambridge: Polity Press, 1989); Jürgen Habermas, "Further Reflections on the Public Sphere," in *Habermas and the Public Sphere*, ed. Craig Calhoun (Cambridge, MA: MIT Press, 1992), 421–461; Jürgen Habermas, *Between Facts and Norms: Contributions to a Discourse Theory of Law and Democracy* (Cambridge, MA: MIT Press, 1996).

13 Habermas, *Between Facts and Norms*, 367.

14 The division between weak and strong publics is taken from Fraser's criticism of Habermas's landmark work examining the structural changes to the public sphere.

also be met. Fraser,[15] based on a critical analysis of the premises of Habermas's ideal public sphere,[16] formulates an alternative model of the democratic public sphere, drawing attention to further normative dimensions.[17]

3.2 *The Normative Model of the Public Sphere*

According to Fraser, the question of open access extends beyond the issue of whether participation is formally and legally guaranteed. Within inclusive public spheres, a much greater degree of emphasis is placed on whether the autonomous members of society possess equal influence. Whereas in her earlier work Fraser regards equal participation in social life as a determinative factor in the democratic public sphere,[18] she later makes participatory parity the focus of her social justice theory, thus eliminating the dichotomy between recognition and distribution.[19] In both works, Fraser highlights that participatory parity is not possible in an arena built upon systemic relations of inequality; equal participation has both objective and intersubjective conditions. The requirement for equal distribution of goods ensures that the resources needed to participate in interactions as equal partners are available to all social groups. Equal participation also requires that institutionalized patterns of cultural value provide equal opportunities for all social groups to achieve social esteem.[20] Therefore, participatory parity can take place only through the elimination of social inequalities and the establishment of "the sort of rough equality that is inconsistent with systematically generated relations of dominance and subordination."[21] The concept of equal participation is closely related to the notion of public affairs. According to Fraser, participants are entrusted with the task of defining what they consider to be a public matter. As an example,

15 Fraser, "Rethinking the Public Sphere."

16 Habermas's early work on the public sphere has remained a point of departure for discourses regarding the public sphere. Originally written as his PhD dissertation in 1962, the English-language translation of this work produced a series of sharp debates, criticisms and revisions, including Habermas's own reflections. Perhaps it was precisely this unceasing interest that prompted Habermas to return to the theme in the work outlined briefly above.

17 In 2007, Fraser formulated a transnational model of the public sphere in which she voiced criticism of the methodological nationalism contained in her own previous work and in the works of Habermas. See Nancy Fraser, "Transnationalizing the Public Sphere: On the Legitimacy and Efficacy of Public Opinion in a Post-Westphalian World," *Theory, Culture and Society* 24, no. 4 (2007): 7–30.

18 Fraser, "Rethinking the Public Sphere."

19 Nancy Fraser, "Rethinking Recognition," *New Left Review* 3 (2000): 107–120.

20 Ibid.

21 Fraser, "Rethinking the Public Sphere," 121–126.

she cites domestic violence, which was regarded as a private affair until the appearance of the feminist subaltern counterpublic.

At the same time, Fraser expresses scepticism regarding the inclusive nature of public affairs. Public affairs framed under the umbrella of "us" frequently do not include the interests of subordinated groups in societies established on inequality. Therefore, she continues the conceptual correction of the public sphere with the critical analysis of the "public" and the "private." The boundary between these two social spheres is defined according to rhetorical labels and cultural classifications. In political discourses, the "public" represents a rhetorical "magic formula" with which certain narratives are delegitimized while others become overvalued. The "private" is defined in contrast to "the public," thus resulting in the transfer of some matters to the realm of private, personal-family life, while other interests are moved to the conceptual field of the public sphere, without any public debate. In the ideal case, the definition of public matters takes place within a discursive arena in which minorities have the opportunity to redefine issues that affect them as public affairs. The concept of subaltern counterpublics is also derived from participatory parity. In those stratified societies in which significant social inequalities prevail, deliberative processes taking place in the public sphere may adversely affect subordinate social groups. In the absence of their own venue for internal consultation, the needs, goals and strategies of these groups may dissolve in the "we" melting pot, which often operates to the advantage of dominant groups.[22] The subaltern counterpublics emerge precisely as a result of their exclusion from the dominant public sphere. They can be regarded as alternative, parallel public spheres in which the subordinate social groups create counter-narratives, which in turn provide them with an opportunity to formulate the interpretation of their own interests and needs. However, this is not an end in itself – the objective of the participants in counterpublics is to disseminate their narratives in ever-widening discursive arenas. The emancipatory potential of counterpublics, the counterbalancing of participatory privileges held by dominant groups, can be perceived in the dialectical relationship between these two functions.[23]

It should be noted here that Habermas has to some degree incorporated this element of Fraser's criticism into his theory of the public sphere. While in his early work Habermas speaks of one, dominant public sphere, in *Between Facts and Norms* he discusses public spheres and attributes to them some of the functions described by Fraser. The difference in Fraser's interpretation is that subaltern counterpublics not only generate discourse but also construct

22 Ibid.

23 Ibid.

the collective identity of participants through participatory parity and create a platform for expressing this identity. However, unequal power relations are also present in the public sphere at the discursive level: "These institutions may be understood as culturally specific rhetorical lenses that filter and alter the utterances they frame; they can accommodate some expressive modes and not others."[24] Nevertheless, with the assertion of the principle of equal participation, the participants are able to speak with their own "voice," thereby "simultaneously constructing and expressing one's cultural identity through idiom and style."[25]

Using the normative paradigm of the public sphere, we have demonstrated how civil society can contribute to deepening democracy. Interpreted as an arena for constructing public affairs, civil society creates a political agency and transmits opinions and interests generated in counterpublics towards wider publics and political decision-making institutions. It initiates political discourse, influences decisions, places issues on the agenda and demands accountability. For Habermas, democratic processes are formed in the interaction between the two public spheres. Since civil society creates the public sphere that provides space for the diversity of opinions and interests and has the potential to assert these in the process of institutional decision-making, political decisions are, in fact, born in the discourses of citizens or, at the very least, made by taking these discourses into account. According to Habermas, the preconditions for this process are, on the one hand, that the public sphere is open to everyone and, on the other, that the various public spheres are interconnected. In other words, political decision-making institutions must give space to particular community interests and opinions articulated in the civil public spheres and integrate them into political discourse and decision-making. Fraser's public sphere model, though including other normative dimensions such as participation parity, reveals an even greater degree of political potential inherent in civil society initiatives and their prerequisites, serving as benchmarks of democracy. In the following section of this study, Fraser's normative model will serve as an orientation point for the analysis of the empirical data.

4 Analysis

Our study – as a descriptive-analytical case study – seeks mostly to provide an interpretive reading of the focus-group discussions rather than to apprehend

24 Ibid., 126.

25 Ibid.

the genealogy and operation of the initiatives. We present what was said during the conversations while taking into account our specific research interests and the limitations imposed by the length of our article. We believe, first of all, that it is important to outline the social and economic environment in which these initiatives are embedded. Subsequently, we present our analysis in five categories. Finally, in the light of our analysis, we also attempt to conduct a critical assessment of the quality of democracy at the local level. We highlight two aspects of this assessment: pluralism in advocacy and participatory parity in discursive processes. It is worth emphasizing that our analysis is paradigm-dependent, as Fraser's approach to critical theory guides our questions and interpretations.

4.1 *The Social and Economic Environment of the Roma Women's Initiatives*

The concept of social exclusion is seen as covering a wide range of social and economic problems.[26] It can be associated with insufficient income, being deprived of social connections and many other determining factors of social existence. At least eight of the Roma women's initiatives possess social and economic characteristics indicating that their communities live in social exclusion and poverty; indeed, at least three of them are among the most disadvantaged communities in Hungary.[27] These communities are in need of urgent socio-economic and infrastructural development and are heavily affected by unemployment. The slum-like environment and segregation significantly impede their access to basic public services. Although a quarter of our interlocutors no longer live in slum-like settlements, it can generally be said that their roots lead back to this milieu. Moreover, of the eleven Roma women's initiatives, ten are implemented in slum-like, segregated settlements. The largest of these settlements has an estimated population of 3,000,[28] and the smallest is

26 Amartya Sen, "Társadalmi kirekesztés: Fogalom, alkalmazás és vizsgálat" [Social exclusion: concept, application, and scrutiny], trans. Judit Kozma, *Esély* 6 (2003): 3–22.

27 See Government Decree No. 105/2015. (IV.23) on the classification of the favoured areas and the conditions for classification in relation to Act XXI of 1996 on Regional Development and Regional Planning.

28 We define a segregated settlement as a section of a settlement consisting of at least one block of houses – on property lying between four streets or public spaces – in which the segregation index, i.e. the proportion of inhabitants who are characterized as low status (those who belong to the economically active population, have no more than an eighth-grade education and have no regular income from work), is above 50 per cent. In the case of those communities that participated in the Regional Operational Programme's capacity increasing or the urban rehabilitation programme and prepared an Integrated Municipal Development Strategy, the segregated residential area must be defined based on the

located in a village that has no transit traffic,[29] electricity or water and where healthcare services are available only once a week and official administrative services twice a week. Public transport is also very limited, as is access to employment. In the case of interlocutors coming from smaller settlements, the public employment programme is the source of almost all income-generating work.[30] With regard to the qualifications of our interlocutors, some have completed secondary or post-secondary education, and at least one staff member of each NGO-based initiative has attained or is pursuing a post-secondary degree (e.g. as a social worker, communications professional or community organizer). With the exception of one who operates a business, all the interlocutors have a low income; some have even joined an initiative producing products and crops in order to supplement their income.

4.2 *The Main Pillars of Participation in the Initiatives*

Based on the narratives of our interlocutors, their involvement in the initiatives rests upon three pillars. On the one hand, (i) a personal *inner drive* manifests itself. This is continually kept in motion by prior knowledge, learning and personal experiences that drive personal aspirations towards the struggle for social equality.

On the other hand, a group-level dynamic also emerges, generated by (ii) the *common objectives* of Roma women and their communities. According to our interlocutors, the issues affecting the Roma community are not adequately addressed by local institutions, including the Roma minority self-governments. In fact, it is precisely this – their exclusion from the dominant public sphere – that gives rise to subaltern counterpublics.

---

segregation map prepared by the Central Statistics Office. See, for example, Integrated Community Development Strategy or Local Equal Opportunity Programme in "Road to Work Programme: Glossary of Terms" [in Hungarian], Employment and Social Affairs Office, March 26, 2009, http://nfsz.munka.hu/engine.aspx?page=full_utamunkahoz (accessed June 16, 2017).

29 Only one single road leads to the settlement, and the settlement can only be approached from one direction.

30 "Public employment is a special form of employment relationship, a supported form of 'transitional employment' that aims to enable public employees to successfully enter or return to the primary labour market. Public employment provides temporary job opportunities for those whose independent search for employment proves to be ineffective for a long period of time." See "Information on the Public Work Scheme" [in Hungarian], Hungarian Ministry of the Interior, January 2016, available at http://kozfoglalkoztatas.kormany.hu/download/f/13/41000/T%C3%A1j%C3%A9koztat%C3%B3%20a%20k%C3%B6zfoglalkoztat%C3%A1s%20rendszer%C3%A9r%C5%91l_2016-01-07.pdf (accessed June 16, 2017). For more details, see Act CVI of 2011 on the Modification of the Act on Public Employment, the Act Related to Public Employment and Other Acts.

> The family support service is the institution that deals with disadvantaged people, children and families to a certain degree, but not the same way we do. (Mediator)
>
> The role of the minority self-government could also be mentioned. But I should say that they – I don't know why – don't do anything here. The fact that the mayor's office organizes an event and a representative of the Roma minority self-government shows up there, in my opinion, does not help the Roma. There are no visible results; in fact, I believe that the Roma minority self-government in this place is useless because it doesn't represent the interests of the Roma, but behaves like a puppet. It dances to the tune of those manipulating it from above. (Association president)

It is important to note, in parentheses, that our interlocutors continue to hold these opinions, in spite of the fact that the amendment of Act LXXVII of 1993 on the Rights of National and Ethnic Minorities in 2005 provided the Roma minority self-governments with the power to independently administer minority public affairs. This allows them to implement individual and collective rights enshrined in the law, voice the interests of their community members and maintain their cultural autonomy – in particular with regard to preserving, safeguarding and enriching their mother tongue.[31] Furthermore, this administrative power includes performing tasks related to guaranteeing their representation in state institutions and minority self-governments and creating the organizational, personal and financial conditions necessary for achieving these aims.[32] The opinion of our interlocutors described above is consistent with the conclusions of social science researchers. For instance, Rátkai's analysis of forty-six minority self-governments concluded that they play an insignificant role and that, in contrast to existing civil society organizations, they do not possess genuine legitimacy. Indeed, these organizations would be able to perform the tasks of the minority self-governments much more effectively.[33] In addition, Koulish has examined the expectations of Roma communities with regard to Roma minority self-governments by surveying 500 individuals using questionnaires. His most significant findings included that, although Roma residents would like to participate in public life, their inadequate skills hamper the successful representation of their interests. In addition, half of

31 See Section 1 of the explanatory provisions of Article 6/A of Act LXXVII of 1993 on the Rights of National and Ethnic Minorities (amended in 2005).

32 Ibid., Section 2.

33 Árpád Rátkai, "A kisebbségi önkormányzatok legitimációhiánya" [Minority self-governments' lack of legitimacy], *Regio* 3 (2000): 113–132.

the respondents were dissatisfied with the work of the Roma minority self-governments, although 90 per cent of them would oppose their elimination.[34] A majority of respondents thus regarded the advocacy of Roma interests as important. However, rather than focusing on cultural activities, they regarded action to tackle discrimination, the implementation of social rights and employment-related training as priorities.

The third pillar common to all initiatives was (iii) an *external individual or organization providing motivation and support*, thus guaranteeing space for these personal and group aspirations.

These opportunity structures open the door that leads from the private sector to the public realm. Representing their initiatives, Roma women act as participants in the public sphere. Local initiatives assume two main forms: informal or formal. In informal groups, Roma women establish community action groups due to an external impetus, while the non-governmental organizational form provides a formal operational framework for grassroots initiatives. In addition, a third alternative form has also emerged in which a local pro-Roma non-government organization directly assists and manages the local women's group. While the three types of initiative display some (albeit minimal) disparities in the representation of interests, the mode of selection of issues for representation is identical in all three cases.

4.3 *Roma Women's Initiatives as Subaltern Counterpublics*

Practice shows that the initiatives always reflect the needs of communities by involving them in the selection of issues. The dusty streets of a Roma settlement, a crowded bus stop in the morning, a shabby room that is transformed into a teahouse on Wednesdays, roundtable discussions organized at regular intervals, a room-sized office and even social-media networks all serve as fora for articulating and hearing the opinions, needs and interests of the community. However, the initiatives do not merely collect individual opinions but also provide diverse arenas for discussing them. Each Roma women's initiative creates its own public sphere, a local arena for discourse operating in parallel to the mainstream public sphere, where community members can formulate their needs and their (counter-)opinions. These initiatives thus create subaltern counterpublics – in the Fraserian sense – for marginalized Roma communities living in rural settlements. In addition to consolidating opinions, the initiatives have raised a series of concrete issues, including the need for house

34 Robert E. Koulish, "What Roma Want Survey: Roma Civic Attitudes in Hungary," in *Partners Studies*, vol. 4 (Budapest: Cicero Press, 2001), also available at http://miris.eurac.edu/mugs2/do/blob.html?type=html&serial=1123850668497.

renovations, mother and baby clubs, sex education for young girls, the alleviation of food shortages, community dances, measures to tackle unemployment, support for young talent, the provision of toys for young children, the establishment of a salt room, the organization of Roma cultural events and the maintenance of local kindergartens. The initiatives address issues that emerge from the routine of everyday life, endowing them with normative elements and presenting them as community matters that subsequently determine their actions and activities. The community therefore participates in these initiatives on two levels: in identifying the issues and by taking part in the actions that are subsequently taken. They create an arena for the community where personal reflections of individual members on social issues gain expression in their own language. The linguistic norms that mainstream public space requires are not valid in these counterpublics. There is not even an implicit obligation to change register, and members of the community can therefore speak in their own voice and act as equal partners in the interaction.

> If an individual providing support comes from the target group, she understands their language, not like the authorities. You don't need to explain yourself. … In this way, confidence is quickly built. (Community action group member)

In these subaltern counterpublics, opinions are realigned in the course of discourse, providing space for the development of common narratives, identities and capacity for collective action. The presence of Roma women plays a vital role in this process.

4.4 *Female Participation as a Springboard*

While emphasizing gender perspectives in their diverse activities and, for the most part, defining themselves explicitly as Roma women's initiatives, the initiatives do not exclusively embrace Roma women's issues. Through activities related to the interests of the female members of the community, such as making handicrafts, establishing a tea house or running a mother and baby club, they create community experiences and discourses. In these emerging micropublics, issues that participants consider important, such as raising children, Roma culture and gender roles, come to the fore. According to our interlocutors, the gender roles of Roma women and men are embedded in the complex context of Roma culture, and any transformation of these roles requires a change in the attitudes of both women and men. Thus, when talking about this issue, they also aim to address men.

> We do not need to live this way. This isn't written anywhere. Women should want and know how to be successful. Her husband should support her, and not put her next to the cooking pot. ... A change is needed. For this to happen, the husband must regard his wife as an equal. ... We must take our husbands into the twenty-first century. (Mediator)

In addition to holding community-organizing programmes for Roma women and implementing activities to raise awareness of the traditional notion of gender roles in Roma culture, all the initiatives, without exception, seek to reach out to children, young people and, indeed, the entire community. They believe that Roma women are key to the inclusion of the wider community.

> Roma women, in this way, play a leading role to some degree also within the family. ... They are the decision-makers on this issue; they can soften up their husbands and lead the family in the right direction. So then, if a Roma woman sees that a Roma community or an organization can be to their benefit and provide them with a service that their family can partake in and from which they can also benefit – and I'm not thinking of financial profit here – ... and can also gain experience, then she will take her family members and the community along with her as well. ... She is the driving force. (Association president)

This reveals the unique nature of women's participation in public affairs, which – according to our interlocutors – underscores the importance of the participation of Roma women in such affairs.

> Within the Roma community, the husband is the breadwinner, while the woman is primarily a community builder. And if a man, a husband, engages in public affairs, he prioritizes the generation of resources regardless of what kind of public affairs we're talking about. But if a Roma woman engages in public affairs, she doesn't focus on resources. She is concerned with how she can rise up, how she can live up to expectations and how she can improve not only her own situation but that of her environment as well. (Association president)

Based on the statements of our interlocutors, it is evident that the leadership of Roma women, as well as their participation in public affairs, promotes not only their own emancipation but also that of their communities. When they have the opportunity to play a role in society, Roma women perform a community-building function. These initiatives are seen by our interlocutors as opportunity structures whose resources can be utilized in order to benefit both the Roma women leading them and their communities.

> I am really happy that I can work for the foundation since it represents … and gives us power to do something that I always wanted to do. … We identify the problems that in fact affect underprivileged people and seek solutions to these issues. [We are concerned with] how we can change these peoples' lives and their circumstances. … We want this to work after a while without our involvement. It would be important if they would be self-sufficient in maintaining this. … Soon it will be necessary for them to break away from us. (Mediator)

By providing the community with decision-making rights, capacity and responsibility, the initiatives are the engine of the emancipation not only of the Roma women leading the initiatives and their female companions but also of the local community. At the same time, we cannot ignore the obstacles faced by Roma women as they take on community and social roles.

4.5 *Factors Inhibiting Participation*

Our interlocutors describe their transition from the margins of local society to the centre of public life as a struggle-filled process. The expectations of their families, the traditions of Roma communities and existing power relations collectively hinder their active presence in public life. These are precisely the factors that cement the disadvantages arising from their status as women and their ethnic origin, preventing their breakout from social invisibility.

Their family members barely notice any changes in their everyday lives. Despite their occasional absence, frequent telephone calls and ever-lengthening work week, they continue, without exception, to fulfil their obligations as homemakers and mothers with absolute devotion. The attitudes their work demands hardly ever enter the intimate family milieu, where they continue to play traditional gender roles.

> Perhaps it is difficult that I cannot just go ahead and forget them. To perform at 100 [per cent at home] and to perform at 100 [per cent] in my work as well is really hard. Perhaps it is somewhat a limitation. (Association employee)
>
> The thing that we must fight with the most is the family background. It's already become somewhat easier for me because the kids are now

> older. But to be able to come here now, I already had to cook at seven o'clock … because we live in a traditional family. My husband is Roma, and, well, there is an expectation that he won't do the cooking, for example. (Association president)

One of our interlocutors described the contradiction between her professional role and her role as a wife in very stark terms.

> When I step out of the house, I must assume a leadership role, and, if necessary, I negotiate and conduct business with men. I am equal with them. Then when I get home, I must immediately put on the style of a Roma housewife. My husband is right whether I like it or not, even if I don't agree with him. And when we go out and we are in the company of friends, then we don't sit among the men. And if somebody says something, if a man starts to say something that I don't agree with, I am not sure that I can express my own opinion, because, if I do, my husband looks at me like, "hey c'mon." So I need to behave in a completely different way – like a Roma wife. I serve all the men while they talk about trivial things, sometimes even nonsense things, and I have to listen to all of it. And I have no say in it. But if it isn't about having fun, but about my work, I can assert my own opinion. So this is why I feel schizophrenic. Do you understand what I mean? (Association president)

They must prove themselves to their community as Roma women and as supporters. Their community leadership clashes sharply with conventional views on the "place" of women, which they can challenge only by demonstrating their aptitude. This requires them to acquire a new skill, namely the ability to speak the language of men.

> They don't accept simply what I would like to do, just like that. … I must explain it to them in an understandable way, in their language. I must translate it. I had to learn how to speak their language. (Association president)

The disillusionment of the disadvantaged Roma communities with self-appointed candidates who want to help them is not unjustified. As a result of their negative experiences, some initially regarded the Roma women's initiatives as a minority affair. The trust and support of the community had to be won through long, patient work and a permanent presence.

> The Roma have started to get used to us. At the beginning, they didn't accept us and attacked us, asking how much I was getting paid for it and claiming that I was just doing it for the money and wanted to steal money. But they now know that this isn't the case and that we're there to do everything we can to promote our common cause. We focus not on issues affecting just one or two families but on changing the situation of the Roma in general, working on something that is good for the community. (Community activist)

Their efforts to navigate the local balance of power are the most demanding. According to our interlocutors, the Roma minority self-governments – which are largely male-dominated political institutions – are seen, particularly in smaller communities, as the custodians of local Roma affairs, and they are not inclined to let Roma women enter the political arena. In many cases, Roma minority self-governments seek to exercise control over the women's grassroots initiatives, while in other cases they work against them as rivals or regard them with suspicion. Only a small number of initiatives reported that they enjoyed largely neutral relationships with the Roma minority self-governments. Furthermore, not a single case of genuine cooperation was reported to have emerged between the initiatives and Roma minority self-governments.

> I try to be open-minded, but I am not going to visit them again. They see me as a rival and they make sure that I feel how they regard me. I don't know; they probably think that I will run for office when the elections take place. But I don't have the slightest intention of doing that. (Association president)

All the initiatives, without exception, currently maintain good relations with local public support offices and educational institutions, although at the time of their establishment they faced numerous difficulties. Due to their ethnic background, gender and lack of professional experience, they were initially pushed to the margins of the municipal institutional system.

> Nobody wanted to talk to us at the local level. Perhaps this was because we were Roma and women. I am not sure – I didn't ask. We had to prove ourselves ... because we are Roma, because we are women, because the leader of the association is a woman. They considered us as inexperienced and uneducated. (Association president)

Currently, the main difficulty faced by the initiatives is to define their role in the institutional matrix while avoiding the establishment of parallel structures.

> One must be careful and pay attention to the fact that we serve as a link between the institutions and disadvantaged people. When there is cooperation with the school, should it be my task, my duty to go out and visit the families? I don't want the institution to sit back and relax and think that our Roma organization will take care of the problems. (Association president)

Two clearly defined patterns emerge regarding the relationship between the initiatives and local decision-makers. On the one hand, as a result of the commitments of municipal governments, some of the initiatives engage in regular communication and interest mediation with the leadership of the municipality.

> The mayor, hats off to him, stands behind us and provides us with the greatest motivation. ... The fact that he supports us shows there is a power behind us and that we can go to him if we need help of any kind, any little thing, and he is there, he stands with us and is a partner. (Mediator)

However, in the majority of cases, there is neither support nor hindrance, but rather a complete lack of contact with the municipal leadership.

> I think that it is really important what kind of cooperation we have with the town leadership. It's really good to hear that you have such a good relationship with the mayor. We have not yet managed to get into the mayor's office. Therefore, [we can] not really [cooperate] with the town leadership. (Association president)

However, balancing between the expectations of different roles in different spheres poses obstacles to the personal and professional achievements of the initiatives. Many describe their activity in terms of serving as a mediator between the minority and the majority, the oppressed and the powerful, the Roma subaltern counterpublic and the wider, non-Roma public sphere.

> We have a responsibility in how we form a bridge between our own people and the majority. (Mediator)

This intermediary role also implies that the initiatives engage in vertical communication – or at least wish to engage in such communication – with a view to bringing community interests to the wider discursive arena. At the same time, their relationship with local decision-makers also has a decisive impact on the nature and effectiveness of their advocacy.

4.6 *Representation of Community Interests*

The initiatives employ two types of advocacy depending on what kind of institutional relationship they have established with municipal leaders. Initiatives that do not receive support from the local leadership channel the interests of the community into their own advocacy activities. As a subaltern counterpublic, they identify local issues and needs through discourse with the local Roma community and offer solutions through focused actions to the best of their abilities. The articulation of interests is thus realized at the community level, but these interests are not channelled into the decision-making process. The interest representation process thus routinely comes to a halt at the intersection of local power relations. The initiatives conduct public advocacy, the primary goal of which is to initiate discourse and construct the public sphere, "actively stimulating citizen voice and engagement in this process."[35]

On the other hand, the two initiatives that have succeeded in establishing good relations with local decision-making institutions can take certain community interests to arenas outside their community, namely to the representatives of relevant local institutions or local decision-makers or, within the framework of joint meetings, to both of them. As a result of institutional advocacy,[36] a portion of community aspirations is absorbed into local decision-making, subsequently altering the life of the communities in the form of policy measures.

> The mayor has supported us from the beginning; he is glad to have us around. … And we have already had many roundtable discussions with institutional leaders and factory directors, and they expect us to help them in everything. I have to go a lot – you really have to go a lot … to the settlement. We did signature collections, and we collected petitions. I visited the job centre to see what kind of training and employment possibilities they have. We sat down with officials from factories and multinational companies. We managed to have them employ Roma. And they [Roma] now also participate in training courses. And I am really happy about this because I feel that if we were not an organization we would not have been able to achieve this. I want us, Roma, not to be oppressed and want everybody to succeed in life. (Community activist)

At the same time, the principle of participatory parity does not prevail in the mechanisms of cooperation and dialogue with local decision-makers.

35 Lang, *NGOs*, 23.
36 Ibid.

> For us, for example, the first major success was that the officials sat down with us to talk, as before we just stood there queuing [in front of the office] and didn't even dare to say anything. We were just happy if we could get in and ask, for example, for some kinds of benefits. We also witnessed how they behave with other Roma. So, for us this was a real achievement. (Community activist)

The women leading the initiatives articulate the interests of the community, but they do not speak with their own "voice." Contrary to subaltern counterpublics, in the course of negotiating with decision-makers an obligation to change registers is prescribed. However, the parties do not have an equal level of standard language norms and argumentation techniques at their disposal. Since political participation materializes in the consultative processes through debate and negotiation, disparities at the discursive level jeopardize the effectiveness of the participation of Roma women.

Access to public discourse and the nature of the dialogue with decision-makers offer a glimpse not only into the mechanisms of participation in local public affairs available to the initiatives but also into the nature of local democratic governance.

4.7 *Local Democratic Governance in the Light of the Initiatives*

In this section of our study, we return to the theoretical framework to compare the relationships revealed in the preceding analysis with the normative prescriptions of the Fraserian model. As we have demonstrated, in the vast majority of cases the boundary between subaltern counterpublics and the dominant public sphere is not porous; they function as parallel structures and closed spheres. Roma communities formulate their interests horizontally, but they cannot represent them vertically. In other words, minority interests are articulated within the community, but the communication channels that would make dialogue with decision-makers possible have not been established. In our view, the role of Roma minority self-governments is not negligible in this process. As a result of their place in the local public sphere, they emerge as the almost exclusive consultative partners regarding Roma-related affairs. At the same time, none of our interlocutors maintain partnerships with the Roma minority self-governments, partly as a result of the latter's desire to retain their authority and position and partly because our interlocutors believe that the representation of community interests by the Roma minority self-governments is inadequate or non-existent. At a certain level, the Roma women's initiatives also emerge as counterpublics opposed to the local Roma minority self-governments. However, while channels of communication have been established between Roma minority self-governments and local decision-makers, none of these decision-makers engage in a genuine dialogue with the Roma women's initiatives. Therefore, decision-makers are not aware of the unequal power relations and conflicting interests within the Roma community.

In other words, instead of plural public spheres, a dominant, monolithic actor has the opportunity to exercise influence over measures affecting the Roma communities in these municipalities. In other cases, Roma women leaders are able transmit the voice of the community to decision-makers, but they are not able to amplify this voice as equal partners. As a result of the requirement to change registers, standard language norms and techniques of persuasion are prescribed, giving rise to inequalities at the discursive level. Political participation, however, materializes through discourse in consultative mechanisms. The question therefore arises how effective their participation can be if the forum that provides space for their participation not only displays but also reproduces the inequalities they voice their objections to. In Fraser's theory of democracy, the intersubjective condition of participatory parity prescribes the normative requirement that institutionalized cultural value patterns provide equal opportunities for all social groups to attain social esteem. If the opportunity to participate is provided but the parties do not participate in their interactions as equal partners, the principle of parity is undermined and democratic participation does not take place.

To summarize, some of the communities represented by the Roma women's initiatives cannot successfully redefine issues affecting them as local public affairs because they cannot even enter the discursive arena that would provide them with an opportunity to do so. The community's participation in interest mediation and consultation with local decision-makers is not only hindered by a lack of necessary resources but also by the fact that the channels of communication for effective dialogue have not been established. In the connection, we have drawn attention to the internal power relations of minority communities and to the fact that participation in consultation mechanisms is limited to those minority representatives who are in a dominant position. In accordance with the principle of pluralism, representation of the interests formulated in the community's counterpublics should also be ensured. On the other hand, we have also highlighted the importance of equal participation at the discursive level. Unequal power relations are also constructed at the discursive level, and communicative interactions reproduce the inequalities that prevail within society. Social inequalities are unavoidably present in acts of speech, and advocates cannot effectively voice the interests of their communities if these inequalities are not counterbalanced.

5 Conclusion

Our study focuses on initiatives launched by Roma women, mothers and wives who, despite facing many obstacles, were able – through their charismatic leadership skills, persistence and commitment – to involve community members in their initiatives and thereby increase their participation in local public affairs. The concept of the public sphere and the normative theory of democracy serve as the guiding principles of our analysis. Although we have interpreted the discourses of our interlocutors by relying on interpretative sociology, the normative dimension of the Fraserian democracy principle serves as a theoretical benchmark for our study.

We have described the initiatives led by Roma women as arenas for internal consultation for Roma communities. They constitute subaltern counterpublics in which the community is able to articulate its needs and interests. Through the discourse that takes place within these initiatives, personal opinions are formulated as common positions and personal needs as public affairs. As common narratives are formulated, the collective identity of each community emerges, and their common understanding is also constructed by the consciousness of the "we." In deliberations based on the particular cultural and linguistic patterns of the community, members of the community participate as equal partners in the discourse. By sharing leadership, the initiatives become workshops for community participation as well as for the internal emancipation of the community. However, despite their efforts, they have only had modest success in transmitting community interests to wider public spheres.

While the Roma women's initiatives provide space for diversity of opinion and equal participation within their communities, they are pounding on closed doors at the gateway to the dominant public sphere. Political indifference, like a daunting wall, blocks the representation of their interests. The wider public sphere and the social elite are not aware of subaltern counterpublics, and the lack of communication channels prevents them from participating in the formulation of local policy measures via consultative frameworks. Although there are Roma women who manage to cross the wide gap separating the subordinated Roma communities and the local power elite, the relationships of dominance and inequality are reproduced through discursive means in the consultative processes. The Roma women's initiatives nevertheless continue to implement their activities with faith, because they wish to provide marginalized Roma communities with a public arena in which to voice their diverse opinions and guarantee their participatory parity – a role that local institutions should fulfil in a state based on democratic principles.

CHAPTER 4

From Victimhood to Citizenship: The Path of Roma Integration, András Bíró, Nicolae Gheorghe, Martin Kovats et al.

Edited by Will Guy

A Review Essay by Angéla Kóczé

This book is an unusual intellectual project that is meant to provoke discussion and critical reflection on the state of Roma identity politics in Europe. As its subtitle indicates, the publication intends to serve as a foundation for an open-ended and perhaps permanent debate on the future of Roma integration among various Roma and pro-Roma activists, scholars and policy-makers. The book begins with three essays, written by András Bíró, Nicolae Gheorghe and Martin Kovats, that provide the conceptual basis for the next section, which summarizes several workshop debates. It ends with a final reflection by Željko Jovanović. The main contributors in this book are Roma and pro-Roma men of distinguished, influential and privileged position. There is a very limited contribution by women in the debate, reflecting the contemporary asymmetrical gender dynamics of Roma identity politics. This book represents a collective effort to find and articulate common ground. It is also an important historical resource on contemporary engagements with Roma identity politics and contains critical reflections on a wide range of issues that shape Roma integration.

The first provocative essay is written by András Bíró, who seeks to highlight some aspects of Roma experience that "might be the stumbling blocks on their side in the integration process" (p. 12). He claims that explaining the situation of Roma solely based on the discrimination and prejudice of the majority population creates a one-sided narrative that overlooks the "Roma's own weaknesses" (p. 12). Bíró argues that ignoring those weaknesses has led to the perpetuation of their victimhood. He suggests that exposing the limitations of the Roma movement with regard to reflection on sensitive issues might change the discourse of victimization. However, confronting internal weaknesses should not blind us from recognizing the degree of external power and oppression that has been imposed on the Roma movement.

Bíró bravely focuses on issues that are rarely discussed in the debate on Roma integration. These issues include, inter alia, the connection between the

 | DOI:10.1163/9789004386426_005

Roma and nomadism, their connection to territoriality, and their exploitative relationship with the "actual as well as the symbolic *gadjo*" (non-Roma). These issues have never been a focus of the Roma movement or political activism. Instead, these topics were conceptualized or dealt with in cultural discourses that describe Roma as an "exotic Other" and as being different from the white European population.

Bíró acknowledges at the very beginning that his conclusions are simple hypotheses based on his own "empirical experience with no claim of being objective or scientific" (p. 11). However, he fails to reflect critically on his position of power as a pro-Roma activist, donor and former influential decision-maker. Bíró ambitiously aims to provide some narratives, based on his experience, about the mentality of Roma, revealing some collective psychological characteristics, such as behavioural and moral group norms. He is perhaps aware of the risky and inevitably essentializing nature of this undertaking, but in order to provoke a debate he nevertheless decides to talk about issues that are usually raised only in racist or racialized discourses about Roma. He deliberately aims to generate a discussion and candidly reflects on various "touchy" or "risky" issues – "taboos" in the words of Nicolae Gheorge – that are usually used by various groups and individuals to justify the subordination of Roma or racism against them. In this first chapter, Bíró covers a wide range of controversial issues and topics to explain the complexities and challenges of Roma integration from his specific, privileged point of view.

Instead of discussing all the topics covered by the author, I will focus on one of the most controversial issues he raises, namely the "code of conduct" among Roma, also known as *shmekeria*. This concept, which originates from a Turkish word meaning cunning, deceit or cheating, is used to refer to the behaviour of Roma in relation to the *gadjo* (non-Roma). The concept becomes a recurring theme in the book and is raised by Gheorghe as well as by other contributors to the debate. Bíró explains persuasively: "The relationship to the actual as well as to the symbolic *gadjo*, who represented the fundamental source of income but simultaneously the barrier impeding free access to needed goods, led Roma to adopt a submissive demeanour where cajolery and deception became a technique of survival" (p. 18). So, *shmekeria*, as Bíró describes it, is a set of specific rules deployed by Roma to gain advantages. Gheorge presents the same argument, although in a different way, in the second chapter. He relies on the same underlying concept but suggests that the Roma, who are caught up in an ambiguous hierarchical power relationship, need to cheat and exploit the *gadjo* in order to succeed. While Bíró conceptualizes *shmekeria* as a kind of innate and universal characteristic of Roma, Gheorghe at least attempts to underline its multiple applications as a survival technique by other subordinated groups. Moreover, Gheorghe emphasizes the importance of contextualization and claims that "*shmekeria* is an ambiguous term as it can be understood and used in very different ways. Its actual meaning only becomes apparent from the context" (p. 59). Contrary to Bíró, Gheorghe elevates *shmekeria* from a stereotypical concept to a concept of social capital. He claims that "Roma leaders, activists and representatives often utilize, justify and eventually legitimize the formal and informal strategies [*shmekeria*] for economic success by explaining this as a 'culture' of the Roma" (p. 59).

In both cases, the logic of argumentation supports some hidden premises based on recycled stereotypes of Roma taking advantage of and exploiting the *gadjo*'s resources. Both authors explain *shmekeria* as an inner cultural characteristic of Roma without connecting it to the larger social systems of power that create the conditions and possibilities for a particular set of habits and rules. In this way, they cannot analyze the process of racialization and the historically situated racial formation through which certain characteristics become culturally coded and connected to racialized individuals. Paul Gilroy draws attention to the danger of "Otherness" when racialized "identity refers to an indelible mark or code which is conceived as somehow written into the bodies of its carriers."[1] In the text, *shmekeria* becomes connected to the bodies of those who are represented and perceived as racialized Roma. Although I understand the intention of the authors to focus on the internal mechanisms that impede the integration of Roma, they seem to lose sight of the external social, political and economic forces that create symbolic and material conditions. Instead of explaining asymmetrical power relations and social conditions that create certain types of behaviours and norms in oppressed groups, Bíró and Gheorghe treat these characteristics as culturally fixed inner features.

Besides controversial "cultural" issues, such as *shmekeria,* Bíró also discusses some "models of enforced integration" and reflects on the empowerment of Roma by the Autonómia Foundation, which he established in 1990. In the final part of the essay, he raises several questions about how the Roma could achieve equal status and how they could create an alternative future on their own. The issues and questions discussed by Bíró suggest that Roma need to take responsibility for their own situation. Even his last sentence reflects this overall message: "It is up to them, to their movements and leaders, to determine what price they are ready to pay for fully-fledged integration" (p. 40).

Nicolae Gheorghe, an activist-scholar and one of the idols of the Roma movement, is the first respondent to Bíró's essay. This is Gheorghe's last publication,

1 Paul Gilroy, "Diaspora and the Detours of Identity," in *Identity and Difference,* ed. Kathryn Woodward (London: Sage Publications, 1997), 308.

written in collaboration with Gergő Pulay, and it can be read as a political manifesto. He emphasizes that the essay is based on discussions with Bíró as well as his own reflections on several disturbing events in Europe that "complicated the relationship between particular Roma groups and majority populations and also their home states or where they migrated" (p. 42). Similarly to Bíró, Gheorghe pulls together various issues and connects them to his own personal experience as a Roma activist. At the outset, he asserts that "recent political developments – particularly the re-emergence of nationalism and populism after EU-accession – suggest that the liberal, human rights-oriented approach to Roma integration failed to achieve many of its expected goals" (p. 44). In order to find a solution and/or design a new path for Roma integration, he intends to construct a new language to talk about the problems and challenges. Gheorghe acknowledges that "the language we are searching for should not arouse hostility towards Roma but instead should provide alternative frames" (p. 44). Gheorghe agrees with Bíró that, in order to change the discourse on Roma, we need to discuss controversial issues, such as "Gypsy crime" or the "genetic force of Gypsy nomadism." However, their invitation to discuss such issues might result in the reappearance of the racialized discourse, which could in turn lead to the validation and legitimization of racism and discrimination against Roma. At the beginning of his essay, even Gheorghe admits the potential pitfalls of this exercise:

> It is hard to take this step because going beyond the limits of political correctness requires a considerable effort. It might be argued that this endeavor is doomed to failure from the start, since no alternatives yet exists to already established discursive frames. Renouncing certain basic elements of the human rights approach to Roma appears dangerous since it could lead to unpredictable consequences both for how we speak and in practice. The natural assumption is that this discursive change opens Pandora's Box, leaving Roma defenceless against racism where the victim is blamed or subsequent pogroms legitimized. (p. 44)

However, this recognition does not stop him from following the same line as Bíró and exposing the Roma's responsibility for hindering their own integration. Although Gheorghe talks about "shared responsibility," his focus still remains on the Roma. He explains:

> What I mean by responsibility is related to the way we think about common concerns. For instance, I am personally not a police officer nor a member of an agency opposing the trafficking of children. Nevertheless,

> I consider it my task to examine the process leading children to beg at Italian churches or railway stations and – with supporters – to raise this an important issue for public debate by creating a language based on solidarity and desire for change. (pp. 45–46)

Gheorghe confronts a broad range of topics, from the fate of trafficked children to predatory lending practices. He offers a provocative view without linking the issue to the restructuring of the global economic order, which facilitates human trafficking and targets vulnerable women and children with the assistance of their own communities.[2] Research suggests that it is not only the darker sides of economic globalization that are responsible for human trafficking but also that racialized people are more likely to become commercialized and exploited for a variety of different reasons as part of the globalization process.[3]

It is important to emphasize that Gheorghe's chapter is not only a contemplation on various issues relating to Roma integration but also an evaluation of and a reflection on his own politics and activism at the local and transnational level.

The second respondent to Bíró's essay is Martin Kovats, whose approach is quite different from that of Bíró and Gheorghe due to his focus on the relationship between Roma identity and the politics of Roma identity. He investigates "how and to what extent Roma identity can be a useful tool for improving the living standards and life chances of 'Roma' people" (p. 102). According to Kovats, Roma identity does not exist as such; rather, it is a politically constructed concept. He recognizes that this construction has important implications for the living Roma subjects whom the authors of the book wish to mobilize. While he does recognize that there are real people who identify themselves – and are perceived – as Roma, he argues that "the meaning of Roma, in the contemporary political context, is not a reflection of an objective reality (of Roma people), but is an ambiguous and malleable, even tendentious abstraction based on belief rather than fact" (p. 104).

Kovats meticulously examines various factors that are conventionally used as a basis for establishing a distinct group identity, such as location, language, religion, traditional practices, citizenship, institutional affiliation, profession/lifestyle, community, racial origin and self-ascription. After carefully

---

2 Kathryn Farr, *Sex Trafficking: The Global Market in Women and Children* (New York: Worth Publishers, 2005).

3 Kevin Bales, "Expendable People: Slavery in the Age of Globalization," *Journal of International Affairs* 53, no. 2 (2000): 461.

considering and scrutinizing these factors in relation to Roma, he concludes that they are a highly diverse group and that there is no single objective characteristic that is shared by all Roma individuals or groups. Indeed, the single issue that applies to all Roma is the fact that all of them are discriminated against. He further argues that, since there is no single characteristic that is shared by all Roma, it is hard to design identity-based policy actions that would address the complex challenges they face. Kovats suggests that, in the current economic and political climate, Roma identity politics cannot succeed alone and thus advises Roma activists to find political common ground with other non-Roma social movements in their fight for social justice.

The second part of the book is a collection of workshop debates relating to various controversial issues, dilemmas and topics raised in the first three essays, including gender issues, the role of the Romani tradition in politics, ethnic and civic nationalism, citizenship and migration within Europe. The final chapter by Jovanović is an inspiring statement that identifies values, leadership and power as essential ingredients for the success of the Roma movement. It is a political manifesto for the emerging young Roma leadership that focuses on how to forge unity on the basis of common values. Jovanović claims that Roma need power in order to recognize and understand that they bear responsibility for their own future.

Finally, this intellectual project is not simply a collection of essays and debates but an important historical source that reflects the state of contemporary Roma political discourse. It is worthy of scholarly analysis to connect it to contemporary social and political theories and events that produced this specific discourse on Roma. Moreover, this book also serves to provoke an important debate on the possible path(s) of Roma emancipation, contemporary Roma representation and the approach to the Roma issues.

My main critique of the book is as follows. Instead of exploring the scale, quality, racialized trajectories and relational nature of Roma integration, particularly during the last two to three decades of globalization, the debates presented here (particularly the arguments of Bíró and Gheorghe) are limited to a repetitive, culturally fixed discussion of the politics of identity and a single-minded focus on "integration failure." The implicit questions asked by the contributors focus on why Roma fail to integrate and what internal cultural characteristics impede their social integration. I think these questions are not productive in the current political discussions. Rather, we should be more interested in finding out what these integration policies and projects actually involve, what local and global conditions affect them and how exactly they contribute to Roma integration. If these questions had been asked, the analysis would not have ignored how the restructuring of the economic and social order has shaped the conditions and opportunities of Roma, especially in the era of Roma integration. Despite these shortcomings, *From Victimhood to Citizenship: The Path of Roma Integration* is a vitally important publication that should serve as a historical resource for scholars to understand current thinking and debates relating to the politics of Roma integration.

PART 2

Jewish Life and Antisemitism

CHAPTER 5

Social Psychology of Intergroup Reconciliation: Moving beyond Guilt and Victimhood

Arie Nadler

Abstract

Conflicts are an integral part of social life. Individuals within groups and groups vis-à-vis other groups go through cycles of conflict and animosity, on the one hand, and cooperation and relative harmony, on the other. This repetitive cycle between conflict and cooperation is due to the fact that people are "social animals" who need to cooperate with other group members to ward off external dangers, while at the same time competing with those members – and other groups – over tangible and intangible scarce resources (e.g. food and status). The present paper examines this movement between conflict and cooperation in *intergroup relations* through a social psychological analysis of processes of intergroup reconciliation.

The paper begins with a brief discussion of the social psychological perspective on intergroup relations and intergroup conflict. It continues with a review of the "real conflict" and "psychological needs" explanations of intergroup conflict and the differences between "conflict settlement," "conflict resolution" and "reconciliation" as ways to end it. The remainder of the paper addresses the social psychological analysis of intergroup reconciliation. After making a distinction between instrumental and socio-emotional processes of reconciliation, the paper addresses the process of socio-emotional reconciliation in greater detail by describing the needs-based model of reconciliation and related research. The final section of the paper is devoted to the destructive role of collective victimhood in intergroup conflict and ways in which it can be alleviated.

A General Background

1 *Social Psychological Perspective on Intergroup Relations*

Social psychology is the science of subjective and active construal of the social world.[1] Unlike other disciplines in the social sciences (e.g. political science,

1 Lee Ross and Richard E. Nisbett, *The Person and the Situation: Perspectives on Social Psychology* (New York: McGraw-Hill, 1991).

DOI:10.1163/9789004386426_006

sociology, economics), the social psychological analysis of social behaviour is based on the premise that *people actively construe* the social world they live in and that these construals determine social behaviour. For example, regardless of whether another person did or did not intend to humiliate me by arriving late to a meeting, my interpretation of his or her tardiness will determine my behaviour towards them. Turning to intergroup relations, the social identity perspective in social psychology[2] asserts that, although groups are objective and "real" (e.g. families, work groups, nations), the "reality" of groups is not the only force that drives intergroup behaviour. From a social psychological perspective, groups constitute a subjective experience expressed in the person's feelings and cognitions about his or her group membership. Under conditions where one's group membership is salient, intergroup relations exist even if one sits alone in a room. For example, when I watch a football match on television between my nation's team and another national team, I feel like a "group member" rather than an individual even though I am sitting alone in the room. This constitutes an intergroup interaction in the sense that I become excited when my group scores and feel sad when the other team does so.

The boundaries of people's self-categorization as group members are flexible and vary across situations.[3] For example, when I am at a conference representing my organization along with others who are representing theirs, my relevant group membership is centred on the organization that is spelled out on my name tag. Yet, when I am at an internal organizational meeting where all other organizational departments are represented, my relevant group membership narrows: from being a member of the whole organization to being a member of the organizational unit I belong to. In these circumstances, my identity as a member of the "marketing," "production" or "accounting" unit rather than my identity as a member of the entire organization dominates. To summarize, social psychological theory tells us that we "carry the groups we belong to in our heads" and that self-categorization as a member in terms of this or that group is situationally determined. This unique view of social psychology of intergroup relations informs the following analysis of intergroup conflict and reconciliation.

2 John C. Turner and Kathrine J. Reynolds, "The Social Identity Perspective in Inter-Group Relations: Theories, Themes and Controversies," in *Intergroup Processes*, eds. Rubert Brown and Samuel L. Gaertner (Oxford: Blackwell, 2001), 133–153.

3 John C. Turner, Michael A. Hogg, Penelope J. Oakes, Stephen D. Reicher and Margaret S. Wetherell, *Rediscovering the Social Group: A Self-Categorization Theory* (Oxford: Basil Blackwell, 1987).

2 *Intergroup Conflict and Its Ending: The "Real Conflict" and "Psychological Needs" Approaches*

The scale of human death and destruction in the twentieth century, which saw two world wars, numerous regional conflicts and various genocidal campaigns (e.g. the Holocaust, massacres in Cambodia and Rwanda), has amplified the need to understand the antecedents of intergroup conflicts and how to end them. Social psychology and related disciplines have given two broad answers to the questions why conflicts occur and how to end them: the "real conflict" and the "psychological needs" approaches.[4]

The "real conflict" approach suggests that intergroup conflicts are due to competition over scarce resources.[5] In international conflicts, these resources can be land or water, while in conflicts between groups within a society (e.g. advantaged and disadvantaged groups) they may be limited governmental budgets. Importantly, this approach holds that, in a bountiful environment in which each group has all it desires, intergroup conflicts would be unlikely. According to this approach, conflicts end when the two groups reach an agreement on how to divide the coveted resources between them. Such an agreement is said to be the result of negotiations between rational negotiators who are motivated to end the conflict. From this perspective, the process of ending a conflict is a calculus of competing interests between relatively rational actors that ends in an agreed-upon formula for the division of these resources. In most if not all cases, this formula gives each of the parties less than they had hoped for, but enough to convince them to lay down their weapons and enter an era of a conflict-free coexistence. Much has been written about the variables that affect this process and conditions under which it is likely to result in a positive outcome.[6] Thus, for example, we are told that the focus on the adversarial *positions of each party* will lead to a distributive bargaining that splits the existing "pie," whereas a focus on the *parties' underlying interests* is likely to expand the "pie" before dividing it.[7] Writings on international, and organizational conflicts

4 Arie Nadler, "Post-resolution Processes: Instrumental and Socio-Emotional Routes to Reconciliation," in *Peace Education Worldwide: The Concept, Principles and Practices around the World*, eds. Gavriel Salomon and Baruch Nevo (Mahwah, NJ: Erlbaum, 2002), 127–143.

5 Muzafer Sherif, O.J. Harvey, B. Jack White, William R. Hood, and Carolyn W. Sherif, *Intergroup Conflict and Cooperation: The Robbers Cave Experiment* (Norman: OK: University of Oklahoma Book Exchange, 1961).

6 Dean G. Pruitt and Peter J. Carnevale, *Negotiation in Social Conflict* (Belmont, CA: Thomson Brooks/Cole Publishing, 1993).

7 Susan Cross and Robert Rosenthal, "Three Models of Conflict Resolution: Effects on Intergroup Expectancies and Attitudes," *Journal of Social Issues* 55 (1999): 561–580.

in the social sciences in general, and social psychology in particular, have been dominated by the "real conflict" approach to conflict.

The "psychological needs" approach is based on the fact that during a conflict the parties hurt and humiliate their adversary and that these conflict-related pains pose a threat to the parties' basic psychological needs (e.g. the need for worthy identity) (Burton 1969). These threats motivate the offended party to restore its sense of worthy identity by actions that perpetuate and intensify the conflict (e.g. taking revenge). Unlike the emphasis on conflicting interests that is at the heart of the "real conflict" approach, here the "high road" to ending conflict is the amelioration of the threats to parties' basic psychological needs. Some of the behaviours that can expedite this amelioration of identity threats include admitting past wrongdoing, apologizing for it and seeking the victim's forgiveness. In interpersonal conflicts this occurs between two individuals, whereas in intergroup conflicts this may take the form of public apologies made by leaders of the offending group to the victimized group.[8]

Recent years have seen an increase in the attention devoted to the "psychological needs" approach in the effort to heal ruptured intergroup relations. In an effort to better intergroup relations, leaders have apologized in the name of their group for the wrongdoings committed against an outgroup. A notable example is Pope John Paul's apology in 2000 to the Jewish people, in the name of the Catholic Church, for two millennia of anti-Semitic persecution. Another notable example is the process established by the South African Truth and Reconciliation Commission, which was intended to facilitate the transition from apartheid to democracy. The essence of this process consisted of perpetrators truthfully owning up to their past wrongdoings in exchange for amnesty for the crimes they had committed. Similar "truth commissions" have been established in many other parts of the world (e.g. South America) with the same goal in mind, namely to facilitate a shift from conflict to a reconciled social existence by addressing past hurts and humiliations.[9] The growing trend to promote restorative justice through methods of alternative dispute resolution (ADR) has been another development that has focused the limelight of ending conflict on ameliorating the psychological damage caused by crime and injustice.

8 Catherine R. Philpot and Matthew J. Hornsey, "What Happens When Groups Say Sorry: The Effect of Intergroup Apologies on their Recipients," *Personality and Social Psychology Bulletin* 34 (2008): 474–487.

9 Edel Hughes, William A. Schabas and Ramesh Thakur, eds., *Atrocities and International Accountability: Beyond Transitional Justice* (New York: United Nations University, 2007).

Similar trends have been evidenced in social psychological research on intergroup conflict. In the mid-1990s, Scheff complained about the dominance of the "real conflict" approach and the complete lack of attention to emotions and psychological needs in the scholarly discussion of intergroup conflicts. He wrote "that one would hardly know that emotions existed from reading the social science analysis of conflict."[10] Recent social psychological work on intergroup conflict has extended the "real conflict" approach to intergroup conflict and has increasingly highlighted the role of emotions and psychological needs in this context.[11] For example, it has emphasized the role of emotions, such as collective guilt or victimhood, in maintaining and intensifying conflict and overcoming them as the path to ending intergroup conflict.[12] Much of our discussion of the needs-based model of reconciliation and victimhood falls within this "psychological needs" approach to conflict and its ending.

3 *Settlement, Conflict Resolution and Reconciliation*

A more refined analysis of ending intergroup conflicts goes beyond the "real conflict" v. "psychological needs" dichotomy to consider the differences between "conflict settlement," "conflict resolution" and "reconciliation."[13]

"Conflict settlement" is similar to the "real conflict" approach in that it views conflicting interests as the root cause of conflict and suggests that the way to end conflict is by settling these *conflicting interests*. Consistent with the previous description of the "real conflict" approach, the way to settle these conflicting interests is by finding an agreed-upon formula to resolve them. The "conflict resolution" perspective on ending conflict suggests that the "broken relationships" between the adversaries are the cause for the ongoing conflict. Conflict is said to be maintained by the mutual lack of trust and negative perceptions of the adversary. According to this approach, the optimal way to end conflict is to remedy the *relationships* between the adversaries. This change is the outcome of an enduring and meaningful cooperative interaction between the two adversaries, who work together to achieve a goal that is important for both. During these cooperative encounters, the parties learn to gradually trust

10 Thomas J. Scheff, *Bloody Revenge: Emotions, Nationalism and War* (Boulder, CO: Westview Press, 1994).

11 Eran Halperin, *Emotions in Conflict: Inhibitors and Facilitators of Peace Making* (New York: Routledge, 2016).

12 Nyla R. Branscombe and Bertjan Doosje, eds., *Collective Guilt: International Perspectives* (New York: Cambridge University Press, 2004).

13 Herbert C. Kelman, "Reconciliation from a Social-Psychological Perspective," in *Social Psychology of Intergroup Reconciliation*, eds. Arie Nadler, Thomas Malloy, and Jeffrey D. Fisher (New York: Oxford University Press, 2008), 15–32.

and respect each other. This results in increasing mutual trust and the amelioration of negative perceptions of the adversary. Examples of this include peace-building projects that engage the adversaries in long-term joint projects to achieve a goal that is important for both (e.g. building a medical facility that will serve both communities). Sometimes these efforts are meant to be a prelude to a peace agreement (e.g. Israeli-Palestinian cooperative projects after the Oslo Agreements in 1993); at other times, they aim to solidify peaceful coexistence after an agreement has already been signed (e.g. community building projects in the Balkans).[14]

The third strategy to end intergroup conflict is "reconciliation." The reconciliation perspective on intergroup conflict suggests that conflict is maintained and intensified because of the damaged identity of each of the parties. Unlike the "settlement" and "resolution" approaches, here the end of conflict is not predicated on addressing conflicting interests or repairing broken relationships but on ameliorating the threat and damage to each of the parties' identities. According to Kelman's analysis, this occurs through a rearrangement of the building blocks of collective identities such that conflict-related elements that have been central to group's identity (e.g. hostility towards the adversary) move to the periphery, while other elements (e.g. commitment to one's group, pride over its achievements) become strengthened as core elements of people's collective identity.

The tripartite distinction between settlement, resolution and reconciliation brings us closer to the main focus of the present paper: intergroup reconciliation. We begin by differentiating between the processes of instrumental and socio-emotional reconciliation, continue by presenting the needs-based model of socio-emotional reconciliation, and conclude by addressing the role of victimhood in this process.

B Processes of Reconciliation: Instrumental and Socio-Emotional Reconciliation

The increasing use of the concept of reconciliation in present-day scholarly discussions on intergroup conflicts is due, among other things, to the

14 See Dinka Corkalo, Dean Ajdukovic, Harvey M. Weinstein, Eric Stover, Dino Djipa and Miklos Biro, "Neighbors Again? Intercommunity Relations after Ethnic Cleansing," in *Justice and Community in the Aftermath of Mass Atrocity*, eds. Eric Stover and Harvey M. Weinstein (New York: Cambridge University Press, 2004), 143–162. Nebojsa Petrovic, "Measurement of Readiness for Reconciliation: An Attempt at the Construction of the Appropriate Scale," *Balkan Social Science Review* 9 (2017): 47–69.

realization that conflicts do not necessarily end with the signing of an agreement. Conflict-related emotions and memories continue to live on and are not erased with the stroke of a pen. Unless they are dealt with, these emotions threaten to plunge the parties into renewed cycles of violence. For example, the perception that one had been unduly victimized by the adversary may leave the embers of the desire to take revenge hot and burning, ready to nourish a renewed cycle of violence. In general, processes of reconciliation are said to address these conflict-related emotions, thereby ensuring stable peaceful relations between former adversaries. In the language of the previous distinctions, processes of reconciliation adopt the "psychological needs" approach to intergroup conflict and seek to go beyond settling the parties' conflicting interests to end it. Thus, processes of reconciliation aim to promote harmonious intergroup relationships by removing conflict-related emotional blocks that separate the parties.[15]

Two major categories of such conflict-related emotional blocks exist: feelings of distrust and animosity towards the adversary and feelings of victimhood and guilt that emanate from being injured by the adversary or inflicting injuries on them. Consistent with this, we have distinguished between instrumental and socio-emotional processes of reconciliation in our work.[16]

Processes of *instrumental reconciliation* centre on repairing "broken relationships" between the adversaries. These broken relationships are expressed in mutual distrust and negative perceptions of the adversary. As noted previously in the description of Kelman's analysis of the concept of "conflict resolution," this process consists of gradually learning to trust the adversary by cooperating with them over an extended period of time. Oftentimes, this cooperative interaction is sustained by a goal that is equally important for both parties. Such goals are superordinate goals that transcend the well-being of one party and address the shared well-being of both. Joint projects that centre on promoting the health of citizens in the two warring groups or working towards a clean environment in the geographical area that they share are examples of such superordinate goals.[17] Because the goals that the parties seek to

15 Nadler, "Post-resolution Processes." See also Arie Nadler, "Intergroup Reconciliation: Definitions, Processes and Future Directions," in *The Oxford Book of Intergroup Conflict*, ed. Linda R. Tropp (New York: Oxford University Press, 2012), 291–309. Arie Nadler and Nurit Shnabel, "Intergroup Reconciliation: The Instrumental and Socio-Emotional Paths and the Needs-Based Model of Socio-Emotional Reconciliation," in *Social Psychology of Intergroup Reconciliation*, eds. Arie Nadler, Thomas Malloy, and Jeffrey D. Fisher (New York: Oxford University Press, 2008), 37–56.

16 Nadler, "Intergroup Reconciliation."

17 Sherif, et al., *Intergroup Conflict.*

achieve during such a process are equally *instrumental* to all, the process of the gradual restoration of intergroup trust and better relations through cooperation is labelled as an instrumental process of reconciliation. Much social psychological research conducted on the "contact hypothesis" has demonstrated the ameliorative value of such interactions on relations between advantaged and disadvantaged groups within a society.[18] Post-conflict peace-building projects follow the same logic in international relations.[19]

Processes of *socio-emotional reconciliation* view the end of conflict as predicated on conflict-related threats to parties' identities. Unlike Kelman's analysis, which views reconciliation as the "rearranging" of collective identities such that conflict-related elements become peripheral, our approach to reconciliation regards it as the process of ameliorating conflict-related feelings of victimhood and guilt. In the course of intergroup conflicts, parties inflict pain, destruction and humiliation on their adversaries, which cause threats to their collective identities (e.g. guilt). Processes of socio-emotional reconciliation consist of the amelioration of the psychological wounds that conflict has inflicted on the victims and the perpetrators of violence. This is oftentimes accomplished when perpetrators acknowledge the harm they have done and seek the victims' forgiveness. In the next section, before we discuss the process of socio-emotional reconciliation and the needs-based model it encapsulates, we draw attention to the major differences between the processes of instrumental and socio-emotional reconciliation.

Processes of instrumental and socio-emotional reconciliation differ in two major aspects: (a) temporal focus and (b) the applicability of each in different social contexts. Regarding the temporal focus, socio-emotional reconciliation is predicated on the assumption that dealing with the painful *past* is the key to a reconciled future, while processes of instrumental reconciliation suggest that a cooperative and friendly contact in the *present* is the key to a reconciled future. The idea behind instrumental reconciliation is to "let bygones be bygones" and learn to coexist in the present. The guiding assumption of socio-emotional reconciliation is that, unless the parties deal with the painful past, it will continue to haunt their relationships and threaten to reignite the conflict.

Regarding the applicability of each process to different contexts, instrumental reconciliation is applicable when the adversaries desire to end the conflict by *separating* from each other (e.g. two states with a border between them) and socio-emotional reconciliation is applicable when they desire to end it by

18 Thomas Pettigrew and Linda R. Tropp, "Meta-Analytic Test of Intergroup Contact Theory," *Journal of Personality and Social Psychology* 90 (2006): 751–783.

19 John P. Lederach, *Building Peace: Sustainable Reconciliation in Divided Societies* (Washington, DC: US Institute of Peace, 1997).

integrating with each other (e.g. black and white South Africans seeking to live together in an integrated South Africa). Instrumental processes will be effective in building trust that will enable parties to *coexist separately in a conflict-free environment*. Yet, when groups desire to end the conflict by creating an *integrated social unit*, this is not enough. The presence of the two adversaries under the roof of the same collective will serve as a constant reminder of the threat to their identities. Perpetrators will remind victims of their powerlessness, and victims will remind the perpetrators of their guilt. Under these conditions, processes of socio-emotional reconciliation need to be implemented to diffuse threats to collective identities.

An example in the context of interpersonal relations is the manner in which two spouses choose to end a conflict that originated when one hurt the other by being disloyal. The parties can decide to resolve the conflict either by separating or by healing their relationship and renewing their intimacy (i.e. separation v. integration). If they decide to separate, they need to build trustworthy relations that will enable them to coexist next to each other in a conflict-free environment and agree on potentially divisive matters (e.g. shared property). However, if they decide to reunite, the wounds of the past need to be openly addressed and an effective and genuine apology-forgiveness cycle needs to be instituted. Turning to the intergroup level, the fact that truth commissions, which seek to implement a socio-emotional process of reconciliation, are common in intra-societal groups (e.g. blacks and whites in South Africa; victims and perpetrators in the fascist regime in Chile) supports this argument.[20]

C Processes of Socio-Emotional Reconciliation: The Needs-Based Model

Our analysis of the process of socio-emotional reconciliation is based on two assumptions: (a) victims and perpetrators experience different conflict-related identity threats and (b) reconciliation is predicated on remedying the threats to the psychological needs of both *the victim and the perpetrator*. What are the different psychological needs of victims and perpetrators?

Psychological theory posits two basic psychological needs that motivate and guide human social behaviour: the need for "agency" and the need for "communion."[21] The need for *agency* consists of people's wish to be efficacious,

20 William J. Long and Peter Brecke, *War and Reconciliation: Reason and Emotion in Conflict Resolution* (Cambridge, MA: MIT Press, 2003).

21 David Bakan, *The Duality of Human Existence* (Chicago: Rand McNally, 1966).

in control, strong and competent. The need for *communion* consists of people's basic psychological need to belong to others and be accepted, liked and loved by others. The pain and humiliation that are experienced by adversarial parties in conflict threaten the *victims' need for agency* and the *perpetrators' need for communion*.[22] This is because being a victim means that one is relatively powerless, and that one's fate is in the hands of the more powerful author of one's victimization. On the other hand, the perpetrator of wrongdoings suffers a threat to its *moral image* and thus to its basic need for *communion*. The emphasis on the threat to the *moral image* underscores the social nature of this threat. While one may perceive the violence one has inflicted as morally justified, the threat to one's morality is anchored in others' disapproval of those actions. If others regard these violent actions as unjustified, the perpetrators' belongingness to the relevant moral community is questioned and they run the risk of being excluded from that community. In the case of an individual perpetrator the relevant community consists of other relevant people, while in the case of a whole nation it is the "community of nations."

Given the critical role of the fulfilment of the need for communion and agency for personal and social well-being, people must ameliorate threats to these fundamental psychological needs. The amelioration of the threats to communion and agency can be accomplished either unilaterally or interactively. In the latter case, each party helps ameliorate the other's threatened need. As the next sections show, the unilateral amelioration of victims' and perpetrators' threatened needs maintains – and even intensifies – conflict, while interactive amelioration promotes reconciliation.

1 *Unilateral Amelioration of Threatened Needs: A Recipe for More Violence*

The unilateral amelioration of victims' and perpetrators' threats to their needs for agency and communion may continue or even intensify the conflict. Victims can try to ameliorate the threat to their "agency" (i.e. loss of power and control) by taking revenge. The act of revenge places the powerless victim in an active and powerful position. Writing on the psychological function of revenge in interpersonal relations, Akhtar notes that "some revenge is actually good for the victim ... it puts the victim's hitherto passive ego in an active position ... [and] imparts a sense of mastery and self-esteem."[23] Yet, what one side regards as justified revenge the other views as unjustified aggression that must

22 Nadler and Shnabel, "Intergroup Reconciliation: The Instrumental."
23 Salman Akhtar, "Forgiveness: Origins, Dynamics, Psychopathology, and Technical Relevance," *Psychoanalytic Quarterly* 71 (2002): 175–212, especially 179.

be avenged. Although palliative to the victim, revenge becomes the prelude to a never-ending cycle of violence.[24] In a similar fashion, perpetrators can try to ameliorate the threat to their need for communion (i.e. a threat to their moral image) by cognitively distancing themselves from their wrongdoings and their victims. They do so by employing the tactic of "moral disengagement."[25] For example, they may justify the violence they have committed by telling themselves and others that they had no choice and acted in self-defence. Alternatively, they may distance themselves from the act and its consequences by belittling the pain they have caused (e.g. "their suffering is nothing") or by blocking any feelings of empathy for their victims' sufferings. As in the case of revenge, the problem is that, while beneficial for the perpetrator, these psychological mechanisms are ruinous to the relationship. For example, feeling no empathy for the victims prepares the ground for inflicting more sufferings on them in the future.

2 *Interactive Amelioration of Threatened Needs: The Apology-Forgiveness Cycle*

The amelioration of threats to parties' identities can also be accomplished in an interactive manner. Such an identity-restoration interaction is expected to promote reconciliation. A paradigmatic example of this is the apology-forgiveness cycle.[26] Commenting on the change that occurs following a successful completion of an apology-forgiveness cycle, Tavuchis writes: "although both victim and perpetrator know that words cannot undo the past, in some magical way this is exactly what they do."[27] The needs-based model of reconciliation suggests the psychological mechanisms that explain this "magic."

The perpetrators' apology, followed by seeking the victims' forgiveness, constitutes a transformation of the power relations between the two parties. Whereas during the victimization episode the helpless victim was at the mercy of the perpetrator, things change after the perpetrator has sought the victim's forgiveness. The victim has the power to grant forgiveness, withhold it or make it conditional on reparations. In the words of Gobodo-Madikizela "the decision to forgive can paradoxically elevate a victim to a position of strength as the one

24 Nico H. Frijda, "The Lex Talionis: On Vengeance," in *Emotions: Essays on Emotion Theory*, eds. Stephanie H.M. van Goozen, Nanne van de Poll, Nanne E. van de Poll, and Joseph A. Sergeant (Hillsdale, NJ: Lawrence Erlbaum, 1994), 263–289.

25 Albert Bandura, "Moral Disengagement in the Perpetration of Inhumanities," *Personality and Social Psychology Review* 3 (1999): 193–209.

26 Nicholas Tavuchis, *Mea culpa: A sociology of Apology and Reconciliation* (Stanford, CA: Stanford University Press, 1991).

27 Ibid., 8.

who has the key to the perpetrator's wish ... the victim becomes the gatekeeper to what the outcast desires."[28] Without the victim's forgiveness, the perpetrator remains morally culpable and at risk of being socially excluded. Thus, under optimal conditions, the apology-forgiveness interaction constitutes a social exchange between victim and perpetrator in which the victim gains empowerment and the perpetrator gains social acceptance and a positive moral image. This interaction remedies threats to the victim's agency and the perpetrator's need for communion, increasing the parties' readiness for reconciliation. It removes the emotional blocks of revenge and moral disengagement that fed the burning fire of conflict. This process is depicted in the chart below.

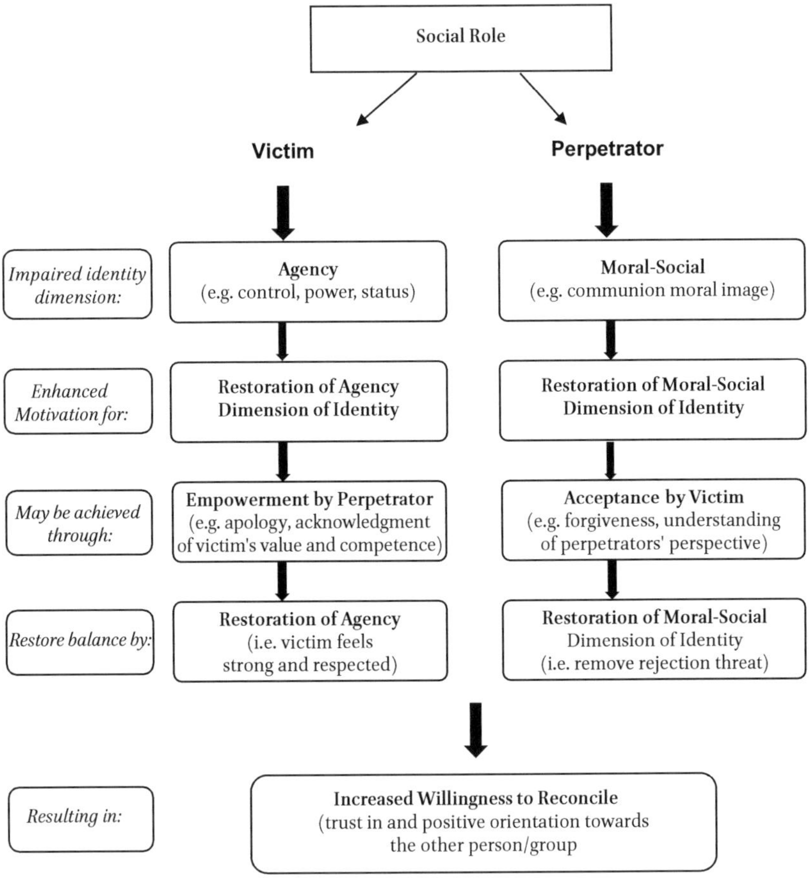

FIGURE 5.1 The needs-based model of reconciliation
SOURCE: NADLER AND SHNABEL, "INTERGROUP RECONCILIATION: THE INSTRUMENTAL," 101.

28 Pumla Gobodo-Madikizela, *A Human Being Died That Night: A South-African Story of Forgiveness* (New York: Houghton Mifflin, 2003).

The needs-based model and its assertions have been empirically supported.[29] In interpersonal contexts, people who had been victimized in a simulated work environment experienced a threat to their sense of power, while the perpetrators experienced a threat to their moral image (i.e. they expected that others would view them as morally inadequate). Importantly, perpetrators' willingness to reconcile was higher after they had received a message of *acceptance* that remedied the threat to their "communion" needs, and victims' willingness to reconcile was higher after they had received a message of empowerment that remedied the threat to their "agency" needs.[30] Another set of studies examined these hypotheses in the context of intergroup conflicts.[31] For example, in one experiment Israeli Arabs and Israeli Jews were reminded of the Kfar Kassem massacre in 1956 in which 56 Arab civilians were killed by the Israeli army (i.e. the Israeli Jews were the perpetrators and the Israeli Arabs were the victims). Subsequently, each group was exposed to a message from a representative of the other group, ostensibly delivered during a memorial ceremony for this tragedy. Israeli Jews (i.e. the perpetrators) were more inclined to reconcile with Israeli Arabs after they received a message from an Arab speaker indicating acceptance (e.g. "we should understand Israeli Jews") than when the message indicated empowerment (e.g. "Jews are competent and successful"). At the same time, Israeli Arabs (i.e. the victims) were more inclined to reconcile following a message of empowerment from an Israeli Jewish speaker than following a message indicating acceptance.[32] Taken together, these findings support the idea that the interactive amelioration of threats to perpetrators' needs for "communion" and victims' needs for "agency" renders adversaries more inclined to reconcile with their enemies.

Before proceeding to discuss the role of victimhood in intergroup conflicts, the distinction between victims and perpetrators needs to be revisited. In some intergroup conflicts, there exists a clear consensus about who is the victim and who is the perpetrator (e.g. following the genocides in Cambodia

29 Arie Nadler and Nurit Shnabel, "Intergroup Reconciliation: Definitions, Instrumental and Socio-Emotional Processes and the Needs-Based Model," *European Review of Social Psychology* 26 (2015): 93–125. See also Nurit Shnabel, and Arie Nadler, "The Role of Agency and Morality in Reconciliation Processes: The Perspective of the Needs-Based Model," *Current Directions in Psychological Sciences* 24 (2015): 477–483.

30 Nurit Shnabel and Arie Nadler, "A Needs-Based Model of Reconciliation: Satisfying the Differential Emotional Needs of Victim and Perpetrator as a Key to Promoting Reconciliation," *Journal of Personality and Social Psychology* 94 (2008): 116–132.

31 Nurit Shnabel, Arie Nadler, Johannes Ullrich, John F. Dovidio, and Dganit Carmi, "Promoting Reconciliation through the Satisfaction of the Emotional Needs of Victimized and Perpetrating Group Members: The Needs-Based Model of Reconciliation," *Personality and Social Psychology Bulletin* 35 (2009): 1021–1030.

32 Ibid.

and Rwanda). Yet, in many conflicts this is not the case and both parties are – and view themselves as being – in the "dual" role of victim *and* perpetrator (e.g. Protestants and Catholics in Northern Ireland, Israelis and Palestinians in the Middle East, etc.). In other words, the clear distinction between victim and perpetrator that forms the basis of the needs-based model is made for the purpose of conceptual clarity and does not reflect the reality of many intergroup conflicts.

Recent research addresses this issue by comparing people who have been induced to view themselves as victims *or* perpetrators to people who have been induced to view themselves as both (i.e. asking them to remember events in which they hurt their adversary *and* events in which they were hurt by their adversary).[33] Consistent with the needs-based model, people who had been induced to view themselves as victims *and* perpetrators (i.e. "duals") experienced a heightened need to be empowered *and* accepted. Yet, their behaviour resembled those who saw themselves exclusively as victims. Like them, when given the chance, they behaved in a vengeful manner towards their adversary, and unlike those who had been induced to view themselves exclusively as perpetrators they did not try remedy the threat to their moral image by acting prosocially towards their adversary. These findings are consistent with the observation that being a victim is a psychologically more profound experience than being a perpetrator.[34] Indeed, when a party has been victimized by an adversary and has victimized them in return during the course of a conflict, said party views itself as a victim and not as a perpetrator and tends to compete with its adversary over victim status.[35] The more significant psychological meaning of victimhood is supported in research showing that it is easier for people to identify themselves as victims than as perpetrators. When recalling an event in which their group attacked an adversary, people immediately stated that this violence had been preceded by prior attacks directed at their group by the adversary.[36] The tendency to view the ingroup as the victim even when recalling its perpetration of an attack against the adversary reflects the ingroup

33 Ilanit SimanTov-Nachlieli and Nurit Shnabel, "Feeling Both Victim and Perpetrator: Investigating Duality within the Needs-Based Model," *Personality and Social Psychology Bulletin* 40 (2014): 301–31.

34 Roy F. Baumeister, *Evil: Inside Human Violence and Cruelty* (New York: Henry Holt, 1997).

35 Masi Noor, Nurit Shnabel, Samer Halabi, and Arie Nadler, "When Suffering Begets Suffering: The Psychology of Competitive Victimhood between Adversarial Groups in Violent Conflicts," *Personality and Social Psychology Review* 16 (2012): 351–374.

36 Agostino Mazziotta, Friederike Feuchte, Nicolay Gausel, and Arie Nadler, "Does Remembering Past Ingroup Perpetration Promote Postwar Cross-Group Contact? Insights from a Field Experiment in Liberia," *European Journal of Social Psychology* 44 (2014): 43–52.

members' need to protect their sense of moral adequacy. As noted previously in the discussion of "moral disengagement," recalling the adversary's aggression against the ingroup renders the aggression committed by the ingroup morally defensible (i.e. "they started and we had to respond").

This "primacy of victimhood" opens the door to the next section, which focuses on the destructive role of victimhood in intergroup conflict and how it can be ameliorated.

D Collective Victimhood: Its Costs and How to Overcome It

1 *Victimhood Self-State and Collective Victimhood*

Being a victim is a psychologically comforting position. When one is a victim one is absolved from responsibility for past wrongdoings. More importantly, victims enjoy a sense of entitlement. Others are indebted to them, while they are not expected to do anything for others. Also, presenting oneself – or one's group – as a victim garners more support from third parties. What are the characteristics of a victimhood self-state? Research has identified four characteristics of individuals who tend to adopt a victimhood self-state in interpersonal interactions. Based on clinical observations and research these individuals (a) constantly seek others' *recognition* of their victimhood, (b) oftentimes *ruminate* about their past victimization, (c) show a *lack of empathy* for others' pain and (d) have a sense of *moral elitism*.[37] These characteristics of victimhood in interpersonal relations characterize collective victimhood in intergroup relations as well. Groups that wear the mantle of collective victimhood want others to *recognize* their victimization, *ruminate* about it, show *little empathy* towards others (including their adversary) and regard themselves as morally better than others (i.e. *moral elitism*).

While psychologically comforting, victimhood inhibits intergroup reconciliation. A major reason for this is the phenomenon of "competitive victimhood" in which adversaries compete over who is the "true victim." Each of the adversaries seeks a monopoly over sufferings and victimhood. This is fuelled by a desire to adopt the psychological position of entitlement and absolve oneself – or one's group – of responsibility for ending the conflict. One can only imagine the negative outcomes of competitive victimhood when it characterizes the

37 Rahav Gabay, Boaz Hameiri, T. Rubel and Arie Nadler, "Tendency for Interpersonal Victimhood (TIV): Theory Development and Scale Validation," (Unpublished manuscript, Tel Aviv University, 2017). See also Ivan Urlic, Miriam Berger, Avi Berman, *Victimhood, Vengefulness and the Culture of Forgiveness* (New York: Nova Publications, 2013).

mindset of both parties to a conflict. It results in neither of them being willing to take responsibility for ending the conflict and both of them showing empathy and understanding for only one victim: themselves.

At the group level, the victimhood self-state has many advantages. It increases solidarity and cohesion within the group. In a sense, it gives the whole group a ready-made social identity of victims who are entitled to do whatever is needed to undo their victimization by others and whatever they see fit to ensure that history never repeats itself. This provides a ready-made rationalization for violence directed at others who are viewed as a threat to the group's well-being. Thus, for example, in an experiment Canadian Jewish participants whose group victimization had been made salient by reminding them of the Holocaust were later more willing to accept as permissible morally dubious acts of the Israeli army against Palestinians.[38] A feeling of collective victimhood is psychologically comforting. It paints a world view in which one's group is innocent, entitled to continuous compensation for its past sufferings and always justified in doing whatever it deems necessary to protect itself.

2 *Hope Leaders and Fear Leaders*

Realizing the psychological benefits of the victimhood self-state, political leaders often nourish and encourage it. Roughly speaking, political leaders can be divided into "hope leaders" and "fear leaders." The first type highlights the future and the possibilities for positive change that it offers. When people are suffering a collective depression in the face of an ominous present, hope leaders ignite people's belief in themselves and their ability to overcome the present difficulties. In short, they draw a picture of a brighter future without losing sight of the dangers in the present. They instil in their followers a sense of efficacy that harnesses their common will and effort to achieve this hopeful future. A prominent example of a hope leader is Winston Churchill during the Second World War. In the darkest times of the war, when the British nation was enveloped in a sense of approaching doom, his speeches gave the British people a picture of a hopeful future and their ability to get there without losing sight or minimizing the dangers that they faced in the present.

A key difference between hope and fear leaders is the way they use the concept of time in their leadership. Whereas hope leaders look towards a *positive future* without losing sight of difficulties in the present, fear leaders look back

38 Michael Wohl and Nyla R. Branscombe, "Remembering Historical Victimization: Collective Guilt for Current Ingroup Transgression," *Journal of Personality and Social Psychology* 94 (2008): 988–1006.

at an *ominous past* without considering the opportunities that may exist in the present. Fear leaders emphasize the past and the dangers that it presents. Such leaders usually focus on a "chosen trauma"[39] around which they organize their messages of victimhood and danger (e.g. the Holocaust, the Nakba, the battle of Kosovo in 1389, etc.). It is not that these traumas did not take place – they did – but the message of the fear leader is that the traumatic past is destined to repeat itself.

However, this is not a black-and-white distinction, and political leaders can move up and down spectrum. Yet, some leaders tend towards the hope-future end of the continuum and others towards the victimhood-past end. The history of the world in general, and that of the Middle East in particular, provides many examples of hope leaders and fear leaders.

3 *Overcoming the Trap of Collective Victimhood*

How can individuals and groups overcome the trap of competitive victimhood and the victimhood self-state?

One answer is that it would be easier for victims to drop the mantle of victimhood and proceed towards reconciliation with their former tormentors if they were to adopt the perpetrators' perspective. The work of Staub and his colleagues in post-genocide Rwanda is an example of this approach.[40] It consisted of making the Tutsi victims of the Hutu's genocidal campaign aware that, if they – the victims – had been exposed to the same intense and vicious propaganda campaigns and social pressures, they might also have succumbed and killed their neighbours. This approach suggests that only by empathizing with one's former tormentor can the victim proceed to forgiveness and reconciliation. It underscores the fact that we are all frail human beings who, given certain circumstances, are capable of committing unthinkable atrocities. Echoing a similar position, Desmond Tutu wrote that victims will forgive their tormentors only if they can understand why they did what they did.[41] In support of this position, research in post-apartheid South Africa indicates that black individuals who agreed that both the white apartheid regime and the black anti-apartheid movements (e.g. the ANC) had committed horrible crimes were more pro-reconciliation than those who assigned all the blame

39 Vamik D. Volkan, *Killing in the Name of Identity: A Study of Bloody Conflicts* (Charlottesville: Pitchstone, 2006).

40 Ervin Staub, "Promoting reconciliation after genocide and mass killing in Rwanda – and other postconflict settings," in *Social Psychology of Intergroup Reconciliation*, eds. Arie Nadler, Thomas E. Malloy, and Jeffrey D. Fisher (New York: Oxford University Press, 2008).

41 Desmond Tutu, *No Future without Forgiveness* (London: Rider, 1999).

to the apartheid regime[42] It is difficult, if not impossible, to reconcile with the representative of ultimate evil and accept that one – or one's own group – could also have committed heinous crimes, thus making it easier to forgive and reconcile with one's former tormentor. Admittedly, stripping oneself of the entitlements that victimhood brings requires a concentrated effort. Yet, when this has been accomplished and victims can see the "perpetrator within," reconciliation is more likely.[43]

A second way to decrease competitive victimhood and its destructive effect on reconciliation is the introduction of a common "victim identity" that unites the two adversaries as victims of the same conflict. In one study, Israelis and Palestinians who had been induced to think of both peoples as victims of the conflict were more willing to forgive their adversary for past wrongdoings and less inclined to be locked into the destructive cycle of competitive victimhood.[44]

Another important process that allows victims to free themselves from the collective victimhood self-state is the acknowledgement of the truth of their victimhood. It is no accident that efforts to promote reconciliation in post-conflict societies have been carried under the auspices of truth and reconciliation commissions.[45] Truth is a cardinal aspect of reconciliation. Victims crave acknowledgement, and when their victimhood is denied they suffer revictimization. As noted above, a key characteristic of the victimhood self-state is the victim's desire for recognition of his or her victimhood. The opposite is also true. Active denial by others nourishes victimhood and the associated negative consequences. For example, the recent efforts of the Iranian leadership to deny the Holocaust form a significant psychological breeding ground for animosity between Israelis and Iranians.

Social psychological research has demonstrated the positive effects that the acknowledgment of a group's victimhood can have in a number of different contexts. Americans of Jewish and Armenian descent evidenced more positive attitudes towards Germans and Turks, respectively, after the Jewish and

42 James L. Gibson, "Overcoming Apartheid: Can Truth Reconcile a Divided Nation?," *Annals of the American Academy of Political and Social Science* 603 (2006): 82–111.

43 Ervin Staub, "Reconciliation after Genocide, Mass Killing, or Intractable Conflict: Understanding the Roots of Violence, Psychological Recovery, and Steps toward a General Theory," *Political Psychology* 27 (2006): 867–894. Elizabeth Levy-Paluck, "Reducing Intergroup Prejudice and Conflict Using the Media: A Field Experiment in Rwanda." *Journal of Personality and Social Psychology* 96 (2009): 574–587.

44 Nurit Shnabel, Samer Halabi, Masi Noor, "Overcoming Competitive Victimhood and Facilitating Forgiveness through Re-Categorization into a Common Victim or Perpetrator Identity," *Journal of Experimental Social Psychology* 49 (2013): 867–877.

45 Hughes, Scabas and Thakur, *Atrocities*.

Armenian genocides had been acknowledged.[46] Similarly, political prisoners expressed lower desire to take revenge on their prison guards after their sufferings in prison had been acknowledged.[47] Our own recent research indicates that denial of the Holocaust undermines reconciliation between Israeli-Jews and Palestinians, while acknowledgment of the Holocaust promotes it. In surveys and experimental research, we found that Israeli Jews who learned that Palestinians acknowledge the sufferings of the Jewish people during the Second World War were more willing to make peace-related compromises on key divisive issues (e.g. Jerusalem as a joint Israeli-Palestinian capital) than when such an acknowledgment was not forthcoming. Similarly, when Palestinians learned that Israeli Jews acknowledge the sufferings of Palestinian refugees, they were more willing to make compromises on key divisive issues (e.g. the "right of return") than when this was not the case.[48] This tells us that reciprocal acknowledgments of the truth of victimhood between Israelis and Palestinians can move us all forward. It is important to note here that Palestinians were not the authors of the Jewish "chosen trauma" (i.e. the Holocaust), while the creation of Israel in 1948 (i.e. the Nakba as a "chosen trauma") is viewed by Palestinians as the event that condemned many of them to a life as refugees. This reinforces the idea that the acknowledgment of the adversary's "chosen trauma," regardless of the identity of the perpetrator, is the driving force behind its positive effect in terms of the willingness to make compromises. Importantly, the beneficial effects of the acknowledgment of victimhood on reconciliation are not restricted to the Israeli-Palestinian context. It is a general phenomenon that is applicable to intergroup relations in other parts of the world.

4 *Jean Amery and the Negative Possession of Identity*

I want to conclude this short paper by referring to the importance of Jean Amery's thinking on victimhood, forgiveness and reconciliation. Amery[49] notes that in many human societies forgiveness is considered to be a morally superior sentiment. Victims' resentment towards their perpetrators is viewed as atavistic, primitive and leading to revenge. Because of this social maxim,

46 Johanna Ray Vollhardt, Lucas B. Mazur, and Magali Lemahieu, "Acknowledgment after Mass Violence: Effects on Psychological Well-Being and Intergroup Relations," *Group Processes and Intergroup Relations* 17 (2014): 306–323.

47 Roman David and Susanne Yuk Ping Choi, "Getting Even or Getting Equal? Retributive Desires and Transnational Justice," *Political Psychology* 30 (2009): 161–192.

48 Boaz Hameiri and Arie Nadler, "Looking Backward to Move Forward: Effects of Acknowledgment of Adversary's Victimhood on Readiness to Compromise for Peace in a Protracted Ongoing Conflict," *Personality and Social Psychology Bulletin* 43 (2017): 555–569.

49 Jean Amery, *At the Mind's Limits: Contemplations by a Survivor on Auschwitz and Its Realities, trans.* Sidney Rosenfeld, Stella P. Rosenfeld (London: Granta Books, 1999 [1966]).

victims are often pressured into granting easy and cheap forgiveness to their perpetrators. Amery asserts that genuine reconciliation can be based only on respect for victims' rights. Victims have a right – an obligation even – to be resentful towards their tormentors, who have violated their most basic human rights. Although at first glance this "sanctification" of the victims' right to resentment may resemble what has been described above as the victimhood self-state, this is far from the case. The key message that Amery conveys is the necessity of replacing cheap forgiveness with genuine forgiveness.

Amery tells us that resentment must be consummated before genuine forgiveness and reconciliation can proceed. How can resentment be consummated? Consummation of resentment occurs when perpetrators accept their past wrongdoings as a *negative possession of their identity*. According to this view, it is not enough for perpetrators to apologize and express sorrow over past wrongdoings. They must convince the victim that they view these wrongful actions as part of who they are. That is the meaning of negative possession of identity (NPI). To use an example, when Germans say that part of who they are (i.e. their identity) includes Beethoven, Goethe and Hitler, they are embracing the negative aspects of their history into their national identity. This requires symbolic and public expressions of contrition (e.g. establishment of memorials, public statements by leaders), but until they occur, suggests Amery, resentment lives – and should live – on.

To return to the example of the Israeli-Palestinian conflict, I also believe that Israelis should embrace the sufferings of Palestinian refugees into their collective identity. Importantly, acknowledging the other side's pain and suffering does not mean taking responsibility for it. It is the *first step* on the long road to genuine reconciliation. For example, if the authorities at Tel Aviv University, my home university, would put up a sign on campus stating that it was once the site of the Arab village Sheikh Munis, they would be publicly accepting this fact as a negative possession of the university's identity in the same way that its academic excellence is viewed as a positive part of its identity. This does not mean that the university should be demolished and returned to pastureland. On the contrary, I truly believe that the willingness to accept one's history of causing pain to others as a negative possession of identity strengthens and solidifies existing identity. I write this as someone who holds Israel close to his heart, but who is also fully aware of the moral and human responsibility to acknowledge that the sufferings of the Palestinians were at least partly due to the realization of the Jewish people's national aspirations.

CHAPTER 6

Towards Negative Possession of Identity

*Gergely Romsics**

Abstract

In this paper, I present an interpretation of German, Austrian and Hungarian politics of memory, with a focus on the emergence and integration of perpetrator legacies into practices of remembrance. Practices of claiming collective ownership of perpetrator roles in genocide represent a more radical approach to memory work than mere acknowledgement of past crimes. I investigate these practices through the concept of "negative possession of identity" (NPI) as proposed by Arie Nadler, who built upon Jean Améry's theorizing on the subject. Sections on Germany, Austria, and Hungary revisit the histories of collective memory in the three countries to determine the social and political conditions that made such radical practices possible and how, if at all, these societies arrived at these conditions. I treat the German case as paradigmatic, representing successive waves of norm entrepreneurship, which have pushed German mnemonic practices towards negative possession of identity. I argue that Austria's relative belatedness in fostering reflection on perpetrator legacies is due to the priority accorded to reconciling the left- and right-wing political traditions in the wake of an interwar cycle of civil violence. In Hungary, as a consequence of the failure to achieve post-civil war reconciliation, memory work about the Holocaust has been mapped onto existing ideological fault lines in society, hampering norm entrepreneurs in their attempts to achieve wider success in integrating perpetrator perspectives into practices of remembrance. Everywhere – including Germany – NPI has remained an ongoing process embedded in heterogeneous national memory landscapes, with many groups in society sustaining alternative modes of remembrance. At the same time, as the main empirical section on Hungary demonstrates, it is possible to identify structural variables, which work against the internalization of perpetrator legacies through mnemonic practices. A comparison of Austria and Hungary suggests that the establishment of common societal values and identities represents a precondition for the configuration of national practices of remembrance through negative possession of identity.

* Research leading to this paper was funded in part by the Trianon 100 Research Group of the Hungarian Academy of Sciences.

 | DOI:10.1163/9789004386426_007

1 Resentment and Negative Possession of Identity

Negative possession of identity (NPI) is a term introduced by Arie Nadler[1] and inspired by Jean Améry's thinking on resentment and reconciliation.[2] It refers to the shift that occurs when perpetrators accept atrocities, committed in their name towards victims of intercommunal crimes, as an integral part of their collective identity.[3] By working towards accepting past wrongdoing, entrepreneurs of identity politics restructure the community's self-definition by embracing the negative aspects of their history. NPI counteracts strategies of temporal distancing, such as the strategy of emphasizing the innocence of postwar generations with regard to crimes committed in the past. In addition, NPI works against the practice of projecting guilt onto a real or fictitious out-group, such as "Nazis" understood as distinct from Germans.

The contours of NPI emerge in the context of Améry's discussion of resentment. Améry argued against enforced forgetting and forgiving in his autobiography *At the Mind's Limits: Contemplations by a Survivor on Auschwitz and Its Realities*.[4] Writing at a time when Germany had negotiated its first compensation agreements under the chancellorship of Konrad Adenauer and Karl Heinrich Lübke, the second president of the Federal Republic of Germany (FRG), had publicly called on Jewish groups – during a visit to Israel – to accept German penitence and look towards the future,[5] Améry contrasted his personal experience of coping with the Holocaust with the political agreement emerging between the two countries. He observed how Germany had been politically rehabilitated due to the Cold War and its support for Israel, and how

1 Arie Nadler, "Intergroup Reconciliation: Definitions, Processes and Future Directions," in *The Oxford Book of Intergroup Conflict*, ed. L. Tropp (London-New York: Oxford University Press, 2012), 291–309. See in this volume, Arie Nadler, "Social Psychology of Intergroup Reconciliation: Moving beyond Guilt and Victimhood."

2 Jean Améry, *At the Mind's Limits: Contemplations by a Survivor on Auschwitz and Its Realities* (Bloomington: Indiana University Press, 1980), 78.

3 Throughout this paper the delineation and referencing of communities (perpetrator, victim, German, Austrian, Jewish, etc.) is functional. This means that the violence forgotten/remembered is taken to have marked out group boundaries in a relational sense by practices of exclusion and genocidal persecution. Germans, Austrians and Hungarians were perpetrating crimes against Jews in this sense. This is in no way intended to deny the right and ability of groups and individuals to inhabit and claim multiple identities. The choice of words in what follows is therefore purely relational and does not engage in the mapping of group identities, unless noted.

4 Stewart Motha, "Reconciliation as Domination," in *Law and the Politics of Reconciliation*, ed. Scott Veitch (Burlington, VT: Ashgate Publishing, 2007), 88.

5 Jeffrey Herf, *Divided Memory: The Nazi Past in the Two Germanys* (Cambridge, MA-London: Harvard University Press, 1997), 333.

political leaders sought to impose reconciliation. He identified these developments, along with the natural processes of forgetting, as a source of personal resentment and discontent.[6]

At the same time, Améry confessed his desire for genuine reconciliation, a "shared moral space" in which the victim and the perpetrator could reunite, but without having to give up their respective relational identities.[7] He argued that such a shared space could only be achieved if the perpetrators were to claim ownership of the crimes committed:

> [The German people] would then, as I sometimes hope, learn to comprehend its past acquiescence in the Third Reich as the total negation not only of the world that it plagued with war and death but also of its own better origins; it would no longer repress or hush up the twelve years that for us others really were a thousand, but claim them as its realized negation of the world and its self, as its own negative possession. On the field of history there would occur what I hypothetically described earlier for the limited, individual circle: two groups of people, the overpowered and those who overpowered them, would be joined in the desire that time be turned back and, with it, that history become moral. If this demand were raised by the German people, who as a matter of fact have been victorious and already rehabilitated by time, it would have tremendous weight, enough so that by this alone it would already be fulfilled. The German revolution would be made good, Hitler disowned.[8]

Améry in effect called for history to be changed by a symbolic, after-the-fact German revolution against Nazi rule. Emphasizing the continuity of history and the importance of acting symbolically within that continuity, he claimed that the protagonist (the German people) can – and indeed must – travel back in time to symbolically change their fate and the *moral* outcome of history through their retroactive rebellion against what their community once was.

As Nadler has emphasized, the voluntary renunciation of self-acquittal through incorporation of past crimes is likely the only gesture on the part of the perpetrator that can enable a dialogue with the victim without adding further injury in the process. This may lead to the creation of a "shared moral

6 Améry, *At the Mind's Limits*, 72.

7 Aleida Assmann, "Two Forms of Resentment: Jean Améry, Martin Walser and German Memorial Culture," in "Taboo, Trauma, Holocaust," special issue, *New German Critique*, no. 90 (2003): 132.

8 Améry, *At the Mind's Limits*, 78.

space." This process unfolds through the victim's response of "radical" forgiveness, that is to say, forgiving the unforgivable, and this is what Nadler terms a "radical apology-forgiveness cycle" and presents as *de facto* reconciliation in the wake of "radical evil."[9]

It should be added that reconciliation is more productively viewed as an ongoing process[10] rather than a terminus,[11] as also shown by the German example, where accepting past wrongdoing and integrating its history into collective identity in the form of a negative "aspect" has unfolded as a cyclical process. Indeed, this integration, as NPI in general, remains an ever-incomplete process, being dependent on the social practices that reinforce it, while also being contested by alternative discourses in the ever-heterogeneous landscapes of collective memory.[12]

In the case studies examined in this paper, the political aspect plays a large and well-defined role. Ideally, the role of political and intellectual leaders is that of norm entrepreneurs, promoters of "ideational change." As Bratberg observes, "[w]here ideational change occurs, and debates enter new territory (thus opening a space for policy change), agency can be traced back to such entrepreneurs."[13] Norm entrepreneurs have a crucial role in dismantling cycles of the reproduction of resentment, which are often fed by competing claims of communities to have suffered in the traumatic event.[14]

Competitive victimhood originally referred to situations in which members of two communities accuse each other of violence against their own group. Current secondary literature increasingly recognizes the role of competitive victimhood in hampering efforts at reconciliation and extends its applicability to asymmetrical cases.[15] Accordingly, in this paper, competitive victimhood refers to the attempts of perpetrator communities to construct secondary victim

9 Assmann, "Two Forms of Resentment," 132. Nadler, "Intergroup Reconciliation," 305.

10 Joanna R. Quinn, "Introduction," in *Reconciliation(s): Transitional Justice in Postconflict Societies*, ed. Joanna R. Quinn (Toronto: McGill-Queen's University Press, 2009), 5.

11 Erik Doxtader, "The Faith and Struggle of Beginning (with) Words: On the Turn between Reconciliation and Recognition," *Philosophy and Rhetoric* 40, no. 1 (2007): 124.

12 Aleida Assmann and Linda Shortt, "Memory and Political Change: Introduction," in *Memory and Political Change*, ed. Aleida Assmann and Linda Shortt (Houndsmills: Palgrave Macmillan, 2012), 5–6.

13 Øivind Bratberg, "Ideas, Tradition and Norm Entrepreneurs: Retracing Guiding Principles of Foreign Policy in Blair and Chirac's Speeches on Iraq," *Review of International Studies* 37, no. 1 (2011): 336.

14 A. Dirk Moses, *German Intellectuals and the Nazi Past* (Cambridge: Cambridge University Press, 2007), 35.

15 Isaac F. Young and Daniel Sullivan, "Competitive Victimhood: A Review of the Theoretical and Empirical Literature," *Current Opinion in Psychology* 11 (2016): 30–34.

roles for themselves, seeking to reclaim moral authority by interpreting history in a way that acknowledges *their* suffering. It is asymmetric in the sense that the suffering of the primary victim group is not denied in the process. Asymmetric competitive victimhood represents one of the chief obstacles to NPI-type practices as the focus on the history of the self as victim precludes memory work on the self as the carrier of perpetrator legacies.

Acknowledgement of the greater moral and physical injury inflicted upon the primary victim group by one's own community, a pre-condition for NPI, might require multiple reframing in the dynamics of competitive victimhood.[16] Norm entrepreneurs need to challenge the narratives sustaining the "victim identities" of perpetrator groups and help their communities accept and internalize perpetrator legacies.[17] Nadler identifies such people as "hope leaders," who, focusing on the hopeful future, propose a way to move forward by abandoning old identity structures that generate a sense of being threatened, for example when perpetrators assume victim roles.[18]

In the following sections of this paper, German, Austrian and Hungarian memory work is analyzed through a qualitative-interpretative framework. Discourses, including written and other representations – predominantly visual and spatial – are investigated as historical products of ideational forces operating through the agency of social and political entrepreneurs, and empirical data are interpreted on the basis of social constructivist ontology.

In particular, the paper aims to explore how discursive resources enable a political elite to move towards restructuring the image of society by incorporating their past wrongdoings as NPI and how "revisionist" counter-language about responsibility and perpetratorship becomes accepted in some but not

16 Marilynn B. Brewer, "Reducing Prejudice through Cross-categorization: Effects of Multiple Social Identities," in *Reducing Prejudice and Discrimination*, ed. Stuart Oskamp (Hillsdale, NJ: Erlbaum, 2000), 165–183. Luca Andrighetto et al., "Reducing Competitive Victimhood in Kosovo: The Role of Extended Contact and Common Ingroup Identity," *Political Psychology* 33, no. 4 (2012): 514. Marilynn B. Brewer and Rupert J. Brown, "Intergroup Relations," in *Handbook of Social Psychology*, 4th ed., vol. 2, ed. Daniel T. Gilbert, Susan T. Fiske and Gardner Lindsey (Boston, MA: McGraw Hill, 1998), 554–594. Miles Hewstone, Mark Rubin and Hazel Willis, "Intergroup Bias," *Annual Review of Psychology* 53 (2002): 576–604.

17 Andreas Huyssen, "Present Pasts: Media, Politics, Amnesia," *Public Culture* 12, no. 1 (2000): 21–38. See also Ruth Wodak and Gertraud Auer Borea d'Olmo, eds., *Justice and Memory – Confronting Traumatic Pasts: An International Comparison* (Vienna: Passagen, 2009). Aleida Assmann and Linda Shortt, eds., *Memory and Political Change* (Houndsmills: Palgrave Macmillan, 2012).

18 Nadler, "Social Psychology of Intergroup Reconciliation."

all cases.[19] First, the paper will investigate how German politicians and intellectuals driving memory work interacted to shape a discursive environment *encouraging* NPI-type practices. Then, it will compare the situation in Austria, where society has been slow to integrate the perpetrator legacy into its collective identity, mainly due to the successful nation-building process, which was based on defining "Austrianness" in opposition to Nazism. Finally, it will demonstrate that in Hungary persistent pre-World War II cleavages in society have proven the largest obstacle to productive memory work.

II Germany: *Schlussstrich* or Struggle?

Interpretations of German collective memory often focus either on political processes associated with mnemonic practices or on the engagement of intellectuals linked to ideational changes.[20] In what follows, these two approaches are combined, with added emphasis on a recurring discourse about a conception of German identity that is based on the memory of World War II.[21]

A. Dirk Moses coined the twin concepts of *non-German Germans* and *German Germans* to explain the dilemmas of collective identity in post-1945 Germany:

> Either Germans could try to convince themselves and others that they had invented a new collectivity, divorced from an unbearable past, or they could defend the viability of their collective identity by making the national past bearable through a variety of displacement strategies.[22]

Memory projects by the *German Germans* sought to salvage an identity of the "good German" by separating Germans and Nazis to preserve a conceptual space for Germanness that is not defined by Nazi crimes. Since they sought to normalize present-day German identity by including its historical antecedents in their identity construct, they rejected displays of contrition as the

19 Michael A.K. Halliday, *Language as a Social Semiotic: The Social Interpretation of Language and Meaning* (Baltimore: University Park Press, 1978). Améry references Hans Magnus Enzensberger's statement according to which "Auschwitz is Germany's past, present, and future." See Améry, *At the Mind's Limits*, 78.

20 Jeffrey K. Olick, *The Sins of the Fathers: Germany, Memory, Method* (Chicago: University of Chicago Press, 2016). See also Herf, *Divided Memory*.

21 Ruth Wittlinger and Steffi Boothroyd, "A 'Usable' Past at Last? The Politics of the Past in United Germany," *German Studies Review* 33, no. 3 (2010): 489–502.

22 Moses, *German Intellectuals*, 9.

fundamental mode of remembering. On the other hand, *non-German Germans* argued that German history represents a whole that needs to be readdressed and rebelled against – an account of how NPI may be integrated as a central aspect into an identity discourse that is closely reminiscent of Améry's.[23] They called for a framework for remembrance that treats the Nazi past as part of the German past that needed to be "worked through." Both approaches have shown remarkable resilience, and, together, they have defined German memory work for nearly seven decades.[24]

The subsequent analysis traces how the country pre-eminently responsible for the Holocaust progressed from the displacement of the perpetrator legacy to creating a memory landscape that permits and even encourages practices of NPI. It should be noted that international pressure was not the primary cause for this; all German mainstream politicians, and none more so than Konrad Adenauer and Helmut Kohl, commanded international respect. Their policies may have been constrained by transnational norm watchdogs and alliance partners, but the opening up of German collective memory to include the perpetrator perspective occurred *despite* and not *because of* their identity politics. Indeed, leaders who gained international approval for post-1945 German projects were the conservatives in the memory struggles of the era, and this is strong evidence in and of itself that *domestic* processes, rather than *international* constraints, created the conditions enabling NPI.

The two main streams of remembrance emerged in German public discourse in the immediate postwar years. Wilhelm Röpke, an important interwar theoretician of social market economics and the Third Way, argued for a rediscovery of the German 19th century identities to imbue society with a new sense of self and overcome the trauma of Nazi rule to normalize the conceptualization of being German.[25] In stark contrast, at roughly the same time, philosopher Karl Jaspers was working towards a concept of a shared, communal sense of perpetrator memory as distinct from juridical and moral guilt.[26]

23 Wittlinger and Boothroyd, "A 'Usable' Past at Last?," 489–502.

24 David Art, *The Politics of the Nazi Past in Germany and Austria* (Cambridge: Cambridge University Press, 2006).

25 Wilhelm Röpke, *The Solution of the German Problem*, trans. Ernest Walter Dickes (New York: G.P. Putnam's Sons, 1947).

26 Karl Jaspers, *Die Schuldfrage: Ein Beitrag zur deutschen Frage* [The question of guilt: a contribution to the German question] (Zürich: Artemis, 1946). See also Christopher Daase, "Apologies as a New Practice in International Relations," in *Memory in a Global Age: Discourses, Practices and Trajectories*, ed. Aleida Assmann and Sebastian Conrad (Houndsmills: Palgrave Macmillan, 2010), 19–31. Hannah Arendt, "Collective Responsibility," in *Hannah Arendt: Responsibility and Judgment*, ed. Jerome Kohn (New York: Schocken, [1968] 2003), 147–158.

The two positions were aligned, by and large, with the emerging discourses among German conservatives and Social Democrats.[27]

During the first years of the FRG, that is to say, roughly from 1949 to 1968, the normalizing framework emerged as the dominant one. Federal President Lübke's aforementioned speech delivered in Israel highlights the logic animating it and faulted by Améry:

> We Germans cannot forget what happened. We hope that the Jews will not leave the goodwill present in our contribution to restitution unanswered. It would be unfruitful, and over time would be paralyzing, if we did not feel that trust grows on the other side as well.[28]

Led by Adenauer, the conservative Christian Democrats (CDU), the winners of the 1949 elections, adopted this approach. The CDU's original identity offer to German society consisted of the acknowledgement of Nazi crimes as distinct from the responsibility of German society and limited prosecution of war criminals, for which the relative generosity in reparations payments and other support provided to victims was intended to compensate.[29] The contradiction between the assertion of a distinction between Nazis and ordinary Germans and the commitment to nevertheless compensate victims was bridged by references to Nazi crimes as acts committed in the name of Germans and the argument that the Nazis had seduced German society.[30] The most important plea in Adenauer's 1949 parliamentary programme speech was the call for a final line to be drawn under the past (*Schlussstrich*) for the purposes of German normalization and national reassertion.[31] This mentality represented the main form of early resistance in mainstream German politics to the adoption of past wrongdoings as NPI.

In opposition to the *Schlussstrich* mentality and the associated displacement of the perpetrator identity onto Nazis, the memory culture of contrition emerged.[32] It rested on the acknowledgement of history as something with

27 Röpke was later an advisor to the CDU. While Jaspers was not a supporter of the SPD, his ideas on the question of responsibility found more resonance there.

28 Herf, *Divided Memory*, 331.

29 Norbert Frei, "L'holocauste dans l'historiographie allemande: un point aveugle dans la conscience historique?" [The Holocaust in German historiography: a blind spot in historical consciousness?], *Vingtième Siècle: Revue d'histoire* 34 (1992): 157–162. See also Herf, *Divided Memory*, 7–10, 331–333. Art, *Politics of the Nazi Past*, 58.

30 Jeffrey K. Olick and Daniel Levy, "Collective Memory and Cultural Constraint: Holocaust Myth and Rationality in German Politics," *American Sociological Review* 62 (1997): 926. Olick, *Sins of the Fathers*, 220–229.

31 Herf, *Divided Memory*, 271–272.

32 Art, *Politics of the Nazi Past*, 10. See also Moses, *German Intellectuals*, 9.

which Germans need to engage in its totality and the Nazi period as the negative part of the new German identity. Its foundations were provided by Karl Jaspers and intellectuals shaping early postwar left-wing discourse.[33] Having returned from exile to the helm of the Social Democratic Party (SPD), Kurt Schumacher reacted to Adenauer's speech:

> It is not only the duty of international socialists to place the fate of the German and European Jews in the forefront of attention and to offer help where it is needed. It is also the duty of every German patriot to do so. ... By the extermination of 6 million Jewish human beings, Hitler's barbarism disgraced the German people. We will have to bear the consequences of this disgrace for the unforeseeable future.[34]

The SPD stance was developed further and articulated by members of its senior cadre, such as Berlin mayor Ernst Reuter and opposition leader Carlo Schmid.[35] It contained the nucleus of the belief that Germans have a moral duty to react especially vigilantly to certain crimes of the present as a result of past (infinitely more serious) crimes.[36] Importantly, powerful liberal politicians and even some conservative ones also aligned themselves with this stance, including the liberal statesman Theodor Heuss of the Free Democrats (FDP)[37] and in some respects CDU party member Franz Böhm, a dissenter within his own party.[38]

German memory politics continued to be determined by these two approaches for three decades. Debates during this era centred on whether to extend the statute of limitations on Nazi crimes, on the reintegration of former Nazis into society and, increasingly, on practices related to burying the past. Increased attention to the confrontation with the Nazi past was originally a part of the New Left's way of challenging German bourgeois society after 1968, but it increasingly found its way into the mainstream.[39]

A media event in 1979, namely the broadcasting of the US-made *Holocaust* miniseries, is usually thought to have had the greatest impact on

33 Daase, "Addressing Painful Memories," 21–24. Herf, *Divided Memory*, 12.
34 Herf, *Divided Memory*, 273.
35 Ibid., 12, 300–312.
36 Olick, *Sins of the Fathers*, 282.
37 Herf, *Divided Memory*, 312–315. Art, *Politics of the Nazi Past*, 56. Olick, *Sins of the Fathers*, 156–159.
38 Herf, *Divided Memory*, 285.
39 Andrei Markovits, "Austrian Exceptionalism: Haider, the European Union, the Austrian Past and Present," in *The Haider Phenomenon in Austria*, ed. Ruth Wodak and Anton Pelinka (New Brunswick, NJ: Transaction, 2002), 104–105.

mainstreaming memory debates in the public discourse. It was seen by approximately 20 million viewers in Germany, and it set off, for the first time, a wave of public engagement with family and local history.[40] These societal processes of working through the past synergized with the efforts of the two Social Democratic administrations of the 1970s. Chancellors Willy Brandt and Helmut Schmidt both pursued the original agenda of the party, making gestures of contrition: the former by famously falling on his knees in 1970 before the monument to the ghetto uprising in Warsaw, while Schmidt delivered a landmark speech at Auschwitz in 1977, taking full responsibility for the crimes that happened there.[41]

However, only in the 1980s did the two coexisting cultures of memory clash openly in the public sphere. The *Historikerstreit* – the controversy about the uniqueness of the Holocaust and the impact of remembrance of the German Nazi past on national identity – was a direct outcome of the attempt of the conservatives to gain domestic and international acceptance of the *Schlussstrich* and normalize German history and identity.

In his most important early statements, CDU chancellor Helmut Kohl emphasized the importance of moving on, notably during his 1984 visit to Israel and the 1985 Bitburg controversy. The latter arose when, to commemorate the victims of the war and express reconciliation between wartime enemies, Kohl and US President Ronald Reagan visited a military cemetery in Bitburg where *Waffen-SS* soldiers were also among the buried. In his speech, Kohl focused on the separation between Nazis and Germans and claimed the Germans were also partial victims, reiterating the CDU memory canon of the late 1940s. The issue of German victimhood was also raised in the *Bundestag* during the debate about the legal sanctioning of Holocaust denial, when some conservative deputies called for a similar sanctioning of the denial of German suffering.[42]

Kohl was able to draw upon a broader coalition of committed public intellectuals, most importantly historians, but also the philosopher Herman Lübbe, for support. They presented at least four radical arguments in opposition to what was perceived as a tendency to overemphasize Germany's Nazi past. Attempts were made to legitimize a reacquisition of the pre-1933 past understood as distinct from the Nazi period (Michael Stürmer), reintroduce comparisons

40 Frei, "L'holocauste dans l'historiographie allemande," 161. See also Daniel Levy and Natan Sznaider, *Erinnerung im globalen Zeitalter: Der Holocaust* [Memory in the global age: the Holocaust] (Frankfurt: Suhrkamp, 2001), 132. Jenny Wüstenberg and David Art, "Using the Past in the Nazi Successor States from 1945 to the Present," *Annals of the American Academy of Political and Social Science* 617 (2008): 77.

41 Herf, *Divided Memory*, 338–346.

42 Ibid., 351. See also Art, *Politics of the Nazi Past*, 69–72. Olick, *Sins of the Fathers*, 349–367.

and causal relationships with Bolshevism into interpretations of Nazism (Ernst Nolte), highlight the ethical aspect of anti-Soviet defensive efforts at the end of the war (Andreas Hillgruber) and plead for a return to factual historiography and an abandonment of the moralizing perspective of German thinking about the past in scholarship (Joachim Fest).

The *Historikerstreit* of the mid-1980s, however, also helped to reformulate and strengthen the *non-German German* identity as formulated first and foremost by Jürgen Habermas in these debates. Following the press scandal, FRG President Richard von Weizsäcker argued in support of accepting liability for Nazi crimes, which would span generations, regardless of personal involvement. He emphasized that German victimhood must never be thought of separately from German aggression.[43] Weizsäcker's abandonment of the competitive victimhood thesis in the midst of a highly visible public debate contributed significantly to shaping a memory framework that prohibits both displacement of blame and the relativization of the suffering of primary victim groups. Buttressed by the moral support of his statements – he was a conservative president in open conflict with a similarly conservative chancellor – a German intellectual majority formed around this second position in the *Historikerstreit*. For the first time in German history, a clear elite preference emerged around accepting responsibility as Germans for the totality of German (not Nazi) history and relinquishing the strategies of *Schlussstrich* and displacement.

Post-unification Germany rejected the arguments of intellectuals and politicians, such as author Günther Grass and the SPD's Oskar Lafontaine, who had expressed reservations about reuniting the country due to Germany's Nazi past. At the same time, these voices reminded Germans that their national triumph, their reunification, came with a moral responsibility. It is often claimed that the German memory bargain consisted of internal support for reunification and a renewed commitment to memory work. However, two pessimistic arguments can be levelled against this interpretation. First, in 1993 Chancellor Kohl succeeded in inaugurating his *Neue Wache* war memorial project, which places victims and perpetrators on the same level by presenting Germans and Jews in quasi-equal roles as victims. It was an important reminder that the *Schlussstrich* mentality and traditions of competitive victimhood had not lost all legitimacy.[44] Furthermore, in the post-reunification years, increased

43 Herf, *Divided Memory*, 352–358. Art, *Politics of the Nazi Past*, 72–73.

44 Bill Niven, "Introduction: German Victimhood at the Turn of the Millennium," in *Germans as Victims: Remembering the Past in the Contemporary Germany*, ed. Bill Niven (Houndmills: Palgrave Macmillan, 2006), 1–25.

attention was paid to German suffering during and after the war, including the Allied bombings and the postwar expulsion of about 15 million Germans.[45] While accounts of German suffering need not be (and in fact are not) in all cases embedded in the phraseology of competitive victimhood, several contributions to the subject brought this aspect to the fore.

In contrast to these examples suggesting that German victimhood roles and displacement strategies have survived intact, a far greater number of at least equally important instances of memory work could be cited. These attest to the continued prevalence of the contrition framework in post-1989 German mnemonic culture. President Roman Herzog (CDU) chose to attend the Jewish commemoration of the liberation of Auschwitz-Birkenau on January 27, 1995 rather than the official governmental commemoration, as a gesture of atonement to the victim community. A year later, the first German national (as opposed to international) day of mourning was held on the anniversary of the liberation of Auschwitz-Birkenau. Most importantly, November 9, the German "Day of Fate" (*Schicksalstag*), has achieved broad acceptance as referring to both the Nazi antisemitic pogroms of 1938, also known as *Kristallnacht* (Night of Broken Glass), and the fall of the Berlin Wall in 1989. Inscribing the memory of Nazi violence into the memory of the reunification presents German history and identity as burdened with perpetrator legacies, an aspect that bears remembering even (or especially) in the context of celebrating democratic unity.[46]

Memory debates, however, remained dominant in the new millennium and were reflected in various public controversies, such as the Walser debate, the *Wehrmacht* exhibition and the Goldhagen controversy. In 1999, author Martin

45 Bill Niven, "The Globalisation of Memory and the Rediscovery of German Suffering," in *German Literature in the Age of Globalisation*, ed. Stuart Taberner (Birmingham: University of Birmingham Press, 2004), 229–245. Stefan Berger, "On Taboos, Traumas and Other Myths," in *Germans as Victims: Remembering the Past in the Contemporary Germany*, ed. Bill Niven (Houndsmills: Palgrave Macmillan, 2006), 210–224. Jie Hyun Lim, "Victimhood Nationalism in Contested Memories: National Mourning and Global Accountability," in *Memory in a Global Age: Discourses, Practices and Trajectories*, ed. Aleida Assmann and Sebastian Conrad (Houndsmills: Palgrave Macmillan, 2010), 138–162. See also Niven, "Introduction," 1–25. Wittlinger and Boothroyd, "A 'Usable' Past at Last?," 490–492. Claus Leggewie and Erik Meyer, *"Ein Ort, an den man gerne geht": Das Holocaust-Mahnmal und die Deutsche Geschichtspolitik nach 1989* ["A place to go to": the Holocaust memorial and German history policy after 1989] (Munich: Hanser, 2005). Gudrun Brockhaus, "The Emotional Legacy of the National Socialist Past in Post-War Germany," in *Memory and Political Change*, ed. Aleida Assmann and Linda Shortt (Houndsmills: Palgrave Macmillan, 2012), 38.

46 Herf, *Divided Memory*, 369–370. Art, *Politics of the Nazi Past*, 78.

Walser, in his controversial acceptance speech on receiving the Peace Prize of German Booksellers, expressed his resentment over the vacuous rituals of remembrance and guilt and argued for self-internalization of the Holocaust memory. While the audience endorsed his speech with applause, Walser's objection to public remembrance of the Holocaust provoked a major public debate, and this in itself demonstrated the commitment not to relinquish these rituals.[47] The *Wehrmacht* exhibition (1999–2002) challenged the myth of the *Wehrmacht* as a professional military organization that should be seen as qualitatively different from the zealous, ideology-driven *SS*. In doing so, it undermined the distinction between Germans who served as soldiers and Germans who were willing Nazis, a cornerstone of Adenauer's and Kohl's identity politics.[48]

Perhaps most illustrative of the state of coming to terms with the past has been the reception of Daniel Goldhagen's book, *Hitler's Willing Executioners*, which explained the Holocaust as a product of the uniquely ardent antisemitism of ordinary Germans. While Goldhagen's claims and methods have remained the subject of scrutiny from a scholarly standpoint, large crowds turned out in several cities during his tour, where he argued his case with moderation in response to the critical observations made by similarly self-restrained German historians.[49] The fact that crowds tended to side with him can be interpreted as a collective acknowledgment, not so much of the absolute truth of his theses but of their potential truth. This mentality was also reflected in the insistence of the German political elite to follow through with the construction of the Holocaust memorial in Berlin despite dissenting voices warning of the effects of a permanent reminder of guilt. The inauguration of the memorial and its acceptance by the German public reveal a climate of opinion that permitted and even facilitated remembrance practices through the role of the perpetrator and reflected a commitment to renounce strategies of displacement and competitive victimhood in memory culture.

In addition, an important intellectual contribution to the post-*Historikerstreit* memory work that contributed to creating the conditions necessary for continued NPI practices should be acknowledged here. The danger of competitive

47 Wittlinger and Boothroyd, "A 'Usable' Past at Last?," 493.

48 Walter Manoschek, "Die Wehrmacht und die Ausstellung 'Vernichtungskrieg. Verbrechen der Wehrmacht 1941 bis 1944' als Thema österreichischer Vergangenheitspolitik" [The Wehrmacht and the exhibition 'War of Extermination: Crimes of the Wehrmacht 1941–1944' as a topic of Austrian politics of the past], *Österreichische Zeitschrift für Politikwissenschaft* 30, no. 1 (2001): 61–77.

49 István Deák, *Essays on Hitler's Europe* (Lincoln-London: University of Nebraska Press, 2001), 102–103.

victimhood discourses emerging between former East Germans, who sensed a lack of acknowledgement of their suffering, and the victims of the Holocaust loomed large after 1990. In reaction, historian Bernd Faulenbach, who was a member of the commission tasked by the *Bundestag* to investigate perspectives for the integration of the memory of the People's Republic of Germany into "West" German mnemonic practices, set up a hierarchy, preserving the primacy of the memory of the Holocaust in identity politics while attempting to prevent victims of the communist dictatorship from being marginalized on the terrain of collective memory.[50] Political and intellectual support for Faulenbach's proposal has largely remained constant since 1993.

In the German case, the initial dominance of the *Schlussstrich* mentality – forgetting and turning the page – was successfully challenged in the 1980s. After the convergence of opinions of intellectuals and support from key political norm entrepreneurs such as President Weizsäcker, reunification provided an additional impetus for critical engagement with the German past and perpetrator legacies. While there are still doubts about the intensive engagement with inherited guilt, mechanistic repetition of contrition rituals and settings pre-configured to force reflection, Germany represents a culture of memory in which political and intellectual norm entrepreneurs have successfully cooperated to create multiple and structured opportunities for reflection. This promotes the culture of internalization of the perpetrator perspective in remembrance. Without overlooking the survival of practices of externalizing guilt, one can contend that the German case may and even should serve as a basis of comparison in measuring the progress of efforts made by perpetrator communities towards reconciliation. It is from this perspective that I now analyse the situation in Austria and Hungary.

---

50 Aleida Assmann, *Das neue Unbehagen an der Erinnerunskultur: Eine Intervention* [The new unease with remembrance culture: an intervention] (Munich: C.H. Beck, 2013), 114. Originally published in an important volume edited by Werner Weidenfeld. See Werner Weidenfeld, ed., *Deutschland: Eine Nation – doppelte Geschichte. Materialien zum deutschen Selbstverständnis* [Germany: one nation – two stories: materials on the German self-image] (Cologne: Verlag Wissenschaft und Politik, 1993). The theses state that "1. The memory of Stalinism must not relativize the memory of the Holocaust. 2. The memory of the Holocaust must not trivialize the memory of Stalinism" (emphasis in original). For an investigation of the difficulties of integrating the memory of the People's Democratic Republic into democratic German politics of identity, see Jan-Werner Müller, "Just Another *Vergangenheitsbewältigung*? The Process of Coming to Terms with the East German Past Revisited," in "From Stasiland to Ostalgie: The GDR Twenty Years After," special issue, *Oxford German Studies* 38, no. 3 (2009): 334–344.

III Austria: From Refusal to Reflection

Austrian engagement with the National Socialist past evolved differently than in (West) Germany, where two competing modes of accepting responsibility prevailed early on. While in Germany the stakes in memory work concerned the displacement or internalization of the perpetrator perspective, in Austria elites opted for forgetting. Postwar leaders, irrespective of party affiliation, seized on the 1943 Moscow Declaration, in which the Allied Powers recognized Austria as a victim of Nazi aggression. In doing so – while disregarding the section of the declaration according to which Austrian society also bore responsibility for Nazi crimes – they disseminated the myth of Austrian victimhood.[51]

A second difference was the degree of antagonism in the non-Nazi segments of society. In Weimar Germany, the 1918–1922 period of violence could at least partially be converted into a fragile truce, whereas Austrian politics had spiralled towards civil war in the interwar period. The opposing political camps were characterized as "substitute nations," since the state lacked an overarching national identity.[52] As a result, Austria, the "state nobody wanted," had to be invented for a second time in 1945–1955, again as the outcome of external pressure rather than a domestic sense of identity.[53] The former enemies – the Christian Socials renamed as the Austrian People's Party (ÖVP) and the Social Democrats under the new name Austrian Socialist Party (SPÖ) – co-constructed the new state in a manner that offered multiple guarantees to the other party that it would not fall victim to its one-time enemy.[54]

---

51 The original theses for the victimhood myth were laid out by Christian Social Austrofascist émigrés during the war, that is to say, by refugees who *were* actual victims of Nazism. See Anton Pelinka, "Der verdrängte Bürgerkrieg" [The repressed civil war], in *Das grosse Tabu: Österreichs Umgang mit seiner Vergangenheit* [The big taboo: Austria's handling of its past], ed. Anton Pelinka and Erika Weinzierl (Vienna: Edition S, 1987), 145–149. Matthew P. Berg, "Challenging Political Culture in Postwar Austria: Veterans' Associations, Identity, and the Problem of Contemporary History," *Central European History* 30, no. 4 (1997): 515. Markovits, "Austrian Exceptionalism," 104. Wüstenberg and Art, "Using the Past," 78.

52 Anton Pelinka, "The Great Austrian Taboo: The Repression of the Civil War," in "Austria," special issue, *New German Critique*, no. 43 (1988): 71, 76.

53 Harry Ritter, "Austria and the Struggle for German Identity," *German Studies Review* 15 (1992): 112–113.

54 G. Bingham Powell, *Social Fragmentation and Political Hostility: An Austrian Case Study* (Palo Alto, CA: Stanford University Press, 1970). Pelinka, "The Great Austrian Taboo," 74–75. Gerhard Botz, "The Short- and Long-Term Effects of the Authoritarian Regime and of Nazism in Austria: The Burden of a 'Second Dictatorship,'" in *Historical Social Research, Supplement*, no. 28 (2016): 201.

The rule of governing in a grand coalition and distributing government and other administrative positions was justified as a means of creating the preconditions for mutual security and forgiveness. Finally, in 1964, the conservative chancellor Alfons Gorbach and his Social Democratic deputy Bruno Pittermann symbolically accepted each other's handshake over the memorial of the 1934 Social Democratic uprising in Vienna.[55]

The Allied Powers also shared a desire to see an Austrian identity emerge, thus they endorsed the separation of the *Ostmark* from the German lands.[56] Consequently, Austrian collective amnesia was uncontested. It represented the shared policy choice of international actors and domestic decision-makers. In the German case, the perpetrator role could be displaced (to the Nazis), but responsibility in its entirety could not. In the case of Austria's first governments, restrained neither by international supervision nor a revisionist opposition, this was precisely what happened, despite formal acquiescence to reparations payments after 1955.[57]

One component of the truce between the mainstream right and left was the limitation placed on the People's Courts (war crime tribunals), which resulted in far fewer sentences than in occupied countries or Germany.[58] Nazi party members temporarily lost the right to vote and many were fired, but they soon found themselves rehired. As the outcome of an agreement between the ruling parties and the occupying powers, they regained their right to vote *en masse* after the 1948 amnesty. While Adenauer's early *Schlussstrich* strategy

55 Heidemarie Uhl, "Von 'Endlösung' zu 'Holocaust': Die TV-Ausstrahlung von 'Holocaust' und die Transformationen des österreichischen Gedächtnisses" [From the 'Final Solution' to 'Holocaust': the TV-broadcast of 'Holocaust' and the transformation of Austrian memory], *Historical Social Research* 30, no. 4 (2005): 34.

56 Ritter, "Austria and the Struggle for German Identity," 113.

57 Herbert Olbrich, "'...was wissen Se, was mir damals alles mitg'macht ham!' Österreich und seine nationalsozialistische Vergangenheit" ['You do not know all the things we suffered back then.' Austria and its Nazi past], in *Die geteilte Vergangenheit: Zum Umgang mit Nationalsozialismus und Widerstand in beiden deutschen Staaten* [The divided past: how to deal with national socialism and resistance in both German states], ed. Jürgen Danyel (Berlin: de Gruyter, 1995), 87–104. Heidemarie Uhl, "The Politics of Memory: Austria's Perception of the Second World War and the National Socialist Period," in *Austrian Historical Memory and National Identity*, ed. Günter Bischof and Anton Pelinka (New Brunswick, NJ: Transaction, 1997), 64–94. Botz, "The Short- and Long-Term Effects," 202.

58 Tony Judt, "The Past Is Another Country: Myth and Memory in Postwar Europe," *Theoria: A Journal of Social and Political Theory* 87 (1996): 45. István Deák, ed., *Europe on Trial: The Story of Collaboration, Resistance, and Retribution during World War II* (Boulder, CO: Westview Press, 2015), 204–206.

was contested by the SPD and to some extent even by President Heuss, in Austria no intra-elite conflict arose, and an actual *Schlussstrich* was drawn.[59]

The complexities of Austrian identity politics became clearly visible when in 1970 Austria's chancellor Bruno Kreisky called Simon Wiesenthal[60] a "Jewish fascist." Kreisky was of Jewish origin, but he became a self-identified Austrian, claiming the "Jews were not a people, or, if so, a *mieses* [sorry] people." Kreisky had also long been the proponent of attracting former Nazi collaborators to the party, and he built strong ties with the FPÖ, the libertarian-nationalists, who had embraced the greater German tradition, as well as various social organizations engaged in "unreconstructed" memory work, *inter alia* about World War II military service and pan-German cultural heritage. When the Socialists lost their absolute majority in 1983, he was quick to invite the FPÖ into a coalition cabinet.[61] Wiesenthal, a self-conscious Jew and Austrian and a conservative supporter of the People's Party, considered Kreisky the archetype of the self-hating Jew. When four former Nazis were to serve in the first purely Socialist cabinet in the history of the second Austrian republic, headed by Kreisky, Wiesenthal made their files public. One, a former *SS* member, was soon replaced, but the others continued to served, some of them for several terms.[62]

Only in the wake of the 1986 Waldheim controversy did the terms of engagement with the past start to shift significantly. The scandal seemed little more than another triumph of Austrian forgetting, culminating in former *SS* member Kurt Waldheim's election to the federal presidency. However, the international and domestic row over Waldheim's election also represented the beginning of the alignment of Austrian memory with international and German patterns of remembrance.

The initial reaction to international criticism included an indignant rejection of "meddling" and the insistence that Austrians were victims, whether they had served in the military or not, as well as, most strikingly, antisemitic remarks.[63] For example, newspapers such as *Die Presse* and *Kronen Zeitung*

59 Pelinka, "The Great Austrian Taboo," 70. Matti Bunzl, "On the Politics and Semantics of Austrian Memory: Vienna's Monument against War and Fascism," *History and Memory* 7, no. 2 (1995): 12. Botz, "The Short- and Long-Term Effects," 202.

60 Wiesenthal was a Holocaust survivor who dedicated his life to documenting the crimes of the Holocaust and finding perpetrators still at large.

61 Pelinka, "The Great Austrian Taboo," 79–81.

62 Heinz P. Wasserman, *Zuviel Vergangenheit tut nicht gut!* [Too much past does not do good!] (Vienna: Studien Verlag, 2000). Art, *Politics of the Nazi Past*, 114. Wüstenberg and Art, "Using the Past," 79.

63 Art, *Politics of the Nazi Past*, 101–144. Ruth Wodak, "Suppression of the Nazi Past, Coded Languages, and Discourses of Silence: Applying the Discourse-Historical Approach to

and many politicians frequently used the word *Ostküste* (East Coast) to refer to people who opposed Waldheim's candidacy[64] and asserted that the *Ostküste* was leading the conspiracy to smear Austria. Given the context and the impossibility of decoding the term in any other way, it has to be understood as a reference to the American Jewish organizational network and media.[65] At the same time, the affair was a catalyst for change. The realignment of the left commenced with the Socialists distancing themselves from their coalition partner, the FPÖ, in 1985, after yet another *SS* scandal, the Reder controversy.[66] During the Waldheim affair, Kreisky's legacy and sway over memory politics finally broke.[67]

The old, interwar Socialist anti-fascism was rekindled first as an intellectual movement (in the Republican Club for a New Austria, a name evoking the interwar struggle for democracy), which attracted the left-wing press and then increasingly involved politicians – both Socialists and the weak but emergent Greens.[68] A coalition had formed, perhaps weaker than what had emerged in Germany, but similar in its dual civilian-political nature and capable of norm entrepreneurship. The shifting patterns of memory and remembrance among intellectuals and parts of the political class became evident during the designated year of remembrance in 1988.[69] Originally, its goal was to commemorate the *Anschluss*, thus reinforcing Austrian victimhood and the Austrian identity based on it. By 1988, however, the discussion had extended to Austrian participation in and support for the Nazi regime. Despite protest on the right, Vienna's Socialist leaders decided to insist on the erection of the occupation memorial in the centre of the city, also featuring the image of the street-sweeping Jew, reminding the Viennese of the task the *citizens* spontaneously imposed on the Jewish population during the heady *Anschluss* days. In addition, with the premiere of *Heldenplatz*, a play reflecting on the circumstances of Jewish protagonists during the *Anschluss*, and the strong statements made by its author,

Post-War Anti-Semitism in Austria," in *Political Languages in the Age of Extremes*, ed. Willibald Steinmetz (Oxford: Oxford University Press, 2011), 358.

64 Bunzl, "On the Politics and Semantics," 14.

65 Richard Mitten, *The Politics of the Antisemitic Prejudice: The Waldheim Phenomenon in Austria* (Boulder, CO: Westview, 1992), 8–10. Bunzl, "On the Politics and Semantics," 16. Art, *Politics of the Nazi Past*, 122. Wodak, "Suppression of the Nazi Past," 356–358.

66 The controversy began when Defence Minister Friedhelm Frischenschlager greeted Walter Reder, a former *SS* major, who had been freed from a life sentence he was serving in Italy, with a handshake. It stirred a political storm in Austria and brought demands for his resignation. See Markovits, "Austrian Exceptionalism," 100.

67 Uhl, "Von 'Endlösung' zu 'Holocaust,'" 32.

68 Bunzl, "On the Politics and Semantics," 16.

69 Wodak, "Suppression of the Nazi Past," 354.

Thomas Bernhard, as well as by playwright and novelist, Elfriede Jelinek, the Austrian intellectual elite was also placing the official memory canon under increasing criticism.[70]

The identity and memory struggles of the late 1980s found their way into politics through landmark speeches by the new Social Democratic[71] chancellor Franz Vranitzky in 1990 and 1991. Vranitzky acknowledged the Austrian role in German history and the crimes committed.[72] In 1991, he made the crucial concession that "many Austrians had greeted the *Anschluss* … and participated in repressive measures and acts of persecution of the Third Reich, in part in leading positions."[73] The primary arena of contestation thus shifted from the territory of Austrian victimhood to debates concerning Austrian perpetratorship, and the terms "Austrian" and "Nazi" were acknowledged as partially overlapping. Finally, the Austrian mode of remembrance became aligned with the German patterns of memory work, if only four decades after the end of the war.

An increasing commitment to facing history led to resentment among some segments of society. The FPÖ and its new national leader, Jörg Haider, strategically capitalized on this, leading to another conflict over memory and Austrian perpetratorship.[74] The "Haider phenomenon," in the context of Austrian memory politics, was not just a populist regression but part of the memory struggles that had been pushed out of the political arena, first by the intra-Austrian reconciliation politics of the permanent grand coalitions and then by Kreisky's conservatism in identity politics.[75]

The foreign reaction to the FPÖ's inclusion in the governing coalition by the incoming conservative chancellor Wolfgang Schüssel in 2000 was met with divergent attitudes domestically. International pressure was not repudiated by a large left-wing coalition but accepted as the consequence of the Europeanization of Austria, in stark contrast to the Social Democrats'

70 Bunzl, "On the Politics and Semantics," 16, 24–28. Steven Beller and Frank Trommler, "Austrian Writers Confront the Past, 1945–2000: An Introduction," in "Austrian Writers Confront the Past," special issue, *New German Critique*, no. 93 (2004): 7. Ritter, "Austria and the Struggle for German Identity," 118–119.

71 In 1991, the SPÖ changed its name from Socialist Party of Austria to Social Democratic Party of Austria.

72 Art, *Politics of the Nazi Past*, 134. Wodak, "Suppression of the Nazi Past," 354–358.

73 Botz, "The Short- and Long-Term Effects," 210.

74 Anton Pelinka, *Austria: Out of the Shadow of the Past* (Boulder, CO: Westview, 1998), 201. Susanna Fröhlich-Steffen, "Die Identitätspolitik der FPÖ" [The identity policy of the FPÖ], *Österreichische Zeitschrift für Politikwissenschaft* 33, no. 3 (2004): 289–291.

75 Lutz Musner, "Memory and Globalization: Austria's Recycling of the Nazi Past and Its European Echoes," in "Holocaust," special issue, *New German Critique*, no. 80 (2000): 78–79. Botz, "The Short- and Long-Term Effects," 210.

reactions during the Waldheim controversy. The movement *We Are Austria* represented a corollary popular dimension.[76] The definitive turn in the Social Democratic approach to the Austrian past came in 2005, when party leader Alfred Gusenbauer "issued a document detailing the party's postwar brown spots," marking its intention to assume a leading role in the reconstruction of Austrian memory.[77] In doing so, Gusenbauer headed an effort that broke the party taboo, namely that the Social Democrats of the interwar period had been pro-*Anschluss* while locked in a life and death struggle with the Austro-fascists. As a result, many party members and even leaders had welcomed the Nazi occupation in 1938.

Another outcome was that the ÖVP-FPÖ coalition under Chancellor Schüssel sought to demonstrate compliance by following the example of Germany in according reparations to forced labourers in the *Ostmark*, declaring Austria's commitment to accepting responsibility. Alongside outside pressure, domestic expectations also contributed to this: the work of the historians' commission set up by Schüssel's Socialist predecessor Viktor Klima in 1998 was starting to exert an influence on historical thinking about the period.[78] Schüssel also accepted President Thomas Klestil's insistence on leaving certain FPÖ candidates out of the government and including a section in the government manifesto about Austrians having been both "victims and perpetrators." In this case, international pressure likely co-determined the outcome, but even so the role played by President Klestil was necessary. Klestil was a cautious norm entrepreneur. He had been Austria's ambassador to the United States during the Waldheim controversy and as *Bundespräsident* had the opportunity to intervene in the largest international controversy involving Austria since the Waldheim case. This meant that international pressure could not be played out against a supposedly "united" Austrian public and domestic critics of the coalition gained legitimacy. While the lack of international pressure contributed to the emergence of an Austrian memory culture of forgetting, this culture could

76 Margaretha Kopeinig and Christoph Kotanko, *Eine europäische Affäre. Der Weisen-Bericht und die Sanktionen gegen Österreich* [A European affair: the wise mens' report and the sanctions against Austria] (Vienna: Czernin, 2000). Beller and Trommler, "Austrian Writers Confront the Past," 16.

77 Art, *Politics of the Nazi Past*, 134.

78 Judith Beniston, "'Hitler's First Victim'? Memory and Representation in Post-War Austria: Introduction," *Austrian Studies* 11 (2003): 3–7. Günter Bischof, "Victims? Perpetrators? 'Punching Bags' of European Historical Memory? The Austrians and Their World War II Legacies," *German Studies Review* 27, no. 1 (2004): 24. Wüstenberg and Art, "Using the Past," 80.

not be overcome by international pressure alone, as the divergent outcomes of the Waldheim case and the coalition controversies demonstrate.[79]

Perhaps the most important statement of the period was made by Klestil's successor, President Heinz Fischer, in an interview in 2006. Fischer directed the public to observe the blatant contradiction between "all historical sources" and the victimhood thesis found in the Austrian *Declaration of Independence* itself. A fundamental revision of the victimhood thesis relating to the *Anschluss* and the acknowledgement that crimes against Jews are not to be relativized were the main focus of the interview – much as Weizsäcker had argued in 1985 in the German context. Fischer was pushing official identity politics far beyond its previous orbit and close to the discourse of advocates of NPI (who constituted a smaller group in Austria than they did in Germany).[80]

While Austrian memory, even within the mainstream, spans a greater spectrum and remains more divergent than patterns of remembrance in Germany, the Fischer-Weizsäcker parallel is perhaps indicative of how the two societies can be compared. The 1980s in Germany were a period in which the reaction to a new conservative identity politics project mobilized *non-German Germans*, whose success in public debates opened the way for practices of NPI. Today, Austrian practices of remembrance also include a strong critical current driven by intellectuals but supported at key junctures by political norm entrepreneurs. NPI is periodically acknowledged by some civic and political leaders, while at the same time traditions of forgetting and displacement of responsibility are proving more resilient and visible than in Germany among some sections of the population. This may be due in no small part to the strength of the post-1945 Austrian identity project, which was based solely on these dynamics of memory. At the same time, this identity project and the overcoming of the civil war memory inherent in it laid the foundations for introspection within political families, including the confrontation of legacies such as Social Democratic acquiescence to the *Anschluss* in 1938. A firm notion of shared Austrian identity functioned as a vantage point from which acceptance of and collaboration with Nazis could be critically assessed. Overcoming internal victimhood narratives dating from the interwar period was a precondition for the consolidation of Austrian identity, and it was this consolidated identity that proved robust enough to bear the weight of memory work.

79 Musner, "Memory and Globalization," 85. Markovits, "Austrian Exceptionalism," 101–102. Bischof, "Victims? Perpetrators?," 23.

80 "Falsche Opferrolle in österreichischer Unabhängigkeitserklärung 1945" [False victim role in the 1945 Austrian declaration of independence], *Der Standard*, June 13, 2006, available at http://derstandard.at/2407834/Falsche-Opferrolle-in-oesterreichischer-Unabhaengigkeitserklaerung-1945 (downloaded on October 17, 2017).

IV Hungary: Culture Wars and the Limits of Memory Work

Hungarian identity politics and memory work have attracted considerable attention in the past fifteen years. This is a consequence of the emergence of post-communist memory studies as a disciplinary subfield,[81] as well as the increasingly conflictual nature of Hungarian mnemonic practices. Examining the Hungarian case requires one to take into account the persistence of competitive victimhood roles predating World War II and the Holocaust. While it is usually accepted that Holocaust memory is tangled up with other traumas of national history, the dynamics of these entanglements are often left undiscussed.[82] This section highlights that pre-World War II political cleavages must also be considered in order to arrive at a more complete interpretation of the memory politics in Hungary. In contrast to Austria, where the rift caused by the interwar civil war was "mended" and the political and social conditions for NPI could crystallize, in Hungary interwar cleavages were rapidly reactivated after 1989, leading to a "frozen" and conflictual social and political environment that has prevented engagement with historical responsibility on a broad social footing.

Central and Eastern European resistance to the adoption of canonical (i.e. Western European) patterns of remembering the Holocaust is often explained by the specific historical trajectory of the region. According to this explanation, communist memory still continues to structure identities, and at least parts of these societies fear that their experience of Stalinism will be marginalized by a European/global memory culture structured around the memory of the Holocaust.[83] This creates a tension with the Western moral imperative requiring sustained Holocaust memory work.[84] In addition, perpetrator memory

81 Gábor Gyáni, "Political Uses of Tradition in Postcommunist East Central Europe," *Social Research* 60, no. 4 (1993): 893–913. James Mark, *The Unfinished Revolution: Making Sense of the Communist Past in Central-Eastern Europe* (New Haven, CN: Yale University Press, 2010).

82 Henriett Kovács and Ursula K. Mindler-Steiner, "Hungary and the Distortion of Holocaust History: The Hungarian Holocaust Memorial Year 2014," *Politics in Central Europe* 11, no. 2 (2015): 54.

83 Regina Fritz and Imke Hansen, "Zwischen nationalem Opfermythos und europäischen Standards. Der Holocaust im Ungarischen Erinnerungsdiskurs" [Between national sacrificial myth and European standards: the Holocaust in Hungarian memory discourse], in *Universalisierung des Holocaust? Erinnerungskultur und Geschichtspolitik in internationaler Perspektive* [Universalization of the Holocaust? Remembrance culture and politics of history in an international perspective], ed. Jan Eckel and Claudia Moisel (Göttingen: Wallstein, 2008), 59–85.

84 Hedvig Turai, "Past Unmastered: Hot and Cold Memory in Hungary," *Third Text* 23, no. 1 (2009): 99.

was suppressed before 1989 with the assistance of the communist parties in power. Acknowledgement of perpetrator legacies once displaced to "Germans," "Nazis" and "fascists" thus threatens national identities rooted in collective victimhood.[85] Central and Eastern European entrepreneurs of memory are in fact proposing a counter-regime to the emerging (Western) European memory canon.[86] This counter-regime centres on the concept of totalitarianism as a common denominator of a universal victim identity. This discourse refers both to the memory of the Holocaust and the memory of the Soviet period, while implicitly attributing responsibility to the imperialist, colonizing great powers bordering the region to the East and the West. Therefore, totalitarianism as the strategic metaphor of remembrance successfully integrates genocidal and oppressive 20th-century regimes into national narratives of history.[87] By linking national histories of suffering at the hands of various imperialists, critical engagement with perpetratorship, chauvinistic and racist aspects of national history, and the underlying ethnic ideologies are avoided and even delegitimized.[88]

However, this explanation fails to account for the fragmentation and dual character of mnemonic practices in Hungary.[89] Neither was the Holocaust made taboo nor were all traces of specifically Jewish victimhood erased before

85 Barbara Zehnpfennig, "Das Ende des ideologischen Zeitalters? Ideologisches Denken vor und nach dem Historikerstreit" [The End of the ideological era? Ideological thinking before and after the *Historikerstreit*], in *Die Gegenwart der Vergangenheit: Der Historikerstreit und die deutsche Geschichtspolitik* [The presence of the past: the *Historikerstreit* and German history policy], ed. Steffen Kailitz (Wiesbaden: VS Verlag für Sozialwissenschaften, 2008), 105–119. John-Paul Himka, "Obstacles to the Integration of the Holocaust into Post-Communist East European Historical Narratives," *Canadian Slavonic Papers / Revue Canadienne des Slavistes* 50, nos. 3–4 (2008): 360–370.

86 Zoltán Dujisin, "Post-Communist Europe: On the Path to a Regional Regime of Remembrance?," in *Thinking through Transition: Liberal Democracy, Authoritarian Pasts, and Intellectual History in East Central Europe after 1989*, ed. Michal Kopeček and Piotr Wciślik (Budapest: Central European University Press, 2015), 558–559. See also Joerg Hackmann, "From National Victims to Transnational Bystanders? The Changing Commemoration of World War II in Central and Eastern Europe," *Constellations* 16, no. 1 (2009): 167–181. Norman J.W. Goda, ed., *Jewish Histories of the Holocaust: New Transnational Approaches* (New York-Oxford: Berghahn Books, 2014). Ferenc Laczó, "Caught between Historical Responsibility and the New Politics of History: On Patterns of Hungarian Holocaust Remembrance," in *Life Writing and Politics of Memory in Eastern Europe*, ed. S. Mitroiu (Basingstoke: Palgrave Macmillan, 2015), 191.

87 Dujisin, "Post-Communist Europe," 568–571.

88 Michael Shafir, "Ideology, Memory and Religion in Post-Communist East Central Europe," *Journal for the Study of Religions and Ideologies* 15, no. 44 (2016): 54–60.

89 Kristian Gerner, "Between the Holocaust and Trianon – Historical Culture in Hungary," in *How the Holocaust Looks Now: International Perspectives*, ed. Martin L. Davies and Claus-Christian W. Szejnmann (Houndsmills: Palgrave Macmillan, 2006).

1989.[90] Forty-three per cent of the postwar trials included accusations concerning crimes committed against Jews, and important relevant documents were published in the late 1940s, including a Black Book on the genocide.[91] Only during the Stalinist period did memory work come to a complete halt. In the post-Stalinist era, first during the Eichmann trials and later with increasing frequency, the Hungarian press regularly reported on news connected to the Holocaust and acknowledged that Jews had been persecuted by Nazis and their Hungarian allies.[92] While international politics – particularly the degree to which Israel was in conflict with the Socialist bloc – influenced the openness of public discourse on the Holocaust,[93] at no time did the intelligentsia's engagement with the past completely cease after the publication of the first editions of official documents relating to the Holocaust during the late 1950s.[94] This may have been facilitated by the decision of the Hungarian ruling regime to pursue a non-nationalist approach to its politics of history after the 1956 revolution. Without attempting to identify the causes, one can conclude that reflection on Hungarian participation in the Holocaust was present in various branches of Hungarian intellectual life prior to the fall of communism. With regard to historiography, for instance, Randolph Braham observed that by the 1980s Hungarian scholarship had made very important inroads into constructing an academic narrative about the Holocaust in Hungary, which conformed to standards of contemporary "Western" scholarship.[95]

90 Gerhard Seewann and Éva Kovács, "Juden und Holocaust in der Ungarischen Erinnerungskultur seit 1945" [Jews and the Holocaust in the Hungarian culture of remembrance since 1945], *Südosteuropa* 54, no. 1 (2006): 24–59. Regina Fritz, "Wandlung der Erinnerung in Ungarn: Von der Tabuisierung zur Thematisierung des Holocaust" [Transformation of remembrance in Hungary: from taboo to the thematization of the Holocaust], *Zeitgeschichte* 33, no. 6 (2006): 303–317.

91 Ildikó Barna and Andrea Pető, *Political Justice in Budapest after WWII* (Budapest: Central European University Press, 2015).

92 Kata Bohus, "Not a Jewish Question? The Holocaust in Hungary in the Press and Propaganda of the Kádár Regime during the Trial of Adolf Eichmann," *Hungarian Historical Review* 4, no. 3 (2015): 737–772.

93 Regina Fritz, *Nach Krieg und Judenmord: Ungarns Geschichtspolitik* [After the war and the murder of Jews: Hungary's politics of history] (Göttingen: Wallstein, 2013).

94 Paul Hanebrink, "The Politics of Holocaust Memory – The Memory of the Holocaust in Postcommunist Hungary," in *Bringing the Dark Past to Light: The Reception of the Holocaust in Postcommunist Europe*, ed. John-Paul Himka and Joanna Beata Michlic (Lincoln, NE: University of Nebraska Press, 2013), 266–267.

95 Braham, "Anti-Semitism and the Holocaust in the Politics of East-Central Europe," in *Anti-Semitism and the Treatment of the Holocaust in Postcommunist Eastern Europe*, ed. Randolph L. Braham (Boulder, CO: East European Monographs, 1994), 1–30.

In fact, memory work started comparatively early even in strongly supervised genres, such as feature films. Despite visual culture being heavily monitored due to its reach, István Szabó's early films, including *Father* (1966), incorporated complex scenes of a society grappling with its past. Their themes focused on the uncertainty of Jewish-Hungarian identity, the forgetting and covering up of Jewish identity in a post-Holocaust society, as well as the memory of the mass murder of Jews by the Hungarian Arrow Cross during the siege of Budapest.[96] By the 1980s, works such as *Job's Rebellion*, a film intended for the broader public that explicitly presented Hungarian complicity, could be produced. The film tells the story of a Hasidic man who adopted a gentile orphan and attempted to save him as he and his wife were being deported. The deportation scene of the film unambiguously depicts Hungarian gendarmes and local authorities – as opposed to Germans – deporting Jews. In 1984, a documentary by Gyula Gazdag, entitled *Package Tour*, reported on a group, many among them survivors, undertaking an organized trip to Auschwitz. The film featured numerous scenes in which survivors reminisced about the Holocaust, and Gazdag abstained from imposing a specific directorial vision about "streamlining" memory. Most strikingly, a documentary film about Italian-Hungarian author and Holocaust survivor Edith Bruck was allowed to have a brief run in cinemas. The film *The Visit* showed Bruck visiting the country and the village from where she had been chased away after returning from the Nazi death camps. This type of portrayal of anti-Jewish violence (by non-Nazi perpetrators who had seized Jewish property) was unique in the Eastern bloc.[97]

While the communist regime certainly never sought to encourage society to reflect on the Holocaust, it passively acknowledged it and partly tolerated the increasing engagement of intellectuals with perpetrator legacies and even allowed such engagement to gain some visibility. As Kata Bohus argues,

96 Joshua Hirsch, "István Szabó: Problems in the Narration of Holocaust Memory," *Journal of Film and Video* 51, no. 1 (1999): 3–11.

97 The only exception being representations of the Holocaust in Northern Transylvania. Increasingly nationalist Romanian communist authorities even encouraged engagement with Hungarian participation in the Holocaust – importantly, while prohibiting all discussion of Romanian complicity. As this makes it clear, the Romanian case of research on Northern Transylvania conducted in the 1980s does not so much constitute an exception, but rather serves as a case in point about how nationalist mnemonic practices manipulate the past.

> The Kádárist narrative tried to incorporate the Holocaust into Hungarian history (rather than just treating it as part of Jewish or German history), but also tried to frame the anti-Semitism of the period as an element of Fascism and something that the communists had defeated, both in 1945 and 1956. This narrative may be ideologically loaded, but it should not be dismissed as complete fiction, much less as entirely tabooizing the Holocaust.[98]

The post-1989 "memory bomb" – as Andrea Pető describes it – exploded not because of an absolute lack of previous memory work, but due to its insular character within a largely passivized society. It was the combination of freedom to reflect and the need to shape a new culture of remembrance that set a broader process of historical contestations in motion.[99]

The pre-1989 taboo thesis thus does not hold in the case of Hungary. The specificity of the Jewish experience during World War II was not marginalized to the same extent as, for instance, had been the case in Poland.[100] The puzzle is therefore why, despite a relatively early start at facing history and perpetrator legacies compared to other states of the Soviet bloc, Hungary has not progressed towards a political culture that facilitates mnemonic practices rooted in NPI. The following sections aim to shed light on parts of this puzzle.

With regard to engagement with its troubled past, post-communist, newly democratic Hungary in the early 1990s followed neither Germany nor post-socialist countries engaged in institutionalized forgetting, such as Romania. The best parallel can be drawn with Austria in the 1980s. In Austria, intellectuals of the left and politicians/norm entrepreneurs at that time engaged in shifting prevailing conceptualizations of perpetrators from an externalized subject (German Nazis) towards their own community (Austrians). At the same time, the prevailing thesis in society and the political mainstream remained based on national innocence and victimhood. In the case of Hungary, a similar minority effort was unfolding, while societal and political majorities still focused

98 Bohus, "Not a Jewish Question," 767.

99 Regina Fritz, "Gespaltene Erinnerung. Museale Darstellungen des Holocaust in Ungarn" [Split memory: museum depictions of the Holocaust in Hungary], in *Nationen und ihre Selbstbilder. Postdiktatorische Gesellschaften in Europa* [Nations and their self-images: post-dictatorial societies in Europe], ed. Regina Fritz, Carola Sachse and Edgar Wolfrum (Göttingen: Wallstein, 2008), 128–148. Andrea Pető, "'Hungary 70': Non-remembering the Holocaust in Hungary," *Culture & History Digital Journal* 3, no. 2 (2014). Available at http://cultureandhistory.revistas.csic.es/index.php/cultureandhistory/article/view/55/210.

100 Joanna Michlic, "Coming to Terms with the 'Dark Past': The Polish Debate about the Jedwabne Massacre," *Acta: Analysis of Current Trends in Anti-Semitism* 21 (2002): 29–32.

on displacing the guilt to the Arrow Cross and Nazi sympathizers, as opposed to "good" Hungarians. Conservative politicians – including József Antall, the first democratically elected prime minister – called for remembrance and acknowledgment of Jewish victimhood during the inauguration of several, nevertheless modest, memorials.[101] However, Antall and other leading politicians shied away from the question of government and non-Jewish Hungarian (majority) participation in the Holocaust.[102]

Also, similarly to Germany and Austria during their quests for acceptance in the international community and NATO membership, the Hungarian political class virtually unanimously supported reparation payments. In conceptual terms, their identity politics were not unlike those of Adenauer in Germany or Renner in Austria. It was the symbolic "Other" of the newly democratic state – the representatives of a foreign, totalitarian imperialism and their Hungarian allies – who was guilty of the crime of genocide.[103] The historical construction underlying this argument was not entirely false. It was the German and not the Hungarian state that created and operated the death camps, and only after the German occupation of the country was the whole machinery of genocide set in motion. However, the proactive and broad participation of the authorities – national and local – and society's bystander behaviour were left largely undiscussed outside the relatively limited circle of intellectuals.

This ambiguity of national history marked out the bifurcation of collective memory with regard to the Holocaust. The twin dilemma could be summarized as an oscillation between partially true claims that are historically valid only together, rather than separately. Relative security for masses of Jews *and* rampant antisemitism characterized the situation in Hungary before March 1944. After March 1944, mass deportations were taking place under German supervision, *but* with a Hungarian government in office and with Hungarian authorities executing the plans. These ambiguities surfaced in intellectual discourses in the early 1990s. They were translated into (fringe) politics by the breakaway radical nationalists of István Csurka, who were excluded from the centre-right main governing party in 1993, as well as by some less significant organizations of the extreme right. These processes generated heated debates in periodicals and occasionally in politics. A broader controversy about Holocaust memory

101 Tim Cole, "Turning the Places of Holocaust History into Places of Holocaust Memory: Holocaust Memorials in Budapest, Hungary, 1945–1995," in *Image and Remembrance: Representation and the Holocaust*, ed. Shelley Hornsten and Florence Jacobowitz (Bloomington, IN: Indiana University Press, 2003), 272–287.

102 Attila Pók, *Scapegoating in Twentieth Century Hungary: History and Historiography* (Szombathely: Savaria University Press, 2009), 148.

103 Laczó, "Caught between Historical Responsibility," 188, 192–193.

arose, but not because the strategy of externalization pursued by Hungarian conservatives was challenged directly by the left or by a coalition of intellectuals. The centre-right government's gestures regarding the Holocaust found acceptance both abroad and domestically. Indeed, post-1989 memory culture was characterized at first by important overlaps across political camps. There was a widely shared sense of imperative to identify the causes of the moral bankruptcy of the socialist dictatorship,[104] and the Holocaust memory fit into this to the extent that it represented an instance of the superiority of democratic Hungary over its socialist predecessor.[105] If it was imperative to bring to light the previously taboo memory of the Stalinist labour camps and other repressive measures, then, for the same reasons, it was necessary to acknowledge a specific Jewish suffering.

In stark contrast to the common ground with regard to victims of totalitarian systems, including Jewish victims of the Holocaust, opinions concerning the political leaders of the 20th century showed radical divergence. The most serious disagreements splitting the mainstream right and left (rather than the mainstream and the fringe) were caused by conflicting interpretations of the interwar period, its intellectual legacies and the memory of the regime named after the regent, Miklós Horthy. These disputes peaked in the autumn of 1993, when Horthy was reburied[106] in Hungary in a private but large-scale ceremony attended by several government officials. Through his figure the issues of modernity, interwar Hungary's political legacies and the Holocaust became entangled.[107]

The quasi-civil war, which took place in 1919, ended in a frozen conflict spanning the interwar years. After 1920, the left – not only the communists – was blamed by the triumphant right for the dissolution of the historical Kingdom of Hungary, for the defeat in World War I and, in general, for importing a cosmopolitan and "Jewish" spirit into the country, which they deemed rootless

104 Ferenc Laczó, "The Many Moralists and the Few Communists: Approaching Morality and Politics in Post-Communist Hungary," in *Past in the Making: Historical Revisionism in Central Europe after 1989*, ed. Michal Kopeček (Budapest: Central European University Press, 2008), 151.

105 Gábor Egry, "A Fate for a Nation: Concepts of History and the Nation in Hungarian Politics, 1989–2010," in *Thinking through Transition: Liberal Democracy, Authoritarian Pasts, and Intellectual History in East Central Europe after 1989*, ed. Michal Kopeček and Piotr Wciślik (Budapest: Central European University Press, 2015), 512.

106 He had died in exile in Portugal in 1957.

107 Victoria Harms, "Living Mitteleuropa in the 1980s: A Network of Hungarian and West German Intellectuals," in *The Politics of Contested Narratives: Biographical Approaches to Modern European History*, ed. Ilse J. Lazaroms and Emily R. Gioielli (London-New York: Routledge, 2015), 28.

and destructive. On the other hand, the discourse on the left depicted the emergent system as preserving the worst elements of the "old," pre-1914 Hungary and mixing it with new right-wing extremism. Regent Horthy had been called a fascist by left-wing émigrés as early as the mid-1920s, and their assessments of interwar Hungary alternated between the tropes of "neo-feudalism" and "white" counterrevolutionary fascism.[108] This polarization within the political class and the intelligentsia reflected the intensification of the ruptures marking the end of the liberal consensus around 1900. With the rise of an authoritarian right and a persecuted and fractured left replacing the pre-1914 hegemonic liberal ruling establishment, cultural and societal antagonism thrived on the separation of the ideas of progress and nationalism, considered a symbiotic relationship within the 19th-century liberal paradigm.

It was the resurrection of this division – that of Hungarian modernity and the memory of the cold civil war defining the interwar period – that was taking place in the form of controversies regarding the role of Regent Horthy in mnemonic practices. This renewed pre-war cleavage in turn led to the reactivation of victimhood roles constructed during the culture wars of the first half of the 20th century, before the experiences of the Holocaust and Stalinist terror. A previously victimized democratic left challenged attempts to reintroduce Horthy into the national pantheon by making references to his role as a counterrevolutionary and a sponsor of "white" violence, antisemitism and authoritarianism, as well as by connecting him with the alliance with Nazi Germany and the persecution of Jews. On the other hand, the emergent, post-1989 right, now reuniting conservatives and populists despite their interwar conflicts,[109] viewed Horthy as a consolidator of the country in the wake of Bolshevik terror, having achieved successful revisions to the Trianon peace treaty (if only through the goodwill of the Axis powers), as an opponent of Nazism, and, ultimately, as the saviour of Budapest's Jews.[110]

The Horthy question and its corollaries, the memory of antisemitic but Anglophile and anti-Nazi Prime Minister Pál Teleki in particular, raised a dilemma similar to the one that had emerged during the *Historikerstreit*.[111] It was accepted that Hungarian history from 1944 (the German occupation) to 1989 (the fall of communism) represented a rupture. But was Hungarian identity to be

108 For an overview of the mutual demonization, see Gergely Romsics, "Hungary in the Journal Foreign Affairs, 1922–1939," *Hungarian Studies Review* 32, nos. 1–2 (2005): 15–41.

109 Egry, "A Fate for a Nation," 509.

110 Karl P. Benziger, "The Trial of László Bardossy: The Second World War and Factional Politics in Contemporary Hungary," *Journal of Contemporary History* 40, no. 3 (2005): 468. Fritz, "Gespaltene Erinnerung," 132–134.

111 Hanebrink, "Politics of Holocaust Memory," 261–263.

constructed out of opposition to these external forces while efforts would be made to find "acceptable" continuities with pre-1944 history, or was it to be constructed out of opposition to the whole of the country's 20th-century history, except for a few brief democratic interludes?[112] Was the Horthy regime a historical stop on the path to the Holocaust? Or was it an imperfect historical product of a lost World War? Or even a quasi-Western, almost democratic, historical optimum of the interwar period, the achievements of which were annihilated by the two imperial, conquering totalitarian regimes?

In part because there was (and is) no consensus among intellectuals or the political class concerning these questions, the first intense conflicts of collective memory arose around the pantheonization of 20th-century figures and not around the right of victims to be remembered or the legacy of perpetratorship. The latter had been partially known. The figure of the gendarme rounding up Jews, the Arrow Cross shootings and the forced labour service to which scores of intellectuals fell victim, along with many thousands of ordinary people, had all been introduced into public memory prior to or around 1989. Similarly, leading intellectuals and politicians taking part in public discussions accepted that non-Jewish Hungarians would also claim a victim role. A late development of the Kádár era driven by certain groups of intellectuals already included the heroization of the common soldier sent to the Soviet front in World War II, who was seen as the victim of the moral failure of the pre-1945 political elite. On the other hand, systematic engagement with the involvement of the majority society, the question of participation in atrocities on the Eastern front and discussion of the precise role of Hungarian authorities in the genocidal actions were not yet on the agenda.

By 1994, increasingly open and later fully liberated public life recreated the interwar cleavages.[113] The strength of these cleavages also became clear during the second democratic elections in 1994, when the most reliable predictor of party preference became the position of the respondent with regard to issues of cultural liberalism.[114] This memory landscape was similar to that of Austria,

---

112 Michael Shafir, "Hungarian Politics and the Post-1989 Legacy of the Holocaust," in *The Holocaust in Hungary: Sixty Years Later*, ed. Randolph L. Braham and Brewster S. Chamberlin (New York: The Rosenthal Institute for Holocaust Studies, 2006), 274–281.

113 Gerner, "Between the Holocaust and Trianon," 101. Hanebrink, "Politics of Holocaust Memory," 271. Harms, "Living Mitteleuropa in the 1980s," 28–29. Laczó, "Caught between Historical Responsibility," 192.

114 Barnabás Rácz and István Kukorelli, "The 'Second Generation' Post-communist Elections in Hungary in 1994," *Europe-Asia Studies* 47, no. 2 (1995): 251–279. Geoffrey Evans and Stephen Whitefield, "Social and Ideological Cleavage Formation in Post-communist Hungary," *Europe-Asia Studies* 47 (1995): 1178–1180. Pók, *Scapegoating in Twentieth Century*

structured by a civil war cleavage, in which the interwar period had generated two opposing memory cultures. The adherents of each culture saw themselves as the victims of the other – as well as of "third parties." As in Austria, the interwar left considered itself and Hungarian modernity at large a victim of the interwar right. In the memory project of the left, the right represented a continuum stretching to the Nazis, by virtue of its antisemitism, its infatuation with the successes of fascist Italy and Nazi Germany, and its wartime alliance with Germany and collaboration in the Holocaust. For the left, memory work therefore could only mean simultaneous engagement with and symbolic rebellion against Nazis proper – whether German or Hungarian – *and* the right-wing authoritarianism of the interwar period. The interwar right, on the other hand, was reborn in a syncretic format. Not without conflicts, it has seen itself as the heir to both the moderates of the authoritarian establishment and its populist-progressive critics. This syncretism has ensured that the emergent right-wing memory culture inherited a fervently anti-liberal bent rooted in a dual legacy of conservatism and populism. Memory work in this milieu focuses on remembering the victims of a fictitious "left," seen also in this case as a continuum from the radical liberals of the pre-World War I period to Muscovite communists of the Kádár era.[115]

The rapid reproduction of the central interwar fault line between two large political families and the integration of earlier "dissenting" traditions – such as that of the populist intellectuals – into this binary structure yielded an outcome that can be compared to the political culture of the Austrian non-nation before the successes of intra-Austrian reconciliation and nation-building.[116] In the case of Hungary, neither international watchdogs nor committed domestic norm entrepreneurs seemed to have an interest in or an effect similar to the incentives that helped along the reconciliation process of the 1950s and 1960s between the ÖVP and the SPÖ. As a result, no single concept of nationhood, be it cultural or civic, has emerged. Displacement of responsibility to Nazis – whether German or Hungarian – implies salvaging some legitimacy for the interwar Horthy regime. On the other hand, engagement with perpetrator legacies of the government and of society at large could not be undertaken without being (mis)understood as referencing the wholesale moral bankruptcy of Hungarian conservative and populist traditions. The resuscitation

Hungary, 131. Brigid Fowler, "Nation, State, Europe and National Revival in Hungarian Party Politics: The Case of the Millennial Commemorations," *Europe-Asia Studies* 56, no. 1 (2004): 57–83.

115 Pók, *Scapegoating in Twentieth Century Hungary*, 130–133.

116 Egry, "A Fate for a Nation," 508–510. Kovács and Mindler-Steiner, "Hungary and the Distortion of Holocaust History," 51.

of competing victimhood roles on the right and the left prevented memory work on the Holocaust from being conducted on a footing that referenced a common national identity that this work would add to rather than threaten. Holocaust memory became mapped onto these "reactivated" pre-World War II cleavages of society. An emergent transnational practice of contrition was rearticulated in Hungary as the continuation of the unresolved, if frozen, civil war by other means.

In the wake of the re-emergence of pre-World War II cleavages in the late 1980s and early 1990s, the subsequent years (also including the first decade of the 21st century) were characterized by subsequent changes in governing coalitions, each of which engaged in memory politics with limited resources and commitments, while sustaining and consolidating the dualist memory structures of the post-1989 period.[117] A much cited reflection of the outcome of these political power shifts was the 2002 inauguration of the museum named House of Terror, followed by the opening of the Holocaust Memorial Centre in 2004. The former conformed to canonical post-communist memory in subsuming both Nazism and Stalinism under the concept of totalitarianism,[118] while focusing in practice far more on the crimes of the latter and instrumentalizing the memory of oppression to delegitimize the post-communist structures supposedly still holding sway over portions of society and politics.[119] This catered to conservative identity politics.

The Holocaust Memorial Centre has been understood widely as a corrective or response to the House of Terror. Commentators have also tended to note the sustained engagement with Hungarian perpetrator legacies in its presentations.[120] At the same time, both projects were initiated, at least formally, by the

117 Egry, "A Fate for a Nation," 516.

118 Dujisin, "Post-Communist Europe," 553–554.

119 Mark Pittaway, "The 'House of Terror' and Hungary's Politics of Memory," *Austrian Studies Newsletter* 15, no. 1 (2003): 16–17. István Rév, "The Terror of the House," in *(Re)Visualizing National History: Museums and National Identities in Europe in the New Millennium*, ed. Robin Ostow (Toronto: University of Toronto Press, 2008), 47–89. Turai, "Past Unmastered," 97–106. Gábor Gyáni, "The Memory of Trianon as a Political Instrument in Hungary Today," in *The Convolutions of Historical Politics*, ed. Alexei Miller and Maria Lipman (Budapest: Central European University Press, 2012), 92–94. Laczó, "Caught between Historical Responsibility," 193.

120 Regina Fritz, "Ungarische Holocaust-Ausstellungen im innen- und aussenpolitischen Spannungsfeld: Das Holocaust Gedenkzentrum Budapest und der ungarische Pavillon im Staatlichen Museum Auschwitz-Birkenau" [Hungarian Holocaust exhibitions from the perspective of domestic and foreign policy: the Holocaust Memorial Centre Budapest and the Hungarian Pavilion at the State Museum Auschwitz-Birkenau], in *Krieg im Museum: Präsentationen des Zweiten Weltkriegs in Museen und Gedenkstätten des östlichen Europa*

conservative government in power from 1998 to 2002, the same government that also instituted a national Holocaust remembrance day.[121] As had been the case with Antall's conservatives, for conservatives of the next generation, Jewish suffering was not to be denied or even marginalized. Based on the different conceptualizations of the two institutions and seeing them as reflections of the two cultures of remembrance, the key difference concerns continuity and rupture in "national" history. The House of Terror displaces perpetratorship to foreign powers (Nazis and, after them, Soviet communists) and their domestic agents (the Arrow Cross and the Hungarian Stalinists). The latter, importantly, are understood in this frame as being outside of the national community proper and in thrall to "alien" ideologies that have no or only weak domestic roots. It is this externalization of guilt that is challenged by various left-wing coalitions of intellectuals and politicians and that is being reversed in the installations of the Memorial Centre.[122]

In stark contrast to the dynamic memory equilibrium of the first two decades of Hungarian democracy, which saw the two traditions build competing Holocaust memory projects, the present decade has been marked by the dominance of the conservative tradition. This permits a better outlining of its fundamental features in the present and expands on observations that Hungarian memory culture has swerved from European patterns of ever more intense engagement with perpetrator legacies.[123] In many ways, if Prime Minister Antall's aims in the early 1990s regarding Holocaust remembrance are interpreted as similar in multiple respects to those of Adenauer, current prime minister Viktor Orbán's project can be seen as approximating that of Helmut Kohl. Orbán, like Kohl, has spearheaded a drive to recast, in more determinative and combative terms, Antall's original project. What the post-1968 left was for Kohl and conservative public intellectuals around him, the loose network of liberal intelligentsia proposing engagement with Hungarian perpetrator legacies, similarly to contemporary German and international practices, is for Viktor Orbán. Orbán's "integrationist" project is an act of resistance to this European

[War in the museum: presentations of the Second World War in museums and memorials of Eastern Europe], ed. Ekaterina Makhotina et al. (Göttingen: Wallstein, 2015), 203–225.

121 Éva Kovács and Gerhard Seewann, "Ungarn. Der Kampf um das Gedächtnis" [Hungary: the fight for memory], in *Mythen der Nationen* [Myths of nations], ed. Monika Flacke (Mainz: Philipp von Zabern Verlag, 2004), 817–846. Seewann and Kovács, "Juden und Holocaust," 56. Fritz and Hansen, "Zwischen nationalem Opfermythos," 73–78. Fritz, "Gespaltene Erinnerung," 128–148.

122 Benziger, "The Trial of László Bardossy," 479. Pók, *Scapegoating in Twentieth Century Hungary*, 147–150.

123 Fritz and Hansen, "Zwischen nationalem Opfermythos," 59–85.

mainstreaming and the emergent Hungarian "culture of contrition." It includes accepting formal responsibility as regards reparations and acknowledging Jewish victimhood, while at the same time searching for a definitive formula that would salvage the "continuity" of national history, a formula that places Jewish victims alongside non-Jewish ones and externalizes guilt for the genocide.[124]

A formal expression of this conceptualization of history is found in the preamble to the new Constitution adopted with the votes of Prime Minister Orbán's ruling conservative-populist party Fidesz in 2011–2012. The preamble defines 1944 and the Nazi German occupation of the country as the year of rupture and the loss of national sovereignty, which was regained only in 1989. The main phase of the Holocaust is thus excluded from the history of the sovereign nation, and responsibility for it is placed squarely on the "usurpers": the occupying Germans and their Hungarian helpers. In one of his numerous interventions, which demonstrate both the commitment among intellectuals to challenging the government and the lack of public impact these efforts have had, historian Krisztián Ungváry has called this formula the "lie in the Preamble."[125]

The historical perspective articulated in the preamble found its most poignant expression in the Occupation Memorial inaugurated as part of the

124 From 2010 to 2015, the conservative identity project faced a dual challenge from proponents of the "contrition framework," on one side, and members and sympathizers of Jobbik, a radical right-wing party, on the other. It should be noted though that this latter challenge existed in separation from the political and cultural mainstream and failed to have a lasting impact. In terms of its characteristics, it was largely a modernized version of the tenets propounded by the 1990s extreme right ideologue István Csurka, at least as far as Holocaust memory was concerned. It also showed similarities with the identity politics of other ultranationalist political formations in the region. It contained an amalgam of tenets – sometimes contradictory – about Hungarian victimhood and innocence in the Holocaust alongside the trivialization of genocide and emphasis on "global" Jewish resentment towards the nation, as well as a drive to dominate Hungarians by breeding a culture of shame in the country. While Jobbik became popular, with popular support for it hovering around 15 per cent for a time, its memory politics could not gain attention beyond a thin layer of ideologically conscious core supporters. As Jobbik started moving towards the political mainstream from 2016 onwards, it abandoned its earlier Holocaust memory politics, which retreated to where they came from: the far-right fringe, which, while vocal, does not tangibly shape society's mnemonic practices. For this reason, this section focuses on the memory struggles animating the conservative right and its liberal left opposition. Their conflict has proven both more impactful and permanent than the periodical far-right challenges against the mainstream.

125 Krisztián Ungváry, *Tettesek vagy áldozatok? Feltáratlan fejezetek a 20. század történetéből* [Perpetrators or victims? Unexplored chapters from the history of the 20th century] (Budapest: Jaffa, 2014). Kovács and Mindler-Steiner, "Hungary and the Distortion of Holocaust History," 53.

Holocaust Memorial Year in 2014. The memorial shows the German imperial eagle (reproduced with artistic license) descending on the figure of the archangel Gabriel, embodying Hungary. The monument is dedicated expressly to all victims: Jewish suffering is to be seen as included in the broader Hungarian suffering, but without clear reference to its specificity. This is evidenced by a positive and a negative fact. First, the inscription on the memorial is also given in Hebrew. Second, no separate memorial to the Jewish victims was created. A separate project named the House of Fates, dedicated to child victims, stalled during the controversy surrounding the memorial year. It is still on hold (in 2018) and therefore a determinative statement regarding the memory language the government relies on when referencing specifically Jewish suffering has remained unrevealed, as well.[126] It has been clear from public statements, however, that Hungarian perpetratorship is not an aspect that the key contributors to the memory work of the Memorial Year have sought to highlight.

The memorial year – as was the case in Austria in 1988 – also saw increased social activism, which again proved that governments and parties are forced to share guardianship over collective memory with non-political actors, usually intellectuals. Most importantly, the counter-memorial, which was spontaneously constructed immediately opposite the Occupation Memorial, succeeded both in contesting the government's narrative and in offering testimony by means of the various personal objects and messages.[127] The protest it symbolized (which included various grass-roots activities, from on-site discussion groups to recurring demonstrations) cowed the government into foregoing an official inauguration ceremony. It also commanded sufficient moral authority to be accepted – by city authorities, the police, etc. – as a *de facto* memorial to be preserved. A boycott of Memorial Year funding by various organizations, activists and cultural entrepreneurs reconfirmed both the fault line cutting across Hungarian elites and the vigour of the counterculture in the face of the conservative identity project.

The main difference between the Austrian case circa 1988–1991 and the Hungarian case today may be seen in the lack of a sustained dynamic and movement towards shared meanings in memory culture and in the memory of the Holocaust in particular. In Austria, first the Greens and some Social Democrats and later, in a piecemeal fashion, the Christian Democrats of the People's Party came to adopt various aspects of the counter-language developed chiefly by artists and activist intellectuals. Important social and elite groups and parts of the FPÖ leadership did hold on to the more traditional patterns of self-acquittal

126 Kovács and Mindler-Steiner, "Hungary and the Distortion of Holocaust History," 59.

127 Pető, "'Hungary 70'."

and the displacement of guilt. A very clear, if heterogeneous, majority coalition nevertheless emerged, generating a self-sustaining dynamic of increasing engagement with the perpetrator legacies of the Nazi period. In Hungary, the situation has been more frozen than transformed. Dissenters from the government party, who played roles similar to the roles of key conservatives in Austria who called for introspection and prevented the critical counter-memory projects from being framed as an ideological manoeuvre of the "left," were rinsed out of the party. Their roles as intragroup norm entrepreneurs were thus stifled. Senior Fidesz cadre who sought to move the government discourse clearly towards engagement with broader Hungarian participation in the Holocaust had included, in late 2013 and early 2014, deputy prime minister Tibor Navracsics, foreign minister János Martonyi and the mayor of Budapest's 12th (traditionally conservative) district, Zoltán Pokorni. Pokorni had already been side-lined by the time of his interjection in the memory struggles, while the former two left the top echelon of the government in 2014. The memory projects of the right and of the left thus preserved their discreet and oppositional character. While the "hot" phase of the memory conflict has subsided for now, there has been little actual transformation.

The key shift in the government's discourse has been the adoption of a phrase referring to the responsibility of the then Hungarian government, but this should be evaluated in the context of the permanent conflict of mnemonic practices. The formal references to the loss of sovereignty and the political innocence implied by this view of history with regard to genocidal violence in the occupied country have not been replaced explicitly with a nuanced interpretation of the country's situation in 1944. The thesis according to which all Hungarians were victims has not been abandoned or refined so as to permit a specific discourse to promote the internalization of perpetrator legacies in society. Hungarian "culpability" is referred to only with regard to the supposed passivity of the government – usually formulated as "not having protected citizens." This is far removed from acknowledging the vigour and proactive role of numerous government, police and civil service officials during the Holocaust. Furthermore, academic discussion of societal responses to the unfolding deportations has not found its way into government discourse.[128] Ongoing projects documenting local and regional attitudes and demonstrating the numerous instances of approval and opportunism, alongside solidarity, remain unacknowledged in this respect.

The stagnant and dual character of Hungarian cultures of remembrance continue to mirror the value-based and historically conditioned opposition of

128 Laczó, "Caught between Historical Responsibility," 188.

the historical right and the historical left. Importantly, neither is heir either to the Nazis or to the Bolsheviks, but in the memory discourses of each side, the other is always defined as existing along some sort of overarching continuum that runs from conservatives to Nazis and from liberals to Bolsheviks. Mapped onto the cultural fault line dividing the elite strata, Holocaust memory work remains valid within the broader political family, but not beyond. This is the cause of the lack of dialogical memory work that Gábor Gyáni *inter alia* has identified as an important marker of the state of memory work on the Holocaust in Hungary.[129]

The disappearance of (public) dissenters from the conservative camp has contributed significantly to the efficiency with which the current conservative-populist government, after mounting international pressure and domestic opposition, has succeeded in freezing the debate. This outcome is different from post-*Historikerstreit* Germany. There, Chancellor Kohl's identity project was largely defeated in intellectual debate. This defeat became canonical in the wake of paradigmatic interventions by conservative norm entrepreneurs, especially President Weizsäcker. The debate itself unfolded in a conservative daily and a liberal weekly to a considerable extent (the *Frankfurter Allgemeine Zeitung* and *Die Zeit*), signalling the imperfect alignment of political-ideological families in the debate. Facing resistance on multiple fronts and increased scrutiny in the context of a possible German reunification, Kohl demonstrated political instinct in largely shelving his identity project and the *non-German Germans* carried the day. In Hungary, freezing the conflict without permitting the mainstream to realign itself around a novel understanding of history and responsibility remained an option for Prime Minister Orbán and his government.[130]

This outcome reconfirms the conclusions of the earlier memory struggles of the 1990s: as long as two opposed grand narratives accommodate specific discourses of remembering, memory work towards the facing of perpetrator legacies and governmental and societal participation in the Holocaust remains problematic on at least two levels. Within the active political camps, mainly composed of middle-class voters and associated elite groups, remembrance remains party-specific and ideology-specific. As far as less politically conscious citizens go, the memory competition naturally undermines the seriousness

129 Gábor Gyáni, "Image and Reality of a Splitting Country: The Case of Hungary," in *Mastery and Lost Illusions: Space and Time in the Modernization of Eastern and Central Europe*, ed. Włodzimierz Borodziej, Stanislav Holubec and Joachim von Puttkamer (Berlin: De Gruyter Oldenbourg, 2014), 53–70. Pető, "'Hungary 70'." Kovács and Mindler-Steiner, "Hungary and the Distortion of Holocaust History," 51.

130 Kovács and Mindler-Steiner, "Hungary and the Distortion of Holocaust History," 55.

and solemnity of remembrance. It is perceived as another politicized controversy, one which has little direct bearing on pressing issues and concerning which the contrary messages are easy to disregard – especially in the countryside.[131] This way, pervasive patterns of forgetting are more easily sustained across the various micro-communities that make up the larger part of Hungarian society. Hungarian memory work has accomplished the miracle of having progressed – as a result of intellectuals' efforts and some support from political actors – while also having stalled. This is a feature that is not explicable in its entirety with reference to regional patterns of remembrance, such as the post-communist memory complex. Understanding how the post-civil war cleavages of pre-Holocaust memory and victimhood prevent overarching coalitions from forming and engaging in memory work towards NPI remains necessary to explain why such practices co-exist in Hungary with other, self-acquitting memory cultures and society at large.

V Conclusions

Negative possession of identity is likely a vanishing point for memory work. Yet, as I have sought to demonstrate, political conditions facilitating practices of NPI can be described and gauged. The actual practice remains dependent on social participation and on the groups that engage in it, but practices of remembering and discourses of the elite can work towards or against creating enabling conditions for NPI. The German case highlighted the primacy of domestic dynamics (over international pressure) in this respect. While German society has made perhaps unique progress towards generating a social identity that can adopt the perpetrator legacy of history, leaders who gained international recognition for the FRG in key instances (such as NATO membership and reunification) were actually at the helm of identity politics projects that counteracted such progress. Adenauer and Kohl both proposed a universal victimhood discourse juxtaposing Jewish and non-Jewish victims and aiming to provide closure by moving beyond the phase of reflection on the Holocaust. Engagement with the self as the perpetrator was primarily a domestically-driven process, not the outcome of international sponsorship, and the outcome is the product of countless debates and controversies.

In Germany, history was not burdened by a civil war between Christian Democrats and Social Democrats. Society's attachment to the democratic "Western" rump state and its values was strengthened further once the nature

131 Ibid., 51.

of the People's Republic under Soviet supervision became known. In Austria, only a thin intellectual stratum had a real attachment to the state, and the feuding interwar parties in many ways had represented stronger identities than citizenship. In this situation, domestic and international actors were in agreement about the primacy of consolidating an Austrian identity over engaging with the past.[132]

It is clear that reconciliation relative to the interwar cycle of violence came first. Was this a necessity? Was Austrian engagement with its wartime past belated in part because the latter presupposed the former? I would argue that this is at least a partial explanation – beyond accidental factors and the different international context if compared with Germany. The hypothetical alternative is an immediate effort at working through the past by challenging the forgetting of intra-group perpetrator histories. Such an undertaking would be challenged by the other group,[133] and it would alienate at least some supporters, weaken group cohesion (were perpetrators to be identified) and undermine the ability of the group to consolidate its positive identity. In the specific Austrian case, the ÖVP carried the burden of Austro-fascism and the socialists that of Greater German sympathies up to and in some ways beyond the *Anschluss*. Both parties included collaborators in great numbers, as well as former Nazis. They both were or could be linked with perpetrators or perpetrator ideologies. Moreover, the international and domestic incentive structure worked directly against pushing Austrian elites to face the past. It was natural – as elsewhere – that "a future-oriented vocabulary of social harmony and material improvement emerged to occupy a public space hitherto filled with older, divisive, more provincial claims and resentments."[134]

Over the course of the past few decades, in no small part as a result of German memory work and its transnational reception, the international normative framework has become more articulate. Both the governmental and transnational dimensions of international politics have shifted towards stronger expectations and less flexibility with regard to engagement with

132 Heidemarie Uhl, "Nur jener, der mit seiner Vergangenheit im Reinen ist, hat die Hande frei fur die Zukunft. Zur Frage der Instrumentalisierung der 'Vergangenheitsbewältigung'" [Only those who are at peace with their past have their hands free for the future: on the question of the instrumentalization of "coping with the past"], in *Gestörte Identitäten? Eine Zwischenbilanz der Zweiten Republik* [Distorted identities? An interim report on the Second Republic], ed. Lutz Musner, Gotthart Wunberg and Eva Cescutti (Innsbruck: Studienverlag, 2002), 10–26. Wüstenberg and Art, "Using the Past," 81.

133 Stuart J. Kaufman, "Escaping the Symbolic Politics Trap: Reconciliation Initiatives and Conflict Resolution in Ethnic Wars," *Journal of Peace Research* 43, no. 2 (2006): 201–218.

134 Judt, "Past is Another Country," 36.

perpetrator legacies.[135] Simultaneously, domestic intellectual elites have both internalized international norms and developed a critical agenda. Their efforts with sympathetic representatives of the political class represent the bottom-up pressure towards creating enabling conditions for NPI.

A comprehensive, multi-dimensional, simultaneously socially and politically driven process aligned to the framework outlined in the previous paragraph – with international and domestic watchdogs and agents of change – started to unfold in Austria when conditions approximated those found in Germany decades earlier. While these observations are based on historical interpretation rather than fully structured process tracing, a comparison of the German and Austrian cases suggests that both a relatively cohesive political class, governing with social assent and bearing a shared identity, and domestic agents of change are necessary to surpass victimhood narratives and facilitate NPI through mnemonic practices. As the success of the FPÖ and recent Austrian memory rows attest, even when movement away from self-acquittal is achieved, such shifts appear as partial, multi-stage and non-linear processes where progress can and should be measured over the medium and longer term rather than from the close-up perspective of cyclically recurring conflicts.[136]

Research on this subject will be enriched by investigations of more societies with unreconciled identity matrixes and cleavages in collective memory. The interpretation of post-1989 Hungarian memory work and the cultural and political obstacles to the acceptance of collective responsibility reveal a society with a perpetrator memory, visible today in its fragments. The emergence of this memory and a culture of remembrance based on it is counteracted and displaced by major political actors, including the right-wing Fidesz government, now in its second consecutive term. The section on Hungary elaborated on and added to important studies on the subject from past years by highlighting the unresolved competitive victimhood cleavage of collective memory: the revolutionary/civil war experience of 1918–1920 and the subsequent frozen civil conflict running up to 1944. This history of a split Hungarian identity has not been "mended" in the Austrian manner, and to the present day there exists no modern Hungarian civic identity comparable to the consolidated sense of being Austrian. As a result, World War II narratives of victimhood and displacements of perpetrator memory are mapped onto the pre-war conflict zones of Hungarian society and politics, causing the cleavage to become deeper and stronger due to the addition of another layer.

135 Elazar Barkan, *The Guilt of Nations: Restitution and Negotiating Historical Injustices* (Baltimore, MD: Johns Hopkins University Press, 2000), xvii.

136 Similar observations are made by David Art in *Politics of the Nazi Past.*

Hungary's travails with its past as a perpetrator society may provide the strongest argument in favour of not passing too harsh a moral judgement on Austrian belatedness of memory work. The construction of a cohesive historical identity, even if based in no small part on the myth of victimhood and the obfuscation or effacement of Jewish suffering, was in all likelihood a prerequisite for recent and current processes of grappling more successfully with perpetrator legacies in Austria. It created the national subject, which could then question the very history created to underpin Austrian identity, face history and assume responsibility as an Austrian – rather than deflect blame on Nazis/Germans or, for that matter, Christian Socials who destroyed Austrian democracy or Social Democrats who welcomed the *Anschluss*. Hungarians, too, likely first need a shared historical identity expressed with the help of an inclusive democratic vocabulary. Such an identity enables those engaging in memory work to connect their work with society as a whole and take possession of the perpetrator's perspective and shame together, so as to be able to effect a symbolical break with it. Without this, memory work will remain limited to groups on one side of the social cleavage and interpreted as part of a left-wing cultural agenda by large segments of society. As the recently deceased Nobel Prize laureate Imre Kertész reminded us on several occasions, Améry should be a trusted guide in navigating the memory of Holocaust for Hungarians as well.

CHAPTER 7

Constructing Memorials, Constructing Memory

A Note by Alex Maws

"History," Margaret Thatcher once wrote, "is an account of what happened in the past."[1]

The former British prime minister was referring to efforts in the 1980s to change the way that history was to be taught in schools in England, and although she may have intended to inject some clarity into an otherwise contentious issue, it is more likely that her statement muddied the waters significantly.

If history is indeed *an* account, one cannot help but ask: which account? Whose account?

The crafting of state-sponsored curricula can often, understandably, provoke dissent; the idea of a government literally writing (or rewriting) its national history raises suspicions of bias towards or even the indoctrination into a particular point of view. But education does not only happen in formal classroom settings. Collective memory is shaped in many ways, in many places. This article looks at some of these other places, specifically sites of Holocaust remembrance, settings which are also typically overseen by governments and also susceptible to bias.

When considering the content and meaning of monuments, memorials and museums, questions about ideological motivations and historical narratives are just as pertinent, but how commonly do we ask them? How publicly? Events in recent years in Hungary, where a proposed site of remembrance became a battleground in a larger "memory war," were noteworthy because they generated international newspaper headlines relating to questions of representation and contested memory – topics more commonly debated in arcane academic journals.

I had an opportunity to witness this debate firsthand on a visit to Budapest in June 2014, leading a study tour for a group of British secondary school teachers.

One evening, we found ourselves walking through Freedom Square, where we witnessed a scene none of us are likely to forget: a cordon of police officers

1 Lucy Russell, *Teaching the Holocaust in School History: Teachers or Preachers?* Google eBook (2006), 85.

 | DOI:10.1163/9789004386426_008

circling what looked like a small construction site, armed with guns and video cameras, keeping a watchful eye on a group participating in a peaceful vigil.

What the police were ostensibly there to protect was a half-built monument. Intended as a memorial to Hungary's occupation by the Nazis starting in March 1944, the now completed sculpture depicts Hungary as an angel being attacked by a German eagle. Hungary's collaborationist wartime government was thus reduced to nothing more than an innocent victim of Nazism. The construction of the monument was one component of the Hungarian government's Holocaust commemorative year, which was so controversial that it was boycotted by the country's own Jewish community.

Monuments are often ideologically questionable, of course, but as these teachers had a chance to learn, there is an even more troubling context to this one. The preamble to Hungary's constitution, which came into effect in 2012, effectively enshrines this type of Holocaust revisionism into law by stating that the country lost its self-determination on March 19, 1944 – the date of the Nazi occupation. In effect, this relieves the Hungarian state of responsibility for its actions during the war, including the ghettoization and deportation of the country's Jews and mass shootings on the banks of the Danube.

Unsettling though this scene was, it did serve to convey an important message: Holocaust memory remains contested throughout Europe. "History" and the commemoration of it cannot be easily separated.

Another construction site of sorts, which I recently visited, serves as a useful and perhaps less contentious case study for understanding some of the complexities associated with commemorating the Holocaust through monuments and memorials.

I recently had occasion, while visiting the Auschwitz-Birkenau Memorial and Museum, to stop by Block 17, the location since 1978 of Austria's national exhibition, but I was unable to enter. This block, which sits alongside eight other national exhibitions, has been under renovation since 2013,[2] a project funded by the Austrian government.

I was pleased to learn that this renovation project had in fact finally begun. The previous occasion I had visited this section of the camp was in 2007. At that time, Block 17 was very much open to the public, albeit with a curious, temporary sign near the entrance, which I photographed. It read:

> The Austrian Memorial in the former death camp in Auschwitz was officially opened in March 1978, 40 years after Austria's *Anschluss* to the

2 See https://www.holocaustremembrance.com/sites/default/files/austria_presentation_sammelmappe.pdf.

> National Socialist German Reich. Its depiction of the years 1938 to 1945 reflects a viewpoint which today is considered too one-sided, and which shows Austria to be simply the "first victim" of the violent expansionist policy of the Nazi regime of terror, whilst not acknowledging the involvement of many Austrians in National Socialist crimes, in particular the Holocaust.
>
> Such a view of history no longer reflects the way present-day Austria understands its past: the recognition of a shared moral responsibility for the involvement of many Austrians in the crimes of National Socialism has led to a much more balanced view of historical events. Such an attitude is also evident in the increased efforts of the Republic of Austria over the last ten years to re-examine the darker episodes in its history.
>
> In tandem with this changed view of its National Socialist past a new approach to commemorating bygone events has emerged in Austria, the central focus of which is to remember the victims of the Nazi regime, especially the victims of the Holocaust and other victims of Nazism.
>
> This changed perspective of how the country views the years of National Socialism will now find similar expression in a new design concept for the Austrian Memorial, which is now being developed.

This text refers to Block 17 as the "Austrian Memorial," but in this case it is far more narrative or "informational" and less interpretive than the Budapest memorial described above. It blurs the line between a museum exhibition and a memorial. At displays such as this one – whether they refer to themselves as a museum or a memorial – what is being "taught" tends to be quite explicit. The experience of visiting is usually predicated on a simple, implicit arrangement between the host institution and the visitor: the museum/memorial represents an authoritative voice that presents certain information, and the visitor is there to receive that information. The visitor hopes to leave the museum/memorial in the most basic sense having learned something from it.

It is rare that any visitor to such a site is encouraged to think critically or metacognitively about the *context* in which the displays were created or about the *process* through which the information was gleaned. For this reason, the densely worded sign at the entrance to the Austrian exhibition – a sign that would have only been seen by a tiny fraction of visitors to Auschwitz – may in fact have been the most important piece of factual information anywhere on the 450-acre site.

Consider just some of the concessions embedded in those four paragraphs:

- Our understanding of historical events evolves over time.
- Our understanding of the same historical events varies from one place to another.

- It is in the interest of perpetrators to depict themselves as something other than perpetrators.
- Political events and changing political climates have an influence on the above points.
- Museums and memorials tend to outlast the political culture in which they were conceived.

The example of Auschwitz also raises other important considerations that can help further our understanding of how sites play a role in shaping collective memory.

Auschwitz is a site that represents many different things to many different people. The formal name given to it by UNESCO is "Auschwitz Birkenau German Nazi Concentration and Extermination Camp (1940–1945)" – a fairly apt description of its historical functions. When nearly two million annual visitors arrive there, however, they enter a place that goes by a different name: "Auschwitz-Birkenau Memorial and Museum".

What exactly, then, is the relationship between Auschwitz the historical site and Auschwitz the contemporary place of remembrance?

Neither of the names applied to Auschwitz is more accurate than the other, and they are not mutually exclusive. Indeed, Auschwitz today is many things simultaneously: an authentic Holocaust site, a re-created Holocaust site, a formal memorial, an informal memorial and a museum. The lines between each of these are blurry.

During its time in operation during the Second World War, Auschwitz also played many different roles for many different classifications of victims: death camp, forced labour camp, POW camp and a place of medical experimentation, to name but a few. Its vast size and many functions were not typical in the Nazi camp system, and perhaps these anomalies are actually what makes it so popular as a destination today. It was horrific in lots of different ways, not just one, thereby multiplying the ways in which we can attempt to derive meaning from it. And it was big, so there remains a lot of it "to see."

Both in the makeup of its visitors and in its content, Auschwitz is an international site. The museum may be formally administered by the Polish government, but the question of who "owns" Holocaust memory is a more nuanced one. It is worth noting when considering the case study of the Austrian exhibition at Auschwitz that relatively few of Austria's Jews died at Auschwitz. And most of those Austrians who did die at Auschwitz – whether they were Jews or Roma and Sinti – would have been sent there precisely because their rights as Austrian citizens had been stripped of them. This conundrum is seemingly addressed by having two memorials that are ostensibly "parallel" to the other national exhibitions. Block 27 is simply called "Shoah" (a memorial to all murdered Jews, administered by Yad Vashem, Israel's national Holocaust remembrance centre), and Block 13 documents the plight of the Roma and Sinti. The responsibility of memorializing a common group of people is claimed by multiple sources, each with different motivations.

Although it is probably not what was intended, a site such as this – where various national and ethnic entities compete with one another in a sort of market place of commemorative spaces to tell their version of the story – serves as a powerful challenge to the notion expressed by Margaret Thatcher that history is by definition something that happened "in the past." Auschwitz existed before the Second World War (as a Polish military barracks), it then served a different function during the war, and today it serves yet another function. Present-day tourists do not merely learn about history by visiting there: they become a part of it.

Auschwitz is but one Holocaust site, albeit one bearing a name that has perhaps become synonymous with "evil." It is a highly popular destination, but by no means is it the "main" Holocaust site or the most important one.

Where else should we commemorate the Holocaust? Perhaps one's response to this question depends on one's perspective on a broader one: where did the Holocaust *happen*?

Is the Holocaust mainly a story that can best be told at famous places or at obscure and private spaces? Is it a story best told through accounts of how people died or accounts of how they lived? Is it a story about victims or a story about perpetrators?

I referred above to informational memorials versus interpretive ones. Depending on any of a number of contextual factors, some memorial sites may feel it necessary to transmit a significant amount of factual information, while visiting other sites can be an experience that tests the visitor's ability to make sense of abstract art. Berlin's Memorial to the Murdered Jews of Europe – an entire city block covered by huge concrete slabs of varying heights – may be on one end of this spectrum (many visitors do not seem to even realize that it is a memorial at all). The United States Holocaust Memorial Museum – by all accounts far more museum than memorial – is perhaps on the opposite extreme. And there is ample middle ground – with Budapest's new memorial to Nazi occupation being an example – consisting of sites that strike some balance of information and interpretation.

But this does not mean that such sites achieve an ideological balance. As we have now learned, this type of balance may be simply impossible.

Throughout Paris, tourists who may have no intention of commemorating the Holocaust as part of their visit will almost invariably pass local schools, many of which have a plaque on the front remembering those students and teachers from the institution who were deported and murdered. The ubiquity of these plaques is a powerful symbol, and emphasising child victims in particular serves as a reminder of the barbarity of Nazi ideology. Translated into English, one such sign on the Rue des Rosiers reads:

> In memory of the director, staff and students of this school, arrested in 1943 and 1944 by the Vichy Police and the Gestapo, deported and exterminated at Auschwitz because they were born Jewish.

I have, however, always found the wording of these plaques to be provocative, specifically the omission of the word "French" to describe either the victims or the perpetrators, the use of the word "exterminated" rather than "murdered" and the reason given for the crime "because they were born Jewish." Even small, sparse sites of remembrance can be ideologically loaded. The transmission of "facts" is seldom straightforward.

The German *Stolpersteine* ("stumbling stones") memorial project, which has expanded into cities throughout Europe, takes the concept of an omnipresent memorial even further. In reducing the transmission of "facts" to the barest minimum, it is perhaps Europe's most noteworthy example of a counter-memorial.[3] The project installs small brass plaques in the pavement in front of the homes of deported Jews. Each plaque contains little commentary other than the words "here lived" followed by the name of a person. As its name suggests, this is not a memorial space that one makes a special trip to visit as a destination, nor is it something that can be seen very easily by casual passersby; rather it is something that we literally stumble across – an acknowledgement that the historical event we seek to commemorate is actually all around us. This is a particularly democratic approach. Who "owns" this memory, it asks? We all do.

Across Europe and beyond, Holocaust memorial spaces present us with competing narratives, driven by ideological factors relating to place, time and much more. Our collective memory of the Holocaust evolves as a result of who is telling the story and why. There can be, of course, no one universally agreed upon standard of what constitutes an acceptable memorial space or an unacceptable one. Ultimately, "history" is not a place that we visit, and "memory" is not a one-way transmission of knowledge. These are shifting concepts that we engage with and become participants in through our own analysis and critique. Even the most politically controversial memorial spaces should spur

3 See http://www.goethe.de/kue/arc/dos/dos/zdk/en204638.htm (accessed August 20, 2014).

such engagement, but this requires a large degree of historical literacy to begin with. Therefore, as we near the end of the era in which survivors and eyewitnesses are alive and able to personally document historical events, we must be very mindful of how collective memory is transferred – whether it be through Holocaust memorial spaces or other forms of education and representation.

Whether one considers Holocaust memorials to be "for the dead" or "for the living," their construction – in both the figurative and the literal sense – undoubtedly comes with great responsibility.

CHAPTER 8

Ki szereti a zsidókat? A magyar filoszemitizmus [Who likes the Jews? Hungarian philosemitism]

Edited by Endre Mózes

Reconsidering the "Jewish Question"
A Review Essay by György Csepeli

In the early years of the post-Communist era, one did not have to wait long for the re-emergence of antisemitism, which was first professed in this era by one of the leaders of a party claiming to be both nationalist and Christian. At first timidly, cautiously and stealthily, then with increasing courage, muddled ideas and thoughts that after 1945 could no longer be read, heard or seen – but before then had been frequent – reappeared in various forms of mass media. Amid this atmosphere, historian László Karsai published a collection of antisemitic texts written in Hungary during the Austro-Hungarian Empire and at the time of the country's independence following the defeat of the monarchy in the First World War. Karsai sought to prove that antisemitism did not disappear but had only become dormant in Hungary between 1945 and 1989.[1] He demonstrated that antisemitic themes resurfaced in the public sphere after it was opened up by Hungary's post-Communist political transformation.[2]

1 László Karsai, ed., *Kirekesztők. Antiszemita írások 1881–1992* [The exclusionists: antisemitic writings, 1881–1992] (Budapest: Aura, 1992).

2 Author and poet Sándor Csoóri triggered the avalanche in 1990, when he wrote the following in his essay "Nappali Hold" (Daytime Moon):

> The possibility for intellectual-spiritual fusion ended with the Hungarian Soviet Republic, the Horthy era and, especially, the Holocaust. Naturally there have always been and always will be people like Antal Szerb, Miklós Radnóti, György Sárközi, István Vas, György Harag, Ottó Orbán, György Konrád, György Faludy and Tamás Zala. But these days it can be felt more and more distinctly that reverse assimilation is happening in the country: liberal Hungarian Jewry wants to "assimilate" Hungarians, both in style and in thought. To achieve this, it constructed a parliamentary springboard for itself of the type that it has never been able to build before.

See Sándor Csoóri, "Nappali hold 2" [Daytime Moon 2], *Hitel* 18 (1990): 4–7. This essay elicited a multitude of responses and counter-responses. The debate has not diminished since then, instead taking increasingly sharp and vehement turns. See Krisztián Ungváry, "Értelmiség és antiszemita közbeszéd" [The intelligentsia and antisemitic public discourse], *Beszélő* (June 2001): 74–92.

 | DOI:10.1163/9789004386426_009

Antisemitism was reborn, though this rebirth took place without antisemites. Even the leader of the new antisemitic party denied that he was an antisemite.[3] The threshold of the Hungarian public was still low enough in the 1990s for Karsai's book to cause general outrage. For this reason, he decided to put together another volume and collect works expressing respect and sympathy for the Jews.[4]

Author and editor Endre Mózes invokes the memory of this dualism in his 2014 book *Ki szereti a zsidókat? A magyar filoszemitizmus* (Who likes the Jews? Hungarian philosemitism), in which he attempts to promote dialogue and cooperation between non-Jews and Jews in Hungary and counterbalance antisemitism. *Who Likes the Jews?* is divided into two parts. The first part is mainly a collection of excerpts from larger works on the history of the Jews in Hungary. It features historical writings focusing on the events of the late modern period, enabling the reader to follow the history of the Jews in Hungary from the Hungarian conquest of the Carpathian Basin at the end of the ninth century until the Holocaust. The detached, analytical approach of these historical texts is counterbalanced by passages from the works of prominent authors and poets expressing sympathy and tolerance towards Jews, epitomizing the humane and receptive side of Hungarian society. The third chapter deals with those rescuers who were brave enough to resist the atrocities aimed at the country's provincial Jewry following Germany's occupation of Hungary on March 19, 1944. Most of Hungary's Jews died at Auschwitz, while others were taken from there to Strasshof (Austria) and other concentration camps.

In accordance with the request of the occupiers, the Hungarian Minister of the Interior, who was appointed on March 22, 1944, issued a decree on April 7 declaring that "the Hungarian royal government will cleanse the country of Jews within a short period of time."[5] Two days before the decree was signed, Jews in Hungary were ordered to wear a yellow star in public. On April 15–16, 1944, the concentration of Jews living in provincial Hungary into ghettos and relocation camps commenced. One month later, the trains began leaving for

3 Author István Csurka (1934–2012) founded the Hungarian Party of Justice and Life (Magyar Igazság és Élet Pártja) in 1993. The rhetoric of this party strongly evoked the antisemitic speech that was not uncommon in the public discourse of pre-1945 Hungary (and other countries of Central and Eastern Europe). Csurka denied that he was an antisemite and generally did not use the word "Jew" in his writings and speeches, instead employing coded versions of this term (e.g. "foreign-hearted," "Ascher Café," etc.).

4 László Karsai, ed., *Befogadók. Irások az antiszemitizmus ellen 1881–1993* [The acceptors: writings against antisemitism, 1881–1993] (Budapest: Aura, 1993).

5 László Karsai and Judit Molnár, *Az Endre-Baky-Jaross per* [The Endre-Baky-Jaross trial] (Budapest: Cserépfalvi, 1994), 484.

Auschwitz. On May 29, 1944, Lieutenant Colonel László Ferenczy of the Hungarian gendarmerie reported that 58 trains had deported 184,049 people from Hungary since May 15. By July 9, 1944, this number had risen to 434,351 people, whose deportation had required 147 trains.[6]

Rescue in 1944 was not a risk-free endeavour. The deportation of Jews living in provincial Hungary was carried out so quickly that there was no time to intervene. In many cases, friends and acquaintances attempted to rescue Jewish children. Guards and commanders attached to military labour battalions often plagued the lives of forced labourers, but Endre Mózes demonstrates that even some of them were kind-hearted and helpful (at 188–195) and the overall survival rate among forced labourers was significantly higher than it was among deportees. The greatest opportunity for rescue existed in Budapest. Regent Miklós Horthy's July 6, 1944 resolution prevented the deportation of the entire Jewish population of Budapest. Following Horthy's forced resignation on October 15, 1944, the Hungarian radical right came to power with German support. The persecutors committed horrible acts against the persecuted, though there were many who helped for personal or moral reasons. The twenty pages listing the names of those from Hungary whom the Yad Vashem International Institute accorded the title of "Righteous Among the Nations" represents one of the assets of Mózes's book. There are 823 Hungarians among the approximately 25,000 people whom the Yad Vashem International Institute for Holocaust Research has recorded as rescuers.[7] This list may serve as good resource material for future researchers attempting to reconstruct the roads, patterns and life paths of victims. Mária Markovics's study sketches the portraits of some of the Hungarian rescuers.

The main venue of rescue was Budapest, which the hand of Eichmann did not manage to reach. Extracts from Géza Komoróczy's monumental work contained in *Who Likes the Jews?* recall the rescue operations of state officials, Christian clerics, monks, nuns, members of the Zionist movement and foreign diplomats that enabled tens of thousands of Jewish adults and children in Budapest to escape.[8] The most widely recognized among the rescuers was Raul

6 László Karsai and Judit Molnár, *A Magyar Qusling-kormány. Sztójay Döme és társai a népbíróság előtt* [The Hungarian quisling government: Döme Sztójay and his associates before the people's tribunal] (Budapest: 1956 KHT, 2004), 890.

7 Kinga Frojimovics and Judit Molnár, eds., *A Világ Igazai Magyarországon a második világháború alatt* [The Righteous among the Nations in Hungary during the Second World War] (Budapest: Balassi Publishing House/Jerusalem: Yad Vashem, 2009).

8 Géza Komoróczy, *Zsidók a magyar társadalomban I–II. Írások az együttélésről, a feszültségekről és az értékekről (1790–2012)* [Jews in Hungarian society I–II: Writings about coexistence, tensions and values (1790–2012)] (Budapest: Pesti Kalligram Kft, 2015).

Wallenberg, whom the Red Army carried off to Moscow following the capture of Budapest. Apostolic Nuncio Angello Rotta and his secretary, Gennaro Verolino, also played a prominent role in rescue operations in the city. Moreover, Swiss Embassy Vice-Consul Carl Lutz provided assistance to Zionist organizations in Budapest, while Italian businessman Giorgio Perlasca posed as the consul-general of Spain in order to save several thousand people among the persecuted.

The second part of Endre Mózes's book presents philosemitism through the writings of contemporary Hungarian authors. While antisemitism presents a simplistic and straightforward discourse, the case of philosemitism is much more complicated. In fact, János Gadó and András Kovács contend that philosemitism may even serve as a mask for antisemitism, inasmuch as it depicts Jews as the homogenized "Other," thereby disguising resentment towards them. However, Gadó and Kovács do not deny that there is also a sincere variant of philosemitism that is based on sympathy towards Jews and rejection of – and outrage against – prejudice and discrimination.

Hungarian liberalism, which emerged during the Reform Era (1825–1848), constituted a powerful counterbalance to antisemitism.[9] For example, the volume cites poet and dramatist Mihály Vörösmarty, who published an article on the "Jewish Question" in *Pesti Divatlap* (Pest fashion magazine) on March 13, 1848.[10] Vörösmarty concluded his article with a call for an emancipation programme that remained in effect until 1920:

> Because if we want neither to dislodge them [the Jews] nor to convert them, nothing can be more intelligent or more just than accepting them into our milieu, opening our schools and our family and social circles to them as well as every profession so that they can live together with us in common liberty and as they grow up can become true and diligent patriots.

9 Members of the Hungarian political and economic elite recognized in the early nineteenth century that Hungary had fallen behind the two great nation states of Western Europe – France and Great Britain – in terms of economic, social and cultural development. The resulting programme of modernization was first presented at the 1825–1827 Diet of Hungary, signalling the beginning of the Hungarian Reform Era. This era ended with the outbreak of the 1848 Hungarian Revolution, which aimed to gain national independence vis-à-vis the Habsburg monarchy. This revolution ended with Hungary's defeat in the subsequent war of independence in 1849.

10 Mihály Vörösmarty (1800–1855) was a giant of Hungarian romantic poetry and the author of *Szózat* (Appeal), the second national anthem of Hungary, which is sung on Hungarian national holidays to this day.

Emil Feuerstein recounts the story of the friendship that developed between poet Sándor Petőfi[11] and composer and violinist Márk Rózsavölgyi.[12] Feuerstein's article reveals that, without Rózsavölgyi, Hungarians would not be able to dance the *Csárdás*, which later became their characteristic dance.

The volume also includes magnificent sociological studies by Péter Tibor Nagy and Viktor Karády on Hungarian-Jewish mixed marriages, which reveal the dynamics of the most intimate dimension of coexistence between Jews and non-Jews. László Végel connects the Jews to the archetype of minority existence. As Végel writes, "Based on [the writings of] Kundera, I pondered in 1991 about whether in Central Europe the role that the Jews once assumed has now fallen to the national minorities. The endless suffering and adversity have made them suitable for this, though I am still uncertain: are the minority cultures prepared for this task?" (at 354). Endre Czeizel writes about Hungarian Nobel Prize winners of Jewish origin who grew up in Hungary but were forced to leave the country due to the antisemitic atmosphere that arose as a result of the Christian-nationalist political order that came to power in 1920.[13] Enikő Bollobás beautifully recalls the friendship of her father, Béla Bollobás,[14] and Sándor Scheiber,[15] who both believed in the "community of Jewish and non-Jewish people and condemned prejudices and stereotypes and the mistrust that stemmed from them regardless of their direction – from non-Jews towards Jews or from Jews towards non-Jews" (at 206).

Endre Mózes's volume aims to sustain the faith and hope that, despite the dreadful atrocities of 1944, the wounds that Hungarian antisemitism inflicted upon Hungarian Jewry can be healed. The success story of Hungarian Jewry came to a tragic end in 1944, though the events of that year cannot retroactively invalidate the good and positive aspects of what had previously taken

11 Sándor Petőfi (1823–1849) was one of the greatest Hungarian poets. He played an active role in both the 1848 Hungarian revolution and the subsequent war of independence. Petőfi was killed fighting in the Battle of Segesvár in 1849.

12 Márk Rózsavölgyi (1789–1849) was born in Balassagyarmat, Hungary, under the name Marcus Rosenthal. Rózsavölgyi was the father of the style of music to which the traditional Hungarian folk dance known as the *Csárdás* is performed.

13 Nobel Prize winners who left Hungary before the Holocaust include: György Hevesy (1885–1966), who won the Nobel Prize in Chemistry in 1943; Dénes Gábor, who won the Nobel Prize in Physics in 1971; and Jenő Wigner, who also won the Nobel Prize in Physics (jointly) in 1963.

14 Béla Bollobás (1911–1985) was a physician and an active member of the Hungarian resistance. He was persecuted during the Arrow Cross period (1944–1945) and the Communist era.

15 Sándor Scheiber (1913–1985) was a linguist and literary historian who served as the director of the Budapest Rabbinical Training Institute.

place. Antisemitism has undoubtedly left its terrible mark on Hungarian national identity, though it could not prevent the birth of the modern Hungarian nation, without which modern Hungarian architecture, fine arts, literature and theatre, and twentieth-century Hungarian science would not have flourished. Indeed, the question arises whether the modern Hungarian nation would have been born without the contribution of Jews.

Political antisemitism has been reawakened in Hungary in the age of globalization, though circumstances today are not the same as they were during the golden age of Hungarian liberalism when it first gained strength. As deportation statistics show, the majority of Hungary's Jews disappeared during the final year of the Second World War, and only the cemeteries, the empty synagogues and the painful memories remained. Only in Budapest did a significant number of Jews survive. If we want to reconstitute the former alliance between Hungarians and Jews, then we must liberate ourselves from the captivity of past mistakes and crimes. Antisemitism represents an aggravated case of discrimination against people on a categorical basis that goes hand-in-hand with disregard for human dignity, demonization of otherness and one-sided deification of one's own group. The phenomenon exists within the individual, though the explanation can be found outside the individual.

The lesson of Endre Mózes's work is that philosemitism is a necessary but not sufficient element of the struggle against antisemitism. The author of the present review believes that the rejection of antisemitism, xenophobia and prejudice is possible only if the inequality that nourishes resentment, collective envy and expropriating passions does not tear the social fabric.[16] The freedom of the present cannot condemn the rising generations to captivity. As in the past, antisemitism remains an illness affecting all of society.

16 György Csepeli, *A meg nem gondolt gondolat. A zsidóellenességtől és a népirtásig* [The unthought thought: from antisemitism to genocide] (Budapest: Kossuth Kiadó, 2016).

PART 3

Hungarian Minorities

CHAPTER 9

Mobilizing Strategies of Hungarian Minority Parties in Romania, Serbia and Slovakia

István Gergő Székely

Abstract

This article analyzes the intra-ethnic political dynamics of Hungarians in Romania, Slovakia and Serbia. The focus is on the competition between the rival political parties of minority communities, a topic which remains underexplored in the literature on both ethnic politics and parties and party systems. The Hungarian minority parties are described in terms of their programmatic goals, political strategies and relations with kin-state actors. As the ethno-political demands of the parties can be positioned in a rather narrow policy space, I argue that the key to understanding their electoral success lies in their differential clientelistic capacity, which, in turn, depends on the parties' strategies in their host-states and their relationships with relevant actors in the kin-state. The Hungarian minority parties represent puzzling cases from the perspective of the well-known outbidding thesis, which predicts that radical parties will successfully outflank moderates when the ethnic cleavage is salient, since the most successful parties are precisely the moderate ones. I argue that the main mechanism behind this phenomenon is the differential ability of these parties to access resources and maintain clientelistic exchanges with the electorate. The moderates are granted access to host-state resources, most importantly through participation in government. The radicals, however, are simply unable to counterbalance the spoils obtainable in the host-state, since they rely primarily on the support of the kin-state, which, however, is of a significantly lower magnitude over the studied period.

1 Introduction

Recent developments in the field notwithstanding,[1] intra-ethnic political competition within minority groups remains a neglected topic in political science,

1 Daniel Bochsler, "Local Politics and Intra-ethnic Party Competition: Multi-party Systems among Ethnic Minorities in Central and Eastern Europe" (paper presented at the 4th ECPR General Conference, Pisa, 6–8 September 2007). See also Daniel Bochsler, "When Two of the

 | DOI:10.1163/9789004386426_010

both in the literature on ethnic politics and in the scholarship about parties and party systems. The dominant tendency is still to view ethnic groups and minorities as compact entities and unitary actors and to focus on the inter-ethnic dimension of politics.

This paper aims to contribute to the dismantling of this oversimplified perspective by examining the political dynamics within minority communities, building on insights from three countries that are home to large Hungarian-speaking communities: Romania, Serbia and Slovakia. Probing the well-known outbidding thesis,[2] this inquiry offers an explanation as to why its predictions do not apply in these countries.

According to the outbidding thesis, where ethnicity is salient, the chances for moderation on ethnic issues are generally diminished. In this view, moderate ethnic parties that are open to compromise with opposing groups are inevitably challenged by more radical in-group parties that generally accuse them of betraying the interests of their community. However, among the parties of the Hungarian minorities in question, it was precisely the more "moderate" ones that were the most successful in much of the period since the fall of communism. In this paper, I argue that the explanation for this apparent puzzle is to be sought in the differential capacity of the minority parties to maintain clientelistic networks. More precisely, the "moderate" parties perform significantly better in this respect, which is due primarily to their ability to extract resources from their host-states through participation in governmental coalitions. Conversely, the more radical minority elites have no access to these resources; hence, they rely preponderantly on patronage sources made available by the kin-state.

In order to substantiate this claim, I will provide an analysis of the Hungarian minority parties in two steps.[3] First, I will describe the parties in terms of

---

Same Are Needed: A Multilevel Model of Intragroup Ethnic Party Competition," *Nationalism and Ethnic Politics* 18, no. 2 (2012): 216–241. John Coakley, "Ethnic Competition and the Logic of Party System Transformation," *European Journal of Political Research* 47, no. 6 (2008): 766–793. Paul Mitchell, Geoffrey Evans and Brendan O'Leary, "Extremist Outbidding in Ethnic Party Systems Is Not Inevitable: Tribune Parties in Northern Ireland," *Political Studies* 57, no. 2 (2009): 397–421. Christina Isabel Zuber, "Beyond Outbidding? Ethnic Party Strategies in Serbia," *Party Politics* 19, no. 5 (2013): 758–777.

2 Alvin Rabushka and Kenneth Shepsle, *Politics in Plural Societies: A Theory of Democratic Instability* (Columbus: Charles E. Merill, 1972). Donald L. Horowitz, *Ethnic Groups in Conflict* (Berkeley, CA: University of California Press, 1985).

3 The characterization of the parties is based on an extensive analysis that cannot be reproduced in this paper due to limitations of space. Readers interested in the Hungarian minority parties of the three countries should consult my doctoral dissertation. See István Gergő Székely, "Dynamics of Party Politics, Electoral Competition and Cooperation within the

their programmatic goals, political strategies and their relations with political actors from the kin-state. This is based on an analysis of party documents, press materials and interviews conducted with party leaders and political analysts in the three countries. The main conclusion of this analysis is that, with few exceptions, the parties are rather similar in terms of their goals, though they differ more in their political strategies and their relations with kin-state actors.

Second, I will discuss the clientelistic capacity of the parties and assess the relative weight of the sources accessible in the host- and kin-states for each of them. It is important to emphasize from the very beginning that we are dealing here with a complex and insufficiently transparent domain. Consequently, it is impossible to provide precise figures concerning the finances of the minority parties or the subsidy systems of Hungary and the host-states. For this reason, the empirical data provided in the paper should be regarded as illustrative, as a tentative assessment of the clientelistic capacity of the parties and of the relative weight of the different sources (i.e. kin-state resources v. various types of assets accessible in the host-state). Despite the limitations of such an endeavour, I believe that the picture that emerges is sufficiently robust to demonstrate that the resources that became accessible in the late 1990s in the host-states (especially Romania and Slovakia) were clearly of a superior magnitude to what the kin-state could offer to its ethnic kin beyond its borders.

My inquiry draws primarily on two strands of political science literature: the scholarship on parties and party systems and, to a lesser extent, on ethnopolitics and nationalism. The timeframe covered is the period between the fall of communism in 1989 and 2012. However, the most relevant developments that have occurred since then will also be addressed briefly. These developments refer primarily to a change in the strategy of Fidesz,[4] Hungary's main centre-right party, which has been in government since 2010. The main arguments of this paper depict the situation in the early 2010s. However, starting from 2013, a paradigm shift seems to be occurring in Hungary, especially in the centre-right governing party's policy towards the Hungarian minority parties in neighbouring countries, which I will briefly address at the end of the study.

The three Hungarian communities analyzed in this paper can be considered fairly similar in many respects. Though they differ in size, all three are large enough to be significant in national politics but too small to render the polity genuinely multi-ethnic. The Hungarian community makes up almost 10 per cent of the population in Slovakia, a bit less than 7 per cent in Romania, and

Hungarian Minorities of Romania, Serbia and Slovakia" (PhD diss., Central European University, 2014).

4 *Fidesz – Magyar Polgári Szövetség* (Fidesz – Hungarian Civic Alliance Forum).

almost 4 per cent in Serbia (without Kosovo). Nonetheless, there is considerable variation in the institutional and political contexts in which the parties of the three Hungarian minority communities have operated both across the cases and over time, and this variation makes a comparative analysis potentially meaningful.[5]

One important feature of all three communities is that their elites have put forward claims for recognition as distinct political subjects since 1989, including demands for various forms of self-government or autonomy. Furthermore, they have defined their communities unequivocally as part of the Hungarian nation in cultural terms, although their relationships with the Hungarian political community have remained more equivocal. The salience of the latter has increased considerably since 2010, when it became possible for members of Hungarian minorities to acquire Hungarian citizenship relatively easily.[6] From the perspective of the internal political dynamics of Hungarian minorities, this important legislative change has made the question of "Hungarian-Hungarian relations" even more salient, by which I mean the relationship of the minority parties with the Hungarian government and political parties from Hungary.

The structure of this paper is as follows. First, I clarify some conceptual issues concerning minorities and their parties. Next, I offer an explanation as to why the predictions of the outbidding theory do not always apply in intra-ethnic party competition. I then analyze the parties of the three Hungarian minority communities according to four considerations: their programmatic goals, their strategies, their relationships with actors from the kin-state and their clientelistic potential. Finally, I use the argument put forward earlier to explain the greater degree of electoral success of the more moderate Hungarian minority parties and to assess the ethno-political model of inclusion of the countries under discussion. The paper ends with a brief discussion of the most recent developments, which seem to indicate a shift in the policies of Hungary's current governing parties.

---

5 The Hungarians in Ukraine (and Austria, Slovenia and Croatia) are not discussed here, as they are too small numerically to be relevant in national politics.

6 On May 26, 2010, the Hungarian parliament adopted Law XLIV on the amendment of Law LV of 1993 on Hungarian citizenship. According to the amendments, applicants no longer need to hold a permanent residence permit to become eligible, nor to have an address or income in Hungary, and the citizenship examination has also been abolished. Applicants have to certify their knowledge of the Hungarian language, that one of their ancestors held Hungarian citizenship, or at least that they are probably of Hungarian ancestry. They must have a clean criminal record and must not pose a security threat to Hungary.

2 Conceptual and Theoretical Considerations

2.1 *Brubaker's Triadic Nexus Meets Political Parties*

Party politics of national minorities are conditioned by what Brubaker[7] describes as the *triadic nexus of nationalisms*. This nexus consists of (1) the nationalizing nationalism of the would-be nation-state or host country; (2) the trans-state or unifying nationalism of the external homeland or kin-state; and, finally, (3) the nationalism of the minority itself. Since the minorities in question are at a level of social-political organization that is comparable to that of established nations, they also engage in nationalist mobilization, asserting demands for certain "collective, nationality-based cultural or political rights."[8] None of these three nationalisms should be viewed as fixed entities but rather as "variably configured and continuously contested political fields." Like the two fully-fledged nations between which it is caught, a national minority is not simply a group but "a family of related yet competing stances."[9]

In this inquiry, I blend Brubaker's triadic framework with the toolkit of the party competition literature. Since political parties are among the most important actors shaping minority politics, contextualizing Brubaker's triadic nexus in the realities of party politics permits a more nuanced analysis of national minority politics, including its transnational and interstate dimensions. I will focus primarily on two sides of the triadic nexus: (1) the actions and strategies of minority parties in their host-states and (2) their relations with actors from their kin-states. The former aspect is fairly straightforward: the parties operate within the party systems of the host countries, and their relative success depends on the actions they undertake in that context. For the latter aspect, however, some further clarifications are in order.

Since the fall of communism, Hungary has engaged in a very active kin-state policy towards its external minorities. Its attitude has generally been one of support of minority rights and aspirations, but the relationship was not always free of tensions. This is mainly due to the fact that this engagement has also been driven by domestic party competition,[10] often leading to conflicts

7 Rogers Brubaker, *Nationalism Reframed: Nationhood and the National Question in the New Europe* (Cambridge: Cambridge University Press, 1996).

8 Rogers Brubaker, "Myths and Misconceptions in the Study of Nationalism," in The State of the Nation: Ernest Gellner and the Theory of Nationalism, ed. John A. Hall (Cambridge: Cambridge University Press, 1998), 272–306.

9 Brubaker, *Nationalism Reframed.*

10 Stephen M. Saideman and William R. Ayres, *For Kin or Country: Xenophobia, Nationalism, and War* (New York: Columbia University Press, 2008). Balázs Ablonczy and Bárdi Nándor,

between minority and kin-state actors. According to Waterbury, kin-state elites may attempt to derive legitimacy from the actions taken for the protection of the minority ("saviours of the nation"), but members of the minority may also influence domestic political outcomes in their kin-states, for instance by gaining the right to vote. As a consequence, kin-state elites will have strong incentives to control the ties with external minorities and their organizations, and they will attempt to establish clientelistic relationships extending across borders.[11] However, this move may be perceived by minority elites as excessive interference in their internal affairs. In addition, it may provide grounds for host-state actors to perceive or simply describe minorities as fifth columns, as agents of the putatively inimical kin-state that aims to undermine their country.

Overall, it can be concluded that the divisions among kin-state parties regarding external minorities considerably influence their competition for the votes of these minorities. Consequently, the internal political dynamics of the minority are structured not only by domestic and party politics in the host-state but also by domestic and party politics in their kin-state. I argue that, in the context of their simultaneous relationships with their host- and kin-states, the strategies of minority political parties can be placed along a continuum with the host-state and the kin-state at the two endpoints, allowing us to consider and assess the trade-offs involved in these orientations of varying intensity. Drawing on this analytical framework, my analysis of the relative success of "moderate" and "radical" Hungarian minority parties considers not only the agency of the parties in their host-states but also the mutually constitutive relationships of the various minority actors with their counterparts in the kin-state. As shown in Figure 9.1, the classic left-right dichotomy is relevant in the case of the political parties in the kin-state, while in the case of the minority parties most of the contestation goes on between the "radical" and "moderate" factions. As the use of quotation marks indicates, these labels are relative, since – as we shall see – whether a party is considered moderate or radical depends not only on its profile but also on the context in which it operates.

2.2 *Parties Making Ethnicity-based Appeals*

The focus of this paper is the political parties of *minorities*. Research on such parties usually takes as its starting point the literature on *ethnic* parties and/or

---

"Határon túli magyarok: mérleg, esély, jövő," in *Határon túli magyarság a 21. Században*, ed. Botond Bitskey (Budapest: Köztársasági Elnöki Hivatal, 2010), 9–32. Myra Waterbury, *Between State and Nation. Diaspora Politics and Kin-State Nationalism in Hungary* (New York: Palgrave Macmillan, 2010).

11 Waterbury, *Between State and Nation.*

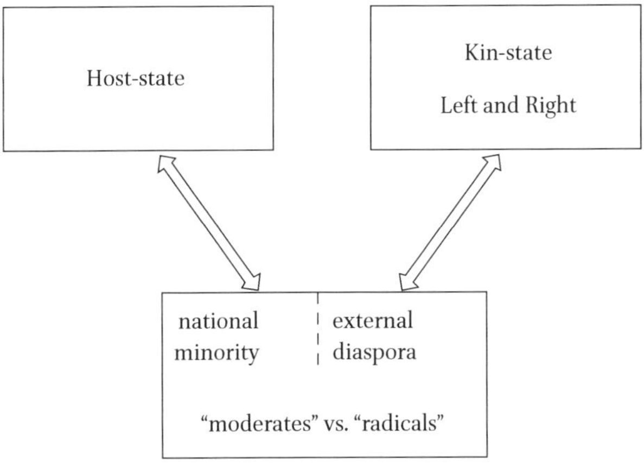

FIGURE 9.1 Brubaker's triadic nexus and the minority parties

the scholarship on (*ethno-*)*regionalist* parties. These two strands of research deal with related phenomena but are only weakly integrated.

There is a broad consensus in the literature that the essential feature of ethnic parties is exclusivism in favour of the ethnic group the party claims to represent. For the most part, this feature is treated as an essential requirement in order to classify a party as ethnic, as it provides the basic criteria for distinguishing between *ethnic* parties, *multi-ethnic* parties or *non-ethnic* parties. For Horowitz, ethnic parties may draw support from multiple ethnic groups, but only if all of these groups are located on the same side of the main ethnic cleavage.[12] Conversely, a party is multi-ethnic only if it spans the major groups in conflict. In other words, what matters is whether the main cleavage is spanned by the party, while secondary cleavages may remain within the electorates covered by the multi-ethnic party. Chandra proposes a similar typology, though her definition of the multi-ethnic party is a bit different and arguably more demanding, since it requires that such parties champion the interests of all significant segments without excluding any.[13] Both Horowitz and Chandra also identify a third type, the non-ethnic party, which does not champion the interests of any ethnic category. While Horowitz notes that it is not clear that such parties are even possible in deeply divided societies,[14] Chandra classifies parties that do not make "an open or a central appeal to an ethnic category, whether exclusive or inclusive," as non-ethnic.[15]

12 Horowitz, *Ethnic Groups in Conflict*.
13 Kanchan Chandra, "What is an Ethnic Party?," *Party Politics* 17, no. 2 (2011): 151–169.
14 Horowitz, *Ethnic Groups in Conflict*, 31.
15 Kanchan Chandra, "A Constructivist Dataset on Ethnicity and Institutions (CDEI)," in *Measuring Identity: A Guide for Social Scientists*, ed. Rawi Abdelal, Yoshiko M. Herrera,

The highly asymmetric demographic proportions between majority and minority populations in the countries studied here have important consequences for the party systems. The minorities are too small to make the ethnic cleavage the main axis of party competition at the national level (as opposed to polities where the balance between groups is more equal, such as Bosnia and Herzegovina, Northern Ireland or Belgium). As a consequence, the party systems in these states can be regarded as a middle ground between the "conventional" party systems of ethnically homogenous societies and the systems of deeply divided societies, which are made up preponderantly of ethnic parties.[16] Given that the ethnic cleavage is of secondary importance in the party system, these systems come closer to the "conventional" party systems, as only some of the parties are organized along ethnic lines. Appeals to ethnicity are central features of a party's identity only in the case of some minorities, and possibly some nationalist radical right parties, but not in the case of all actors in the party system. The most important parties usually refrain from explicit ethnic identification, though occasionally they may play the "ethnic card."

The distinction between ethnic, multi-ethnic and non-ethnic party appeals is important, because minority representation may also be undertaken by multi-ethnic parties. In this inquiry, my characterization of a party as "Hungarian" (or not) is not based on the degree to which the parties conform to the requirements of theoretical typologies (e.g. ethnically exclusive or inclusive appeals) but rather on an assessment of which ethnic community can be considered the "owner" of the party as a political project. The decisive criterion is whether or not a given party is perceived as (primarily) representing Hungarian minorities both by the electorate and by the politicians themselves. This warrants the classification of the multi-ethnic party *Most-Híd* in Slovakia, which is the project of a predominantly Hungarian elite (and is regarded as such both by Slovak politicians and by its Hungarian opponents), as a "party of the Hungarians."[17] Conversely, the same criterion excludes the multi-ethnic parties from Serbia – most importantly the regionalist Social Democratic League of Vojvodina (LSV) and the Democratic Party (DS) – which obtain significant numbers of votes

Alastair Iain Johnston and Rose McDermott (Cambridge: Cambridge University Press, 2009), 250–275, especially 259.

16 Maria Spirova, "The Ethnic Parties as Democratic Actors: An Analytical Framework. Part I: Beyond Numbers? The Electoral Strategies of Ethnic Parties" (paper presented at the ECPR Joint Sessions of Workshops, Antwerp, April 10–15, 2012).

17 An important argument for considering *Most-Híd* a party of the Hungarians is the fact that the politicians of the rival ethnic party, *Magyar Koalíció Pártja* (MKP, Party of Hungarian Coalition), and the political analysts and experts I interviewed during my fieldwork in Slovakia all agreed with this classification.

from ethnic Hungarians and even run ethnic Hungarian candidates in areas with high concentrations of Hungarian speakers but nevertheless remain parties with a Serbian core into which Hungarian (and other minority) politicians have been co-opted.

Hungarian minority elites involved in ethnic or multi-ethnic parties hold very different conceptions of the nature of the minority community. Leaders of multi-ethnic parties generally subscribe to a multicultural view of society or an overarching identity transcending ethnic ties with members of the minority community integrating as individuals in the wider society. Conversely, the elites of Hungarian ethnic parties mostly regard their group as a distinct political community or a self-standing society that needs to be integrated into the polity in a collective and vertical fashion (as a pillar). One could say that the elites of ethnic parties tend to favour accommodationist or power-sharing arrangements, while the elites of multi-ethnic parties are more inclined to content themselves with integrationist solutions to ethnic conflict resolution.[18] Framed within Brubaker's triadic nexus, a multi-ethnic party strategy also implies that political integration into the host-state is prioritized over ties to the kin-state.

Though the idea of bridging the inter-ethnic divide generally implies downplaying the salience of ethnicity, the appeal is still targeted at voters who attribute some importance to the fact that an ethnic cleavage exists. In a society with an asymmetric distribution of ethnic groups (which often results in asymmetric access to power), such voters will be found preponderantly (though not exclusively) within the minority. Thus, a programme of inter-ethnic reconciliation has to be interpreted as primarily targeting minority voters, even if it entails a denial of ethnic exclusiveness, since a non-ethnic programme would be most appealing for the majority, as it is more in line with their taken-for-granted "ownership of the state."[19]

18 The integrationist approach aims for equal citizenship, but is reluctant to endorse the different cultures on an equal footing, relegating the differences to the private sphere. Conversely, accommodation requires the public recognition of more than one ethno-cultural community on an equal footing, with safeguards for all. Accommodationists argue that the integrationist approach fails where divisions are deep and enduring, since it implies a choice in favour of only one (usually the dominant) community. (See John McGarry, Brendan O'Leary and Richard Simeon, "Integration or Accommodation?," in *Constitutional Design for Divided Societies: Integration or Accommodation?*, ed. Sujit Choudhry (Oxford and New York: Oxford University Press, 2008), 41–88, especially 41–53).

19 Andreas Wimmer, "Who Owns the State? Understanding Ethnic Conflict in Post-colonial Societies," *Nations and Nationalism* 3, no. 4 (1997): 631–665.

2.3 *The Outbidding Thesis and Its Limitations*

The theoretical model of competition in ethnic party systems that probably continues to enjoy the most widespread acceptance is the ethnic outbidding thesis. The argument originates in the rational choice-inspired model developed by Rabushka and Shepsle.[20] Horowitz proposes a similar argument based on a sociologically grounded analysis in his seminal book *Ethnic Groups in Conflict*.

As noted before, the essence of the outbidding thesis is that where ethnicity (or race, religion, etc.) is salient, moderation on ethno-cultural issues will not prevail. In this view, multi-ethnic parties do not stand a chance, because they will be outflanked by exclusivist ethnic parties. Furthermore, moderate ethnic parties, open to compromise with opposing groups, will inevitably be challenged by more radical parties within their own group for betraying the interests of their community. As a consequence, politics evolves according to a centrifugal dynamic, whereby the society becomes increasingly polarized, eventually leading to the breakdown of democracy and peace. Without appropriate institutions to prevent this, the outcome can be catastrophic. Majorities will permanently exclude minorities, while minorities might engage in pre-emptive violence to avoid this outcome. Outbidding is considered to be the most convenient strategy for mobilization, since intransigence is seen as the easiest way for challengers to set themselves apart from the incumbent elites. Rabushka and Shepsle conclude on a very pessimistic note, stating that: "[m]oderation on the ethnic issue is a viable strategy only if ethnicity is not salient."[21]

However, more recent research has demonstrated that outbidding is not necessarily the only possible scenario when ethnicity is salient. Parties claiming to represent ethnic groups may engage in alternative strategies, radicalization does not always occur and the more radical parties are not necessarily the most successful.[22] Overall, more recent research shows that intra-ethnic challenger parties are neither necessarily more radical nor more moderate than their predecessors. Rather, their position depends on the interplay of a number of conditions, and outbidding platforms are not always more successful than moderate platforms.

---

20 Rabushka and Shepsle, *Politics in Plural Societies*.

21 Ibid., 86.

22 Coakley, "Ethnic Competition." Zuber, "Beyond Outbidding?" Daniel Bochsler and Edina Szőcsik, "Building Inter-ethnic Bridges or Promoting Ethno-territorial Demarcation Lines? Hungarian Minority Parties in Competition," *Nationalities Papers* 41, no. 5 (2013): 761–779. Mitchell, Evans and O'Leary, "Extremist Outbidding."

Arguments in the literature on possible strategies to avoid successful outbidding can be summarized as the "moderation through inclusion" thesis, which is based on the idea that inclusion in the various structures of political power (most importantly, participation in government) will motivate ethnic elites to adopt moderate stances. However, the mechanisms that ensure that ethnic electorates will accept such compromising stances is less evident.

3 Clientelistic Potential as an Explanation for Unsuccessful Outbidding

Building on the theory of alternative party-voter linkage types and the nature of ethno-political inclusion models prevalent in Central and Eastern Europe (CEE), I attempt to sketch a possible mechanism to explain why more moderate positions prevailed over more radical ones at the electoral level in the case of the Hungarian minorities in question. I argue that the dynamics of intra-ethnic competition can be better understood if, in addition to the programmatic appeals of the parties, their capacity to maintain clientelistic linkages with the minority electorate is also considered. The key to the immunity of moderate parties against outbidding challengers is their superior ability to secure constant and safe access to public resources, which, for parties or groups with more radical platforms, is extremely difficult to counterbalance.

Of the existing theories, the closest to my argument is the *ethnic tribune parties* model of Mitchell, Evans and O'Leary,[23] since it attributes as much significance to the parties' access to state resources as it does to programmatic commitments anchored in minority nationalism. The essence of this model is that even radical parties are willing to become more pragmatic in order to gain increased access to public resources. However, they still strive to maintain their image as the most credible defenders of the ethnic cause by conveying radical messages to their constituency.

The argument presented here is different from the ethnic tribune parties model, however, because the political context of the countries under discussion is different from that of power-sharing systems such as the one in Northern Ireland. None of the three countries that are home to the largest Hungarian minorities have institutionalized guarantees for power-sharing. This means that the bargaining power of the minority parties is greatly reduced compared

23 Ibid.

to a consociationalist setting. In other words, there are limitations on the pursuit of a classic ethnic tribune party strategy.[24]

Following their integration into the European Union, the political and economic exclusion of minorities is no longer an acceptable strategy in CEE countries. However, the EU accession process has had some unintended consequences that are disadvantageous for minorities. Since nation-states had to relinquish sovereignty to the European Union in a significant number of policy domains, they became less flexible in matters over which the Union has little or no say. Minority protection is one such domain. During the accession process, which was informed by the Copenhagen criteria,[25] the situation of minorities improved significantly in all three countries. However, in the late 2000s, the process arguably plateaued. In the three countries under discussion, no significant minority-friendly measures have been adopted recently, while in a few issue areas setbacks have even occurred.[26]

Given the narrow room for manoeuvre in their programmatic goals, minority elites have limited ability to reinforce their legitimacy through policy achievements in the ethno-political domain. Thus, they are compelled to turn to alternative mechanisms. Clientelistic exchanges are the best avenue for maintaining their electoral support, since access to state resources is more readily accommodated by the majority than concessions relating to the restructuring of the state. The availability of this avenue is further conditioned by the political systems of CEE, which generally exhibit a higher inclination towards

---

24 For a discussion of the case in Romania, see Tamás Kiss and István Gergő Székely, "Shifting Linkages in Ethnic Mobilization: The Case of RMDSZ and the Hungarians in Transylvania," *Nationalities Papers* 44, no. 4 (2016): 591–610.

25 According to the Copenhagen criteria (or accession criteria), candidate countries must satisfy the following political conditions: stability of institutions guaranteeing democracy, the rule of law, human rights and *respect for and protection of minorities.* While the EU acquis does not elaborate on this condition, in practice the EU has required candidate countries to ratify and implement the minority protection documents of the Council of Europe.

26 The following is presented for the sake of illustration only. In Romania, the last significant piece of minority-friendly legislation was the education law, adopted in January 2011. However, even the implementation of this law is deficient. In 2009, Slovakia adopted a controversial language law, which basically renders communication solely in the minority language punishable. In 2010, the country's citizenship law was amended in response to Hungary's citizenship law. Under this law, persons applying for Hungarian citizenship will lose their Slovak citizenship. In Serbia, the adoption of the law on national minority councils in 2009 was a significant positive development. In 2014, however, the Constitutional Court declared a number of provisions of the law unconstitutional. A similar decision was reached in 2013 concerning the statute of the Autonomous Province of Vojvodina, where the Hungarian population is concentrated.

clientelism.[27] Under these circumstances, the capacity to deliver concrete results to the ethnic constituency will become the key marker of competence and credibility in the competition between rival minority parties. However, due to the lack of institutional guarantees for participation in power, access to resources through participation in power compels ethnic parties to tone down ethno-political demands. “Moderate” elites that are willing to do this will be able to secure resources of a magnitude that their “radical” challengers will be unable to counterbalance. Given their own reluctance to cooperate, combined with their exclusion by majority actors, minority “radicals” have to rely mostly on resources from the kin-state. However, as I will show below, despite the unquestionable increase in the financial aid provided by the kin-state over the studied period, these resources are of a clearly inferior magnitude compared to what became available to minority parties after they were accepted as legitimate coalition partners in their host-state’s governments. My argument differs from the ethnic tribune parties model on two important counts. While I agree with the importance attributed to resource allocation, I propose, first, that the lack of institutional guarantees for inclusion in power means that minority parties are only accepted as partners at the price of more moderation. Second, I include the kin-state in the equation as an alternative, albeit inferior, source of patronage.

The most important implication of this model of inter-ethnic cooperation is that this state of affairs can be characterized as a mixed model of minority incorporation, combining elements of informal power-sharing and co-optation/hegemonic control, in the sense of the concept as described by Lustick and O’Leary and McGarry.[28] The essence of the mixed model is that particularistic demands involving a significant restructuring of the nation-state are not accommodated, so the minority elites must either tone down their demands or find alternative avenues to secure resources. According to Rothchild, the holders of central power provide some degree of status, autonomy, power or economic resources to minority leaders in exchange for their support and compliance with the policies (and ideology) of the state.[29]

27 Petr Kopecky and Gerardo Scherlis, “Party Patronage in Contemporary Europe,” *European Review* 16, no. 3 (2008): 355–371. Conor O’Dwyer, “Runaway State Building: How Political Parties Shape States in Postcommunist Eastern Europe,” *World Politics* 56, no. 4 (2004): 520–553. Clara Volintiru, “Institutional Distortions, Clientelism and Corruption: Evidence from Romania,” *CCREI Working Papers Series 1* (Bucharest University of Economic Studies, 2010).

28 Ian Lustick, “Stability in Deeply Divided Societies: Consociationalism versus Control,” *World Politics* 31, no. 3 (1979): 325–344. Brendan O’Leary and John McGarry, “The Political Regulation of National and Ethnic Conflict,” *Parliamentary Affairs* 47, no. 1 (1994): 94–115.

29 Donald Rothchild, *Managing Ethnic Conflict in Africa: Pressures and Incentives for Cooperation* (Washington, DC: Brookings Institution Press, 1997).

Although initially elaborated for post-colonial settings, the idea of control through co-optation or hegemonic exchanges has also been applied to the post-communist CEE region, for instance in the case of Estonia[30] and Romania.[31] As these authors emphasize, control or hegemonic exchanges are not a stable feature of the system in this region, and the level of control may vary considerably. Nonetheless, the use of some elements of control provides majority elites with a way to accommodate minority claims that is less costly than institutionalizing any form of power-sharing. A mix of control and moderate accommodation does not require a redefinition of the nation-state.[32] Under the asymmetric conditions that prevail in the countries under discussion, most minority elites tend to accept that a softer version of co-optation provides relatively easy access to state resources, although it significantly limits their opportunities to further ethno-political claims rooted in minority nationalism.

A second consequence of this state of affairs is the low incidence of intra-ethnic cooperation among minority elites. Minority elites interested in gaining access to power will not necessarily aim for vote and seat maximization for the ethnic segment, which, arguably, may provide better chances for restructuring the state. Majority parties will refuse to invite minority elites that are perceived (or characterized) as "extremist" into power. Hence, the more "radical" minority elites become a liability for the more compromising ones, which believe they will have easier access to resources if they do not bring the radicals along into the institutions of power.[33]

4 A Framework of Analysis for Political Parties of Minorities

The dichotomy between "moderates" and "radicals," a foundational assumption underlying theories of ethnic party competition, is a conceptual simplification that is needed to keep the theory parsimonious. A more nuanced analysis of intra-ethnic political dynamics, however, requires a more sophisticated conceptualization of differences between parties.

A description of Hungarian minority parties in terms of the economic left-right is largely irrelevant, since intra-ethnic competition has little to do with

30 Vello Pettai and Klara Hallik, "Understanding Processes of Ethnic Control: Segmentation, Dependency and Co-optation in Post-communist Estonia," *Nations and Nationalism* 8, no. 4 (2002): 505–529.

31 Narcisa Medianu, "Analysing Political Exchanges between Minority and Majority Leaders in Romania," *The Global Review of Ethnopolotics* 1, no. 4 (2002), 28–41.

32 Ibid.

33 Székely, "Dynamics of Party Politics."

political ideologies. I argue that the pattern of party competition is better understood if we pay attention to several aspects relating primarily to the agenda of minority rights and identity politics. These include: (1) the ethno-political goals of the parties, including their positions on various forms of autonomy; (2) their strategies in the politics of the host-state, outlining their attitudes towards mainstream political parties and participation in power; and (3) their relationships with the political parties and the government of the kin-state, in this case Hungary. In addition to these three dimensions relating primarily to identity politics, a fourth aspect on which parties may differ needs to be considered. This concerns the different types of party-voter linkages and, most importantly, the relative weight of the clientelistic linkage mechanisms. I discuss these four aspects in more detail below, since they will guide my analysis of Hungarian minority parties.

4.1 *Programmatic Goals*

The goals of minority parties are usually grasped with the help of typologies of ethnic or ethno-regionalist mobilization demands.[34] A common feature of such typologies is that they consist primarily of programmatic goals with a heavy symbolic load related to the ethno-cultural or linguistic domain and to the standing of the groups as "societal cultures."[35] Such demands usually range from cultural protectionism to claims for the "reorganization of the existing national power structure,"[36] including various types of autonomy, as well as irredentism or secessionism.

From the full spectrum of ethno-political demands usually included in these typologies, only some are relevant for the Hungarian minority parties discussed here. For the most part, their demands are located between the moderate end and the middle of the continuum, with the most radical claim being the demand for territorial autonomy. While ethnic extremism exists in the shape of calls for secession, irredentism or incitement to violence, it is

34 Janusz Bugajski, "The Fate of Minorities in Eastern Europe," *Journal of Democracy* 4, no. 4 (1993): 85–99. Lieven De Winter, "Conclusion," in *Regionalist Parties in Western Europe*, ed. Lieven De Winter and Huri Türsan (London and New York: Routledge, 1998), 204–247. Erin K. Jenne, *Ethnic Bargaining: The Paradox of Minority Empowerment* (Ithaca, NY: Cornell University Press, 2007).
Régis Dandoy, "Ethno-regionalist Parties in Europe: A Typology," *Perspectives on Federalism* 2, no. 2 (2010): 194–220.

35 Will Kymlicka, *Multicultural Citizenship: A Liberal Theory of Minority Rights* (Oxford: Clarendon Press, 1995).

36 De Winter, "Conclusion."

generally marginal. On the other hand, the most moderate demands (e.g. non-discrimination, respect for individual rights only, cultural protectionism) are also irrelevant from the perspective of party competition, because all parties aim for something more substantial.

Some typologies of ethnic claim-making assume that the different types of autonomy can be ordered on a scale, ranging from the mildest claims for decentralization to functional autonomy, cultural or personal autonomy, regional autonomy and, ultimately, territorial autonomy and federalism.[37] Indeed, territorial autonomy requires a more robust reorganization of state power than arrangements based on the personality or functional principle. In my assessment, however, an ordering of the parties based on whether they regard territorial or other types of autonomy as the main goal (e.g. personal or functional) would be misleading. The main reason for this is that the settlement structure of the Hungarian minorities is such that, even if the creation of territorial autonomy was feasible for the territorially concentrated segment of the Hungarian population, a significant part of the community living in a scattered way would remain outside the borders of the autonomous region. Moreover, claims for other types of self-government may also display significant variation in terms of institutional design or competences, and in some cases it is precisely the design or the underlying philosophy of the institutions on which the rival parties disagree. Under these circumstances, I suggest a classification of parties according to their conception of the preferable model for the social and political organization of the minority community, which includes, but cannot be reduced to, the issue of autonomy. In this vein, the simplest classification draws on the dichotomy between autonomist and non-autonomist parties, but in most cases it implies differences in the institutional architecture of the proposed form of self-government and/or differences in the underlying ideology or tradition (i.e. liberal or communitarian, national-conservative) from which they derive their ethno-political claims.

4.2 *Political Strategies in the Host-state*

In addition to the substance of ethno-political demands, the means parties are willing to deploy in order to achieve their aims are also critical. De Winter[38] identifies three types of strategies employed by ethno-regionalist parties that are also relevant in the context of minority parties: *anti-system*, *tribune*, or

37 See, for example, Milton J. Esman, *Ethnic Politics* (Ithaca: Cornell University Press, 1994) and Jenne, *Ethnic Bargaining*.

38 De Winter, "Conclusion."

governmental strategies.[39] An anti-system strategy implies non-adherence to democratic rules and often goes together with violence. While this strategy is characteristic of regions such as Northern Ireland or the Basque Country, and has also been used in the Western Balkans (e.g. Bosnia and Herzegovina, Macedonia or Kosovo), none of the Hungarian minority parties have ever embraced it. A tribune strategy[40] involves a refusal to participate in government and a preference to exercise pressure from opposition, often by employing extra-parliamentary means and by seeking support from international organizations and the kin-state. Governmental strategies, finally, provide the best access to public resources in the host-state, and policy leverage may be higher as well. However, this strategy also implies programmatic concessions, often coupled with the complete shelving of critical demands.

The goals located in the rather narrow policy space discussed in the previous section are compatible in theory with both governmental and tribune strategies, even if in practice it has often proved difficult for the parties to reconcile autonomy demands with participation in power. Furthermore, it should be pointed out that an anti-system or tribune strategy may not be adopted by choice but as a reaction to the refusal by other parties to cooperate.

4.3 *Relationships with Kin-state Actors*

Minority participation in power in the host-state captures only one side of the interlocked triadic nexus of nationalisms.[41] For the purposes of analyzing minority party competition, it is equally important to consider the dimension that captures the relationship between minority parties and actors from the kin-state.

In Brubaker's framework, national minorities are viewed as a community caught between two states and political communities. This specific situation conditions minority parties to manoeuvre in a political space that can be represented as a continuum on which one endpoint is integration into the host-state and the other is a robust orientation towards the kin-state. Since 2010, the mass naturalization and enfranchisement of members of Hungarian minorities implied a degree of political integration with Hungary, making this dual political orientation more visible. Depending on relevant interstate relations, there are trade-offs between the two orientations, which at times can

39 The use of these strategies is certainly not limited to minority parties, but due to the central importance of the issue of the reorganization of the state power structure the difference between these strategies becomes especially trenchant in their case.

40 Not to be confused with the previously discussed ethnic tribune parties model of Mitchell, Evans and O'Leary.

41 Brubaker, *Nationalism Reframed*.

become antagonistic. Closer ties to actors from one polity may require greater distance from, or even a break with, the other. More concretely, if a minority party chooses a governmental strategy, this choice may not be compatible with the actual goals of the government of the kin-state. But it is also not necessary that an anti-system strategy or even a tribune strategy be backed by the kin-state's government.

While it never included irredentist aspirations, Hungary's "virtual nationalism" was one of the most systematically pursued kin-state policies in Central and Eastern Europe.[42] It entailed not only external lobbying activity of varying intensity[43] but also the provision of financial subsidies for external minorities. However, there have been considerable differences between parties on the left and the right concerning policies towards ethnic kin beyond the country's borders. After a brief period of consensus following the regime change in 1989, the Hungarian right started portraying itself as the "owner" of the Hungarian minority issue, while the left adopted an increasingly anti-nationalist discourse that prioritized foreign policy considerations over minority issues.[44] In general, right-wing governments have tended to regard Hungarian minorities as part of the Hungarian cultural nation and, since the adoption of the new law on Hungarian citizenship in 2010, of the Hungarian political nation as well. Conversely, parties on the left regard Hungarian minorities primarily as citizens of their host-states, encouraging integration in their host-states through the participation of their parties in host-state governments. The right has often backed more radical minority party voices demanding autonomy, while distancing itself from more moderate and cooperative factions. A failed referendum on dual citizenship for Hungarian minorities in 2004 has had devastating consequences for Hungary's left-wing parties, whose campaign against dual citizenship alienated Hungarian minorities in the adjacent countries.

After returning to power in 2010, Fidesz, the major centre-right conservative political party in Hungary, was eager to pass a law concerning dual citizenship as one of its first acts. Although the law had the support of the parties on the left, as the initiator Fidesz once again reinforced its image as the party

---

42 Zsuzsa Csergő and James M. Goldgeier, "Virtual Nationalism in Comparative Context: How Unique Is the Hungarian Approach?," in *Beyond Sovereignty: From Status Law to Transnational Citizenship?*, ed. Osamu Ieda (Sapporo: Slavic Research Center, Hokkaido University, 2006), 281–302.

43 Jenne, *Ethnic Bargaining: The Paradox of Minority Empowerment.*

44 See Zsuzsa Csergő, *Talk of the Nation: Language and Conflict in Romania and Slovakia* (Ithaca, NY: Cornell University Press, 2007). See also Nándor Bárdi, *Tény és való. A budapesti kormányzatok és a határon túli magyarság kapcsolattörténete* (Pozsony: Kalligram, 2004).

that cares most about the fate of Hungarian minorities. However, Fidesz also departed from the so-called Antall doctrine[45] of the early 1990s, according to which the Hungarian government should treat all legitimate minority parties as partners and refrain from making important policy decisions without their consent. After it formed a government in 1998, Fidesz aimed to turn Budapest into the single most important power centre of the "unified Hungarian nation." Minority parties were expected to adapt to the new situation. The policies of the first Orbán government (1998–2002) only led to minor confrontations with some (factions within) Hungarian minority parties, since there was only one umbrella minority party in both Romania and Slovakia at that time. Hence, the minority factions close to Fidesz were part of these unified parties. However, the second Orbán government, which came to power in 2010, adopted a policy characterized by a previously unseen intolerance towards those Hungarian minority parties that were reluctant to embrace the course set in Budapest. While favouritism towards one or several organizations was not necessarily a new policy for Hungarian governments (and was sometimes also characteristic of the left), what was certainly a novelty after 2010 was the unequivocal hostility towards minority organizations that were seen as incompatible with Fidesz's conception of the ethnic kin beyond the borders. Not surprisingly, the organizations that were most irritated by this new policy direction were precisely the ones that were best integrated into their host-states' political community. Occasionally, they had participated in the governments of their host-states, and they expected support, not interference, from their kin-state in their ethnopolitical struggles.

4.4 *Clientelistic Capacity*

Given that all the minority parties concerned have put forward relatively similar programmatic goals, an assessment of their clientelistic capacity greatly improves our understanding of intra-ethnic party competition. By clientelistic capacity I mean the ability of parties to engage in three types of particularistic behaviour, as described by Kopecky and Scherlis:[46] *patronage* (the distribution of public sector jobs or contracts among individuals close to the party); *pork-barrel* or political pork (the direct channelling of public funds and state resources to a specific territory by the parties in the form of infrastructural developments, e.g. roads, schools, sewage, etc.); and *clientelism* (direct exchange of material goods, e.g. food or presents, for votes).

45 Named after József Antall, Hungary's first prime minister after 1989.

46 Kopecky and Scherlis, "Party Patronage."

The high propensity of minority parties to rely on clientelistic linkages is a central idea in the literature on ethnic parties. Interestingly, it is almost completely absent from the Western ethno-regionalist perspective, which emphasizes programmatic party goals related to the restructuring of state power. According to Gunther and Diamond,[47] the main goal of ethnic parties is "to secure material, cultural, and political benefits (and protections) for the ethnic group in its competition with other groups," while their programmatic commitment and coherence is "extremely low." Moreover, as the ethnic party primarily aims to channel resources to its exclusively defined electorate, it will not be interested in transforming the state power structure (devolution, autonomy or secession). Rather, it will prefer to maintain existing state structures, which can be exploited to extract resources. According to Fearon (1999), ethnicity is a very solid basis for keeping the size of the winning coalition minimal (so that the spoils of office can be divided among fewer individuals).[48] Ethnicity provides a simple way for identification and monitoring, since it is not easily chosen or changed by individuals.

While the low salience of programmatic goals postulated by the authors cited above is questionable, I believe that clientelistic capacity is indeed crucial in the case of Hungarian minorities, especially in light of the very similar programmatic profile of the rival parties.

Given the difficulty of measuring clientelism,[49] I will attempt to characterize the clientelistic capacity of the parties based on an assessment of their access to various types of resources. Parties of national minorities can be considered special in this sense, as they may rely on multiple sources. First, through participation in the government of their host-state, they secure access to patronage and, most importantly, pork-barrel opportunities. Second, they can also control resources from regional or local government structures that are under their control or in which they participate, depending on the level of decentralization of their host-sate. While the first two types are relevant for any

47 Richard Gunther and Larry J. Diamond, "Species of Political Parties. A New Typology," *Party Politics* 9, no. 2 (2003): 167–199, especially 183–184.

48 James D. Fearon, "Why Ethnic Politics and 'Pork' Tend to Go Together" (Working paper, Stanford University, 1999).

49 See Herbert Kitschelt, Kent Freeze, Kiril Kolev and Yi-Tang Wang, "Measuring Democratic Accountability: An Initial Report on an Emerging Data Set," *Revista de Ciencia Politica* 29, no. 3 (2009): 741–773. See also Wolfgang Muno, "Conceptualizing and Measuring Clientelism" (paper presented at the workshop "Neopatrimonialism in Various World Regions," German Institute of Global and Area Studies (GIGA), August 23, 2010). Volintiru, "Institutional Distortions."

type of party, in the case of minority parties there are two additional and more specific sources. The third source consists of budgetary funds allocated by the host-states specifically for the financing of minority cultures. Finally, national minorities may also receive resources from the kin-state. Obviously, the access of the parties to these resources will depend to a large extent on their political strategies and their orientations towards their host- and kin-state.

The financial aspects of minority party competition are a delicate and insufficiently transparent domain. Consequently, it is not possible to provide a thorough analysis of or precise figures concerning the finances of minority parties or the resources accessible to them in both Hungary and the host-states. For this reason, empirical data will be provided for purposes of illustration only, as a tentative assessment of the clientelistic capacity of the parties and the relative weight of the different sources (i.e. host-state *versus* kin-state) in these activities.

Of these four types of resources, only the last two can be measured with satisfying precision. The funding from the kin-state can be documented relatively well for the 1990–2012 period.[50] The funding provided by the host-states for minority cultures are a more elusive and less transparent domain,[51] though some accounts of the systems of financing for the cultural activities of the minorities are available.[52] Conversely, the first two types of resources are virtually impossible to measure. However, for the sake of my argument, it is sufficient to establish that the magnitude of the resources flowing from the kin-state is clearly of an inferior magnitude compared to what can be accessed by minority politicians in their host-states, especially through participation in power.

50 Bárdi, *Tény és való.* Nándor Bárdi, "Magyar-magyar párbeszéd a támogatáspolitikáról (2004–2007)," *Regio* 18, no. 4 (2007): 128–164. Nándor Bárdi and Tibor Misovitz, "A kisebbségi magyar közösségek támogatásának politikája," in *Határon túli magyarság a 21. Században*, ed. Botond Bitskey (Budapest: Köztársasági Elnöki Hivatal, 2010), 66–76. Papp, Z. Attila, "Határon túli magyar oktatási támogatások és hasznosulásuk 2006–2010 között," *Educatio* 19, no. 1 (2010): 88–110.

51 Bárdi and Misovitz, "A kisebbségi magyar."

52 For Romania, see Magdolna Mohácsek, "Analiza finanţărilor alocate organizaţiilor minorităţilor naţionale," *Working Papers in Romanian Minority Studies 16* (Cluj: Romanian Institute for Research on National Minorities, 2009). For Slovakia, see Károly Tóth, "A kulturális intézményrendszer," in *Magyarok Szlovákiában III. kötet, Kultúra (1989–2006)*, ed. Gábor Csanda and Károly Tóth (Somorja/Dunaszerdahely: Fórum Kisebbségkutató Intézet/Lilium Aurum Könyvkiadó, 2006), 223–240. See also Myrtil Nagy and Károly Tóth, "A kulturális intézményrendszer forrásai és finanszírozása," in *Magyarok Szlovákiában. III. kötet. Kultúra (1989–2006)*, ed. Gábor Csanda and Károly Tóth (Somorja: Fórum Kisebbségkutató Intézet, 2006), 241–256. For Serbia, I know of no such studies.

5 Understanding Intra-Ethnic Party Competition

In the remainder of this paper, I will discuss the development of the Hungarian minority party systems in the three countries concerned (Romania, Slovakia and Serbia) and characterize the relevant parties[53] according to the four criteria presented above. First, I will discuss each party according to its programmatic goals, political strategies and ties to kin-state actors, then I will turn to an assessment of their clientelistic capacity.[54]

5.1 *The Hungarian Minority Parties: Goals, Strategies and Cross-border Relations*

In Romania, there was a single relevant Hungarian minority organization between 1989 and 2003, namely *Romániai Magyar Demokrata Szövetség* (RMDSZ, Democratic Alliance of Hungarians in Romania). However, the tensions between its more moderate and more radical factions came to a head in 2003, leading to the creation of two challenger parties in the following years: *Magyar Polgári Párt* (MPP, Hungarian Civic Party) and *Erdélyi Magyar Néppárt* (EMNP, Hungarian People's Party of Transylvania).[55]

In the early 1990s, RMDSZ pursued an emphatically autonomist agenda, which proved difficult to reconcile even with the sensitivities of the more liberal Romanian democratic opposition parties, let alone the post-communist parties in power and their nationalist allies. But, since 1996, RMDSZ has almost continuously been part of, or provided support for, various governing coalitions in Romania. This required shelving the party's demands for autonomy, which, in turn, contributed to growing tensions between moderates and radicals. This eventually led to the splintering of the umbrella party. Both of the emerging Hungarian challenger parties defined themselves as autonomists and adopted a tribune strategy. They also failed to acquire relevance in national politics, which prevented them from developing significant coalition potential

53 Only the Hungarian parties that contested at least two consecutive elections (regardless of type) and obtained at least 2 per cent of the overall votes cast for Hungarian parties are covered in this study.

54 For a detailed analysis of the Hungarian minority parties that were active in the three countries, see Székely, "Dynamics of Party Politics."

55 MPP was registered as a political party in 2008 after having functioned as a minority NGO for five years. EMNP was registered in 2011. The reasons for the delay in MPP's registration can be found primarily in Romania's rather restrictive party law. The emergence of two challenger parties instead of a single one can be explained by the internal tensions within the "autonomist" camp, which were rendered more serious by the clashing ambitions of leaders connected to different factions within Fidesz.

with majority parties. Furthermore, both challenger parties were created with significant help from Hungary's right-of-centre Fidesz, while RMDSZ tried to maintain a politics of "equal proximity" towards both left- and right-wing parties in Hungary. Resenting Fidesz for its interference in minority politics, the relationship between RMDSZ and Fidesz reached its nadir after the latter came back to power in 2010, which had negative consequences for RMDSZ's access to resources from Hungary. However, since 2013, there has been a rapprochement between the two parties, which will be discussed briefly at the end of the paper.

In Slovakia, there were two periods of organizational pluralism. The first began right after the regime change, when three Hungarian minority parties were created: *Magyar Polgári Párt* (MPP, Hungarian Civic Party),[56] *Együttélés* (Coexistence) and *Magyar Kereszténydemokrata Mozgalom* (MKDM, Hungarian Christian Democratic Movement). In 1998, the three parties merged, creating the *Magyar Koalíció Pártja* (MKP, Party of Hungarian Coalition), which immediately joined the government. However, MKP's tenure in power ended in 2006.[57] This created tensions in the party and resulted in a leadership change that culminated in a split in 2009, when the internally marginalized former leadership established a new party, *Most-Híd*.

In the first phase of political pluralism, the rival Hungarian parties also distinguished themselves from each other in terms of classical ideologies. MPP was a liberal party, which prioritized democratization over minority rights, approaching the minority issue from a general human rights perspective, and envisaged organizational pluralism along ideological lines for the minority. In contrast, *Együttélés* was a national conservative party, which proposed autonomist models with a corporatist flavour and militated for the merger of all Hungarian parties. Finally, as its party label indicates, MKDM was a Christian-democratic organization. Despite their differences, all three parties developed conceptions of autonomy, but after a large-scale rally in Komárom/Komárno in 1994, where the parties were unable to reach consensus, the issue of autonomy gradually disappeared from the political agenda. While MPP advocated cooperation with the Slovak democratic parties and was part of government between 1990 and 1992, *Együttélés* followed a consistent tribune strategy. In the early 1990s, in particular, MKDM was closer in its strategy to *Együttélés*.[58]

56 Until January 1992, the organization was called *Független Magyar Kezdeményezés* (Hungarian Free Initiative).

57 Between 1998 and 2006, the country was led by a centre-right coalition, with Mikuláš Dzurinda as prime minister. However, the 2006 elections were won by the centre-left Direction – Social Democracy (SMER) party, led by Robert Fico, who became prime minister.

58 László Öllös, "A magyar pártok programjai," in *Magyarok Szlovákiában (1989–2004) Összefoglaló jelentés: A rendszerváltástól az Európai Uniós csatlakozásig. I. kötet,* ed. József

Against the background of this ideological diversity, the links of the minority parties with political actors in Hungary were also based primarily on ideological proximity. Hence, *Együttélés* cooperated mainly with the national-conservative Hungarian Democratic Forum (MDF),[59] MPP with the Hungarian Liberals (SZDSZ),[60] and MKDM initially with the Hungarian Christian Democrats (KDNP).[61] Later, during their tenure in government between 1994 and 1998, the Hungarian Socialists chiefly supported MKDM, which gradually distanced itself from *Együttélés*.[62]

The second phase of organizational pluralism, which started in 2009, is characterized by the prevalence of *Most-Híd*. Unlike the other Hungarian parties, *Most-Híd* is not an ethnic party but a multi-ethnic one, combining a programme of Slovak-Hungarian reconciliation with a rather moderate ethnopolitical rhetoric. At the same time, MKP re-emerged in a somewhat more radical form, sporadically even engaging in autonomist rhetoric, a topic which had been shelved since 1998.

Since 2010, only *Most-Híd* has been represented in the Slovak parliament, but MKP has remained relatively strong at the local level. While *Most-Híd* participated in government between 2010 and 2012, MKP did not pursue a tribune strategy, but its exit from parliament brought about some degree of political isolation.[63] In terms of cross-border relations, however, the main feature of the second phase of minority multi-partyism has been Fidesz's unequivocal support for MKP and its consistent refusal to treat *Most-Híd* as a legitimate Hungarian organization, due to its multi-ethnic character.[64]

Fazekas and Péter Hunčík (Somorja/Dunaszerdahely: Fórum Kisebbségkutató Intézet/Lilium Aurum Könyvkiadó, 2004), 51–78. László Szarka, "Kisebbségi többpártrendszer és közösségépítés: A szlovákiai magyar politikai pártok működése 1990–1998," in *Magyarok Szlovákiában (1989–2004) Összefoglaló jelentés: A rendszerváltástól az Európai Uniós csatlakozásig. 1. kötet*, ed. József Fazekas and Péter Hunčík (Somorja/Dunaszerdahely: Fórum Kisebbségkutató Intézet/Lilium Aurum Könyvkiadó, 2004), 79–104.

59 *Magyar Demokrata Forum* (Hungarian Democratic Forum).

60 *Szabad Demokraták Szövetsége* (Alliance of Free Democrats).

61 *Kereszténydemokrata Néppárt* (Christian Democratic People's Party).

62 This was motivated primarily by the desire of the Socialists to counterbalance *Együttélés*, which was in a privileged position during the previous centre-right coalition in Hungary (Interview with Nándor Bárdi, on file with author).

63 In September 2012, MKP changed its name to *Magyar Közösség Pártja* (Party of the Hungarian Community). Following the 2016 elections, *Most-Híd* is once again part of the governing coalition.

64 In 2013, a third Hungarian party was registered in Slovakia, *Magyar Kereszténydemokrata Szövetség* (Hungarian Christian-Democratic Alliance). So far, it has failed to become a relevant actor.

In Serbia, Hungarian political pluralism unfolded in the 1994–1997 period, when the *Vajdasági Magyarok Demokratikus Közössége* (VMDK, Democratic Community of the Hungarians of Vojvodina) split into three parties in two phases. In the first phase, a more moderate party, *Vajdasági Magyar Szövetség* (VMSZ, Hungarian Union of Vojvodina) was created in 1994–1995, inheriting most of the organizational assets of VMDK. In the second phase, the *Vajdasági Magyar Demokrata Párt* (VMDP, Hungarian Democratic Party of Vojvodina), which emerged in 1996, pledged to stay faithful to the predecessor organization's principles and strategy. By the end of the 1990s, after a few years of fierce electoral competition, VMSZ consolidated itself as the strongest party, while both VMDK and VMDP gradually lost popularity and became marginal. In subsequent years, the fragmentation increased further. At certain points, there were no less than seven Hungarian political parties. In the period preceding the 2012 elections, this number decreased to five. In addition to those already mentioned, two small, even more radical parties were active: *Magyar Polgári Szövetség* (MPSZ, Hungarian Civic Alliance) and *Magyar Remény Mozgalom* (MRM, Hungarian Hope Movement).

One of the main factors leading to the split of the original VMDK was the self-isolating tribune strategy pursued by its leadership. Conversely, VMSZ has been clearly seeking participation in power since its creation, yet it did not have sufficient coalition potential at the national level until 2014 (with the exception of a brief period in 2001–2003), due to its relatively weak representation in parliament. VMDP returned to the same tribune strategy that was characteristic of the original VMDK,[65] while the remainder of VMDK mixed opportunistic behaviour[66] with sometimes blatant criticism of what they characterized as the compromises in VMSZ's strategy. MPSZ and especially MRM were unable to obtain important positions even at the local level (the latter suspended operations in 2014 due to a shortage of human resources).[67]

An interesting (and until 2014 unique) feature of the trans-border relationships between the Hungarian parties of Vojvodina and the parties in Hungary was that Fidesz had already been backing the strongest Hungarian party (VMSZ) since the tenure of the first Orbán government. However, they also considered VMDP a partner, while ignoring the other smaller parties, although

65 VMDP was created by VMDK's first president.

66 By this I mean coalitions at the local level with parties regarded as hostile to minorities, such as the Serbian Radical Party.

67 In 2013, another small party was created by a splinter from VMDK, called *Magyar Egység Pártja* (Party of Hungarian Unity). In 2015, a more serious split occurred, when a number of prominent and public intellectuals from VMSZ created *Magyar Mozgalom* (Hungarian Movement).

some of the latter were also seeking their favour. Mentioning MRM in the analysis is justified primarily by its uniqueness as the only avowed partner of Hungary's far-right *Jobbik Magyarországért Mozgalom* (Jobbik, Movement for a Better Hungary).

In programmatic terms, all the Hungarian parties in Vojvodina have been autonomist and have drafted more or less elaborate plans for various forms of self-government. In 2008, VMSZ, VMDP and VMDK even agreed on a joint autonomy plan, which was later endorsed by the other two parties too.[68] Basically, all parties are in favour of both territorial and personal autonomy, with some qualifications. First, VMDP insists that personal autonomy is the only way forward, regarding territorial autonomy claims as futile. Second, as a consequence of the fact that Vojvodina has regained some of its competences as an autonomous province since the fall of Slobodan Milošević, VMSZ shifted its focus to the expansion of the autonomy of the province instead of territorial autonomy for the Hungarian-majority areas. The other parties consider that the autonomy of Vojvodina is the business of the Serbs, who constitute over two-thirds of the population. Third, after the implementation of (a limited form of) cultural autonomy through the Hungarian National Council (*Magyar Nemzeti Tanács* – MNT)[69] in 2010, one of the main points of contention between VMSZ, which has been dominating the MNT, and its challengers relates precisely to the institutional features of personal autonomy. While VMSZ emphasizes the need to develop the MNT, the smaller and more radical parties are demanding a reform of the law on national councils, and some of them (especially VMDP) even question the legitimacy of the MNT.

5.2 *A Rather Narrow Policy Space*

Having described the Hungarian minority parties, I now turn to some conclusions about the patterns of their competition. The first important thing to note is that ethno-political demands range from proactive protectionism or cultural revivalism (at the moderate end) to territorial autonomism (as the most radical demand). On the one hand, parties putting forward demands that fall short of some sort of autonomy are rather exceptional. In fact, only the multi-ethnic *Most-Híd* from Slovakia can be classified as such (but even *Most-Híd* mentions autonomy in some of its documents, although it emphasizes the issue to a significantly lesser extent than the other parties). On the other hand, the most "radical" demand of any Hungarian minority party is territorial autonomy.

68 Available online in Hungarian at http://www.corvinuslibrary.com/autonom/bacska.pdf (accessed 14 August, 2017).

69 The Hungarian National Council is the elected body of the Hungarian cultural autonomy.

No claims challenging the territorial integrity of the host-states have ever been tabled. Even calls for federalization have emerged only sporadically. In this respect, even the "radical" Hungarian minority parties are more moderate in their goals than the average Western European ethno-regionalist parties, as Ishiyama and Breuning (1998) also point out.[70] Second, if we compare the substance of "radicalness" of the main Hungarian minority parties across the countries in question, it becomes obvious that this is highly contextual matter, as it is always defined in relation to the demands tabled by other Hungarian minority parties in the host-state concerned. For instance, the emergence of a multi-ethnic party, such as *Most-Híd* in Slovakia, renders its counterpart, the MKP, radical in the same country, while in terms of its aspirations it is less demanding than even the "moderate" RMDSZ in Romania, where the focus on autonomy is far more emphatic.

Overall, the array of demands put forward by Hungarian minority parties demarcates a rather narrow policy space, which means that the Hungarian minority party systems are primarily characterized by *valence competition*[71] with regard to the overarching issue of autonomy. Slovakia seems to be an exception, especially in the second phase of organizational pluralism. However, this is clearly the case in Romania, where the newly founded challenger parties all justified their creation as a return to the original goals and organizational principles of RMDSZ, from which the latter had putatively departed. The situation is similar in Serbia. Even if the rival parties have emphasized different types of autonomy, they all agree on the overarching importance of autonomy, while accusing each other of not doing enough in support of it.

As noted above, the Hungarian community of Slovakia is somewhat different. Although all three relevant parties elaborated autonomy plans in the early 1990s, classical political ideologies also played an emphatic role in their competition, and there was a more fundamental divide concerning the preferable principles of the community's social and political organization, pitting a

70 Probably one of the main reasons for this is that the changing of the borders was excluded from the toolkit of the parties through the signing of bilateral treaties as early as 1992 through the Balladur Plan.

71 *Valence* issues involve some condition that is regarded as good or bad by the electorate in general but is linked to the parties in different ways. The classic example is corruption: no party would campaign for more corruption, and all voters would agree that corruption must be fought; however, some parties may be associated more with corruption than others, and some parties may claim more credibly that they will fight corruption. The issue of autonomy is similar: the parties (and most of the electorate) agree that it is a desirable goal, and they fight each other on how credible it is that they will be able to deliver on the issue. See Donald E. Stokes, "Spatial Models of Party Competition," *American Political Science Review* 57, no. 2 (1963): 368–77.

liberal-pluralist alternative (MPP) against a corporatist-nationalist conception (*Együttélés*). In the second period of pluralism, the divide between MKP and *Most-Híd* can be regarded as even more fundamental, as the consensus among the Hungarian political elites about the desirability of representation through exclusively ethnic parties has been broken.

Given this rather narrow policy space (even in Slovakia), it is evident that programmatic goals on their own are insufficient to differentiate between the parties in question. Against this fairly homogenous substantive background, an analysis of political strategies and attitudes towards the actors of both the host- and kin-state has a distinctive value. Of the ideal-typical strategies identified by De Winter,[72] pure participationist/governmental strategies are more prevalent in reality than pure tribune strategies. Consistent opposition strategies were more characteristic of the early 1990s (e.g. VMDK, *Együttélés*), when minorities were more optimistic about opportunities for exerting pressure on their host-states through the international community, they enjoyed more kin-state support for their political goals and the political revival of majority nationalism in their host-states legitimized their aspirations for autonomy as a legitimate response. However, these strategies did not yield the expected results, and they consequently lost their appeal. Presently, opposition strategies are pursued by small parties only. However, in their case, in addition to their principled position on their political goals, there is a more practical explanation for the vociferous rejection of participation in power: they are too small to have coalition potential, except at the local level. None of the minority parties could be classified as pursuing an anti-system strategy, apart from occasionally engaging in non-conventional types of political participation, such as protests. Yet, this does not prevent some of the mainstream parties (or the majority media) from labelling them as extremists and refusing to cooperate with them. Sometimes the more moderate minority parties also engage in this kind of strategic labelling.

The most important feature of the Hungarian-Hungarian relationships is that the connections between the minority parties and their counterparts in Hungary are highly asymmetrical. While the ties with the parties on the right (Fidesz and, partly, the far-right Jobbik) are rather clear and openly assumed by the minority parties, no such partnerships are assumed to exist with the Hungarian left (perhaps with the exception of MPP in Slovakia). Some "moderate" parties, as the largest (or only) minority parties in their host-states (RMDSZ in Romania and VMSZ in Serbia), were interested in maintaining good ties with any party that was governing in Budapest, thus also with the left-of-the-centre

72 De Winter, "Conclusion."

socialist and liberal parties. But even in these cases they framed the relationship as being with the Hungarian government and not with a specific party, while on the right the "special partnerships" were framed as being with Fidesz, even while the latter was in opposition. The case of *Most-Híd* in Slovakia is special, as this multi-ethnic party is less interested in maintaining close ties with any party in Hungary. The example of *Most-Híd* also shows that very low-intensity ethno-political demands are incompatible with orientation towards the kin-state.

The three features of the parties discussed so far (their programmatic goals and their relationship with the parties from the host- and kin-state) are closely, albeit not perfectly, interrelated. At the risk of gross simplification, the main divide in all three countries can be described as being between a more "radical" and a more "moderate" camp. Radical parties oriented more emphatically towards the kin-state (and within it, towards political parties on the right, most importantly Fidesz) were advocating autonomy more vocally and were less likely to prioritize participation in their host-states' governments. Often, these parties were prone to depict their rivals within the minority community as "not sufficiently Hungarian" or even anti-national. *Együttélés* in Slovakia, VMDK and later VMDP in Serbia, and MPP and EMNP in Romania belong to this group. Conversely, the "moderates" or pragmatics were more open towards inter-ethnic cooperation, believed that the problems of the minority should be solved in the host-state through participation by the minority community in power and relied less on the support of Hungary. The principal examples in this category are RMDSZ in Romania (especially after 1996) and *Most-Híd* in Slovakia, while VMSZ in Serbia represents a somewhat special case, as the party was able to maintain the support of Fidesz while also pursuing a participationist strategy.[73]

5.3 *Clientelistic Potential*

It is important to note that within all three communities there was only a single instance when a party was able to be more successful than its intra-ethnic rivals on a more radical platform. This party is *Együttélés* in Slovakia, which was the dominant Hungarian minority party until the mid-1990s. Conversely, the emergence of VMSZ against VMDK in Serbia and of *Most-Híd* against MKP in Slovakia were successful instances of underbidding, while the challenge of MPP and EMNP in Romania and VMDP, MPSZ and MRM in Serbia were

73 As discussed at the end of the paper, the situation of RMDSZ in Romania also developed in this direction after 2013.

unsuccessful cases of ethnic outbidding. Thus, the question arises: why were the more radical parties unable to prevail among the Hungarian minorities?

I argue that the key to this phenomenon lies in the relative importance of clientelistic linkages, that is, the different levels of access that the parties have to resources that can be deployed for clientelistic purposes. Starting in the late 1990s, the "moderate" parties were able to access increasingly substantial resources (especially in Romania and Slovakia; in Serbia this process began much later). At the same time, a process of decentralization also began in both Romania and Slovakia, while in Serbia the province of Vojvodina, where most Hungarians live, regained some of the competences lost during the Milošević era.[74]

As a consequence of these processes, the moderate Hungarian parties of Romania and Slovakia were able to access resources of a magnitude that the radical challengers were unable to counterbalance. Although the issue of finances is very complex and insufficiently transparent, a rough comparison of the clientelistic potential of the parties is possible based on an assessment of the access of the parties to various types of resources and the magnitude of those resources.

Figures 9.2 and 9.3 present information about the approximate amount of financial aid provided by the kin-state to external minorities and by Romania and Slovakia for the development of Hungarian minority culture.[75] Unfortunately, no such graph could be created for Serbia due to a lack of data. Yet, based on the financing features of the Hungarian National Council (MNT), it is reasonable to state that between 2010 and 2014 financial aid from Hungary still accounted for 65–75 per cent of the budget of the MNT,[76] despite a significant improvement in host-state financing after 2009.[77]

These graphs show that funding for minorities has increased in both Hungary and the host-states over the past two decades, although the trends were not continuous and some of the deviations are quite significant. Clearly, the resources from Hungary still represent higher amounts of money than the allocations of

74 On these developments, see Katinka Beretka, "Fragile Autonomy Arrangements in the Republic of Serbia: The Territorial Autonomy of Vojvodina and the National Minority Councils," in *Autonomy Arrangements around the World: A Collection of Well and Lesser Known Cases*, ed. Levente Salat Sergiu Constantin, Alexander Osipov, and István Gergő Székely (Cluj: Romanian Institute for Research on National Minorities, 2015), 247–274.

75 The figures for kin-state funding do not include the allocations for pupils in Hungarian-language schools (*oktatási-nevelési támogatás*) and the subsidies for higher education at Sapientia University and Selye János University. These were subtracted because their beneficiaries are clearly defined and the minority elites cannot exert any influence on their destination.

76 Based on the budgets of the MNT, available at www.mnt.org.rs (accessed August 14, 2017).

77 Based on interviews I conducted in 2010 with leaders of VMSZ and the MNT.

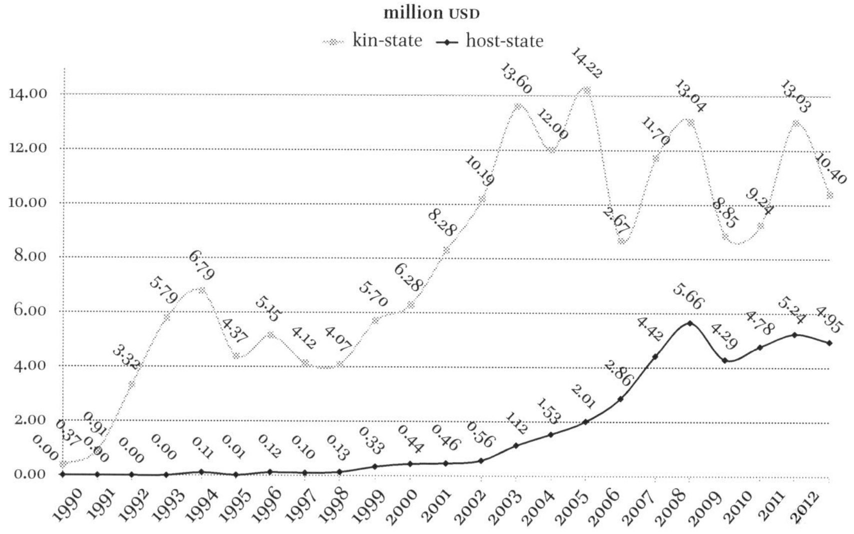

FIGURE 9.2 The evolution of funding from the kin-state and cultural subsidies in Romania, Author's computations.
SOURCES: FOR HUNGARY: BÁRDI AND MISOVITZ, "A KISEBBSÉGI MAGYAR," PAPP, "HATÁRON TÚLI MAGYAR" (2010), AND HTTP://WWW.BGAZRT.HU (ACCESSED JULY 12, 2017); FOR ROMANIA: MOHACSEK, "ANALIZA FINANŢĂRILOR," YEARLY LAWS ON ROMANIA'S BUDGET.

the host-states for minority cultures, and as such they are very important for the sustainability of the institutional system of all three Hungarian communities (especially in the case of Serbia, where, as we have seen, host-state financing of minority cultures remains unsatisfactory).

However, this is not the main point. First, what is really important is that the total subsidies provided by Hungary (aggregated for all Hungarian communities beyond the borders) represented a rather small amount of money over the period studied here (between 0.1–0.2 per cent of Hungary's budget, the highest value in the period covered being $74.6 million in 2008[78]). Second, the gap between kin-state funds and host-state subsidies for minority culture had decreased to some extent by the late 2000s, as compared to the early 1990s (when host-states were allocating virtually nothing or very little for these purposes).

Third, and probably more important than the arguments about the amount of money, is the fact that the influence of minority elites over the distribution of kin-state resources (and, implicitly, the clientelistic potential that follows

78 The value of the financing was converted to US dollars according to average yearly exchange rates.

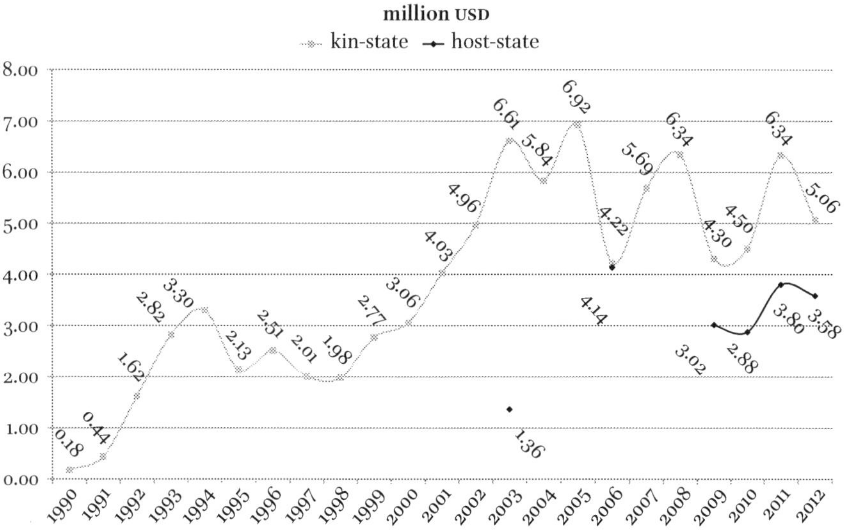

FIGURE 9.3 The evolution of funding from the kin-state and cultural subsidies in Slovakia, Author's computations.
SOURCES: BÁRDI AND MISOVITZ, "A KISEBBSÉGI MAGYAR," PAPP, "HATÁRON TÚLI MAGYAR," AND HTTP://WWW.BGAZRT.HU (ACCESSED JULY 12, 2017); FOR SLOVAKIA: NEWSPAPER ARTICLES FROM WWW.MEDIASPAJZ.INFO (ACCESSED JULY 12, 2017).

from it) is much more limited than in the case of funds provided by the host-state. The bulk of the kin-state funding is earmarked and not channelled to the minority parties, and some of the other beneficiaries are strong interest groups over which the parties have little influence (e.g. the churches). Thus, the opportunities for clientelistic network-building are mostly indirect for the minority parties. They can only exert some influence over the distribution of funds meant for civil society by using their personal ties to lobby kin-state decision-makers. In addition, non-governmental organizations (NGOs) with close ties to the minority parties may undertake administrative tasks on behalf of the kin-state (e.g. processing applications for dual citizenship or the distribution of subsidies for the minority education system), which provides them with a number of jobs and infrastructure that the parties may also deploy for other purposes, the running costs being covered from kin-state resources. A third important type of funding that is not channelled to the minority parties is the funding of minority media.

I would like to stress once again that it is not only the amount of the resources that matters but also their type, more precisely the manner in which they can be used by the parties. As compared to kin-state funding, the resources allocated by the host-states for minority culture provide much more leeway for minority parties, due to the simple fact that the state grants them greater discretion to decide how they wish to distribute these funds (while, in the case of funds from Hungary, decision-makers in Budapest also have their own agenda). In Romania, the funds allocated through the Council of National Minorities[79] are almost totally at the discretion of minority elites,[80] which in the case of the Hungarians means the largest moderate party, RMDSZ. In Slovakia, until 2012, the most important actor in the distribution of state subsidies for culture was the Deputy Prime Minister responsible for Minorities. Since then, it has been the Governmental Commissioner for Minority Issues. The appointments to these positions were made by the Hungarian minority parties whenever they were part of the government coalition. (In fact, the Commissioner was appointed by *Most-Híd* after the 2012 elections as well, despite the fact that the party was formally in opposition.) Only Serbia can be considered different in this respect, due to the generally problematic nature of financing minority national councils.[81] However, even here, there has been some improvement in host-state allocations. For instance, since 2010, the Hungarian National Council also receives some funding from the central, provincial and municipal budgets.

All in all, although the funds allocated by host-states for minority cultures still represent significantly less in absolute terms than the finances flowing from Hungary, the fact that minority elites have much more discretion with regard to the former compensates for the difference in absolute numbers. That is, the allocations for minority culture in Slovakia and Romania can be regarded as providing a clientelistic capacity that is quite comparable to, if not more substantial than, what can be derived from the funding provided by the kin-state.

Moreover, and most importantly, it is not the subsidies for minority culture that represent the relevant point of reference to which kin-state resources should be compared but the spoils that can be secured through participation in the governments of the host-states (and secondarily by controlling local

79 A consultative body of Romania's government, whose members are delegated by the organizations of the minorities represented in parliament.

80 See Dan Oprescu, "Politici publice pentru minoritățile naționale din România (1996–1998)," in *Relații interetnice în România postcomunistă*, ed. Lucian Nastasă and Levente Salat (Cluj: Ethnocultural Diversity Research Center. 2000), 73–82. See also Andrea Cârstocea, "Ethno-business: The Manipulation of Minority Rights in Romania and Hungary," in *Perpetual Motion? Transformation and Transition in Central and Eastern Europe and Russia*, ed. Tul'si Bhambry Clare Griffin, Titus Hjelm, Christopher Nicholson and Olga G. Voronina (London: University College, 2011) 16–28.

81 Beretka, "Fragile Autonomy."

governments). Moreover, participation in government enables not only softer forms of clientelism, and a number of jobs or contracts that can be employed for patronage purposes, but also pork-barrel projects (i.e. public investments directed to areas with a high proportion of Hungarians). Precise data are not available for the resources obtainable through governmental participation, but a single example suffices to illustrate the magnitude of these resources. In the years when the funding provided by Hungary was at its highest for Romania ($13–14 million), this aid would have sufficed to build about 2–3 kilometres of motorway or to rehabilitate approximately 30 kilometres of national roads.[82] Obviously, this is a very small sum compared to what can be obtained by controlling certain ministries (especially through pork-barrel projects). Furthermore, as already mentioned, starting in the late 1990s/early 2000s significant decentralization processes occurred in all three countries, resulting in a significant increase in sub-national budgets.[83]

Based on these considerations, we are now able to assess the clientelistic capacity of the rival Hungarian parties. Note that what we are trying to assess here is their clientelistic capacity relative to each other. In other words, we will only look at the periods when more than one relevant Hungarian party existed in each country.

In Romania, by the time of its splintering into several parties, the moderate RMDSZ was already regarded as a trusted coalition partner by all mainstream parties.[84] During its tenure in government, RMDSZ was able to obtain some ministries with fairly high budgets and provide significant opportunities for clientelistic exchanges, especially of the pork-barrel kind.[85] Furthermore,

82 The total cost of the rehabilitation of a county-level road in 2015 in Harghita county amounted to about $16.3 million for 26.6 kilometres, a figure higher than the typical annual sum total of kin-state in the early 2010s. See http://www.szekelyhon.ro/aktualis/udvarhelyszek/iden-befejezik-a-132-es-megyei-ut-felujitasat (accessed August 14, 2017). I am indebted to Nándor Bárdi for drawing my attention to the possibility of expressing the magnitude of financial flows in terms of the cost of infrastructural projects.

83 For details on Serbia (Vojvodina), see Beretka, "Fragile Autonomy." For Romania, see, Ana Maria. Dobre, "Romania: From Historical Regions to Local Decentralization via the Unitary State," in *The Oxford Handbook of Local and Regional Democracy in Europe*, ed. John Loughlin, Frank Hendriks and Anders Lidström (Oxford: Oxford University Press, 2011), 685–714. For Slovakia, see Soňa Čapková, "Slovakia: Local government. Establishing Democracy at the Grassroots," in *The Oxford Handbook of Local and Regional Democracy in Europe*, edited by John Loughlin, Frank Hendriks and Anders Lidström (Oxford: Oxford University Press, 2011), 552–575.

84 RMDSZ was part of a centre-right coalition between 1996 and 2000 and provided parliamentary support to a centre-left government between 2000 and 2004.

85 Between 2004 and 2008, RMDSZ appointed various ministers, including the ministers of public works, telecommunications and environmental protection, and for a short period

RMDSZ remained solely in charge of the distribution of the subsidies provided by the Romanian state for Hungarian cultural activities. As regards the kin-state, during the socialist-liberal governments in Hungary (2002–2010), but especially after the unsuccessful 2004 referendum on Hungarian citizenship for Hungarians abroad, RMDSZ was able to exert considerable influence over the distribution of kin-state funding.[86] However, the change of government in Hungary in 2010 brought about some important adjustments. RMDSZ lost control over some of the resource flows from Hungary, some of which have been redirected by Fidesz towards the challenger parties and others towards NGOs. As opposed to RMDSZ's access to multifarious resources, its more radical challengers could rely almost exclusively on the backing of the kin-state, more precisely of Fidesz, while being categorically weaker with regard to host-state resources.[87]

In summary, the Hungarian party system of Romania is characterized by programmatically very similar parties competing around the concept of autonomy. For a long time, RMDSZ enjoyed an unequivocal advantage in what concerns clientelistic capacity, due to its integration into the Romanian party cartel, while the two smaller and more radical parties tried to mount a challenge against it relying mostly on resources from Hungary. However, since late 2013, Fidesz has shifted its strategy again, leading to a rapprochement with RMDSZ in the aftermath of the challengers' disappointing electoral results.

In Slovakia, in the first phase of multiparty minority politics, only the liberal and moderate MPP had governmental experience, but only for a short period (1990–1992). In local governments, the more radical *Együttélés* was initially the strongest party, but by the mid-1990s MKDM grew to a similar strength. MPP failed to enter parliament in 1992, and only managed to re-enter by accepting very strict conditions to run as part of a coalition with the other two Hungarian parties in 1994. Concerning relations with Hungary, *Együttélés* was the primary

---

was even in charge of the ministry of regional development, which has one of the highest budgets in Romania. Between 2009 and 2012, and later in 2014, RMDSZ was in charge of the ministries of culture and the environment.

86 Bárdi and Misovitz, "A kisebbségi magyar."

87 While MPP was able to obtain majority in some – mostly rural – local governments, EMNP controlled no local governments at all. Of the two challenger parties, EMNP outpaced MPP in the kin-state dimension, as Fidesz entrusted the network of offices set up to deal with citizenship applications to an NGO closely associated with EMNP. For MPP, the only channel of patronage from Budapest is its former president, Jenő Szász, who has been appointed head of the Research Institute for National Strategy (*Nemzetstratégiai Kutatóintézet*). On the funding of EMNP, see http://itthon.transindex.ro/?cikk=20082. The budget of the Research Institute for National Strategy was €4.3 million in 2013. See http://vilag.transindex.ro/?cikk=23238 (accessed August 14, 2017).

partner of the government in the early 1990s (while the national-conservative MDF was in power), but after the socialists came to power in 1994 they increasingly preferred MKDM, boosting its clientelistic capacity with regard to the kin-state (although certain key personalities within *Együttélés* maintained their influence). Thus, the first phase of Hungarian multi-partyism can be characterized by the presence of two parties of approximately equal clientelistic capacity (with *Együttélés* on the decline and MKDM on the rise) and a third party (MPP) struggling for survival. As access to government opened up for the Hungarian parties only after their merger in 1998, this first phase is less interesting from the perspective of the comparison of clientelistic potential. Furthermore, of all instances of intra-ethnic party competition within the various Hungarian minorities, it was during the 1990–1998 period in Slovakia that party competition came closest to competition based on programmatic (as opposed to clientelistic) linkages.

In the second phase, which started in 2009, *Most-Híd*'s governmental participation, which occurred in parallel with MKP's exit from parliament, obviously tilted the balance in favour of the former, even if the latter was able to remain relatively strong at the local and county level.[88] However, patronage opportunities based on kin-state resources remained almost completely in the hands of MKP, due to Fidesz's hostile attitude towards *Most-Híd*. Still, all this backing was insufficient for MKP to enter parliament at three subsequent elections. If we also attempt a cross-country comparison, MKP's clientelistic capacity deriving from its strong backing by Fidesz is diminished by the fact that Slovakia's civil society can be regarded as the most developed of the three countries, and thus less tied to political parties, which means that a smaller part of civil society depends on politically distributed funds.[89]

88 Between 2010 and 2012, *Most-Híd* was in charge of two very important ministries in the government, namely the environment and agriculture and rural development. Although the party was in opposition between 2012 and 2016, it still nominated the governmental commissioner in charge of minorities (and implicitly of distributing Slovakia's subsidies for minority cultures). Since 2016, *Most-Híd* holds three portfolios in Robert Fico's third government: the ministry of transport, construction and regional development, the ministry of justice and the ministry of the environment.

89 Károly Tóth, "A magyar intézményrendszer fejlődése." in *Magyarok Szlovákiában (1989–2004) Összefoglaló jelentés: A rendszerváltástól az Európai Uniós csatlakozásig. I. kötet*, ed. József Fazekas and Péter Hunčík (Somorja/Dunaszerdahely: Fórum Kisebbségkutató Intézet/Lilium Aurum Könyvkiadó, 2004), 247–270. See also Károly Tóth, "A kulturális intézményrendszer," in *Magyarok Szlovákiában III. kötet, Kultúra (1989–2006)*, ed. Gábor Csanda and Károly Tóth (Somorja/Dunaszerdahely: Fórum Kisebbségkutató Intézet/Lilium Aurum Könyvkiadó, 2006), 223–240.

In Serbia, in the early 1990s, VMDK was able to gain access to very few resources due to its self-isolating tribune strategy, which sometimes implied a refusal to enter multi-ethnic coalitions even at the local level. After the split, the more moderate VMSZ adopted a cooperative strategy, primarily at the local and the provincial level (Vojvodina) and, after the end of the Milošević era, also at the national level, increasing its access to resources. However, it was never able to develop the same kind of clientelistic potential based on host-state resources as the major Hungarian parties of Romania or Slovakia, primarily because of its small size.[90] Still, even this sufficed for VMSZ to clearly outperform all other Hungarian parties in Vojvodina in this respect, as the latter remained relevant only in a few local strongholds after 2000, providing them with very limited opportunities for patronage. The position of VMDP was arguably somewhat stronger, as it was able to maintain the support of Fidesz, which meant access to some kin-state resources. However, the other three parties had no partners in the kin-state.

VMSZ is unique among the Hungarian minority parties in that it has enjoyed uninterrupted support from Hungarian governments (regardless of colour) since the party's creation and is regarded in Budapest as the primary partner (even though VMDP has also maintained close ties with right-wing governments). This position is even more interesting, as in this case it is the party that is most integrated into the Serbian party system that has been prioritized by Budapest. The reasons why the situation of VMSZ has differed from that of the major Hungarian parties in Romania and Slovakia are complex, but it probably matters that, by the time Fidesz came to power in 2010, all other Hungarian parties in Serbia were already quite insignificant. Furthermore, mainstream or Vojvodina-based regionalist parties consistently obtain quite a significant proportion (sometimes more than half) of the votes cast by ethnic Hungarians. Also, funding from Hungary has generally remained much more important in Serbia. This prompted VMSZ to behave in a very conflict-averse manner with Fidesz, while also avoiding isolation in Serbia thanks to the fact that the issue of autonomy has not been treated as a taboo subject there (due to the situation of Vojvodina).

Based on this assessment of the different types of resources accessible to minority parties, one can conclude that relying solely or overwhelmingly on funding from Hungary is not sufficient to mount a challenge against the parties

90 The highest share of MPs ever held by VMSZ was 2.4 per cent, which did not enable the party to obtain portfolios in government. For a short time (2001–2003), VMSZ held the position of deputy prime minister, but its next participation in national government only occurred in 2014, and then only at the state secretary level.

that are able to control host-state resources while in government. However, despite the relatively low weight of kin-state funding compared to host-state resources, the interplay of the various types of resources discussed above has two important implications.

First, kin-state resources were more important in the early years, when the mechanisms for subsidizing minority culture were not yet institutionalized and, even more importantly, minority parties were considered incompatible with a position in the central government. This is one of the reasons why more radical platforms were more successful in the early 1990s. Note that we have only a single example of a successful radical party within the studied period, namely *Együttélés* in Slovakia in the early 1990s. However, the still unified RMDSZ in Romania and VMDK in Serbia were also operating on more radical platforms by that time. Second, funding from the kin-state becomes more important for the minority parties when they are not in government. Furthermore, it can become crucial in special situations or in times of crisis, modifying the balance of forces between rival minority elites. This is what happened during the split of MKP in Slovakia in 2009, when the faction that enjoyed the support of Hungary engineered a replacement of the leadership after the party ended up in opposition and lost access to host-state resources.

6 Concluding Remarks

I have argued that the key to the success of the "moderate" minority parties is their superior clientelistic capacity compared to that of their "radical" intra-ethnic rivals. Furthermore, this is a consequence of the different magnitude and types of resources obtainable from the host-state and the kin-state. Although financial flows from the kin-state are clearly on the rise, they do not provide minority elites with such good opportunities for clientelistic exchanges, especially compared to the resources available in their host-states.

In the host-states, the really relevant resources are not the subsidies provided for minority culture but the spoils that can be obtained primarily through participation in government and secondarily by controlling local governments. These are evidently of a higher magnitude and can often be deployed more flexibly for patronage activities than what the kin-state can offer. As a consequence, relying solely or overwhelmingly on funding from Hungary is not sufficient for mounting a challenge against the parties that are able to control host-state resources while in government.

However, the price of access to government is moderation. In both Romania and Slovakia, this entailed shelving more radical ethno-political demands, such as autonomy.[91] The ability of the minority parties to push for stronger ethno-political goals is reduced by the lack of guarantees for their participation in power, as in all three countries their inclusion in government depends on ad hoc political deals and the need of the mainstream parties to secure a majority in parliament. Their only important asset is that, relative to a mainstream party of similar size, they may be cheaper coalition partners.[92]

The record of the Hungarian parties that were included in governing coalitions in Romania (RMDSZ) and especially Slovakia (MKP and later *Most-Híd*) also demonstrate that minority parties have made little progress in efforts to restructure the state, at least compared to the ethno-regionalist parties of Western Europe.[93] The most that the majority ethnic groups are willing to guarantee (especially in Romania and Slovakia) is individual rights for minorities, but demands that would require redefining the nation-state or neutralizing the ownership of the state by the majority segment (which is what formalized power-sharing arrangements or autonomy with real competences would imply) have been rejected. Under such conditions, moderate minority elites that participate in power are less and less able to reinforce their legitimacy through policy achievements in the ethno-political domain, so they turn to clientelistic exchanges instead. For the moderate minority elites the situation is convenient because they can access resources and can also feel safe from challengers within their own segment. The fact that the moderates can reinforce their position within the minority by relying on public resources is also convenient from the standpoint of the majority elites, since it ensures that minority radicals will remain marginalized. While this model of minority incorporation has so far been able to prevent inter-ethnic conflict, the asymmetrical nature of inter-ethnic cooperation and the fact that certain fundamental aspects of the state are not open to negotiation render it reminiscent of arrangements based on a mix of elite co-optation and control. The moderate minority elites receive some degree of status, power and access to economic resources in exchange for compliance with the state's regulation and their agreement not to broach certain "delicate" issues. Most importantly, these "delicate" issues include autonomy. However, in Romania, for instance, the issue of a state-funded Hungarian-language university was also regarded as a "delicate" issue.

91 Nándor Bárdi, "Cleavages in Cross-Border Magyar Minority Politics, 1989–1998," *Regio: A Review of Studies on Minorities, Politics and Society* 1, no. 1 (2000): 3–36. Csergő, *Talk of the Nation.*

92 The main reason for being a "cheaper" partner is the difficulty, or even inability, of minority parties to supply personnel for public positions at the subnational level outside the regions inhabited by the minority. For details, see Kiss and Székely, "Shifting Linkages."

93 However, in the case of VMSZ, it is perhaps too early to judge.

A further consequence of this model of minority incorporation is that intra-ethnic cooperation is not the default within Hungarian minorities. On the contrary, the "moderates" regard electoral coalition with the "radicals" as undesirable, as any such cooperation would decrease their chances of participating in power and securing resources. However, this reluctance to cooperate has clearly contributed to the slow yet constant downward trend in electoral results, which is evident in all three countries. It is questionable how long this type of behaviour will continue to secure the "moderates" sufficient weight in parliament to maintain their potential as coalition partners.

While the magnitude of funding from the kin-state is clearly insufficient to shift the balance of power in favour of the more radical parties, these resources still suffice to "keep alive" some of the more radical minority elites (i.e. the leadership of the challenger parties). The strategy of Fidesz can also be interpreted as indicating a desire to sustain competing elites in the minority communities in order to keep the mainstream elites of the strongest minority parties in each country in check. Furthermore, kin-state support may become crucial under special circumstances, such as crises.

7 Epilogue

The bulk of the research behind the present article was carried out between 2011 and 2013, and the arguments put forward here were formulated based on data gathered in this period. Since then, however, some important changes have occurred, which may seem to be at odds with the argument concerning the trade-off between orientation towards the kin-state and integration into the power structures of the host-state.

The first development relates to Romania. In 2013, a rapprochement between the moderate RMDSZ and Fidesz began to take shape. Furthermore, RMDSZ entered into an electoral cooperation agreement with MPP in 2016, which was not independent of developments in Budapest, while the other more radical party, EMNP, seems to be gradually losing Budapest's support. Thus, the relationship between the Hungarian parties of Romania and kin-state actors increasingly resembles the model that I have described above as being characteristic only of Serbia. The explanations for this rapprochement are manifold, but in my view the crucial reason is that both radical challenger parties failed to achieve an electoral breakthrough.[94] This also casts doubts on the capacity

94 Since 2012, support for the two smaller parties taken together stands at approximately 15 per cent of the votes cast by ethnic Hungarian voters.

of the challenger parties to mobilize a sufficiently high proportion of the newly enfranchised Transylvanian Hungarian voters in Hungary's parliamentary election, prompting Fidesz to seek RMDSZ's assistance for this purpose. Later, other factors also contributed to Fidesz's reorientation towards RMDSZ, such as Romania's increased interest in a rapprochement with Hungary after a relatively tense period. In this context, RMDSZ has the potential to act as an intermediary towards Romanian mainstream parties.

A second important event occurred in Serbia, where VMSZ was shaken by a major split. In 2015, the former president of the Hungarian National Council, joined by a number of important public intellectuals and notable local politicians, created a new Hungarian organization, *Magyar Mozgalom* (Hungarian Movement). Although the new organization (which joined forces with the rather marginal VMDK) obtained the best result of any newcomer Hungarian organization in the Vojvodina Assembly and the municipalities since the rise of VMSZ, it was unable to run in the parliamentary elections. It also failed to secure the support of Fidesz, which made it clear that VMSZ remained its partner of choice.

Thus, in the three countries discussed in this paper, it is only in Slovakia that Fidesz is sticking to its strategy of hostility towards the minority party that is most integrated into the polity of the host-state. In other words, Fidesz still refuses to recognize *Most-Híd* as a legitimate representative of the Hungarian minority, despite the fact that MKP also failed to get back into parliament in the 2016 elections.[95]

The last significant development is that the magnitude of the financial flows directed beyond Hungary's borders has increased substantially in recent times. In 2015, the Hungarian government announced an economic development plan for Vojvodina worth 50 billion Hungarian forints (approximately $179 million), followed in 2016 by a similar plan worth 30 billion Hungarian forints (about $107 million) for Subcarpathia in Ukraine. The motivation behind these plans was the precarious development situation in these regions, coupled with outright neglect by their host-states. No similar announcements have been made for the other regions so far, but the resources channelled to Romania have also been significantly increased. However, it appears that these resources are no longer being deployed with the intention of shifting the balance between rival minority elites or parties. If such an intention does exist, it is still difficult to detect.[96]

95 The attitude of Fidesz towards the two rival Hungarian organizations in Ukraine remains similar, as only one is regarded as a partner and the other is ignored.

96 See the analysis of the Atlastzo.hu independent journalism forum on this topic: https://erdely.atlatszo.hu/2017/03/20/hataron-tuli-tamogatasok-2-az-allando-tetelek-es-a-legjobb-baratok (accessed August 14, 2017).

CHAPTER 10

Mono-ethnic Transnationalism? Romanian Public Perceptions of Hungarian Ethno-political Claims and Kin-state Policies

Tamás Kiss

Abstract

In 2010, Hungary modified its citizenship legislation, making it possible for Hungarians living in neighbouring countries to obtain extra-territorial citizenship. In this paper, I seek to explain the lack of Romanian resistance and countermeasures to the Hungarian legislation, suggesting that Romania has moved towards a post-Westphalian concept of sovereignty and away from a territorially-bounded notion of what constitutes a national community. I investigate the Romanian public perception of existing minority rights and Hungarian ethnic claims, as well as the relationship between the Hungarian citizenship legislation and the claims of the Transylvanian Hungarian political elite for minority rights and autonomy. Relying on empirical studies and surveys on how the ethno-national majority in Romania perceives the minority rights of Transylvanian Hungarians and the Hungarian kin-state policy, I assert that it is primarily an empirical question whether national majorities see minority autonomy and extra-territorial citizenship offered by the kin-state as conflicting strategies.

1 Introduction

Several commentators have argued that the Hungarian-Romanian debates over kin-state involvement and minority accommodation are connected to competing notions of sovereignty.[1] Scholars analyzing Hungarian citizenship policy and kin-state involvement have often presumed that, (at least) at an interstate level, Romania tends to use a concept of territorial sovereignty

1 Zsuzsa Csergő and James Goldgeier, "Nationalist Strategies and European Integration," *Perspectives on Politics* 2, no. 1 (2004): 21–37; Zsuzsa Csergő, *Talk of the Nation: Language and Conflict in Romania and Slovakia* (Ithaca, NY and London: Cornell University Press, 2007); Szabolcs Pogonyi, "Dual Citizenship and Sovereignty," *Nationalities Papers* 39, no. 5 (2011): 685–704.

 | DOI:10.1163/9789004386426_011

prevalent in the nineteenth and early twentieth century.[2] This concept would be connected to the Westphalian paradigm,[3] where states have legitimate authority over bounded territorial units and the population inhabiting those territories without any interference by external actors. In the classic version of the Westphalian paradigm, territorial units and communities of citizenry generally coincided, while dual citizenship was considered an anomaly. Due to the growing importance of transnational organizations and increased transnational mobility, the Westphalian paradigm is no longer in a hegemonic position.[4] However, according to this argument, concerns over territorial sovereignty connected to it still exist and can lead to interstate and inter-ethnic tensions in cases where external citizenship or enfranchisement is offered to kin communities.

These (explicit or tacit) assumptions shaped expectations concerning the consequences of the modification of Hungarian citizenship legislation in 2010, which made it possible for Hungarians living in neighbouring countries to obtain extra-territorial citizenship. There was widespread concern that the law allowing external citizenship would provoke diplomatic and political debates between Hungary and neighbouring countries with large Hungarian communities and that nationalist parties would benefit from these debates, while Hungarian minorities would become the losers of the process.[5] These murky forecasts were partially confirmed when the Slovak Citizenship Act was modified on May 26, 2010, the same day that Hungary adopted its new citizenship legislation. The relevant amendment provided that, if a Slovak citizen acquired the citizenship of another state "by an act of will", he or she would automatically lose Slovak citizenship. Slovakia made direct reference to territorial sovereignty and invoked (at least rhetorically) Westphalian principles when, in

2 Mária Kovács, "The Politics of Dual Citizenship," in *Dual Citizenship in Global Perspective: From Unitary to Multiple Citizenship*, ed. Thomas Faist and Peter Kivisto (New York: Palgrave Macmillan, 2007), 92–112; Myra Waterbury, *Between State and Nation: Diaspora Politics and Kin-State Nationalism in Hungary* (New York: Palgrave Macmillan, 2010); Pogonyi, "Dual Citizenship and Sovereignty," 694.

3 See Stephen Krasner, *Sovereignty: Organized Hypocrisy* (Princeton, NJ: Princeton University Press, 1999).

4 On the territorially-bounded concept of society and its transnational alternatives see Thomas Faist, "Diaspora and Transnationalism. What Kind of Dance Partners?," in *Diaspora and Transnationalism: Concepts, Theories and Methods*, ed. Thomas Faist and Rainer Bauböck (Amsterdam: Amsterdam University Press, 2010), 9–35.

5 Pogonyi, "Dual Citizenship and Sovereignty," 694; Szabolcs Pogonyi, Mária Kovács and Zsolt Körtvélyesi, *The Politics of External Kin-State Citizenship in East Central Europe* (EUDO Citizenship Observatory, 2010), available at http://eudo-citizenship.eu/docs/ECEcompreport.pdf (consulted February 24, 2011).

response to Hungary's creation of extra-territorial citizenship, it outlawed dual citizenship.[6] Several observers predicted that Romania – even if not so harshly as Slovakia – would also take countermeasures if Transylvanian Hungarians opted in considerable numbers for Hungarian citizenship.[7] However, this has not happened so far. Romania (along with Serbia and Croatia) was among the states neighbouring Hungary that barely opposed the new Hungarian citizenship legislation. The Social Democrats (PSD), who at the time were in opposition, criticized Hungary, and some lower-ranking politicians of the party publicly proposed countermeasures. According to these proposals, dual citizens would have been prohibited from holding public office. However, these initiatives did not even reach the level of an official parliamentary petition. The first aim of this paper is to explain this lack of Romanian resistance and countermeasures. I argue that – contrary to the presumptions of scholars studying Hungarian citizenship policy – Romania moved towards a post-Westphalian concept of sovereignty and a less territorially-bounded notion of what constitutes a national community. In this framework, multiple memberships are tolerated and are no longer perceived as a threat to state sovereignty.

At the intrastate level, there was a debate between Transylvanian Hungarian elites and Romanian political actors on the desirable forms of popular sovereignty. Among Romanian political elites, a consensus had taken shape according to which the state should be reconstructed on the basis of national sovereignty and "the people," whose will was the underlying principle of democratic legitimacy, should be defined in ethnic and cultural terms (as the Romanian people).[8] According to this concept, the titular majority owned all state institutions,[9] which were designed to underpin national reproduction.[10]

---

6 See Rainer Bauböck, "Dual citizenship for transborder minorities? How to respond to the Hungarian-Slovak tit-for-tat" (European University Institute Working Papers 75, 2010); Ágnes Vass, "Szlovák-magyar kettős állampolgárok szlovák állampolgárság nélkül" (Slovak-Hungarian dual citizens without Slovak citizenship), *Magyar Kisebbség*, nos. 3–4 (2013): 129–151.

7 To cite Levente Salat, "[Romanian political actors] would certainly not remain passive if Hungarian citizens occupied Romanian state offices and functions in considerable numbers." See Levente Salat, "A politikai közösség kérdése a többségkisebbség viszonyának a nézőpontjából II" (The question of the political community from the perspective of majority-minority relations), *Korunk*, no. 2 (2012): 63.

8 Csergő, *Talk of the Nation*, 25; Sherrill Stroschein, *Ethnic Struggle, Coexistence and Democratization in Eastern Europe* (New York: Cambridge University Press, 2012).

9 See Andreas Wimmer, *Nationalist Exclusion and Ethnic Conflict: Shadows of Modernity* (Cambridge: Cambridge University Press, 2002).

10 See also Brubaker's concept of a nationalizing state: Rogers Brubaker, "Nationalizing States in the Old 'New Europe' and the New," *Ethnic and Racial Studies* 19, no. 2 (1996):

Majority elites often relied on the Westphalian concept of state sovereignty at intrastate level too. In this framework, the emphasis was on strong central government control, while regional and minority claims for self-government (or even administrative decentralization) were depicted as challenging state sovereignty.[11] Hungarian elites also (re)defined their community in national terms and claimed institutions and minority rights that would guarantee cultural reproduction and the community's "share of popular sovereignty".[12] The ultimate goal of the Hungarian minority elites and RMDSZ[13] (the dominant party representing the Hungarian community) was autonomy or, in other words, the recognition of the Hungarian population as a self-standing political community. In the late 1990s, a process of reconciliation between the Hungarian and Romanian elites started. As a consequence, the Romanian minority policy regime[14] adopted some pluralistic characteristics, while the representatives of the Hungarian community were co-opted into executive power. My second research question refers to the Romanian public perception of existing minority rights and Hungarian ethnic claims. I argue that, contrary to some expectations,[15] the repeated participation of the Hungarian minority in executive power in the Romanian government has not increased the legitimacy of minority rights/claims within the Romanian majority.

As a third research question, I investigate the relationship between the Hungarian citizenship legislation, on the one hand, and the claims of the Transylvanian Hungarian elites for minority rights and autonomy, on the other. Political scientists often emphasize that in the context of the Westphalian paradigm

411–437; Rogers Brubaker, "Nationalizing States Revisited: Projects and Processes of Nationalization in Post-Soviet States," *Ethnic and Racial Studies* 34, no. 3 (2011): 1785–1814.

11 Zsuzsa Csergő, "Kosovo and the Framing of Non-Secessionist Self-Government Claims in Romania," *Europe-Asia Studies* 65, no. 5 (2013): 889–991.

12 Csergő, *Talk of the Nation*, 25.

13 Romániai Magyar Demokrata Szövetség. In Romanian, UDMR (Uniunea Democratică a Maghiarilor din România). In English, DAHR (Democratic Union of Hungarians in Romania).

14 By "minority policy regime" I mean the totality of legal and institutional norms and political practices aiming to manage ethno-cultural diversity. See Bernd Rechel, "Introduction," in *Minority Rights in Central and Eastern Europe*, ed. Bernd Rechel (New York: Routledge, 2009), 3–16.

15 See István Horváth and Marius Lazăr, "Dinamica relaţiilor interetnice din ultimul deceniu" (The dynamics of inter-ethnic relations during the last decade), *Altera* 16 (2001): 120–136; Valér Veres, "Analiza comparată a identităţii minorităţilor maghiare din Bazinul Carpatic. A Kárpát-medencei magyarok nemzeti identitásának összehasonlító elemzése" (A comparative analysis of the Hungarian minority identities in the Carpathian Basin) (working paper, National Institute of Minority Research, Cluj-Napoca, 2008), 44; Salat, "A politikai közösség kérdése."

there is a trade-off between autonomist claims of minority elites and extra-territorial citizenship offered by an external ethnic homeland. According to Bauböck, national majorities are sensitive to the issue of state sovereignty; as a consequence, it is less likely that they would accept both autonomy and external citizenship. From a Westphalian perspective, this would weaken and practically "virtualize" state sovereignty over minority populations.[16] My approach is an empirical one, and I argue that it is primarily an empirical question whether national majorities tolerate external citizenship or autonomy. In my analysis, I present Romanian public perceptions concerning both Hungarian ethno-political claims and kin-state policy measures. I rely on ten surveys representative of the adult population of Romania carried out between 1995 and 2016.[17]

16 Rainer Bauböck, "The Trade-off between Transnational Citizenship and Political Autonomy," in *Dual Citizenship in Global Perspective*, ed. Thomas Faist and Peter Kivisto (London: Palgrave Macmillan, 2007), 69–91.

17 In 1995 and 1996, one of the major public opinion firms, namely the Institute of Marketing and Polls (Institutul de Marketing și Sondaje – IMAS, http://www.imas-inc.com) conducted quantitative studies concerning ethnic relations in Romania. In 1995, a total of 1,376 subjects were interviewed, and in 1996 this number grew to 1,582. The number of ethnically Romanian respondents was, respectively, 1,032 and 1,098. We did not succeed in acquiring the databases. Only the research report was accessible in the archives of the Ethno-Cultural Diversity Resource Centre (IMAS, *Relații interetnice în România. Sondaje de opinie 1994–1996*, April 1996). The 2000, 2001 and 2002 surveys were part of the Etnobarometer project run by the Ethno-Cultural Diversity Resource Centre (Centrul de Resurse pentru Diversitate Etnoculturală – CRDE, http://www.edrc.ro), a Cluj-based NGO engaged in promoting intercultural peace and justice. In 2000, the Research Centre on Inter-Ethnic Relations (Centrul de Cercetare a Relatiilor Interetnice – CCRIT, http://www.ccrit.ro), a Cluj-based research centre run by the Sociology Department of the Babeș-Bolyai University, was the research institute in charge of the fieldwork, while in 2001 and 2002 Metro Media Transilvania (a major public opinion firm based in Cluj, http://www.mmt.ro) took over this role. In 2000, a total number of 2,051 people were interviewed, including 1,253 ethnic Romanians. Different subgroups (ethnic Hungarians, ethnic Romanians living in Hungarian-majority counties) were represented by separate sub-samples. In 2001 and 2002, the national representative sample was 800 respondents. Separate sub-samples for Roma (600) and Hungarian (600) populations were created, and an additional 200 Transylvanian ethnic Romanians were interviewed. The 2006 survey was carried out by CCRIT and financed by the Department for Inter-Ethnic Relations of the Romanian Government. The survey was carried out using a sample representative for Romania of 1,170 respondents. In 2008, 2012, 2014 and 2016, the Romanian Institute for Research on National Minorities (Institutul pentru Cercetarea Minorităților Naționale – ISPMN, http://www.ispmn.gov.ro), a Cluj-based research institute subsidized by the Romanian Government, carried out empirical studies concerning the same issue. In 2008, the national sample consisted of 1,189 respondents, and a sample of 537 Transylvanian Hungarians was added. In 2012, the size of the national sample was 1,200. Transylvanian Hungarians were represented by a separate sample of 1,991, and an additional 491 Transylvanian Romanians were interviewed. In 2014, there was a national sample of 1,200 and a Transylvanian

A longitudinal approach allows me to investigate whether the modification of the Hungarian citizenship legislation had a discernible impact on the attitudes of the Romanian majority and raised concerns regarding state sovereignty. The attitudes prevalent among the wider public are important, as they can shape political processes and push political actors in specific directions.

This paper is divided into six sections. In the first section, I present the conceptual tools used during the analysis. The second section presents the main aspects of the Romanian minority policy regime affecting the integration of Transylvanian Hungarians in the Romanian polity. The third section presents Romanian attitudes towards different Transylvanian Hungarian ethno-political claims and existing minority rights. The fourth section outlines the evolution of Hungarian and Romanian citizenship policies. The fifth section presents Romanian perceptions of Hungarian kin-state policy measures, including measures relating to extra-territorial citizenship. In the sixth and final section, I present my concluding remarks.

2 Analytical Framework: Ethno-political Actors and Minority Strategies

This paper does not provide an analysis of Hungarian kin-state policy or Hungarian minority politics in Romania but focuses exclusively on the perceptions and attitudes of the Romanian majority towards these issues. However, before presenting the Romanian majority perceptions on Hungarian minority claims, we have to define the relevant ethno-political actors and classify their possible strategies. For this purpose, I will rely on two (complementary) analytical models that are both closely connected to the Westphalian paradigm of inter-state relations and nation-building.

The first one is Roger Brubaker's well-known triadic-nexus model,[18] which focuses on the interrelationship between nationalizing states, minority elites and external homelands. These are conceived by Brubaker as social fields in a Bourdieusian sense, and their dynamics cannot be properly interpreted without considering the interrelationship among them. According to Brubaker's model, more than one power centre attempts to exert an influence on minority

Hungarian sample of 668 respondents. In 2016, the size of the national sample was 1,138 respondents and an additional 1,023 were interviewed.

18 Rogers Brubaker, *Nationalism Reframed: Nationhood and the National Question in the New Europe* (Cambridge: Cambridge University Press, 1996); Rogers Brubaker, "Accidental Diasporas and External Homelands in Central and Eastern Europe: Past and Present" (Political Science Series no. 71, Institute for Advanced Studies, Vienna, October 2000).

populations (in our case Transylvanian Hungarians). The first one is the nationalizing state. From a Romanian perspective, Transylvanian Hungarians constitute a national minority or a minority ethnic group[19] that should be integrated or accommodated. Of the factors shaping ethno-political processes, the Romanian minority policy regime (as institutionalized by the state) is certainly the most important. The second power structure trying to exert an influence on the minority population is the minority elites or in this case the Transylvanian Hungarian political class. Brubaker's model draws neither an analytical nor a normative distinction between the position of minority elites and majority political actors, as both are characterized as trying to exert their influence on the minority population.[20] The dominant discourse produced by the Transylvanian Hungarian political class assumes that Transylvanian Hungarians are or should be a self-sufficient (political) community[21] and that, as such, they should be integrated into the Romanian polity in communitarian terms through segmental and territorial autonomies. The last factor in Brubaker's model is the so-called external homeland, which regards the minority population as part of its politically divided nation or even an as external diaspora.

19 In Romania, the terms ethnic group and national minority are used interchangeably for official purposes. For instance, until 2002, the census asked about people's "ethnicity" and not "nationality." Furthermore, the Romanian government has a Department of Inter-Ethnic Relations. However, the Romanian parliament includes a fraction of national minorities, and the Romanian Institute for Research on National Minorities was established as a governmental body in 2007. In addition, several official documents use the term national minority.

20 The ethnicity without group thesis is of central importance here (see Rogers Brubaker, *Ethnicity without Groups* (Cambridge: Harvard University Press, 2004), 7–28). Brubaker reinterprets the old distinction between category and group, which he traces back to Marx and Weber and which plays a central role in the sociology of Bourdieu (see Pierre Bourdieu, *Language and Symbolic Power* (Cambridge: Polity Press, 1991), 229–252) and Jenkins (Richard Jenkins, *Rethinking Ethnicity: Arguments and Explorations*, 2nd ed. (London: Sage, 2008)). Categories are created by (powerful) external observers, while members of categories do not necessarily share any sense of belonging to them. And from the contrary perspective, groups need an internally shared sense of belonging and solidarity. Brubaker took a rather radical step by suggesting that we avoid considering ethnic categories groups at all. He argues that by considering ethnic categories groups we reify the perspective of ethnic elites (ethnic entrepreneurs) who seek to (re)present these entities as mobilized, internally solidary and ready to act collectively. Brubaker's analytical perspective obviously deconstructs and delegitimizes the position of ethnic elites and treats them (along with the majority political actors) as external observers.

21 In this respect, the idea of parallel minority society is of key importance. This is not only an analytical category, but a political programme. On this issue, see Tamás Kiss and István Székely, "Shifting Linkages in Ethnic Mobilization: The Case of RMDSZ and the Hungarians in Transylvania," *Nationalities Papers* 44, no. 4 (2016): 591–610.

Brubaker emphasizes that the term diaspora (like the terms ethnic/national minority and self-sufficient political community) constitutes a political claim and programme. Diaspora implies that the primary reference point of the minority population should be its external homeland.[22]

Brubaker's model has been revised[23] and criticized by several commentators. Some of the critiques focus on the connections between the model and the Westphalian paradigm. Peter Vermeersch, for instance, argues that the process of nation-building in post-communist Europe cannot be properly understood in a Westphalian framework and therefore adds a fourth dimension to the triadic nexus, namely transnational organizations and their norms.[24] Others argue that the nationalizing strategies of the actors competing for the loyalty of the minority communities should also be reconceptualized. Csergő and Goldgeier[25] keep Gellner's[26] famous definition of nationalism as a project urging for congruence between national and political units; however, they argue that, in a "post-Westphalian" international environment no longer dominated exclusively by states, "political units" should not necessarily be understood in territorial terms. Thus, under peaceful conditions (e.g. without relying on irredentism and renouncing territorial claims), a new strategy of nation-building, namely "trans-sovereign" or "virtual" nationalism, can evolve. In other words, trans-sovereign nationalists strive for national reunification not through border changes or the repatriation of co-nationals but rather by "virtualizing" state borders and establishing a non-territorial institutional framework aimed at underpinning the reproduction of the national community.[27] The concept of trans-sovereign or virtual nationalism underscores that, in a post-Westphalian environment, the distinction between irredentist territorial claims, on the one hand, and the search for alternative non-territorial forms of nation-building, on the other, is important both from an analytical and a normative perspective. In this view, not all national projects that contain extra-territorial elements can be described as actions potentially conducive to violent intra-state conflict.[28]

---

22 Rogers Brubaker, "The 'Diaspora' Diaspora," *Ethnic and Racial Studies* 28, no. 1 (2005): 1–19.

23 Rogers Brubaker, "Nationalizing States Revisited: Projects and Processes of Nationalization in Post-Soviet States," *Ethnic and Racial Studies* 34 (2011): 1785–1814.

24 Peter Vermeersch, "Minority Policy in Central Europe: Exploring the Impact of the EU's Enlargement Strategy," *Global Review of Ethnopolitics* 3, no. 2 (2004): 3–19.

25 Csergő and Goldgeier, "Nationalist Strategies and European Integration."

26 Ernest Gellner, *Nations and Nationalism* (Ithaca, NY: Cornell University Press, 1983).

27 Csergő and Goldgeier, "Nationalist Strategies and European Integration," 26.

28 As a contrary example, Saideman and Ayres could be cited. They carried out an important comparative inquiry on the factors promoting and hindering irredentism. While also

Another important frame of reference is the aforementioned article by Rainer Bauböck,[29] in which he discusses the trade-off between autonomist minority claims and external citizenship policies. Bauböck outlines a general typology of minority strategies that is useful for interpreting our empirical results concerning the acceptance of these strategies by the Romanian majority. The typology distinguishes between several actors and levels of action. Minority actors can pursue different strategies at the intrastate level, while their external homeland can support these strategies at the interstate level. The model, which is strongly connected to the Westphalian concept of state sovereignty, also emphasizes that in some cases there could be an incompatibility between the strategies of the minority elites, on the one hand, and kin-state policy, on the other.

Bauböck distinguishes between four basic minority strategies and three additional intermediate options. The four basic strategies are: mass exodus, assimilation, autonomy and secession. The first intermediate option is the diasporic identity, which is based on the reproduction of a collective identity focused on the external homeland (this focus being its *differentia specifica*). The second intermediate option is the maintenance of a separate ethnic identity. This is similar to the diaspora identity in that it tries to maintain ethnic boundaries vis-à-vis the majority. In this case, however, "internal" resources, such as community-building by ethnic elites, are more important. The third intermediate option is condominium, which in the classic sense means divided/shared sovereignty over a given territory and population.

Like Bauböck, political scientists used to consider assimilation and emigration as collective strategies of minority populations seeking to escape the disadvantages of belonging to a minority category.[30] However, one should note that assimilation and emigration (and to a certain degree diasporic and ethnic

focusing on cases in which irredentism has failed, they did not make a conceptual distinction between irredentist and non-irredentist claims. For them, irredentism is more a "continuum than a binary opposition" ranging from "doing nothing to full-out war." See S. Saideman and W. Ayres, *For Kin or Country: Xenophobia, Nationalism, and War* (New York: Columbia University Press, 2008), 46.

29 Rainer Bauböck, "The Trade-off between Transnational Citizenship and Political Autonomy," in *Dual Citizenship in Global Perspective*, ed. Thomas Faist and Peter Kivisto (London: Palgrave Macmillan, 2007), 69–91.

30 It suffices to refer to the classic typology of minority strategies presented by Kymlicka, which enumerates assimilation, mass exodus, renegotiating the terms of integration into the polity and marginalization as the potential alternatives of minority populations facing asymmetric power relations produced by the institutional order of the nation-state. See Will Kymlicka, *Politics in the Vernacular: Nationalism, Multiculturalism, and Citizenship* (Oxford: Oxford University Press, 2001).

identity) differ in an essential way from struggles for autonomy, on the one hand, and secession and condominium, on the other. Autonomy, secession, and condominium are political programmes that are developed by ethnic elites and require ethnic mobilization in order to be implemented. They can only be conceived as proposals for collective action. In contrast, in the majority of cases, assimilation and emigration do not require collective action but are rather consequences and aggregates of individual decisions. Their primary drivers are not political programmes articulated by elites but individual status-aspirations.[31] In this respect, I agree with Brubaker,[32] who criticizes political theorists conceptualizing assimilation and emigration as collective strategies. He argues that emigration and assimilation are rarely strategic alternatives sustained by minority elites.[33] Nevertheless, they are important in ethnic politics, as the collective strategies of ethnic elites (struggling for ethno-cultural reproduction or segmental autonomy) can be undermined by the individual decisions of group members to emigrate or assimilate. It is also important that, as individual strategies, they can exist simultaneously among different members and strata of minority populations: some may seek to assimilate into the majority group, some may emigrate and others may develop a sense of ethnic or diaspora identity.

Bauböck's main thesis is that there is a trade-off between claims for autonomy and extra-territorial citizenship. These are mutually exclusive political programmes, and, as such, they cannot be realized simultaneously (see: Table 10.1).

31 Laitin's micro-model concerning assimilation and/or minority cultural reproduction is instructive. See David Laitin, *Identity in Formation: The Russian Speaking Populations in the Near Abroad* (Ithaca, NY and London: Cornell University Press, 1998).

32 Rogers Brubaker, "National Homogenization and Ethnic Reproduction on the European Periphery," in *La teoria sociologica e lo stato moderno: Saggi in onore di Gianfranco Poggi*, ed. Marzio Barbagli and Harvie Ferguson (Bologna: Il Mulino, 2009).

33 Assimilation and mass emigration could be conceptualized as an aggregate consequence of individual decisions in the majority of cases. Nevertheless, we know of a few cases in which they can be interpreted as collective strategies, proposed and sustained by ethnic elites. In the case of emigration, the most important example is that of the Zionist movement, which aimed to solve the problem of the *Galut* through mass emigration to Palestine/Israel. As for assimilation as a collective strategy, Alba and Nee refer to the case of the Mississippi Chinese (see Richard Alba and Victor Nee, *Remaking the American Mainstream: Assimilation and Contemporary Immigration* (Cambridge, MA: Harvard University Press, 2003), 39–45). A geographically closer example is that of Hungarian Jews in the nineteenth century. Here the collective strategy of assimilation induced liturgical changes and led to a religious schism between the Neolog and Orthodox wings of Judaism (see János Gyurgyák, *A zsidókérdés Magyarországon* (The Jewish question in Hungary) (Budapest: Osiris, 2001), 211–243).

TABLE 10.1 Minority strategies and potential external homeland support

Basic strategic possibilities	Intermediate alternatives	Type of external homeland support
Emigration		Supporting "return" (repatriation)
	Diaspora identity	Maintenance of linkages to the ethnic homeland and the possibility of "return"
Assimilation		–
	Ethnic identity	Cultural support
Autonomy		Political support
	Condominium	Offering external citizenship
Secession		Territorial incorporation

SOURCE: RAINER BAUBÖCK, "THE TRADE-OFF BETWEEN TRANSNATIONAL CITIZENSHIP AND POLITICAL AUTONOMY," IN *DUAL CITIZENSHIP IN GLOBAL PERSPECTIVE*, ED. THOMAS FAIST AND PETER KIVISTO (LONDON: PALGRAVE MACMILLAN, 2007), 75.

According to Bauböck, autonomy can be perceived as a type of "vertical dual citizenship," which – in opposition to the integrationist perspective of universal citizenship – recognizes and institutionalizes the minority population as a distinct political community. Under such circumstances, it is highly unlikely (also from a normative point of view) that the majority would accept both autonomy (vertical dual citizenship) and extra-territorial citizenship (horizontal dual citizenship). The acceptance of both would mean the nearly complete loss of the sovereignty of the state over its minority population.

Bauböck's thesis, which is evidently connected to the presumption that national majorities are attached to a Westphalian notion of state sovereignty, was widely accepted and reproduced by Transylvanian Hungarian political actors and social scientists. A prominent example is political scientist Levente Salat,[34] who elaborated a communitarian critique of Hungarian kin-state policies.[35] According to Salat, external Hungarian citizenship undermines all minority efforts to obtain forms of autonomy and power-sharing in Romania, as

34 Levente Salat is a political scientist and a former vice-chancellor of the Babeș-Bolyai University in Cluj.

35 Salat, "A politikai közösség kérdése"; Levente Salat, "Cei 25 de ani ai UDMR – în oglinda obiectivelor" (Twenty-five years of RMDSZ – in the mirror of the objectives) (manuscript, 2016).

> it is less likely that the representatives of the Romanian state, who have been reluctant to enter into a bargaining process with Hungarian political actors concerning the issue of autonomy or other forms of power sharing, would do so with representatives of a community whose members held Hungarian citizenship in considerable numbers.[36]

Furthermore,

> paradoxically, this result of the extension of citizenship abrogated also those de facto forms of autonomy of the Hungarian minority, which had been – tacitly – accepted by the Romanian authorities.[37]

In the next section, I will systematically present the evolution of Romanian attitudes towards the political claims of the Hungarian minority elites, minority rights in general and Hungary's kin-state policy involvement (e.g. citizenship policy, different forms of financial support). I will also outline the relevant political and institutional framework, including the main characteristics of the Romanian minority policy regime and the evolution of Romanian and Hungarian citizenship policies.

3 Main Aspects of the Romanian Minority Policy Regime

On the basis of a recent analysis by Székely and Horváth (2014), one can offer a comparative characterization of Romanian minority policy in a central and south-eastern European context.[38] The typology outlined by Székely and Horváth reveals the dual character of the Romanian institutional settings and shows that it is difficult to place Romanian minority policy on the frequently-used accommodationist-integrationist scale.[39]

---

36 Salat, "Cei 25 de ani ai UDMR."

37 Ibid.

38 István Székely and István Horváth, "Diversity Recognition and Minority Representation in Central and Southeast Europe: A Comparative Analysis," *Nationalities Papers* 42, no. 3 (2014).

39 Integration and accommodation are distinct political philosophies concerning the management of ethnic and cultural diversities. As tools to characterize and classify minority policies, they obviously represent ideal types in the Weberian sense. Accommodation denotes political and institutional solutions that allow for public expression and representation of group identities and help protect these identities against the homogenizing efforts of the majority. In an accommodationist institutional order, communities could autonomously manage their internal affairs. In contrast, integration calls for "common"

First, relying on the constitutional definition of the Romanian political community (as the source of sovereignty) and the lack of any general recognition of cultural diversity, Romania can be characterized as a *mono-ethnic* state.[40] According to the Romanian constitution, the Romanian people – in an ethnic sense – are the source of sovereignty, and the state is designed to protect their culture and interests. As a consequence, the main characteristic of the Romanian institutional order is an asymmetry between the categories of minority and majority, which is obviously reproduced in various everyday settings.[41] It is worth emphasizing that the hegemonic control of the state by the dominant ethnic group is (almost) univocally supported by Romanian political actors. None of the political parties in the Romanian parliament (except for RMDSZ) have criticized this set-up.

Second, the Romanian minority policy regime has some pluralistic characteristics, the most important of which concern minority political representation. Generally speaking, the Romanian institutional and legal order not only tolerates but even promotes the political representation of ethnic identities and political participation through ethnic parties. There are several (more or less explicit) provisions in Romanian electoral legislation that support ethnic politics. The first (indirect) factor is that ethnic parties are not legally banned.[42] The second (also indirect) factor is that there are no provisions creating unfavourable conditions for ethnic parties (most importantly RMDSZ). From the perspective of the Hungarian community, the maintenance of the proportional character of the Romanian electoral system is of central importance.[43] The third (explicit) factor is that small minorities can obtain preferential seats

---

loyalties and a political culture that transcends the particularities of ethnic communities. As a consequence, integrationists favour political institutions that block the political engagement of ethnic groups. Integrationism is obviously the mainstream perspective as transnational organizations, such as the European Commission, the OSCE High Commissioner on National Minorities, the United Nations, the International Monetary Fund and the World Bank favour integration over accommodation. See John McGarry, Brendan O'Leary and Robert Simeon, "Integration or Accommodation? The Enduring Debate in Conflict Regulation," in *Constitutional Design for Divided Societies: Integration or Accommodation?*, ed. S. Choudhry (Oxford: Oxford University Press, 2008), 41–88.

40 Székely and Horváth, "Diversity Recognition and Minority Representation," 134.

41 The institutional asymmetry has harsh demographic consequences. It is the principal factor causing the aforementioned assimilatory processes, and it is among the key factors causing emigration. The system of ethnic stratification is also determined by these institutionalized asymmetries.

42 Bulgaria and Turkey are contrary examples in this respect in the South-Eastern European region.

43 With a Westminster-type electoral system, the political representation of the Hungarian community could be reduced to the Székely Land (an area inhabited overwhelmingly by Hungarians but consisting of only one-third of the community).

under quite favourable conditions. This provision, however, is less relevant from the perspective of the almost 1.5 million Transylvanian Hungarians. The fourth (quasi-explicit) factor favouring ethnic politics relates to the alternative thresholds, which were introduced in 2008[44] and modified in 2015[45] in a manner that further favours ethnic parties. These mechanisms were not explicitly designed to promote ethnic parties, but they obviously benefit RMDSZ (which is the only relatively small party with a territorially concentrated electorate). According to the 2008 Electoral Law, parties that won a plurality in six constituencies for the Lower Chamber and three constituencies for the Senate were able to enter parliament even if they had not surpassed the 5 per cent threshold. According to the 2015 Electoral Law, parties that obtain more than 20 per cent of the vote in at least four constituencies are able to enter parliament even if they have not passed the 5 per cent threshold. A fifth factor relates to the fact that the borders of individual constituencies in the 2008 and 2012 elections also favoured ethnic parties (more precisely RMDSZ). Hungarian speakers constituted a majority in fifteen constituencies for the Lower Chamber and seven constituencies for the Senate. Ethnic politics is also promoted by non-legislative elements in the Romanian political system. The most important of these is the simple fact that the mainstream parties do not target Hungarian voters. In counties inhabited overwhelmingly or significantly by Hungarians, these parties act as titular ethnic parties in that they are practically reserved for local Romanian elites and exclusively promote the interests of the local Romanian community (against Hungarians and RMDSZ).[46]

One can also mention language and education policies as additional pluralistic characteristics of the Romanian legal environment. Stroschein emphasizes that intensive Hungarian ethnic mobilization focused in particular on language and educational policy in the early 1990s and that the Romanian state made important concessions to Hungarians on these issues in the context of Euro-Atlantic integration.[47] With regard to language policies, it is important to underscore that – in spite of these concessions – there remains a basic asymmetry in the public use of Romanian and minority languages. According to the Constitution, Romanian is the sole official language of the country, and no other languages are mentioned as having any kind of special status. However, according to Local Administration Law 215/2001, minority groups can use their mother tongue in oral and written communications with the local administration in

44 Law No. 35/2008.
45 Law No. 208/2015.
46 Stroschein, *Ethnic Struggle, Coexistence and Democratization*; Kiss and Székely, "Shifting Linkages in Ethnic Mobilization."
47 Stroschein, *Ethnic Struggle, Coexistence and Democratization*; see also Csergő, *Talk of the Nation*.

local administrative units where their proportion reaches 20 per cent of the population. According to Governmental Ordinance 1206/2001, moreover, people able to communicate in minority languages should be employed in jobs involving interaction with the public in these administrative units. Romania has also ratified the European Charter for Regional and Minority Languages, which creates quite favourable conditions for the use of the Hungarian language in public. However, these legal provisions have been implemented only selectively and have failed to create meaningful and effective bilingualism in local administration. In addition, provisions prescribing the employment of officials with competence in minority languages have not been systematically implemented, and other preconditions of bilingualism (especially written bilingualism) have not been met.[48] In the field of education, Education Law 1/2011 is of primary importance, as it contains quite favourable provisions concerning minority language education. However, these provisions have also not been systematically implemented.[49] It is important to highlight this legal uncertainty regarding linguistic rights and education. The fact that relevant legal provisions are not (or only partially) implemented creates severe difficulties and unfavourable conditions for the enforcement of (theoretically existing) minority rights.

To summarize, the Romanian minority policy regime is characterized by duality. On the one hand, the privileges of the titular category are deeply anchored in the legal and institutional order. On the other hand, this order also expressly supports the political representation of ethnic identities and in practice allows for a high degree of ethnic parallelism.[50] This duality also shapes the integration of Transylvanian Hungarians in the Romanian polity. Due to factors favouring ethnic parties, RMDSZ has managed to maintain a monopoly over the resources set aside for the Hungarian community. However, in the

48 See Tibor Toró, "Detached Implementation: Discourse and Practice in Minority Language Usage in Romania" (manuscript, 2017).

49 The fifth article of the forty-fifth paragraph stipulates that, in administrative units in which instruction is held in minority languages in more than one school, a separate minority educational institution should be created. This provision has not been systematically implemented. A notorious example is that of Târgu Mureș/Marosvásárhely University of Medicine and Pharmacy, where paragraph 363 concerning "multicultural and multilingual" universities has not been implemented.

50 The idea of ethnic parallelism (i.e. a *pillar* or *verzuiling*, in the terminology of the literature on divided societies) played a central role in the processes of institution- and community-building in which Hungarian elites have engaged since 1989. In the political rhetoric and self-representation of the Hungarian elites, institutionalized ethnic parallelism appears under the notion of "minority society" (*kisebbségi társadalom*). Transylvanian Hungarian political thinkers envisaged an ethnically integrated institutional structure that would enable members of the community to live their lives inside a "Hungarian world" (without having to constantly face the fact that they physically live in Romania).

absence of legally codified forms of ethnic power-sharing, the main Hungarian ethnic party is involved in a deeply asymmetric relationship with majority political actors. This institutional setting has hampered the emergence of political pluralism inside the Hungarian community.

4 Romanian Public Perceptions Concerning Minority Rights and Hungarian Ethno-political Claims

While the minority policy regime is characterized by a degree of ambivalence, the vast majority of the Romanian public is unanimous in its views on the regime. Romanians overwhelmingly support and take for granted the characteristics of the institutional environment that affirms the mono-ethnic nature of the state (or at least the dominance of the titular nation) and reject most characteristics that tend towards ethnic pluralism. From their majoritarian perspective, the politically active nature of the Hungarian ethnic minority and ethnic parallelism are anomalies. In the next two subsections, I will present an overview of Romanian public perceptions of Hungarian claims. First, I will present some general perceptions on stereotypes of Hungarians, Hungarian-Romanian relations and minority rights. Second, I will examine the perceived legitimacy of various types of minority rights/claims from the perspective of the majority.

4.1 *General Perceptions Concerning Hungarians and Minority Rights*

Stereotyping processes in Hungarian-Romanian relations have been studied by several social scientists.[51] Two general aspects of these studies merit mention. First, they use a social-psychological framework, and, second, they all take the notion of parallel processes of nation-building as a common point of departure. As a consequence, the conclusions of the studies are based on general and decontextualized models of intergroup relations and on the assumption that Romanian stereotypes concerning Hungarians and Hungarian stereotypes concerning Romanians mirror each other. This approach rests on

51 See Irina Culic, István Horváth and Cristina Raţ, eds., *Reflecţii asupra diferenţei* (Reflections on differences) (Cluj-Napoca: Limes, 2000); György Csepeli, Antal Örkény and Mária Székelyi, *Nemzetek egymás tükrében: interetnikus viszonyok a Kárpát-medencében* (Nations in the mirror of each other: Inter-ethnic relations in the Carpathian Basin) (Budapest: Balassi, 2002); Valér Veres, *Nemzeti identitás Erdélyben – szociológiai olvasatban* (National identities in Transylvania – a sociological reading) (Budapest: Akadémiai Kiadó, 2005); Gabriel Bădescu, Mircea Kivu and Monica Robotin, eds., *Barometrul relaţiilor etnice 1994–2002. O perspectivă asupra climatului interetnic din România* (Barometer of ethnic relations 1994–2002: A perspective on the inter-ethnic climate in Romania) (Cluj: CRDE, 2005).

the presumption that stereotyping takes place in an environment characterized by symmetric relations. This is not entirely unreasonable, since Romanian and Hungarian identity structures are in many respects analogous and the Hungarian-Romanian relationship is *unranked* in the sense in which Horowitz uses this term.[52] However, in the Hungarian-Romanian context, stereotyping takes place in a social environment characterized by a deeply asymmetric discursive order and deeply asymmetric power relations. The 2014 survey conducted by the Romanian Institute for Research on National Minorities contained open-ended questions regarding the perceived characteristics of the major ethnic categories in Romania. These open-ended questions (respondents could mention three possible attributes in the case of each ethnic category[53]) were post-coded in two phases. Our previous analysis highlights that, in the case of Romanian stereotypes of minority Hungarians, the process was determined by two types of power asymmetries.[54] First, stereotyping is embedded in globally produced and locally reproduced civilizational/developmental discourses. Second, it is strongly affected by the institutional order of the Romanian nationalizing state outlined above.

National self-perceptions and stereotyping are powerfully shaped by civilizational/developmental discourses (see: Table 10.2). Attila Melegh uses the term *East-West slope* to describe a global-hierarchical evaluative scheme (or discursive framework) in which Western countries and actors are positioned at the peak of the hierarchy and all other actors are evaluated on the basis of their distance from/proximity to this Western core.[55] One major aspect of the Romanian stereotyping of Hungarians is that Hungarians are located in a relatively advantageous position on this "slope." In other words, with regard to civilization and development, positive stereotypes dominate.[56]

---

52 Ranked and unranked systems of ethnic relations are ideal types. In the case of ranked relations, belonging to an ethnic category also marks one's social status, and channels of social mobility are not controlled by ethnic elites (see Donald Horowitz, *Ethnic Groups in Conflict* (Berkeley: UCLA Press, 21–22)). The relationship between Roma and non-Roma in Eastern Europe is quite close to the ideal type of a ranked system of ethnic relations, while Hungarian-Romanian relations – in spite of the existing asymmetries – is closer to the opposite end of the spectrum.

53 Romanians, Hungarians, Roma and Germans.

54 Tamás Kiss, "Escaping the 'Balkanizing' Gaze? Perceptions of Global and Internal Developmental Hierarchies in Romania," *East European Politics and Societies* 31, no. 3 (2017): 565–595.

55 See Attila Melegh, *On the East-West Slope: Globalization, Nationalism, Racism and Discourses on Central and Eastern Europe* (Budapest: CEU Press, 2006).

56 In fact, Hungarians have an intermediate position and are in a competitive relationship with Romanians. The Germans are at the top of this internal ethnic hierarchy, while Roma are at the bottom. See Kiss, op. cit., note 54.

TABLE 10.2 Stereotypes concerning Hungarians (national sample, 2014) (N=1200)

Second level code	First level code	Number[a]	%
Civilized/ developed	Laborious/hard-working/diligent, honest/trustworthy, civilized/developed/cultured, rich, Western-oriented, disciplined/well-organized, punctual/ precise, courteous/well-educated	555	32.2
Partially interpretable as developed/ civilized	Egoistic/individualistic, intelligent/ clever/rational, decided/persistent, reserved	112	6.5
Backward/ underdeveloped	Backward, poor, lazy/slothful, dirty, traditionalist	14	0.8
Politically active group	Nationalistic (80), Romanian-hating (55), inimical/hostile (to Romanians) (79), separatist/autonomist (53)	267	15.6
Partially interpretable as politically active group	Unfriendly/closed (to/towards Romanians) (87), showing solidarity with one another (71), privileged (22), opportunistic (18)	176	10.2
Other stereotypes	Bad person/people, hospitable/friendly, good people, proud, arrogant, stubborn, nervous, tolerant, skilful/adept, melancholic, etc.	600	37.9

a All respondents could mention three attributes, thus the number of stereotypes exceeds the number of respondents.

SOURCE: ROMANIAN INSTITUTE FOR RESEARCH ON NATIONAL MINORITIES (2014).

Another important aspect of the stereotypes concerning Hungarians is related to the fact that Romanians perceive Hungarian as a politically active ethnic group and that they oppose this type of political engagement. The mention of attributes such as nationalistic, Romanian-hating, inimical/hostile to Romanians and autonomist/separatist is arguably a symptom of the political aspects of intergroup perception. Sixteen per cent of the stereotypes concerning Hungarians fall into this category. An additional 10 per cent of the attributes mentioned could be interpreted in part as being related to the politically active character of the Hungarian minority. Characteristics such as unfriendly, showing solidarity with one another and privileged also belong in this category. The mention of these attributes is connected to the perception that

RMDSZ is willing to go into coalition with any political party and has no ideological or moral constraints. All in all, more than 25 per cent of the stereotypes refer to the politicized character of the Hungarian minority in a negative way. This data shows that Hungarian political agency is regarded as quite illegitimate and is opposed by the larger Romanian public.

Seven of the ten surveys contained an identical question concerning the general perception of Romanian-Hungarian relations (see: Figure 10.1). This was a closed-ended question: respondents had to decide what term best described relations between Hungarians and Romanians: conflict, cooperation or mutual ignorance. Over the period under review, the proportion of those who chose conflict oscillated between 18 and 28 per cent, and no linear trend emerged. It is also worth noting that many of the respondents (between 31 and 55 per cent) characterized these relations as cooperative. These findings highlight the duality of Hungarian-Romanian relations (which has been emphasized by many other social scientists). Romanians oppose and refuse Hungarian ethno-political claims, but on a more general level they describe Hungarian-Romanian relations in more pragmatic terms and perceive them as being mostly cooperative.

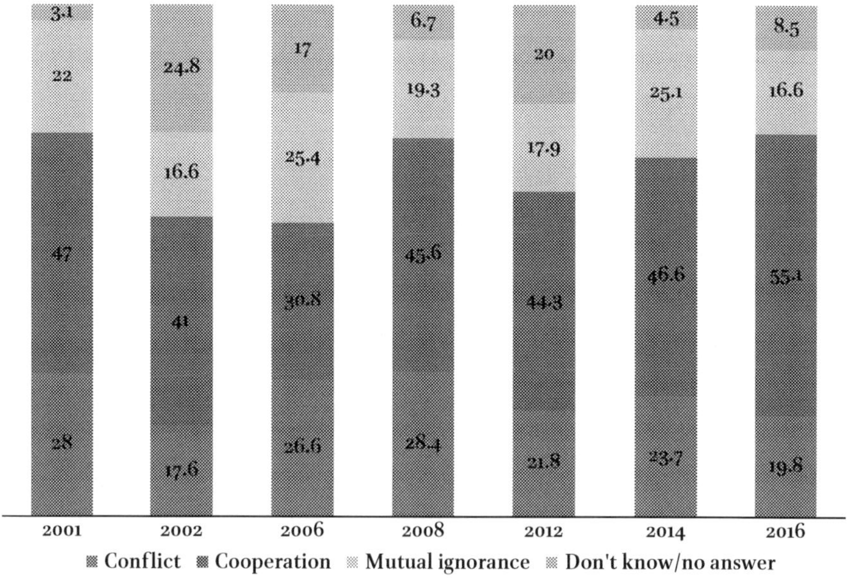

FIGURE 10.1 In your opinion how can relations between Romanians and Hungarians be characterized? (national samples, 2001–2016)
SOURCES: METRO MEDIA TRANSILVANIA (ETNOBAROMETER 2001, 2002); ROMANIAN INSTITUTE FOR RESEARCH ON NATIONAL MINORITIES (2008, 2012, 2014, 2016).

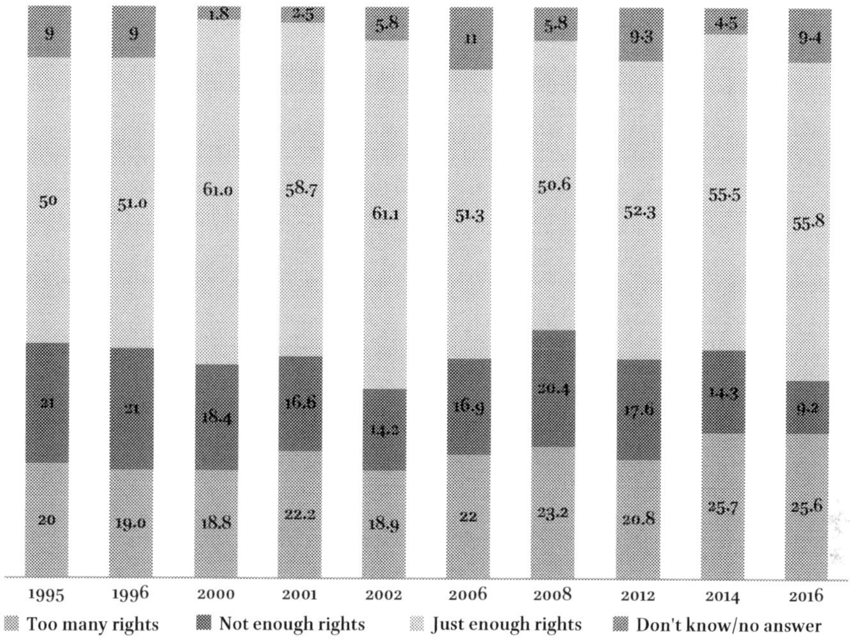

FIGURE 10.2 In your opinion minorities in Romania have ... (national samples, 2000–2014)
SOURCES: IMAS (1995, 1996); CCRIT (2000, 2006); METRO MEDIA TRANSYLVANIA (ETNOBAROMETER 2001, 2002); ROMANIAN INSTITUTE FOR RESEARCH ON NATIONAL MINORITIES (2008, 2012, 2014, 2016).

A standard question concerning general perceptions of minority rights in Romania was included in each of the ten surveys to which I refer in my paper (see: Figure 10.2). Between 1995 and 2016, the proportion of respondents who felt that "minorities have too many rights" increased slightly, while the proportion of those who felt that "minorities do not have enough rights" decreased. The majority of the respondents (50–61 per cent) felt that minorities have "just enough rights."

4.2 *Acceptance of Different Hungarian Ethno-political Claims and Existing Rights*

The 1995, 1996, 2012, 2014 and 2016 surveys contained a similar block of questions regarding the acceptance of different existing minority rights and ethno-political claims (see: Figure 10.3). The questions referred specifically to the rights granted to the Hungarian community (and not to minority rights in general).

The majority of the questions fall under the heading of minority language rights. In the typology outlined by Bauböck, minority language rights can be

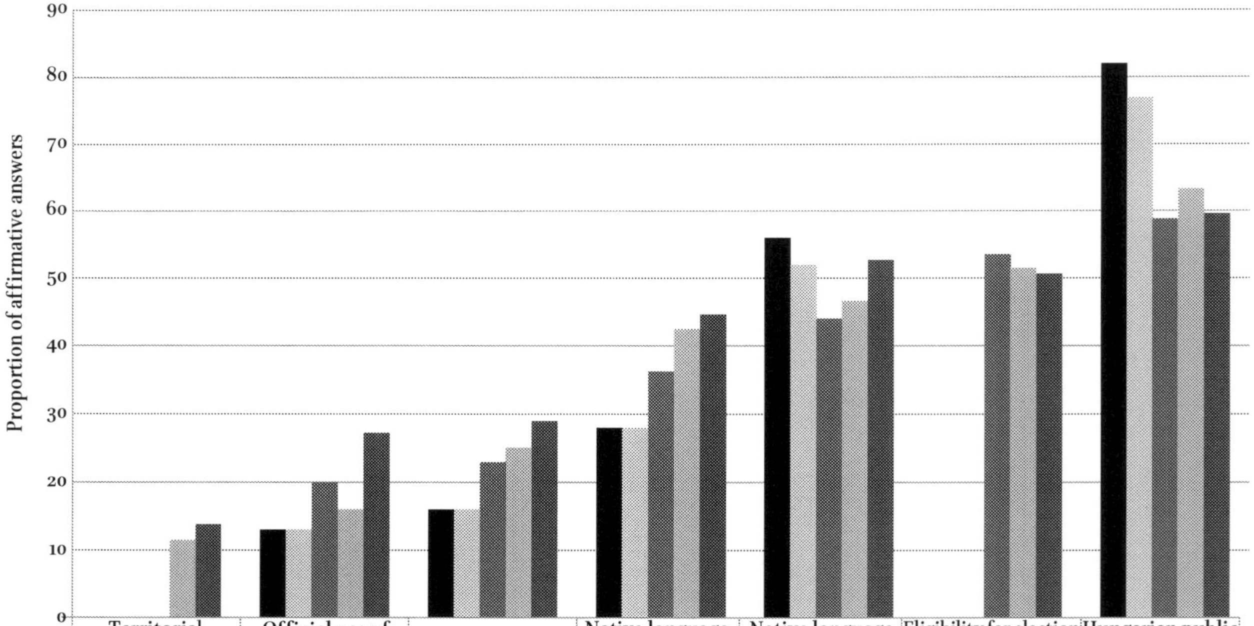

	Territorial autonomy	Official use of Hungarian	Separate schools	Native language university	Native language education	Eligibility for election to public office	Hungarian public broadcasting
1995		13	16	28	56		82
1996		13	16	28	52		77
2012		20	23	36	44	54	59
2014	12	16	25	43	47	52	63
2016	14	27	29	45	53	51	60

FIGURE 10.3 Do you or would you support allowing Hungarians in Romania to enjoy the following rights? Proportion of affirmative/positive answers (national sample, Romanians, 1995, 1996, 2012, 2014, 2016)

SOURCES: IMAS (1995, 1996); ROMANIAN INSTITUTE FOR RESEARCH ON NATIONAL MINORITIES (2012, 2014, 2016).

linked to the strategy of maintaining ethnic identity. Our questions referred to the acceptance of the following minority language rights:

- native-language primary and secondary education (*Do you support allowing Hungarians to attend primary and secondary schools in which instruction is conducted in their mother tongue?*);
- native-language university education (*Do you support allowing Hungarians to pursue university studies in their mother tongue?*);
- separate educational institutions (*Do you support allowing Hungarians to have separate schools and universities?*);
- official use of the Hungarian language (*Do you support allowing Hungarians to use their mother tongue in their interactions with public institutions such as local government bodies and courts of justice?*); and
- Hungarian-language TV programmes on state-financed channels (*Do you support allowing TV programmes targeting Hungarians to be produced by state-financed channels?*).

As already mentioned, the law regulating the use of minority languages in local administration was passed in 2001. In other words, the official use of Hungarian had not yet been legally codified in 1995 and 1996, meaning that only Romanian could be used in official settings. Another question refers to the acceptance of Hungarian claims for territorial autonomy (*Would you support granting Hungarians autonomy in regions in which they constitute a majority?*). This relates to more than minority language rights. According to Bauböck, it implies the recognition of the Hungarian community as a distinct and autonomous political subject in a way that is rather distant from the present Romanian legal-institutional order. This question was asked only in the 2014 and 2016 surveys. We added another question to the 2012, 2014 and 2016 surveys concerning eligibility for elected public office (*Do you agree that Hungarians should be eligible for election to public office, for example as a mayor or a deputy in the Romanian Parliament?*). Responses to this question offer a way of gauging the general acceptance of the principle of equality among citizens. The acceptance of eligibility for elected public office could be considered an integrationist minimum, and as such it is not included in the typology outlined by Bauböck (it is a taken for granted as a foundational element of any democratic institutional order).

The 2000, 2001, 2002 and 2006 surveys also included statements referring to different minority rights/claims (see: Table 10.3). The responses to statements concerning Hungarian-language education and autonomy were as listed in the table below. They are not directly comparable to the questions described above but may be useful as indications of general trends in the acceptance of Hungarian minority claims.

TABLE 10.3 Acceptance of Hungarian-language education and territorial autonomy among Romanians in Romania (2000, 2001, 2002)

	2000	2001	2002	2006
The Romanian state should provide Hungarian-language education at all levels.	42.6	31.6	51.6[a]	47.3[a]
Hungarians should have a larger degree of autonomy in counties where they constitute a majority.	-	20.4	19.1	18.6

a In 2002 and 2006, the wording of the statement was different: "The Romanian state should provide native-language education for Hungarian children."

SOURCES: CCRIT (2000, 2006); METRO MEDIA TRANSILVANIA ETNOBAROMETER (2001, 2002).

The first obvious conclusion is that the degree of acceptance of various existing rights and further claims is quite low. Romanians not only perceive autonomy as an illegitimate claim but also consider existing minority language rights as illegitimate privileges. Around half of them believe that it is not appropriate for Hungarians to be educated in their mother tongue. Only one-third of Romanians accept Hungarian-language education at the tertiary level, and only 13–27 per cent accept the use of Hungarian in official settings. The widespread rejection of minority language rights considerably hinders the implementation of legal provisions in this area. Two-thirds of Romanians accept public broadcasting in Hungarian, but acceptance of autonomy claims barely exceeded 14 per cent in 2016. It is also worth noting that nearly half of Romanians do not accept that Hungarians should be eligible for election as a mayor or a deputy, reflecting popular support for (a quite hegemonic version of) the dominant ethnic model of governance.

The second conclusion is that there is no linear trend concerning the acceptance of minority rights. In the case of Hungarian-language public broadcasting (i.e. minority-language education), acceptance has decreased compared to the mid-1990s. In the case of Hungarian-language university education and separate schools, there has been an increase in the degree of acceptance. The acceptance of autonomist claims has also dropped. Consequently, survey results do not support the interpretation/narrative that (due to the repeated governmental participation of RMDSZ) Romanian public opinion has become increasingly tolerant of moderate Hungarian ethno-political claims or minority language rights.

The third finding of our study is that different socio-demographic and political segments of Romanian society have rather similar perceptions of Hungarian claims. As one can observe in Appendix 1, there is little difference between major subgroups in terms of their acceptance of the official use of a minority language, Hungarian-language education, autonomy and eligibility for election to public office. We used region, type of settlement, size of settlement, age group, sex, educational attainment, income, religion, personal migratory experience, emigrant household member, electoral activity and political choice as independent variables. In addition to using cross-tabulations, we also ran binary logistical regression models to identify the determinants of the acceptance of Hungarian ethno-political claims and minority rights. It emerged that Nagelkerke R^2 was rather low in each case (0.148, 0.137, 0.134 and 0.127), meaning that different strata of Romanian society have similar attitudes towards Hungarian claims.

Nevertheless, there are some significant differences, for example based on certain contextual variables, such as region and type of settlement. Higher proportions of Romanians living in Transylvania (who thus come into contact with Hungarians) accept linguistic rights. However, this is not true for autonomy or eligibility for election to public office. Rural inhabitants are more tolerant of autonomy and native-language education. As for settlement size, small and medium-sized towns are less tolerant of every type of minority right/claim.

Individual-level basic demographic variables have less of an effect. There is a slight tendency (above a certain threshold of significance) for young people to be less tolerant concerning native-language education and eligibility for election to public office, but they also accept autonomist claims in slightly higher proportions. Differences in sex and educational attainment are insignificant.

Religion also influences perceptions of minority rights. Non-Orthodox Romanians are more inclined to accept every type of minority right/claim. Politically passive people are more tolerant (or ignorant) of Hungarian claims. Supporters of Victor Ponta[57] and supporters of Klaus Iohannis[58] (the two presidential candidates in 2014) have rather similar perceptions of autonomist claims, native-language education and official use of Hungarian, while Ponta's supporters were less inclined to accept Hungarian eligibility for election to public office.

57 Ponta was the candidate of the Social Democrats (Partidul Social Democrat – PSD).
58 Iohannis was the canditate of the National Liberal Party (Partidul Național Liberal).

5 Hungarian and Romanian Citizenship Policies

Romanian citizenship laws today show a high degree of similarity to Hungarian ones. As Iordachi points out,[59] the Romanian law served as a model for Hungarian legislators when they modified regulations in Hungary concerning the acquisition of citizenship. This was motivated in part by the desire to avoid anticipated Romanian objections. While the citizenship laws in the two countries are quite similar, the Hungarian and Romanian political processes that led to them differ significantly. It is also important to note that the discursive framings of these laws diverge.

5.1 *Hungarian Citizenship Legislation and Its Reception among Transylvanian Hungarians*

In Hungary, intensive classificatory struggles concerning the official definition of the national community have dominated the post-socialist political scene. For instance, right-wing parties have tried to codify their vision of the virtual reunification of the culturally and linguistically defined and politically divided Hungarian nation. The 2001 Status Law (and the Hungarian Card[60] it created) was the first attempt to establish legal-bureaucratic ties between the Hungarian state and individual members of Hungarian minority communities. The Status Law was interpreted by many observers as an example *par excellence* of trans-sovereign nation-building[61] and a form of quasi-citizenship.[62] However, it is worth highlighting that for the mainstream Hungarian right (Viktor Orbán's Fidesz) it was a substitute for dual citizenship and a way for the government to respond to pressure from various sectors of the electorate without having to radically modify citizenship legislation.[63] Fidesz had opposed external citizenship until 2004, when a referendum was held on the issue. The major Hungarian right-wing party ultimately decided to back the initiative. The Hungarian left-wing and the liberal intelligentsia in particular presented a very different vision of the Hungarian nation. Their ideal was constitutional patriotism,

59 Constantin Iordachi, "From Disentanglement to Interdependence: State Citizenship in Romania and Hungary: 1945–2012," in *Hungary and Romania beyond National Narratives*, ed. A. Blomquist, C. Iordachi and B. Trencsenyi (Bern: Peter Lang, 2013).

60 The Hungarian Card was a special identity card issued by Hungarian authorities for Hungarians living across the border, proving that its holder was ethnically Hungarian.

61 Csergő and Goldgeier, "Nationalist Strategies and European Integration," op. cit.

62 See Zoltán Kántor, Balázs Majtényi, Osamu Ieda, Balázs Vizi and Iván Halász, eds., *The Hungarian Status Law: Nation Building and/or Minority Protection* (Sapporo: Hokkaido University/Slavic Research Center, 2004).

63 Szabolcs Pogonyi, *Extra-Territorial Ethnic Politics, Discourses and Identities in Hungary* (Cham: Palgrave Macmillan, 2017), 84.

according to which neither ethnic nor cultural links were conditions for belonging to the nation.[64] This ideal of constitutional patriotism provided a discursive framework for a militant anti-ethnicist stance.[65] As a consequence, the liberal left vehemently opposed any attempt to redefine the Hungarian nation and legally embrace trans-border Hungarians. This question has become the focus of political struggles on many occasions, the most notorious being the aforementioned campaign on dual citizenship in 2004. In the end, the 1993 Citizenship Law was modified by the right-wing dominated parliament in 2010, following the political collapse of the Hungarian left. The 2011 Electoral Law made it possible for extra-territorial citizens to vote in parliamentary elections.

As already mentioned, many actors of the minority field[66] in Transylvania considered the new citizenship legislation, enfranchisement and the growing kin-state activity of Hungary as a major challenge. Initially, the political class was divided on this issue. Some RMDSZ leaders made a deliberate show of applying for Hungarian citizenship immediately after the new legislation had come into effect.[67] But Béla Markó, the then president of RMDSZ, declared that he would not apply for Hungarian citizenship.[68] Later he openly criticized the enfranchisement of the trans-border Hungarians.[69] It seems obvious that most of the top leaders of RMDSZ and the members of the party's intellectual entourage were critical of the introduction of dual citizenship. However, the

64 Comparisons to Germany seem to be quite important here. The term constitutional patriotism also has roots in post-World War II German political philosophy, and it was elaborated by authors such as Jaspers, Stemberger and Habermas. These philosophers argued against the so-called "normalization" of German national identity (implying a return to its pre-Nazi forms). Instead, they sought to cultivate a new (post-national and post-ethnic) form of identity rooted in a supportive relationship towards democratic institutions and critical publicity. On this topic, see Jan-Werner Müller, *Constitutional Patriotism* (Princeton: Princeton University Press, 2007).

65 On the classificatory struggles between actors pushing for de-ethnicization and re-ethnicization of the citizenship regimes, see also Cristian Joppke, *Selecting by Origin: Ethnic Migration in the Liberal State* (Cambridge, MA: Harvard University Press, 2005), 219–250.

66 Brubaker uses the term minority field in the Bourdieusian sense of a social field composed of different actors struggling for definite positions and sharing a common frame of reference. In our understanding, the Transylvanian Hungarian minority field includes not only the political class but also a sub-elite level of ethnic activists (teachers, clerics, journalists, etc.) who are interested in the maintenance of the minority institutions, the internal solidarity of the group and the programme of ethnic parallelism. See Brubaker, *Nationalism Reframed*, op. cit.

67 See http://www.szatmar.ro/Kettos_allampolgarsag__vegyes_a_megiteles/hirek/37445.

68 See http://nepszava.hu/cikk/380701-marko-bela-egyelore-nem-igenyel-magyar-allampol garsagot.

69 See http://www.szatmar.ro/Marko_a_magyaorszagi_szavazati_jog_ellen/hirek/42622.

Transylvanian Hungarian political class (and most importantly RMDSZ) did not draft any coherent response to it.

The arguments of the Transylvanian Hungarian elites opposing the "trans-national"[70] or "trans-sovereign"[71] nation-building efforts of the Hungarian right-wing government (including external citizenship, enfranchisement and the establishment of other institutional ties) can be grouped in several categories.[72] (1) The first argument is that extra-territorial citizenship weakens the claim-making potential of the Hungarian elites towards the Romanian state. As already mentioned, Bauböck's argument concerning the trade-off between autonomy and extra-territorial citizenship has been widely accepted and reproduced by Transylvanian Hungarian political elites and social scientists. At a more general level, there was a fear that, if Transylvanian Hungarians were to rely on kin-state support and become oriented towards politics in Hungary, they would become less mobilized and less interested in making claims on the Romanian state through their own political parties. As a consequence, they would become more and more dependent on kin-state support and even more marginalized in their country of residence.[73] (2) The second argument focuses on migration and posits that extra-territorial citizenship eases entry into Hungary, thus accelerating the process described as "ethnic un-mixing" by Brubaker.[74] (3) Third, Transylvanian Hungarian elites also feared a general cultural and political reorientation towards Hungary. In Bauböck's typology, this would be a shift from an (internally oriented) ethnic identity to a (kin-state oriented) diaspora identity. Salat argues in a similar vein, saying that the programme for building a parallel minority society might transform into a programme for building a diaspora community dominated by kin-state actors.[75]

Among top RMDSZ leaders, these opposing views have been predominant. However, since there was widespread popular support for the new Hungarian citizenship policy among Transylvanian Hungarians, political pragmatism gained ground and RMDSZ adopted a supportive stance on the issue. As a result, since January 2015, rmdsz has been an official partner of the Hungarian

70 Pogonyi, "Dual Citizenship and Sovereignty."

71 Csergő and Goldgeier, "Nationalist Strategies and European Integration."

72 For an inventory of their arguments, see Myra Waterbury, "National Minorities in an Era of Externalization," *Problems of Post-Communism* 64, no. 5 (2016): 228–241; Pogonyi, *Extra-Territorial Ethnic Politics*, 105–111.

73 Pogonyi, *Extra-Territorial Ethnic Politics*, 190.

74 Rogers Brubaker, "The Migration of Ethnic Unmixing in the New Europe," *International Migration Review* 32, no. 4 (1998): 1047–1065.

75 Salat, "A politikai közösség kérdése," op. cit.

government in the implementation of the citizenship legislation. The widespread public support among Transylvanian Hungarians for dual citizenship is shown by survey results. While 9 per cent of Transylvanian Hungarians were against the new legislation in 2012, by 2014 this number had dwindled to less than 3 per cent (see: Figure 10.4).[76]

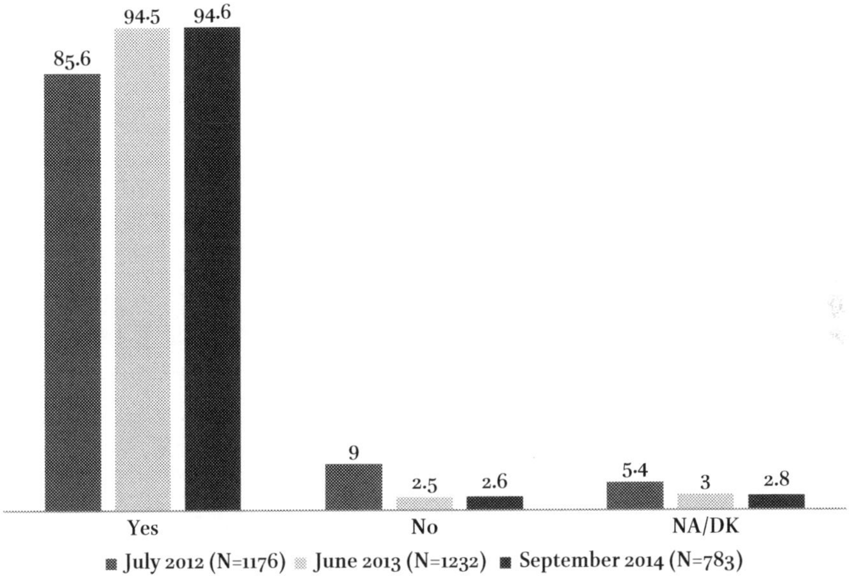

FIGURE 10.4 The Hungarian state offers citizenship to Hungarians living in neighbouring countries. As a consequence many Transylvanian Hungarians have applied for and obtained Hungarian citizenship. Do you support this? (Transylvanian Hungarian sample)
Note: "NA, DK" refers to "Not applicable/Don't know"
SOURCE: ROMANIAN INSTITUTE FOR RESEARCH ON NATIONAL MINORITIES (2012, 2013, 2014).

According to the results of a June 2016 survey, 44 per cent of adult Transylvanian Hungarians obtained Hungarian citizenship and an additional 5 per cent applied for it. A further 21 per cent intended to apply. As a consequence, the proportion of Hungarian citizens among Transylvanian Hungarians will probably reach 50 per cent in the near future (see: Figure 10.5).

76 It is important to underscore that Hungarian citizenship legislation is a much more divisive issue within the Hungarian community in Slovakia as well. See Ábel Ravasz, "Szlovákiai magyarok mint választók, 2009–2013" (The Hungarian electorate in Slovakia, 2009–2013), *Magyar Kisebbség*, no. 2 (2013): 42–68.

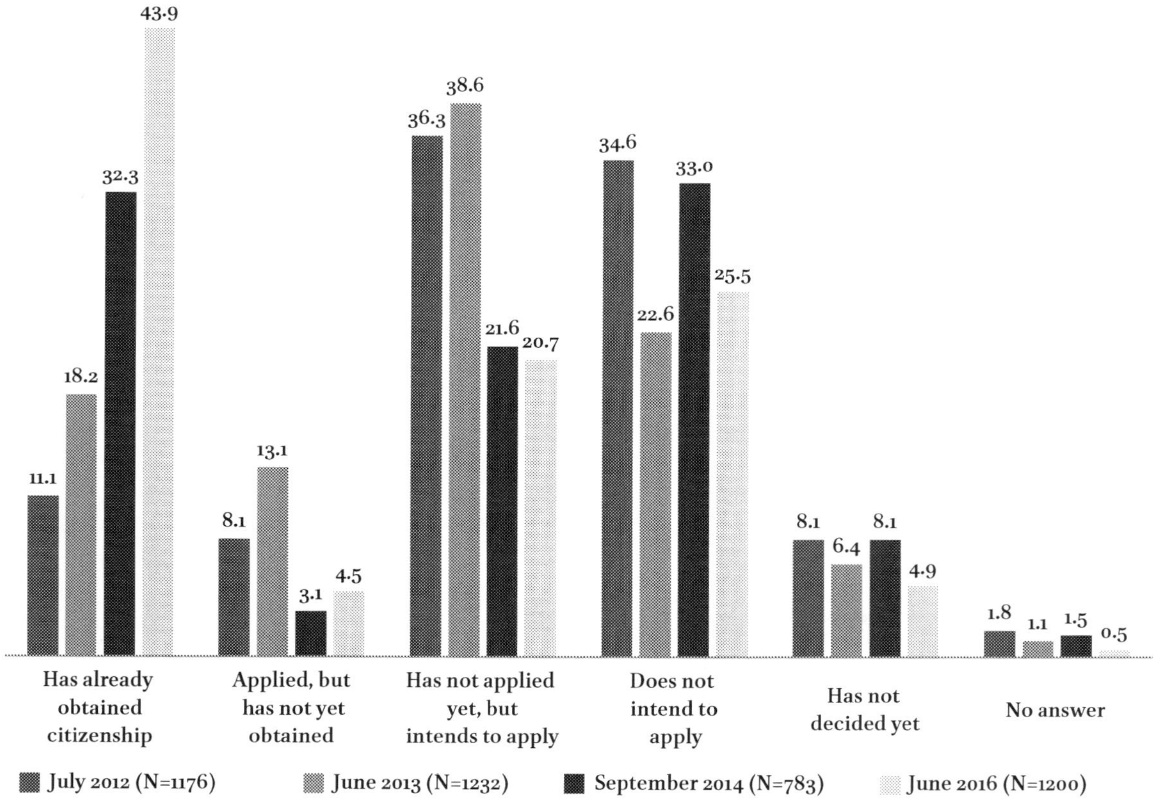

FIGURE 10.5 Did you apply for Hungarian citizenship? (Transylvanian Hungarian sample)
SOURCES: ROMANIAN INSTITUTE FOR RESEARCH ON NATIONAL MINORITIES (2012, 2023, 2014); KVANTUM RESEARCH (2016).

5.2 *Romanian Citizenship Legislation and the Redefinition of the Nation*

As already mentioned, many commentators expected that the amendment of Hungarian citizenship legislation would create tensions between Romania and Hungary. This was anticipated even by those observers who explained these amendments as a possible reconceptualization of the territorially-bounded notion of sovereignty. Csergő and Goldgeier argue that Hungarian attempts to establish an institutional framework enabling and sustaining national reproduction across existing state borders could be labelled as "virtual" or "trans-sovereign" nationalism and, as such, that it should be distinguished from irredentist claims. However, they also underscore that there is a high potential for conflict between states trying to virtualize state borders unilaterally, on the one hand, and states claiming exclusive sovereignty over their minority populations, on the other.[77] In what follows, I will first outline some aspects of Romanian citizenship legislation and then present Romanian perceptions of the multiple national membership of Transylvanian Hungarians. I will argue that Romania also took important steps towards a trans-sovereign strategy of nation-building and a more de-territorialized concept of the Romanian nation, although these notions still compete with more traditional, territorially-bounded concepts and strategies.

The relatively favourable Romanian reception of the changes in Hungarian citizenship legislation can be explained by the earlier redefinition of Romanian citizenship, which also represented a move away from the Westphalian paradigm. However, as already mentioned, the discursive and political contexts of the changes in citizenship legislation were markedly different in Romania and Hungary. In Romania, no political and public debates took place regarding the official (re)definition of the political/national community. Changes concerning the acquisition of Romanian citizenship seemed to be a matter of consensus among different political actors.

Nevertheless, citizenship legislation and the official definition of the Romanian nation have changed radically in Romania too. Iordachi[78] emphasizes Romania's difficult position, which can be interpreted in the framework of Brubaker's triadic nexus. First, Romania has a national/ethnic minority (Transylvanian Hungarians) that aspires to autonomous status and is backed by an external homeland. Second, Romania is also the external homeland

77 Csergő and Goldgeier, "Nationalist Strategies and European Integration."

78 Constantin Iordachi, "Politics of Citizenship in Post-Communist Romania: Legal Traditions, Restitution of Nationality and Multiple Memberships," in *Citizenship Policies in the New Europe*, Expanded and Updated Edition, eds. Rainer Bauböck, Bernhard Perchinig, Wiebke Sievers, (Amsterdam: Amsterdam University Press, 2009), 177–211.

for Romanians living abroad, most importantly in the Republic of Moldova, Ukraine and Serbia. One could also add that Romania has been affected by a significant outflow of migrants. Thus, the existence of increasingly numerous Romanian diaspora communities has also affected the (re)definition of the national community.

Before 1989, a rather extreme version of the Westphalian paradigm had been propagated by the Romanian regime. However, Romania's position gradually changed in many dimensions. First, Romania initially supported nationalizing policies of an increasingly mono-ethnic character,[79] which focused on the assimilation of internal minorities (with a rhetorical emphasis on the Hungarians).[80] Hungarian-Romanian relations reached their nadir in the 1980s, as Hungarian foreign policy increasingly demanded respect for the human and minority rights of Transylvanian Hungarians, while Romania accused Hungary of interfering in its internal affairs and violating its sovereignty.[81] From this Romanian perspective, any form of Hungarian kin-state activism was absolutely unacceptable. This standpoint changed gradually over the course of the last decade of the twentieth and first decade of the twenty-first century, culminating in a relatively favourable official reception of Hungary's External Citizenship Law in 2010.

Second, Romania's relations with its own trans-border ethnic kin have also changed considerably.[82] The former regime's nationalist rhetoric did not

79 On the nationalist turn of the Romanian communist regime see Katherine Verdery, *National Ideology under Socialism: Identity and Cultural Politics in Ceausescu's Romania* (Berkeley: University of California Press, 1991).

80 Other important minority groups, such as Jews who survived the Holocaust or Germans (Saxons and Swabians), have not been directly targeted by the increasingly ethnicist official propaganda. However, selective emigration policies were implied. While the regime practically prevented the outflow of other ethnic groups, it allowed Jews and Germans to emigrate. Ethnically selective Israeli and German emigration policies were unquestionably the most important factor in the mass exodus of Romanian Jews and Germans (see Brubaker, "Migration of Ethnic Unmixing"). However, the ethnic selection of the emigrants by the Romanian state should not be considered anything other than a non-violent form of ethnic cleansing.

81 See Iordachi, "From Disentanglement to Interdependence."

82 On this issue, see Cristian Ghinea, István Horváth, Liliana Popescu and Victoria Stoiciu, *Republica Moldova în conștiința publică Românească* (The Republic of Moldova in the Romanian public consciousness) (Bucharest: Soros Foundation Romania, 2011); Constantin Iordachi, Ștefan Leonescu, Alexandra Toderiță, Claudia Silaghi and Cristian Ghinea, eds., *Redobândirea cetățeniei române* (Reacquiring Romanian citizenship) (Bucharest: Cureta Veche, 2012); Sergiu Panainte, *Redobândirea cetățeniei române: o politică ce capătă viziune?* (Reacquisition of citizenship: A policy gaining vision?) (Bucharest: Soros Foundation Romania, 2013); Irina Culic, "From Restitution to Privileged Re-Naturalisation: The

focus on Romanians living in neighbouring countries, instead encouraging a politics of forgetting with regard to Bessarabia and Northern Bukovina.[83] Nevertheless, Romania was among the first Eastern European states to grant extra-territorial citizenship to its trans-border co-ethnics.[84] It is important to emphasize that, in spite of this important step, Romania engaged in low-profile kin-state activism until its accession to the European Union in 2007.[85] Most importantly, there was no public debate in Romania concerning its relationship with trans-border ethnic kin, which could have raised the public visibility of the issue. As Dumbrava highlights, there was "a careful wrapping in civic clothing"[86] of Romanian citizenship legislation. This proved to be a successful strategy of discursive framing. The 1991 Citizenship Law did not refer directly to former citizens of Greater Romania (but rather to those who lost their citizenship "against their will or for any other reason for which they cannot be blamed"). The law (framed as an act that addressed injustices committed by the communist regime) also made it possible for people belonging to certain other categories (e.g. emigrants and politically persecuted persons) to regain Romanian citizenship. An important consequence of the "non-ethnic" framing of this issue has been that Romania did not offer citizenship to Romanians living outside the former territories of Greater Romania (the most important group being the Vlachs of Serbia). Furthermore, the decision to grant extra-territorial citizenship to Romanians living in the Republic of Moldova and Ukraine was clearly subordinated to other foreign policy goals, notably EU accession. During the EU pre-accession period between 2002 and 2007, provisions granting citizenship to former citizens of interwar Greater Romania were not just publicly invisible but their implementation was practically suspended. The process of reacquiring Romanian citizenship was restarted

Expansive Politics of Dual Citizenship in Romania after 1989," *Minority Studies* 16 (2012): 125–152.

83 Romania lost these territories in 1940, following the Molotov-Ribbentrop Pact and again following the Second World War. The situation of the Romanian-speaking population living in the Soviet Union was mostly a taboo subject during the former regime.

84 See Myra Waterbury, "Making Citizens beyond the Borders: Nonresident Ethnic Citizenship in Post-Communist Europe," *Problems of Post-Communism* 61, no. 4 (2014): 34–49; Costică Dumbrava, *Nationality, Citizenship and Ethno-National Belonging: Preferential Membership Policies in Europe* (Basingstoke: Palgrave Macmillan, 2014).

85 Zsuzsa Csergő and James Goldgeier, "Kin-State Activism in Hungary, Romania and Russia," in *Divided Nations and European Integration*, ed. T. Marby, J. McGarry, M. Moore and B. O'Leary (Philadelphia: University of Pennsylvania Press, 2013), 89–126.

86 Costica Dumbrava, "Rolling Back History: The Romanian Policy of Restoration of Citizenship to Former Citizens," CITSEE Story, Edinburgh, June 2013, http://www.citsee.eu/citseestory/rolling-back-history-romanian-policy-restoration-citizenship-former-citizens.

immediately after the country joined the European Union. Following Romania's EU accession, this issue has gained considerable public visibility, most importantly because former president Traian Băsescu has repeatedly raised it.

Third, to understand the Romanian move towards a post-Westphalian concept of the nation, one needs to take into account, as emphasized by Knott[87] and Waterbury,[88] that the Romanian concept of diaspora includes both recent emigrants and the historic category of Romanian national minorities or ethnic kin. For example, the country's electoral legislation[89] does not differentiate between these categories. The resulting process of extra-territorial voting is leading to the increasing inclusion of both historical kin minorities and Western diaspora in a de-territorialized Romanian nation.[90] It is also worth mentioning that the emerging emigrant or expatriate communities have shaped popular concepts of the Romanian nation far more emphatically than the existence of the historic kin minorities. In spite of the quick modification of the citizenship legislation, everyday trans-border connections between Romanians have been far less frequent than in the Hungarian case, where such relationships are common. The vast majority of Romanians have never visited the Republic of Moldova.[91] Everyday practices of national classification do not necessarily follow official definitions. In May 2014, the Romanian Institute for Research on National Minorities conducted a focus group discussion with Moldovan students in Cluj. Moldovan-Romanians reported strong negative attitudes on the part of the Romanian population. They mentioned that they were regarded as outsiders among Romanian students and were strongly discriminated against in the labour market. According to a survey conducted by the Romanian Soros Foundation, 59 per cent of Romanians agreed that the Republic of Moldova was more backwards than Romania proper.[92] Furthermore, Romania has never been a major recipient country of Moldovan emigrants. The largest communities of Moldovan emigrants were in Russia (277,527 Moldovan-born persons in 2002) and Italy (123,147 Moldovan citizens in 2012). According to the 2011 Romanian census, only 37,370 persons born in Moldova and 8,099 persons

87 Eleanor Knott, "Extra-Territorial Voting Practices and the Asymmetry of Charisma: Băsescu and His Moldovan Constituents" (paper presented at the annual meeting of the MPSA, Chicago, March 2015).

88 Myra Waterbury, *The Challenges of and Responses to Intra-EU Emigration in Central and Eastern Europe* (manuscript, 2016).

89 Law No. 35/2008 and Law No. 208/2015.

90 Knott, "Extra-Territorial Voting Practices"; Waterbury, *Challenges and Responses*; Eleanor Knott, "The Extra-Territorial Paradox of Voting: The Duty to Vote in Extra-Territorial Elections," *Democratization* 24, no. 2 (2017), 325–346.

91 See Ghinea et al., *Republica Moldova în conștiința publică.*

92 Ibid.

born in Ukraine resided in the country. Moreover, a significant portion of them were persons born before 1944.

Large-scale emigration seems to be a far more important factor in the official and popular redefinition of the nation. During the communist period, emigrants were both legally and rhetorically excluded from the Romanian nation. As in the other countries in the former Eastern Bloc, the act of emigration was regarded as an implicit critique of the regime and was thus incompatible with "socialist patriotism." Dual citizenship was legally banned, and emigrants obtaining citizenship in host countries lost Romanian citizenship.

The 1991 Citizenship Law also explicitly allowed for multiple citizenship in the case of emigrants. It is worth highlighting that the Romanian (ethnic/national) community has become increasingly transnational due to large-scale emigration. Sizeable Romanian emigrant communities have appeared, especially since 2000. The largest ones are those in Italy, Spain and Germany (see: Table 10.4). The issue of the political participation of these Romanian emigrant communities (and the resulting transnational character of the Romanian political community) was intensely debated during the 2009 and the 2014 presidential elections.[93] It seems that the de-territorialization of the Romanian nation also weakened the exclusivist claims of loyalty towards Transylvanian Hungarians. Contrary to Slovakia, Romania has not objected to Hungary's "simplified naturalization" procedure.[94] Moreover, according to representative surveys, a majority of Romanians accept that the Hungarian state grants citizenship to Hungarians in Romania.

6 Romanian Public Perceptions of the Hungarian Kin-state and Its Citizenship Policy

As regards perceptions of Hungarian kin-state involvement and its citizenship policy, we can consider three statements or blocks of statements. In the 2000, 2001, 2002, 2006 and 2012 surveys, respondents were asked to evaluate several areas of Hungarian kin-state activity. In all five surveys, respondents were asked to indicate whether or not they accepted extra-territorial citizenship (*The Hungarian state should provide Hungarian citizenship for Hungarians*

93 See Toma Bueran, *Migrant Political Participation and Voting Behavior in Romania* (paper presented at APSA, San Francisco, September 3–6, 2015).

94 Simplified naturalization (*egyszerűsített honosítás*) is the official name of the procedure through which transborder Hungarians can acquire extra-territorial citizenship.

TABLE 10.4 Number of Romanian immigrants in the main recipient countries

	1980	1990	2000	2010	2013
Italy	3,886	15,725	123,957	813,037	1,008,169
Spain	930	765	47,854	810,471	800,400
Germany	74,251	1,144,848	324,085	134,911	438,000
Hungary	160,423	139,690	133,077	189,055	232,793
United States	69,349	101,256	140,085	171,253	188,638
Israel	193,905	151,154	139,278	182,099	105,488
United Kingdom	3,481	4,031	21,684	53,081	103,421
Canada	19,193	29,887	59,644	96,209	95,499
Austria	3,223	28,723	24,647	56,932	73,900
France	13,143	15,725	123,957	54,305	57,689
Belgium	168	168	2,487	21,634	52,700
Greece	610	4,762	21,132	45,289	38,597
Turkey	19,840	9,324	20,853	23,232	30,706
Portugal	128	76	3,008	3,954	23,513
Sweden	1,971	7,991	11,646	16,184	23,299
Australia	5,652	10,932	12,700	17,449	18,130
Ireland	469	423	5,264	12,682	17,800
Switzerland	2,576	29,152	3,146	7,914	14,624
Denmark	208	952	2,017	4,186	13,615
Netherlands	1,645	2,361	4,822	8,716	13,606
Czech Republic	121	852	12,066	12,083	12,800
Norway	138	290	1,105	2,045	10,278
Slovakia	48	147	3,178	2,751	5,300
Poland	6,841	4,986	3,623	3,632	2,659
Total (countries above)	**582,199**	**1,704,220**	**1,245,315**	**2,743,103**	**3,381,624**
Total (worldwide)	**632,334**	**1,761,648**	**1,307,973**	**2,769,053**	**3,430,476**

SOURCE: WORLD BANK BILATERAL MIGRATION DATABASE (1980, 1990, 2000, 2010, 2013).

in Romania). In the 2001, 2002, 2006 and 2012 surveys, they were asked to evaluate the political support provided to Hungarian ethnic parties (*The Hungarian state should strengthen its relations with the Hungarian political organizations in Romania*). Two measures relating to cultural support were also included, namely the promotion of Hungarian-language university education (*The Hungarian state should support Hungarian-language universities in Romania*) in 2001 and 2012 and the provision of scholarships for Hungarian students from Romania (*The Hungarian state should offer bursaries for Hungarian students from Romania*) in 2000, 2001 and 2012 (see: Figure 10.6).

It should be pointed out that tolerance towards Hungarian kin-state activism increased considerably in the period between 2000 and 2014. In 2002, 33.4 per cent responded positively to the statement on extra-territorial citizenship. By 2012, this figure had reached 58.7 per cent. The acceptance of the external homeland's political support has also increased considerably. In 2012, 62.3 per cent of Romanians were willing to tolerate Hungary's maintenance of strong relations with Hungarian ethnic parties in Romania. Romanians have also become more tolerant of Hungarian state support for native-language university education. However, it is also important to emphasize that Romanians were tolerant of Hungarian extra-territorial citizenship in larger proportions than they were of Hungarian-language universities in Romania, even though it is financed by the Hungarian state (state-financed native-language university education is less tolerated). The acceptance among Romanians of the practice of offering scholarships for Transylvanian Hungarian students by Hungary has been consistently high (above two-thirds of those who had this as an option) in all three surveys.[95]

In the 2012, 2014 and 2016 surveys conducted by the Romanian Institute for Research on National Minorities, we asked respondents more directly to evaluate the new Hungarian citizenship legislation. Their responses confirmed our conclusion above: 55, 54 and 60 per cent of the (ethnically Romanian) respondents supported the new Hungarian citizenship policy and accepted the dual citizenship of Hungarians living in Romania (see: Figure 10.7).

It is worth noting that the socio-demographic and political profile of Romanians who accept Hungarian extra-territorial citizenship is more clear-cut than that of those who accept minority rights. This is shown by the higher value of the Nagelkerke R^2 of the regression model concerning the determinants

95 It is worth noting that offering scholarships is the most substantial element of Romanian kin-state activism and the promotion by the Romanian state of "Romanianism" in neighbouring countries. In 2010, more than 5,000 Moldovan students received scholarships to pursue studies in Romania. See Irina Culic, "From Restitution to Privileged Re-naturalisation: The Expansive Politics of Dual Citizenship in Romania after 1989," *Minority Studies* 16 (2012): 125–152.

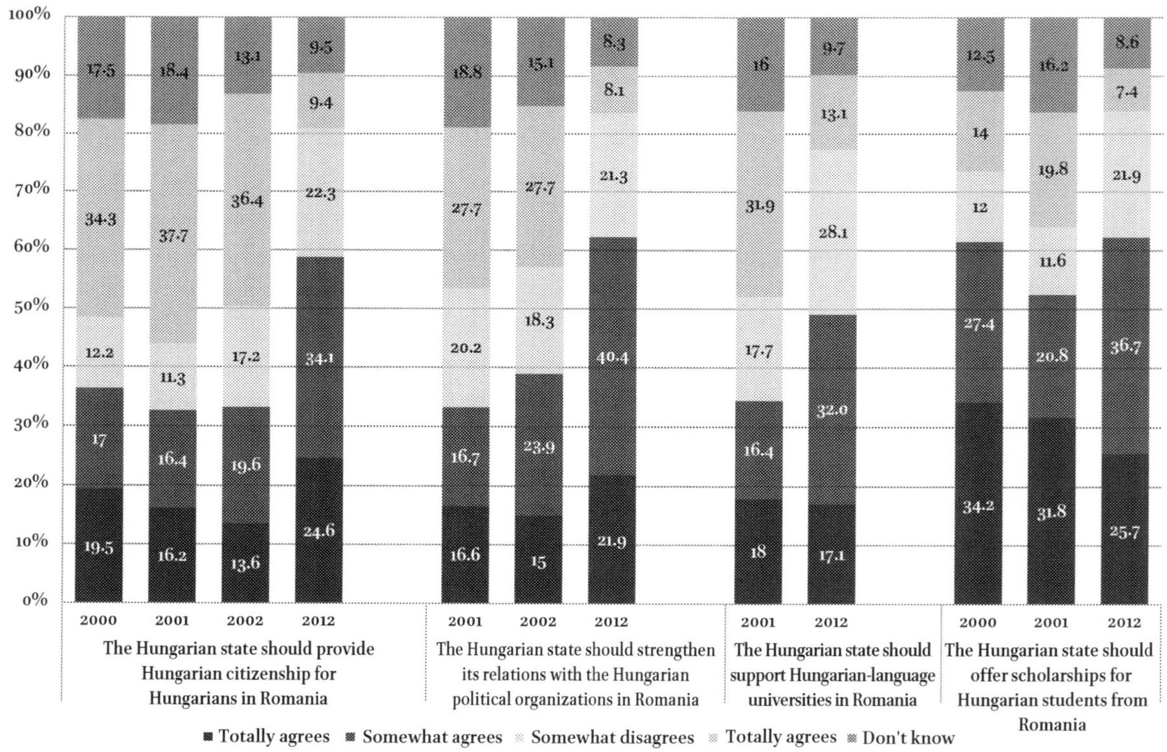

FIGURE 10.6 Do you agree with the following? (national sample, Romanians)
SOURCES: CCRIT (ETNOBAROMETER 2000); METRO MEDIA TRANSILVANIA (ETNOBAROMETER 2001, 2002); ROMANIAN INSTITUTE FOR RESEARCH ON NATIONAL MINORITIES (2012).

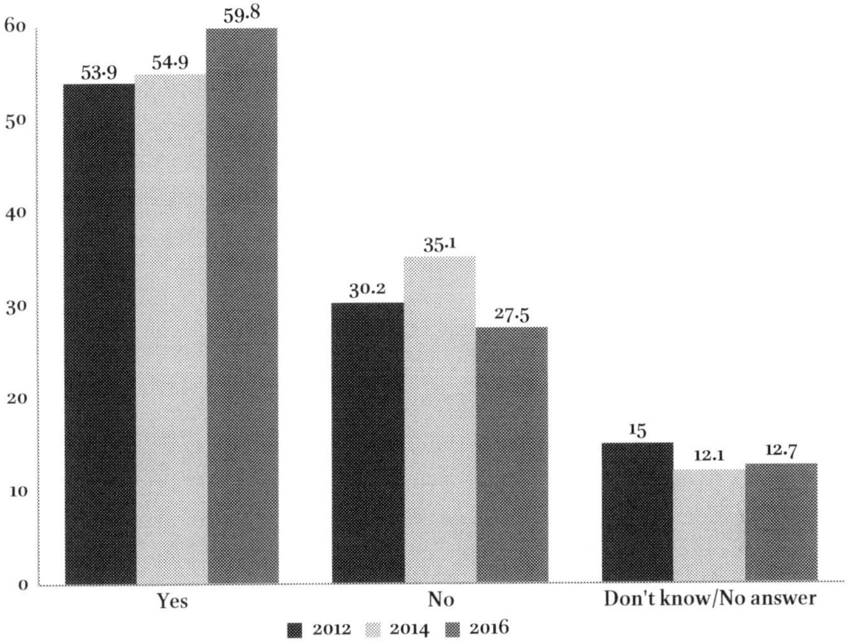

FIGURE 10.7 The Hungarian state has made it possible for Hungarians living in neighbouring countries to obtain Hungarian citizenship. In the wake of this change, many Hungarians in Romania have become Hungarian citizens. Do you agree that Hungarians living in Romania should be entitled to obtain Hungarian citizenship? (national sample, Romanians)
SOURCE: ROMANIAN INSTITUTE FOR RESEARCH ON NATIONAL MINORITIES (2012, 2014, 2016).

of acceptance (0.186, see Appendix 1). As one can observe, the so-called "progressive" (or highly ranked) segments of Romanian society[96] have a more favourable view on this issue, but this is evidently not the case when it comes to minority rights/claims (ranging from cultural rights to autonomy). According to our 2014 results, Transylvanian Romanians are much more tolerant of Hungarian citizenship legislation (69 per cent of them accept it). Attitudes are also significantly more favourable in Bucharest and cities with more than 100,000 inhabitants. There is a split between members of older generations and members of the middle and younger generations. The latter accept dual citizenship in significantly higher proportions. We note that Romanians with

96 We adopt an analytical (and rather critical) stance towards the developmental discourses shaping internal hierarchies. However, it is obvious that ideas shared by more prestigious societal segments have a better chance of spreading.

less formal education are more tolerant of Hungarian ethno-political claims and minority rights (even if not significantly according to the regression model). This is not true in the case of external citizenship. The least educated strata reject it in significantly higher proportions than people with a university degree. Belonging to a non-Orthodox religion, having personal migratory experience or supporting Klaus Iohannis in the second round of the 2014 presidential election also significantly increases the likelihood that a person will accept Hungarian citizenship legislation.

The last block of statements to be presented relates to support for possible countermeasures to be taken by the Romanian state against Romanian citizens of Hungarian ethnicity who have obtained Hungarian citizenship. We asked about the revocation of Romanian citizenship (*The Romanian state should revoke the Romanian citizenship of Hungarians who have obtained Hungarian citizenship*), the revocation of voting rights (*The Romanian state should revoke the voting rights of Hungarians who have obtained Hungarian citizenship*) and the revocation of eligibility for public office (*The Romanian state should revoke the eligibility of Hungarians who have obtained Hungarian citizenship to be elected mayor or deputy*). Although the 2012 and 2014 surveys show a slight increase in support for these measures a clear majority of Romanians rejects radical countermeasures (see: Figure 10.8).

7 Concluding Remarks

The main question of my paper is how the ethno-national majority in Romania perceives the minority rights and claims of the Transylvanian Hungarians as well as Hungarian kin-state policy. I accept the arguments of observers who emphasize the importance of conflicting visions of sovereignty at the level of both inter-ethnic[97] and interstate relations.[98] However, my own argument is that majoritarian concepts of sovereignty cannot be taken for granted or defined *a priori* but should be investigated empirically. These concepts and perceptions are shaped by historical legacies, particular social contexts and political processes. It is also important to note that concepts of sovereignty can change over time. As a consequence, we need empirically grounded case studies in order to arrive at general statements and theoretically relevant

97 See Csergő, *Talk of the Nation*.

98 Csergő and Goldgeier, "Nationalist Strategies and European Integration"; Pogonyi, "Dual Citizenship and Sovereignty"; Pogonyi, *Extra-Territorial Ethnic Politics*.

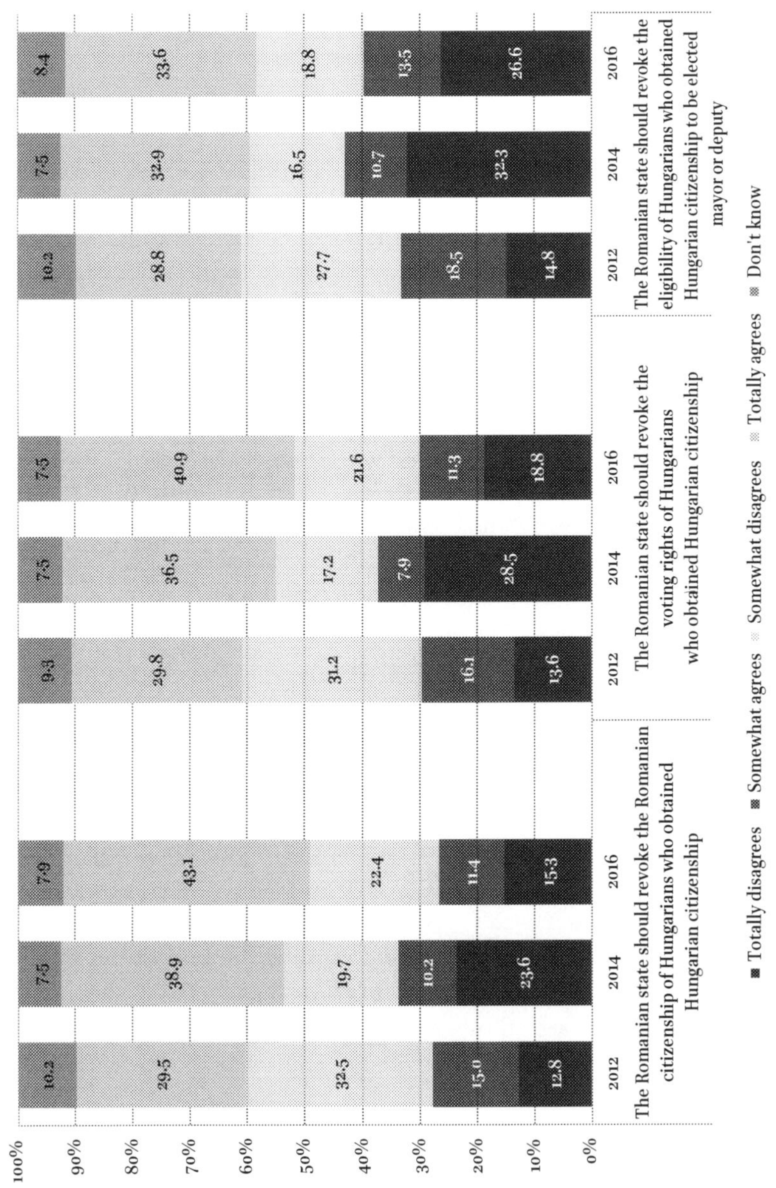

FIGURE 10.8 Do you agree with the following statements? (National sample, Romanians)
SOURCE: ROMANIAN INSTITUTE FOR RESEARCH ON NATIONAL MINORITIES (2012, 2014, 2016).

conclusions. In my paper, I have outlined such a case study based on longitudinal survey results concerning majoritarian perspectives.

At the intrastate level, the conflict between the Transylvanian Hungarian claims for territorial autonomy, on the one hand, and the Romanian notion of a unitary and highly centralized nation-state, on the other, is obvious. There is a consensus among Romanian political parties (except RMDSZ) that autonomy would violate the exclusive sovereignty of the state over its territory and be conducive to ethnic separatism. Another important question is whether the perception of minority language rights is also connected to conflicting notions of sovereignty. According to Arzoz, "the purpose of these rights is to enable speakers of the minority language to use their own language rather than the majority language."[99] This is necessary because nation-building and the institutional order of the nation-state create a hierarchy between majority and minority languages. Arzoz argues that it is misleading to link minority language rights to human rights; however, it is also obvious that (contrary to territorial autonomy) they can be conceptualized not only as collective rights but also within the framework of individual rights. It is important that the Hungarian elites have used multiple (and in some instances competing) discursive framings to legitimize their ethno-political claims. One the one hand, they have demanded territorial autonomy and the recognition of Transylvanian Hungarians as a self-standing and autonomous political community. On the other hand, however, they have also used the discursive framework of minority (language) rights. This duality made it possible for RMDSZ to reformulate its claims in the late 1990s, effectively leaving out the passages referring to collective rights and autonomy and focusing on educational policy and minority language rights.[100] In parallel, as several observers argue, Romanian political actors have also reformulated their ideas concerning the integration of the Hungarian minority into the Romanian polity, allowing for a more pluralistic model.[101] It was widely expected that the larger Romanian public would also

99 Xavier Arzoz, "The Nature of Language Rights," *Journal on Ethnopolitics and Minority Issues in Europe* 6, no. 2 (2007): 1–35.

100 See Toró, "Detached Implementation: Discourse and Practice." It is important to note that RMDSZ relied on a two-pronged rhetoric after 2004 in the context of intra-ethnic completion. It presented itself as intransigent towards its own electorate, on the one hand, while using de-ethnicized language in its relations with majority political partners, on the other. See Tibor Toró, "Ethnicization or De-ethnicization? Hungarian Political Representation in the Romanian Parliament," *Nationalities Papers*, published online on June 23, 2017, available at http://www.tandfonline.com/doi/full/10.1080/00905992.2017.1318122.

101 As Csergő highlights, the Romanian model does not include elements of a symmetric linguistic pluralism. She argues that Romania shifted from a hegemonic model towards a model of linguistic predominance, which allows for several languages but establishes a clear hierarchy between them. See Csergő, *Talk of the Nation*, 117–118.

move towards a more tolerant attitude concerning minority language rights and the presence of Hungarians in the public sphere. However, contrary to expectations, this has not happened: there is no discernible linear trend in the acceptance of minority language rights. Only a tiny minority of Romanians accepts the official use of the Hungarian language, and almost half of them oppose the right of Hungarians to native-language education. Furthermore, only 51 per cent of Romanians agree that Hungarians are eligible for election to public office. In sum, not only is territorial autonomy firmly rejected by the larger Romanian public but minority language rights have no substantial legitimacy either.

Conflicting visions of sovereignty can affect interstate relations too. In this respect, many observers fear that Hungarian attempts to establish a non-territorial institutional framework in order to reproduce the national community (or, in other words, to foster the virtual reunification of their national community cross-cut by existing state borders) could provoke severe interstate tensions. For instance, Csergő and Goldgeier argue that, in spite of the increasing transnationalization of the international environment, the more traditional strategies of nation-building and the notion of territorial sovereignty are still dominant in Eastern Europe. Thus, unilateral attempts to "virtualize" state borders could provoke counter-reactions by nation-states that claim exclusive sovereignty over their minority populations. From this perspective, attempts at trans-sovereign nation-building could be perceived as a soft form of irredentism, as they question the exclusive sovereignty of the neighbouring states over their citizens. Following the modification of Hungarian citizenship legislation, this argument was used primarily by Slovak diplomats and provided the ideological foundation for an amendment of the Slovak Citizenship Law to ban dual nationality.[102]

The presumption that Romania is also attached to this notion of territorial sovereignty was taken for granted by many observers. Some of them even predicted that Romania would also take countermeasures if Transylvanian Hungarians opted for Hungarian citizenship in considerable numbers.[103] However, this has not been the case. Romania was among the neighbouring states that barely opposed the new Hungarian citizenship legislation. My argument is that Romania abstained from countermeasures because its concepts of sovereignty and nation have moved increasingly towards transnationalism. From a historical perspective, the Romanian progression is quite spectacular. Before 1989, the regime propagated an extreme version of the Westphalian paradigm. This standpoint gradually changed, finally resulting in a relatively

102 See Bauböck, "Dual citizenship for transborder minorities?"

103 Salat, "A politikai közösség kérdése."

favourable official reception in Romania of Hungary's External Citizenship Law in 2010.

Empirical data shows that both official definitions and public perceptions of national membership have become more tolerant towards multiple memberships. The table below shows the distribution of the responses to a more abstract block of questions concerning the duties of Romanian citizens. As we can see, support for exclusive membership is largely rejected by the Romanian public.

Data indicating the increasing public acceptance of Hungarian kin-state activity should be interpreted in this context. Most Romanians have accepted that Hungarians in Romania are eligible for Hungarian citizenship because both Romanian citizenship legislation and public opinion have distanced themselves from the Westphalian paradigm. It is also important that the Romanian concept of diaspora refers to emigrants as well as national

TABLE 10.5 Do you think that every Romanian citizen should ... (national sample, 2014)

	Totally agree	Somewhat agree	Somewhat disagree	Totally disagree
pay all his/her taxes in Romania?	62.0	25.4	8.5	4.0
exercise his/her voting right at every opportunity?	65.7	27.2	4.9	2.2
manifest solidarity with citizens in vulnerable positions (poor, etc.)?	50.7	41.3	6.5	1.5
be active in NGOs?	38.4	42.9	15.3	3.4
respect the Romanian Orthodox Church?	20.7	35.6	19.2	24.4
be able to speak fluent Romanian?	48.7	35.4	10.1	5.7
transmit respect for the Romanian people to his/her children?	30.6	44.8	17.2	7.4
respect the history and the traditions of the Romanians?	28.5	45.0	15.2	11.3
respect the national anthem and flag?	34.8	46.1	10.9	8.2
be ready to defend the country in case of a war?	35.6	38.4	15.0	10.9
not apply for the citizenship of another country?	5.3	4.5	12.0	78.3

SOURCE: ROMANIAN INSTITUTE FOR RESEARCH ON NATIONAL MINORITIES (2014).

minorities across borders. As a consequence, Romanians conceptualize the situation of Transylvanian Hungarians in this framework and regard it as similar to that of Romanian expatriate communities. This also serves as a possible explanation for the acceptance of kin-state involvement alongside the rejection of minority rights.

A complementary argument that I have presented refers to Bauböck's thesis concerning the trade-off between autonomist claims of minority elites and extra-territorial citizenship offered by an external homeland. According to Bauböck,[104] autonomy could be perceived as a kind of "vertical dual citizenship." Under such circumstances, it is highly unlikely that the majority would accept both autonomy and dual citizenship, as the acceptance of both would mean a near-complete loss of the state's sovereignty over its minority population. Echoing this argument, a communitarian critique of Hungarian kin-state policy has also been articulated by some Transylvanian Hungarian political actors and political scientists. This standpoint expressly favours autonomy over dual citizenship and declares that the renegotiation of the terms of integration of the Transylvanian Hungarian community into the Romanian polity should be prioritized over the Budapest-centred programme of virtual national reunification, as these two strategies are seen as being mutually exclusive. According to this view, the new Hungarian citizenship legislation not only weakens the chances for territorial or segmental autonomy but could also lead to an identity shift among Transylvanian Hungarians from an ethnic identity that prioritizes the internal efforts of minority elites to build an institutional framework sustaining the minority society towards a diaspora identity that looks to Budapest for support and inspiration.[105]

I believe that Bauböck's thesis and the related communitarian critique of kin-state involvement can be misleading, since they are based on the untested assumption that national majorities are attached to a concept of territorial sovereignty prevalent in the nineteenth and early twentieth century. In my view, given the increasingly diverse and highly contextual practices described in this paper, it is primarily an empirical question whether national majorities see minority autonomy and extra-territorial citizenship offered by the kin-state as conflicting strategies. For instance, every person born in Northern Ireland has the right to acquire both British and Irish citizenship, while Northern Ireland also has considerable autonomy within the United Kingdom.[106] Contrary to

104 Bauböck, "Transnational Citizenship and Political Autonomy."

105 Salat, "Cei 25 de ani ai UDMR." op. cit.; Pogonyi, *Extra-Territorial Ethnic Politics.*

106 John McGarry and Brendan O'Leary, *The Northern Ireland Conflict: Consociational Engagements* (Oxford: Oxford University Press, 2004).

this practice, all major political actors in Slovakia vehemently rejected both the autonomy claims of the minority Hungarian political elites and the decision of the Hungarian state to grant dual citizenship to Hungarians in Slovakia.[107] In the case of Romania, however, the modification of the Hungarian citizenship legislation has not had a substantial impact on the national majority's acceptance of minority rights and autonomy claims.

On a more general level, the problem – as Margaret Moore[108] and John McGarry and Brendan O'Leary[109] have pointed out – is that statist theories of justice rooted in the Westphalian paradigm fail to deal with the problem of political loyalties that transcend existing state borders This is the case in both the integrationist and the accommodationist perspective. Although the latter is accepting of multiple or diverging political loyalties connected to ethno-cultural differences, it seeks their accommodation inside a territorially delimited polity. Furthermore, it perceives the existence of cross-border ties and loyalties as an anomaly and a threat to the territorially-bounded political community.

107 Bauböck, "Dual citizenship for transborder minorities?"

108 Margaret Moore, "Divided Nations and Challenges to Statist and Global Theories of Justice," in *Divided Nations and European Integration*, ed. T. Marby, J. McGarry, M. Moore and B. O'Leary (Philadelphia: University of Pennsylvania Press, 2013), 33–55.

109 See John McGarry and Brendan O'Leary, "Introduction," in *Divided Nations and European Integration*, ed. T. Marby, J. McGarry, M. Moore and B. O'Leary (Philadelphia: University of Pennsylvania Press, 2013), 1–33.

Appendix

TABLE 10.A1 Factors affecting the acceptance of different types of minority rights, ethno-political claims, and kin-state policy measures among ethnic Romanians (2014)

		Official language use			Native-language education			Autonomy			Eligibility to be elected			Hungarian citizenship		
		%	OR*	Sig	%	OR*	Sig	%	OR*	Sig	%	OR*	Sig	%	OR*	Sig
Region	Muntenia	10.0	.243	.000	40.7	.525	.000	9.6	1.022	.937	46.1	1.022	.937	45.5	.338	.000
	Moldavia	16.6	.450	.001	53.6	.921	.679	11.8	.888	.699	58.3	.888	.699	50.7	.474	.000
	Oltenia	8.8	.187	.000	36.8	.396	.000	17.6	1.186	.632	56.0	1.186	.632	51.2	.460	.001
	Transylvania (ref.)	*27.6*			*55.1*			*11.3*			*51.9*			*68.6*		
Type of settlement	Rural	17.4	1.755	.106	50.2	3.506	.000	14.3	2.123	.040	50.8	1.230	.524	52.8	.690	.164
	Urban (ref.)	*14.5*			*41.6*			*9.3*			*51.5*			*55.2*		
Size of settlement	Bucharest	13.8	1.178	.749	49.1	.493	.066	4.6	.245	.030	57.4	.531	.235	57.5	1.999	.064
	Above 100,000	19.1	.946	.891	59.8	.642	.176	8.5	.466	.110	69.9	.922	.811	67.3	1.849	.051
	20–100,000	5.1	.155	.001	29.9	.147	.000	4.4	.195	.005	32.1	.399	.005	34.8	.442	.020
	5–20,000	9.7	.374	.041	42.7	.293	.001	10.7	.588	.304	38.8	1.163	.704	42.9	.664	.239
	1,000–5,000	22.7	1.906	.012	42.7	.732	.115	22.2	2.211	.005	43.5	.414	.001	51.2	.719	.088
	Below 1,000 (ref.)	*14.5*			*46.6*			*10.2*			*53.2*			*56.1*		

TABLE 10.A1 Factors affecting the acceptance of different types of minority rights, ethno-political claims, and kin-state policy measures among ethnic Romanians (2014) (*cont.*)

		Official language use			Native-language education			Autonomy			Eligibility to be elected			Hungarian citizenship		
		%	OR*	Sig	%	OR*	Sig	%	OR*	Sig	%	OR*	Sig	%	OR*	Sig
Age group	18–34	16.1	1.083	.746	**44.3**	.719	**.064**	13.4	**1.675**	**.061**	**45.9**	.675	.061	**58.1**	**1.384**	**.066**
	35–54	16.2	1.158	.515	45.6	.769	.106	11.9	1.373	.225	54.4	1.373	.225	**57.9**	**1.424**	**.029**
	55+ (ref.)	*14.9*			*49.1*			*9.1*			*52.2*			*46.3*		
Sex	Men	14.8	.861	.410	45.4	.898	.417	11.3	.901	.615	50.3	.897	.600	54.7		
	Women (ref.)	*16.5*			*47.5*			*11.6*			*52.0*			*53.0*		
Educational attainment	Primary, lower secondary	18.7	1.625	.139	48.8	1.018	.939	12.6	1.726	.175	43.5	1.816	.136	**45.9**	**.556**	**.043**
	Vocational	17.9	1.490	.185	52.0	1.347	.174	13.4	1.614	.200	57.9	1.640	.184	58.0	1.204	.401
	Upper secondary	14.0	1.173	.552	42.0			11.6	1.645	.137	49.3	1.695	.115	53.9	.983	.928
	University, college (ref.)	*13.4*			*46.5*			*6.9*			*55.0*			*57.0*		
Income poverty	No	15.3	.890	.620	45.1	1.289	.150	14.9	.948	.835	53.1	.948	.835	55.1	.797	.195
	Yes (ref.)	*17.0*			*51.1*			*10.9*			*44.3*			*49.4*		

Religion	Other	**24.5**	**1.890**	**.048**	63.2	**1.870**	**.014**	**21.6**	**2.246**	**.011**	**70.1**	**2.246**	**.011**	**75.8**	**2.145**	**.002**
	Romanian Orthodox (ref.)	*14.9*			*45.1*			*10.6*			*49.5*			*51.1*		
Personal migratory experience	Does not have	**15.1**	**.633**	**.086**	51.2	.748	.162	10.3	.619	.086	50.9	.631	.098	**51.3**	**.448**	**.000**
	Has (ref.)	*20.5*			*45.9*			*18.6*			*53.1*			*72.2*		
Emigrant household member	No	**15.2**	**.623**	**.075**	47.1	1.022	.930	10.9	.748	.389	50.0	.792	.486	52.2	.724	.210
	Yes (ref.)	*22.2*			*46.5*			*17.4*			*64.4*			*65.2*		
Political/ electoral activity	Passive	**18.9**	**1.608**	**.065**	**52.5**	**1.735**	**.006**	**18.6**	**1.814**	**.018**	49.2	1.065	.847	52.7	1.019	.924
	Likely to vote	16.3	1.100	.703	41	.872	.467	9.6	1.065	.847	44.6	.814	.018	58.8	1.169	.402
	Surely will vote	14.6			46.3			10.2			53.2			53.7		
Political option (2nd round of 2014 presidential elections)	Ponta	13.5	.981	.934	45	1.271	.172	12.2	1.622	.094	48.0	1.622	.094	**47.3**	**.518**	**.020**
	Iohannis	15.4	1.134	.601		1.671	.005	13.5	1.717	.075	**57.6**	**1.921**	**.026**	60.4	1.300	.148
	Passive, without option	18.9			45.6			8.2			49.9			56.5		
Nagelkerke R^2		R 148			R 137			R 134			R 127			R 186		

PART 4

General Issues

CHAPTER 11

The Congress of European Nationalities and the International Protection of Minority Rights, 1925–1938

Ferenc Eiler

Abstract

The Congress of European Nationalities (hereinafter, the Congress) was the only organization in the interwar period that aimed to create an international forum encompassing all organized national minorities in Europe. In the fourteen years of its existence, the Congress continued to see itself as a unified movement despite several national minorities turning their back on it due to internal conflicts. In this study, I first describe the organizational structure of the Congress and analyze its official and public activities. I then discuss the causes of tensions and the complexities of cooperation among the national minorities. I also examine the efforts of Germany and Hungary – the kin-states of the two most active national minority groups in the Congress – to use the institution to serve the interests of the Hungarian-speaking and German-speaking minorities.

1 Events Leading Up to the Formation of the Congress

The peace treaties ending the First World War radically transformed the political map of Central and South-Eastern Europe. The Paris treaties recognizing the new borders more or less satisfied the aspirations for self-determination of nations able to form their own independent states (such as Poland and the Baltic states). They also satisfied, more or less, the claims of those national minorities that were able to join their kin-state as a result. Based on the size and ratio of the national minorities in the successor states, the new political map unquestionably corresponded more closely to the principle of the nation-state than the sprawling empires ruling the territories before the war. Nonetheless, almost every state in the region was home to minority communities of significant sizes.[1] Furthermore, many of these minority communities lived

1 On the sizes of the minority groups, see Wilhelm Winkler, *Statistisches Handbuch der europäischen Nationalitäten* [Statistical Handbook of European Nationalities] (Vienna, Leipzig: Wilhelm Braumüller Verlag, 1931).

 | DOI:10.1163/9789004386426_012

in ethnically homogenous concentrated territories and often directly adjacent to the new borders. This was mainly due to the fact that the great powers approved the holding of referendums, perhaps the most effective and obvious means of enforcing the principle of self-determination, only in exceptional cases before the borders of disputed territories were drawn.

During their preparations for the peace conference, the great powers agreed that, in order to ensure the stability of the region, it would be necessary to find some means of protecting the national minorities of the new states. However, no clear concept of how these protections would actually be ensured in practice was agreed upon before the delegations arrived in Paris.[2] They were perfectly well aware of the fact that the discontent of the new national minorities, which regarded themselves as bound nationally to their kin-states (in particular the German, Hungarian and Bulgarian minorities), could easily destabilize the new states – and with it the new European peace. Therefore, with the intention of strengthening the internal stability of the new states, the great powers decided to develop a system for protecting the rights of national, religious and linguistic minorities under the auspices of the League of Nations (hereinafter, the League).[3] The system of minority protections of the League left the states the power to pass laws positively impacting minority communities, while also establishing and enforcing (more or less) a minimum standard of minority rights protection for the Central and South-Eastern Europe countries through its system of minority guarantees. This was a major step forward in the history of international minority protections.

The German minorities reacted quickly to the changed situation, and in 1922 they founded the Verband der deutschen Minderheiten in Europa (Association of German Minorities in Europe) in Vienna.[4] With the encouragement of the German Ministry of Foreign Affairs, including financial support provided in secret, it created an institutional framework for supranational cooperation. The most important activities of the organization's Berlin office involved lobbying

2 On the ideas and visions for the region of the Entente Powers, see Erwin Viefhaus, *Die Minderheitenfrage und die Entstehung der Minderheitenschutzverträge auf der Pariser Friedenskonferenz 1919* [The Minorities Question and the Emergence of Minority Protection Treaties at the Paris Peace Conference 1919] (Würzburg: Holzner, 1960), 56–74.

3 On the terminological question, see Theodor Veiter, *Das Recht der Volksgruppen und Sprachminderheiten in Österreich* [Rights of Nationalities and Minorities in Austria] (Vienna, Stuttgart: Braumüller, 1970), 44–88.

4 The Verband der deutschen Minderheiten in Europa became the Verband deutscher Volksgruppen in Europa (Association of German Peoples in Europe) in 1928. Both are hereinafter referred to as the Verband.

ministries and civil society organizations interested in minority affairs. Delegates of the German political communities in the various states convened several times a year as committee members to discuss concrete problems and potential solutions. The organization recognized the League as the body that guaranteed international minority protection, and it requested the League to improve the effectiveness of its system of minority guarantees. It expected the individual states to implement laws guaranteeing minority protection and, in the long term, to allow for the establishment of cultural autonomy. The establishment of the system of minority protections of the League and the activities and political and social objectives of the Verband created the direct political background for the formation of the Congress.[5]

In late May 1925, Ewald Ammende, a German journalist from Estonia,[6] who also played a significant role in the creation of the Verband, embarked on a journey across Europe. He set out on his travels in large part to share his notion of international cooperation among minorities with influential representatives of minority groups who could be important from the perspective of an organization that would bring together minorities of the continent. In particular, he wanted to persuade them to take part in a conference that he would organize. He met with leading politicians of the larger national minorities in the Baltic states, Poland, Romania, Yugoslavia, Austria, Italy, Germany, Spain and Hungary.[7]

5 On the Congress of European Nationalities, see Rudolf Michaelsen, *Der Europäische Nationalitäten-Kongreß 1925–1928. Aufbau, Krise und Konsolidierung* [Congress of European Nationalities 1925–1928: Structure, Crisis and Consolidation] (Frankfurt am Main: Verlag Peter Lang, 1984); Sabine Bamberger-Stemmann, *Der Europäische Nationalitätenkongreß 1925 bis 1938. Nationale Minderheiten zwischen Lobbyistentum und Großmachtinteressen* [Congress of European Nationalities from 1925 to 1938: National Minorities between Lobbyists and Great Power Interests] (Marburg: Verlag Herder-Institut, 2000); Ferenc Eiler, *Kisebbségvédelem és Revízió. Magyar törekvések az európai Nemzetiségi Kongresszuson (1925–1939)* [Minority Protection and Revision: Hungarian Aspirations at the Congress of European Nationalities (1925–1939)] (Budapest: Gondolat, 2007); Martyn Housden, "Ewald Ammende and the Organisation of National Minorities in Inter-war Europe," *German History* 18 (2000): 439–460; Martyn Housden, *On Their Own Behalf: Ewald Ammende, Europe's National Minorities and the Campaign for Cultural Autonomy 1920–1936* (Amsterdam: Rodopi, 2014).

6 Ewald Ammende (1892–1936) was a Baltic German journalist and minority politician. He was one of the pivotal leaders in the founding of the Verband. He convened the Congress of European Nationalities, of which he then became the Secretary-General. In the 1930s, he became active in the propaganda war against the Soviet Union. In 1936, in the course of a trip around the world, he had a stroke. He died in Beijing.

7 In May, Ammende began his trip after gaining the approval of Axel de Vries, president of the Baltic German Party in Estonia. Michaelsen, *Der Europäische Nationalitäten-Kongreß*, 71.

The German Ministry of Foreign Affairs firmly rejected the idea, and it did everything in its power to hamper the organization of the first conference.[8] The organizational work in which Ammende was engaged was taking place at the same time as the Locarno conference and the negotiations concerning preparatory measures for Germany's entry into the League. The Ministry of Foreign Affairs feared that the conference might degenerate into an irredentist demonstration, which would have complicated Germany's negotiating position.[9] The reason most often given for the rejection of Ammende's request, however, was that his initiative threatened the domestic political situation of some of the German minorities.[10] Furthermore, Ammende did not have a good reputation within the ministry's bureaucratic circles. According to a 1923 document, although he spoke several languages and was both bold and helpful, Ammende was seen as unsuitable for any leading role within an organization or institution. His most serious flaws were his "unsuitability for proper parliamentary debate", "his lack of self-restraint" and his tendency to indulge in "uninhibited chatter."[11] Ammende nonetheless managed to organize and hold the first conference, the efforts of the Ministry of Foreign Affairs notwithstanding.[12] The German government only began to support the cooperation envisioned by Ammende, which in the meantime had taken on institutional form, in 1928, after having realized that it did not pose a threat to the interests of German minorities or Germany itself.

The fact that Hungarian Prime Minister István Bethlen saw considerable potential in Ammende's idea, in particular its potential advocacy power, played an important role in enabling Ammende to transform his plan into a reality. Bethlen also hoped that the cooperation envisioned by Ammende would promote revisionist-oriented cooperation between the Hungarian and German minorities in the states neighbouring Hungary. (There had not been any such cooperation up to that point, nor would there be later.) On August 18, 1925,

8 Political Archives of the Ministry of Foreign Affairs (PA AA), R 60462, unnumbered, Freytag's report to the German Ministry of Foreign Affairs, Bucharest, September 18, 1925.

9 PA AA, R 60492, unnumbered, Welczeck's report to the German Ministry of Foreign Affairs on his conversation with István Bethlen, Budapest, August 27, 1925.

10 PA AA, R 60462, unnumbered, Gen. Konsul Müller's memo concerning events pertaining to the international minority Congress, September 5, 1925.

11 In 1923, the advisory opinion on Ammende (author unknown) became widely known in the bureaucratic circles of the ministry. The document is presented in detail in Bamberger-Stemmann, *Der Europäische Nationalitätenkongreß*, 74.

12 The only German organization to offer support was the Deutsche Stiftung, which provided 2,000 German marks to defray the costs of the German delegates' travel to Geneva. The Stiftung provided no funding, however, to help cover the costs of the Congress. See Bamberger-Stemmann, *Der Europäische Nationalitätenkongreß*, 149.

Bethlen and Ammende met in person at Bethlen's private estate. Bethlen immediately pledged to have the Hungarian Ministry of Foreign Affairs call the attention of the Hungarian minority parties to the event. He also promised to provide financial support to cover some of the organizational costs of the Congress, which would be held in September in Geneva. He told Ammende that he would provide 5,000 German marks, which would be made available by the Hungarian Ministry of Foreign Affairs.[13]

The first conference, which was held on October 15–16, 1925, was attended by fifty delegates representing twenty-eight minority communities (twelve nationalities in total) from twelve states. Since the response to the conference in the international press was positive, or at the very least neutral, the participants decided to convene again the following year in Geneva. The conference was held every year until 1938, with recognized minority politicians, experts and journalists participating. In 1933, forty-four minority groups representing a total of eighteen nationalities sent representatives to the conference, which was held in Bern that year. These numbers clearly illustrate the appeal of the organization.[14]

In founding the Congress, Ammende had two fundamental goals. He wanted to create an organization that would be able to represent and effectively lobby on behalf of the interests of minorities in the League, the international press and the actual states themselves. He was convinced that sooner or later the League would be compelled to take into consideration the resolutions that were adopted at the conferences, which were held either right before or right after the League's General Assemblies. He also believed that, in time, the League would recognize the organization as an equal negotiating partner. In addition, Ammende wanted to promote the recognition of and support for the idea of autonomy – more precisely the notion of cultural autonomy – which was enjoyed by minorities in Estonia in the 1920s and was remarkably successful.

II Legitimacy, Scope of Action and Organizational Frameworks

The Congress strove to establish its legitimacy by only permitting national minorities that showed a degree of organization and commitment to the

13 National Archives of Hungary (MNL OL) K 64 (documents of the political division of the Ministry of Foreign Affairs) 1925-47-503, 369, Coded telegram sent by the Hungarian Ministry of Foreign Affairs to Emich, Budapest, September 11, 1925.

14 On the national minorities that took part in the work of the Congress see Table A1 in the appendix.

preservation of their national cultures to delegate representatives. They also placed restrictions on the individuals who could participate as representatives of a minority group. One fundamental requirement was that the person lived in the country in question. In other words, mere knowledge of the problems faced by the minority group was not sufficient. The person had to accept responsibility back home for what he or she said at the Congress. In exceptional cases, representatives who did not live in the country in question could participate if the political circumstances in the country made travel to Geneva potentially dangerous or difficult. However, they were only granted consultation rights. In 1929, a resolution was accepted according to which the loss of citizenship for political reasons did not disqualify someone from taking part in the Congress.[15]

In the interests of averting the outbreak of internal or external conflicts that might threaten the very existence of the Congress, the organization always adhered closely to two basic principles: participants were prohibited from raising the idea of redrawing state borders (i.e. territorial revision), and no state-specific assessments of minority situations were made. The first principle was intended to ensure that the Congress would be able to function peacefully within the international order that had emerged after the First World War. The second was intended to protect the unity of the Congress by preventing clashes between representatives of different minorities.

Formally, the most important body of the Congress was the General Assembly, which was convened once a year. The decisions of the General Assembly ensured the legitimacy of all of the other bodies of the Congress. Although representatives of any national minority group were allowed to participate as observers in the sessions of the General Assembly, only representatives of minorities that had been accepted as members of the organization were allowed to vote. The minority groups that the three-member Steering Committee of the first Congress had invited to Geneva in 1925 could remain members in subsequent years. However, tensions concerning the question of the admittance

15 Resolution: *1929/Report of the Organising Committee/7.* (The resolutions can be found in the final pages of the so-called *Sitzungsberichte*, the published reports of the annual conferences.) The real reason for this resolution was that the President of the Congress was facing an increasingly impossible situation in Italy. After an impassioned exchange of words with Mussolini on September 25, 1928, he left Italy for good, settling in Vienna. See Jože Pirjevec, "Die politische Theorie und Tätigkeit Josip Vilfans" [The Political Theory and Activity of Josip Vilfans], in *Die Minderheiten zwischen den beiden Weltkriegen* [Minorities in the Interwar Period], ed. Umberto Corsini and Davide Zaffi (Berlin: Duncker and Humblot, 1997), 172.

of new members made it necessary to establish criteria for their acceptance.[16] Candidates had to demonstrate that they were representatives of organized minority groups and show "signs of enduring collective cultural life." Moreover, a majority of member organizations had to support their participation in the Congress, or at least not oppose it.[17]

The primary task of the General Assembly was to discuss the items on the agenda prepared by the Steering Committee and accept resolutions concerning individual agenda items, which were presented to the public as the position of the European minorities. Reports and supplementary reports were read concerning each agenda item. With regard to the passage or rejection of a resolution, each individual minority group had one vote. The General Assembly also decided on the composition of the Chairmanship of each conference, and it consistently adhered to the system that had been adopted in 1925. Josip Vilfan, the representative of the Slovenian minority in Italy, was chosen as president, and five or six vice-presidents were assigned to serve alongside him, depending on attendance.[18] The issue of the composition of the Chairmanship was a matter of consensus among the groups. Every larger national minority group could delegate one representative, but the Congress also took care to ensure that no minority would feel that it had been left without representation. Alongside the German, Hungarian, Jewish, Ukrainian, Russian and Catalan vice-presidents, Vilfan himself represented the Croatian, Slovenian

16 The problem began at the very first Congress with remarks made by the representatives of the Polish minorities in Germany in support of the acceptance of the Frisians as members. Since the German minority leaders did not consider the Frisians an independent minority, a three-member committee was created in 1926 to decide the question. The members of the committee were Romanian German Rudolf Brandsch, German Pole Jerzy Kaczmarek and Italian Slovene Josip Vilfan. The committee could not reach a consensus. The situation was complicated in part by the fact that the two official organizations of the Frisian minority had opposing views on the matter. Bundesarchiv (BA), Nachlass Vilfan, Josip (N 1250), Fasz. 32, 16–18, Vilfan's memo on the Frisian question, undated (probably from late 1926). Ultimately, in order to gain time, the preparatory Steering Committee for the third Congress decided to postpone the admission of all new applicants until the charter had been approved. In response, the minority groups in Germany resolved as a group to withdraw from the Congress. The German Ministry of Foreign Affairs did not consider it desirable for the Congress to accept the Frisians, and it proposed waiting to provide financial support for the year (1928) until after having learned the final decision of the Steering Committee. PA AA, R 60467, unnumbered, Transcript of communication from the fourth division to the sixth division of the German foreign ministry, undated.

17 Resolution: *1928/Charter Rule/II/2*.

18 The list of names of the members of the Chairmanship and the Steering Committee can be found in the *Sitzungsberichte*. For a list of names including short biographical sketches, see Table A2 in the appendix.

and Czech-Slovak minorities. The Chairmanship was entrusted with the task of ensuring that the proceedings of the Congress went smoothly and without disturbance. It was also responsible for scheduling the plenary sessions and the sessions of the temporary committees (of which there were always three of four) that were assigned the task of preparing the texts of the resolutions concerning individual agenda items. Finally, it was responsible for overseeing the sessions themselves. With the close of the Congress, the Chairmanship ceased to function, with the exception of the activities of Vilfan, who served continuously as president.

Immediately before the close of the conference, the General Assembly entrusted a Steering Committee with the task of addressing the issues that would arise before the Congress met again the following year. Although the Steering Committee was formally independent of the Chairmanship and was a completely separate body in terms of the period of time in which it met and was active, starting from the very first Congress a practice emerged according to which the General Assembly proposed members of the Steering Committee to serve as members of the Chairmanship.[19] The main task of the Steering Committee was to make the necessary preparations for the next Congress. It chose the optimal time and place, drew up an agenda and selected presenters from among the participants. In addition, during the first round of meetings, the Steering Committee made decisions concerning the acceptance or rejection of minority groups that were seeking membership of the Congress. On essential issues, the Steering Committee had to be unanimous in its decisions, while for technical matters a simple majority was sufficient. For the first three years, the Steering Committee met four times a year: once immediately after the conference, once on the day before the next conference and twice in between. Beginning in 1928, one of the meetings was held by the Council, a body that had been created in the meantime.[20] In contrast to the Steering Committee, every minority group had three representatives on the Council. The Council's primary task was to ensure that the individual groups familiarized themselves with questions concerning preparatory measures and that they arrived at decisions on these questions. Minority communities that belonged to the same nationality had a single vote. The Council reached its decisions in a similar manner to the Steering Committee.

The organization also included a few permanent committees. The oldest (which existed for almost the entire history of the Congress) were the

19 Members of the Steering Committee were permitted to send people to the sessions to act in their stead if they had to tend to other obligations. Resolution: *1926/7/I*.

20 Resolution: *1928/Charter Rule/IV/3–5*.

Organizing Committee and the Finance Committee, with the latter functioning continuously alongside the Chairmanship from 1929 onwards. The Organizing Committee was responsible for developing a strategy that would be adopted by the Congress. The Finance Committee's main task was to hold the Secretary-General financially accountable. Over time, other committees were formed, but the available sources provide only fragmentary information concerning their responsibilities, the regularity with which they met and the periods during which they were active. The Nationality Studies Committee was one such body. It was entrusted with the task of investigating the possibility of creating an institute of nationality studies. Examples also include a permanent committee dealing with petitions (formed in 1932) and the so-called Committee of Experts, which was created in 1935, at the suggestion of Elemér Jakabffy,[21] to examine alleged infringements of minority rights.[22] However, without exception, these committees had little power or influence, and they either did no real work or were not active for very long.

At their first conference, the minority group representatives elected Ammende as the secretary responsible for the coordination of the practical tasks related to the sessions. In doing so, they laid the foundation for the office of the Secretary-General. Ammende did the preparatory work for the first two Congresses without being able to rely on any real infrastructure.[23] In April 1927, the Congress opened a permanent office in Vienna, and this made it significantly easier for Ammende to address the tasks that awaited him as Secretary-General. This was true in no small part because one or two paid employees were able to take some of the administrative tasks off his shoulders. Ammende held this position until his death in 1936. His personality, vision, aspirations and connections fundamentally shaped the work and political orientation of the entire

21 Elemér Jakabffy (1881–1963) was a Romanian Hungarian politician, lawyer and editor. He was a corresponding member of the Hungarian Academy of Sciences (1938–1949). In 1922–1938, he served as the vice-president of the National Hungarian Party in Romania. He founded the periodical *Magyar Kisebbség* (Hungarian Minority) and was the only actual editor of the periodical almost until 1942, when it was banned. He was the vice-president of the Society of the Romanian Hungarian Folk League and one of the more prominent members of the Congress of National Minorities.

22 BA N 1250, Fasz. 6, 135, The founding session of the expert committee of the Congress of European Nationalities, May 4, 1935.

23 Until 1927, the Secretary-General's seat was in the Hotel Victoria in Geneva, not just for the duration of the conferences but continuously. Herbert Plesse, *Organisation und Arbeit der Kongresse der organisierten nationalen Gruppen in den Staaten Europas (Inaugural Dissertation zur Erlangung der Doktorwürde)* [Organization and Work of the Congress of European Nationalities (Inaugural Dissertation for Obtaining a Doctoral Degree)] (Leipzig, 1930), 57.

organization. After Ammende's death, Ferdinand von Uexküll-Güldenband, also a German journalist from Estonia, was appointed temporary Secretary-General of the Congress, and his appointment was made permanent in 1938.[24]

Fundamentally, the Secretary-General was responsible for two tasks. During the conferences, he had to address the administrative and technical questions that arose. When the conferences came to an end, he had to help the Steering Committee perform the preparatory work for the next conference. With regard to its fundamental functions, the office of the Secretary-General was a body that had to maintain the ties and the flow of information between the individual member groups, on the one hand, and the Congress itself, on the other. It had to establish and cultivate relationships with the press and with international organizations that dealt with minority issues and also, when possible, with the League. Before sessions of the Steering Committee, it had to determine whether or not minority groups seeking to become members of the Congress met the admission criteria. The office of the Secretary-General published the official periodical of the organization, as well as Congress reports. Financial questions, including income and costs, also fell within the scope of its authority.[25]

The Congress was a very loose organization. Indeed, by its own definition, it was a "Congress community." It is hardly surprising that, in an organization whose members live several hundreds and sometimes several thousands of miles from one another, the influence of the Secretary-General, who holds a full-time position, will grow with time, even if officially he does not have the final say on any question of importance. This was the case with Ammende's Congress. After the 1926 conference, even the German minority leaders no longer called into question Ammende's suitability, and thus his position as Secretary-General was firmly consolidated. He exerted a far greater influence on the organization than one might think based on the powers given to him

24 Before becoming Secretary-General of the Congress, Uexküll-Güldenband was the editor-in-chief of the periodical *Nation und Staat*, which dealt with issues faced by the German-speaking minorities. Before he became part of the editorship of the journal, the German foreign ministry informed itself about him through the embassy in Estonia. According to the report, he was a remarkably talented journalist and editor. PA AA, R 60426, K 435709–K 435710. Since before his departure, Ammende had entrusted him to serve in his stead, and after the Secretary-General's death the 1936 Congress asked him to head the Secretariat temporarily. *Sitzungsbericht des Kongresses der Organisierten Nationalen Gruppen in den Staaten Europas: Genf 1936* [Meeting of the Congress of European Nationalities: Geneva 1936] (hereinafter, *Sitzungsbericht 1936*) (Vienna/Leipzig: Braumüller, 1937), 70.

25 From 1926 until 1930, the title of the publication was *Mitteilungen der Geschäftsführung*. In 1930, it was changed to *Pressewochenschau zur Nationalitätenfrage* and in 1932 to *Europäische Nationalitätenkorrespondenz*.

by the resolutions of the Congress. The primary reason for this is unquestionably related to the nature of the organization itself. However, other factors also contributed to the consolidation of his position and the strengthening of his influence and role.

Ammende was elected Secretary-General simply because the notion of creating a forum for international cooperation among the minorities had been his idea and because the success of the first gathering had indisputably been the result of his dedicated organizational work. His energetic and ambitious personality and his talents as an organizer made him indispensable, as did his background knowledge pertaining to the Congress. Naturally, his interpersonal capital, which was rooted in the relationships he managed to develop over the years, also contributed to the consolidation of his position. Well before 1925, Ammende was known as a journalist who was unusually knowledgeable about minority affairs and not only followed the fate of the German minorities closely but also paid close attention to its international nexus. When he served as Secretary-General, his network of relationships continued to grow, since he not only came into contact with people who worked at international organizations that were important from the perspective of minority affairs (e.g. the International Federation of League of Nations Societies and the Inter-Parliamentary Union) but also met with influential politicians in the course of his travels.[26] In addition, he maintained continuous ties with influential constituents of the minority groups connected to the Congress, both through correspondence and sometimes via personal visits.[27] This gave him a kind of monopoly on information that further strengthened his position. His good working relationship with Vilfan, the President of the Congress and head of the Steering Committee (who

26 Ammende did not only have ties to staff members at the German Ministry of Foreign Affairs. He also met with influential politicians, including Hungarian Prime Minister István Bethlen, Romanian Prime Minister Iuliu Maniu, various members of the government of Yugoslavia and even Scandinavian politicians in the course of his travels in northern Europe.

27 He wrote a detailed, two-part report of his travels that also testifies to this. The most important stops in the course of his travels between July 1 and July 14, 1930 were Berlin, Sombor/Zombor, Novi Sad/Újvidék, Belgrade, Vršac/Versek, Timișoara/Temesvár, Oradea/Nagyvárad, Sibiu, Bucharest, Silistra, Varna, Sofia, Belgrade, Budapest and Vienna. He began the second part of his trip on July 19 and ended it on August 4. He stopped in Berlin, Tilsit (now Sovetsk), Kowno (now Kaunas), Riga, Pärnu, Reval (now Tallinn), Riga, Vilnius, Warsaw, Vienna and Gottschee (now Kočevsko). Both the Hungarian and the German foreign ministries received the report. PA AA, R 60528, unnumbered, Ammende: Bericht über meine Reise nach Ungarn, Rumänien, Jugoslavien und Bulgarien vom 1. bis 14. Juli 1930 (II. Teil: Ostpreussen, Litauen, Estland, Polen und die Gottschee) [Ammende: Report on my trip to Hungary, Romania, Yugoslavia and Bulgaria from 1 to 14 July 1930 (Part II: East Prussia, Lithuania, Estonia, Poland and Gottschee)].

moved to Vienna in 1928), facilitated cooperation between the two bodies of the Congress. This was particularly important for the Secretary-General, since any conflict with Vilfan would have weakened his position. For Ammende, the good relationship with the President was important for another reason as well. In the Chairmanship and on the Steering Committee, Vilfan represented the Croatian, Slovenian and Czech-Slovak minorities and sought to maintain good ties with the Slavic groups remaining in the Congress after 1927. Furthermore, Vilfan ensured that the Congress enjoyed the support (including financial support) of the leaders of the Yugoslav foreign ministry.[28] Ammende's position, however, was strengthened most by the moral backing and secret financial support he was given by the German and Hungarian foreign ministries.

Following Ammende's death, his successor, Uexküll-Güldenband, did not play nearly as dominant a role in the life of the organization. Uexküll-Güldenband's contributions were essentially limited to the principles expressed in the resolutions of the Congress. The primary reason for this was simply that, beginning in 1933, serious changes took place in German "ethnic politics," and attempts were made to establish central control over civil society organizations in Germany.[29] As a consequence of these centralization efforts, the position of the head of the Berlin office of the Verband became significantly stronger.[30]

28 The available sources contain no concrete data concerning the amount of financial support provided to the Congress, nor does Vilfan's bequest contain any references to it. However, the files of the Ministry of Foreign Affairs in Belgrade may offer an answer to this question.

29 On the centralization of ethnic politics, see Hans-Adolf Jacobsen, *Nationalsozialistische Außenpolitik 1933–1938* [National Socialist Foreign Policy 1933–1938] (Frankfurt am Main/ Berlin: A. Metzner, 1968).

30 Carl Georg Bruns, the previous head of the office, died in February 1931. Even before his death, the question of his successor had already led to a rift between the Germany-focused organizations that dealt with providing support for minorities and the leaders of the German minorities. There were people (for instance Paul Schiemann) who sought at all costs to avoid doing anything that would strengthen the position of the Schutzbund and its leader, Christian von Loesch, while others (Hans Otto Roth) supported von Loesch. Hasselblatt, in any event, was considered someone with close ties to the Schutzbund. The debate between Ammende and Schiemann became acrimonious. Ammende sought to put a confrontational leader at the head of the office who had himself lived as a member of a minority community. Schiemann preferred a sober, judicious, impartial expert, as Bruns had been. In the end, the debate was decided in favour of Hasselblatt. Because of his stance on this question, the principles to which he had alluded (on occasion quite publically) in his opposition to the concentration on minority politics and his theory of the a-national state (which was unpopular both in the Ministry of Foreign Affairs and among most of the minority leaders), Schiemann, who at one time had been an influential politician with a profound belief in bourgeois democracy, rapidly lost favour in Berlin following the rise to power of the national socialists. For more on the

Thus, Werner Hasselblatt,[31] the head of the office of the Verband, not only began to supervise the international activities of the German minorities but also took over a significant share of the behind-the-scenes organizational and negotiating work of the previous Secretary-General.[32]

III The Public Face of the Congress on the Basis of Its Resolutions

During the fourteen years of its existence, the Congress passed a total of sixty-three resolutions. Eight of these resolutions dealt with organizational issues, while the other fifty-five specified the position of the member groups on issues that were of importance to the minorities. There were questions on which the organization managed to pass only a single resolution, but there were also many to which the Congress often returned or which continuously remained on the agenda (as was often the case at the League of Nations).

It could be foreseen from a note that Ammende committed to paper in the spring of 1925 that the organization would devote particular attention to the international protection of minority rights guaranteed in principle by the League. This was indeed the case. At eleven Congresses, resolutions were passed that focused very specifically on the work and activities of the League.[33] The first two conferences gave a clear vote of confidence to the international organization as "the most important forum for the resolution of conflicts between peoples and preserving peace in the world."[34] After this, however, assessments of the work and effectiveness of the League became more critical and, in some cases, even harsh.

The point of departure for this criticism was the realization that the League was unable to compel the governments of its member states to comply with the obligations stipulated in the treaties. In general, in its critical assessments, which were framed in the context of European peace, the Congress

fight for control of the office following Bruns's death, see Bamberger-Stemmann, *Der Europäische Nationalitätenkongreß*, 181–197.

31 Werner Hasselblatt (1890–1958) was a German Estonian minority politician. In 1923–1932, he was the head of the Baltic-German and German-Swedish parliamentary caucus. He played a key role in the framing of the law guaranteeing minorities cultural autonomy and in the successful efforts to get it passed. In 1931, he became a legal advisor to the Verband and the director of its Berlin office.

32 As is clear from the materials in Vilfan's bequest, Hasselblatt was given a very important role in shaping the life of the organization.

33 Resolutions: *1925/3; 1926/6; 1927/1, 2; 1928/1; 1929/1; 1931/1; 1932/1, 3; 1933/4; 1934/4, 6, 7; 1936/2; 1937/1*.

34 Resolution: *1926/6*.

concentrated on the question of enforcement of minority guarantees and only rarely gave voice to expectations that went beyond the obligations specified in the minority treaties.

With regard to the mechanisms and procedures of the League's system of minority guarantees, the second Congress raised the objection that the League Council was in practice the first and last forum for debates concerning infringements of minority rights. It also objected to the fact that the activities of the League were not public and transparent and that a minority that approached the League with a complaint was not recognized as a party to the discussions and was not even given the chance to respond to the answers given by the relevant government. The essential principles of these objections did not change over time; indeed, in 1932, the Congress openly questioned the objectivity of the League Council.[35] It criticized the failings of the League's bodies participating in the minority guarantees system one by one, objecting first and foremost to the lack of familiarity of the Secretariat and the Committee of Three with minority affairs and their bias in favour of the governments against which the complaints were brought.[36]

A recurrent theme of the resolutions concerning the League was the clarification of the attitude towards the recommendation of the third General Assembly of September 21, 1922.[37] This recommendation called on the member states to demonstrate the same degree of patience and commitment to justice in their dealings with their minorities as the minority treaties required of their signatories. From the perspective of its purpose, the recommendation was little more than a gesture for the sake of appearances. It avoided the question of general international protection and entailed no sanctions of any kind. The Congress, however, could not avoid appealing to it, since there were minority groups among its members (e.g. the Catalans and the Slovenians of Italy) that lived in states that were not actually bound by any obligations to implement

35 Resolutions: *1932/3, 7*.

36 The petitions were sent to the Secretariat. If they met the necessary criteria regarding form and content, the Secretary-General forwarded them to the Council. If a member of the Council wanted to take action on the basis of a petition, he or she had to call the attention of the other members of the Council to the infringement of rights that had been committed or to the fact that an infringement of rights was imminent. Although the Council was the body responsible for discussing such alleged infringements, in time it became common practice for the members of the Committee of Three that was formed to examine the given case to deal with a given complaint. Christoph Gütermann offers an analysis of the structure, development and functioning of the Secretariat in *Das Minderheitenschutzverfahren des Völkerbundes* [The Minority Protection Procedure of the League of Nations] (Berlin: Duncker and Humblot, 1979) 273–287.

37 Resolutions: *1925/3; 1926/6; 1927/2; 1938/1; 1934/6*.

minority rights. Naturally, the frequent references to the 1922 recommendation were an expression of the desire and aspiration to secure genuine international recognition and protection of minority rights. In 1932 and 1934, the Congress took a concrete stance on this question.[38]

In addition to passing resolutions on the procedures of the League relating to the implementation of minority guarantees, the Congress also took positions on questions concerning the League that clearly pertained to international politics. The first such instance was a resolution passed in 1928, in which the Congress expressed its doubts concerning the suitability of Spain's Aguirre de Carcer as a candidate for the position of director of the Minorities Section of the League Secretariat.[39] The second instance was a letter written to Aristide Briand, the Prime Minister of France, in which the Congress essentially expressed its opposition to France's vision for Europe, the Briand Plan.[40] The third was a resolution passed in 1934 in which the Congress called on the League to accept among its members only states whose minority policies left little or no room for complaint. Though the resolution made no mention of any specific states, it was quite clear to everyone involved that the Congress was taking a position against the admission of the Soviet Union to the League.[41]

Ammende clearly wanted to get the Secretariat of the League of Nations to recognize the Congress as an authentic organization that faithfully represented the views of the minorities of Europe. Before the first conference in Geneva, however, the Minorities Section of the Secretariat adopted an unambiguously

38 In the 1934 resolution, the Congress responded to the steps taken by the Polish government, which had suspended all cooperation with the League of Nations on this question until the minority rights treaties had been accepted as general standards of minority protection. In addition to this measure taken by the Polish government, the states of the Little Entente also strove, in the debates that took place within the League, to link the reform of the procedure by which minority rights were guaranteed to the question of making the minority rights treaties generally valid. In its resolution, the Congress supported the general standards created by the treaties, but it considered it crucial not to allow the politicization of this question to weaken the existing commitments.

39 Resolution: *1928/1*.

40 Resolution: *1930/2*. The 1929 version of the Briand Plan for Europe focused very clearly on European economic integration as a means of countering emerging US dominance. However, in the version that was submitted to the League of Nations in 1930, the focus had shifted from economic issues to questions of politics and security. This was undoubtedly influenced in part by the fact that the French foreign ministry had realized in the meantime that the creation of a strong, unified single market would also mean a stronger German economy. Emma Kövics, *Az európai egység kérdése és Németország 1919–1933* [The Question of European Unity and Germany 1919–1933] (Budapest: Akadémiai Kiadó, 1992), 152.

41 Resolution: *1934/7*.

dismissive stance towards the Congress. Erik Colban, the director of the Minorities Section, did not attend the first session, although he had been invited, and he also forbade his colleagues from receiving the participants of the conference as a delegation.[42] In spite of this, Pablo Azcárate, one of the staff members of the section, followed the events closely, though not in an official capacity.[43] The stance of the Minorities Section later changed slightly, as reflected in the fact that on several occasions the director paid a courtesy visit to the sessions of the Congress and that each conference was attended by one staff member of the section. The neutral but curious attitude of the Secretariat towards the Congress became particularly evident in the first half of the 1930s, when the name of Danish staff member Ludvig Krabbe, who regularly attended the conferences, was included in the published minutes.[44] In 1931 and 1934, the chairman of the League Council even met with a delegation of the Congress.[45] These meetings, however, were little more than polite gestures. The organization never managed to attain recognition as a potential partner in Geneva.

From the perspective of their contents, the resolutions of the Congress concerning organizations that dealt with minority rights protection were also tied to the resolutions concerning the League.[46] They did not go any further than the expressions of acknowledgment addressed to the International Federation of League of Nations Societies and the Inter-Parliamentary Union and the declaration affirming the need to cooperate with them. Given the nature of Ammende's efforts, it is hardly surprising that the Secretary-General and the Steering Committee wished to deepen cooperation between the organizations. A significant number of Congress delegates were also members of one of the two organizations (mostly of the International Federation of League of

42 PA AA, R 96559, K 431876, Aschmann's report to the German Ministry of Foreign Affairs, Geneva, October 22, 1925. Erik Colban (1876–1956) was a Norwegian diplomat. In 1919, he became a member of the staff in the Secretariat of the League of Nations. In 1919–1927, he served as the director for the "Administrative Affairs (Saar, Danzig) and Minorities Section." In 1928–1930, he headed the Commission for Reduction of Armaments.

43 Ibid. Pablo de Azcárate y Flórez (1890–1971) completed his university studies and then taught administrative law at universities in Spain. In 1915–1922, he was a parliamentary representative. In 1922, he became a member of the staff in the Secretariat of the League of Nations and a colleague in the minority section. He was Erik Colban's right hand. In 1931, he became the head of the section. In 1933–1936, he served as the deputy Secretary-General of the League.

44 On Krabbe's report see *Sitzungsbericht 1932; 1933; 1934*, Introduction and presidential opening speeches. In 1936, Peter Schou, the Danish president of the minorities section of the Secretariat also took part in the conference. See *Sitzungsbericht 1936*, Introduction.

45 *Sitzungsbericht 1931; 1934*, Introductions.

46 Resolutions: *1925/4; 1928/3; 1929/3; 1934/5*.

Nations Societies). Ammende was particularly active in his attempts to further cooperation among the organizations during the discussion of potential reforms to the enforcement procedures for minority guarantees, when he lobbied for resolutions that would lead to substantial reforms.[47] Both Ammende and Vilfan corresponded with leading figures in both organizations, and on several occasions these influential personalities were guests or even presenters at the conferences.[48]

Some of the resolutions of the Congress concerning the League of Nations called attention to the failure to implement treaty obligations. Some of them made note of the general deterioration of the situation, but others closely examined issues that were of key importance from the perspective of minority rights, including citizenship, the right to vote, the use of minority languages and religious and economic equality.[49] Since the Congress could not make any single state the subject of its critical assessments, its resolutions offered only summaries of general tendencies. In certain cases, however, it formulated claims that went beyond the minority rights recognized in the treaties. A resolution concerning the right to vote and a resolution on the question of language are perhaps the best examples of these normative claims. In the first resolution, the Congress called for the proportional representation of minorities in legislative bodies and bodies of local government. In the second, it proposed the recognition of the minority language as the official language instead

47 He was able to build, first and foremost, on the International Federation of League of Nations Societies (hereinafter, the Federation), which in comparison to the other organizations was more actively involved in the minority question. At the general assembly of the Federation that was held in The Hague on July 2–7, 1928, the suggestion was made that the League form a permanent committee whose authority would extend to the minority problem in its entirety, much as was later suggested by the Congress (in Resolution: *1929/2*). At the subsequent general assembly, which was held in 1929 in Madrid, the Federation called on the League to create a committee of experts (a so-called "Studienkommission") to study the minority problem in Europe. László Buza, *A kisebbségek jogi helyzete* [The Legal Situation of Minorities] (Budapest: Magyar Tudományos Akadémia, 1930), 390.

48 For the Congress, the support of the following individuals was most important: Théodore Ruyssen (Secretary-General of the Federation), Willoughby Dickinson (president of the permanent minority committee of the Federation), Christina Bakker van Bosse (member of the permanent minority committee of the Federation) and Leopold Boissier (Secretary-General of the Inter-Parliamentary Union). On their participation, presentations and telegrams of congratulations, see Vilfan's opening speeches in the Congress's annual reports.

49 Resolutions: *1926/2–5; 1932/2; 1933/2; 1935/3*.

of the majority language of the state in the case of minorities living in homogenous blocks.[50]

On several occasions, the Congress suggested an academic study of the circumstances of the minorities. In 1928 and 1929, for instance, it passed two resolutions on the necessity of the publication of a handbook of statistics on national minorities.[51] It also made efforts to establish an institute of nationality studies.[52] In 1931, a handbook was published by Wilhelm Winkler, a professor at the University of Vienna, although it was essentially independent of the work of the Congress. The envisioned institute never made it beyond the planning stages, but in 1931 the Congress did manage to publish a book compiled by the minorities entitled *Nationalities in European States: A Collection of Reports on Their Situation.*[53]

The Congress regarded the idea of cultural autonomy as the most suitable means to address relations between minority and majority populations, and in its resolutions it often made reference to the question of various concepts of autonomy.[54] However, since it immediately became clear at the first conference that some of the groups present did not support such claims, the Congress made its expectations of the states more precise in 1926. In the interests of maintaining unity within the organization, it emphasized that cultural self-determination through self-government could only be implemented with the support of the affected minorities. Once minorities from Germany left the Congress because they suspected that Germany was behind the organization and they did not agree with the idea that they themselves, as communities with only limited financial resources, should have to establish and maintain the necessary institutional frameworks for culturally autonomy, the resolutions dealing with the question no longer stirred up discord.

The dual loyalties that were expected from the national minorities inevitably compelled the Congress to address the question of the relationship between the national minorities and their so-called kin-states. A resolution passed in 1928 entitled "The Cultural Relationships among Co-National Groups and between these Groups, the Nation as a Whole, and the Kin-State," which was addressed to the states, emphasized the essentially natural character of

50 Resolution: *1926/4–5.*

51 Resolutions: *1928/4; 1929/4.*

52 Resolutions: *1929/4; 1932/4.*

53 Ewald Ammede, ed., *Die Nationalitäten in den Staaten Europas. Sammlung von Lageberichten* [Nationalities in European States: A Collection of Reports on Their Situation] (Vienna: Wilhelm Braumüller Verlag, 1931).

54 Resolutions: *1925/2; 1926/1; 1931/2; 1933/3.*

these ties.[55] It provided the basis for one of the most prominent issues of the first half of the 1930s, namely the question related to conceptions of nationhood. Naturally, the inclusion of the concept of transborder nations was closely intertwined with the fact that the belief in the primacy of cultural community (which at the time did not yet mean racial community) was gaining ground among German minority organizations and minority rights theorists.[56] On several occasions, the Congress emphatically insisted on a strictly cultural understanding of the notion of national community, and it also identified the limits of this concept. Membership in a national community could never undermine the loyalty of citizens to their host-state, nor could it be used in the service of the interests of other states. The Congress passed several resolutions touching on this subject.[57] When the agenda for the 1935 Congress was being drawn up, however, Hasselblatt objected to the inclusion (again) of this question for several reasons. He was certain that the states affected never thought for a moment that the activities of a national community were restricted simply to cultural affairs. Furthermore, he feared that, if the Congress were to raise the question, it would draw attention to the fact that the issue was being pushed primarily by the German minorities.[58]

The espousal by the Congress of the notion of the national community was itself arguably a sign of the growing strength and influence within the organization of the German minorities and, through them, the German government. The ability of the Germans to use the organization to further their interests had significantly influenced the workings of the Congress before, but from 1933 onwards resolutions were passed that made this influence evident, even to an outside observer. The decision of the Jewish group to leave the Congress in 1933 and the stance adopted by the Congress in 1935 with respect to authoritarian systems were clear signs that this tendency was growing in strength.

Cooperation between the German and Jewish minority groups within the Congress had in fact been essentially problem free until the early 1930s, and

55 Resolution: *1928/2*.

56 Paul Schiemann discerned this increasingly strong tendency and took a stand against it at the 1932 conference of the Verband: "We cannot elevate service of racial 'völkisch' character above ethical laws unless we wish to do away completely with the significance of ethical laws. Nor can we place service of ethnic character a priori above the relations that grow out of other communities. It is as wrong to ask about the order of rank of the relations among various human communities as it was of the Pharisee to ask the question he put to which Jesus replied, 'Render therefore unto Caesar the things which are Caesar's; and unto God the things that are God's.'" Paul Schiemann, "Die neue nationalistische Welle" [The New Nationalist Wave], *Nation und Staat* 6 (1931–1932): 802.

57 Resolutions: *1931/5; 1934/3; 1935/4*.

58 BA N 1250, Fasz. 6, 125, Hasselblatt's letter to Ammende, Berlin, April 15, 1935.

the Jewish minority groups always sent highly respected and well-prepared individuals to represent them at the sessions.[59] Indeed, cooperation between the delegates representing the two groups was so close that they were able to put up sufficient resistance to the efforts of the Hungarian representatives seeking to promote more confrontational advocacy strategies.[60] In 1932, however, the Jewish leaders lost faith in the organization, especially in its Secretary-General and German members. In October 1932, an article was published in *Nation und Staat* which in their assessment constituted an unambiguously anti-Semitic outburst.[61] Leo Motzkin, the Jewish member of the Steering Committee of the Congress, immediately lodged a protest with Ammende and demanded that the German minority leaders denounce the article.[62]

At the session of the Steering Committee in Vienna on April 1, it became clear that the Jewish group would not simply allow the Congress to sweep the problem under the rug.[63] The situation was clear: the Jewish leaders sought to pressure the Congress to adopt a position condemning the events taking place in Germany, which would have put the representatives of the German minority groups in a very awkward position for several reasons. First, they depended on Germany's financial support. Had they taken any steps to condemn Germany, they would have faced serious financial consequences.[64] Second, most

59 "Particularly close cooperation developed between the German and Jewish groups. Dr Motzkin, the representative of the Jews on the Chairmanship, was remarkably loyal even in the preparatory stage of the Congress. During the Congress, alongside Motzkin, it was first and foremost Robinson (Lithuania) who worked in close cooperation with the Germans, contributing decisively to the resolution of the question of autonomy in favour of German interests." PA AA, R 60464, unnumbered, Junghann's report on the second Congress of National Minorities, Geneva, October 25–27, 1926.

60 National Széchényi Library, Manuscript Collection, bequest of Géza Szüllő (Fond X), X/27, 5. Szüllő's report to the foreign ministry on the Berlin session of the International Federation of League of Nations Societies (1928), undated.

61 Norbert Gürke, "Der Nationalsozialismus, das Grenz- und Auslanddeutschtum und das Nationalitätenrecht" [National Socialism, Border and Foreign German Nationality and Nationality Law], *Nation und Staat* 6 (1931–1932): 7–30.

62 BA N 1250, Fasz. 32, 490, Motzkin's letter to Ammende, Paris, November 16, 1932.

63 Szüllő and Jakabffy suggested that the conference not be held that year, but the German and Jewish members of the Steering Committee did not agree. Emil Margulies emphasized that he did not wish to overwhelm the new German regime with an inundation of complaints, but the Congress definitely had to discuss the question. BA N 1250, Fasz. 5, 1114–1115, Protocol, The April 1 (Saturday) 1933 session of the Steering Committee in Vienna.

64 A letter written by Ammende to Vilfan at the end of June also clearly illustrates the difficult position of the German minorities. Ammende informed Vilfan that he was travelling to Berlin in order to meet with Goebbels and intervene on behalf of the Jews of Germany. His argument sheds light on the assessment of the situation given by the German

of the leaders of the German minorities hoped that the new regime would strengthen Germany's international position, which in turn would lead to improvements in the circumstances of the German minorities.[65] At the July 2–3 session of the Steering Committee, an agreement was reached to discuss the issue, which would be included as an agenda item with the title "Dissimilation and Nationality Rights." An agreement was even reached concerning the manner in which the question would be discussed.[66] According to this agreement, both the German representatives and the Jewish representatives would make a clear declaration, while the other minority groups would not participate in the debate. Paul Schiemann composed the text of the declaration on behalf of the German representatives, and Emil Margulies composed the text of the declaration for the Jewish representatives.[67] They both emphasized the struggle of the group in question against assimilation, and neither questioned the right of any group to decide who belongs among its members. Schiemann insisted that

minority politicians and their perception of the circumstances. He sought to call the attention of the German minister of propaganda to the fact that the measures that had been taken against the Jews in Germany seriously endangered the foreign policy interests of the Reich and the interests of the German minorities. He continued: "Or Mr Motzkin, do you believe that I, or any other person from the German circles, would still have a chance to intervene directly in Berlin, if we let ourselves … to be pressured to make open declarations on the Jewish Question?" BA N 1250, Fasz. 5, 1124, Ammende's letter to Vilfan, Vienna, June 21, 1933.

65 In his aforementioned critical speech, Schiemann offered the following characterization of the relationship between national socialism and the German minorities: "In national socialism, however, the concept of the state is so closely interlinked with the concept of the *Volk* [people] that for it [national socialism] the preservation of the German people outside of the country only seems possible through their incorporation into the territory of the German state, or at least through the direct intervention of the will of the state power." Schiemann, "Die neue nationalistische Welle," 804.

66 BA N 1250, Fasz. 5, 1129–1132, Vilfan: Notes on the 2–3 July 1933 report of the Steering Committee and the Council.

67 Paul Schiemann (1876–1944) was a Latvian German minority politician and journalist. In 1919–1933, he was the editor-in-chief of *Rigasche Rundschau*. In 1920–1933, he was the head of the German caucus of the Latvian parliament. He was one of the founders of the Verband, as well as a member of the Chairmanship. Until 1933, he served as one of the editors of the Verband's periodical, *Nation und Staat*. He was also one of the creators of the Congress of National Minorities and a member of the presidium. He was an implacable opponent of national socialism from the outset. In 1937, he founded the Deutscher Verband zur Nationalen Befriedigung Europas, together with Eduard Pant. Emil Margulies (1877–1943) was a Czechoslovak Jewish politician and lawyer. He organized most of the Zionist societies in the German-speaking territories of Czechoslovakia. In 1924, he founded the Czechoslovak Jewish League of Nations Society. In 1927, he was one of the founders of the Jewish Party, and he served as its president in 1931–1935. He was also a member of the Czechoslovak Jewish National Council. In 1939, he moved to Palestine.

"one must not make the rights of the citizens of a state dependent on membership in a religious or national community."[68] Margulies, for his part, considered it perfectly natural that Zionist politicians could not remain indifferent to the fate of Jews who chose assimilation, and without mentioning Germany by name he condemned the continuous humiliation of some 550,000 Jews and the deprivation by the state of their rights as citizens.[69]

The Jewish representatives from Poland, Romania, Czechoslovakia, Bulgaria and Latvia again discussed the question at the Second Preparatory World Jewish Conference, which was held at the beginning of September in Geneva. Taking a stance that contradicted the earlier agreement, they decided to send representatives to Bern only if the Congress were to accept a resolution clearly condemning the acts of the German government depriving its Jewish citizens of their rights. They also demanded a free, open discussion of the issue, with no restrictions.[70] The Steering Committee unanimously rejected this demand, justifying its decision with reference to the rules of its charter. In response, the Jewish delegates did not attend the session on September 16. In his opening speech, Vilfan made very cautious reference to the situation and specifically announced that "Dissimilation and Nationality Rights," which was one of the items on the agenda, would not be discussed as part of the session. (Schiemann was not present on account of illness.) Hans Otto Roth, a Romanian German politician, unexpectedly read aloud a declaration in the name of the German group that aggravated the situation even further. According to Roth,

> this kind of exclusion of other people, in particular people who belong to another race/ethnic group, from the culture of the Volk,[71] as one could observe in recent times, we consider fundamentally justified ... we vigorously state that we will stand up again in the future in firm defence of the fundamental principles of our Congress, principles to which we have already shown our commitment on many occasions.[72]

68 BA N 1250, Fasz. 32, 583, Paul Schiemann: Dissimilation und Minderheitenrecht [Paul Schiemann: Dissimilation and Minority Rights].

69 BA N 1250, Fasz. 32, 578–580, Emil Margulies: Vorschläge zum Inhalt der jüdischen Ausführungen zum Programmpunkt: "Dissimilation und Nationalitätenrechte" [Emil Margulies: Proposals on the Content of the Jewish Statements on the Agenda Item: "Dissimilation and Nationality Rights"]. Margulies emphasized that the plan reflected his personal stance and that it also had to be accepted by the Jewish group.

70 BA N 1250, Fasz. 32, 494–495, Motzkin's letter to Vilfan, Geneva, September 8, 1933.

71 Roth used the word "Volk," which over the course of the second half of the nineteenth century and the first half of the twentieth century was increasingly used in a racial sense, in particular in the discourse of German conservative and right-wing politics.

72 For Roth's speech, which he made before the gathering began to address the items on its agenda for the meeting, see *Sitzungsbericht 1933*, 26.

This proclamation, for which – at least according to the available sources – Roth had neither sought nor been given any preliminary approval by the Congress, added oil to the fire. On the afternoon of September 18, the President of the Congress read the response of the Jewish group, stating that the group considered further cooperation impossible.[73] Roth spoke again, announcing that, while he recognized the very painful nature of the process of dissimilation, the Congress had to remain faithful to its charter and could not take any position concerning concrete events. He again added that they could not violate the spirit of the resolutions of the Congress.[74] The mood was already tense, but then the situation exploded: the Ukrainian, Lithuanian, Catalan and Hungarian groups refused to accept the text of the resolution as it was.[75] They were only prepared to accept it with the following addition: "We consider the wave of particularly anti-Semitic measures that have recently been observed in some states, violations of general human rights and irreconcilable with the principles of our Congress."[76]

A resolution entitled "National Minorities in the Authoritarian State," which was passed in 1935, was another clear indication of the increase in German influence. In this resolution, the Congress declared that it did not identify itself with any particular political system and that it was prepared, in the interests of addressing questions of minority rights, to work together with any state. It nonetheless expected authoritarian states to respect minority rights.[77] There was clearly no question concerning the immediate relevance of the issue, since by the middle of the 1930s authoritarian regimes or even dictatorships had replaced parliamentary democracies in many European states. The position of the speakers at the session was founded on the (perfectly accurate) contention that no single political system was in and of itself a clear guarantee of respect for minority rights. The final conclusion was that in any given case it might well be possible to expect improvements in the circumstances of a minority living in an authoritarian state. The primary problem with these statements and the comments added in response was not that they implied that minorities always had to seek to assert their interests in cooperation with the prevailing system at any given time, but rather that they seemed to deliberately blur the

73 BA N 1250, Fasz. 5, 1223–1224, Letter of Motzkin, Rosmarin, Margulies and Farchy to the President of the Congress, Bern, September 17, 1933.

74 *Sitzungsbericht 1933*, 69–70.

75 "The Congress has determined that, in the case of the introduction and implementation of national dissimilation, all of the freedoms and rights must remain untouched, in support of which the Congress of European Nationalities has taken a stance in its declarations and resolutions since its founding." Resolution: *1933/1*.

76 *Sitzungsbericht 1933*, 70.

77 Resolution: *1935/2*.

fundamental difference between democratic systems and dictatorships and ignored the examination of tendencies involving human rights violations. Dénes Strelitzky, a Hungarian politician from Yugoslavia, was the only person who was willing to go beyond this terminological framework.[78] In his assessment, the rights of minorities were under far greater threat in authoritarian systems, since, as he himself had experienced, authoritarian regimes were disrespectful of and hostile to not only the right to political representation but also freedom of the press, freedom of association and the right to use one's mother tongue. It was telling, at the very least, that not a single German delegate offered a response to the question.

In summary, 1933 was a pivotal moment in the evolution of the Congress – both politically and, arguably, ethically – but not in its efforts to catalogue the challenges faced by minorities. Of the various questions it raised, "only" the two above-mentioned issues were particularly politically sensitive because of the growing strength of national socialism. The organization continued to deal with the primary questions of the relationship between states and minorities (e.g. language use, education, culture, churches, religious life, etc.) on a theoretical level, as it had before.

IV The Complexities of Cooperation

1 *Financing*

After the 1925 General Assembly had reached agreement in support of holding the conference again the following year, the preliminary meeting of the Steering Committee was charged with the task of establishing the specific amounts that the individual groups would pay in order to provide the necessary funds.[79] The German, Jewish and Hungarian groups were asked to pay 2,000 Swiss francs each, while the Poles and the other minorities in Germany were expected to pay a total of 2,200 Swiss francs, in two instalments. The Slovenian and Croatian groups were asked to pay 750 Swiss francs. These amounts changed several times over the following years, as did their proportions to one another. In 1928, the system of finances reached its final form (at least from this perspective):[80]

78 For Strelitzky's supplementary paper, see *Sitzungsbericht 1935*, 38–41.

79 BA N 1250, Fasz. 2, unnumbered, Excerpt from the report on the 1926 preparatory Steering Committee session of the organized national groups, Dresden, April 6–7, 1926.

80 At the time, a Hungarian ambassador to Paris, Berlin or Rome was paid a salary of roughly 4,000 Swiss francs. See Pál Pritz, *Magyar diplomácia a két világháború között* [Hungarian Diplomacy in the Interwar Period] (Budapest: Magyar Történelmi Társulat, 1995), 59. In the years in which Ammende brought a total of 18,000 Swiss francs from Budapest

the German group would pay a total of 12,000 Swiss francs per year in four annual instalments, the Hungarian group would pay 8,000, the Jewish group would pay 7,000, and the Catalan group and Slovenian group (which included the Croatians) would pay 5,000 each.[81]

Immediately after the first Congress, the Steering Committee set the salary of the Secretary-General at 1,000 Swiss francs per month. This sum, which included the salaries of the assistants who worked in the office of the Secretary-General, did not change.[82] Officially, Ammende was obliged to use whatever was left of this money, once it had been used to pay salaries, to cover the costs of office space, office supplies, postage, official travel, Congress publications and conference-related expenses.[83] In principle, the Secretary-General's salary provided a respectable living, but it was by no means enough to live sumptuously. Ammende, who travelled a lot, enjoyed the pleasures of life and supported both his mother and a sibling living in Estonia, would quite clearly never have been able to support this lifestyle without the additional monies he was sent once a year by Berlin and Budapest.[84]

The member groups of the Congress were often late in making their payments, which hampered administrative affairs and also placed a strain on Ammende's finances. The situation was made even direr by the withdrawal of some groups and the announcement by others that they were unable to pay their dues. Indeed, financial issues threw the future of the organization into question.[85] The first blow came in 1927, when all of the minorities from Germany were joined by the Polish minorities in their decision to withdraw from the Congress. Next, following the 1929 conference, the Jewish minorities informed Vilfan and Ammende that they were no longer able to meet the

(including extraordinary subventions) in order to defray the costs of organizational operations, the Hungarian contribution was roughly 1/200 of the financial support provided in secret by Budapest for the Hungarian minorities (which in 1928–1929 amounted to 3.6 million Swiss francs). On the support provided for the Hungarian minorities, see Nándor Bárdi, "A Keleti Akció II" [An Eastern Action II], *Regio* 6 (1995): 121.

81 PA AA, R 60528, L 497565, Ammende's letter to Graebe, Vienna, March 14, 1931.

82 PA AA, R 60528, L 497561, Ammende's letter to Graebe, Vienna, February 8, 1930.

83 At the session of the Steering Committee that was held in early February 1927, the finance committee warned Ammende about the necessity of proper book-keeping. MNL OL K 64 1927-47-78, Flachbarth's report to Masirevich, Prague, February 8, 1927.

84 Officially, these funds, which were naturally kept secret, were intended to help defray travel costs and costs involved in the preparations for the conferences.

85 Because of delays in payment, Ammende often found himself in a seemingly hopeless position, since the Secretariat was unable to cover its financial liabilities. On several occasions, Vilfan provided loans that saved Ammende from immediate grief. Michaelsen, *Der Europäische Nationalitäten-Kongreß*, 246–248.

financial obligations of membership, and so were compelled to withdraw from the Congress. Although they nonetheless regularly attended every meeting until 1933, they were never able to pay more than a fraction of the amounts they were supposed to provide.[86] By 1933, the Catalan minority was insolvent, and the Ukrainian group, which in 1927 had become a permanent member (until then it had only had observer status), never provided more than a negligible contribution to the costs of maintaining the organization.[87] By 1933–1934, only three groups paid their dues more or less as required: the Germans, the Hungarians and the Slovenes.[88]

The German Ministry of Foreign Affairs adopted a position in support of the Congress. After 1933–1934, the Congress was the only international forum in and through which the German minorities could hope to secure the attention of a relatively substantial international audience for their alleged grievances.[89] Furthermore, the organization could be used as an arena to promote and further – or when expedient downplay – German foreign policy endeavours. For instance, in 1933, the German group managed to have a resolution passed concerning the potential justification of the principle of dissimilation, and in 1935, approaching the question from the perspective of minority politics, it blurred the distinction between authoritarian regimes and democratic systems of government. Ammende also openly played a role in the propaganda war against the Soviet Union.[90] Thus, since the organization and its survival were increasingly important in eyes of the German Ministry of Foreign Affairs from 1932 onwards, it regularly covered a significant share of the payments that had been

86 Ammende and Vilfan contacted the Jewish representatives on several occasions in order to pressure them to pay their debts. BA N 1250, Fasz. 3, unnumbered, Vilfan's circular to the leaders of the Jewish minority groups, Belgrade, December 22, 1930. The Secretary-General and Schiemann also sought to obtain help from influential German Jews, though their efforts were unsuccessful. PA AA, R 60529, L 497595–L 497596, Ammende's letter to Julius Hirsch, Vienna, November 27, 1931.

87 PA AA, R 60531, L 497732, Graebe's letter and attached summary report to the sixth division of the German Ministry of Foreign Affairs on the financial circumstances of the Congress, undated.

88 MNL OL K 64 1935–47, unnumbered, Elemér Jakabffy's report to the Chairmanship of the National Hungarian Party on the tenth Congress of European Nationalities, undated.

89 PA AA, R 60531, L 497732, Graebe's letter to the sixth division of the German Ministry of Foreign Affairs, Berlin, February 21, 1934.

90 Ammende was also swept along by the tide of affairs in politics and built up ties with the Rosenberg office. In 1933 and 1934, the Congress passed a resolution concerning the famine in Russia. The Secretary-General maintained a press campaign and wrote a book on the subject, and in 1935–1936 he set off on a trip around the world whose real (and also secret) purpose would have been to map the spread of communist influence. Bamberger-Stemmann offers a detailed analysis of the question in *Der Europäische*

left in arrears by other groups. By 1934–1935, Germany provided 32,850 German marks to support the Congress, and by 1935–1936 this sum had grown to 38,600 marks. Of this, 19,100 marks came from funds that had been set aside for the Verband. The rest was paid by the Ministry of Foreign Affairs as an extraordinary allocation, which, however, was becoming a regular practice.[91]

In contrast to Berlin, the Hungarian Ministry of Foreign Affairs and the Office of the Prime Minister had been committed from the outset to providing financial support for the new organization. However, while Berlin decided in 1928–1929, after an initial period of cautiousness, to provide adequate support for the Congress to survive, and essentially never changed its position on this question, after September 1932 the Hungarian foreign minister revised the policies according to which the government had provided support for such initiatives. From that point onwards, Hungary did not actually make the payments it had agreed to in principle until the conference in a given year had actually begun. This left the leaders of the organization in a state of constant uncertainty.

Following the second Congress, the annual payment for the Hungarian group was raised to 4,000 Swiss francs, and then 8,000 Swiss francs after they decided to establish a permanent office. This amount never changed, at least not officially, in the remaining eleven years of the organization's history. From the moment this decision was made until September 1932, the Hungarian Ministry of Foreign Affairs regularly sent the funds on behalf of the Hungarian group (two payments of 4,000 Swiss francs each) to Ammende, sometimes with slight delays. The only change that took place came in July 1928, when at Ammende's request the funds were sent to the Secretary-General through the embassy in Vienna, though in some cases Ammende was given the money in person in Budapest.[92] The Hungarian Ministry of Foreign Affairs made the payments contingent on at least one condition. Ammende had to enter each payment in the records of the office in Vienna as a "contribution made by the Hungarian minorities," since even a minor indiscretion could have put the Hungarian government in an extremely awkward position.[93] After the Hungarian contact had

Nationalitätenkongreß, 325–349. Ammende received 8,000 German marks annually, in quarterly instalments, for the "Russia Operation." PA AA, R 60496, K 262362, Hasselblatt's letter to Twardowski, Berlin, May 19, 1936.

91 Ammende's "Russia Operation" was presumably one of the things covered by the extraordinary allocations, as was covering the costs of the groups that either had withdrawn or could not pay. PA AA, R 60496, K 262361–K 262363, Hasselblatt's letter to Twardowski, Berlin, May 19, 1936.

92 MNL OL K 64 1935–47 (403/1928), Instruction of the foreign ministry to Ambassador Lajos Ambrózy, Budapest, June 20, 1928.

93 Ibid.

convinced himself that the Secretary-General was proceeding in accordance with the requests of the Hungarian government, the deputy minister gave his consent to allow the funds to be transferred through the embassy.[94]

Between 1925 and 1938, the financial support provided to the Congress definitely exceeded 140,000 Swiss francs, taking into considerations the various payments (e.g. annual membership fees and extraordinary allocations made by the foreign ministries). These payments, however, were by no means the only state costs of membership in the organization. For instance, the Hungarian Ministry of Foreign Affairs covered the travel costs of the delegates.[95] Furthermore, in the years immediately following the founding of the Congress, the Office of the Prime Minister also provided extraordinary allocations to support the annual conferences (in the amount of 5,000 Swiss francs per conference).

2 *Representativeness and Solidarity*

The founders of the Congress were guided in their efforts by the goal of creating a unified organization in which all national minorities of Europe were represented. They sought to create a forum founded on a belief in the complete equality of individual minorities, a forum that recognized and accepted differences arising from their various backgrounds but was still able to develop unified strategies in relation to fundamental issues and represent them effectively. While the Congress enjoyed the participation of a significant share of the minorities of Europe, full representation and complete consensus on issues of importance among members proved to be an illusion.

The first group to withdraw from the Congress consisted of members who disagreed with its official position (more precisely the position of the majority of its members) on cultural autonomy as a long-term goal. The notion of cultural autonomy was attacked from two sides. The representatives of the political organizations of the Lithuanian, Ukrainian and Belarusian minorities in Poland were not satisfied with the Congress's stance, which they regarded as too moderate. As numerically significant minorities living in relatively homogenous blocks, they strove to assert their right to self-determination. For this reason, they participated in the first three congresses only as observers.[96]

94 MNL OL K 64 1935–47 (322/1928), György Lukács's letter to Khuen-Héderváry, Vienna, July 20, 1928.

95 For instance, MNL OL K 64 1927-47-430, Costs of the travels of Péter Matuska, the foreign ministry's chargé d'affaires, to Prague, Budapest, September 15, 1927; MNL OL K 64 1927-47-385, Kristóffy, Pro domo, Budapest, August 17, 1927.

96 Elemér Jakabffy, *Adatok családunk történetéhez* [Information concerning the History of Our Family], Manuscript, National Széchényi Library Manuscript Collection, F 625/3066, 9–10.

(In 1928–1929, they became permanent members of the organization, although they maintained their stance on the issue of cultural autonomy.) The minorities in Germany were critical of the concept for an entirely different reason. They did not find it acceptable for the Congress to focus in its strategic goals on an idea whose implementation would compel the so-called "weaker minorities" to bear costs that exceeded their means.[97] Their opposition, however, may also have been a sign of their discontent with some of the details concerning the manner in which the Congress functioned. The Danish, Polish and Serb minorities, which formed the Alliance of Minorities in Germany, found the influence wielded by the German minorities – an influence that exceeded their numerical proportion in the Congress – overwhelming. They felt that the German minorities had created the organization as a tool to promote pan-German interests. When they withdrew from the Congress in 1928, the explanation (or pretext) for their decision was the fiery debate concerning the possible admission of the Frisian minority and the official decision of the Congress to reject its application.[98] Out of solidarity with the Frisians, all the Polish minority groups withdrew from the organization.

While the admission of the Frisians to the Congress was blocked by the German minorities, the admission application of the Slovak minorities in Hungary (or rather the application of a Czechoslovak emigrant organization because the Slovak minorities were "hindered" in their efforts to join the Congress) was hampered by the Hungarian minorities or, more precisely, by the Hungarian Office of the Prime Minister.[99] In cases like this, it was already obvious that the states were striving to instrumentalize the Congress as a forum to assert their interests. Likewise, their financial support of the Congress was dependent on whether or not the decisions reached at the sessions of the Steering Committee on individual issues served their interests.

On several occasions in the 1930s, questions surrounding the identity of specific individuals who represented the various minorities at the Congress became a source of tension between the German, Hungarian and Slovenian groups, which until then had managed to cooperate with one another relatively effectively. For instance, in 1930 and 1931, following the dissolution of the political parties in Yugoslavia, the Yugoslav state sought to prevent the leading politicians of the Hungarian minority from reaching the sessions of the

97 Remarks of Ernst Christiansen, Danish German minority politician. *Sitzungsbericht 1925*, 54–56.

98 PA AA, R 60426, K 435450, Lutz Korodi's confidential report to the German Ministry of Foreign Affairs on the session of the German minorities that took place after the conference, Berlin, undated.

99 BA N 1250, Fasz. 5, 706, Szeberényi's letter to Ammende, Miskolc, July 12, 1931.

Congress in time by making the process of obtaining a passport more complex and burdensome. Instead, they supported a politician who had never been recognized by the Hungarian minority as a legitimate political representative and had shown himself to be willing to cooperate with the regime (and even facilitated his travel to the Congress). In the meantime, however, the politicians who represented the German minorities in Yugoslavia were able to travel and attend the annual conference without any difficulty. It was not until Hungarian delegates from Transylvania and Czechoslovakia and the Office of the Hungarian Prime Minister issued an ultimatum threatening the withdrawal of the Hungarian group from the organization that the President of the Congress managed to persuade Belgrade not to create any more obstacles preventing the Hungarian politicians from travelling abroad.[100]

The relationship between the German and Hungarian groups was fraught with complexity and tension between 1936 and 1938 because of the question surrounding the representation of the German minorities in Hungary. Until 1936, the German minority in Hungary had been represented in the Congress by one of the leading officials of the *Ungarländischen Deutschen Volksbildungsverein* (German Folklore Association in Hungary), who was recognized by the Hungarian government. However, when Jakob Bleyer, the leader of the *Volksbildungsverein*, died in 1933, a fight for control broke out in which the leaders of the *Verband*, the Office of the Hungarian Prime Minister and even the German Ministry of Foreign Affairs took part. After 1935, the *Verband* supported the more radical wing of the *Volksbildungsverein* and insisted that it represent the German minority in Hungary at the conferences. However, the Office of the Hungarian Prime Minister did not allow an internal opposition figure to travel from Hungary to the conferences instead of the more moderate official leaders, who had the support of the Hungarian government. The stance of the Hungarian government was hypocritical, since no one could represent the Hungarian minorities without the preliminary approval of the state secretary of the Office of the Prime Minister. For years, the Office of the Prime Minister had taken advantage of the influence of Géza Szüllő, the Hungarian member of the Steering Committee, to prevent the radical wing of the German minorities in Hungary from representing the German minorities at the conference. Hasselblatt, however, blocked the active participation of the wing of the *Volksbildungsverein* supported by the Hungarian government in the work of the Congress. Even in the last years of the existence of the Congress, this conflict remained unresolved, and the relationship between the Hungarian delegates and the German delegates became increasingly tense.[101]

100 BA N 1250, Fasz. 5, 1174, Ammende's letter to Vilfan, Vienna, August 10, 1933.

101 On the representation of the Hungarian Germans, see Eiler, *Kisebbségvédelem*, 251–279.

The principle of solidarity, however, had already suffered a major blow in 1933, when the Jewish group called on the Congress, in particular the German representatives, to publically condemn the persecution of the Jews of Germany and the deprivation of their rights. The German representatives were not willing to condemn the measures that had been implemented by the German government, so the Jewish group broke its ties with the Congress. A declaration was added to the relevant resolution expressing the limited solidarity of the other groups of the Congress with the Jewish group, but this did not suffice to persuade the Jewish group to remain. The debate, which took place behind the scenes, had at least one other consequence: relations between the German and Hungarian groups continued to worsen. The German delegates regarded the events as a manifestation of disloyalty to them.[102] In his conversation with Romanian Hungarian politician Elemér Jakabffy, Hans Otto Roth, who was serving as president of the Verband, made no effort to mask his disappointment or anger:

> Sir! You have stabbed us. Even here you have isolated the German nation. Papen recently travelled to Budapest to introduce a far-reaching programme for German-Hungarian cooperation. You have now made this impossible. With your decision, you have delved deeply into European politics, and this will have consequences. We did not expect this of you.[103]

Jakabffy described to Roth the motivations underlying the steps that had been taken by the Hungarian group, and he could not resist giving the Saxon politician a lesson on the minority organization's limited influence on the German government: "With regard to international politics – concluding ironically – I don't think that we are such big players that our declarations will influence the decisions of the Berlin government."[104]

3 *Divergent Goals and Means*

With regard to the work of the Congress and the tactics it adopted, two basic viewpoints came into conflict: the cautious German stance, which did not wish to endanger the situation of the minorities in their host-states, on the one hand, and the confrontational Hungarian stance, which urged more radical steps and sought to attain as much influence as possible through advocacy, on

102 PA AA, R 60530, L 497705, Junghann's report on the ninth Congress of European Nationalities, undated.

103 Jakabffy, *Adatok*, 52.

104 Ibid., 53.

the other.[105] The members of the Steering Committee tended to side with the more cautious Germans.

Immediately after the first conference, the Hungarian minority leaders were already entertaining visions of an influential organization with a firm institutional framework, an organization that would have its own periodical and serve as a tool of effective international advocacy, first and foremost in Geneva, the seat of the League of Nations. Otto Junghann, one of the deputy chairmen of the International Federation of League of Nations Societies and an observer at the conference, described the viewpoint of the German leaders, which was hardly compatible with the Hungarian stance, as follows:

> The German group is unanimously of the view that a rigid organization of the European minorities is not desirable. ... However convinced they may be that the Congress should be used as an instrument in the future, they fear that a permanent organization with permanent tasks may cause complications that eventually and inevitably will lead to its disintegration.[106]

After the second Congress, a kind of compromise was reached with regard to the structure of the organization and the independent periodical – a compromise with which both the German group and the Hungarian group were temporarily content. The Germans essentially regarded the organization that took form after 1926 as a movement that did not function continuously, as the organs of the Congress only met occasionally, with the exception of the Secretariat. The official tasks of the Secretariat, which had a permanent office but only a minimal staff, consisted only of preparatory and publication work.[107] Furthermore, the official organ of the Congress, which was created in November 1926, ended up under the control and oversight of Ammende, who besides being German was concerned about the future of the organization and

105 The primary cause of the differences between the German and Hungarian stances on this question was the fact that all the Hungarian minorities supported territorial revision. The circumstances of the German minorities were more complicated. The German minorities that lived directly next to the border with Germany also supported territorial revision, while for those living in south-eastern Europe this was not a "life or death" question, since they would in any case remain distant from Germany and under the power of another state.

106 PA AA, R 60464, unnumbered, Junghann's report on the second Congress, undated.

107 BA N 1250, Fasz. 2, unnumbered, Werner Hasselblatt: Denkschrift zur Anregung der Begründung einer Europäischen Gesellschaft für Nationalitätenrecht [Werner Hasselblatt: A Memorandum on the Foundation of a European Law on Nationality Minorities], Geneva, August 1927.

therefore clearly cautious.[108] Thus, the organization managed to avoid a situation in which "the bulletin would offer an opportunity for some of the minority groups adopting shrewd tactics to create a broad platform for their advocacy goals with this periodical."[109]

From the Hungarian viewpoint, however, the mere fact that a Secretariat with a permanent seat had come into being at all was viewed as a positive development, in particular considering that Ammende, who was on good terms with the Hungarian Ministry of Foreign Affairs, was at its head. While only three people worked in the office in Vienna, this did not necessarily mean that the office would not later undergo further development. Since the composition of the Steering Committee had been made permanent, the Hungarian group would always be represented, and without its consent no decisions could be made on any issue of importance. With regard to the periodical, while the Congress had not decided in favour of a publication that would be put under Hungarian editorship and could be used for confrontational advocacy, the new situation nonetheless was regarded as a step in the right direction, at least from the Hungarian perspective. The new publication would be made available to influential officials in the League of Nations and some of the politicians who took part in its sessions, and this was clearly better than nothing. Furthermore, the Verband launched its own periodical – *Nation und Staat* – the same year, with secret support from the German Ministry of Foreign Affairs. Naturally, the limits that applied to the Congress's bulletin did not apply to the journal of the Verband. The Congress's periodical regularly presented accounts of the situation of the individual minority communities in Europe, and Hungarian minority politicians published articles in it.[110]

---

108 The first issue of the bulletin was published in November 1926. It was entitled *Mitteilungen der Geschäftsführung*. The periodical, which was initially disseminated only in small circles, provided a summary of the new minority petitions, the sessions of the Congress and the legal regulations in force in individual states. It also made reference to the most important publications on the question of minority rights. In 1930, it was supplanted by *Pressewochenschau zur Nationalitätenfrage*, which was published for six years, and (from 1932 onwards) *Europäische Nationalitätenkorrespondenz*, which was unambiguously supportive of German interests from the outset. Initially, Ammende edited the periodical entirely on his own. At the beginning of the 1930s, however, he was joined by his journalist sibling Erich. Bamberger-Stemmann provides a detailed discussion on the publications of the Congress in light of the efforts of Germany to use it as an instrument of German aims in *Der Europäische Nationalitätenkongreß*, 203–233.

109 PA AA, R 60464, unnumbered, Junghann's report on the second Congress, undated.

110 At the end of April, Ammende informed the Hungarian foreign ministry that there would be a section in the periodical being launched by the German minorities on August 1 dealing with the circumstances of the other national minorities in Europe, and that he would be responsible for compiling it. He indicated that he would be happy to include news

A few years later, however, a quarrel again broke out between the German and Hungarian members of the Steering Committee because of their differing strategic goals. Géza Szüllő, one of the Hungarian members, urged the Congress on several occasions to present the actual conditions under which the minorities lived to the wider public. He summarized his criticism regarding the Congress as follows:

> a minority conference is not here to promulgate academic principles, nor should it sink to the level of a botanical Congress. … I assert that I do not see any need for us to take part in this kind of academic institution since our goal must be first to demonstrate to Europe that we are dissatisfied and, second, that we are a fire trap in the middle of Europe.[111]

The other Hungarian representatives did not lend their unanimous support to this vision until the period immediately preceding the next conference. They did not want to cause a scandal that might disturb the official programme, but they did authorize Leó Deák to "suggest," in his remarks, the drafting and publication of a book presenting in detail the circumstances faced by the minorities belonging to the organization before the next session of the Congress.[112] While the Germans were irritated by the Hungarian's suggestion, they gave in after considerable negotiations. The book was eventually published in 1931. It met with little interest in the arena of international politics.

Earlier in the year, Ammende and Vilfan had been engaged in serious international advocacy efforts, and this may have prompted the Hungarian group, in spite of the threats, to content itself with the publication of a book presenting concrete infringements of minority rights. At a session in December 1928, Rauol Dandurand, a member of the Council of the Congress delegated by Canada, announced that at the next session of the Congress, which was to be held in March 1929, his government would suggest a detailed debate concerning possible reforms to the complaint procedure.[113] Ammende then threw himself into the fight to win the favour and support of the leading politicians of

concerning the problems faced by the Hungarian minorities. MNL OL K 64, 1927-47-181, Ammende's letter to Khuen-Hédervàry, Budapest, April 25, 1927.

111 National Széchényi Library Fond XX/27, 5, Szüllő's report on the inter-parliamentary conference in Berlin, Bratislava, September 5, 1928.

112 Leó Deák, "A Népszövetség és kongresszusunk jövő feladatai" [The Future Tasks of the League of Nations and Our Congress], *Magyar Kisebbség* 8 (1929): 670–679.

113 On the session of the Council, see Bastian Schot, *Nation oder Staat? Deutschland und der Minderheitenschutz* [Nation or State? Germany and Minority Protection] (Marburg/Lahn: J.G. Herder-Institut, 1988), 208–213.

the neutral states. On December 13, he informed the permanent deputy of the Hungarian Ministry of Foreign Affairs that, having been given authorization by the Steering Committee, he was going to travel with Vilfan for a short time to Switzerland, the Netherlands, Sweden, Norway and Denmark at the invitation of the member organizations of the International Federation of League of Nations Societies. The purpose of the trip, he explained, was to establish ties with the "relevant authorities" and urge them to take more active steps in support of reforms.[114] At the end of December and the beginning of January, the Secretary-General travelled to Finland by himself, where according to the Hungarian ambassador he created quite a stir. In February, Vilfan held a presentation in Geneva at an event led by William Martin, the editor of *Journal de Genève* and a man of considerable esteem.[115] They then travelled together to the Netherlands and the Scandinavian states.

At the March session of the Council, Dandurand and German Minister of Foreign Affairs Gustav Stresemann held a speech on the importance of reforming the minority rights protection procedures. While they may have listened to the speeches politely, the other members of the Council clearly sought to sweep the question under the rug.[116] It was quite clear that it would be necessary to reach a compromise, and this was indeed what happened. The Council entrusted a committee consisting of three people, chaired by the Japanese delegate Mineitciro Adatci, to compile a thorough report on the issues Dandurand and Stresemann had raised by the time of the session scheduled for June.[117] It also called on the states to inform the committee of their views concerning the protection of minority rights and made it possible for international organizations dealing with questions of minority rights to share their ideas and visions with the committee members.

The Steering Committee drew up a memorandum calling for complete transparency of the minority rights protection procedure, the participation of minority complainants in the procedure, improvements to the procedures governing the functioning of the Committee of Three, systematic requests for the opinion of the Permanent Court of International Justice (hereinafter, the Court) in The Hague and the creation of a committee of experts that would

114 MNL OL K 64 1928-47-757, Ammende's letter to Khuen-Héderváry, Vienna, December 13, 1928.

115 PA AA, R 60527, L 497516, Ammende's letter to Consul Reinebeck, undated (arrived on February 22, 1929).

116 Schot, *Nation*, 227–229.

117 Hugo Wintgens, *Der völkerrechtliche Schutz der nationalen, sprachlichen, und religiösen Minderheiten* [Protection of National, Linguistic and Religious Minorities under International Law] (Stuttgart: Verlag von W. Kohlhammer, 1930), 456.

operate alongside the League. In addition, the memorandum called on states with no treaty obligations to protect minority rights to respect the spirit of the minority protection treaties in cases involving minority complaints.[118]

In light of these expectations, the outcome of the June session of the Council was disappointing. The reforms that were passed brought some improvements to the procedures, but Dandurand's and Stresemann's suggestions, which would have significantly redrawn the framework for the minority rights protection procedure, were essentially ignored.[119] The Court in The Hague was not handed a larger role, and nothing came of the idea of involving minority plaintiffs in the procedure, improving transparency or creating a committee of experts. From the perspective of the Congress, it was an unambiguous failure.[120]

In 1934, the Hungarians again sought to exert pressure on the Secretary-General and the President (and thus on the Steering Committee), as well as on the other members of the Congress. They hoped that the Congress, instead of busying itself with theoretical analyses of infringements of minority rights, would engage in genuine awareness-raising efforts to influence and inform public opinion, identify the problems faced by minority communities and take a clear stance on concrete violations of rights. This demonstration of determination on the part of the Hungarians in the mid-1930s differed from their earlier attempts to influence the Congress in the late 1920s in two major ways. In 1929, the Hungarians had threatened to withdraw from the organization, but this threat had been little more than a bluff. In 1934, however, it was quite real. No one could know for sure when the Hungarian foreign minister might arrive at a potentially irrevocable decision concerning the withdrawal of the Hungarian minority groups from the Congress. The other difference concerned the conditions for remaining in the organization. In 1929, Szüllő and those in his circle had contented themselves with the Congress's pledge to publish a book containing reports on the state of affairs of the minorities, but in 1934 they set their sights considerably higher. They made demands that would have fundamentally transformed the operations of the organization if they had been met immediately.

However, the other two conditions set by the Hungarian group created serious difficulties for the leaders of the Congress. One of them was a request

118 Denkschrift des Ausschußes der Europäischen Nationalitätenkongressen [Memorandum from the Steering Committee of European Congress of National Minorities], *Nation und Staat* 2 (1928–1929): 583–589.

119 For the text and an analysis of the resolution, see Wintgens, *Der völkerrechtliche Schutz*, 461–463.

120 MNL OL K 64 1935–47 (575/1929), Ammende's letter to Bethlen, Vienna, July 22, 1929.

to transform the office in Vienna into a bureau that would operate continuously and examine complaints concerning concrete infringements on minority rights. If it determined that the complaints were well-founded, it would submit a petition to the Secretariat of the League of Nations. The other condition was that, if the Vienna office were to be restructured, a Hungarian representative would be made part of its staff. Although the two conditions were related – in their arguments the Hungarians explained the necessity of the second with reference to the first – they quite clearly served different goals. The transformation of the scope of the duties of the Secretariat would have resulted in fundamental changes to the essential functioning of the Congress, which at that point was ten years old. The second condition was merely meant to increase the influence of the Hungarian minority groups within the organization.

Naturally, Jakabffy already knew whom he wanted as the Hungarian member of the staff in the Vienna office: Imre Prokopy, who had been active as a Yugoslav Hungarian politician and enjoyed the confidence of the Office of the Prime Minister.[121] According to Vilfan, this demand could have been met, but only if three conditions were satisfied first. The Hungarians would have to name someone they considered suitable for the position, they would have to cover the additional costs and under no circumstances would the appointment of a Hungarian assistant be allowed to serve as a precedent for other national minorities to make similar demands.[122]

In the end, no Hungarian was actually appointed to serve as a member of the staff in the office in Vienna. There were several reasons for this. First and foremost, it is doubtful that the Office of the Prime Minister or the Ministry of Foreign Affairs would have been willing to cover any additional costs, but they were certainly not willing to do so once the Steering Committee had essentially torpedoed Jakabffy's suggestion concerning the transformation of the Secretariat.

The essential part of the Hungarian ultimatum of 1934 concerned the changes that the Hungarians hoped to make to the role and work of the Congress. However, Vilfan had serious reservations – and indeed anxieties – concerning this suggestion.[123] He cautioned Jakabffy that the positions adopted by the Congress could easily give rise to tensions among the individual national minority

121 MNL OL K 64 1935–47, unnumbered, Elemér Jakabffy's report to the Chairmanship of the National Hungarian Party, undated.

122 BA N 1250, Fasz. 8, 856, Vilfan's letter to Jakabffy, Vienna, June 23, 1934; BA N 1250, Fasz. 30, 7, Minutes of the session of the Congress of European Nationalities' Steering Committee, Vienna, June 29, 1934.

123 BA N 1250, Fasz. 8, 855–856, Vilfan's letter to Jakabffy, Vienna, June 23, 1934.

groups. He also felt it was worth keeping in mind that, if the submission of petitions to the League of Nations were to become a central part of the Congress's endeavours, minorities that did not fall under its protection would no longer have any interest in becoming or remaining members of the Congress, since no one would be able to submit complaints to Geneva on their behalf.

The session of the Steering Committee that took place on June 29, 1934 was decisive from the perspective of the fate of the Hungarian proposal. Szüllő represented the Hungarian group.[124] Those who made remarks essentially agreed that it would be inappropriate for the office in Vienna to draft or even offer an opinion on petitions and then submit them to the League of Nations. The inadequacy of the existing infrastructure made this practically impossible, not to mention the other complications it raised. Vilfan spoke out, first and foremost, in the interests of members of the Congress who did not enjoy the protections of the minority treaties. The President called Szüllő's attention to the fact that the representatives of these minorities would find themselves in a difficult position vis-à-vis their constituencies if they were to support complaints submitted by other minorities with their signatures, since those other minorities had no way of reciprocating the gesture given the nature of the mechanisms involved.

Tibor Pataky, a state secretary in the Office of the Prime Minister who dealt with minority affairs, was clearly aware that these objections were well founded, much as he knew that the Congress would have collapsed relatively rapidly if it had accepted the proposal without any changes. However, the Hungarian group did manage to achieve something, as the Steering Committee showed some willingness to deal with concrete infringements of minority rights, in addition to its theoretical work, and did not refuse from the outset to make efforts to influence and inform public opinion. Presumably, they succeeded in part because Jakabffy stopped insisting on his request that the Vienna office draft and submit petitions.

Eventually, the Congress was swept from the stage of history by the Second World War. The German group planned to call a conference in 1939, and the Secretary-General and Hasselblatt had both taken steps in preparation for the conference. However, the occupation and partition of Czechoslovakia and the invasion of Poland (which signalled the outbreak of war) made the conference logistically virtually impossible.[125] Furthermore, given the resulting

124 For details concerning the events of the session of the Steering Committee, see BA N 1250, Fasz. 30, 3–9, Minutes of the session of the Congress of European Nationalities' Steering Committee, Vienna, June 29, 1934.

125 BA N 1250, Fasz. 11, unnumbered, Uexküll-Güldenband's letter to Vilfan, Vienna, January 27, 1939.

rapid and drastic shift in international relations, it clearly would have been preposterous to hope that the national minorities would be able to work together with one another as they had in the past.

v The Congress's Place in the International Arena

During the years of the interwar period in which it was active, there were basically two opposing views on the role of the Congress. These assessments did not change in the decades following the Second World War, long after it had ceased to function.

Many people saw the Congress as little more than a tool of the German government – and to a lesser extent of the Hungarian government – whose activities contributed, even if only on a small scale, to the disintegration of post-First World War European order. According to this assessment, the politicians who were active in the organization were at fault for at least two reasons. First, their efforts in the framework of the Congress weakened the League of Nations. Second, the demands they made and the attention they attracted on the international stage further poisoned relations between majority groups and national minorities, which were hardly free of tension to begin with. Finally, they did this with the goal of helping the two states that had lost the war (Germany and Hungary) achieve their revisionist aspirations.[126]

Others, however, had an entirely different – or rather contradictory – assessment of the Congress. In their view, during the fourteen years of its existence, the Congress had striven to minimize the harm caused by the peace treaties. It had been an initiative from below that aimed to promote and foster stability and create a sense of solidarity among the minorities, and it had basically managed to preserve its independence, even if, towards the end of the 1930s, minority politicians who sympathized with national socialism had acquired roles of some influence.[127] Each of these assessments of the Congress focuses on a different aspect of the actual situation and offers categorical statements from

126 Maria Rothbarth, *Der Europäische Minderheitenkongreß als Instrument imperialistischer deutscher "Revisionsstrategie." Grenzrevision und Minderheitenpolitik des deutschen Imperialismus (1919–1932)*, Dissertation zur Erlangung des akademischen Grades Doktor der Wissenschaft [The Congress of European Nationalities as an instrument of imperialist German "revisionist strategy": Border revision and minority policy of German imperialism (1919–1932), Doctoral dissertation] (Rostock: Wilhelm-Pieck-Universität, 1982).

127 Plesse, *Organisation*; Erwin Kelmes, *Der Europäische Nationalitätenkongreß 1925–1938* [The Congress of European Nationalities, 1925–1938], Dissertation (Cologne: University of Cologne, 1958).

a single perspective without actually examining the organization's activities and the work in which it engaged or the motivations of the politicians who accepted roles in it and their interactions with one another and with forces outside the Congress. The truth, not surprisingly, lies somewhere between these two extremes.

The Congress can indeed be regarded as an initiative from below, but it was never – not for a moment – entirely independent of state influence, not least because of the tension between the need to cover its operational costs and the continuous financial difficulties faced by the minority groups. However, it is not true that the German Ministry of Foreign Affairs was behind the founding of the Congress from the outset. The years 1927–1928 constituted a turning point in the life of the "Congress community," although this was not necessarily entirely obvious to an outside observer. It was at this time that the German Ministry of Foreign Affairs decided that, all things considered, the Congress could be used in support of German foreign policy interests, and so it guaranteed the necessary funds to ensure that the organization would be able to cover its operating costs. In exchange, however, it required the German leaders to coordinate with the ministry on a continuous basis, especially prior to Congress gatherings. This by no means meant that from then on everything went just as the German government desired. The organization maintained some of its freedom of movement, which was due in part to Ammende himself and in part to the fact that the various steps that were taken were motivated by various interests. In other words, on basic questions, the Secretary-General also had to come to an agreement with the leaders of the other national groups.

The fourteen-year history of the Congress came to an end in 1938. It was hardly a success story, as the organization was unable to bring about enduring improvements in the circumstances of the minorities. But its failure was not the consequence of a lack of commitment, theoretical preparation or political experience on the part of the delegates. The realities of European power relations limited its scope for action from the outset. Even the League of Nations did not officially recognize it as the foremost international organization representing the interests of the national minorities of Europe and certainly never considered it a possible partner.

The minority politicians, who were well prepared for the challenges they faced, and the many minority lawyers, who had established reputations across Europe and provided the theoretical/legal background for the work of the Congress, did everything possible to strengthen the organization's prestige and authority on the international stage and help it develop into a prominent forum for the discussion and resolution of minority affairs. Their efforts, however, proved unsuccessful. From the 1930s onwards, the organization became increasingly marginalized, and this, along with political events at the international level, only hastened its internal collapse. After 1933, there were significant changes in the leadership, and many of the original figures who had supported cultural autonomy passed away or left and were replaced by others. Ammende died in 1936, and many of the more prominent members of the organization, who were troubled to see the ideas of national socialism gaining ground rapidly within the German group, subsequently decided to leave.[128]

The real significance of the Congress lay in the tremendous and genuinely valuable theoretical work in which it engaged, which resulted in the creation of a kind of catalogue of the various problems arising in connection with the existence of minorities – problems to which the members of the Congress were compelled to adopt position that in their assessment were – or should have been – understood as normative. To this day, the writings published by the Congress remain important sources in the scholarship on minorities and minority rights, and the resolutions that were passed, with the exception of a few that were clearly shaped by political exigencies, continue to embody important viewpoints on the complex question of minority rights.

128 Even individuals who had played important roles in the founding of the organization later turned their backs on the Congress. For instance, Paul Schiemann left the organization in 1934, followed by Elemér Jakabffy in 1937.

Appendix

TABLE 11.A1 Participation of the minorities in the annual conferences of the Congress (1925–1938)[a]

Minorities/Countries	Participation in the annual conferences
Germans	
Poland	1925, 1926, 1927, 1928, 1929, 1930, 1931, 1932, 1933, 1934, 1935, 1936, 1937, 1938
Czechoslovakia	1925, 1926, 1927, 1929, 1930, 1931, 1932, 1933, 1934, 1935, 1936, 1937, 1938
Estonia	1925, 1926, 1927, 1928, 1929, 1930, 1931, 1932, 1933, 1934, 1935, 1936, 1938
Romania	1925, 1926, 1927, 1928, 1929, 1930, 1931, 1932, 1933, 1934, 1935, 1937, 1938
Hungary	1925, 1926, 1927, 1929, 1930, 1931, 1932, 1933, 1934, 1935, 1936, 1938
Yugoslavia	1925, 1926, 1927, 1928, 1929, 1930, 1931, 1932, 1934, 1935, 1937
Latvia	1925, 1926, 1927, 1928, 1929, 1930, 1931, 1932, 1934, 1937, 1938
Denmark	1925, 1926, 1927, 1932, 1934, 1936, 1937, 1938
Italy	1925, 1926, 1928, 1937
Belgium	1934, 1935
Lithuania	1926, 1932
Jews	
Czechoslovakia	1925, 1926, 1927, 1928, 1929, 1931, 1932
Latvia	1925, 1926, 1927, 1928, 1929, 1930, 1932
Poland	1925, 1926, 1927, 1929, 1931, 1932
Bulgaria	1926, 1927, 1929, 1930, 1932
Lithuania	1925, 1926, 1927, 1928, 1930
Romania	1927, 1928, 1929, 1931
Estonia	1927
Poles	
Czechoslovakia	1925, 1926, 1927
Latvia	1925, 1926, 1927
Lithuania	1925, 1926, 1927
Germany	1925, 1926, 1927
Romania	1926

Minorities/Countries	Participation in the annual conferences
Russians	
Estonia	1926, 1927, 1928, 1929, 1930, 1931, 1932, 1933, 1934, 1935, 1936, 1937
Poland	1926, 1927, 1928, 1929, 1930, 1931, 1932, 1933
Romania	1929, 1930, 1931, 1935, 1936, 1937
Latvia	1932, 1933
Hungarians	
Yugoslavia	1925, 1926, 1927, 1928, 1929, 1930[c], 1931[c], 1932, 1933, 1934, 1935, 1936, 1937, 1938
Czechoslovakia	1925, 1926, 1927, 1928, 1929, 1930, 1931, 1932, 1933, 1934, 1935, 1936, 1937, 1938
Romania	1925, 1926, 1927, 1928, 1929, 1930, 1931, 1932, 1933, 1934, 1935, 1936, 1937, 1938
Ukrainians	
Poland	1925, 1926[b], 1927[b], 1928, 1929, 1930, 1931, 1932, 1933, 1934, 1935, 1936, 1937, 1938
Romania	1927, 1928, 1929, 1930, 1931, 1932, 1933, 1937, 1938
Slovenes	
Italy	1925, 1926, 1927, 1928, 1929, 1930, 1931, 1932, 1933, 1934, 1935, 1936, 1938
Austria	1925, 1926, 1927, 1928, 1929, 1930, 1931, 1932, 1933, 1934, 1935, 1936
Bulgarians	
Romania	1928, 1929, 1930, 1931, 1932, 1933, 1937
Yugoslavia	1929, 1930, 1933, 1934
Lithuanians	
Poland	1925, 1926[b], 1929, 1930, 1931, 1933, 1935
Germany	1930, 1931, 1934
Catalans	
Spain	1926, 1927, 1928, 1929, 1930, 1931, 1932, 1933, 1934, 1935, 1936, 1937

TABLE 11.A1 Participation of the minorities in the annual conferences of the Congress (1925–1938)[a] (*cont.*)

Minorities/Countries	Participation in the annual conferences
Czechs	
Austria	1926, 1927, 1928, 1929, 1930, 1931, 1932, 1933, 1934, 1935
Carpatho-Ukrainians/ Ruthenians	
Czechoslovakia	1925, 1928, 1929, 1930, 1931, 1932, 1934
Belarusians	
Poland	1925, 1926[b], 1927[b], 1928, 1931, 1933
Croats	
Austria	1926, 1927, 1929, 1930, 1932, 1935
Basques	
Spain	1930, 1931, 1932, 1934
Danes	
Germany	1925, 1926, 1927
Swedes	
Estonia	1930, 1937, 1938
Sorbs	
Germany	1925, 1926, 1927
Greeks	
Italy	1931
Gaus	
Spain	1933[c]

a The author compiled this table on the basis of the Congress's reports.
b Only as observers.
c Arrived late.

TABLE 11.A2 The members of the Steering Committee[a]

Members	Political work and endeavours
German group	
Kurt Graebe (1874–1952)	A German Polish minority politician. In 1922, he was made a member of the foreign affairs committee of the Sejm. In 1924–1934, he was a key figure in acquiring secret financial support from Germany for Posen-Pomerellen. He was a member of the Chairmanship of the Verband. In 1930–1933, he was the head of the German caucus in the Sejm. After 1933, he began to lose political influence and prominence. He was the main representative of the older generation and, as such, often came into conflict with members of the younger generation. In 1937, he moved to Berlin. He never joined the Nazi party.
Jewish group	
Leo Motzkin (1867–1933)	Zionist politician. He began his political career as a leading Zionist in Russia. In 1897, he gained recognition as one of the youngest members of the first Zionist Congress. During the First World War, he represented the interests of the organization in Copenhagen. As one of the leaders of the Zionist delegation, he took part in the Paris Peace Conference. He settled in Paris, and in Geneva he often represented Jewish interests at the League of Nations. He was the Jewish vice-chairman of the European Congress of National Minorities. He was also one of the most influential leaders of the World Jewish Congress.
Hungarian group	
Géza Szüllő (1873–1957)	Czechoslovak Hungarian minority politician. In 1901–1908, he was a representative in the Hungarian parliament. From 1925 until his resignation in 1932, he was the president of the National Christian Socialist Party. In 1925–1938, he was a representative in the national assembly. In 1927, he became the president of the parliamentary club of Hungarian parties. He was the honorary president of the Czechoslovak Hungarian League of National Societies. After the so-called First Vienna Award, he served as a member of the Hungarian upper house until 1944.

TABLE 11.A2 The members of the Steering Committee[a] (*cont.*)

Members	Political work and endeavours
Ukrainian group	
Dymitr Levickij (1877–1940)	Ukrainian Polish minority politician. In 1927–1939, he was the head of the Ukrainian National Democratic Society. From 1928 to 1935, he was a representative in the Sejm. He was also one of the leaders of the Ukrainian caucus in the Polish parliament.
Polish group	
Stanisław Sierakowski (1891–1939)	Polish German minority politician. One of the founders of the Polish Alliance of Eastern Prussia. In 1922, this organization evolved into the Alliance of German Poles, and he served as its first president (and as its honorary president until 1932). In 1922, he became a member of the Prussian parliament. He served as president of the Association of National Minorities in Germany, which was founded in 1924 (ditto). In 1939, he and his wife were murdered by German soldiers.
Catalan group	
Juan Estelrich i Artigues (1896–1958)	Catalan Spanish writer and politician. He sought to draw international attention to the Catalan problem. He was a parliamentary representative in 1931–1939. He was a member of the governing council of the Catalan League. During the civil war, he edited a periodical. In 1952–1958, he represented his county in UNESCO.
Slavic group (after 1928)	
Josip Vilfan (1878–1955)	Slovenian Italian minority politician. He began his political career in 1906, when he became the secretary of Edinost, an organization of the Slovenians of Trieste. In May 1921, he became a parliamentary representative in Rome. In 1922, he became active in the work of the Inter-Parliamentary Union. In 1925–1938, he served as the President of the Congress of National Minorities. On September 25, 1928, he quarrelled with Mussolini. A few days later, he moved permanently to Vienna. In 1939, he moved to Belgrade.

a The author compiled these brief biographical summaries based on a selection of national and subject-specific encyclopaedias, as well as data found scattered in the secondary literature.

CHAPTER 12

Group Identities and Human Rights: How Do We Square the Circle in International Law?

Gaetano Pentassuglia

Abstract

The identity of groups of an ethno-cultural variety has long fallen within the remit of international human rights law. In this context, discussions have been largely concerned with the legal status of groups and/or the nature of the legal right(s) in question. While acknowledging the importance of these dimensions, in this article I seek to provide an alternative account by discussing the continuities and discontinuities in articulating the very concept of group identity. I first examine the potential, limitations and eventual hybridity of human rights practice across the spectrum of minority/indigenous identities. Then, I critique a range of instabilities in human rights discourse relating to the idea of group identities, their personal scope and the role of international law. I argue that such instabilities do not merely mirror the ambivalent outlook of the relationship between human rights and group identities; they raise the broader question of whether there is a relatively more coherent way to capture the legitimacy of group claims. I conclude by pointing to the outer limits of identity claims, the understated interplay of sovereignty and inter-group diversity, and the need to unpack the reasons why certain groups merit protection in the way they do.

1 Introduction: Ethno-cultural Identity as a Human Rights Concern

From the proliferation of indigenous claims to land and natural resources to European anxieties about national belonging and the challenge of migration to attempts to bring several ethnic or sub-national conflicts to an end, the theme of group identities of a cultural variety has recently rekindled public discourse in a number of significant ways. Yet, the collective story of ethno-cultural identities goes much further back in time to a point where the articulation and

 | DOI:10.1163/9789004386426_013

defence of those identities, or some of them, becomes deeply entangled with the very existence and functioning of states as we know them today.[1]

This article examines one important dimension of this broader phenomenon: the conceptual continuities and discontinuities in articulating ethnic, linguistic and/or religious identities within international human rights law. The role of ethno-cultural group identities in this context has been largely shaped by discussions about the legal status of groups and/or the nature of the right(s) in question. Despite the importance of these dimensions, it has not been uncommon for them to appear as obstacles to, rather than opportunities for, a deeper understanding of the field. The following sections seek to develop an alternative account by looking at selective dimensions of human rights practice across the spectrum of minority/indigenous identities and what their comparative outlook tells us about the concept of group identities in international law.[2] I will first capture a range of developments affecting ethno-cultural identities (subsection 2.1), followed by an assessment of the uncertainties and potential of human rights discourse (subsections 2.2 and 2.3). Then, I will provide a critique of the conceptual instabilities of such discourse by discussing prominent narratives that question, directly or indirectly, the legitimacy of group interests, the ability of international law to relate meaningfully to group identities and/or its ability to do so in distinctive ways (Section 3). Finally, I will argue that the ever-expanding body of practice in the field is not only cause to rejoice but should also give us pause to reflect on the normative purposes of human rights interventions in relation to group identities. I will point to the outer limits of identity claims, the understated interplay of sovereignty and inter-group diversity, and the need to unpack the reasons why certain groups merit protection in the way they do (Section 4).

1 For several strands of this debate, see *Ethno-Cultural Diversity and Human Rights: Challenges and Critiques*, ed. G. Pentassuglia (Leiden: Brill Nijhoff Publishers, 2018); G. Pentassuglia, "Self-Determination, Human Rights, and the Nation-State: Revisiting Group Claims through a Complex Nexus in International Law," *International Community Law Review* 19 (2017): 443.

2 I will mainly deal with cross-cutting dimensions of protection regarding "national minorities" or "minorities" and "indigenous peoples" and will assume some basic starting points concerning the protection of such groups against genocide or other international crimes. The comparative thrust of the analysis moves beyond compartmentalized visions of the field in order to explore synergies and tensions within human rights discourse and to recognize (conceptually at least) the correlation between legal classifications and historical contingencies (for commentary from a broader angle, see e.g. N. Berman, "The International Law of Nationalism: Group Identity and Legal History," in *International Law and Ethnic Conflict*, ed. D. Wippman (Ithaca and London: Cornell University Press, 1998), 25).

2 Group Identities and International Human Rights Law: A Bumpy Road to Somewhere

2.1 *Tracing Developments: A Selective Account*

That the sort of group identities considered in this article have been traditionally associated with the notion of equality is not at all surprising. As early as 1935, the Permanent Court of International Justice held that combining "perfect equality" (equality in law) within the political community with the protection of cultural differences brought about by the minority population within the state would lead to "true equality" between the majority and the minority, including most notably securing the minority's own institutions.[3] What was relatively predictable (yet innovative) in the pre-human rights era driven by the 1919 Versailles settlement became almost entirely unpredictable in an area (post-1945) where the language of human rights was essentially meant to replace, rather than augment, the international legal protection of group identities.

In this sense, the recent renewal in equality-based group protections is undoubtedly remarkable. A few brief examples can illustrate the point. Both the Inter-American human rights bodies (Court and Commission) and the African human rights structures under the African Charter on Human and Peoples' Rights (ACHPR) have increasingly worked on the premise that there is something inherently unfair or unjust in the way that the groups concerned have been treated in matters of land title and natural resources, cultural identity as well as wider participation in public life. The Inter-American Court, in particular, has treated the standard of non-discrimination in this context as a fundamental basis for progressive readings of indigenous rights.[4] For its part, the European Court of Human Rights has engaged in a major re-conceptualization of Article 14 of the European Convention on Human Rights (ECHR) that is focused on the effects of seemingly neutral measures adopted by the state on

3 *Minority Schools in Albania* (Advisory Opinion) 6 April 1935, P.C.I.J. Series A./B., No. 64, p. 3.

4 See e.g. *Yakye Axa Indigenous Community v. Paraguay*, Judgment of 6 February 2006, Series C, No. 125 (2005), para. 51; *The Saramaka People v. Suriname*, Judgment of 28 November 2007, Series C, No. 172 (2007), para. 103. For similar readings under the ACHPR, see *Centre for Minority Rights Development (Kenya) and Minority Rights Group International on behalf of Endorois Welfare Council v. Kenya*, Comm. No. 276/2003, 4 February 2010, para. 149; *Advisory Opinion of the African Commission on Human and People's Rights on the United Nations Declaration on the Rights of Indigenous Peoples*, adopted by the African Commission on Human and Peoples' Rights at its 41st session, Accra, Ghana, May 2007, para. 19. For a similar line from the African Court on Human and People's Rights, see recently *African Commission on Human and Peoples' Rights v. Republic of Kenya*, App. No. 006/2012, Judgment of 26 May 2017 (hereinafter, the *Ogiek* case).

certain religious or ethnic groups. The notion that "a general policy or measure that has disproportionately prejudicial effects on a *particular group* may be considered discriminatory notwithstanding that it is not specifically aimed at that group"[5] has reverberated through several cases in which claims of indirect discrimination against Roma groups generated a platform for a groundbreaking reflection on some form of substantive and procedural inter-group equality.[6]

Whether it is through the notions of "equality in fact," "indirect discrimination," "full and effective equality" and/or "positive action,"[7] it now seems rather undisputed that the expansion of the scope of equality in recent human rights case law and legislation requires domestic authorities to evaluate the real or potential impact of public policies on the position of particular groups (including, for example, in matters of language or education) and whether there is a need for corrections and improvements, or even (narrowly construed) forms of "reasonable accommodation."[8] As implied by the 1992 UN Declaration on the Rights of National or Ethnic, Religious and Linguistic Minorities (Articles 4(2) and 8(3)), state-generated special arrangements for all or specific minority groups are presumed to be compatible with the principle of equality, subject to a challenge on proportionality grounds.[9]

Apart from articulating group issues through the lens of anti-discrimination law, group identities are most obviously integral to discussions about the scope of cultural protections in human rights law. For example, the Inter-American

5 *Kelly v. United Kingdom*, App. No. 30054/96, Judgment of 4 May 2001, para. 154 (emphasis added).

6 For commentary, see G. Pentassuglia, "The Strasbourg Court and Minority Groups: Shooting in the Dark or a New Interpretive Ethos?," *International Journal on Minority and Group Rights* 19 (2012): 1 at 6–7, 12–13.

7 *Supra* notes 3 and 4; Framework Convention for the Protection of National Minorities (FCNM), 1 February 1995, CETS No. 157, Article 4(2); Committee on the Elimination of Racial Discrimination, *The meaning and scope of special measures in the International Convention on the Elimination of Racial Discrimination*, General Recommendation No. 32 adopted by the Committee on the Elimination of Racial Discrimination at its 75th session, 24 September 2009, UN Doc. CERD/C/GC/32 (2009); Council Directive 2000/43/EC of 29 June 2000 implementing the principle of equal treatment between persons irrespective of racial or ethnic origin, *OJ* 2000 L180/22, Article 5.

8 For the concept of "reasonable accommodation" in Canadian legislation and case law, see J. Woehrling, "L'obligation d'accommodement raisonnable et l'adaptation de la société à la diversité religieuse," *McGill Law Journal* 43 (1998): 325.

9 Judicial practice reflects this line of thinking by upholding the overall legitimacy of the arrangement, arguing against its withdrawal and/or criticizing particular aspects of it. See G. Pentassuglia, *Minority Groups and Judicial Discourse in International Law: A Comparative Perspective* (Leiden: Martinus Nijhoff Publishers, 2009), 149–180.

Court on Human Rights has developed its multidimensional jurisprudence on indigenous rights on the basis that indigenous communal property under Article 21 of the American Convention on Human Rights (ACHR) must be grounded in a broader and conceptually "transversal" right of indigenous communities to culture, particularly the identity and spirituality tied to traditional indigenous lands and resources.[10]

Crucially, it has noted that the connection between land and (indigenous) culture should be taken as a particular articulation of an underlying right to "cultural identity" grounded in the "collective dimension of the cultural life of native, indigenous, tribal and minority peoples and communities."[11] In a similar vein, Article 27 of the International Covenant on Civil and Political Rights (ICCPR) affirms rights of cultural integrity to the benefit of ethnic, religious and linguistic minority groups, which encompass but are not limited to indigenous ways of life associated with the use of land and its resources. Together with other leading global and regional human rights instruments,[12] this body of practice has resulted in converting the cultural rights-based argument into a discussion about the extent to which particular state measures impact the level of cultural access and enjoyment for the group and/or the cultural rights and interests of non-members and dissenting members within the group.[13]

To the extent that group identities are treated solely as cultural issues, one can hardly deny the broad resonance of this approach with a variety of individuals and communities. The European Court of Human Rights, for instance, has recognized cultural pluralism as an important value to be protected under the ECHR, for the sake of particular groups and society as a whole, in the context of narrower or broader aspects of minority and majority identity.[14] It

10 *The Kichwa Indigenous People of Sarayaku v. Ecuador*, Judgment of 27 June 2012, Series C, No. 245 (2012), para. 213; *Mayagna (Sumo) Awas Tingni Community v. Nicaragua*, Judgment of 31 August 2001, Series C, No. 79 (2001).

11 *The Kichwa Indigenous People of Sarayaku v. Ecuador*, *supra* note 10, para. 216.

12 United Nations Declaration on the Rights of Persons Belonging to National or Ethnic, Religious and Linguistic Minorities, UN GA Res. 47/135 (1992); United Nations Declaration on the Rights of Indigenous Peoples (UNDRIP), UN Doc. A/61/L.67 (2007); FCNM (*supra* note 7); International Labour Organisation (ILO) Convention on Indigenous and Tribal Peoples in Independent Countries (No. 169), available at http://www.ilo.org/dyn/normlex/en/f?p=NORMLEXPUB:12100:0::NO::P12100_ILO_CODE:C169.

13 For cases discussing the individual rights implications of Quebec's commercial sign policy and legislation and of a comprehensive agreement with the Maori in New Zealand, see *Ballantyne et al. v. Canada*, Comm. Nos. 359/1989, 385/1989, Views of 31 March, 1993, UN Doc. CCPR/C/47/D/385/1989 (1993); *Apirana Mahuika et al. v. New Zealand*, Comm. No. 547/1993, Views of 27 October 2000, UN Doc. CCPR/C/70/D/541/1993.

14 See G. Pentassuglia, *supra* note 6; T. Koivurova, "Jurisprudence of the European Court of Human Rights Regarding Indigenous Peoples: Retrospect and Prospects," *International*

has effectively called for relevant general and particular decision-making processes to be able to respond to particular groups' practices in ways that are consistent with an underlying entitlement to cultural recognition.[15] In many ways, this is part of the background to the recent rise of cultural rights as exemplified by General Comment 21 adopted in 2009 by the Committee on Economic, Social and Cultural Rights, which is charged with overseeing compliance with the International Covenant on Economic, Social and Cultural Rights (ICESCR).[16] In providing a coherent account of the right to take part in cultural life set out in Article 15(1)(a), the Committee employs an expanded and dynamic (anthropological) concept of "culture" to include ways of life, language and other manifestations of relevance to individuals, groups of individuals and communities, including (among others) "minorities," "migrants" and "indigenous peoples."[17] All of them are regarded as being entitled to core rights of choice, non-discrimination and participation in relevant decision-making.[18]

Although there is an inevitably cross-cutting dimension to group cultural interests, some of them actually blend with very specific claims to political and legal authority. The latter's conceptual (and legal) thrust can be traced back to early "national" self-determination claims made against the domination of European empires or early articulations of claims to indigenous self-government levelled against settler states' colonization. In the aftermath of the First World War, United States President Woodrow Wilson's commitment to the recognition of new states in "indisputably" national territories[19] proved only part of a wider treaty-based and institutional structure designed to empower international law over and above other sources of authority, whether state or nation, in addressing inter-group diversity issues from within the system, including a measure of group autonomy.[20] In the second post-war period, the

Journal on Minority and Group Rights 18 (2011): 1; *Lautsi v. Italy*, App. No. 30814/06, Judgment of 18 March 2011.

15 See e.g. *Chapman v. United Kingdom*, App. No. 27238/95, Judgment of 18 January 2001; *Muñoz Díaz v. Spain*, App. No. 49151/07, Judgment of 8 December 2009.

16 Committee on Economic, Social and Cultural Rights, *Right of everyone to take part in cultural life*, General Comment No. 21 adopted by the Committee on Economic, Social and Cultural Rights at its 43rd session, 21 December 2009, UN Doc. E/C.12/GC/21 (2009).

17 Ibid., at paras. 12–13.

18 Ibid., at Sections B-C.

19 US President Wilson's Fourteen Points Address to Congress, 8 January 1918, point XIII (regarding Poland); see also similar references, including point IX (regarding Italy) and point XI (regarding several Balkan states).

20 *The Aaland Islands Question (On Jurisdiction)*, Report of the International Committee of Jurists, League of Nations Official Journal, Special Supplement No. 3 (1920); *The Aaland Islands Question (On the Merits)*, Report by the Commission of Rapporteurs, League of

reformulation of the right to self-determination as a human right – indeed, as a fundamental precondition for the enjoyment of human rights as such – first became primarily synonymous with independence within colonial (predefined) boundaries and later on began to be further reconfigured in connection with broader notions of participation and recognition of group diversity within established states.[21]

In fact, self-determination's entrenchment in common Article 1 of the UN Covenants on Human Rights, coupled with a string of developments in distinct areas of group protection (minority and indigenous rights featuring prominently among them), have gradually added to postcolonial extensions of the concept by viewing specific forms of "effective" participation in, or control over, decision-making processes as the most significant ways of enriching the minimum legal standard of "representative government" within the wider polity, which was upheld by the 1970 United Nations Declaration on Friendly Relations.[22] This was implicitly confirmed by the Supreme Court of Canada in the 1998 *Reference* case.[23] As the Court noted that "the right to self-determination of a people is normally fulfilled through internal self-determination," it also delved into the ways in which the constitutional framework, as defined by the interplay of federalism, democracy, the rule of law and the protection of minorities, could embody or enable a "meaningful" exercise of that right to the benefit of all the parties concerned, including groups and individuals within. It ultimately spoke to a wider practice concerned with equal rights, rights of participation in decision-making and a measure of territorial or cultural autonomy for distinctive ethno-cultural identities. The 2007 United Nations Declaration on the Rights of Indigenous Peoples (UNDRIP) importantly

Nations Council Document B7 21/68/106 (1921). For a broader assessment, see G. Pentassuglia, "Self-Determination, Human Rights, and the Nation-State," *supra* note 1.

21 H. Hannum, *Autonomy, Sovereignty and Self-Determination: The Accommodation of Conflicting Rights* (Philadelphia: University of Pennsylvania Press, 1996); A. Cassese, *Self-Determination of Peoples: A Legal Reappraisal* (Cambridge: Cambridge University Press, 1995).

22 Declaration on Principles of International Law Concerning Friendly Relations and Co-operation among States in accordance with the Charter of the United Nations, GA Res. 2625, UN GAOR, 25th Sess., Supp. No. 28, UN Doc. A/8028 (1970). See e.g. United Nations Declaration on the Rights of Persons Belonging to National or Ethnic, Religious and Linguistic Minorities, Article 2(2)-(4); UNDRIP, Articles 3, 4, 18 and 19; FCNM, Article 15; see generally G. Pentassuglia, "Ethnocultural Diversity and Human Rights: Legal Categories, Claims, and the Hybridity of Group Protection," *The Yearbook of Polar Law* 6 (2015): 271–280; M. Weller, ed., *Political Participation of Minorities: A Commentary on International Standards and Practice* (Oxford: Oxford University Press, 2010).

23 *Reference Re Secession of Quebec* [1998] 2 S.C.R. 217 (hereinafter, the *Reference* case).

recognizes the right of internal self-determination while still articulating the overall protective framework as an intertwined bundle of entitlements to cultural protection within the state that are rooted in patterns of historical and persistent injustice.

2.2 *On the Edges of the System*

These are no doubt important developments. Yet, they can as much illuminate as obscure what is at stake when it comes to grappling with the role of group identities in human rights discourse. In fact, there is no shortage of uncertainty about the limits of the legal categories that generally underpin the relationship between group protection and human rights. However significantly more progressive and open-ended than in the past, the equality-based approach still leaves the degree of "sameness" or "difference" that can or should be derived from general norms in any particular case unclear. For example, the grounding of indigenous property rights in circumstances of inequality raises the question of whether conditioning such rights on traditional social and economic activities may partly inhibit rather than empower indigenous communities' autonomy within their land.[24] Moreover, it is not clear that such an approach can consistently support group identities or even generate positive obligations to that effect. In *Thlimmenos v. Greece* and *Chapman v. United Kingdom*,[25] part of the argument before the European Court of Human Rights revolved around exemptions on religious or cultural grounds for members of the group. In the first case, the Court took the view (partly under Article 14 ECHR) that Greece had in the circumstances failed "to introduce appropriate exceptions" within the legislation in question for Jehovah's Witnesses, whereas in the second case it dismissed the notion that exemptions from planning laws could be treated as the subject of positive duties or indeed derived from the principle of equality itself. It is quite significant that Protocol 12 to the ECHR, which prohibits discrimination beyond the narrow context of ECHR rights, does not resolve the matter, nor has it been widely ratified.[26] Indirect discrimination claims have

---

24 See e.g. L. Rodríguez-Piñero Royo, "El impacto international de la sentencia," in *El caso Awas Tingni: Derechos Humanos entre lo local y lo global*, ed. F. Gómez Isa (Bilbao: Universidad de Deusto, 2013), 178–181.

25 *Thlimmenos v. Greece*, App. No. 34369/97, Judgment of 6 April 2000; *Chapman v. United Kingdom*, App. No. 27238/95, Judgment of 18 January 2001.

26 11 April 2000, CETS No. 177; established Council of Europe states are conspicuously absent from the list of those members who have ratified the protocol. In the context of European Union equality law, see also J. Marko, "Five Years After: Continuing Reflections on the Thematic Commentary on Effective Participation: The Interplay between Equality and Participation," in *Minorities, Their Rights, and the Monitoring of the European Framework*

remarkable potential but may be difficult to trigger unless state legislation is in place (as has invariably been the case before the Strasbourg Court), and their individual, collective, contingent or structural consequences may or may not inform particular equality considerations or may not derive from the equality argument alone.

While the articulation of group identities as quintessentially cultural claims partly removes that uncertainty, it still appears unable to make sense of a variety of individual and communal identities that could arguably qualify for protection. The Inter-American Court of Human Rights has firmly embraced the cultural argument in relation to indigenous communities and even extended it to non-indigenous groups such as Afro-descendants who are linked to patterns of abuse and exploitation dating back to European colonization. However, whether the Court might be prepared to extend similar protection to *every* conceivable ethno-cultural grouping within the state remains an open question. Tellingly, broad interpretations of general terms, such as "family" under the ICCPR and the ACHR, have been informed by cultural considerations, though in a context specific to indigenous identity.[27] The European Court of Human Rights has acknowledged the cultural dimension of certain minority claims, and even of certain majority traditions, but it has appeared less than forthcoming in using the cultural argument as a transversal category that is able to support reasonable accommodation in matters of religious or ethnic diversity in the public sphere in response to state defences based on respect for secularism, democracy or gender equality.[28]

Similar ambiguities surround the capacity of Article 27 ICCPR to effectively address identity claims. One of the early commentators on this provision went as far as to suggest that it was unclear what its specific contribution really was other than "avoiding the consequences of an unenlightened interpretation of

---

Convention for the Protection of National Minorities – Essays in Honour of Rainer Hofmann, ed. T. Malloy and U. Caruso (Leiden: Martinus Nijhoff Publishers, 2013), 97 at 110 (noting that "[u]ntil today, neither primary nor secondary EU law prescribe a 'positive duty' to take positive measures which must – by definition – be group-oriented").

27 G. Pentassuglia, *supra* note 8, 73–74.

28 See e.g. S. Borelli, "Of Veils, Crosses and Turbans: The European Court of Human Rights and Religious Practices as Manifestations of Cultural Diversity," in *Cultural Heritage, Cultural Rights, Cultural Diversity: New Developments in International Law*, ed. S. Borelli and F. Lenzerini (Leiden: Martinus Nijhoff Publishers, 2012), 55. A similar reluctance is reflected in the recent case law of the Luxemburg-based European Court of Justice operating under EU law in relation to religious clothing in the workplace: *Achbita v. G4S Secure Solutions NV*, Case C-157/15, Judgment of 14 March 2017.

other provisions."[29] While the prevailing reading of Article 27 has largely outweighed the provision's negative formulation, including positive duties in the private sphere or positive rights to effective participation, critical questions remain about the ability of this norm to operate meaningfully across the wide(r) spectrum of group diversity, including minority languages, minority education and/or minority religions. For example, in the recent case of *Leonid Raihman v. Latvia* concerning a claim by a Russian-Jewish minority member to have his name on his passport spelled in its Russian-Jewish form, the Human Rights Committee found a breach of Article 17 ICCPR, but two Committee members argued that the case should have been considered under Article 27 on the basis that the Committee's jurisprudence on indigenous cultures applied, in their view, to minority religious cultures as well.[30] In short, below the surface of unquestionably positive developments lies a deeper sense of incompleteness in the construction of this specialized provision, as the Human Rights Committee struggles to reconcile generic accounts of rights with more targeted views of the field informed by historical or context-specific circumstances.

One typical critique of the cultural argument in this context is that it encourages the "essentialization" of group cultures at the expense of politically and legally more ambitious narratives, including (where appropriate) autonomy or self-government. As the debate over legal pluralism shows, there is certainly merit in the notion that too "culturalist" an approach may be in tension with other interests, such as internal communal reform or the protection of the rights of individuals.[31] Nevertheless, it is difficult to argue that cultural groups, particularly those attached to a homeland, can ground a claim

---

29 N. Rodley, "Conceptual Problems in the Protection of Minorities: International Legal Developments," *Human Rights Quarterly* 17 (1995): 48 at 65.

30 Comm. 1621/2007, Views of 30 November 2010, UN Doc. CCPR/C/100/C/100/D/1621/2007 (2010), Appendix, Individual opinion of Committee members Mr. Rafael Rivas Posada and Mr. Krister Thelin (dissenting), para. 8.6. More broadly, the Human Rights Committee has been seemingly reluctant to recognize positive obligations in the context of the status or special protection of minority languages, minority education or minority religions. See e.g. the *Ballantyne* case, *supra* note 13; *Waldman v. Canada*, Comm. No. 694/1996, Views of 5 November 1999, UN Doc. CCPR/C/67/D/694/1996 (1996); N. Ghanea, "Are Religious Minorities Really Minorities?," *Oxford Journal of Law and Religion* 1 (2012): 1. However, in *Rakhim Mavlonov and Shansiy Sa'di v. Uzbekistan*, Comm. No. 1334/2004, Views of 19 March 2009, UN Doc. CCPR/C/95/D/1334/2004 (2009), the Committee conceded, without further elaboration, that "education in a minority language is a fundamental part of minority culture" in the context of Article 27 (para. 8.7).

31 See e.g. H. Quane, "Legal Pluralism and International Human Rights Law: Inherently Incompatible, Mutually Reinforcing or Something in Between?," *Oxford Journal of Legal Studies* 33 (2013): 675; for conceptual debates over domestic approaches, see N. Bankes, "Recognising the Property Interests of Indigenous Peoples within Settler Societies: Some Different Conceptual Approaches," in *The Proposed Nordic Saami Convention: National*

to self-determination (or autonomy) *solely* in their communal identity. As the post-1945 international law of self-determination gradually emerged out of United Nations practice, those groups claiming to have suffered discrimination at the hands of settler states or new sovereigns were left with the option of aligning with the decolonization paradigm or, later on, seeking redress for gross human rights violations committed against them by the state. Retrospectively, such groups, particularly indigenous communities, did not pursue the former argument with any degree of consistency. And as the recent case of Kosovo shows, international law has hardly endorsed separate statehood as a general international legal remedy for group-based human rights violations.[32] Whatever dilemmas affect the substance of the right, self-determination has traditionally attracted a variety of claimants arguing for their status as "peoples." Yet, the concept of "peoplehood" as a freestanding and identity-based human rights category has been generally met with resistance in international legal doctrine and practice.

2.3 *Legal Hybridity as a Synthesis*

The interplay of legal developments and conceptual fluidity in the field paradoxically results not in inhibiting further progress but in the proliferation of hybrid sites of protection for group identities. More specifically, rigid dichotomies between the individual and the group in human rights law are giving way to complex, yet practical, articulations of what is loosely perceived as a bundle of claims pervasively linked to one another, the hybrid outlook of which opens up possibilities for various degrees of protection. Valid analytical distinctions among individual rights that can be activated on a group basis, group rights in the sense of jointly held rights of group members (collective rights) and group rights in the sense of rights held by groups as such (corporate rights)[33] broadly resonate with practical dimensions of human rights but do not necessarily work as sharply separate categories as one might assume from a purely conceptual point of view.

---

and International Dimensions of Indigenous Property Rights, ed. N. Bankes and T. Koivurova (Oxford: Hart Publishing, 2013), 21 at 24–30.

32 *Accordance with International Law of the Unilateral Declaration of Independence in Respect of Kosovo*, Advisory Opinion, 22 July 2010, I.C.J. Reports 2010, p. 403, paras. 51, 56, 82. In the *Reference* case (*supra* note 23), the Supreme Court of Canada noted that "external" self-determination in the form of "remedial secession" would be contingent upon the state failing to respect "internal" self-determination, though it did question whether remedial secession could be considered an established international law standard (ibid., paras. 134–135).

33 P. Jones, "Groups and Human Rights," in *Human Rights: The Hard Questions*, ed. C. Holder and D. Reidy (Cambridge: Cambridge University Press, 2013), 100; P. Jones, "Human Rights, Group Rights, and Peoples' Rights," *Human Rights Quarterly* 21 (1999): 80.

For example, the relationship between Article 27 ICCPR rights as collective rights and certain collective dimensions of freedom of religion – such as the viability of religious communities or the protection of religious sites[34] – arguably defies a strict operational distinction between rights that are possessed and exercised collectively and rights that are possessed by individuals severally but still enable group activity. In this sense, the European Court's comparatively more timid approach to group issues under the ECHR still retains an important space for recognizing the legitimacy of collective interests deriving from cultural – notably religious – communities and even for fostering group-oriented readings of discrimination cases. Tellingly, the Committee on Economic, Social and Cultural Rights has very loosely framed cultural rights under the ICESCR as *both* rights of individuals and rights of groups built around entitlements to freely choose a specific set or multiple sets of cultural goods in order to facilitate access to such goods and participation in the design and implementation of laws affecting them.[35] The Committee has indicated that such a participation should involve "their free and informed prior consent" when their "cultural resources ... are at risk."

This level of hybridity is anything but unique to these more general human rights instruments; in reality, it has become something of a hallmark of much of human rights practice, including more complex cases. For all its significance and transformative potential, the recognition of indigenous autonomy in the UNDRIP, for example, still requires the group to engage in negotiations with the state (and vice versa) over the exact terms of its political status, its cultural autonomy and/or legal systems where they exist, as well as to work out regimes that are consistent with the rights of individual members and non-members. Some of these uncertainties tap into the relational philosophy of the UNDRIP and the consequent demand on all the parties concerned to engage in what the Supreme Court of Canada called "a continuous process of discussion"[36] – a process that is designed to work out the terms of the indigenous peoples-state relationship. Other global and regional practice has similarly developed a discourse whereby formally individual and group rights not only meet but are *explained* in light of each other's cross-cutting and intertwined dimensions, be they religion, culture, property, self-determination, participation or a combination of these. Certain individual rights have been re-read to incorporate group

34 See e.g. the European Court of Human Rights' decision in *Metropolitan Church of Bessarabia and Others v. Moldova*, Appl. No. 45701/99, Judgment of 13 December 2001; P. Jones, "Groups and Human Rights," *supra* note 33, 107.

35 See *supra* note 16, para. 15(a).

36 See the *Reference* case, *supra* note 23, para. 68.

rights at sub-state level, and group rights (e.g. rights to natural resources) have been re-read to partly endorse the logic of the individual rights (e.g. property rights) to which they are said to be intimately related as a matter of substance and process.[37] Ambitious peace settlements equally appeal to "hybrid" ideas of self-determination resulting from cumulative views of standards in an attempt to govern competing individual and group claims.[38] In a non-conflict scenario, the Draft Nordic Saami Convention, produced in 2005 by Norway, Finland and Sweden together with the respective Nordic Saami parliaments, exemplifies a major attempt at institutionalizing aspects of the Saami legal order as a central component of Saami self-determination within wider state systems,[39] including conflicts of law norms, forms of territorial and cultural autonomy and weaker translations of Saami legal practices into state law.[40]

In sum, the role of group identities in human rights discourse is increasingly multi-layered, and increasingly hybrid at that. In some cases, human rights practice will enable vitally important group activity. In other cases, it will protect the distinctive collective interest of the group through measures that target specific rights. In still other cases, it will create a framework for institutional and policy action to be worked out at the local level. For all the progress that has been undisputedly made on several fronts of human rights law, there is, however, a sense that the international human rights regime leaves space for conceptual ambiguity vis-à-vis the pathways on which it needs to be set for ethno-cultural group identities to be taken seriously. More specifically, the limitations and uncertainties surrounding the field have simultaneously fed into – and are probably a function of – broader (conceptual, non-doctrinal) perspectives on the very significance of group identities, their personal scope and the ways in which international (human rights) law can or should respond to them.

37 G. Pentassuglia, "Toward a Jurisprudential Articulation of Indigenous Land Rights," *European Journal of International Law* 22 (2011): 165 at 187–190, 198.

38 For an excellent discussion in conflict contexts, see C. Bell, *On the Law of Peace: Peace Agreements and the Lex Pacificatoria* (Oxford: Oxford University Press, 2008), chs. 5, 11 (arguing that hybrid self-determination, including autonomy arrangements, from the Bougainville to the Belfast agreements, can be pursued as "the best application of the law in situations of intrastate ethnic conflict," p. 225).

39 The unofficial version of the Draft Convention is available from the Saami Council website at http://www.saamicouncil.net. For an extensive commentary, see N. Bankes and T. Koivurova, *supra* note 31.

40 For this gamut of models, see J.W. Hamilton, "Acknowledging and Accommodating Legal Pluralism: An Application to the Draft Nordic Saami Convention," in N. Bankes and T. Koivurova, *supra* note 31, 45–77.

The remainder of this article provides an illustration and critique of some of these conceptual instabilities.

3 The Conceptual Instabilities of Human Rights Discourse

3.1 *Identity Matters*

It can be argued, first, that certain ambivalences in the field are in part the upshot of narratives that question the very validity of claims relating to ethno-cultural group identities. Much of this thinking essentially seeks to deconstruct the meaning(s) of such identities from a critical, "post-cultural" (post-modern) or cosmopolitan angle.

Martti Koskenniemi, for example, has argued that, since there is no natural standard to assess the existence of "national" communities, "national" self-determination claims (and, by analogy, group identity claims more broadly) should be understood essentially as ways "to enlist popular support for the struggle against political oppression," be they in the form of anti-colonialism as we have known it or some other form of resistance or reaction as a legitimate process of political contestation.[41] Others have gone as far as to question the plausibility of coherent cultural, national or identity claims as significant drivers of human identity in an era of globalization and mobility. For them, if there is any culture or identity at all, it is a global one that dissolves, not affirms, differences built around "natural languages" and "natural cultures"; it is one that operates in circumstances of "radical heterogeneity and fragmentation," which are no longer capable of sustaining any serious concept of (group) identity within or across state boundaries.[42] Needless to say, several of these perspectives also exemplify concerns about essentialism and varying degrees of hostility or suspicion towards right claims attached to a community defined in (broadly understood) ethno-cultural terms (be it a minority or majority group).[43]

41 M. Koskenniemi, "National Self-Determination Today: Problems of Legal Theory and Practice," *International and Comparative Law Quarterly* 43 (1994): 241 at 262.

42 For discussion and critique of this line, see e.g. J. Tully, *Strange Multiplicity: Constitutionalism in an Age of Diversity* (Cambridge: Cambridge University Press, 1995), 45–47 (citing the work of James Clifford and Peter Emberley).

43 F. Tesón, "Ethnicity, Human Rights, and Self-Determination," in *International Law and Ethnic Conflict*, ed. D. Wippman (Ithaca and London: Cornell University Press, 1998), 86; F. Tesón, "Introduction: The Conundrum of Self-Determination," in *The Theory of Self-Determination*, ed. F. Tesón (Cambridge: Cambridge University Press, 2016), 1.

However, while it may be historically accurate to link several group claims to positive emancipatory projects, and others to more destructive projects of political manipulation, aggressive chauvinism and/or cultural essentialism, it would be wrong to assume either that group identities can be reduced to patterns of discourse or that all identity claims involve a fundamental re-engineering of the state as opposed to more limited forms of recognition. For one thing, social science research has convincingly shown that, whatever their origins and form, and whatever their openness and potential for negotiation and revision, group identities must be taken seriously, as they are no less real as underlying social determinants than the political projects or priorities that help mediate them (or some of them).[44] On the other hand, virtually no states are home to homogenous socio-cultural "nations," yet most states seek to secure one version or another of a uniform public culture or uniform cultural paradigm that poses a threat (in principle or in practice) to inter-group diversity. The very emergence of new states in the name of "national" independence or the continuing running of states as nation-states – from Europe to the Americas to Africa and Asia – has consistently raised very real questions about the rearrangement of authority within the newly constituted or established entity in order to meet certain group demands. While not all nation-building projects have proved wholly incapable of recognizing some form of group diversity within (at least in some of their founding documents), they certainly indicate the salience of community identity of one form or another *across* the fabric of emerging or established states. They speak to a constant interplay of homogenizing tendencies and group representation, on the one hand, and cultural claims and the state's own pursuit of social and cultural protection or integration, on the other.[45]

An arguably more subtle way of deconstructing the role of group identities is by making identity claims overwhelmingly dependent upon strictly

44 See e.g. the insightful analyses of I. Berlin, "Nationalism: Past Neglect and Present Power," in *Against The Current: Essays in the History of Ideas*, ed. H. Hardy (London: The Hogarth Press, 1979), 333; C. Geertz, *The Interpretation of Cultures* (London: Fontana Press, 1973); C. Geertz, *Mondo globale, mondi locali: cultura e politica alla fine del ventesimo secolo* (Bologna: Il Mulino, 1995), chs. II and IV; J. Tully, *supra* note 42; M. Walzer, *The Paradox of Liberation: Secular Revolutions and Religious Counterrevolutions* (New Haven, CT and London: Yale University Press, 2015).

45 See generally M. Walzer, *supra* note 44; *Ethno-Cultural Diversity and Human Rights*, ed. G. Pentassuglia, *supra* note 1 (e.g. chapters by Chris Chapman, Dwight Newman, Tom Hadden, and Ephraim Nimni and Lucia Payero); for a review of similar debates in South East Asia, see e.g. J. Castellino, "Autonomy in South Asia: Evidence for the Emergence of a Regional Custom," in *Minority Accommodation through Territorial and Non-Territorial Autonomy*, ed. T. Malloy and F. Palermo (Oxford: Oxford University Press, 2015), 217.

individual choice. Obviously there are different facets to this dimension, and some of them can be treated as relatively uncontroversial (at least as a matter of principle). Individual self-identification acquires particular salience vis-à-vis claims made by the group and/or assumptions about group identities made by the state. While such claims normally presuppose a legitimate institutional agent that is capable of making them (or at least individuals who can legitimately voice the shared collective interest), each putative member of the group is in principle free to opt out of her/his putative group membership and/or to challenge any group status, or lack of it, imposed upon them by the state.[46] One can thus argue that, under international human rights law, compulsory individual identifications with (or membership in) the group are not permitted, be they enacted through legislation or other domestic practices. It is also the case that group arrangements, like certain power-sharing agreements whereby individuals, including members of smaller minorities, must either declare their affiliation with any of the dominant groups or accept certain legal consequences (e.g. in relation to certain political offices or types of employment) resulting from their free identification as belonging to a group other than the dominant one(s), or to no particular group, pose especially difficult challenges to the most appropriate way of articulating group identities that reconciles effectively with individual interests.[47] In *Sejdić and Finci v. Bosnia and Herzegovina*, for example, the European Court of Human Rights concluded that Bosnia's power-sharing agreement signed at Dayton in 1995 was incompatible with Article 14 ECHR insofar as it excluded members of communities other than the Bosniak, Croat and Serbian ones (who had freely so self-identified) from certain political offices.[48]

However pressing these concerns are – some of them have long been canvassed by international standards – a strand of expert analysis has gone on to draw the unwarranted conclusion that "group identity" is little more than shorthand for the individual's subjective choice. In its latest Thematic Commentary on "The Scope of Application of the Framework Convention for the Protection of National Minorities," the FCNM Advisory Committee has argued that Article 3 (right to free self-identification) is "necessarily applicable to

46 Document of the Copenhagen Meeting of the Conference on the Human Dimension of the CSCE, 29 June 1990, para. 35; *Ciubotaru v. Moldova*, App. No. 27138/04, Judgment of 27 April 2010; *Sandra Lovelace v. Canada*, Comm. No. 24/1977, Views of 30 July 1981, Human Rights Committee, *Annual Report* (1981), 166; UNDRIP, Articles 33(1), 44, 46(2)-(3).

47 See e.g. FCNM Advisory Committee, Third Opinion on the United Kingdom, 30 June 2011, paras. 44–47; Third Opinion on Cyprus, 19 March 2010, para. 39; Fourth Opinion on Cyprus, 18 March 2015, paras. 11–12; Third Opinion on Italy, 15 October 2010, para. 53.

48 Apps. Nos. 27996/06 and 34836/06, Judgment of 22 December 2009.

everyone, as every person must have the right to identify freely as a member of a specific group, or to choose not to do so." Although the Explanatory Memorandum attached to the Convention points to objective criteria as a way of supporting (or disproving) subjective claims, the Committee notes that:

> [It] has intentionally refrained from interpreting what such objective criteria may be, as it is clear from the wording of the Explanatory Report that they must only be reviewed vis-à-vis the individual's subjective choice. Thus, objective criteria do not constitute elements of a definition.[49]

It can be questioned whether this is a correct reading of the Explanatory Memorandum. Paragraph 35 of this document states in no uncertain terms that the subjective choice is "inseparably linked" to objective criteria, and one would have thought the gist of those criteria to be drawn (however imperfectly) from the Convention's scope itself and the basic principles underpinning the field in international law. In *Ciubotaru v. Moldova* before the European Court of Human Rights,[50] Judge Mijović went as far as to contend that self-identification was primarily "a matter of personal perception rather than a matter based on objective grounds." He argued that "[in] Moldova, just as in Bosnia and Herzegovina, ethnic affiliation is not to be regarded as a legal and objective concept, but a political and subjective one." Judge Mijović concurred with the majority's finding of a breach of Article 8 (private and family life) not on the basis (upheld by the Court) that Moldova had failed to provide the applicant with an opportunity to adduce evidence in support of his identity claim but rather on the basis that the applicant's self-identification choice should have been respected *regardless* of any objective parameters to establish affiliation with a particular group. These lines of thinking hardly fit in with established international law and human rights practice,[51] though they most certainly offer a critique of such practice. It is one thing to mark out the limits of state

49 Thematic Commentary No. 4, *The Scope of Application of the Framework Convention for the Protection of National Minorities*, 27 May 2016, ACFC/56DOC(2016)001, para. 10.

50 *Supra* note 46.

51 See generally G. Pentassuglia, *Minorities in International Law: An Introductory Study* (Strasbourg: Council of Europe Publishing, 2002), 72–74; it can also be argued that the European Court of Human Rights does not regard self-identification as an exclusive criterion: see the Chamber's ruling in *Ciubotaru* (*supra* note 46, paras. 57–58) and *Gorzelik and Others v. Poland*, App. No. 44158/98, Judgment of 17 February 2004 (for commentary, see G. Pentassuglia, "Protecting Minority Groups through Human Rights Courts: The Interpretive Role of European and Inter-American Jurisprudence," in *The Cultural Dimension of Human Rights*, ed. A.F. Vrdoljak (Oxford: Oxford University Press, 2013), 104–106).

action in recording and classifying group identities, and it is quite another to re-conceptualize group identities in ways that break them down into a highly variable set of subjective views or discourses. By reconfiguring those identities as a mirror of "externally imposed markers,"[52] such a re-conceptualization effectively essentializes "atomized" choices at both the point of exit from and the point of *entry* into an indeterminate number of legal regimes, as opposed to engaging with the legitimacy of core interests that attach to individuals *and* groups alike.[53]

3.2 *Whose Identity?*

A parallel source of instability is generated by the chronic uncertainty affecting the status of ethno-cultural groups in international law. Much of this instability is a reflection of certain – not uncommonly competing – ideas about how group identities (or some of them) relate or ought to relate to human rights. A prime example of this is the rather complex debate over so-called "new" minorities as distinct from "old" or traditional (national) minorities. The argument in favour of extending the concept to include immigrants and similar groupings rests essentially on the notion that cultural identities or cultural differences inhere in all individuals regardless of communal or situational circumstances. As long as access to a cultural "context of choice"[54] affects virtually everyone, there would be no reason, so the argument goes, for denying minority status to immigrants while granting it to other groups within the state. In terms of the legal categories mentioned earlier in this article, the point appeals to the necessarily universal scope of rights to culture in (explicit or implicit) conjunction with the principle of equality.

While the argument has become increasingly popular in some expert circles, it still faces a range of rather formidable legal and policy challenges. For one thing, there is virtually *no* empirical evidence that indicates an emerging international consensus on the above extension as a matter of law. Take, again, the FCNM. Although the Advisory Committee has consistently supported the

---

52 *Supra* note 49, para. 37.

53 Indeed, the logical, and quite extraordinary, implication of this conceptual approach is that individual choice would be (ontologically and legally) *constitutive* of the identity phenomenon itself, not (or not only) an ex post facto safeguard against certain pre-existing socio-cultural communities that people are born into (whatever their legal characterization) and that they can perceive as a significant part of their core identity. From a different (negative) angle, the essentialization of choice can even go as far as to justify restrictions on basic identity rights in the name of public "neutrality" (see *supra* note 28).

54 W. Kymlicka, *Multicultural Citizenship: A Liberal Theory of Minority Rights* (Oxford: Oxford University Press, 1995).

idea of a broader application of this treaty, a large number of the current states parties that have taken a stance on this matter (*at least* more than half of the current treaty membership) has equally consistently held on to a more restrictive understanding of the concept of "national minority." As I suggested in my earlier work,[55] it is entirely possible (and in some cases perhaps even advisable) for individual states to provide extended protection on a de facto (discretionary) rather than de jure (obligatory) basis, as evidenced by a limited number of later cases. Equally, it is *not* permissible for states to make group status dependent upon exceedingly restrictive (discrimination-inducing) criteria, such as state recognition, territorial concentration or state kinship, which lie beyond the minimum parameters supplied by international human rights law. For present purposes, though, the key point is that, while the cultural argument can (indeed must) support essential elements of protection under general human rights norms (e.g. access to non-discrimination tout court or to basic religious rights), it struggles to make sense of those largely contextual considerations that underpin the *prioritization* of certain group interests over others within state jurisdictions, including specific levels of decision-making authority involving minority and majority communities.[56]

An adapted cultural argument that has proved relatively more successful so far has emerged in the context of debates over indigeneity. As I mentioned in subsection 2.2, the Inter-American Court of Human Rights has broadly interpreted that concept to include certain non-native and land-dependent traditional communities. Similarly, the African Commission on Human and Peoples' Rights has linked selective "peoples' rights" under the ACHPR – mainly the right to existence and self-determination (Article 20), the right to natural resources (Article 21) and the right to development (Article 22) – to an expansive concept of indigeneity that is not dependent upon "prior occupancy" of traditional communal lands and resources.[57] In the ground-breaking *Endorois*

55 G. Pentassuglia, *supra* note 51, 65–66.

56 The FCNM Advisory Committee, for example, has encouraged the enjoyment of specific language and education rights under the FCNM irrespective of traditional residency or numerical requirements, in the name of promoting multilingualism and diversity as well as equality (see *supra* note 49, paras. 31, 42 and 79). For commentary on the national minority/immigrants divide and the implications for *both* national minorities and majorities, see D. Newman, "Why Majority Rights Matter in the Context of Ethno-Cultural Diversity: The Interlinkage of Minority Rights, Indigenous Rights, and Majority Rights," in *Ethno-Cultural Diversity and Human Rights*, ed. G. Pentassuglia, *supra* note 1; A. Patten, *Equal Recognition: The Moral Foundations of Minority Rights* (Princeton: Princeton University Press, 2014), ch. 8. See also Section 3 below.

57 Report of the African Commission's Working Group of Experts on Indigenous Populations/Communities, submitted in accordance with the Resolution on the Rights of

case against Kenya, for example, the Commission recognized the pastoralist community in question as an indigenous community on account of the group's long-standing cultural and land tenure practices, "beyond the "narrow/aboriginal/pre-Colombian" understanding of indigenous peoples."[58] In addition to criteria of self-identification, territorial connection and cultural distinctiveness, notions of social marginalization, discrimination and non-dominance have informed such rethinking to a significant degree.

Despite a measure of relative jurisprudential success, questions have nonetheless been raised as to the longer-term sustainability of this particular way of (re-)conceptualizing certain group identities. For example, legal theorists such as Patrick Macklem and Dwight Newman have warned against the danger of over-emphasizing generic non-dominance at the expense of a more coherent account of the normative purposes of the field,[59] while other prominent voices such as Will Kymlicka and Benedict Kingsbury have, in different ways, exposed critical dimensions of the ambivalent relationship between "indigenous peoples" and "national minorities" or otherwise traditional ethno-cultural communities.[60] It can be argued that, while a flexible legal concept of "indigenous peoples" is fast gaining ground, this concept, rooted as it is in international law, does not surrender the task of identifying the groups to state legislation or purely (not infrequently unfavourable) domestic practices, nor does it surrender it to the group through a notion of self-identification that does away with socio-historical evidence appropriate to the case.[61] In fact, the flexible

---

Indigenous Populations/Communities in Africa, IWAGIA (Copenhagen) and ACHPR (Banjul) (2005), Section 3.2.

58 *Supra* note 4, para. 159. In the *Ogiek* case (*supra* note 4), the African Court on Human and Peoples' Rights situated a broadly similar line on indigenous groups within the much broader context of how to read the specific notion of peoples' rights under the ACHPR (see *infra* note 70).

59 P. Macklem, *The Sovereignty of Human Rights* (Oxford: Oxford University Press, 2015), ch. 6; D. Newman, *supra* note 56; see also F.M. Ndahinda, *Indigenousness in Africa: A Contested Legal Framework for Empowerment of "Marginalized" Communities* (The Hague: T.M.C. Press, 2011).

60 B. Kingsbury, "Reconciling Five Competing Conceptual Structures of Indigenous Peoples' Claims in International and Comparative Law," *New York University Journal of International Law and Politics* 34 (2001): 189 at 233, 244; W. Kymlicka, *Multicultural Odysseys: Navigating the New International Politics of Diversity* (Oxford: Oxford University Press, 2007), 273–291.

61 For concerns relating to an open-ended approach to "indigenous peoples" as a legal concept, see P. Macklem, *supra* note 56, 156–162; domestic policy and legislation in Africa frequently involve issues of group recognition and land security against the backdrop of restrictive internal requirements: see ILO/ACHPR, *Overview Report of the Research Project by the International Labour Organization and the African Commission on Human and*

view reflected in the Inter-American and African case law seeks to render international human rights law more responsive to the position of the groups concerned. However, in ways that are highly reminiscent of the old/new minorities debate in Europe, the deployment of the cultural argument in connection with broader social equality concerns does not ipso facto settle group status issues, nor does it invite to address the underlying reasons why certain ethno-cultural groups merit protection in the way they do.

Probably the holy grail of legal discussions about group status is tied to popular claims to "national" self-determination made by groups that perceive themselves as fairly coherent cultural communities linked to a traditional homeland. In terms of legal developments post-1945, the right to self-determination was deliberately narrowed primarily to the (identity-blind) right of dependent territories (and "peoples") to achieve political and legal independence,[62] although the simultaneous reshaping of self-determination as a human right laid the foundations for the later broader articulation of the right in common Article 1 of the UN Covenants on Human Rights ("all peoples have the right to self-determination"), at least within the institutional (constitutional and political) framework of the state.[63]

However, it is still relatively unclear how international law (and the international community) should respond to sub-state groups' claims to self-determination that are seemingly in conflict with this (largely territorial) paradigm. The problem is unlikely to be resolved through precise definitions or judicial or quasi-judicial pronouncements over the status of a claimant as a "people" or a "nation" within an emerging or established state. For example, the then European Community Arbitration Commission on Yugoslavia located the position of the Bosnian Serbs around hybrid notions of "population,"

Peoples' Rights on the Constitutional and Legislative Protection of the Rights of Indigenous Peoples in 24 African Countries (2009), paras. 117–121.

62 In this sense, it was a way of prioritizing certain communities (territorially defined) over other communities (however defined); it did not reflect a conscious "cherry-picking" act from a pre-set of universally recognized "ethnic" or "cultural" nations. See G. Pentassuglia, "Self-Determination, Human Rights, and the Nation-State," *supra* note 1, Section 2.1. See also A. Anghie, "Nationalism, Development and the Postcolonial State: The Legacies of the League of Nations," *Texas International Law Journal* 41 (2006): 447 (noting that, if anything, the new "culture" of the postcolonial state was to transcend local cultures altogether).

63 Human Rights Committee, *CCPR General Comment No. 12: Article 1 (Right to Self-determination), The Right to Self-Determination of Peoples,* adopted by the Human Rights Committee at its 21st session, 13 March 1984, para. 4, available at http://www.refworld.org/docid/453883f822.html.

"minority" and "ethnic group" for purposes of self-determination within Bosnia.[64] The International Court of Justice, for its part, held that Kosovo's Declaration of Independence was not, in and of itself, at odds with international law, but still refrained from recognizing the population of Kosovo, let alone the Kovosar Albanians, as a people in a legal sense.[65] Critics have suggested that the awkwardness surrounding these rulings reflects a failure to recognize sub-unit claims from within the internal federal boundaries of collapsing Yugoslavia or a failure to genuinely engage with self-determination issues from within Serbia as an established state.[66] Yet, it can be argued that these pronouncements underscore a deeper tension between human rights law and claims to self-determination made by "national" groups, one that can be resolved neither by carving out entire states out of a "national" *droit acquis* in "abnormal" circumstances of territorial and political transition,[67] nor through outright rejection of such claims or some alternative version of them.[68]

Remarkably, in the 1998 *Reference* case, the Supreme Court of Canada noted in no uncertain terms that determining the exact status of the French-speaking community of Quebec, or indeed of any other group within Quebec, as a "people" was not necessary in the case at hand. Given that much of the judgment situates Quebec's position in the context of a wider process of internal self-determination and even the possibility of Quebec's secession,[69] such an

64 European Community Arbitration Commission, Opinion No. 2, 11 January 1992, *International Legal Materials* 31 (1992): 1497.

65 *Supra* note 32, paras. 51, 56, 82, 89, 105, 109.

66 See e.g. R. Falk, *Human Rights Horizons: The Pursuit of Justice in a Globalizing World* (New York and London: Routledge, 2000), 115–116 (commenting on H. Hannum, "Self-Determination, Yugoslavia, and Europe: Old Wine in New Bottles?," *Transnational Law and Contemporary Problems* 3 (1993): 59).

67 Just as in the *Aaland Islands* case (*supra* note 20), the international community's intervention to address the claims in those transitional circumstances did not use the "nation" as the ultimate controlling legal principle, so the European Community's heightened competence in Yugoslavia did not buttress the equation between "natural" (national) communities and nation-states.

68 However arguably clumsily, the so-called Badinter Commission's Opinion No. 2 (*supra* note 64) still sought to reconcile sovereignty, self-determination and human rights by looking at minority protection and possible dislocations of power across national boundaries. See more broadly G. Pentassuglia, "Self-Determination, Human Rights, and the Nation-State," *supra* note 1.

69 The Court ruled out the possibility of remedial secession on human rights grounds, even though it was unclear (a) how that reconciled with the Court's silence as to who was entitled to remedial secession – or indeed whether there was such an entitlement – in the first place, and (b) whether Quebec would have been entitled to remedial secession as a distinct "people" or some other entity, had denial of access to government and gross human rights abuses been proven.

agnostic line says more about the ambiguities of the "peoplehood" (or "nationhood") argument than it says about the substance of self-determination. By adapting from the 1970 United Nations Declaration on Friendly Relations, the Court did not prioritize group status issues but instead focused on the "whole of the people or peoples resident within the territory" as a basis for proper constitutional (internal) arrangements. What does come into view is thus an acknowledgment of the coexistence of various "national" groups within the state and the requirement of complex constitutional conversations designed to achieve accommodation of that diversity, *regardless* of precise communal classifications.

These decisions may struggle to fit rigid patterns of doctrinal coherence or fully match expectations on the ground. Still, they seem to be able to make space for a constructive, though tentative, response of international (human rights) law to group identities (or some of them) in ways that arguments built squarely around "peoplehood" (or "nationhood") per se cannot, as they tend to be either implausible or incomplete. The point here is not that some subnational groups can never be viewed as "peoples" for legal purposes, however hybrid and highly contingent such a recognition may be,[70] but rather that national legislators, adjudicators or policy-makers are hardly keen to make this sort of determination.[71] If anything, constructive responses of the kind mentioned above should be taken to represent particular participation-based articulations of underlying (general) issues of group protection and inter-group

70 Some such groups have gradually come within the purview of the ACHPR as being entitled to "peoples' rights," and indigenous groups have been recognized as "peoples" entitled to self-determination under the UNDRIP. In the *Ogiek* case (*supra* note 4, para. 198), the African Court on Human and Peoples' Rights broadly read the beneficiaries of specific ACHPR rights to include "sub-state ethnic groups and communities" in addition to the whole population of the state. See generally *supra* note 57, ch. III, and note 58. However, as I have discussed elsewhere (G. Pentassuglia, "Do Human Rights Have Anything to Say about Group Autonomy?," in *Ethno-Cultural Diversity and Human Rights*, ed. G. Pentassuglia, *supra* note 1, Section 2.4.2), neither of these cases reflects a strict terminological coherence or a quest for group status precision, either within the context of the same treaty or across the field. Crucial components of indigenous rights come from legal settings where matters of group status are either irrelevant or have been deliberately omitted, and practice under the ACHPR suggests, if anything, the hybrid capacity of this instrument to protect a variety of minority groups, regardless of how to translate their communal pedigree into legal discourse.

71 Indeed, the reluctance by international bodies to engage in such classifications matches a similar reluctance in domestic settings: see e.g. M. Suksi, "On the Entrenchment of Autonomy," in *Autonomy: Applications and Implications*, ed. M. Suksi (Dordrecht: Kluwer Law International, 1998), 151 at 165 (noting that very few groups enjoying autonomy through domestic arrangements have been recognized as "peoples" for such purposes).

diversity within plural societies, rather than the effect of some kind of logical or normative necessity, let alone an international legal requirement, regarding sub-state "peoplehood."

3.3 *Between Effectiveness and Individuals' Cosmopolis*

In addition to critiques of the very substance of such identities and their personal scope, the oscillations of legal and policy discourse unsurprisingly resonate with broader narratives questioning the ability of international law to relate to complex socio-cultural realities, or its ability to do so in distinctive ways. Recent analyses of group claims to secession or autonomy arrangements, on the one hand, and to democratic participation in governance, on the other, best illustrate the point.

At one end of the scale is what I might call the "effectiveness" approach to self-determination. It is essentially based on the notion that, because international law does not or cannot regulate matters such as unilateral secession or autonomy regimes within a state, the law of self-determination is inevitably hostage to facts on the ground. Fernando Tesón, for example, has argued that the principle of self-determination and the principle of territorial integrity prevail over one another depending on whether or not a secessionist movement is successful in overcoming resistance from the territorial state and the international community. Based on this model, the annexation of Crimea by Russia or the independence of Kosovo – both of which involved, for better or for worse, strong assertions of group identities – is *legally* a matter of self-determination (*vel non*) depending on whether or not Ukraine, Serbia and/or the rest of the world are factually capable of reversing it.[72] As a rule of thumb, international law's clearly hostile, yet deregulatory, approach to unilateral secession can thus be overtaken by new political and military realities on the ground and can possibly become entrenched by some degree of international recognition. In a broadly similar fashion, international support for groups seeking autonomy arrangements (short of independence) within a state based on their sense of distinctiveness can be exceptionally vocal in response to new "facts" on the ground – the reality of territorial control and/or loss of life often coupled with the abolition of previous forms of self-government – and, conversely, more cautious and tentative (though not necessarily hostile) where these circumstances have not (or have never) been met.[73]

72 F. Tesón, "Introduction: The Conundrum of Self-Determination," *supra* note 43, 7–8.

73 See e.g. the review of practice by J. Ringelheim, "Considerations on the International Reaction to the 1999 Kosovo Crisis," *Revue Belge de Droit International* 2 (1999): 475.

Leaving aspects of general international (or human rights) law aside,[74] what is important for present purposes is to emphasize that the extent of the legal outcome in those circumstances is deemed to be largely a function of factual realities – "secession [or autonomy] in the streets," to borrow (and paraphrase) from the Supreme Court of Canada in the *Reference* case.[75] Insofar as group identities are cast in the language of independence or autonomy, the "effectiveness" approach generally displaces human rights considerations in the name of security (*realpolitik*) priorities or, in a more attenuated form, tends to value group identities as valid human rights matters *only* by reference to regimes that already exist(ed) within a state.[76]

At the other end of the scale is a minimalist concept of participation in governance within states. As I noted earlier, international law's gradual shift away from colonial self-determination towards the notion of internal self-determination based on "representative government" has suggested an alternative avenue for addressing sub-state group identities. Nevertheless, prominent calls for equating internal self-determination with a distinct "right to democracy" under international law – the right of a people to engage in meaningful decision-making within the state – have raised concerns about the empirical accuracy of the claim and, more crucially, the different ways in which the requirement of democracy can or ought to be articulated. Leading proponents of narrow electoral views of democracy have emphasized general collective aspects of voting rights and internationally-backed processes of election monitoring rather than any additional requirement to rearrange decision-making authority for the benefit of particular groups.[77] And yet, a "right to democracy" understood as a mere entitlement to inclusion in the political community on a non-discriminatory

74 Tesón's view, for example, seems to downplay international law's a priori resistance to validating facts that are deemed incompatible with peremptory rules of general international law. See e.g. J. Vidmar, "Crimea's Referendum and Secession: Why it Resembles Northern Cyprus More Than Kosovo," available at www.ejiltalk.org/crimeas-referendum-and-secession-why-it-resembles-northern-cyprus-more-than-kosovo.

75 *Supra* note 23, para. 142.

76 The FCNM Advisory Committee has commended autonomy arrangements "in States parties where they exist" (*Commentary on the Effective Participation of Persons Belonging to National Minorities in Cultural, Social and Economic Life and in Public Affairs*, 27 February 2008, paras. 133–137).

77 See e.g. T. Franck, "The Emerging Right to Democratic Governance," *American Journal of International Law* 86 (1992): 46; G. Fox, "The Right to Political Participation in International Law," *Yale Journal of International Law* 17 (1992): 539; G. Fox and B. Roth, ed., *Democratic Governance and International Law* (Cambridge: Cambridge University Press, 2000). But see also United Nations Millennium Declaration, GA Res. 55/2, UN Doc. A/55/L.2 (2000), Section V, paras. 24–25.

basis does little to engage with group claims, including claims to specific involvement in decision-making and/or political autonomy.[78]

Indeed, this view often chimes with a deep-seated suspicion towards group identities and a preference for cosmopolitan views that deconstruct those identities in law and policy into generic accounts of multiple and cross-cutting identities attached to individuals as such within the political and global community.[79] In the aforementioned FCNM Advisory Committee's latest Thematic Commentary, for instance, identities are not only decoupled from objective criteria; they are also linked up with highly fluid views of simultaneous individual belonging to multiple "minorities" and/or free association across the spectrum of available (minority or majority) identities within the state.[80] What begins as a plausible claim to diversifying legal protections by safeguarding individual choice and circumstances ultimately takes the form (conceptually at least) of an open-ended endorsement of cosmopolitan perspectives

78 Conceptually, a similar view is reflected in the so-called Pellet Report – a study on the legal impact of Quebec's possible secession from Canada prepared in 1992 by five international lawyers in response to a request from the Committee of the Quebec National Assembly. Regardless of any legitimate interests that Quebec may have in pursuing independence from Canada, the Report considered indigenous opposition to Quebec's independence from within the province by restating a generic right of indigenous groups to participate in democratic governance and to assert their own identity rather than advancing any entitlement to a robust consultation process with Quebec's authorities. See "Territorial integrity of Quebec in the event of the attainment of sovereignty," para. 3.08, available at https://english.republiquelibre.org/Territorial_integrity_of_Quebec_in_the_event_of_the_attainment_of_sovereignty#lien_121. For a critique of generic approaches to democratic governance, see e.g. S. Marks and A. Clapham, *International Human Rights Lexicon* (Oxford: Oxford University Press, 2005), 61–70. From a different angle, see also D. Orentlicher, "Separation Anxiety: International Responses to Ethno-Separatist Claims," *Yale Journal of International Law* 23 (1998): 1 at 44–78 (cautioning that a rapid move to free elections or referenda, and nothing else, might paradoxically support certain ethno-separatist claims and/or entrench ethnic divisions where a strong civic culture is still in the making; a similar point is made by B. Kingsbury, "Reconciling Five Competing Conceptual Structures of Indigenous Peoples' Claims in International and Comparative Law," *New York University Journal of International Law and Politics* 34 (2001): 232).

79 See e.g. T. Franck, *The Empowered Self: Law and Society in the Age of Individualism* (Oxford: Oxford University Press, 2001).

80 *Supra* note 43, para. 13. Apart from more predictable overlapping identities across minority/majority lines or across a whole variety of human activities below and above the surface of the state, the notion that individuals *consciously* move *across minorities* within the meaning of international law (as opposed to exiting a minority group by way of voluntary assimilation into the wider society or rejoining a minority group at a later stage) remains untested. Moreover, we do not seem to have enough empirical data to suggest that this specific phenomenon occurs on such a scale so as to involve a proliferation of legal minority claims under human rights law.

that assume hybridized or mixed (ethno-cultural) identities to be the norm and understate (wittingly or unwittingly) the legitimacy of core group interests across (minority and majority) communities.

4 Conclusions: Unpacking Identity Claims

I would argue that the conceptual instabilities discussed in Section 3 do not merely mirror the ambivalent outlook of the relationship between human rights and group identities; they raise the broader question of whether there is a relatively more coherent way for international law in general, and human rights discourse in particular, to capture the legitimacy of group claims, including those made by sub-state groups who view themselves as somehow distinct communities.

As human rights practice yields a significant, and well-documented, measure of progress in addressing dimensions of group protection, including dimensions of group identities, the field is bound to face critical challenges not only at the level of practical implementation but also in terms of (re-) conceptualizing the normative purposes of legal interventions. An expansive approach to non-discrimination and cultural rights, primarily (though by no means exclusively) on the basis of general human rights norms, provides a refreshing cluster of legal developments but inevitably begs the question of whether norms specific to ethno-cultural groups correspondingly serve the main purpose of reaffirming levels of protection that can be afforded (perhaps even more comfortably at times) on broader grounds. Ideas of non-dominance that are so engrained in human rights accounts of ethno-cultural identities are intuitively essential to addressing certain sub-state group claims, yet an excessive focus on non-dominance may lead to obscuring the legitimacy of group interests across minority and majority communities at both state and regional levels. Emerging overly individualist ("cosmopolitan") views of identity add further pressure to the field. At the high end of the scale, self-determination claims built around cultural understandings of "peoplehood" (or "nationhood") in legal and/or public discourse may prove exorbitant or inconsistent with international human rights law, especially where taken in isolation from the rights of others within the political community. These are some of the conundrums that are considerably amplified by perennial debates over the legal status of groups and the attendant scramble by groups themselves (or some of them) to achieve recognition in one form or another depending on the rights claims involved. While the resulting increasing levels of hybridity involved in the human rights protection of group identities, as examined in subsection

2.3, are definitely cause to rejoice, they should also give pause to reflect on the normative underpinnings of the field, as well as the potential and limitations of human rights discourse.

While traditional views of human rights have focused on the role of minority cultures within a universal code of human rights standards that values (at least in principle) cultural differences across the wide spectrum of human identity, the field's general concerns for non-discrimination and diversity have been invariably shaped by the historical circumstances of groups, including their distinctive character and treatment. For constitutional purposes, for example, major constitutional courts have consistently distinguished between general human rights protection and special (targeted) forms of group protection, such as language or education rights.[81] The fact that various international human rights bodies have engaged in different ways with group identities informs the creation of hybrid and sophisticated sites of legal analysis and discussion but should not obscure the reasons why certain groups merit protection in the way they do.

What tends to remain under the (human rights) radar is the close interface between the protection of groups such as "national minorities" and "indigenous peoples" and the ways in which sovereignty relates to international law-making. The several rearrangements of sovereign authority that have been buttressed by international law throughout history have been constantly punctuated by efforts to mitigate the effects of those redistributions on groups who found themselves within wider political communities with which they had little or no affiliation. From the Westphalia settlement, to the Versailles and League of Nations settlement, to the rise of indigenous rights post-decolonization, to more recent attempts to govern the demise of the USSR and Yugoslavia and other processes of state reconfiguration, the mitigating impact of these multilayered regimes of group protection underscores a series of "pathologies" or "anomalies" that arises from those rearrangements of authority and not from the issue of cultural difference alone.[82]

81 J. Woehrling, "'Droits', 'liberté' et 'accommodements' linguistiques dans la jurisprudence de la Cour suprême du Canada," in *Humanisme et Droit: Ouvrage en Hommage au Professeur Jean Dhommeaux*, ed. L. Hennebel and H. Tigroudja (Paris: Pédone, 2013), 447; J. Woehrling, "Les trois dimensions de la protection des minorités en droit constitutionnel comparé," *Revue de droit de l'Université de Sherbrooke* 34 (2003–04): 93.

82 A strand of scholarship has, implicitly or explicitly, drawn attention to this key "systemic" or "constitutional" dimension. See e.g. N. Berman, "'But the Alternative is Despair': European Nationalism and the Modernist Renewal of International Law," *Harvard Law Review* 106 (1993): 1792; P. Macklem, *supra* note 59, chs. 5–7; S. Krasner and D. Froats, "Minority Rights and the Westphalian Model," in *The International Spread of Ethnic Conflict: Fear, Diffusion, and Escalation*, ed. D. Lake and D. Rothchild (Princeton: Princeton University

The underlying *inter-group* (majority-minority) dynamics linked to the creation and subsequent functioning of states arguably helps explain the problematic role of positive human rights obligations benefiting minority or majority identities and their legitimate collective interests, on the one hand,[83] and the recurrent oscillation between creative institutional exercises in problem-solving and deference to contingent realities, on the other.[84] More specifically, it tells us that, although in several cases the group's demands can be met by respecting, protecting and fulfilling the rights of persons belonging to the group to their identity, greater forms of protection beyond essential association and cultural rights do *not* automatically derive from identity claims but instead rest on the prioritization of certain interests in human rights discourse. To the extent that group accommodation is primarily designed to mitigate the impact of group-related pathologies that arise from multiple (re-)allocations of sovereign power actively pursued or validated by international law, special protection of national minorities and indigenous peoples can only, relatedly, serve the purpose of remedying or offsetting those pathologies, that is, certain forms of majoritarian (cultural) domination or oppression – such as exclusion from state-formation, forced assimilation, abolition of self-government and/or state-sponsored violence – that have emerged (or might emerge) as a result of those (re-)allocations. International human rights law should actively engage with the legitimate interests of state-wide majorities but should nonetheless situate those interests within a framework of mutual – and mutually proportionate – inter-group accommodation tied to broader relational processes of self-determination.[85]

What is important is not (or not only) whether any particular form of group accommodation proves acceptable in any particular case but rather

Press, 1998), 227; C. Reus-Smit, *Individual Rights and the Making of the International System* (Cambridge: Cambridge University Press, 2013), 97–105; J. Nijman, "Minorities and Majorities," in *The Oxford Handbook of the History of International Law*, ed. B. Fassbinder and A. Peters (Oxford: Oxford University Press, 2012), 100; C. Bell, *supra* note 38; R. Kuppe, "The Three Dimensions of the Rights of Indigenous Peoples," *International Community Law Review* 11 (2009): 103.

83 See e.g. the *Lautsi* case (allowing for a *majority* religious symbol to be maintained in public schools subject to proportionality criteria, *supra* note 14) and the debate over the cultural rights of immigrants (*supra* note 56); see also, in parallel, the limits of ICCPR Article 27 rights of *minorities*, *supra* note 30. For an articulation of aspects of this tension in human rights discourse from a jurisprudential perspective, see G. Pentassuglia, *supra* note 9, 248–256.

84 See e.g. N. Berman, *supra* note 82; J. Nijman, *supra* note 82; C. Bell, *supra* note 82.

85 For fuller human rights-based accounts of self-determination and group autonomy, see G. Pentassuglia, *supra* notes 1 and 70.

the capacity of international human rights law to distinguish claims that are ultimately a (rebuttable) call for certain (re-)configurations of the state from more generic claims that only question the outer limits of particular measures within a state's jurisdiction. Definitional debates and a focus on group status or formal right-holding aspects do not greatly advance matters in that they either obscure the reasons for seeking protection or encourage potentially distorting images of who is (or is not) entitled to such protection. Equally, legal narratives that force the large diversity of groups through the needle's eye of single and self-contained human rights categories (culture/equality) or deconstruct groups into little more than a replaceable set of individuals fail to capture the normative complexities involved or to recognize the distinct legitimacy of core group interests that result from the concrete (direct or indirect) interventions and legacies of international law in matters of decision-making authority. In the wake of remarkable developments in the field, the future of group identities in international human rights law ultimately hinges on illuminating and unpacking what is actually at stake, not on shrouding it in a well-intentioned conceptual fog.

CHAPTER 13

Policing the Public Sphere: Regulating Religion in Europe

Kathleen Cavanaugh

Abstract

At both the national and European level, there is a move to secularize the public square; privatizing religion by ensuring that freedom of religion is protected in the private sphere but controlled in its outward (public) manifestation. This secularization of the public sphere cannot be understood without acknowledging the rootedness of Christianity in the European project. The intertwining of a secular hegemonic regime and Christianity shapes and forms how states (and indeed courts) read secularism. Secularism is, in this context, no longer the absence of religious involvement in government affairs and, conversely, the absence of government involvement in religious affairs, but rather an ideology or belief with a hegemonic knowledge regime of what is compatible with the traditions and values of European states and what is not. As this paper will argue, where questions of freedom of religion arise, at both state and European Court level, religion is protected in the private sphere. Where religion pricks the public square, however, we find an illiberal secularism expressed in illiberal restrictions on religion in the public square – a religious pluralism grafted to traditional (and dominant) European norms and values.

1 Introduction

The contestation over the relationship between religion and democracy weighs heavily in Europe.[1] Although questions as to whether, or the extent to which, religion should extend into the public sphere[2] also exist within democratic or

---

1 The idea of Europe embraces wider political and cultural alliances that transcend geographic or physical boundaries. References to Europe are therefore inclusive of both European Union and Council of Europe member states.

2 German social theorist Jürgen Habermas is most closely associated with the use of this term. The concept itself is derived from the German word *Öffentlichkeit*, which has two meanings. The first is "the public" – a collective of speakers and listeners present in the public sphere – and

 | DOI:10.1163/9789004386426_014

quasi-democratic states beyond European borders, the debates within Europe on multiculturalism and pluralism are particularly rife. Where these debates interface with law – at the domestic or international level – what emerges is a hegemonic contestation over European cultural identity.

As a consequence of significant demographic changes, immigration and Islam have become almost synonymous[3] within Europe.[4] This new demographic reality has tested the secular political order and exposed deep divisions over Europe's cultural identity. It is heavily contested whether "European unity, and therefore its external and internal boundaries should be defined by the common heritage of Christianity and Western civilization or by its modern secular values of liberalism, universal human rights, political democracy and tolerant and inclusive multiculturalism".[5]

This ambiguity over Europe's cultural identity is reflected at both the national and regional level, and what emerges as a response is a move to secularize the public sphere. Religion is privatized by ensuring that freedom of religion is protected in the private sphere but controlled in its outward (public) manifestation. This secularization of the public sphere, however, cannot be properly understood without acknowledging the fact that the understanding of the role of religion in public life is shaped by the rootedness of Christianity in the creation of a shared European identity.

Most Europeans self-identify as Christian, but what it means to be Christian is indeed diffuse. Empirical data suggest that self-identification as Christian may be less about religiosity but rather a reflection of a type of a "fuzzy fidelity."[6] As David Voas notes, many people who consider themselves Christian have only a "few or no discernible Christian beliefs." They self-identify as Christian

---

the second is "publicness" – the state of being publicly visible and therefore subject to scrutiny by the public.

3 José Casanova, "Immigration and the New Religious Pluralism: A European Union/United States Comparison" (paper presented at the Conference on "The New Religious Pluralism and Democracy," Georgetown University, Washington, DC, April 2005).

4 For a breakdown of the Muslim population in Europe, see Conrad Hackett, "5 Facts about the Muslim Population in Europe," Pew Research Center, November 29, 2017, http://www.pewresearch.org/fact-tank/2016/07/19/5-facts-about-the-muslim-population-in-europe. For Christian population trends, see David Masci, "Europe Projected to Retain Its Christian Majority, But Religious Minorities Will Grow," Pew Research Center, April 15, 2015, http://www.pewresearch.org/fact-tank/2015/04/15/europe-projected-to-retain-its-christian-majority-but-religious-minorities-will-grow.

5 Casanova, "Immigration and the New Religious Pluralism," 9.

6 David Voas, "The Rise and Fall of Fuzzy Fidelity in Europe," *European Sociological Review* 25, no. 2 (2009): 161.

based on perceived shared values and traditions, and in order to differentiate themselves from other groups associated with another religion.[7] This

> point[s] to an implicit, diffused, and submerged Christian cultural identity. … In this respect, "secular" and "Christian" cultural identities are intertwined in complex and rarely verbalized modes among most Europeans.[8]

Such constructive ambiguity is also present in relation to the concept of secularism. In this context, secularism is no longer the absence of religious involvement in government affairs, and, conversely, the absence of government involvement in religious affairs; rather, it is an ideology or belief that polices what is compatible with the traditions and values of European states and what is not.

The intertwining of secular and Christian cultural identities – as this article shows – has impacted how the requirements of secularism and freedom of religion are legally accommodated in European states. The article explores the various techniques used by European states, and replicated by the European Court of Human Rights (ECtHR), to accommodate and regulate religious diversity. Section II provides an overview of how freedom of religion is regulated at the national level. It begins by detailing how the varied church-state models are mapped out in a number of states and then examines the different constitutional and legislative ways through which European states both protect and regulate religious freedom. Section III provides a brief summary of how government restrictions on the manifestation of religion have been mapped out in European states. As the debates on the role of religion in public life at the national level are often revisited within the European regional system, Section IV turns to the case law of the ECtHR. As this section shows, while freedom of religion in the private sphere has been protected by the ECtHR, when religion pricks the public sphere the results have been mixed. The final section argues that some of the underpinnings of the current liberal debates on religion and democracy serve to reinforce a dominant political culture at the expense of minority communities in Europe.

II Regulating Freedom of Religion

States are given wide discretion as to how they establish and regulate relations between religious communities and the state. Most European states have

7 Ibid., 162–163.

8 Casanova, "Immigration and the New Religious Pluralism," 6–7.

formalized this relationship either constitutionally or legislatively through a freedom of religion bill. In addition, some states also regulate the position of particular religious communities. They may constitutionally designate a particular religious denomination as a state church or conclude an agreement that gives preference to a particular religion. States may also regulate religious activity through a state registration process, designating religious communities with different legal statuses or providing a religious group with additional or specific guarantees. The next section provides a brief overview of each method.

A *Different Church-State Models in Europe*

The degree to which religious institutions are accommodated or excluded in various church-state models moves between states that have an official state religion and those that are actively secular. So while there are states that structurally and legally maintain a state church, the opposite end of the spectrum is occupied by the French model of *laïcité*, with its enforced separation between religion and state and the complete isolation of religion to the private sphere.

Although most official state-church relationships have disappeared, and a variety of other models of church-state relations have emerged, a few European states still retain a state church. Five traditionally Protestant states have a state church: the Anglican Church in England, the Evangelical Lutheran Church in Finland,[9] the Evangelical Lutheran Church in Iceland, and the Evangelical Lutheran Church in Denmark. In addition, the Roman Catholic Church remains a state church in Liechtenstein and Monaco, and the Greek Orthodox Church remains so in Greece.

Constitutional provisions in many of these states have led to significant entanglements between church and state, often at the expense of minority religions. In Greece, for example, the constitution provides for freedom of religion but also establishes the Eastern Orthodox Church of Christ (Orthodox Church) as the state church. As the prevailing religion, the government recognizes the Orthodox Church's canon law, both within the church and in such areas of civil law as marriage.[10] Moreover, the clergy of the Orthodox Church receive their remuneration and pensions from the state and are exempt from taxation.

9 The Evangelical Lutheran Church of Finland is included in this list although it is defined in the country's general legislation as a public organization. However, it has a close relationship with the state and is domestically referred to as both a state church and a folk church (or church for the people).

10 Since 1999, the Catholic Church has unsuccessfully sought government recognition of its canon law.

The Orthodox Church also has a visible role in state affairs, as the Archbishop presides over each opening session of parliament and church and state leaders often jointly preside over state functions and national holiday celebrations. Furthermore, the statutory charter of the Orthodox Church must be passed by the plenary session of parliament. It has also been accorded privileges over non-Orthodox religious minorities with regard to the building and operation of places of worship and the application of legal provisions against proselytism.[11]

The situation is similar in Denmark, where Sections 70 and 71(1) of the Constitutional Act[12] protect freedom of religion, while Section 4 of the Act designates the Evangelical Lutheran Church (the *Folkekirke*) as the state church of Denmark and Section 6 mandates that "the King shall be a member of the Evangelical Lutheran Church."[13]

European states that have concluded a church-state agreement that gives preference to a particular religion include Germany, Poland, Spain, Hungary, Italy and Austria. These treaties generally take the form of concordats with the Holy See and confer a special status and privileges on the Roman Catholic Church. Although the exact nature of these privileges varies from state to state, their existence casts doubt on the notion of an official separation of church and state in these countries.

In Spain, for example, the 1979 Concordat provides for state financing through taxation.[14] Spanish citizens are obliged to "choose between allocating 0.5239 percent of their income to the Roman Catholic Church or to the government's welfare and culture budget, while the state makes up the remaining part of the Catholic Church's finances."[15] While the state is required to provide religious education for all recognized religions, it only fully funds Catholic education and all other religious education must be financed by the religious communities themselves.

11 This issue has even led to a number of cases against Greece at the ECtHR. See *Larissis et al. v. Greece*, Apps. Nos. 140/1996/759/958-960, Judgment of February 24, 1998; *Manoussakis and Others v. Greece*, App. No. 18748/91, Judgment of September 26, 1996; and *Kokkinakis v. Greece*, App. No. 14307/88, Judgment of May 25, 1993.

12 Constitutional Act of Denmark of 1953, available at http://www.thedanishparliament.dk/Publications/The_Constitutional_Act_of_Denmark.aspx.

13 This has led commentators to argue that this differential treatment is a form of discrimination. See Marie Vejrup Nielsen and Lene Kühle, "Religion and State in Denmark: Exception among Exceptions?," *Nordic Journal of Religion and Society* 24, no. 2 (2011): 175.

14 There is some debate over the use of this term, as the agreement in question is not officially a "concordat." However, it is continually referred to as such because it is an international treaty between the Vatican and Spain.

15 Cathelijne de Busser, "Church-State Relations in Spain: Variations on a National-Catholic theme?," *GeoJournal* 67 (2006): 291.

In Italy, the state's relations with the Catholic Church[16] are governed by the 1984 revision of the Concordat, which formalized the principle of a secular state but maintained the practice of state support for religion. This support could be extended, if requested, to non-Catholic confessions by enacting an accord (*intesa*) between the government and the religious confession. While an *intesa* is not required for a religious group to worship freely, it is essential for a group to benefit financially from the voluntary check-off on taxpayer returns. An *intesa* also provides for ministers of religion to have access to state hospitals, prisons and military barracks. It also allows for civil registry of religious marriages, facilitates special religious practices regarding funerals and exempts students from school attendance on religious holidays. It should be added the revised Concordat of 1984 accords the Catholic Church certain privileges. For example, the Church is allowed to select Catholic teachers, paid by the state, to provide instruction in "hour of religion" courses taught in the public schools.[17]

In sharp contrast to these models of church-state relations stands the French model of *laïcité*. France's history of religious conflict, which led to the break of the state's ties to the Catholic Church in the early 1900s, serves as a backdrop for understanding its current and very strong commitment to maintaining

16 It is worth noting here that, although Roman Catholicism is no longer the state religion, its close relationship to the state is still evident. In 2004, for example, the Italian Parliament passed legislation (strongly supported by the Vatican and Catholic legislators) that equates an embryo with a human life, prohibits the use of donated sperm for artificial insemination, restricts the production of embryos and limits scientific research on embryos. See Law No. 40 of February 19, 2004 on Rules on Medically Assisted Procreation, *Official Gazette of Italy* 45 (February 24, 2004), available in English at http://www.ieb-eib.org/en/pdf/loi-pma-italie-english.pdf. For details of the law and subsequent debates, see Andrea Boggio, "Italy Enacts New Law on Medically Assisted Reproduction," *Human Reproduction* 20, no. 5 (2005): 1153–1157.

In addition, the continued public display of Catholic symbols, such as crucifixes, in courtrooms, schools and other public buildings has drawn criticism and led to a number of legal challenges. In an April 2005 case brought by the president of an Islamic association, a court ruled that crucifixes do not have to be removed from polling stations. Previously, in December 2004, the Constitutional Court of Italy held that a 1928 regulation providing for the display of crucifixes in public classrooms was constitutional. This approach to religion in the public sphere is consistent with the state's support of public displays of Catholic symbols. In March 2005, the Interior Minister, Giuseppe Pisanu, argued publicly that the crucifix was a symbol of great value that represented 2,000 years of civilization and culture In 2003, the President, Carlo Azeglio Ciampi, argued that the crucifix was a symbol of national identity and not only a religious emblem.

17 See US State Department's Annual Report on International Religious Freedom 2004, available at https://www.state.gov/j/drl/rls/irf/2014religiousfreedom/index.htm#wrapper.

a completely secular public sphere. A 1905 law[18] cements the separation of church and state, protects religious freedom and prohibits discrimination on the basis of religion. France's policing of the public sphere, however, has raised questions regarding the protection of freedom of religion of minority communities. In a highly controversial decision in March 2004,[19] the French government passed a law prohibiting public school employees and students from wearing conspicuous religious symbols, including the Muslim headscarf, the Jewish skullcap and large crosses. This was followed in 2010 by a law[20] that imposed a ban on the wearing of face coverings, including the niqab and burqa, which extended to the social sphere.[21]

Certainly, this bifurcation – between states that have an official religion or concordats and other states that are actively secular – is reflective of some of European states, but there are a number of other models of church-state relations found in between. These include, for instance, the Dutch-Belgian version of *laïcité*, which differs from the French model in that it is less about removing religious symbols from public view and more about providing an equality of space for confessional and non-confessional organizations (for example, allowing humanists to provide moral guidance in hospitals, the army and prisons), and the Swiss church-state model, which leaves the responsibility for defining the exact nature of the church-state relationship to individual cantons.

B *Regulating Religious Activities*

One method used by states to regulate religious activities is through the process of granting status through state registration. The state registration process is usually governed by a specific law, and in most cases there is a right of judicial review of the decision made by the state agency. While the requirements for registering varies between states, there are three main conditions that are broadly shared. Firstly, the religious community must be able to show that it has a designated number of followers, although the exact number differs significantly

18 See Loi du 9 décembre 1905 concernant la séparation des Eglises et de l'État [Law of December 9, 1905 on the Separation of the Churches and the State], *Journal Officiel de la République Française*, December 11, 1905, Arts. 1–2, current version available at http://www.legifrance.gouv.fr/texteconsolide/MCEBW.htm.

19 The legislation took effect at the beginning of the school year in September 2004.

20 See Loi n° 2010-1192 du 11 octobre 2010 interdisant la dissimulation du visage dans l'espace public [Law No. 2010-1192 of October 11, 2010 prohibiting concealment of the face in public], *Journal Officiel de la République Française* 237, October 12, 2010, available at https://www.legifrance.gouv.fr/affichTexte.do?cidTexte=JORFTEXT000022911670&categorieLien=id.

21 In 2016, the Council of State (*Conseil d'État*) struck down a ban on the wearing of the "burkini" that was instituted by the commune of Villeneuve-Loubet and subsequently adopted by other coastal towns throughout France. Although the Council deemed the ban to have "dealt a serious and clearly illegal blow to fundamental liberties such as the

between states. Secondly, the internal statute or mission statement of the religious community must be compatible with other fundamental freedoms of the state. Lastly, registration documents must provide details on the composition and operation of their religious authorities or management boards.

Only in a small number of European states – Slovakia, Macedonia and Lithuania – are religious communities required to register in order to operate. In most European states, state registration is not obligatory for a religious community to operate but might be necessary in order to obtain legal personality or receive benefits. For instance, while Spain does not have a mandatory registration process per se, since religious communities can be established without initial authorization or registration, registration with the Ministry of Justice is required in order to be granted legal status. Similarly, in Germany, religious organizations are not required to register but must do so if they wish to be treated as non-profit associations enjoying a degree of tax-exempt status.

A second type of regulation is when the state designates a religious organization as belonging to one of three legal categories conferring a distinct set of rights, privileges and responsibilities. These legal categories include religious societies, religious confessional communities and associations (listed in descending order of status).

In Austria, for instance, under an 1874 law, recognition as a religious society provides religious organizations with certain rights and privileges. These include the authority to participate in the mandatory church contributions programme, provide religious instruction in public schools and bring religious workers into the country as ministers, missionaries or teachers. Religious societies have public corporation status, permitting them to engage in a number of public or quasi-public activities that are denied to other religious groups, such as confessional communities and associations. Moreover, they are provided with government financial support for religious teachers at both public and private schools.

The 1998 Law on the Status of Religious Confessional Communities[22] imposed new criteria on religious groups to obtain the status of a religious

---

freedom of movement, freedom of conscience and personal liberty," it remained in force in at least twenty towns. See Angelique Chrisafis, "French Mayors Refuse to Lift Burkini Ban Despite Court Ruling," *The Guardian*, August 28, 2016, https://www.theguardian.com/world/2016/aug/28/french-mayors-burkini-ban-court-ruling. It is worth noting that this ruling was followed by an administrative court ruling in the town of Bastia in Corsica, which upheld a ban instituted by a local mayor on the grounds that it was necessary to maintain public order. See "Burkini Ban Issued on French Island of Corsica Upheld by Court," *The Guardian*, September 6, 2016, https://www.theguardian.com/world/2016/sep/06/burkini-ban-corsica-upheld-by-french-court.

22 See BGBl. Nr. 19/1998: Bundesgesetz über die Rechtspersönlichkeit von religiösen Bekenntnisgemeinschaften [Federal Law No. 19/1998 on the Status of Religious Confessional

society, although it allowed previously recognized societies to retain their status. These include a twenty-year period of existence (at least ten years of which must be as a group organized as a confessional community under the law) and membership equalling at least two thousandths of the country's population (approximately 16,000 persons). Only four of the thirteen previously recognized religious groups met this membership requirement – the Catholic, Protestant, Eastern Orthodox and Islamic communities – though all other previously recognized religious communities were able to retain their status. Of the non-recognized religious groups, only the Jehovah's Witnesses met this new requirement. Additionally, this law allows non-recognized religious groups to seek official status as confessional communities without the fiscal and educational privileges available to religious societies. However, such a status grants them legal standing. To be recognized as confessional communities, religious organizations must have at least 300 members, submit documentation to the government outlining their mission statement and prove that their organization differs from already recognized religious societies or confessional communities.

Another example of this type of regulation is found in France, where, under the aforementioned 1905 law, groups that wish to receive tax-exempt status must register as an *association cultuelle*.[23] This association status allows the group to avail itself of various privileges, including financial incentives. In 2001, under the About-Picard Law,[24] increased restrictions were imposed on religious associations, allowing the state to dissolve groups, including religious groups, if certain conditions existed.[25]

Communities], *Bundesgesetzblatt für die Republik Österreich*, January 9, 1998, available at https://www.ris.bka.gv.at/Dokumente/BgblPdf/1998_19_1/1998_19_1.pdf.

23 See Section C(2) of the 1905 Law. Religious communities that wish to register do so under one of two categories: *associations cultuelles* (associations of worship), which are exempt from taxes, and *associations culturelles* (cultural associations), which are normally not exempt from taxes.

24 It is named after French Members of Parliament Nicolas About and Catherine Picard. See Loi n° 2001-504 du 12 juin 2001 tendant à renforcer la prévention et la répression des mouvements sectaires portant atteinte aux droits de l'homme et aux libertés fondamentales [Law No. 2001-504 of June 12, 2001 intended to reinforce the prevention and repression of sectarian (cultic) movements that infringe on human rights and on fundamental freedoms], *Journal Officiel de la République Française* 135, June 13, 2001, available at https://www.legifrance.gouv.fr/affichTexte.do?cidTexte=JORFTEXT000000589924&dateTexte=&categorieLien=id.

25 These conditions included: endangering the life or the physical or psychological well-being of a person; placing minors at mortal risk; violation of another person's freedom, dignity or identity; the illegal practice of medicine or pharmacology; false advertising; and fraud or falsification.

A third type of regulation is found in states that conclude an agreement with a particular church or religious organization that provides that religious group with additional or specific guarantees. This is the case in Germany, where, despite the separation between church and state, there remains a special partnership between the state and those religious communities that have the status of a corporation under public law. Under Article 137 para. 5 of the Weimar Constitution, "Religious societies shall remain corporations under public law insofar as they have enjoyed that status in the past. Other religious groups shall be granted the same status upon application, if their constitution and the number of their members give assurance of their permanency." The status of a corporation under public law is granted when certain requirements are met, including size, date of establishment, likelihood of permanence and, importantly, an assurance/indication that the organization is not hostile to the constitution or fundamental rights. Religious groups that have achieved this status are entitled to levy taxes on the basis of the civil taxation list. Those religious communities that are given public law corporation status are therefore granted certain entitlements, including a levy or tithe (averaging 9% of income tax) on its members that the state collects.[26]

III Policing Freedom of Religion in the Public Sphere

A state may seek to regulate religion in the public sphere by placing some restrictions on the manifestation of religion in order to reconcile the interests of various groups or when public order is affected. While the modes of regulation may differ from state to state, what is shared across all European states is that the right to manifest one's religion is not absolute and may be restricted under certain circumstances. This is reflected in Article 9(2) of the European Convention on Human Rights (ECHR), to which all Council of Europe (CoE) member states are signatory:

> Freedom to manifest one's religion or beliefs shall be subject only to such limitations as are prescribed by law and are necessary in a democratic society in the interests of public safety, for the protection of public order, health or morals, or for the protection of the rights and freedoms of others.

26 Another example of this type of regulation is found in Switzerland, where the relationship between church and state takes the form of recognition of religious communities as corporations under public law. The Swiss case is somewhat unique as there are 26 cantons, each independently having the authority to recognize religious communities. What is notable, however, is that only Judeo-Christian communities have been recognized within the cantons, leaving other religious groups (including *inter alia* Muslim, Hindu,

In practice, restrictions on the manifestation of religion in the public sphere are often framed as necessary to protect religious freedom, gender equality and secular traditions or to combat terrorism. For example, Italy,[27] Denmark,[28] Bulgaria,[29] Germany,[30] Russia,[31] Switzerland,[32] France,[33] Turkey,[34] the

Buddhist, Free Church organizations, etc.) subject to private law. Liechtenstein and Portugal also fall under this model. In both states, the Catholic Church is conferred a unique status, while other religious communities and churches must adopt private law forms.

27 Italy does not have a national ban, but several towns in Italy, including Novara and Lombardy, have local bans on face-covering veils.

28 In 2008, the government announced it would bar judges from wearing headscarves and similar religious or political symbols, including crucifixes, Jewish skull caps and turbans, in courtrooms.

29 Bulgaria's Parliament banned the burqa in September 2016.

30 In 2016, the German Chancellor, Angela Merkel, endorsed a partial ban on the burqa and the niqab, stating: "The full facial veil is inappropriate and should be banned wherever it is legally possible." See Philip Oltermann, "Angela Merkel Endorses Party's Call for Partial Ban on Burqa and Niqab," *The Guardian*, December 6, 2016, https://www.theguardian.com/world/2016/dec/06/angela-merkel-cdu-partial-ban-burqa-niqab-german. In February, the 2017 the German Bundestag debated a draft act that would prohibit federal civil servants from performing official duties and soldiers in general from wearing burqas and niqabs. See Gesetzentwurf der Bundesregierung, Entwurf eines Gesetzes zu bereichsspezifischen Regelungen der Gesichtsverhüllung [Draft Act of the Federal Government, Draft Act to Regulate Certain Aspects of Face Veils], *Deutscher Bundestag: Drucksachen und Protokolle* BT-Drs 18/11180, February 15, 2017, Arts. 1–4., available at http://dip21.bundestag.de/dip21/btd/18/111/1811180.pdf. This draft act followed a similar act proposed by the state government of Bavaria banning face veils for civil servants and people working in public service on elections boards, in universities and in schools and kindergartens, as well as for students. Bavaria's Parliament approved the ban on the full Islamic face veil in July 2017. See Josh Lowe, "Why Southern Germany Has Declared War on Burqas and Muslims," *Newsweek*, July 8, 2017, http://www.newsweek.com/bavaria-burqa-ban-europe-muslims-islam-633616. This was followed shortly after by the German Bundesrat's approval of a law banning face coverings while driving in Germany. See Jefferson Chase, "German Bundesrat Approves 'Burqa Ban' for Drivers, Beefs up Road-Race Sanctions," *Deutsche Welle*, September 22, 2017. In April, the German Lower House approved a partial ban on face covering by supporting the draft law prohibiting anyone in the civil service, military or working for an election from covering their faces in Germany. See Lizzie Dearden, "German Parliament Votes in Favour of Partial Burqa Ban," *The Independent*, April 28, 2017, http://www.independent.co.uk/news/world/europe/germany-burqa-ban-law-vote-favour-angela-merkel-islam-muslim-civil-servants-judges-military-a7706781.html.

31 Russia's Stavropol region has a ban on hijabs, the first of its kind imposed by a region in the Russian Federation. The ruling was upheld by Russia's Supreme Court in July 2013.

32 In September 2013, 65% of the electorate in the Italian-speaking region of Ticino voted in favour of a ban on face veils in public areas by any group. The ban came into force in 2016.

33 See discussion of the French bans in Section II.

34 Although the political landscape in Turkey has changed with the election of the AK Party in 2002, Turkey has historically pursued a policy of strictly enforced secularism. The Constitution establishes the country as a "secular state" and provides for freedom of belief, freedom of worship and the private dissemination of religious ideas. However,

Netherlands,[35] Spain,[36] Austria[37] and Belgium[38] have all imposed or proposed legislation limiting the wearing certain religious clothing in the public realm, focusing mainly on the Muslim veil.

These attempts to restrict religious dress to the private sphere have taken place alongside an increase in government restrictions on religion in general (i.e. government harassment or intimidation). A 2017 study of government restrictions[39] on religion published by the Pew Research Center on Religion and Law[40] found that, in 2014–2015, 53% of the forty-five countries surveyed experienced "an increase in government harassment or use of force against religious groups."[41] While it is important to situate the increase in government restrictions on and social hostility toward religion within the wider "refugee crisis" that unfolded in Europe during this period, deeply rooted fears of threats posed by the "other" – a rhetorical proxy for Muslims in Europe – was already embedded in the debates taking place in Europe on multiculturalism and the need to assimilate minority communities.[42]

these protections were coupled to other constitutional provisions that restricted these rights for the purpose of preserving the integrity and existence of the secular state. Until October 2013, when the government lifted the ban, public officials were not permitted to wear religious head scarves in government offices and state-run institutions (including universities). Universities also imposed such restrictions on students.

35 In March 2015, the Dutch government approved a partial ban on face-covering Islamic veils on public transport and in public areas. The ban does not apply to the wearing of the burqa or the niqab in the street, except when there are specific security reasons for doing so.

36 Several parts of Catalonia have laws against burqas and niqabs. For instance, a law has remained in place in Reus, despite a decision of the Spanish Supreme Court in 2013 overturning the ban in some parts on the grounds that it "limits religious freedom." See Tribunal Supremo, Sala de lo Contencioso-Administrativo, Sección: Septima, Recurso Casación Num.: 4118/2011, February 14, 2013.

37 In January 2017, the ruling coalition agreed to prohibit full-face veils (niqab and burqa) in public spaces such as courts and schools. It said it was considering a more general ban on state employees wearing the headscarf and other religious symbols.

38 A law banning the full-face veil came into effect in Belgium in July 2011.

39 They define government restrictions as "laws, policies and actions that restrict religious beliefs and practices."

40 See *supra* note 4.

41 The report went on to state that 27 European countries (60%) saw widespread government harassment or intimidation of religious groups in 2015, up from seventeen countries in 2014. And the governments of 24 countries in Europe (53%) used some type of force against religious groups, an increase from fifteen (33%) in 2014.

42 See Shaista Gohir, "The Veil Ban in Europe: Gendered Equality or Gendered Islamophobia," *Georgetown Journal of International Affairs* (Winter/Spring 2015): 24–33.

Unsurprisingly, the number of legal challenges has also arisen – at both national and regional level – as a consequence of these restrictions. In restricting religious manifestation in the public sphere, states have frequently invoked the concept of secularism. Often, enforced secularism was argued to be necessary to ensure equality (and prevent discrimination), preserve the stability of the state, guarantee public safety or promote social integration. While national courts have pushed back (Spain[43] and Germany[44] are two cases in point) against these injunctions limiting religious freedom in some cases, individuals subject to these restrictions have increasingly turned to the ECtHR for redress, with mixed results. This public sphere dilemma, namely where to draw the line between the suppression of religious expression in the public sphere and free exercise of religion, which is taking place at the national level and being replayed at the regional level in the ECtHR, suggests that this line is moving decidedly closer to the suppression of the public face of religious pluralism. As the next section details, in leaning heavily on the "margin of appreciation" principle in these cases, the ECtHR's approach to drawing that line is best understood as a political settlement that reflects the different meanings and forms of secularism adopted in certain European states.

IV The Case Law of the European Court of Human Rights

In a number of cases, the ECtHR has engaged with the question how much regulation on religious freedom is permitted in a democratic society. The Convention itself provides an unqualified right to the protection of freedom of thought, conscience and religion (observed in the "private sphere"). The right to manifest (i.e. outwardly conduct) that religion or belief, however, is subject

43 A 2013 decision by Spain's Supreme Court repealed the prohibition against wearing the burqa in public spaces in the Catalonian city of Lleida on the grounds that it "limits religious freedom." See Mónica Ceberio Belaza, "El Supremo anula la prohibición del 'burka' en Lleida" [Supreme Court annuls the prohibition of "burqa" in Lleida], *El País*, February 28, 2013, http://sociedad.elpais.com/sociedad/2013/02/28/actualidad/1362051859_884570.html.

44 A 2003 ruling by the Federal Constitutional Court favoured a teacher who wanted to wear an Islamic scarf to school. That being said, the judgment also noted that states within Germany could change their laws locally to allow such a ban. See Judgment of the Second Senate of September 24, 2003 on the basis of the oral hearing of June 3, 2003 of case No. 2 BvR 1436/02, available at http://www.bundesverfassungsgericht.de/SharedDocs/Entscheidungen/EN/2003/09/rs20030924_2bvr143602en.html. Despite the ruling, a number of states in Germany went on to ban teachers from wearing headscarves. In the state of Hesse, the ban included civil servants.

to restrictions under Article 9(2) of the Convention. The "margin of appreciation" doctrine plays an important role in the ECtHR's approach to qualified rights, including the right to manifest one's religion.[45] While not codified in the text of the Convention, the doctrine was first introduced in the case of *Handyside v. the United Kingdom*.[46] It allows a contracting state "a certain measure of discretion, subject to European supervision, when it takes legislative, administrative or judicial action in the area of a Convention right."[47] When considering whether a state has overstepped its margin of appreciation (for example in relation to religious freedom), the ECtHR asks three questions:

1. Was the interference prescribed by law?
2. Did it pursue a legitimate aim?
3. Were the measures necessary in a democratic society?

The specific meaning of each of these questions within the context of religious freedom under the Convention has been developed in the ECtHR's Article 9 case law, which reveals a number of trends. When religion is contained within the private sphere, a review of case law indicates that it is likely to be protected. Where religion pinpricks the public sphere, however, the ECtHR has adopted two distinct approaches for determining whether to allow or challenge a state's limitation on the right to manifest one's religion. The first approach is a type of benign secularism.[48] In these cases, the ECtHR has tended to rule in favour of the individual conscience of the applicants over claims by the state that restrictions were necessary to maintain public order or protect the rights of others. The second trend is toward an enforced secularism.[49] In these cases, the ECtHR has more actively policed the public sphere and prioritized the state's right to protect secularism over an individual's right to publicly manifest his or her religion by invoking a particular formulation of the principles of neutrality and non-identification.

45 It has also been used when Article 15 of the Convention (derogation during a state of emergency) has been invoked.

46 App. No. 5493/72, Judgment of December 7, 1976. In this judgment, the ECtHR stated (in para. 48): "By reason of their direct and continuous contact with the vital forces of their countries, State authorities are in principle in a better position than the international judge to give an opinion on the exact content of those requirements [of morals] as well as on the 'necessity' of a 'restriction' or 'penalty' intended to meet them. ... Consequently, Article 10 para. 2 ... leaves to the contracting states a margin of appreciation. This margin is given both to the domestic legislator ('prescribed by law') and to the bodies, judicial amongst others, that are called upon to interpret and apply the laws in force."

47 D.J. Harris, M. O'Boyle, and C. Warbrick, *The Law of the European Convention on Human Rights* (Oxford-New York: Oxford University Press, 1995), 12.

48 See, for example, *Kokkinakis v. Greece*, App. No. 14307/88, Judgment of May 25, 1993, and *Eweida and Others v. the United Kingdom*, App. No. 48420/10, Judgment of January 15, 2013.

49 See *infra* note 56.

The principle of neutrality flows from the idea that there must be a separation of church and state. It is often reflected either in the state's constitution or in its domestic laws. It is closely linked to the principle of non-identification, which is embedded in the notion of religious pluralism and entrenches the notions of impartiality and equality. States must be impartial to existing religions and ideologies and respect the principle of freedom and equality. In order to ensure that a state does not favour or unjustly hinder a religious group, there must be a clear division between the functioning of the state and the functioning of its religious institutions.[50]

At UN level, these principles have been understood to have two requirements: (1) any restriction on a religious belief should not disproportionality affect one religious faith over another; and (2) courts, states and government bodies should refrain from determining what constitutes a manifestation of religious belief.[51] In relation to this requirement, the UN Special Rapporteur on freedom of religion or belief has specifically argued that the determination whether the wearing or display of religious clothing or a symbol is an "observance" (i.e. compulsory) or a "practice" (i.e. an authorized but not prescribed religious expression) should be left to the believer:

> A certain appearance or exhibition of a symbol may or may not be linked to any religious sentiment or belief. It would therefore be most inappropriate for the State to determine whether the symbol in question was indeed a manifestation of religious belief.[52]

However, the ECtHR has adopted a very different approach to secularism – both in how it is read and how it is applied. In contrast to UN bodies, the ECtHR does not look at the various models of secularism that are applied at the national level to determine whether the limitations imposed on religious

50 For this principle to be fully realized, states must not have a state or "official" religion, nor can they privilege a particular religion.

51 Report of the Special Rapporteur on Freedom of Religion or Belief, Heiner Bielefeldt, UN Doc. A/HRC/16/53, December 15, 2010; Note by the Secretary-General on the Elimination of All Forms of Religious Intolerance (transmitting Interim Report of the Special Rapporteur on Freedom of Religion or Belief, Heiner Bielefeldt), UN Doc. A/66/156, July 18, 2011, para. 46. See also Report by United Nations Special Rapporteur on Freedom of Religion or Belief, Asma Jahangir: Civil and Political Rights, Including the Question of Religious Intolerance, UN Doc. E/CN.4/2006/5, January 9, 2006, para 41.

52 Report by United Nations Special Rapporteur on Freedom of Religion or Belief, Asma Jahangir: Civil and Political Rights, Including the Question of Religious Intolerance, UN Doc. E/CN.4/2006/5, January 9, 2006, para 41.

freedom are proportionate[53] and non-discriminatory.[54] Instead, the ECtHR has emphasized the principle of subsidiarity and allowed states a wide margin of appreciation to determine whether limitations on manifestations of religious freedom are necessary to ensure stability, security, cohesion and protection of the rights and freedoms of others. Secondly, the ECtHR has also allowed states to determine whether the symbol in question is a manifestation of religious belief. Indeed, the ECtHR has produced an opinion on religious symbols that largely supports the states' view. For the ECtHR, secularism – in and of itself – is required by the values of the Convention and should therefore be considered a valid justification for limiting the right to religious freedom,[55] particularly where contestations over the right to manifest religious symbols arise in the public realm.

The ECtHR cases involving freedom of religion are varied,[56] although a substantial part of the relevant case law has involved restrictions on religious

53 The principle of proportionality appears across a number of areas of public international law but is a prominent feature of ECtHR case law. The principle is applied when the ECtHR seeks to determine whether a state's action has violated a particular right. In particular, it asks whether the action taken by the state was proportionate to achieving a legitimate aim (public order, morals, etc.). If the ECtHR believes the state was pursuing a legitimate aim, it will ask whether lesser measures could have been taken. In cases concerning religious dress, this could include the wearing of alternative head coverings. Where no lesser measure could be taken (e.g. in the *Eweida* case), the ECtHR asks other questions, including whether the measure was necessary in a democratic society or to protect the rights of others or for public safety.

54 The principle of non-discrimination is enshrined in Article 14 of the Convention, which applies to all 47 states parties to the Convention, and Protocol 12 to the Convention (2000), which has not yet been ratified by all Council of Europe member states (to date, it has been ratified by twenty member states). It is important to note that unlike Protocol 12, Article 14 is not a stand-alone right, which means that it must be invoked in conjunction with another right. When this happens, the ECtHR often finds (or rejects) a violation of a particular Convention right but for various reasons (article not applicable, applicant's complaint already satisfied, etc.) does not address Article 14 separately and/or find a separate violation under Article 14.

55 See, in particular, *Şahin v. Turkey*, App. No. 44774/98, Judgment of November 10, 2005, para. 115; *Dogru v. France*, App. No. 27058/05, Judgment of December 4, 2008, paras. 17–22.

56 Topics covered include: the obligation to disclose religious convictions; the organization of churches and religious communities; the obligation to swear religious oaths; proselytism; the granting of religious permits; religious holidays; and the refusal to provide public services in religious matters. See *Metropolitan Church of Bessarabia v. Moldova*, App. No. 45701/99, Judgment of December 13, 2001; *Serif v. Greece*, App. No. 38178/97, Judgment of December 14, 1999; *Agga v. Greece*, App. No. 33331/02, Judgment of July 13, 2006; *Supreme Holy Council of the Muslim Community v. Bulgaria*, App. No. 39023/97, Judgment of December 16, 2004; *Hasan and Chaush v. Bulgaria*, App. No. 30985/96, Judgment of October 26, 2000; *Jehovah's Witnesses of Moscow v. Russia*, App. No. 302/02, Judgment of June

symbols, clothing and observance in the public realm and has been primarily (although not exclusively) related to Islamic dress or practice.[57]

One of the earliest attempts to challenge a state's limitation on religious manifestation arose in the case of *Dahlab v. Switzerland* (hereinafter *Dahlab*).[58] While the case was declared inadmissible, the ECtHR's reasoning begins to reveal how it understands the requirements of secularism. In this case, school authorities had prohibited the applicant from wearing the hijab when teaching (although the state acknowledged that the applicant had at no time attempted to disseminate her religious teachings to her students). The principle of *laïcité* (neutrality) was invoked by the state and upheld by the Federal Court of Switzerland. The state argued that, in order to preserve religious peace in the community, some restrictions on the right of civil servants to manifest their religion were necessary. In declaring the case inadmissible, the ECtHR noted that this neutrality argument presented by the state was even more compelling in an educational setting. Students may be more easily influenced and "religious peace" must be protected with extreme care in such settings. The ECtHR paid special attention to the young age of the applicant's students and characterized the headscarf as a "powerful external symbol" that was "imposed on women by a [religious] precept" that was "hard to square with the principle of gender equality",[59] thereby weighing in on the debate as to whether this particular religious manifestation was one of free choice or coercion.

The ECtHR adopted a similar approach in *Şahin v. Turkey* (hereinafter *Şahin*).[60] The case involved a 24-year-old woman enrolled in the Faculty of

---

10, 2010; *Magyar Keresztény Mennonita Egyház and Others v. Hungary*, Apps. Nos. 70945/11, 23611/12, 26998/12, 41150/12, 41155/12, 41553/12, 54977/12 and 56581/12, Judgment April 8, 2014; *László Magyar v. Hungary*, App. No. 73593/10, Judgment of May 20, 2014.

57 See, for example, *Dahlab v. Switzerland*, App. No. 42393/98, Decision of February 15, 2001; *Şahin v. Turkey*; *Phull v. France*, App. No. 35753/03, Decision of January 11, 2005; *Kurtulmuş v. Turkey*, App. No. 65500/01, Decision of January 24, 2006; *El Morsli v. France*, App. No. 15585/06, Decision of March 4, 2008; *Dogru v. France*; *Kervanci v. France*, App. No. 31645/04, Judgment of December 4, 2008; *Bayrak v. France*, App. No. 14308/08, Decision of June 30, 2009; *Gamaleddyn v. France*, App. No. 18527/08, Decision of June 30, 2009; *Ghazal v. France*, App. No. 29134/08, Decision of June 30, 2009; *Jasvir Singh v. France*, App. No. 25463/08, Decision of June 30, 2009; *Ranjit Singh v. France*, App. No. 27561/08, Decision of June 30, 2009; *Aktas v. France*, App. No. 43563/08, Decision of June 30, 2009; *Lautsi and Others v. Italy* [GC], App. No. 30814/06, Judgment of March 18, 2011; *Eweida and Others v. the United Kingdom*; *S.A.S. v. France* [GC], App. No. 43835/11, Judgment of July 1, 2014; *Ebrahimian v. France*, App. No. 64846/11, Judgment of November 26, 2015.

58 App. No. 42393/98, Decision of February 15, 2001.

59 Ibid.

60 App. No. 44774/98, Judgment of November 10, 2005. The judgments and decisions of the European Court of Human Rights are available online at http://www.echr.coe.int.

Medicine at the University of Istanbul. The applicant challenged a decision of the university that stated:

> By virtue of the Constitution, the law and regulations, and in accordance with the case-law of the Supreme Administrative Court and the European Commission of Human Rights and the resolutions adopted by the university administrative boards, students whose "heads are covered" (wearing the Islamic headscarf) and students (including overseas students) with beards must not be admitted to lectures, courses or tutorials.[61]

Şahin was subsequently denied entry to the university on several occasions for defying the ban on wearing the hijab. She filed a case with the ECtHR, arguing that the ban on the Islamic headscarf in higher education institutions in Turkey violated her rights and freedoms under several ECHR provisions, including Article 9 (freedom of thought, conscience and religion). A 2004 decision by a seven-judge chamber of the ECtHR found that there had been no violation since "the University of Istanbul's regulations imposing restrictions on the wearing of Islamic headscarves and the measures taken to implement them were justified in principle and proportionate to the aims pursued and, therefore, could be regarded as necessary in a democratic society."[62] The case was later referred to the Grand Chamber, where the decision was upheld.

The judgment in the *Şahin* case has attracted significantly scholarly attention for good reason.[63] Here the ECtHR supported a particular reading of the hijab as an instrument of proselytism that undermined the values of democracy. In contrast to the French cases that would follow, this particular case involved the regulation of a majority religion. In arriving at its decision, the ECtHR accepted the Turkish state's argument that applying the principles of neutrality and equality, in the specific context of Turkey's socio-political landscape,[64] required state institutions to restrict the manifestation of religion (in this case religious clothing). Given that Turkey was a Muslim majority country,

61 Ibid., para. 12.

62 Ibid., para. 114.

63 See, for example, Jill Marshall, "Freedom of Religious Expression and Gender Equality: Şahin v. Turkey," *Modern Law Review* 69, no. 3 (May 2006): 452–461; Cindy Skach, "Şahin v. Turkey. App. No. 44774/98; 'Teacher Headscarf.' Case No. 2BvR 1436/02," *American Journal of International Law* 100, no. 1 (2006): 186–196; Aernout Nieuwenhuis, "European Court of Human Rights: State and Religion, Schools and Scarves: An Analysis of the Margin of Appreciation as Used in the Case of *Leyla Şahin v. Turkey*, Decision of 29 June 2004, Application Number 4477498," *European Constitutional Law Review* 1, no. 3 (2005): 495–510.

64 Although the political landscape in Turkey has changed with the election of the AK Party in 2002, Turkey has historically pursued a policy of strictly enforced secularism.

the ECtHR argued that these measures were necessary to protect the secular nature of the state and ensure that pluralism and public order prevailed in public institutions.[65] As Judge Tulkens notes in his dissenting opinion, however, the majority of judges were of the view that the wearing of the hijab was a non-prescribed practice and that the ban did not impact an individual's ability to "manifest their religion in accordance with habitual forms of Muslims observance."[66] In doing so, Tulkens argues:

> they [the ECtHR] take position on an issue that has been the subject of much debate, namely the signification of wearing the headscarf and its relationship with the principle of secularism.[67]

In both *Şahin* and *Dahlab*, the ECtHR disregarded the meaning attributed to the wearing of the headscarf by the applicants and instead took the view that it was a gender equality issue. The ECtHR argued that the wearing of the hijab "appears to be imposed on women by a precept which is laid down in the Koran and which ... is hard to square with the principle of gender equality."[68] Yet, as Judge Tulkens reminds us:

> It is not the Court's role to make an appraisal of this type – in this instance a unilateral and negative one – of a religion or religious practice, just as it is not its role to determine in a general and abstract way the signification of wearing the headscarf or to impose its viewpoint on the applicant.[69]

Although the context of the series of French cases that followed differs significantly from the Turkish case, the ECtHR's judgments would draw extensively on the reasoning of the *Şahin* case. Unlike the Turkish case, where the state argued (and the ECtHR accepted) that ridding the public sphere of religious symbols was necessary to protect secularism and plurality in a Muslim

---

The Constitution establishes the country as a "secular" state and provides for freedom of belief, freedom of worship and the private dissemination of religious ideas. However, these protections were coupled to other constitutional provisions that restricted these rights for the purpose of preserving the integrity and existence of the secular state. At the time of this case, public officials were not permitted to wear religious head scarves in government offices and state-run institutions (including universities). Universities also imposed such restrictions on students. In October 2013, the government lifted this ban.

65 *Şahin v. Turkey*, para. 115.

66 Ibid., para. 118.

67 Ibid., Dissenting Opinion, para. 7.

68 *Dahlab v. Switzerland*, para. 1.

69 *Şahin v. Turkey*, Dissenting Opinion, para. 12.

majority country (where the Muslim majority could eventually pose a threat to the minority), the French cases involved the regulation of the practices of religious minorities.

The 2008 admissibility decision in *Mann Singh v. France* (hereinafter *Mann Singh*)[70] involved a Sikh whose application to obtain a duplicate driving licence after the original had been stolen was rejected because he submitted photographs in which he appeared wearing a turban. The ECtHR declared the case manifestly ill-founded and thus inadmissible. In arriving at its conclusion, the ECtHR argued that the requirement to appear bareheaded on the identity photograph was necessary for safeguarding public order and safety, since the authorities must be able to identify the driver and check whether he or she is allowed to drive a vehicle. In this case, the ECtHR highlighted that the requirement to appear bareheaded on identity documents was even more relevant since there was a higher risk of fraud and falsification where driving licences were concerned.[71] Finally, the ECtHR stressed that the restriction concerned an occasional measure that fell within the ambit of the state's margin of appreciation.

The *Mann Singh* case is interesting because the ECtHR's reasoning in this case differs sharply from the approach taken by the UN Human Rights Committee in a similar case. In *Ranjit Singh v. France*,[72] a case which also involved a Sikh, the French authorities refused to accept photographs submitted by the applicant for the renewal of a permanent residence permit because he was wearing a turban. The authorities argued that the photographs failed to meet the requirements applying to foreign nationals' admission to and residence in France, which stipulate that individuals must appear full face and bareheaded in photographs destined for residence permits. The applicant's request for an exemption from this provision was rejected. In contrast to the ECtHR, the focus of the Committee was not whether the identity check was necessary to protect public safety (from fraud and falsification) but rather whether wearing a turban on an identity document made it more difficult to identify the person. When it turned to this question, the Committee observed that:

---

70 App. No. 24479/07, Decision of November 27, 2008.

71 "La Cour souligne, à cet égard, que la règlementation litigieuse s'est montrée plus exigeante en la matière en raison de l'augmentation des risques de fraude et de falsification des permis de conduire." (The Court emphasizes, in this respect, that the disputed regulations have been more demanding in this respect because of the increased risk of fraud and falsification of driving licenses.)

72 Human Rights Committee, Communication No. 1876/2000, Views of July 22, 2011, UN Doc. CCPR/C/102/D/1876/2009.

> the State party has not explained why the wearing of a Sikh turban covering the top of the head and a portion of the forehead but leaving the rest of the face clearly visible would make it more difficult to identify the author than if he were to appear bareheaded, since he wears his turban at all times. Nor has the State party explained how, specifically, identity photographs in which people appear bareheaded help to avert the risk of fraud or falsification of residence permits. Consequently, the Committee is of the view that the State party has not demonstrated that the limitation placed on the author is necessary within the meaning of article 18, paragraph 3, of the Covenant.[73]

The ECtHR's deference to the state is even clear in cases involving religious dress where concessions were made by the applicants, for example by replacing headscarves with hats or bandanas or other head coverings when entering school grounds or participating in sports classes,[74] agreeing to remove head coverings for identity checks (if undertaken by female staff)[75] or agreeing to remove head coverings when entering school classrooms.[76] In these cases, the ECtHR failed to scrutinize whether the concessions made by the applicants were sufficient to meet the state's claim under Article 9(2) (protecting public order, public safety or the rights of others) or indeed whether the reasons given by the state justified any restriction. Rather, the ECtHR shifted these questions back to the state and in the end uncritically accepted that these alternative forms of head cover were simply new ways to signal religiosity, which fell under the limitations imposed by the 2004 French law on secularity.[77]

In contrast to the aforementioned cases, the following cases concern the regulation of Christian symbols. In the 2011 case of *Lautsi and Others v. Italy*

---

73 Ibid., para. 8.4.

74 See, for example, *Dogru v. France*; *Kervanci v. France*; *Gamaleddyn v. France*; *Bayrak v. France*; *Aktas v. France*; *Ghaza v. France*; *J. Singh v. France*; *R. Singh v. France*.

75 See *El Morsli v. France*.

76 See *Aktas v. France*.

77 Loi n° 2004-228 du 15 mars 2004 encadrant, en application du principe de laïcité, le port de signes ou de tenues manifestant une appartenance religieuse dans les écoles, collèges et lycées publics [Law No. 2004-228 of March 15, 2004 on secularity and conspicuous religious symbols in schools] *Journal Officiel de la République Française* 65, March 17, 2004, available at https://www.legifrance.gouv.fr/affichTexte.do?cidTexte=JORFTEXT000000417977&categorieLien=id. This law bans the wearing of conspicuous religious symbols in French public primary and secondary schools. This was followed by the French Law No. 2010-1192, which banned face coverings of all kinds, including masks, niqabs and the full body dress known as the burqa, in public spaces, except under specified circumstances.

(hereinafter *Lautsi*),[78] the applicant argued that the presence of a crucifix in an Italian public school classroom interfered with her children's freedom of conscience. Allowing these religious symbols to be displayed in public schools, the applicant argued, was a violation of the principles of neutrality and impartiality. The Italian Constitutional Court rejected this argument and agreed with the state. The state argued that, while crucifixes were religious symbols, they were also symbols of the country's history, culture and identity and that they represented the democratic principles of equality, liberty and tolerance. At the ECtHR, the case was heard by a Chamber and subsequently by the Grand Chamber with different results. In the first case to come before the ECtHR in 2009, it was the applicant and not the state that framed the arguments in terms of secularism. As the ECtHR observed:

> The approach advocated by the applicants was thus clearly distinct from State atheism, which amounted to denying the freedom of religion by imposing a secular viewpoint in an authoritarian manner. Seen in terms of the State's impartiality and neutrality, secularism was on the contrary a means of securing the religious and philosophical freedom of conscience of all.[79]

In its first ruling, the ECtHR agreed with the applicant that, for non-Christian students (including atheists), the presence of a crucifix in the classroom could suggest that the state was expressing a particular belief and, in placing dissenters "in a situation from which they cannot extract themselves",[80] could influence the private conscience of students. This, the ECtHR argued, was "incompatible with the State's duty to respect neutrality in the exercise of public authority, particularly in the field of education."[81]

An appeal was lodged and accepted by the Grand Chamber, which held, by a 15-2 majority, that there had been no violation of Article 2 of Protocol No. 1 (right to education).[82] Crucially, while the requirements of secularism were central to its judgment, the Grand Chamber departed quite significantly from the reasoning of the Chamber in two ways. Firstly, the Grand Chamber argued

78 App. No. 30814/06, Judgment of March 18, 2011.

79 *Lautsi and Others v. Italy*, para 44.

80 Ibid., para. 55.

81 Ibid., para. 57.

82 The decision to depart from the 2009 ruling cannot be disassociated from the significant attention that this case received from both state and non-state actors, many of whom contributed opinions and briefs to the ECtHR. The ECtHR authorized written submissions from the governments of Armenia, Bulgaria, Cyprus, Greece, Lithuania, Malta, Monaco, Romania, the Russian Federation and San-Marino; 33 members of the European Parliament (jointly); Greek Helsinki Monitor; Associazione Nazionale del Libero

that there was no European consensus regarding the displaying of religious symbols on the walls. Therefore, it fell within a state's margin of appreciation. Secondly, like in other cases involving religious symbolism, the Grand Chamber formed an opinion as to the nature of the symbol and, from that particular understanding, went on to determine whether its presence in the public domain transgressed the principle of neutrality. A majority in the Grand Chamber viewed the crucifix as:

> an essentially passive symbol and this point is of importance in the Court's view, particularly having regard to the principle of neutrality (see paragraph 60 above). It cannot be deemed to have an influence on pupils comparable to that of didactic speech or participation in religious activities.[83]

In this case, the crucifix was understood to be part of the state's cultural heritage and tradition, and the ECtHR therefore did not view its presence as having a signalling effect on the children. This contrasts sharply with the ECtHR's reading of the headscarf in *Dahlab*. Rather than seeing the wearing of the headscarf as a mark of observance, the ECtHR viewed it as a "powerful external" sign that could directly influence students and could disturb the educational environment.[84] In both *Lautsi* and *Dahlab*, the ECtHR was asked, by the applicant and the state respectively, whether the religious symbol in question jeopardized the principle of neutrality. In making a determination in each case, the ECtHR's reading of the nature (and indeed ostensible influence) of the religious symbol rested heavily on the state's understanding of how that particular symbol related to the national identity and dominant Christian culture in each state. Where the symbol was seen as being part of the tradition of the state, it was considered passive. However, in cases where the symbol or attire represented the "otherness" of Islam (even if the wearing of attire such as hats or bandanas would not normally be ascribed a religious symbolism), the ECtHR's view has been that the principle of secularism or neutrality was threatened.

However, the ECtHR took a different approach in 2013, when it heard the case of *Eweida and Others v. the United Kingdom* (hereinafter *Eweida*).[85] The applicant in this case, who worked for a private employer, British Airways, had

Pensiero; European Centre for Law and Justice; Eurojuris; International Commission of Jurists, Interights and Human Rights Watch (jointly); and Zentralkomitee der deutschen Katholiken, Semaines sociales de France and Associazioni Cristiani Lavoratori Italiani (jointly).

83 *Lautsi and Others v. Italy*, para. 72.

84 Ibid., paras. 73–74.

85 App. No. 48420/10, Judgment of January 15, 2013.

faced disciplinary measures when she wore a cross that was visible to customers. The company argued that wearing religious symbols was in breach of its uniform policy. The ECtHR held that, while the UK courts had correctly applied a proportionality test, which examined the right to manifest the applicant's religious belief against the company's interest in preserving its corporate image, it had failed to strike a "fair balance" and had accorded the factor of the company's image too much weight. This approach by the ECtHR was distinct from earlier cases involving religious expression in two ways. Firstly, much like in the other cases, the ECtHR acknowledged that, when applying Article 9(2) in a particular case, the state had a margin of appreciation in deciding whether and to what extent interference was necessary. That said, in this case, the ECtHR did not give the state a blanket margin and examined the justification offered by the state for restricting the religious manifestations of the applicant. Secondly, the ECtHR made proportionality a key component of the test. The judgment initially suggested a turning point in the ECtHR's approach to Article 9 in that it recognized that the right of an individual to manifest religious beliefs in the public realm could outweigh secular interests. There were certain distinct factors in this case (e.g. the fact that it concerned a private rather than a public employer). Nevertheless, the ECtHR examined whether the limitation was necessary and endeavoured to define and attribute weight to the harm produced when religious expression is suppressed, something that it had failed to do in earlier cases.

That being said, if the *Eweida* case gave some indication that the ECtHR had changed it approach when examining the limitation of expressions of controversial or contestable religious belief in the public sphere, the case of *S.A.S. v. France* (hereinafter *S.A.S.*)[86] put us back in familiar territory, albeit with some notable detours. In the *S.A.S.* case, the applicant challenged a 2010 French law (also referred to as the "burqa ban") that prohibits the covering of the face in public.[87]

In its submission, the state argued that the ban was necessary to ensure public safety and "respect for the minimum set of values of an open and democratic society", which included three separate elements: gender equality, human dignity and "respect for the minimum requirements of life in society" or "living together." While the ECtHR recognized that gender equality and human dig-

86 App. No. 43835/11, Judgment of July 1, 2014.

87 It is worth noting here that this case differs from other ECtHR cases that arose out of the 2004 French law. While the applicant invoked several articles, including Article 3 (prohibition on torture), Article 8 (right to respect for private and family life), Article 9 (freedom of thought, conscience and religion), Article 10 (freedom of expression), Article 11 (freedom of assembly and association) and Article 14 (prohibition of discrimination), the ECtHR limited its review to Articles 8, 9 and 14, focusing much of its attention on Article 9.

nity were legitimate aims under the Convention, it took the view that, in these circumstances, "a State Party cannot invoke gender equality in order to ban a practice that is defended by women – such as the applicant – in the context of the exercise of the rights enshrined in those provisions."[88] The ECtHR also did not accept that the limitation in this case was necessary to protect human dignity and argued that the state failed to provide evidence to support its assertion that:

> women who wear the full-face veil seek to express a form of contempt against those they encounter or otherwise to offend against the dignity of others.[89]

The ECtHR did, however, accept that public safety and/or respect for the minimum requirements of life in society (which fall under the protection of the rights and freedoms of others) may, in certain circumstances, justify restricting an applicant's freedom of religion. However, the ECtHR did not accept that there was "a general threat to public safety" that warranted a blanket ban. On the other hand, it accepted that the ban pursued the legitimate aim of "living together" under "the protection of the rights and freedoms of others" and that it therefore did not violate the Convention.[90] While the decision did not depart from its earlier case law concerning the rights of Muslim women to wear religious attire, the ECtHR did take a few interesting detours in its reasoning that are worth noting. First of all, the ECtHR refrained from making value judgments on religious attire (e.g. whether it was optional or what it was meant to express), something it had previously done in the *Dahlab* case. Secondly, the ECtHR seemed to move away from a reductionist reading of Islam to recognize

> the expression of a cultural identity which contributes to the pluralism that is inherent in democracy. It notes in this connection the variability of the notions of virtuousness and decency that are applied to the uncovering of the human body.[91]

While this goes some way toward addressing its value-laden language in earlier decisions, the ECtHR's reasoning in this case still remains state-centred. The ECtHR did not attempt to define the notion of "living together," which, as Judges Nussberger and Jäderblom argue, "seems far-fetched and vague."[92] Thus, it failed

88 *S.A.S. v. France*, para. 119.
89 Ibid., para. 120.
90 Ibid., para. 139.
91 Ibid., para. 120.
92 Ibid., Dissenting Opinion, para. 5.

to prioritize a careful examination of the arguments offered by the state above the wide margin of appreciation it was afforded. Without such an examination, the ECtHR could not strike a fair balance between the pursuit of the aim of living together and the harm that may be produced by limiting the religious expression of the applicant. Moreover, the ECtHR continued to invoke pluralism, tolerance and broadmindedness as hallmarks of a democratic society, but its judgments conveyed "a selective pluralism and restricted tolerance."[93] In framing its understanding of the requirements of secularism within a liberal political order that subscribes to a Christian conception of the "collective good," the ECtHR "can be seen to be acting not only as an independent protector of rights but also as instrument of governance maintaining a particular social order."[94]

Finally, in the case of *Osmanoğlu and Kocabaş v. Switzerland*,[95] the ECtHR again was asked to consider the question as to what limitations should be placed on state interference in the religious freedom of minority religions. While the aforementioned Article 9 cases concerned the need to protect the collective national identity against religious signalling, in this particular case the limitation on religious freedom was allegedly required to ensure that a national identity (including the adoption of customs and mores) was cultivated. In this case, two Turkish-Swiss parents refused to allow their daughters to attend compulsory mixed swimming lessons on the grounds that it contravened their religious beliefs. The ECtHR accepted that the authorities' refusal to grant the children an exemption from swimming lessons interfered with their freedom of religion but held, unanimously, that there had been no violation of Article 9 as the interference pursued the legitimate aim of "social integration."

In arriving at this decision, the ECtHR stated that the school had a "special role in facilitating their [the children's] successful social integration according to local customs and mores."[96] It argued that this consideration "prevailed over the parents' wish to have their children exempted from mixed swimming lessons."[97] As in other cases where the actions taken by an individual deviate from the actions of the collective, the ECtHR's approach suggests that:

> the court has generally construed individual rights in terms of the collective good of the majority as against that of minority religious groups. This approach does not prevent minority religious groups from freely

93 Ibid., Dissenting Opinion, para. 14.

94 Peter G. Danchin, "Islam in the Secular Nomos of the European Court of Human Rights," *Michigan Journal of International Law* 32, no. 4 (2011): 708.

95 App. No. 29086/12, Judgment of January 10, 2017.

96 Ibid.

97 Ibid.

> practicing their beliefs as guaranteed under article 9 – at least not in those "private" spaces of the private sphere such as homes or places of worship.... [I]t [does] mean [...] that in cases of conflict, the court will prefer the majority nation's conception of the collective good including the limits to individual freedom implied by that conception.[98]

In contemporary Europe, this conception of the collective good is increasingly shaped by the anti-immigration and anti-Muslim sentiments of right-wing populism and a kind of liberal-secular nationalist discourse that continues to travel seamlessly across contemporary Europe. Situating the ECtHR's case law on religious freedom within this socio-political landscape, we find a residue of this discourse, in which the "otherness" of Islam is understood to be a "threat to the secular political order."[99] From there, then, it is easier to understand the inconsistencies that arise in the ECtHR's case law:

> first, finding a danger of pressure or proselytizing when a medical student wears an Islamic headscarf to a public university (*Şahin*) but not when a state officially adopts a majority religious symbol in its public schools (*Lautsi*); and second, finding the (democratic) decision "whether or not to perpetuate a religious tradition" in the public sphere to be a violation of the principle of secularism in a Muslim-majority state (*Refah*) but within the margin of appreciation in a Christian majority state (*Lautsi*).[100]

V Concluding Remarks

In March 2017, the European Court of Justice (ECJ) issued rulings in two cases concerning religious dress that merit some mention. Both cases – one from Belgium (*Achbita*)[101] and one from France (*Bougnaoui*)[102] – involved women who were fired from their positions after refusing to remove their headscarves

98 Peter G. Danchin, "Of Prophets and Proselytes: Freedom of Religion and the Conflict of Rights in International Law," *Harvard International Law Journal* 49, no. 2 (2008): 287.

99 Danchin, "Islam in the Secular Nomos," 689.

100 Ibid., 723.

101 See ECJ, Case C-157/15: *Samira Achbita and Centrum voor gelijkheid van kansen en voor racismebestrijding v. G4S Secure Solutions NV*, Judgment of March 14, 2017 (hereinafter *Achbita*).

102 See ECJ, Case C-188/15: *Asma Bougnaoui, Association de défense des droits de l'homme (ADDH) v. Micropole Univers SA*, Judgment of March 14, 2017 (hereinafter *Bougnaoui*).

at work. Although the situations were similar, the ECJ was asked a different question in each case, which in turn led to different findings. In the first case, the Belgian *Cour de Cassation* asked whether a ban on wearing a headscarf at work constituted direct discrimination. In the second case, the French *Cour de Cassation* asked whether a client's wish not to have services provided by an employee wearing a visible religious symbol or attire contravened EU law. In the *Bougnaoui* case, the ECJ held that employers cannot discriminate between employees who wear religious symbols and those who do not based on a customer's demand.[103] However, in the case of *Achbita*, the ECJ ruled that employers banning the visible display of "any political, philosophical or religious sign in the workplace, does not constitute direct discrimination."[104] Although this ruling gives employers the option – not the obligation – to impose a ban on visible religious symbols, it suggests that an individual cannot cite religious beliefs in order to avoid complying with generally applicable norms. In arriving at its decision, the ECJ invoked the principle of religious neutrality as a legitimate ground for restricting religious freedom. However, just what is necessary to achieve such neutrality is left to the subjectivity of a particular employer. This, in turn, allows for a majority view to prevail.

Although ECJ and ECtHR cases are different in scope, both courts have juridically guarded the norms of the dominant political culture in cases concerning the regulation of religion in the public sphere. This raises:

> critical questions about the possibility, and limits, of religious freedom in increasingly diverse polities, within the European Union and beyond. On the one hand, [European court cases] signify a growing tension between a "coming world order" that aims at the "cultural extension and legal enforcement of human rights," including freedom of religion and belief. On the other hand, the cases reflect both an increased vigilance of religious practices that are considered indicative of a "clash of civilizations," and the resulting restrictions on religious freedom in the name of public order. The cases also demonstrate the growth of a pan-European legal discourse of religious symbols not only as text, but as a mechanism, however broad and ambiguous, of social control.[105]

Religious practices that fall outside the secular *nomos* of Western religious traditions have come to occupy our imaginations in ways that encapsulate a

103 Ibid., para. 41.
104 *Achbita*, para. 44.
105 Skach, "Şahin v. Turkey," 186.

culture. Within Europe, such essentialist thinking about Islam has reduced it to a belief system that is intolerant, pre-modern and rigid. And if believers express a choice (to the veil for example) this is only a derivative of the "coercive" influences of powerful religious expressions.[106] The decisions of the ECtHR, then, merely reflect what is now firmly embedded in Europe: an illiberal secularism expressed in illiberal restrictions on religion in the public sphere; a religious pluralism grafted to traditional (and dominant) European norms and values where the "dominant reading of religion as a private belief … justifies active intervention in the faith of subjects ensuring that their faith conform to this homogenous conception of religion."[107]

The reality of multicultural Europe will continue to push against the gates and demand a re-examination of the public sphere. Cases that place courts at the centre of Europe's identity crisis will continue to be raised at national and European level.[108] In negotiating this contested terrain, we will need to unthink the "hegemonic knowledge regime of secularism"[109] and create a space where faith and reason can be accommodated. And until we do, this European political project will remain conflicted and incomplete.

---

106 This view is mapped out in the Muslim veil cases discussed in this paper, in which the wearing of the veil was read as a political rather than a religious act. The same view was also clearly expressed by the ECtHR in the *Refah* case (*Refah Partisi (The Welfare Party) and Others v. Turkey* [GC], Apps. Nos. 41340/98, 41342/98, 41343/98 and 41344/98, Judgment of February 13, 2003), in which the Court opined (para. 123): "that sharia, which faithfully reflects the dogmas and divine rules laid down by religion, is stable and invariable. Principles such as pluralism in the political sphere or the constant evolution of public freedoms have no place in it. … It is difficult to declare one's respect for democracy and human rights while at the same time supporting a regime based on sharia, which clearly diverges from Convention values, particularly with regard to its criminal law and criminal procedure, its rules on the legal status of women and the way it intervenes in all spheres of private and public life in accordance with religious precepts."

107 Amélie Barras, "Transactional Understanding of Secularisms and Their Impact on the Right to Religious Freedom: Exploring Religious Symbols Cases at the UN and ECHR," *Journal of Human Rights* 11, no. 2 (2012): 273.

108 While it is beyond the scope of this article, some interesting work has been done on the effect that the different approaches to religious freedom issues of the ECtHR and the UN bodies have had on plaintiffs. See Barras, "Transactional Understandings of Secularisms," 273–274.

109 Casanova, "Immigration and the New Religious Pluralism," 6.

CHAPTER 14

Identity and Human Rights in a "Populist" Era: Urging Caution and Pragmatism in Minority Rights Protection

Joshua Castellino

Abstract

Recent years have been marked by a rise in "populism" and frenzied identity-based politics, and the continued exclusion of minority groups from meaningful participation in addressing problems faced by society. In this article, I assert that the only pragmatic way to address these issues is to guarantee the genuine social inclusion of all people, and to ensure that those seeking to build inclusive societies understand the role that human rights, minority rights, and identity should play in this process. Building upon these assertions, I identify the roots of minority rights protection, as well as the importance placed on identity in generating egalitarian societies. I also examine the UN human rights approach to minority protection, and highlight the backlash to identity-based politics. Finally, I advocate for the use of pragmatism in working to build inclusive societies, and offer a number of starting points towards such an approach.

1 Introduction

Protest seems rife all over the world. Some of it is manifest in legitimate democratic processes where "protest" candidates gain traction against "institutional" candidates.[1] Some of it is evident in mass, pseudo-legitimate decisions to undermine, leave, or weaken international institutions.[2] Other protests are being launched through armed struggle aimed at undermining incumbent powers,[3] leading to migratory population flows in search of security.[4] Still others take

1 See Matthew C. MacWilliams, *The Rise of Trump: America's Authoritarian Spring* (Public Works: Amherst College Press, 2016).

2 Harold D. Clarke, Matthew Goodwin and Paul Whitely, *Brexit: Why Britain Voted to Leave the European Union* (Cambridge: Cambridge University Press, 2017).

3 Michael Weiss and Hassan Hassan, *ISIS: Inside the Army of Terror* (London: Regan Arts, 2015).

4 Elizabeth W. Collier and Charles R. Strain, eds., *Global Migration: What's Happening, Why, and a Just Response* (Winona, MN: Anselm Academic, 2017).

 | DOI:10.1163/9789004386426_015

the form of dastardly attempts to sow terror into ordinary populations. It could be argued that all of these protests are driven by a single commonality: the failure of contemporary politics to address the key governance challenges of the day.

In the last few decades, the acute failure of politics has come into sharper focus: its failure to redress deep structural inequalities within society,[5] to address the challenge of how to generate full and meaningful employment in an increasingly technology-driven world[6] and, in many cases, to combat uncertainties caused by the wanton destruction of the environment that has contributed to climate change.[7] In the 1990s, the salutary demise of totalitarian regimes was cause for much optimism concerning the birth of a new democratic era,[8] in which the consent of the people would provide legitimacy to all governance.[9] That optimism has faded dramatically, in part as a result of the failure of democratically elected governments and others to generate meaningful answers to legitimate contemporary questions faced by many populations.

In unpicking the cause of this failure, one fact stands out in contrast to others. Despite progress on all fronts, "growth," "prosperity" and "success" have not been achieved in a manner that is inclusive.[10] In every country in which it is possible to review data in a meaningful way, the trappings of "modernity" and "success" appear to have accrued far more significantly to males from dominant ethnic, linguistic and religious groups. The "Other" has been excluded, either directly through discriminatory policies or indirectly through a failure to remedy systemic biases that favour "Us" over "Them." What has emerged as a consequence is a throwback to a different age – that of the "ruling" class and the "ruled" class. Democracy, the game of numbers rather than values, has fuelled protest and thrown up pseudo-legitimate results of dubious value. Yet popularity contests are hardly the way to get to grips with contemporary challenges.

5 See *Combatting Poverty and Inequality: Structural Change, Social Policy and Politics* (New York: United Nations, 2011).

6 See *Work Anywhere, Anytime: The Effects on the World of Work* (Geneva: ILO, 2017), available at http://www.ilo.org/global/publications/books/WCMS_544138/lang--en/index.htm (consulted May 30, 2017).

7 See Johan Rockstrom and Mattias Klum, *Big World, Small Planet: Abundance within Planetary Boundaries* (New Haven, CT: Yale University Press, 2015).

8 See Francis Fukuyama, *The End of History and the Last Man*, reissue edition (New York: Free Press, 2006).

9 See Thomas Franck, "Democratic Legitimacy," *American Journal of International Law* 86, no. 1 (1992): 46–91.

10 Ken Wytsma, *The Myth of Equality: Uncovering the Roots of Injustice and Privilege* (London: IVP Books, 2017).

The challenges of the day need urgent and creative solutions that are arrived at through design rather than by chance, are based on understanding and respond to complexity. Contemporary politics appears to be throwing up simple solutions to address these complexities in the naïve belief that, like an application on a smartphone, the problem will simply vanish if we "swipe" it away. This hinders efforts to arrest global warming through technology and behavioural change and to find rapid solutions-to-scale that can mitigate its fast-flowing impact. In order to tackle incessant global unrest, it is imperative that identity-based disparities are addressed and that a new compact of mutual trust is harnessed to create an environment that fosters solutions. Populations across the planet need to feel a sense of a shared future if they are to be expected to engage more deeply in its unfolding.

Despite a commendable belief in democracy, global societies still only rely on a small proportion of the vast human potential at their disposal. For the most part, fifty per cent of the population, based on gender, has been actively prevented from fully realizing its potential in a manner that can contribute to addressing contemporary problems.[11] Elsewhere, subconscious and conscious bias has created barriers to entry for "Them" into "Our" institutions, be they educational, commercial, political or socio-cultural.[12]

If urgent problems are to be solved, it is imperative that everyone who may have an answer is involved. Otherwise, the excluded masses can only react in protest, which despite its importance only gives rise to withering critique, not creative solutions. The only pragmatic way forward is to seek genuine social inclusion in the entire gamut of human interactions. At a time like this, social exclusion is not a luxury that humanity can afford. Against this backdrop, and in a spirit of pragmatism, it is equally important for those seeking to build inclusive societies, including minority rights advocates, to understand the role that human rights and identity ought to play.

This brief paper seeks to address this question, first, by identifying the identity-oriented roots of minority rights protection, especially in post-colonial contexts. The second section aims to show the importance placed on identity in a bid to generate egalitarian societies. This is mirrored by the UN human rights approach in seeking to protect minorities and other groups located far from sites of power, as highlighted in the third section. The fourth section

11 See *Women, Gender and Work: Social Choices and Inequalities*, vol. 2 (Geneva: ILO, 2017).

12 See e.g. Malcolm Langford and Ananda Mohan Bhattarai, "Constitutional Rights and Social Exclusion in Nepal," *International Journal of Minority and Group Rights* 18 (2011): 387–411; and Marilyn Carr and Martha Chen, "Globalization, Social Exclusion and Gender," *International Labour Review* 143 (2004): 129–160.

calls attention to the backlash to identity-based politics and advocates greater pragmatism, while the fifth and final section identifies some starting points towards such an approach. This paper calls for reflection and an active quest to design multi-layered approaches, driven by the need to ensure that those far from sites of power are effectively protected in an era of frenzied identity-based politics.

II Grounds for Protection: The Roots of Minority Rights in a Post-Colonial Space

Despite the rich pedigree of the protection of minorities in the development of international law, the United Nations has taken a cautious approach in seeking to build standards concerning minority rights.[13] While the entire edifice of UN human rights law was built on the experience of the Holocaust and the Second World War, the UN Charter emphasized "human rights for all" rather than any special measures to protect minorities.[14] In conceptual terms, the reason for this is clear: if a legal and political system could be built that ensured the inherent dignity and worth of every individual, the specific identity of that individual would become less relevant over time. Such a system would emphasize commonalities rather than differences. As the United Nations developed and countries began to emerge from colonial rule, the need for unity rather than dissonance became even stronger. Most post-colonial countries were emerging within externally constructed boundaries based on the interests of hegemons.[15] These often bore little relation to the demographics of the ethnic, linguistic or religious communities that fell within them.[16] As a result, new post-colonial states emerged with a mass of communities, including some that were historically antagonistic towards each other and others nurturing new antagonisms construed, constructed and even nourished by years of colonial "divide and rule" policies. These new states were required to achieve coherence through the adoption of smart nation-building policies that would reify

13 Mark Mazower, *No Enchanted Place: The End of Empire and the Ideological Origins of the United Nations* (Ithaca: Princeton University Press, 2013).

14 See Joshua Castellino, "The Protection of Minorities and Indigenous Peoples in International Law: A Comparative Temporal Analysis," *International Journal on Minority and Group Rights* 17, no. 3 (2010): 393–422.

15 See Joshua Castellino, *International Law and Self-Determination* (The Hague: Brill Publishers, 2000).

16 See J.D. Hargreaves, "From Strangers to Minorities in West Africa," *Transactions of the Royal Historical Society* 31, no. 1 (1981): 95–113.

an imagined national identity and construct effective symbols and histories in support of that identity.[17]

With decolonization in most parts of the world resulting in the capture of the new state by certain powerful groups with close ties to the ruling regimes, the question of what nuances this "national" identity would take on became, perhaps inevitably, polarized.[18] The adoption of a unified "national identity" effectively meant that identities that were "Other" to the emerging consensus had to be accommodated, moderated, challenged or even eliminated. While the accommodation of identity may have been the most pragmatic way to build viable states, pragmatism, as in the current era, was sacrificed on the altar of intense competition and feelings of insecurity, for example over boundaries, identity and territorial and other claims from rival emerging states. Instead, post-colonial states across the globe adopted majoritarian identities as "national" identities, with minorities seen as a potential threat. This also meant that the need for minority protection could be strategically subsumed under the need to create, protect and promote general human rights.

III The UN Approach: Special Regimes and Special Measures

Now entering its eighth decade, the UN-based international human rights machinery can boast many successes. It has made the discourse on human rights the cornerstone of state policy,[19] it has contributed to the building of (albeit imperfect) mechanisms for the scrutiny of states at international level,[20] it has contributed to the establishment of state-based institutions mindful of the need for the protection of human rights,[21] and it has established a strong moral basis for the protection of individual human rights in times of peace and war.[22]

17 See Karl Deutsch and William Folz, *Nation Building* (New York: Atherton Press, 1963).

18 See Husamettin Inac and Feyzullah Unal, "The Construction of National Identity in Modern Times: Theoretical Perspectives," *International Journal of Humanities and Social Sciences* 3, no. 11 (2013): 223–232.

19 See Thomas Risse, Stephen C. Ropp and Kathryn Sikkink, eds., *The Power of Human Rights: International Norms and Domestic Change* (Cambridge: Cambridge University Press, 1999).

20 See Elvira Domínguez Redondo, "The Universal Periodic Review – is there life beyond naming and shaming in human rights implementation?," *New Zealand Law Review* 4 (2012): 673–706.

21 See e.g. Principles Related to the Status of National Institutions (Paris Principles), adopted in UN General Assembly resolution 48/134 of December 20, 1993.

22 See Samuel Moyn, *The Last Utopia: Human Rights in History* (Cambridge: Belknap Press, 2012).

On the other hand, it has also experienced some stark failures. It has failed to address questions of how collective rights can be protected,[23] it has not been able to find ways to ensure that groups far from sites of power gain access to justice,[24] and it has been of limited utility in articulating solutions that emphasize the socio-economic and developmental needs of communities.[25]

Today, the UN approach towards human rights is still based on creating a system that protects the inherent dignity and worth of every human being. However, in recognition of the enormous implementation gaps for groups located far from sites of power, it has encouraged the creation of "special regimes" of protection,[26] including instruments pertaining to indigenous peoples,[27] minorities,[28] women,[29] children,[30] migrant workers (documented

23 See Dwight G. Newman, "Collective Interests and Collective Rights," *American Journal of Jurisprudence* 49, no. 1 (2004): 127–163. For an older but nonetheless relevant view, see also Philip Alston, "A Third Generation of Solidarity Rights: Progressive Development or Obfuscation of International Human Rights Law?," *Netherlands International Law Review*, vol. 39 (1982), 307–322.

24 For an interesting econometric analysis of social exclusion and the law in the context of the United States, see Giorgio Rampa and Margherita Saraceno, "Beliefs, Precedent, and the Dynamics of Access to Justice: A Bayesian Microfunded Model," *American Law and Economics Review* 18, no. 2 (2016): 272–301.

25 See David Bilchitz, "Socio-economic Rights, Economic Crisis, and Legal Doctrine," *International Journal of Constitutional Law* 12, no. 3 (2014): 710–739.

26 David B. Lewis and Joshua Castellino, "Establishing a Different Dimension of Citizen Security: The Case for Special Protection for Whistleblowers," *Beijing Law Review* 4, no. 4 (2013): 185–197.

27 See Convention Concerning Indigenous and Tribal Peoples in Independent Countries (ILO No. 169), 72 *ILO Official Bulletin* 59, entered into force September 5, 1991; United Nations Declaration on the Rights of Indigenous Peoples, General Assembly resolution 61/295, UN Doc. A/RES/47/1 (2007); Proposed American Declaration on the Rights of Indigenous Peoples, approved by the Inter-American Commission on Human Rights, February 26, 1997, Doc. no. OEA/Ser/L/V/II.95 Doc. 6 (1997).

28 Declaration on the Rights of Persons Belonging to National or Ethnic, Religious or Linguistic Minorities, General Assembly resolution 47/135, annex, 47 UN GAOR Supp. (No. 49) at 210, UN Doc. A/47/49 (1993).

29 Convention on the Elimination of All Forms of Discrimination against Women, General Assembly resolution 34/180, 34 UN GAOR Supp. (No. 46) at 193, UN Doc. A/34/46, entered into force September 3, 1981; Optional Protocol to the Convention on the Elimination of All Forms of Discrimination against Women, General Assembly resolution 54/4, annex, 54 UN GAOR Supp. (No. 49) at 5, UN Doc. A/54/49 (Vol. I) (2000), entered into force December 22, 2000; and, in the context of war, Declaration on the Protection of Women and Children in Emergency and Armed Conflict, General Assembly resolution 3318 (XXIX), 29 UN GAOR Supp. (No. 31) at 146, UN Doc. A/9631 (1974).

30 Convention on the Rights of the Child, General Assembly resolution 44/25, annex, 44 UN GAOR Supp. (No. 49) at 167, UN Doc. A/44/49 (1989), entered into force September 2, 1990; Convention concerning the Prohibition and Immediate Action for the Elimination

and undocumented),[31] refugees[32] and the disabled.[33] In each context, international treaties that have been signed and ratified contain a series of general human rights, a list of specific rights pertaining to the class of persons in question and, in some cases, an additional mechanism designed to overcome the problem of the group's lack of access to general rights.[34] This trend is also mirrored at European level, where a special regime, though not identity-based in the same sense, has been created to protect human rights defenders, on the grounds that their rights would otherwise be difficult to guarantee.[35]

of the Worst Forms of Child Labour (ILO No. 182), 38 ILM 1207 (1999), entered into force November 19, 2000; Optional Protocol to the Convention on the Rights of the Child on the involvement of children in armed conflicts, General Assembly resolution 54/263, Annex I, 54 UN GAOR Supp. (No. 49) at 7, UN Doc. A/54/49, Vol. III (2000), entered into force February 12, 2002, and Optional Protocol to the Convention on the Rights of the Child on the sale of children, child prostitution and child pornography, General Assembly resolution 54/263, Annex II, 54 UN GAOR Supp. (No. 49) at 6, UN Doc. A/54/49, Vol. III (2000), entered into force January 18, 2002. In addition there are also guidelines concerning juvenile offenders, such as United Nations Rules for the Protection of Juveniles Deprived of their Liberty, General Assembly resolution 45/113, annex, 45 UN GAOR Supp. (No. 49A) at 205, UN Doc. A/45/49 (1990); United Nations Guidelines for the Prevention of Juvenile Delinquency (Riyadh Guidelines), General Assembly resolution 45/112, annex, 45 UN GAOR Supp. (No. 49A) at 201, UN Doc. A/45/49 (1990); and the United Nations Standard Minimum Rules for the Administration of Juvenile Justice (Beijing Rules), General Assembly resolution 40/33, annex, 40 UN GAOR Supp. (No. 53) at 207, UN Doc. A/40/53 (1985).

31 International Convention on the Protection of the Rights of All Migrant Workers and Members of Their Families, General Assembly resolution 45/158, annex, 45 UN GAOR Supp. (No. 49A) at 262, UN Doc. A/45/49 (1990), entered into force July 1, 2003.

32 Convention relating to the Status of Refugees, 189 UNTS 150, entered into force April 22, 1954; Protocol Relating to the Status of Refugees, 606 UNTS 267, entered into force October 4, 1967; Guiding Principles on Internal Displacement, UN Doc. E/CN.4/1998/53/Add.2 (1998); and the Cartagena Declaration on Refugees, *Annual Report of the Inter-American Commission on Human Rights*, OAS Doc. OEA/Ser.L/V/II.66/doc.10, rev. 1, at 190–193 (1984–85), April 17, 1998.

33 Declaration on the Rights of Disabled Persons, General Assembly resolution 3447 (XXX), 30 UN GAOR Supp. (No. 34) at 88, UN Doc. A/10034 (1975); International Convention on the Protection and Promotion of the Rights and Dignity of Persons with Disabilities, General Assembly resolution 61/106, Annex I, UN GAOR, 61st Sess., Supp. No. 49, at 65, UN Doc. A/61/49 (2006), entered into force May 3, 2008; First Optional Protocol to the International Convention on the Protection and Promotion of the Rights and Dignity of Persons with Disabilities, General Assembly resolution 61/106, Annex II, UN GAOR, 61st Sess., Supp. No. 49, at 80, UN Doc. A/61/49 (2006), entered into force May 3, 2008.

34 For a general explanation of the UN treaty-based system, see P. Alston, ed., *United Nations Human Rights: A Critical Reappraisal* (Oxford: Oxford University Press, 1996).

35 See "Ensuring Protection: EU Guidelines on Human Rights Defenders," available at http://www.consilium.europa.eu/uedocs/cmsUpload/GuidelinesDefenders.pdf (last accessed February 1, 2010).

The approach taken in these special protection regimes is to create specific protection for a class of persons, in order to enable them to enjoy the fruits of human rights without discrimination. The International Convention for the Elimination of Racial Discrimination typifies this approach, requiring that:

> States Parties shall, when the circumstances so warrant, take, in the social, economic, cultural and other fields, special and concrete measures to ensure the adequate development and protection of certain racial groups or individuals belonging to them, for the purpose of guaranteeing them the full and equal enjoyment of human rights and fundamental freedoms. These measures shall in no case entail as a consequence the maintenance of unequal or separate rights for different racial groups after the objectives for which they were taken have been achieved.[36]

Thus, the elements of the envisaged protection consist, first, of a clear identification of a specific class of individuals who suffer as a result of a lack of means to access their rights. Second, it advocates that states pay special attention to creating social policy mechanisms designed to assist in their advancement. Third, these mechanisms are envisaged as creating affirmative action measures that give preference to this class of individuals. Fourth, the objective of this special preference is to generate greater access than that achieved through a pure "human rights based approach," which treats everyone the same. However, in order to ensure that such measures do not serve as justification for apartheid-style measures, the Convention also encompasses a caveat:

> Special measures taken for the sole purpose of securing adequate advancement of certain racial or ethnic groups or individuals requiring such protection as may be necessary in order to ensure such groups or individuals equal enjoyment or exercise of human rights and fundamental freedoms shall not be deemed racial discrimination, provided, however, that such measures do not, as a consequence, lead to the maintenance of separate rights for different racial groups and that they shall not be continued after the objectives for which they were taken have been achieved.[37]

There are a limited number of socio-legal policy-oriented tools that are in use worldwide to seek to provide remedies to groups, such as minorities, that

---

36 Article 2(2) ICERD.
37 Article 1(4) ICERD.

remain far from power. They include political mechanisms (e.g. federalism,[38] autonomy,[39] identity-based electoral policies and representative quotas);[40] administrative mechanisms (providing special access to justice, legal aid, special courts and tribunals, ombudsman services, educational policies and employment quotas);[41] and judicial mechanisms (access to lawyers and language protection). In the specific case of minorities, however, the vast majority of global measures tend to emphasize the importance of the protection of their cultural rights.[42] This is manifested in the right sought by – and in some cases granted to – minorities to celebrate their own culture, practice their own religion and propagate their own language.[43]

IV The Backlash: Populism and Minorities

One significant impact of this focus on minorities in more recent, populist times has been a backlash based on the belief that "minorities get special privileges." This paper accepts that the contours of what constitutes "populism" remain to be defined.[44] The concept is particularly nebulous in the legal arena, where it may refer to sweeping legal reforms driven by popular leaders,[45] processes by

38 See S. Choudhry, ed., *Constitutional Design for Divided Societies: Integration or Accommodation?* (Oxford: Oxford University Press, 2008).

39 See especially Y. Ghai and S. Woodman, eds., *Practising Self-Government: A Comparative Study of Autonomous Regions* (Cambridge: Cambridge University Press, 2013).

40 See e.g. M. Alagappa, ed., *Political Legitimacy in Southeast Asia: The Quest for Moral Authority* (Stanford: Stanford University Press, 1995).

41 Discussed in country-specific case studies in J. Castellino and E. Domínguez Redondo, *Minority Rights in Asia: A Comparative Legal Analysis* (Oxford: Oxford University Press, 2006); J. Castellino and D. Keane, *Minority Rights in the Pacific: A Comparative Legal Analysis* (Oxford: Oxford University Press, 2009); and J. Castellino and K. Cavanaugh, *Minority Rights in the Middle East: A Comparative Legal Analysis* (Oxford: Oxford University Press, 2013).

42 See e.g. Will Kymlicka, *The Rights of Minority Cultures* (Oxford: Oxford University Press, 1995); W.K. Barth, *Cultural Rights: The Equality of Nations and the Minority Legal Tradition* (Leiden/Boston: Martinus Nijhoff/Brill, 2008); and Alan Patten, *Equal Recognition: The Moral Foundations of Minority Rights* (Ithaca: Princeton University Press, 2016).

43 See e.g. Marion Vargaftig, *Cultural Rights, Media and Minorities* (Strasbourg: Council of Europe Publishing, 1998).

44 For one source that addresses these issues in the sphere of political governance, see Jan-Werner Muller, *What is Populism?* (Philadelphia: University of Pennsylvania Press, 2016).

45 See e.g. Marten Brienen, "A Populism of Indignities: Bolivian Populism under Evo Morales," *Brown Journal of World Affairs* 23, no. 1 (Fall/Winter 2016): 77–93.

which constitutions are made more amenable to the "popular will,"[46] or the extent to which adequate protection can be brought to bear based on the effective articulation of this will.[47] However, the treatment of populism in this paper focuses on the trends through which the will of the masses may be mobilized in a political system and the fact that the nature of that mobilization may constitute an existential threat to minorities because they are not included among the masses or – worse yet – because the masses are mobilized on the basis of a perceived hostility against a particular group. This may take the form exhibited in the Indian context, where sustained efforts to provide minority rights were traditionally posited as a basic constitutional principle in support of equality. In recent decades, however, there has been a slow erosion of the value of this principle, and instead minority rights have been portrayed in the popular media and by leading politicians as nothing more than the "appeasement of minorities"[48] or the granting of special privileges to people somehow less deserving.

This sentiment is equally prevalent in discussions in Europe concerning "benefits for migrants,"[49] in crises concerning access to university education for Latinos in the United States,[50] and in exemptions from the one-child policy for Chinese Muslims.[51] The narrative often portrayed in the mainstream media tends to construct these attempts to unravel entrenched structural discrimination as providing a perceived "less-deserving" Other with "benefits" that are not available to majority populations. At a time of limited economic growth or heightened socio-economic competition, these measures come under increased pressure, creating enmity and building new rifts in society. In many cases, the poor design of such policies often means that they do not always have the mass positive effect that they are envisaged as achieving. Instead, they may privilege only an elite group within a specific minority and discriminate

46 See J.M. Balkin, "Populism and Progressivism as Constitutional Categories," *Yale Law Journal* 104, no. 7 (May 1995): 1935–1990.

47 See Terry Carney, "Protection, Populism and Citizenship," *Law in Context: A Socio-Legal Journal* 17, no. 2 (2000): 54–76.

48 For more on this discussion see Catarina Kinnvall and Ted Svensson, "Hindu Nationalism, Diaspora Politics and Nation-Building in India," *Australian Journal of International Affairs* 64, no. 3 (2010): 274–292.

49 See Michael Blauberger and Susanne K. Schmidt, "Welfare migration? Free movement of EU citizens and access to social benefits," *Research and Politics* 64, no. 3 (2014), available at http://journals.sagepub.com/doi/pdf/10.1177/2053168014563879 (consulted 30 May, 2017).

50 See *Affirmative Action in American Law Schools*, Briefing Report of the US Commission on Civil Rights (Washington, DC: US Commission on Civil Rights, 2007).

51 Yuanyuan Feng and Monit Cheung, "Public Policies Affecting Ethnic Minorities in China," *China Journal of Social Work* 1, no. 3 (2008): 248–265.

against the more deprived or economically marginalized members of this community. In cases of public anxiety or hysteria, these measures, which are often designed to afford no more than basic minimal standards, are easily aggrandized by vested interests as providing substantial privileges to "undeserving" groups. When these "undeserving" groups further seek to articulate their distinctiveness, this is seen as a further attempt to undermine the national narrative. Thus, societies seem to be locked in a zero sum game whereby the provision of limited remedies is portrayed as the problem, ignoring the wider socio-economic context of the crises that underpin societal pressures in the first place.

Intelligently designed but time-bound affirmative action measures[52] with very specific goals and a regular review to test their effectiveness may prove the optimal way of disrupting structural discrimination in the short and medium term. The only long-term guarantee against structural discrimination is a full understanding and articulation of the value of equality and the importance of social inclusion, delivered to all in an imaginative manner via the education system. However, this long-term goal is unrealizable in the short and medium term, where more concerted social engineering is required to ensure that the value of diversity is not completely lost from public life. Among the variety of measures that could be used, legally enshrined and fairly administered affirmative action measures probably serve the purpose best. In the medium to long term, it is only when society begins to realize and accept that group identity is not particularly relevant to an individual's talent or ability that it will be possible to create an egalitarian society. It is exclusion itself that propagates further exclusion and isolation, and when that exclusion is based on a personal identifier, such as gender, race, ethnicity, religion or language, it reifies existing structural hierarchies. An emphasis on equality of opportunity, measured sector by sector, yields startling results. In societies that believe themselves to be meritocratic, people bemoan the fact that there are not as many "qualified" women or ethnic minority candidates.[53] The argument proffered lays the blame at the feet of societies, communities, families or individuals themselves for having failed to encourage or inspire people from within specific socio-ethnic or gendered groups to acquire the skills and attributes necessary to be successful. Yet this argument fails to address the manner in which the attributes for success

52 For more on affirmative action measures and the elements behind constructing an effective one, see Marc Bossuyt, *The Concept and Practice of Affirmative Action*, UN Doc. E/CN.4/Sub.2/2000/11 (June 19, 2000).

53 See e.g. Anne Sweigart, "Women on Board for Change: The Norway Model of Boardroom Quotas as a Tool of Progress in the United States and Canada," *Northwestern Journal of International Law and Business* 32, no. 4 (2012): 81.

are determined or how individual achievements are calibrated against these indicators. It also fails to pay adequate attention to conscious and unconscious biases. In societies that may be less progressive, candidates from “Other” backgrounds may be barred from even competing.

Minority rights advocacy has focused overwhelmingly on the politics of difference in seeking greater cultural autonomy and recognition of rights. While calls for redistributive justice, through an emphasis on substantive equality and participation in socio-economic life, have been part of the narrative of minority rights, they have usually been met in the field of social policy through concessions based on cultural autonomy and recognition of rights. In other words, states appear to have found it easier to agree to cultural rights than to make the necessary changes to societal structures that are necessary to achieve redistributive justice.[54] While this approach has its merits in combating group exclusion, it has in some contexts set “minorities” apart as being somehow more deserving than other excluded populations. With societies being unable to generate meaningful solutions-to-scale in terms of employment and public participation, many from the majority communities have fallen on equally hard times. The emphasis on “cultural rights based” advocacy alienates these people and turns them into competitors rather than allies. One of the facets most visible in the failure in democracies to accept and endorse political processes that promote values is mass hysteria, which is often generated within excluded majority communities towards minorities. Turning democratic processes into a strict game of numbers means that well-fuelled anger, even when mobilized through questionable facts and with significant cynicism, can generate unity in a common cause and comprehensively “win” the day. If large sections of the population, often drawn from the majority community, feel excluded, it is easy to convince them that the “privileges” afforded to other excluded communities are the cause of their suffering.

It is therefore unsurprising that, rather than revolting against the increased concentration of wealth and influence among the few, these few are now also given the “democratic legitimacy” to act, thus constructing societies where the tyranny of the many can prevail. To be able to engineer such an outcome requires significant media capture, which is usually achieved by identifying convenient scapegoats who are blamed for taking scarce resources rather than

54 For instance, the Framework Convention on National Minorities (1995) takes a programmatic approach to minority rights that emphasizes cultural rights rather than focusing on entitlements to socio-economic rights and redistributive justice. See also Claudia Tavani, *Collective Rights and the Cultural Identity of the Roma: A Case Study of Italy* (Leiden: Martinus Nijhoff, 2012).

by attributing failures to the lack of impetus in the job creation machinery of the state. Many recent developments, including Donald Trump's victory in the US presidential election and Brexit, were based on questionable interpretations of socio-economic difficulties, which were attributed to inflows of outsiders rather than flawed economic modelling and increased automation, which is making it even harder to create jobs. The relative accumulation of greater wealth within the super-elite did not merit as much attention, not even during Trump's election campaign. If it had, it might have created allegiances between excluded communities, be they members of the urban or rural poor from the majority community or members of equally disenfranchised minority communities. Instead, the orchestration of the "Other" as a scapegoat served to galvanize the tyranny of the majority (especially the socio-economically excluded) over minority communities.

The challenge for those advocating for minority rights lies in the extent to which the specific cultural aspects of minorities can be put aside in a bid to unite in common cause with others who also face exclusion. Many will articulate concerns that such an approach may lead to assimilation, and it is equally clear that emphasizing difference at a time of unrest has its own problems. The quest to create a society where difference is a point of interest rather than a cause for exclusion requires significant imagination. Not only does it need to draw on the skills of people who may not have had the widest exposure to solutions but it also has to be achieved against the backdrop of historic structures that are exclusionary and in an era of frenzied identity politics, where identity issues seem central to heated political discussions. This is a particularly steep gradient to overcome in a bid to create a "level playing field," which therefore requires pragmatism, reflection and context-specific but widely derived solutions, as articulated in the concluding section.

V Towards a Pragmatic Approach

The nature of pragmatism dictates that solutions should be guided by the context rather than the approach. The following strands of thought are therefore offered as starting points for a pragmatic approach, with the caveat that some are more likely to be effective than others.

A *Using the Tags: Cultural Rights versus Human Rights*

In many societies, minority identity is a source of difference, suspicion and enmity. These antagonisms are often historically derived, and overcoming them has proved difficult even in better, more collaborative times. Seeking to overcome them in times of heightened strife and scarcity may prove to be an ineffectual strategy. Instead, an emphasis on the shared sense of isolation and deprivation of human rights among disenfranchised populations, irrespective of their different identities, may serve as a basis for new alliances and constituencies that could generate meaningful results, especially in countries where periodic democratic processes yield opportunities for change. This necessitates working across identity barriers and reaching out to communities that may traditionally have been considered the "enemy." It is instructive to note, however, that most societies have changed well beyond the binary distinction between the pre-constructed "Us" and "Them" of historical lore. It remains to be seen how effectively non-ethnic and non-religious politics can be engaged without sacrificing the ethnic and religious identities that many consider to be of fundamental importance.

B *Emphasizing Administrative Measures for Equality*

All constitutions remain committed to the idea of equality in terms of international and domestic law. This has usually meant that states have an obligation to undertake legislative, judicial and administrative measures that would go a long way towards promoting such equality. Traditionally, emphasis has been placed on seeking change by amending laws or "winning" court cases through judicial pronouncements. This presupposes that minorities and others from excluded communities have access either to the levers of legislative power or to well-meaning and passionate advocates who will be able to persuade, cajole or coax justice for individual victims out of a reluctant system. For most people from the Bottom Billion,[55] including many minorities, neither option is feasible due to their traditional lack of access. An emphasis on legal reform that targets administrative legal systems is much more likely to achieve social inclusion, since it is more likely to enable access to rights as a matter of course than an antagonistic struggle through the courts. Paying particular attention to social policy and ensuring that it is "exclusion proof" is far more likely to yield benefits. It will engage the people most in need and design solutions that are more accessible without recourse to the upper echelons that sit far from those excluded and engage in inflated political debate.

C *Creating a Sector-based Approach*

Any quest to tackle social exclusion needs to have the benefit of significant engagement with the details of that exclusion. This requires a full understanding

55 See Paul Collier, *The Bottom Billion: Why the Poorest Countries Are Failing and What Can Be Done about It* (Oxford: Oxford University Press, 2007).

of the nature of exclusion in the socio-economic, cultural, civil and political space on a sector-by-sector basis. It is only by determining the nature of exclusion in access to education, health, public sector employment, finance, legal status and land, among others areas, that specific measures and policies can be designed to address the exclusion. These determinations may vary depending on the setting (rural or urban) or variations within such settings. Creating alliances between excluded populations through local, issue-driven advocacy that cuts across identity gaps may be more likely to yield results, as it enables communities to bond over a common local cause rather than through dramatic debates at national level that are inevitably politicized and in which rhetoric and drama count for more than substance.

D *Focusing on the Pragmatic and the Need to Rebuild Social Cohesion*

The rupture in the social fabric of societies lies at the heart of many of these discussions (or rather the fierce ranting that characterizes the modern political space). These episodes are designed to cause shock, horror and moral outrage. They focus on intense scrutiny and attempt to appoint blame for current problems, with little energy left over for addressing solutions. Focusing political discussion on the shape of the future, say 2030 and beyond, requires a degree of calm discussion and clinical focus that is inconceivable in the middle of a shouting match. Mobilizing people, irrespective of their identity tags, to imagine a shared future can help rebuild the social fabric, renew awareness of the nature of historical exclusion and commence the detailed and complex design work needed to achieve a common vision.

E *No One Size Fits All*

When examining post-colonial societies, it is remarkable to see how specific structures designed in one context are simply reconstructed in others. For instance, most legal systems around the world remain influenced by the few "northern" systems from which they are derived. These predesigned systems have been reproduced on a massive scale in post-colonial states and are often ill-suited to the local context, creating new problems and failing to address long-standing ones. In seeking designs for more inclusive societies, it is imperative to understand that there is unlikely to be one system that works everywhere. Instead, it is from a multiplicity of efforts, informed by experiences from around the globe, that better solutions are likely to emerge.

CHAPTER 15

Comments for a Roundtable Discussion on "Transnational Activism: Impact of Populism on Minorities, Indigenous Peoples and Refugees"

A Note by Fiona McConnell

The diversity of populism is often overlooked. The focus of many scholars and policy-makers in recent years has been on the rise of an exclusionary mode of populism across Europe and the United States,[1] which discriminates against particular vulnerable groups and leads to a curtailment of the rights of minorities, and the more inclusive mode of populism that has dominated in Latin America.[2] However, it is also important to remember that there is a *geography* to populism: it is a mode of politics that has different manifestations in different places and at different times. Populism might be most common in democratic states,[3] but populist elements are also apparent in authoritarian regimes.[4] In many ways, populist parties and leaders disregard democratic norms in their invocation of the "will of the people" and use this to intimidate those deemed to be "others." We can, for example, trace elements of populism in contemporary Chinese Communist Party rhetoric, with their promotion of a harmonious (read "homogenous") society, which is deemed to be threatened by dangerous "others," in particular the Muslim Uyghur community in the west of the country. In thereby recognizing that populism is a mode of politics that can manifest in a number of different guises and in a wide range of cultural

1 Daniel Gros, "Is Globalisation Really Fuelling Populism?" *CEPS Commentary*: 11 May, 2016 [Policy Paper], available at http://www.ceps.eu. See also Ruth Wodak, Majid KhosraviNik, Brigitte Mral, eds., *Right-Wing Populism in Europe* (London: Bloomsbury, 2013). Michael Kazin, "Trump and American Populism," *Foreign Affairs* 95, no. 6 (2016): 17–24.

2 Juan Grigera, "Populism in Latin America: Old and New Populisms in Argentina and Brazil," *International Political Science Review* 38, no. 4 (2017): 441–455.

3 Daniele Albertazzi, and Duncan McDonnell, eds., *Twenty-First Century Populism: The Spectre of Western European Democracy* (Basingstoke and New York: Palgrave Macmillan, 2008). Cas Mudde, "The Populist Zeitgeist," *Government and Opposition* 39, no. 4 (2004): 542–563.

4 Peter Fritzsche, *Rehearsals for Fascism: Populism and Political Mobilization in Weimar Germany* (Oxford: Oxford University Press, 1990).

 | DOI:10.1163/9789004386426_016

contexts, we need to be alert to its effect on minority communities in a range of geographical settings.

However, highlighting the diversity of populism also has drawbacks. In essence, populism is a timely and powerful concept, but it is also a messy, fuzzy term. There is a danger of it becoming a loose, catch-all concept that is too broad to be useful. One way to have leverage on populism is to focus on what it opposes: pluralism.[5] As Robert Dahl has argued, pluralists assert that politics should reflect the preferences of as many groups as possible through processes of consensus and compromise.[6] The mainstream understanding of populism, on the other hand, sets up a framework of a "pure people" versus a corrupt elite and thereby denies the legitimacy of a multiplicity of different groups. In this context of increasing discrimination against and silencing of minority communities in a diverse range of contexts, I want to suggest that it is important both to think creatively about how marginalized voices can be amplified and to turn attention to how and where alternative political discourses are being promoted: discourses of pluralism, cosmopolitanism and internationalism. My specific focus is on how this amplification of minority voices to counter populism can happen not just on the ground but also on the international stage.

When we think about how minority groups frame their cause to external audiences, and in particular how they seek to use international law and the institutions of the United Nations to garner support, then we run up against the perennial tension between group rights and individual rights. This is a tension that has been discussed at considerable length in academic literature,[7] with the following questions prompting considerable debate: Should group rights and human rights be distinguished from each other? Are human rights borne only by individuals? Are group rights a threat to individual rights? Or can human rights take collective as well as individual forms? These questions are beyond the scope of this short essay, but it is important to highlight the fact that minority groups are, of course, not immune from elements of populist politics. A fine line always needs to be tread when advocating for group rights, whether they be minority rights, indigenous rights or the right to self-determination, and this is particularly the case when identity politics are prioritized and when there is thus a danger of essentializing and homogenizing identity, denying diversity and reproducing discourses of fear and insecurity. The challenge for

5 Jan-Werner Müller, *What is Populism* (Philadelphia: University of Pennsylvania Press, 2016).

6 Rober A. Dahl, *Dilemmas of Pluralist Democracy: Autonomy vs Control* (New Haven: Yale University Press, 1982).

7 Peter Jones, "Human Rights, Group Rights, and Peoples' Rights," *Human Rights Quarterly* 21, no. 1 (1999): 80–107.

minority communities is therefore to maintain their cultural identity while not going down the route of tribal politics: a balancing act at the intersection of human rights and identity politics. There are several ways that marginalized groups are seeking to do this: from lobbying for specific human rights as well as collective or group rights to creatively forming coalitions across regional and cultural boundaries. It is the latter I want to focus on here.

If the rise of populism is resulting in the shutting down of spaces for minority communities to exercise their rights, then one way for such groups to start to carve out space to challenge these policies and assert a presence on the international stage is through forging coalitions. Networks of transnational solidarity across marginalized communities are certainly nothing new. For example, we can think back to the anticolonial movements that emerged after the First World War, which included Pan-Islamism, Pan-Arabism (which in many ways failed to gain backing from the new states of the Middle East) and the more influential Pan-Asianism and Pan-Africanism.[8] In the contemporary period, networks of transnational solidarity are arguably more fragmented and ad hoc, but I want to suggest that they are also instructive in challenging populist narratives both in terms of how they seek to engage in the international arena and the discourses of universal human rights, internationalism and subaltern cosmopolitanism that they promote. I will focus briefly on three examples here: transnational indigenous activism, regional alliances of minority groups and marginalized communities that come together under the auspices of the Unrepresented Nations and Peoples Organization (UNPO).

The notion of unity in diversity and the forging of alliances across communities from a wide range of regions have been at the core of indigenous advocacy at international level. Indeed, in many ways indigenous communities have led the way in coalition-building in recent years. The present form of indigenous organization at the United Nations emerged from an inter-ethnic meeting in a Sioux reserve in 1974, which brought together 98 delegates from North and South American Indian nations. This led to the creation of the International Indian Treaty Council, the first indigenous organization registered with the United Nations Economic and Social Council (ECOSOC), in 1977.[9] A series of regional level councils and parliaments have since been established (from the 1980s onwards), including the Indian Council of South America (CISA), which

8 Mark Mazower, *No Enchanted Palace: The End of Empire and the Ideological Origins of the United Nations* (Princeton: Princeton University Press, 2009).

9 Irène Bellier, "'We Indigenous Peoples…' Global Activism and the Emergence of a New Collective Subject at the United Nations," in *The Gloss of Harmony: The Politics of Policy-Making in Multilateral Organisations*, ed. Birgit Muller (London: Pluto Press, 2013), 177–201.

was created in 1980, the Sami Parliament, which brings communities together across the Arctic, the Asian Indigenous Peoples Pact (AIPP), which incorporates local organizations from fourteen countries, and the Indigenous Peoples of Africa Coordinating Committee (IPACC), which covers the whole continent and includes 150 organizations in twenty countries. Working in trans-regional alliances, such coalitions have contributed to solidarity-building between indigenous peoples, have overcome linguistic and political divisions and were key to drafting the UN Declaration on the Rights of Indigenous Peoples, which was adopted in 1995.[10]

At the regional level, we have also seen the formation of coalitions of minority communities from the same state that come together to lobby on common rights issues. An illustrative example is the Congress of Nationalities for a Federal Iran, a diaspora-based alliance of political parties and advocacy groups representing the Baloch, Kurdish, Turkmen, Ahwazi Arab and Azerbaijani minorities in Iran. Their aim is not only to publically represent the presence of non-Persian communities within the state but also to lobby for a range of rights by calling for the establishment of a secular, democratic and federal government in Iran. We can also think of marginalized communities in Ethiopia – the Oromo, Somalis in Ogaden and the Sidama – lobbying together at the European Union, and minorities in China – the Uyghurs, Tibetans and Southern Mongolians – who frequently share a platform to lobby China at the United Nations, including writing joint shadow reports and issuing joint press statements.

Indeed, it was the Allied Committee of the Peoples of Eastern Turkestan, Inner Mongolia, Manchuria and Tibet that was the precursor to the UNPO. The Allied Committee was founded in 1985 as a coalition of indigenous and marginalized communities in China that came together to highlight their shared cause at the international level. Members of the Committee then extended their gaze to other unrepresented peoples and nations, realizing that a global platform that generated solidarity and collaboration with other oppressed peoples was needed in order to make an impact on global geopolitics.[11]

At first glance, UNPO members appear to be unlikely bedfellows. Not only do they span all continents, they also cover a wide constitutional spectrum, with their political demands ranging from full recognition of statehood (e.g. Somaliland) to claims to self-determination (e.g. Iranian Kurdistan) and demands for the protection of cultural rights (e.g. Afrikaners). They are a group

10 Ibid.

11 UNPO, *Twenty Years of Promoting Nonviolence, Human Rights and Self-Determination: UNPO 20th Anniversary Publication* (The Hague: UNPO, 2011).

of polities that would likely not, under other circumstances, share a lobbying platform. Yet they have come together through a series of shared experiences of marginality: exclusion from forums of international diplomacy and common struggles to protect human rights – often challenging the policies of populist governments.[12] Indeed, through membership of UNPO, we see the creation of a level playing field among actors of varying sizes, resources and political clout. Although nationalism underpins the politics of most of the member communities, within UNPO events this is tempered by a collective pan-community solidarity.

This solidarity is manifest in drafting joint shadow reports (e.g. on the protection of the rights of indigenous peoples with respect to their cultural heritage[13]), organizing side events and sharing a platform at joint conferences (e.g. on minorities and humanitarian crises that brought together representatives from Southern Mongolia, Balochistan, the Chittagong Hill Tracts and Ogaden[14]) and using social media to raise awareness of each other's causes. On the one hand, there are practical advantages to forming advocacy coalitions: spreading scarce financial and human resources as far as possible, pooling expertise, learning from other groups, sharing best practices and thereby maximizing lobbying opportunities. On the other hand, forming such coalitions also makes a broader political statement about human rights running parallel to identity politics. In essence, this is about drawing out connections across regions, cultures and religions, highlighting common challenges and struggles and bringing common values and interests among diverse communities to the fore. By thus reframing causes that are conventionally seen in terms of ethnic nationalism, forming advocacy coalitions catches the attention of the international community. This establishes minorities as promoters of a different set of discourses: of solidarity and internationalism from below, of pluralism and unity in diversity, and of subaltern cosmopolitanism – an ability to negotiate difference and traverse geographical and cultural boundaries.[15]

In these brief comments, I have offered just a snapshot of solidarity-building between marginalized communities. We can also think, *inter alia*, of networks among liberation movements and connections between sub-state governments. It is also important to recognize that there are significant limitations to coalition-building and solidarity. There are limits to how far internationalism

12 Fiona McConnell, "Liminal Geopolitics: The Subjectivity and Spatiality of Diplomacy at the Margins," *Transactions of the Institute of British Geographers* 42, no. 1 (2017): 139–152.

13 http://unpo.org/article/17985.

14 http://unpo.org/article/19628.

15 Vinay K. Gidwani, "Subaltern Cosmopolitanism as Politics," *Antipode* 38, no. 1 (2006): 7–21.

as articulated by minority and indigenous communities extends, as there is always a perceived danger of diluting a group's cause, with the voice, identity politics and specific grievances of a particular community being lost in a coalition. At the end of the day, it is often a compromise and a balancing act between advocating for universal human rights alongside other marginalized communities and preserving and promoting your own identity politics. But if populism rests on discourses of fear and insecurity, then hope lies in the notion of unity in diversity and the practices of forging alliances across communities.

PART 5

Report

CHAPTER 16

Human Rights Education in the Visegrád Countries: A Difficult Journey

Louise Métrich

Abstract

This report deals with human rights education (HRE) in the Visegrád countries: the Czech Republic, Hungary, Poland and Slovakia. The analysis focuses on public policies and discourses on HRE in this region, in the context of the growing institutionalization of HRE on a global scale and new efforts to converge educational policies at EU level, as well as increasing overt criticism of the human rights movement. To this end, the paper presents the historical background to the emergence of the field of HRE and situates current strategies on and approaches to HRE in a European[1] framework. The study focuses exclusively on policies aimed at the formal education system, including the primary and secondary school levels; pre-school, tertiary, vocational, non-formal and informal education, as well as lifelong learning and youth policies, are beyond its scope. The paper aims to shed light on the concepts and approaches used and promoted by institutional actors responsible for designing and implementing HRE, putting them in perspective by comparing them to existing education traditions, such as citizenship education. It also touches upon the role of civil society in the development of HRE and investigates the possibility of the existence of an epistemic community on HRE in the Visegrád region.

1 Introduction

The report originates from the empirical observation that it is difficult for HRE to establish a foothold in the Visegrád countries. In the course of three seminars on HRE in these countries organized by the Tom Lantos Institute, Pro Humanum and Tandem[2] in Budapest and Warsaw in late 2015 and 2016,

1 In this context, "European" refers to the member states of the European Union and the Council of Europe.

2 These three civil society organizations are respectively based in Budapest (Hungary), Warsaw (Poland) and Komárno (Slovakia). Two of the seminars were organized in the framework of a project supported by the International Visegrád Fund.

 | DOI:10.1163/9789004386426_017

participants from various backgrounds and responsibilities, working in formal and non-formal education, civil society organizations, universities and public institutions, gathered to share their experiences as practitioners and policy-makers. The seminars were aimed at mapping existing practices in HRE and discussing obstacles encountered by HRE practitioners in the Visegrád countries. Participants pointed out the similar challenges and dilemmas they were facing and expressed analogous concerns regarding the development of HRE in their respective countries, including: the generally low interest of governments in HRE and the discrepancy between their formal commitment and the real implementation of HRE in schools; the suspicion of the educational community and population at large towards human rights and HRE; and the undemocratic and hostile climate in most schools.

The first section of this paper provides a theoretical framework and discusses the emergence of HRE as an institutionalized field. The second section analyzes policies and strategies on HRE developed and implemented by the governments of the Visegrád countries within the ET2020 context. The assumption underlying this study is that human rights and education are indispensable to each other and cannot be regarded as two distinct spheres of policy-making if HRE is to develop purposefully and coherently. Human rights provide a secure framework for education, and the right to education itself is an overarching, enabling right.[3] Education is a condition for the existence of human rights and their effective implementation, since it opens up the possibility of claims. But education may also be oppressive and lead to human rights violations.[4] Furthermore, education *per se* is not a guarantee against undemocratic, discriminatory or violent behaviours in adulthood.[5] Only education based on human rights and emancipatory values may provide a strong enough framework for social justice and respect for human rights in society. The main finding of this study is that human rights and education are not embedded, while education in the EU – and thus in the Visegrád region – is justified mostly as a foundation

3 Audrey Osler, *Human Rights and Schooling: An Ethical Framework for Teaching for Social Justice* (New York and London: Teachers College Press, 2016); Tristan McCowan, "Human Rights within Education: Assessing the Justifications," *Cambridge Journal of Education* 42 (2012).

4 Osler, *Human Rights and Schooling*; McCowan, "Human Rights within Education"; Duncan Wilson, "A Human Rights Contribution to Defining Quality Education" (Background Paper prepared for the Education for All Global Monitoring Report 2005, UNESCO, Paris, 2004); Katarina Tomaševski, *Human Rights in Education as Prerequisite for Human Rights Education* (Lund and Stockholm: Raoul Wallenberg Institute and SIDA, 2001); Paulo Freire, *Pedagogy of the Oppressed* (New York and London: Continuum, 2005).

5 James A. Banks, "Teaching Literacy for Social Justice and Global Citizenship," *Language Arts* 81 (2003).

for the economic development of society and individuals. When addressed in education, human rights are subsumed under this neoliberal agenda. Hence, the conditions for substantial and meaningful HRE in the Visegrád countries are not being met. However, some countries attempted to develop comprehensive strategies for HRE in the early 2000s, and civil society organizations remain major contributors in this field.

In terms of methodology, the study is based on a review of primary and secondary literature sources on human rights, education and pedagogy, HRE, citizenship education and multicultural education, as well as on a substantive analysis of legal and policy documents, including international human rights documents, acts of the European institutions, national strategies, curricula and other official statements. In addition, sixteen semi-structured in-depth interviews were conducted with public and civil society actors involved in HRE in their respective countries. These interviews, as well as the outcomes of the discussions conducted during the above-mentioned seminars, proved useful for understanding the general context and identifying patterns of attitudes across the four countries. Participants in the discussions and interviews included: representatives of national human rights institutions, representatives of ministries of education and public agencies working in the educational field (inspectorates, in-service teacher training institutions, curriculum development institutions), representatives of civil society organizations working in HRE and related fields, independent experts on HRE and educational actors in formal, non-formal and higher education settings.

II Human Rights and Education: Two Sides of the Same Coin

HRE currently has two internationally acknowledged definitions. One stems from the Council of Europe's 2010 Charter on Education for Democratic Citizenship and Human Rights Education (Article 2b):

> "Human rights education" means education, training, awareness raising, information, practices and activities which aim, by equipping learners with knowledge, skills and understanding and developing their attitudes and behaviour, to empower learners to contribute to the building and defence of a universal culture of human rights in society, with a view to the promotion and protection of human rights and fundamental freedoms.

The other definition was adopted in the 2011 UN Declaration on Human Rights Education and Training (Article 2) and states:

1. Human rights education and training comprises all educational, training, information, awareness-raising and learning activities aimed at promoting universal respect for and observance of all human rights and fundamental freedoms and thus contributing, inter alia, to the prevention of human rights violations and abuses by providing persons with knowledge, skills and understanding and developing their attitudes and behaviours, to empower them to contribute to the building and promotion of a universal culture of human rights.
2. Human rights education and training encompasses:
   (a) Education about human rights, which includes providing knowledge and understanding of human rights norms and principles, the values that underpin them and the mechanisms for their protection;
   (b) Education through human rights, which includes learning and teaching in a way that respects the rights of both educators and learners;
   (c) Education for human rights, which includes empowering persons to enjoy and exercise their rights and to respect and uphold the rights of others.

These two rather recent definitions are an important outcome of nearly seven decades of developments, which have seen the slow but steady emergence of HRE at the crossroads of various dynamics dating back to the nineteenth century. Firstly, the elitist field of education has spread to the masses, while becoming more and more institutionalized and a matter of international concern.[6] Secondly, human rights themselves have been institutionalized and codified, expanding from grassroots movements to nation-states and international organizations.[7] Lastly, popular education movements have attempted to democratize education through human rights values and make human rights relevant and accessible to the people once again. This intermingling of traditions is reflected in the complex relationship between education and human rights, whose essence the UN definition, in particular, manages to capture.

---

6 Universal primary education was one of the Millennium Development Goals, while quality education is one of the Sustainable Development Goals.

7 On the institutionalization of human rights, see Michael A. Elliott, "The Institutional Expansion of Human Rights, 1863–2003: A Comprehensive Dataset of International Instruments," *Journal of Peace Research* 48 (2003). Elliott shows that the earliest international human rights instruments date back to the middle of the nineteenth century but that a tremendous expansion of international human rights norms has taken place since the end of the Second World War, both in terms of the amount of adopted texts and the diversity of their subjects.

1 *Education in Human Rights – Human Rights in Education*

During the nineteenth century, mass education became a traditional state mission in Europe, and nowadays constitutes a core prerogative globally. States understand that it is an efficient tool of standardization and socialization that helps guarantee the continued existence of the nation in addition to establishing its authority.[8] Education systems contribute to the development of the national identity of a given state and its economy and are sometimes even a matter of national pride. For instance, even in a highly integrated interstate organization such as the EU, states jealously protect their education policies. According to Article 6 of the Treaty on the Functioning of the European Union (TFEU), in the field of education, the EU only has the competence to "support, coordinate or supplement the actions of the Member States". This means that it cannot require member states to harmonize their educational policies. However, the global spread of mass education since the second half of the twentieth century has largely contributed to the diffusion of education models.[9] In a mimetic process, and even without pressures, states frequently borrow education policies and reforms from each other when they consider it appropriate, albeit with local variations.[10] Interstate socialization through membership in intergovernmental organizations has an impact on norm diffusion for a variety of reasons – compliance, policy-convergence, world society effect, mimicry – and this also affects human rights and education policies.[11] Several authors suggest the existence of a strong social and cultural process on a global scale, or even "standardized models of society",[12] if not a "single world culture",[13] revealed by similarities in beliefs and practices relating to teaching and longer historical trends in the structure of curricula.[14]

8 John Boli, Francisco O. Ramirez and John W. Meyer, "Explaining the Origins and Expansion of Mass Education," *Comparative Education Review* 29 (1985); Yasemin Nuhoglu Soysal and David Strang, "Construction of the First Mass Education Systems in Nineteenth-Century Europe," *Sociology of Education* 62 (1989).

9 David F. Suárez, "The Institutionalisation of Human Rights Education," in *The Impact of Comparative Education Research on Institutional Theory*, ed. David P. Baker and Alexander W. Wiseman (Oxford: Elsevier, 2006), 97.

10 Ibid., 98.

11 Brian Greenhill, "The Company You Keep: International Socialization and the Diffusion of Human Rights Norms," *International Studies Quarterly* 54 (2010).

12 Suárez, "Institutionalisation of Human Rights Education," 98.

13 Greenhill, "The Company You Keep," 130.

14 Boli, Ramirez and Meyer, "Explaining the Origins."

A The Right to Education

Since the adoption of the Universal Declaration of Human Rights (UDHR) in 1948, education has been a universally recognized human right. Article 26 of the UDHR proclaims that everyone has the right to an education and further details the purpose of education. Yet the UDHR only has moral force, and it was nearly two decades later that the right to education was finally enshrined in a legally binding document, namely in Article 13 of the International Covenant on Economic, Social and Cultural Rights (ICESCR) in 1966. It was later reiterated in Articles 28 and 29 of the Convention on the Rights of the Child (CRC) in 1989.

At European level, education remained little addressed in core human rights documents. The 1950 European Convention on Human Rights (ECHR) did not include the right to education, which was added two years later in its first Protocol. But unlike Article 26 of the UDHR, Article 2 of the Protocol is formulated as a negative right[15] and does not contain any statement on the aim of education. The European Social Charter (ESC), adopted a decade later, addresses education only indirectly and for specific purposes: in relation to the employment of children (Article 7), the right to vocational training (Article 10) and education for the promotion of health (Article 11). Its 1996 revised version introduces two articles that address education more explicitly, although there is still no right to education *per se.* Article 17 provides for the right of children and young people to social, economic and legal protection, which includes a commitment from signatory states to ensure that children receive the education they need and are encouraged to attend school regularly, and that education in the fundamental stages is free of charge. The article states that measures of social, legal and economic protection of children, including education, shall ensure "the effective exercise of the right of children and young persons to grow up in an environment which encourages the full development of their personality and of their physical and mental capacities". Article 30 on the right to protection against poverty and social exclusion requires states to promote effective access to education for persons living in, or at risk of, poverty. More recently, the European Union's 2000 Charter of Fundamental Rights (hereinafter, the EU Charter) enshrined the right to education in its Article 14, again without specifying its purpose.

Common concerns raised in the above-mentioned documents are the availability of and access to education. All of them, except for the ECHR, inscribe basic education as compulsory and free of charge. Furthermore, the CRC and the ESC pay specific attention to the access to education of children with

---

15 "No person shall be denied the right to education."

disabilities and economically vulnerable persons. The CRC, the ICESCR and the EU Charter also guarantee the right of non-state actors to establish educational institutions. According to the former (and first) UN Special Rapporteur on the Right to Education, Katarina Tomaševski, making education available and accessible represents two of the four obligations that states must commit to in order to ensure full and effective realization of the right to education.[16] She also includes acceptability and adaptability of education in her so-called "4-A scheme."[17] Availability reconciles two visions of the right to education: (1) as a civil and political right, through the freedom of establishment of non-state educational institutions, and (2) as a social and economic right, through the obligation on states to establish and fund educational institutions for all.[18] Accessibility is about the effective availability of schools for all children, i.e. the real possibility for all children to reach and enter school buildings and take part in the education process. For Osler, it is not only about free (compulsory) or affordable (post-compulsory) education but also about inclusion of vulnerable groups and the prohibition of segregation and discrimination in the access to education.[19] Acceptability and adaptability go even further, but are only marginally addressed in the aforementioned core human rights documents. They refer to the quality, relevance, suitability and flexibility of education, both in terms of content and methods. They imply an obligation not only to refrain from indoctrination, discrimination and the violation of children's dignity but also to actively respect pupils' religious, ideological or cultural beliefs and needs by adjusting and adapting programmes and facilities.[20] It is clear from this scheme that the right to education also encompasses rights *in* education and education *through* rights, i.e. the effective realization of human rights within the education system.

B Rights in Education and Education through Rights

For Tomaševski, education requires a human rights framework in order to ensure consistency between curricular content and messages, on the one hand, and the educational process and teaching methods, on the other.[21] As

16 Katarina Tomaševski, *Human Rights Obligations: Making Education Available, Accessible, Acceptable, and Adaptable* (Lund and Stockholm: Raoul Wallenberg Institute and SIDA, 2001).

17 Tomaševski, *Human Rights Obligations*, 13.

18 Ibid.

19 Osler, *Human Rights and Schooling*, 20.

20 Ibid. See also Tomaševski, *Human Rights Obligations*, 13–15.

21 Tomaševski, *Human Rights in Education*. She bases part of her argument on recommendations published by the UNESCO in the early 1990s. UNESCO, *Guidelines and Criteria for*

she recalls, education is not "inherently good,"[22] and so it is far from enough to merely focus on "getting all children to school."[23] Human rights violations do happen within the education system, from policy-making to textbooks to school practices, and hence the question of the realization of rights in education must be addressed. For McCowan, "human rights violations in education are … a serious concern,"[24] yet they are less strenuously addressed than violations of the right *to* education. Schools are often places of oppression and abuse, ranging from corporal punishment to humiliation to extreme stress due to high-stakes examinations.[25] Violence and human rights infringements may occur at all levels and in many directions: towards learners, teachers and specific groups of learners (such as minority and minoritized groups) but also among students themselves. Indoctrination, biased textbooks, marginalization through the use of a specific language and hidden curricula also breach the human rights of learners.[26]

Nonetheless, rights *in* education and education *through* rights are missing in the aforementioned documents, although they are present in other human rights instruments. For instance, Article 7 of the 1965 Convention on the Elimination of All Forms of Racial Discrimination (CERD) refers to acceptability of education and, in particular, combating prejudices and promoting understanding in the field of teaching. Article 10 of the 1979 Convention on the Elimination of All Forms of Discrimination Against Women (CEDAW) relates to both acceptability and adaptability of education, since it aims at eliminating discrimination against women and promoting stereotype-free education through coeducation. Lastly, Articles 8 and 24 of the 2006 Convention on the Rights of Persons with Disabilities (CRPD) reassert the right to education and affirm the need to ensure inclusive education for persons with disabilities. In so doing, the CRPD encompasses all four As of Tomaševski's scheme and pays specific attention to the realization of the rights of persons with disabilities within the education system.

McCowan discusses several ways of justifying support for human rights within education and distinguishes between a deontological and a consequentialist

---

the Development, Evaluation and Revision of Curricula, Textbooks and other Educational Materials in International Education in Order to Promote an International Dimension in Education (1995), 12, available at: http://www.unesco.org/education/pdf/34_71.pdf.

22 Tomaševski, *Human Rights in Education*, 9.

23 Ibid.

24 McCowan, "Human Rights within Education," 6.

25 Ibid., 5; Osler, *Human Rights and Schooling*, 106–108; Tomaševski, *Human Rights in Education*; bell hooks, *Teaching to Transgress* (New York and London: Routledge, 1994), 1–22.

26 McCowan, "Human Rights within Education," 5–6; Tomaševski, *Human Rights in Education.*

approach, whereby the former is based on the status of human rights (i.e. their legal, moral or natural form) and the latter derives from an instrumental view of human rights.[27] Thus, human rights may be justified *per se*, because of the intrinsic attributes of human beings – such as rational thought or dignity – and regardless of any consequences. In contrast, human rights may be regarded as tools and justified "on the basis of the positive consequences that will accrue to individuals and society."[28] Applying these two different approaches to the educational field, McCowan argues that both present pitfalls but should be seen "as part of a single process" rather than being mutually exclusive: "the upholding of human rights in practice in educational experiences provides significant opportunities for learning [while] the learning gained may ensure that those rights will be more effectively upheld."[29]

The status-based justification has two aspects. On the one hand, the "instantiation argument" posits that educational institutions are components of society in themselves and that human rights are thus applicable as they are anywhere else. On the other hand, the indivisibility of human rights implies interrelatedness between the right to education and other rights. The fulfilment of the right to education necessitates the fulfilment of other rights, not only in schools and within the education system, as suggested by Tomaševski's scheme, but also upstream as "prerequisites to education,"[30] such as access to food, housing, healthcare and so forth. Thus, while the right to education is an enabling right, it cannot be fully and effectively realized if other rights are disregarded. Yet the weakness of this status-based justification is that it can easily be dismissed by those who already contest the very possibility of human beings having fundamental rights. Moreover, financial constraints and pressure lead some governments to focus on cost-effectiveness arguments for human rights in education.

27 McCowan, "Human Rights within Education," 1–2. He leaves aside objections to human rights in general, such as questioning the possibility of their implementation or even their very validity, criticizing their Western roots, patriarchal nature, universalist ideal, etc. Such objections have been mentioned several times by HRE actors participating in the aforementioned seminars, as well as in the interviews, and they reflect a very concrete challenge faced by HRE actors in their everyday work at all levels. At best, governments show little interest in human rights, but HRE actors may also face overt hostility from some parents' organizations that might attempt to bring proceedings against human rights programmes offered at their children's school. Thus, several interviewees did not expect state actors to be actively engaged in favour of HRE but wished that the state would refrain from putting obstacles in the way of their work.

28 Ibid., 3.

29 Ibid., 13.

30 Ibid., 7.

Within the instrumental approach, McCowan differentiates between rights-based and non-rights-based objectives. In the first case, the assumption is that students will learn democratic and human rights values and attitudes more efficiently if they see them implemented in their learning environment,[31] i.e. in "both the formal curricula, through explicit teaching, and throughout the hidden curriculum, as embodied in school structures, codes of conduct, mission statements, and classroom interactions."[32] In addition, learners will understand better the scope of their own actions and how to adjust them so as to respect and uphold the rights of others. Indeed, learning about, and having the opportunity to exercise, rights may enhance learners' self-esteem and perceived status, which in turn "enables greater respect for others and guards against victimization of minorities."[33] This approach promotes participation of learners in the decision-making process and sees schools and classrooms as a laboratory or training opportunity for the subsequent practice of democracy and citizenship in adulthood. Moreover, educational institutions also become a place where otherwise marginalized children may be empowered through such experience of effective participation.

While cautious about treating human rights in education as a tool to improve the process of democracy and human rights learning, McCowan finds that other, non-rights-based instrumental justifications may be at best irrelevant and at worst even destructive to the advancement of human rights. Instrumental justifications include the improvement of cognitive outcomes and the reduction of drop-out rates, but also broader societal goals such as economic development. Seeing human rights as a more efficient means to an end is risky, because they could easily be dismissed if new methods or approaches are seen as more successful. In some cases, instrumentalist arguments might even lead to the restriction of rights in schools. As a matter of fact, there is no proven causality between rights-based approaches and better economic results, while economic growth has often happened simultaneously with, or even as a consequence of, human rights abuses.[34] One may also argue that economic growth in the current neoliberal context is a cause of human rights abuses. Furthermore, rights-based approaches are less likely to be understood and become deeply rooted on the basis of consequentialist intentions, because they will be implemented only superficially and for purposes unrelated

31 Ibid., 8–10.

32 Brian R. Howe and Katherine Covell, *Empowering Children: Children's Rights Education as a Pathway to Citizenship* (Toronto: University of Toronto Press, 2005), 12.

33 McCowan, "Human Rights within Education," 10.

34 Ibid., 10–12.

to human rights. Lastly, a further danger is that core concepts, such as participation, might be misused or even abused by governments that do not have a genuine intention to promote human rights. With manipulative or tokenistic intentions, participation can easily become a way to legitimize an authority and its oppressive practices without learners having a real possibility to influence the decision-making process.[35]

C The Purpose of Education

For Claude, the very existence of a right to education implies that "education is not value-neutral,"[36] implying that education is more than about mere cognitive achievements. Thus, the question of human rights in education can also be approached from the perspective of the purpose of education.

Banks and Banks argue for "equity pedagogy" as "teaching strategies and classroom environments that help students from diverse racial, ethnic, and cultural groups attain the knowledge, skills, and attitudes needed to function effectively within, and help create and perpetuate, a just, humane, and democratic society."[37] They criticize a vision of education that merely consists of preparing students to adapt to, and move within, the existing structures, divisions and stratification of society. Their concern goes beyond violations of children's rights in the education system, as they clearly argue that students should learn to question hegemonic discourses and be able to use the acquired skills "to become effective agents for social change."[38] Their model is transformative in essence and poses the question of the purpose of education, both for students as individuals and for society. Banks suggests that education focusing on traditional literacy skills is a necessary but insufficient condition for a democratic, peaceful and fair society, recalling that some of the worst crimes in human history were committed by "highly literate individuals, groups, and nations."[39]

---

35 Ibid., 12. See also Helen Trivers and Hugh Starkey, "The Politics of Critical Citizenship Education: Human Rights for Conformity or Emancipation?," in *Politics, Participation and Power Relations: Transdisciplinary Approaches to Critical Citizenship in the Classroom and Community*, ed. Richard C. Mitchell and Shannon A. Moore (Rotterdam: Sense, 2012), 14.

36 Richard Pierre Claude, "The Right to Education and Human Rights Education," *International Journal on Human Rights* 2 (2005): 37. See also Tristan McCowan, "Reframing the Universal Right to Education," *Comparative Education* 46 (2010). McCowan analyzes the notion of education that underpins the right to education.

37 Cherry A. McGee Banks and James A. Banks, "Equity Pedagogy: An Essential Component of Multicultural Education," *Theory into Practice* 34 (1995): 152.

38 Ibid.

39 Banks, "Teaching Literacy for Social Justice." Also McCowan makes the point that "it is absolutely possible for one to develop a high level of basic skills and simultaneously develop more intolerance for human rights." McCowan, "Human Rights within Education," 11.

Similarly to McCowan, Banks advocates multicultural literacy, understood as critical attitude towards knowledge with the purpose of advancing human rights and social justice.[40]

Human rights and their realization are regarded as one of the two aims of education in international human rights documents, and education *for* human rights has been a central element of the right to education since the adoption of the UDHR in 1948. Among the documents that specify the purpose of education (UDHR, ICESCR, CRC and ESC), two components are recurrent, though to a different extent. Firstly, education aims to promote and strengthen respect for human rights, peace and other cultures.[41] Human rights are universal, but they must also become part of local and popular culture, and education has a major role to play in this area.[42] Universal human rights start at home, in small, local places, in the "world of the individual person," as noted by Eleanor Roosevelt in 1958.[43] And education is therefore also aimed at individuals, in particular the development of their personality, their physical and mental capacities (CRC and ESC) and their sense of dignity (ICESCR). Hence, the purpose of education is emancipation, both in its individual and collective dimensions.

Contributors from Latin America had a major influence on the conceptualization and formulation of the right to education in the UDHR.[44] Value-based education, popular empowerment and the development of people's faculties are important elements that were kept in the final wording of the Declaration thanks to them. The connections between these elements, in particular between the collective and the individual dimension, "between popular empowerment and self-realization as the consequence of people learning and exercising their human rights,"[45] have had a major impact on the development of HRE. The practice and analytical work of Brazilian educationalist Paulo

40 Banks, "Teaching Literacy for Social Justice." On the five dimensions of multicultural education, see Banks and Banks, "Equity Pedagogy," 152.

41 Article 26 of the UDHR states that education "shall be directed … to the strengthening of respect for human rights and fundamental freedoms. It shall promote understanding, tolerance and friendship among all nations, racial or religious groups, and shall further the activities of the United Nations for the maintenance of peace."

42 Sergio Vieira de Mello, Statement to the 59th Session of the UN Commission on Human Rights, available at http://www.universalrights.net/heroes/display.php3?id=67.

43 Eleanor Roosevelt, Excerpt from a speech made at the presentation of *In Your Hands: A Guide for Community Action for the Tenth Anniversary of the Universal Declaration of Human Rights* (New York: United Nations, 1958), available at http://www.udhr.org/history/biographies/bioer.htm.

44 Claude, "Right to Education," 40–42. He explicitly mentions Argentina, Brazil, Cuba, Ecuador and Mexico.

45 Ibid., 41.

Freire, a leading figure of popular education movements in Latin America and a founder of critical pedagogy, contributed considerably to the theorization of HRE.[46] In his most influential work, he describes the intrinsic oppression and violence in education and the necessity of a "pedagogy of the oppressed."[47] He rejects the commonly used educational concept of "banking,"[48] which consists of treating children (or learners in general) as empty bank accounts that need to be filled up with information, knowledge, skills, behaviours, rules, social norms and so forth. This practice puts learners in a position of inferiority and submission, assuming their lack of intellectual faculty and capacity to think and learn by themselves. Learners (and even more so children)[49] assume an asymmetric relationship of subordination towards teachers, who possess the undisputable authority, legitimacy and power of producing, spreading and controlling knowledge. Such an oppressive pattern leads to the dehumanization of learners,[50] as they are denied their inherent dignity and rational thought. Hence, Freire elaborates a pedagogical framework in which he sees

46 Claude sees in the link made between the self-development of individuals and emancipation of the people a prefiguration of Freire's work. Claude, "Right to Education," 40–41. See also Kathleen Modrowski, "Paulo Freire and Popular Education in the 20th Century," in *Human Rights Learning: A People's Report*, ed. Upendra Baxi and Kenny Mann (New York: People's Movement for Human Rights Learning (PDHRE), 2006): 65–75; Monisha Bajaj, "Human Rights Education: Ideology, Location, and Approaches," *Human Rights Quarterly* 33 (2011): 490; McCowan, "Human Rights within Education"; Osler, *Human Rights and Schooling*; Felisa Tibbitts, "Understanding What We Do: Emerging Models for Human Rights Education," *International Review of Education* 48 (2002): 164; Claudia Lohrenscheit, "International Approaches in Human Rights Education," *International Review of Education* 48 (2002): 177; David F. Suárez, "Education Professionals and the Construction of Human Rights Education," *Comparative Education Review* 51 (2007): 61–62; hooks, *Teaching to Transgress*, 45–58; Lee Jerome, Lesley Emerson, Laura Lundy and Karen Orr, *Teaching and Learning about Child Rights: A Study of Implementation in 26 Countries* (Queen's University Belfast and UNICEF, 2015), 19.

47 Freire, *Pedagogy of the Oppressed*.

48 Ibid., 71–86.

49 Freire's *Pedagogy of the Oppressed* focuses mainly on adult education among working-class populations and must be placed within its geographical and historical context. Some would surely argue that his concept of oppression would not be applicable to today's European context. For instance, in his introduction to Freire's book, Donaldo Macedo recounts the rejection of the use of words like "oppression" by what he calls mainstream academia (Donaldo Macedo, "Introduction," in Freire, *Pedagogy of the Oppressed*, 21–22). However, even without using such language or the concept itself, numerous authors have shown how children are systematically denied their rights and that schools are still places of violence and abuse, as discussed in the previous section.

50 In his general theorizing of oppression, Freire argues that oppressors, as they "dehumanize others and violate their rights, … themselves also become dehumanized." See Freire, *Pedagogy of the Oppressed*, 56.

education as "the practice of freedom,"[51] "which must be forged *with*, not *for*, the oppressed (whether individuals or peoples) in the incessant struggle to regain humanity."[52] Criticizing both "verbalism" (theory and intellectual work for its own sake) and "activism" (action without reflection), Freire shapes the concept of "praxis: reflection and action upon the world in order to transform it."[53] Thus, a key element in his theory is the participation of learners, which he warns should not be "pseudo-participation, but committed involvement."[54] Participation in knowledge creation and in the educational process means (re)gaining self-awareness, dignity and hope; it opens up the opportunity for self-emancipation and transforming the world. This is reminiscent of Banks's definition of "multicultural literacy" as the "skills and ability to identify the creators of knowledge and their interests, to uncover the assumptions of knowledge, to view knowledge from diverse ethnic and cultural perspectives, and to use knowledge to guide action that will create a humane and just world."[55]

D Education for Human Rights

Education aims at the full realization of human rights but also requires a human rights framework and practices and methodologies based on human rights values. At the same time, human rights need informed and emancipated citizens who have the capacity to protect and claim them. For Hannah Arendt, neither the moral nor the natural nor the legal justifications of human rights are enough to secure them.[56] In her understanding, human rights are primarily social constructs: they exist because of "our decision to guarantee ourselves mutually equal rights."[57] They are "conventions, forms of recognition produced by human agreement, fragile artefacts of human living together."[58]

51 Ibid., 81.

52 Ibid., 48.

53 Ibid., 51, see also 65 and 87–88.

54 Ibid., 69, see also 48. Other important and closely connected elements include: the dialogical and problem-posing approach; the relevance of education and its necessary rooting in learners' everyday life experience; and the construction of an equalitarian relationship between learners and teachers, which shall solve the inherent contradiction and violence of the teacher-student relationship "by reconciling the poles of the contradiction so that both are simultaneously teachers *and* students." Ibid., 72. All these elements are championed by HRE theorists and practitioners, albeit to various degrees.

55 Banks, "Teaching Literacy for Social Justice," 18.

56 Jeffrey C. Isaac, "A New Guarantee on Earth: Hannah Arendt on Human Dignity and the Politics of Human Rights," *The American Political Science Review* 90 (1996).

57 Hannah Arendt, *The Origins of Totalitarianism* (Cleveland and New York: Meridian Books, 1962), 301.

58 Isaac, "Hannah Arendt on Human Dignity," 64.

In her writing about totalitarianism, Arendt analyzes the deep paradox and fragility of human rights revealed from the experience of the Holocaust and the post-war situation in Europe. It is exactly when people are merely human beings that they face the greatest danger of rightlessness, because "a man who is nothing but a man has lost the very qualities which make it possible for other people to treat him as a fellow-man."[59] Deprived of all their rights, such bare individuals are expelled from humanity, i.e. not only does their individuality become irrelevant, because they are denied the possibility of expression and action in the world, but they are relegated to the condition of savagery, which is the biggest fear and perceived threat of highly civilized societies.[60] Reflecting on the experiences of the Holocaust, but also slavery and statelessness, she concludes that "the fundamental deprivation of human rights is manifested first and above all in the deprivation of a place in the world which makes opinions significant and actions effective."[61] Thus, the very first human right is "the right to have rights,"[62] that is to say, the right to belong to a polity, which implies not only the right to freedom but the right to action, not only the right to think but the right to express an opinion that matters. These experiences show that human rights do not speak for themselves and that they remain inexistent until they are demanded and "made actionable"[63] by citizens. Understanding human rights as natural entitlements belonging to everyone because they are human is problematic, since it ignores the question of the capability of rights-holders to claim them. In fact, human rights do not exist outside politics; they "rest on political commitment and artifice rather than anything given in the human condition."[64]

Such politics is what Arendt calls "action," i.e. participation in public life that is derived from human interrelations in society: men and women in their plurality acting as citizens and not merely as workers.[65] In her view, human rights are incompatible with national sovereignty and the nation-state, but neither do international treaties guarantee their realization. Only citizens

59 Arendt, *The Origins of Totalitarianism*, 300.

60 Ibid., 300–302.

61 Ibid., 296.

62 Ibid.

63 Isaac, "Hannah Arendt on Human Dignity," 67.

64 Ibid.

65 Arendt differentiates between three human activities: labour, work and action. Action is based on the plurality of human beings, i.e. the fact that "men, not Man, …inhabit the world" and that each of us share the same human characteristics of being unique and never the same as any other human being. Action is the "political activity par excellence" as it "engages in founding and preserving political bodies." Hannah Arendt, *The Human Condition* (Chicago and London: University of Chicago Press, 1998), 7–9.

organized in a strong civil society can act.[66] In this respect, she agrees with Freire, who argues that no change in power relations can be expected from dominant elites – which he describes as oppressors – for "they cannot find in this power the strength to liberate either the oppressed or themselves. Only power that springs from the weakness of the oppressed will be sufficiently strong to free both."[67] Citizenship, in this case, cannot be understood solely as a legal status that entails rights and duties but rather encompasses a feeling of belonging and the practice or "engagement in the life and affairs of the community."[68] Participation in public life is essential for the advancement of human rights, and thus education *about* rights must be completed by education *for* and *through* rights if citizens, no matter their status, are to meaningfully take part in decision-making processes and negotiate, monitor, insist upon and defend human rights.

Both education *through* rights and education *for* rights are crucial aspects of the right to education. Education through rights protects children and fosters their emancipation at individual level in order to become agents of change, and education for rights adds a collective dimension, where learners, as part of the citizenry, fight for social justice and the rights of others against state oppression and structural inequalities. Osler warns against the danger of exclusion and irrelevance that lies within citizenship education programmes rooted in a patriotic approach and focused solely on the rights of citizens rather than human rights. By simplifying the experience of citizenship and reducing the national experience to one dominant version, such programmes tend to ignore the realities of an important part of society – and thus the classroom – such as linguistic, religious, ethnic or national minorities, as well as migrants, refugees and their descendants.[69]

2 *The Institutionalization of HRE*

As discussed in the previous section, the relations between education and human rights are complex and the right to education is multifaceted. HRE has been present in several international documents from the very beginning in the form of elements of education about, for and through rights incorporated in the right to education. Yet it is only in the past two decades that HRE has become a field, supported by a UN Decade, a World Programme, a Declaration,

66 As a matter of fact, the human rights movement is deeply rooted in the social and civil society movements that started in the late eighteenth century, and up until today civil society has played a major role in the protection and advancement of human rights.

67 Freire, *Pedagogy of the Oppressed*, 44.

68 Osler, *Human Rights and Schooling*, 114.

69 Ibid., 70–80.

a European Charter and a wide range of other documents, programmes and activities.[70] Moreover, the two most important documents that are fully and exclusively dedicated to HRE – the UN Declaration and the Council of Europe Charter – date back less than ten years.

One of the earliest institutional actors in the field of HRE was UNESCO, interestingly enough through its first popular education programme in 1953 and later on in the 1970s.[71] At this time, UNESCO started promoting human rights as "curricular reform"[72] and to this day remains a major contributor to the development of HRE through its numerous programmes, resolutions and guidebooks.[73] At European level, the Council of Europe started its work on HRE with the adoption of a resolution of the Committee of Ministers on the Teaching of Human Rights in 1978, only four years after the General Conference of UNESCO adopted a Recommendation concerning Education for International Understanding, Co-operation and Peace and Education relating to Human Rights and Fundamental Freedoms. In the Council of Europe's resolution, the Committee of Ministers considers teaching human rights a "valuable, and indeed necessary, means of ensuring that human rights are protected as effectively as possible," adding that individuals should know as early as possible about their rights. The Committee recommended that HRE be part of curricula, including for teacher training and development. These documents represented a milestone in the institutionalization of HRE, in so far as that, for the first time, HRE was not at the margins but the core subject. According to Osler, the Council of Europe's 1985 recommendation on "Teaching and Learning about Human Rights in Schools" was an "important step in standard setting"

70 See the list published on the website of the Office of the UN High Commissioner for Human Rights (OHCHR): "The Right to Human Rights Education – A compilation of provisions of international and regional instruments dealing with human rights education," 2014, http://www.ohchr.org/EN/Issues/Education/Training/Compilation/Pages/Listofcontents.aspx.

71 Suárez, "Construction of Human Rights Education," 49. In 1953, UNESCO launched its still existing Associated School Project Network while working on a programme entitled "Education for Living in a World Community," which consisted of experimental national educational projects and activities focusing on human rights, women's rights, cultural diversity and the UN system. See UNESCO, *UNESCO Associated School Project Network (ASPnet): Historical Review 1953–2003* (Paris: UNESCO, 2003) and UNESCO, *Education for Living in a World Community*, UNESCO/ED/127 (Paris: UNESCO, 1953), http://unesdoc.unesco.org/images/0012/001261/126122EB.pdf.

72 Suárez, "Institutionalisation of Human Rights Education," 105.

73 Important initiatives include the 1984 guidebook on "Teaching for international understanding, peace, and human rights," and the "Education for All" movement launched at the 2000 World Forum on Education in Dakar.

that helped put HRE "firmly on the agenda."[74] Indeed, in addition to recalling and reaffirming key human rights documents, commitments to HRE made by member states and the need to teach human rights to young people "throughout their school career," the recommendation's appendix provides concrete suggestions. Though not very detailed, the suggestions go beyond a list of topics to be included in human rights teaching and touch upon the importance of the learning environment, the possibility of mainstreaming human rights in the curriculum, the diversified nature of knowledge and skills relating to human rights, expected outcomes of human rights teaching, and the attitude of teachers, as well as their training and professional development.[75] The appendix also affirms key principles of HRE, such as participation, freedom of expression of teachers and pupils, fairness, justice, self-reflection and empowerment. However, despite many documents, programmes and initiatives from various international organizations and agencies, HRE faced resistance from major Western democracies from the very beginning. It was only later, with the impulse of the UN Decade for Human Rights Education that HRE became a stand-alone policy goal.[76] Indeed, many observers see the 1990s as a turning point for HRE.

Foyn describes the year 1993 as a "breakthrough for education for human rights and democracy"[77] because of the numerous events happening simultaneously in different places. In March 1993, UNESCO adopted a World Plan of Action for Education for Human Rights and Democracy, and a few months later, in June, the Second UN World Conference on Human Rights took place. This conference emphasized "the importance of establishing programmes for human rights education,"[78] as well as the responsibility of member states in doing so, and reasserted the purpose of education as a contribution to a broader and stronger respect for human rights and fundamental freedoms. A few months later, the 48th session of the UN General Assembly requested several relevant international governmental and non-governmental actors and bodies to consider the idea of a "Decade for Human Rights Education."[79] At the same time, at European level, several steps were taken by the Council of Europe and the CSCE in the field of education, particularly HRE. In late 1993, the Council

74 Osler, *Human Rights and Schooling*, 22.

75 Council of Europe, Recommendation No. R (85) 7 of the Committee of Ministers to Member States on Teaching and Learning about Human Rights in Schools.

76 Suárez, "Institutionalisation of Human Rights Education," 112.

77 Syssel Foyn, "1993 – A Breakthrough for Increased Focus," *European Journal of Education* 29 (1994): 355.

78 Ibid., 356.

79 Ibid., 357.

of Europe organized a "coordination meeting of cooperation programmes for Central and Eastern European countries in the field of HRE, including education for democratic values at school level and teacher training," which included representatives of ministries of education and NGOs, including from Western Europe.[80] The idea of establishing a regional centre for HRE emerged for a second time after the failed attempt to set up a European Centre for HRE in Prague at the initiative of Vaclav Havel and with the support of UNESCO.[81] In March 1994, the Council of Europe's Standing Conference of European Ministers of Education adopted a resolution on "Education for democracy, human rights and tolerance," which focused in particular on the role of actors such as ministers and the Council of Europe but also on the role of schools and civil society organizations. It recalled the need for a "coherent and sustained approach in schools," with the incorporation of HRE in both the formal curriculum and extra-curricular activities, as well as the need for appropriate teacher training.[82] Furthermore, the Polish Minister of Education suggested establishing a European Information Centre on Civic Education in Warsaw.[83] It is in this context of great enthusiasm and apparent political commitment, at least at the international level, that the UN Decade for HRE was launched in 1995, which was also proclaimed the UN Year of Tolerance. After the end of the Decade, the need for further development of HRE was exemplified by the launch of the UN World Programme for HRE in 2004. The programme is currently in its third phase and regular monitoring and mid-term evaluations are carried out by the United Nations, relying on information provided by governments.[84]

Overall, Suárez notices that the influence of several global processes and social movements has contributed to the wide diffusion of HRE.[85] He describes the threefold process of democratization and professionalization of HRE as follows:

80 Ibid., 358.

81 Ibid., 359–360.

82 Council of Europe, Resolution on "Education for democracy, human rights and tolerance," adopted at the Standing Conference of European Ministers of Education 18th session, March 23–24, 1994, point 6.

83 According to point 9 of the Resolution, the Centre would be a place for sharing curricula and teaching materials, training relevant actors, such as curriculum planners, educational administrators and teacher trainers, and promoting national associations of civics teachers in Central Europe.

84 Evaluations of the programme as well as some of the national initiative questionnaires filled out by member states can be found here: http://www.ohchr.org/EN/Issues/Education/Training/Pages/Programme.aspx.

85 Suárez, "Institutionalisation of Human Rights Education," 104.

> First, over time [HRE] moves from the periphery to the centre of education discourse in many organizations. Second, [HRE] transitions from a grassroots, popular education movement to a formal education project for students and professionals. Third, [HRE] moves downwards, from elite discourse at abstract levels, to curricular practice in nations.[86]

He considers the development of HRE to be rooted in the human rights movement through the "curricular movement,"[87] i.e. the evolution of HRE as a subject of textbooks and training courses, both in formal and non-formal education. The shift of the human rights movement – from promoting rights, to protecting them, to preventing abuses through education – has gone hand in hand with the "transformation of human rights from a radical social movement to a component of national curricula."[88] Suárez sees one reason for this expansion in "the shift from an emphasis on international law to an emphasis on formal education and schooling"[89] driven by the desire of lawyers to help spread newly created international human rights norms.

Historically a leading force in the human rights movement, civil society has been a major player in the field of HRE, including in the Visegrád countries. Civil society organizations (CSOs) have played a central role in putting HRE on the political agenda, providing teaching resources to schools and teachers, training teachers on HRE and designing HRE strategies and curricula. Albeit mostly associated with non-formal education, CSOs often operate in formal settings and work in close cooperation with public institutions in charge of formal education. Despite divergences of approach, tensions and difficulties during cooperation, and sometimes overt conflict, it is clear that the work of public institutions cannot be separated from the work of CSOs. The former rely heavily on the resources and expertise of civil society, while the latter conduct an important part of their HRE activities in schools, i.e. within a framework that is primarily designed and managed by public authorities. Furthermore, some CSOs also monitor public policies, do advocacy work and take part in consultations with public authorities. There is indeed a general consensus among CSOs that, in order to be most effective, HRE needs to fully enter the

86 Ibid., 96.

87 Suárez, "Construction of Human Rights Education," 48; see also Suárez, "Institutionalisation of Human Rights Education," 100, 104 and 109–110.

88 Suárez, "Institutionalisation of Human Rights Education," 100.

89 Ibid., 104. Meyer, Bromley and Ramirez show the increasing presence of human rights in social science textbooks at secondary school level, especially since 1995. John W. Meyer, Patricia Bromley and Francisco O. Ramirez, "Human Rights in Social Science Textbooks: Cross-national Analyses, 1970–2008," *Sociology of Education* 83 (2010).

formal education system and be mainstreamed in the curriculum, despite the contradictions and dilemmas this might cause.[90] CSOs are thus aware of the necessity to establish working relationships with public institutions, schools or local authorities if they want their voice to be heard and their resources and programmes to be used by teachers. At the same time, the lack of real political will on the part of governments and the gap between formal commitment and real implementation are striking.[91] Despite its institutionalization, HRE thus remains more in the field of civil society than public policy.

As discussed above, the United Nations and the Council of Europe have been major players[92] in the institutionalization of HRE, and countries in Central Europe have also contributed, including through attempts to set up HRE centres. In practice, the EU never adopted this approach to education.[93] Instead, EU institutions promote "active citizenship," a phrase that has become fashionable in the past decade but which has no internationally acknowledged, let alone legally binding, definition. Because there was no "central actor pushing a particular model,"[94] HRE has been accompanied from the very beginning

90 A common question is whether HRE is compatible at all with formal education settings, in particular when such settings threaten or even violate children's rights and dignity, for instance due to acts of bullying, corporal punishment or segregation. Another dilemma is the difficulty of teaching universal values in a system that is framed by a national – if not nationalist – approach to education.

91 On the reluctance of states to implement HRE in a meaningful manner and the reasons why states would engage in HRE at all, see Sonia Cardenas, "Constructing Rights? Human Rights Education and the State," *International Political Science Review/Revue internationale de science politique* 26 (2005).

92 For more detailed analyses of the role of the UN, the Council of Europe and UNESCO, see Suárez, "Institutionalisation of Human Rights Education," 105–106; Osler, *Human Rights and Schooling*, 22–23 and 87; Upendra Baxi, "Human Rights Education: The Promise of the Third Millennium?," in *Human Rights Education for the Twenty-First Century*, ed. George J. Andreopoulos and Richard Pierre Claude (Philadelphia: University of Pennsylvania Press, 1997), 142–154.

93 The EU has adopted a few non-binding documents that include some references to issues related to HRE. See OHCHR, "The Right to Human Rights Education – A compilation of provisions." The only document that has clear connections to HRE (although without stating so explicitly) is the Resolution of the Council and of the Representatives of Member States' Governments meeting within the Council of 23 October 1995 on the response of educational systems to the problems of racism and xenophobia, *OJ* C 312 (1995), 1. Human rights are mentioned only once throughout the document, which states that, in order to foster pluralism and "encourage equality of opportunity," "European educational systems should continue as well as enhance their efforts at promoting education in values which encourage attitudes of solidarity and tolerance, as well as respect for democracy and human rights."

94 Suárez, "Institutionalisation of Human Rights Education," 104.

by discussions on its essence, content and purpose, often mirroring similar debates on the nature and substance of human rights and their relationship to other concepts and theories, such as democracy, citizenship or social justice.[95] For instance, one important discussion has been about the hierarchy of rights, in particular the difference between civil and political rights, on the one hand, and social, economic and cultural rights, on the other. The Western European tradition tends to consider the former as more fundamental, leading to the development of citizenship education and its primacy over HRE.[96] Many other approaches have been placed on a par with HRE, such as intercultural education, global education and citizenship education. As early as 1969, Hines and Wood discussed HRE content and methodology in an American context, providing a historical and philosophical account of human rights and revealing what would become major issues of debate, such as the teaching of values and the risk of indoctrination and, by extension, the role and responsibilities of teachers.[97] Such has not been the case with "active citizenship," a concept that is barely defined, even in policy papers and programmes using it. In this context, and under increasing pressure for more policy coordination between EU member states, how do the Visegrád countries shape their education policies and what place do they give human rights in formal education? The next section analyzes public policies and strategies on HRE in the light of EU perspectives.

III Human Rights Education Policies in the ET2020 Context

The Visegrád countries are required to adapt to EU requirements, while also participating in various other international settings and facing constraints and pressures from numerous actors at home. Furthermore, they must navigate through a complex web of policies, concepts and perspectives on education,

95 See, for instance, Tom Campbell, "Human Rights: A Culture of Controversy," *Journal of Law and Society* 26 (1999); George J. Andreopoulos and Richard Pierre Claude, eds., *Human Rights Education for the Twenty-First Century* (Philadelphia: University of Pennsylvania Press, 1997); Ali A. Abdi and Lynette Shultz, eds., *Educating for Human Rights and Global Citizenship* (Albany: SUNY Press, 2008); Doutje Lettinga and Lars van Troost, eds., *Can Human Rights Bring Social Justice? Twelve Essays* (Amnesty International Netherlands, 2015).

96 In this school of thought, HRE is considered part of citizenship education, which is regarded as an all-encompassing educational approach. This is the case in Poland and the Czech Republic, for instance.

97 Paul D. Hines and Leslie Wood, *A Guide to Human Rights Education* (Washington: National Council for the Social Studies, 1969).

which at times contradict each other. They have to juggle two contradictory models of education that echo the different origins and directions taken by the human rights movement and the spread of mass education. On the one hand, the United Nations and the Council of Europe have long supported a model of education that is deeply rooted in the struggle for human rights, people's emancipation and social justice. On the other hand, in recent years, the EU has endorsed an approach that subsumes education under economic priorities and reduces it to a tool of the labour market. Neoliberal in its essence, this vision encourages competitiveness and a productivist way of learning and seeks to reduce inequalities in terms of educational outcomes for the sole purpose of bolstering labour market performance and improving employment rates among so-called disadvantaged populations. These philosophies diverge considerably from each other and rely on different principles and values. At the same time, the EU has focused increasingly on building up European citizenship and fostering citizens' participation in the EU integration process, for instance through its 2007–2013 Europe for Citizens grant programme. In the framework of the Lisbon process, the European Commission aimed to increase social cohesion and reduce the democratic deficit across Europe through the use of the concept of "active citizenship."[98] However, it did not rally to the long-time expertise of the Council of Europe on education for democratic citizenship and human rights education, and to this day cooperation between the two international organizations remains limited, despite the launch of a joint programme on "Human Rights and Democracy in Action" in 2013.[99] Instead, following the attacks in France and Denmark in early 2015, the EU is shaping its own model of education to match its new agenda on radicalization prevention. Thus, as opposed to UN or Council of Europe documents, the EU's educational strategy – the Education and Training 2020 (ET2020) programme – uses language that reflects the securitization of education in a neoliberal context.

98 Massimiliano Mascherini, Anna Rita Manca and Bryony Hoskins, *The Characterization of Active Citizenship in Europe* (Luxembourg: European Communities, 2009), 5.

99 European Commission, "Social inclusion and citizenship through formal and non-formal learning," accessed February 22, 2017, http://ec.europa.eu/education/policy/strategic-framework/social-inclusion_en; Council of Europe, "Presentation of the project 'Competences for Democratic Culture,'" accessed February 22, 2017, http://www.coe.int/en/web/education/competences-for-democratic-culture. This programme specifically addresses citizenship and human rights education, and one of its outcomes was the establishment of the Council of Europe's Reference Framework of Competences for Democratic Culture. The exact role played by the European Commission and other EU institutions is unclear, and not very visible at first sight.

1 *Growth and Security, the Two Legs of Education in the EU*

Although it is a strong prerogative of member states, the EU has paid increasing attention to the field of education – and thus potentially HRE – within its general aim of policy convergence. In its attempt to modernize member states' educational policies and make them more cohesive and more responsive to current common challenges, the Commission and the Council have been working with member states on the development of work programmes and strategic frameworks for education.[100] The first one – Education and Training 2010 – was adopted in 2002 in the context of the Lisbon strategy, which was concerned with social exclusion,[101] and focused on active citizenship, equal opportunities, democratic participation and social cohesion. Whereas the work programme[102] adopted by the Commission and the Council of Ministers of Education included no explicit reference to human rights, the EU's socio-economic stance on education soon became clearer. In early 2004, the Council and the Commission adopted a joint interim report on the implementation of the ET2010 work programme, whose first key message clearly highlights the need for more "synergies and complementarity"[103] between education, employment and macroeconomic policies. It states: "Investment in education and training is a key factor of the Union's competitiveness, sustainable growth, and employment and therefore a prerequisite for achieving the economic, social and environmental goals set in Lisbon for the European Union."[104] Within the "package of key competences" that learners are meant to acquire by the end of compulsory schooling, and in addition to traditional literacy skills, the report suggests "civic competences, entrepreneurship and cultural awareness."[105]

---

100 See, for instance, European Parliament, "Education and Vocational Training," last modified October 2016, http://www.europarl.europa.eu/atyourservice/en/displayFtu.html?ftuId=FTU_5.13.3.html; European Commission, "Strategic framework – Education & Training 2020," accessed February 27, 2017, http://ec.europa.eu/education/policy/strategic-framework_en.

101 See the conclusions of the Lisbon European Council: http://www.consilium.europa.eu/en/uedocs/cms_data/docs/pressdata/en/ec/00100-r1.en0.htm.

102 "Work programme on the follow-up of the objectives of education and training systems in Europe," last modified September 28, 2006, http://eur-lex.europa.eu/legal-content/EN/TXT/HTML/?uri=URISERV:c11086&from=EN.

103 Council of the European Union, "Education and Training 2010": The success of the Lisbon strategy hinges on urgent reforms. Joint Interim Report of the Council and the Commission on the implementation of the detailed work programme on the follow-up of the objectives of education and training systems in Europe, 14358/03 EDUC 168 – COM (2003) 685 final, March 3, 2004, 4.

104 Ibid.

105 Ibid., 25.

In 2009, the EU adopted the more comprehensive ET2020 strategic framework, which included working groups, clearly defined priorities and a wide range of resources. Following the ET2010 work programme and in line with the general Europe 2020 strategy for smart, sustainable and inclusive growth, the new work programme keeps its focus on socio-economic issues and active citizenship. One of its four objectives, which focuses on equity, social cohesion and active citizenship, states as follows: "Education should promote intercultural competences, democratic values and respect for fundamental rights and the environment, as well as combat all forms of discrimination, equipping all young people to interact positively with their peers from diverse backgrounds."[106] But none of the five European benchmarks and the three other work areas refer to human rights literacy, which is only indirectly touched upon within the eight key competences. Next to "traditional skills," the European Commission wants learners to acquire "horizontal skills," including "social and civic responsibility" and "cultural awareness."[107] Overall, despite the 2006 Recommendation of the European Parliament and the Council on key competences for lifelong learning,[108] which mentions concepts such as gender equality, non-discrimination, civil rights, democracy, participation and diversity and explicitly refers to the EU Charter of Fundamental Rights, ET2020 does not contain a substantial reference to HRE or human rights.[109] In its 2012 Communication on "rethinking education," the Commission focuses exclusively on productivity and employment. Europe needs to invest in skills to "boost growth and competitiveness" and even horizontal skills like critical thinking or objectives like active citizenship and inclusion are meant to be a tool to help individuals face a flexible and unpredictable labour market and ultimately protect European industry's competitiveness.[110] Thus, until 2016, none of the seventeen working groups established in the ET2020 framework

106 Council Conclusions of 12 May 2009 on a strategic framework for European cooperation in education and training ("ET 2020"), *OJ* C 119 (2009), 2, 4.

107 European Commission, "Key competences," accessed February 27, 2017, http://ec.europa.eu/education/policy/school/competences_en.

108 Recommendation of the European Parliament and of the Council of 18 December 2006 on key competences for lifelong learning (2006/962/EC), 16–17.

109 As a matter of fact, "HRE" does not belong to the language of the EU: "human rights" does not appear in the 2009 Council Conclusions and is only mentioned once in the 2006 Recommendation.

110 European Commission, Rethinking Education: Investing in skills for better socio-economic outcomes. Communication from the Commission to the European Parliament, the Council, the European Economic and Social Committee and the Committee of the Regions, COM (2012) 669 final (November 2012), 2.

adopted a consistent human rights perspective on education that went beyond ad hoc, group-targeted and economy-driven steps.[111]

The year 2015 marked a new step for EU education policy.[112] Following the attacks in France and Denmark, an informal meeting of EU ministers of education was convened in Paris in March 2015 with the aim of "promoting citizenship and the common values of freedom, tolerance and non-discrimination through education." The so-called Paris Declaration[113] was adopted, establishing four overarching priorities: (1) the acquisition by young people of social, civic and intercultural competences through the promotion of democratic values, fundamental rights, social inclusion, non-discrimination and active citizenship; (2) the enhancement of critical thinking and media literacy with a view to developing "resistance to discrimination and indoctrination"; (3) the advancement of education of disadvantaged pupils; and (4) the promotion of intercultural dialogue.[114] The Paris Declaration called for "renewed efforts to reinforce the teaching and acceptance of these common fundamental values and laying the foundations for more inclusive societies through education" at both EU and national level, insisting that "the primary purpose of education is not only to develop knowledge, skills, competences and attitudes and to embed fundamental values, but also to help young people – in close cooperation with parents and families – to become active, responsible, open-minded members of society." A few months later, a mid-term evaluation report on the ET2020 strategy was issued by the Council and the Commission. New priority areas were defined, in line with the above-mentioned declaration, including: "inclusive education, equality, equity, non-discrimination and the promotion

111 For instance, the "whole-school" approach is mentioned only with a view to preventing early school leaving and inclusive education is listed as a priority for learners with special needs. On the other hand, the three expert groups working on horizontal key competences focused on languages, ICT and entrepreneurship education.

112 Emblematic of this turning point is the fact that European Commission reports on the application of the EU Charter of Fundamental Rights dedicated a specific section to the right to education for the first time in 2015, highlighting that EU policies and programmes "aim at promoting and enacting the right to education." Previously, education was addressed within the sections on non-discrimination and equality policies, usually referring to segregation of Roma or inclusion of children with disabilities. European Commission, *2015 Report on the Application of the EU Charter of Fundamental Rights* (Luxembourg: Publications Office of the European Union, 2016), 70.

113 European Union Education Ministers, Declaration on promoting citizenship and the common values of freedom, tolerance and non-discrimination through education, March 17, 2015.

114 European Commission, "Social inclusion and citizenship through formal and non-formal learning," accessed February 27, 2017, http://ec.europa.eu/education/policy/strategic-framework/social-inclusion_en.

of civic competences."[115] The report highlights the negative impact on educational outcomes of the high level of inequality in most European countries and underlines the essential role of education "in promoting social cohesion, equality, non-discrimination and civic competences."[116] Thus, in 2016, new working groups were established, with one of them focusing on "promoting citizenship and the common values of freedom, tolerance and non-discrimination through education."[117]

Since the 2009 Council Conclusions on ET2020, the EU's views on education have started to evolve towards a more consistent and comprehensive approach towards the right to education, including more and more elements of HRE. For example, the 2015 joint report took into consideration the importance of pupils' experience of democracy, inclusion and equality in school, as well as the role to be played by a broad range of educational actors, including school leaders,[118] while references to inclusive education, preventing discrimination through education and introducing Roma history into school curricula are also more frequent. However, it is questionable whether such rhetoric forms part of a newly emerging policy framework for HRE. For instance, inclusive education is not thought of as a strategic goal necessitating reform of the education system but as a measure targeted at Roma children, children with disabilities and children with a migrant background who are categorized as "disadvantaged learners" and thus most at risk of being unemployed.[119] Furthermore, Holocaust education and education on discrimination and hatred is brought up in the context of antiziganism, antisemitism and anti-Muslim sentiment. Rather than displaying a willingness to reassess and rethink mass education, intentions to adopt educational policies akin to HRE are driven by the need to respond to a specific situation (e.g. gaps in educational outcomes), context (e.g. increasing level of intolerance against Roma) or most recently the perceived

115 2015 Joint Report of the Council and the Commission on the implementation of the strategic framework for European cooperation in education and training (ET 2020) – *New priorities for European cooperation in education and training*, *OJ* C 417 (2015), 26.

116 Ibid., 29.

117 European Commission, "Working group on promoting citizenship and the common values of freedom, tolerance and non-discrimination through education," accessed February 27, 2017, http://ec.europa.eu/education/policy/strategic-framework/expert-groups/citizenship-common-values_en.

118 2015 Joint Report of the Council and the Commission, 28. In the 2009 Council Conclusions, high-quality teaching and efficient and equitable education systems were deemed "crucial for Europe's success and for enhancing employability," Council Conclusions of 12 May 2009, 3.

119 See, for instance, European Commission, Rethinking Education, 11, but also all the European Commission's reports on the application of the EU Charter of Fundamental Rights.

threat of radicalization.[120] The European Commission's 2015 report on the application of the EU Charter of Fundamental Rights highlights the links between human rights, education and counter-terrorism policies, affirming that the "Agenda on Security seeks to address the root causes of extremism through education."[121] It is clear from the document and from other EU strategies, communications and programmes that the rhetoric on combating discrimination, encouraging intercultural dialogue and youth participation and fostering tolerance and diversity at school serves a broader strategy on preventing radicalization and terrorism.[122] Not only is this securitization of human rights and education at odds with the very philosophy of HRE, but anti-radicalization programmes in schools have been criticized for posing a threat to children's rights and the human rights of learners.[123]

Until recently, human rights, children's rights, value-based education, participation and other key concepts of HRE were absent from the discourse of the ET2020 working group on citizenship, while policy aims remained vague and

---

120 European Commission, 2015 Report on the Application of the EU Charter of Fundamental Rights; European Commission, "Joining forces against antisemitic and anti-Muslim hatred in the EU: Outcomes of the first Annual Colloquium on Fundamental Rights, October 9, 2015," accessed February, 28, 2017, http://ec.europa.eu/justice/events/colloquium-fundamental-rights-2015/files/fundamental_rights_colloquium_conclusions_en.pdf.

121 European Commission, 2015 Report on the Application of the EU Charter of Fundamental Rights, 10.

122 On the anti-radicalization strategy of the EU, see Communication from the Commission to the European Parliament, the Council, the European Economic and Social Committee and the Committee of the Regions: "Preventing Radicalisation to Terrorism and Violent Extremism: Strengthening the EU's Response," COM (2013) 941 final, January 15, 2014; Council of the European Union, Revised EU Strategy for Combating Radicalisation and Recruitment to Terrorism, Brussels, May 19, 2014, 9956/14; Communication from the Commission to the European Parliament, the Council, the European Economic and Social Committee and the Committee of the Regions: "Supporting the prevention of radicalisation leading to violent extremism," COM (2916) 379 final, June 14, 2016; Didier Bigo, Laurent Bonelli, Emmanuel-Pierre Guittet and Francesco Ragazzi, *Preventing and Countering Youth Radicalisation in the EU: Study for the LIBE Committee* (Brussels: European Parliament, 2014).

123 See Osler, *Human Rights and Schooling*, 127; Bigo et al., *Preventing and Countering Youth Radicalisation*, 8–9; Francesco Ragazzi, "Policed Multiculturalism? The Impact of Counter-Terrorism and Counter-Radicalization and the 'End' of Multiculturalism," in *Counter-Radicalisation: Critical Perspectives*, ed. Christopher Baker-Beall, Charlotte Heath-Kelly and Lee Jarvis (New York: Routledge, 2015); Francesco Ragazzi, "Towards 'Policed Multiculturalism'? Counter-Radicalization in France, the Netherlands and the United Kingdom," *Les Études du CERI* 206bis (September-December 2014).

their wording sometimes unfortunate.[124] Nonetheless, a new step was made during a peer-learning activity in October 2016, where the policy interventions that were proposed were clearly inspired by existing HRE theories and practices. For instance, the resulting document emphasized that "learning should … be about, through and for human rights," that building a democratic school culture is essential and should be based especially on learners' participation and that curricula should "reflect multiperspectivity" while teachers should become aware of their unconscious biases.[125]

2 *Education in the Visegrád Countries*

This section examines the legislative and policy frameworks for education in the Visegrád countries, including recent and current national reform programmes, general policy documents addressing education and, where relevant, HRE strategies and curricula. General policy documents usually do not cover HRE and rarely address human rights. Nonetheless, they provide a useful tool for understanding the context in which education reforms take place and thus aid reflection on the existence of the proper conditions for the realization of HRE.[126]

Because HRE is located at the intersection of the fields of public education, human rights and popular education, a wide range of actors with a diversity of institutional backgrounds and functions are involved in designing, implementing, monitoring and advocating HRE. Focusing on the area of education, these are typically ministries of education,[127] state agencies such as school inspectorates, institutes in charge of curriculum development and institutes in

124 On the webpage of this expert group, one can read about "enhancing critical thinking and media literacy to develop resistance to all forms of discrimination and indoctrination," although it is unclear what "resistance to discrimination" means. The 2016 Council Conclusions on media literacy and critical thinking dropped all reference to discrimination and used the exact phrase of the Paris Declaration: "to resist all forms of indoctrination and hate speech." A 2015 report on the first Annual Colloquium on Fundamental Rights that addressed, *inter alia*, the role of education in preventing discrimination, speaks of "encourag[ing] a culture of inclusive tolerance and respect."

125 European Commission, *Policies to Promote Social and Civic Competences – From the Paris Declaration to Global Citizenship Education: Key messages from the PLA, Vienna, 26–28 October 2016* (Luxembourg: Publications Office of the European Union, 2017), 9.

126 On the beginning of HRE in the post-communist Central European context, see Felisa Tibbitts, "Human Rights Education in Schools in the Post-Communist Context," *European Journal of Education* 29 (1994). Specifically on the Slovak context, see Miroslav Kusy, "Human Rights Education, Constitutionalism and Their Interrelations in Slovakia," *European Journal of Education* 29 (1994).

127 In Hungary it is a state secretariat in charge of public education within the Ministry of Human Resources.

charge of in-service teacher training, as well as schools, of course. Institutes working in the field of child psychology may also contribute to the development of HRE.[128] In the area of human rights, national human rights institutions (NHRIS) can also play an essential role in HRE, since their mandate includes educational activities, for example according to the 1993 Paris Principles.[129] In the Czech Republic, the Public Defender of Rights does not have NHRI status and is thus not bound by law to engage in HRE. While she rarely engages in HRE activities in formal settings, the Czech Defender has been part of several HRE activities initiated by civil society. In Hungary, Poland and Slovakia, however, NHRIS do contribute to HRE, though each one does so to a different extent. In Poland, the Commissioner for Human Rights[130] does not have an explicit mandate to deal with HRE, yet the office has developed a strong expertise and is particularly engaged in antidiscrimination education (ADE) in schools. The 2015 report on the activities of the Polish Commissioner in the area of equal treatment dedicates one page to the why and how of implementing ADE in schools, justifying it on the grounds that "shaping appropriate attitudes – in particular those respecting the dignity of every human being – is one of the basic tasks of the educational process."[131] Contextualizing the role of ADE in the current migration wave, the Commissioner also emphasizes the need to pass on "the knowledge on human rights and measures to protect them, as well as the skills to act according to principles of solidarity, democracy, tolerance, justice and freedom,"[132] clearly referring to education *about* and *for* human rights. Children are symbolically granted the role of actors for social change in their communities, where they can act as multipliers by influencing the attitudes of their families and peers.[133]

---

128 Such is the case in Slovakia, for instance.

129 Article 3(g) reads that NHRIS have the responsibility "to publicise human rights and efforts to combat all forms of discrimination, in particular racial discrimination, by increasing public awareness, *especially through information and education* and by making use of all press organs" (emphasis added).

130 Interestingly, the literal translation of "Rzecznik Praw Obywatelskich" is "Commissioner for Civil Rights." In the mission statement, human rights and civil rights are both mentioned.

131 Report on the activity of the Commissioner for Human Rights in the area of equal treatment for 2015 and on the observance of the principle of equal treatment in the Republic of Poland, 45, https://www.rpo.gov.pl/sites/default/files/Equal_Treatment_in_2015.pdf.

132 Ibid.

133 The Act on the Ombudsman for Children reiterates the right to education of every child and specifies the duty of the Children's Ombudsman to promote the rights of the child and their protection (Articles 3.2 and 5). In practice, both institutions cooperate.

A Legislative Frameworks

The right to education is enshrined in the constitutions of all four countries, albeit in different ways. While the Czech Republic, Poland and Slovakia guarantee the right to education to everyone, in Hungary it is guaranteed only to Hungarian citizens.[134] All countries stipulate that education is compulsory and available for free at primary and secondary level, thus securing the availability of education. With the exception of Hungary, the right to establish non-public schools – possibly with tuition fees – is constitutionally enshrined, and Poland also guarantees the right of parents to choose their children's education. That covers the availability and accessibility of education. In addition, the Polish constitution specifically guarantees the accessibility and adaptability of education through measures of financial or organizational assistance.[135] National and ethnic minorities enjoy a constitutional right to education in their own language in the Czech Republic, a constitutional right to establish their own educational institutions in Poland and a constitutional right to do both in Slovakia.[136] The acceptability of education has thus also been addressed.

National education acts[137] further specify the content of the right to education, as well as its purpose and principles. Overall, the acts of the four countries are similar in content, reiterating basic principles already stated in their constitutions and in international human rights instruments, such as equal and free access to compulsory education, respect for and promotion of human rights and respect for other cultures. They also refer to the following common principles: taking account of individual educational needs; the development of personality; respect for values such as tolerance, solidarity, dignity, justice and freedom; the development of social and civic competences and responsibility; the idea of the development of a national identity; and protection against physical and psychological violence. But some go further than others. For instance, Slovakia explicitly prohibits segregation, corporal punishment and the spread of information aimed at inciting racial hatred. Both Hungary

134 In Article 33 of the Charter of Fundamental Rights and Basic Freedom of the Constitution of the Czech Republic, Article 70 of the Polish Constitution, Article 42 of the Slovak Constitution and Article XI of the Hungarian Constitution.

135 Article 70 of the Constitution. Article 33 also guarantees accessibility of education in equal terms for both men and women.

136 In Article 25 of the Czech Charter, Article 35 of the Polish Constitution, and Article 34 of the Slovak Constitution. In Hungary, the right to education of national and ethnic minorities is addressed in the National Education Act.

137 In the Czech Republic: Article 2 of the 561/2004 Sb. Act on preschool, primary, secondary, vocational and other education; in Hungary: Articles 1 and 27 of the 2011 CXC Act on national public education; in Poland: Article 1 of the 1991 School Education Act; in Slovakia: Articles 3 and 4 of the Act 245/2008 Coll. on Upbringing and Education.

and Slovakia list the rights of students and teachers. While the Hungarian Act provides that pupils should have access to the Commissioner for Educational Rights, the Polish Act guarantees respect for the rights of the child and highlights the duty of the education system to disseminate knowledge about these rights. The Slovak Act stipulates that children should be informed about their rights but also that they should have the capacity to implement them. According to the Czech, Polish and Slovak Acts, pupils should be able to understand and apply principles of democracy and the rule of law, human rights, gender equality and sustainable development. Poland and Hungary explicitly refer to teachers' attitudes and their duty to respect the dignity of children and nurture their moral and civic attitudes.[138] Only the Polish and Slovak Acts mention specific international agreements, including the UDHR, the ICCPR, the CRC and the ECHR, in addition to referring to universal ethical principles. The Polish Act also states that education and teaching shall be respectful of Christian values. National values, heritage, traditions and patriotism are mentioned in all four acts, usually in the framework of respect for minorities and knowledge of and respect for the cultures of Europe and the world.

B General Policy Strategies

Within the ET2020 framework, member states are required to submit a national reform programme (NRP) and regularly update it based on the recommendations of the Commission and the Council. The NRPs of the Visegrád countries all view education through a socio-economic lens.[139] Mitigating socio-economic inequalities, tackling early school-leaving and supporting inclusive education for Roma students and pupils with disabilities are common measures of these NRPs, based on an acknowledgement that the skills of citizens need to be raised and better adapted to labour market requirements, in particular among groups facing higher unemployment risks. This clearly echoes EU concerns about the impact of low educational attainment and lack of appropriate skills[140] on employment, productivity and innovation; the possible negative social and economic consequences of educational inequalities and

138 In 1982, Poland adopted a Teachers' Charter that remains part of the legislative framework on education to this day. The duties of teachers are listed in Article 6, including the education of young people in an atmosphere of freedom of conscience and respect for every human being.

139 It is illustrative that the Czech NRP addresses education in the section on the labour market, social policies and employment. Office of the Government of the Czech Republic, National Reform Programme of the Czech Republic 2016.

140 In particular, "transversal skills" are seen as necessary for pupils to adapt to a "rapidly changing labour market." European Commission, Country Report Poland 2016, Commission Staff Working Document, SWD (2016) 89 final (February 2016), 22.

the segregation of Roma pupils; and the generally weak responsiveness of educational systems to labour market needs.[141] On the other hand, each NRP has its own priorities and deals with the various features of the right to education in a very different manner.

The Czech NRP's main objective is to improve quality and equality in education through better conditions for pupils, teachers and schools. Indeed, the programme is concerned with reinforcing accessibility and acceptability of the right to education. On the one hand, pupils with special educational needs are entitled to a wide range of supportive measures; on the other, the programme wants schools to cultivate relationships and mutual cooperation between and among teaching staff, pupils and parents and thereby "actively create a healthy educational climate."[142] The NRP also addresses inclusion in education, which is understood as "collective education in regular mainstream schools."[143]

The Hungarian NRP limits itself to listing a few educational programmes (scholarships and after-school or talent programmes) aimed at advancing the school attendance and success "of vulnerable, disadvantaged and multiply-disadvantaged – including Roma – learners" in order to reduce the risk of drop-out.[144] The National Core Curriculum (NCC) is being reviewed with the same intention, and Hungary is implementing the recommendations of the Council and the Commission to tackle the gaps between Roma and non-Roma pupils and increase the participation of disadvantaged groups in inclusive education. The objective is twofold: "increasing the fairness of public education and the competitiveness of the economy."[145] Overall, the primary concern in Hungary is the accessibility of education.

Poland adopted its first NRP in 2011 and updated it in 2016. In both versions, the main concern of the government is the accessibility of education for children from socially excluded communities (in a context of severe inequality in terms of educational achievements correlated to socio-economic background). The NRP also pays attention to media, cultural and civic education, but again within an economy-driven perspective, stating that pupils

141 European Commission, Country Report Czech Republic 2016, Commission Staff Working Document, SWD (2016) 73 final (February 2016); European Commission, Country Report Hungary 2016, Commission Staff Working Document, SWD (2016) 85 final (February 2016); European Commission, Country Report Poland 2016, Commission Staff Working Document, SWD (2016) 89 final (February 2016); European Commission, Country Report Slovakia 2016, Commission Staff Working Document, SWD (2016) 93 final (February 2016).

142 Office of the Government of the Czech Republic, *National Reform Programme of the Czech Republic* (2016), 15.

143 Ibid.

144 Government of Hungary, *National Reform Programme 2016 of Hungary*, March 2016, 14.

145 Government of Hungary, *Annex 1: Incorporation of country-specific recommendations*, 34.

need to "develop attitudes conducive to creativity, cooperation and flexibility in using the acquired knowledge and skills in a variable labour market."[146] This dual view on education, which seeks to promote both active and informed citizenship and "pro-business and pro-innovation attitudes,"[147] with the ultimate purpose of boosting creativity, innovation and competitiveness, is present in numerous other strategic documents, including the 2020 and 2030 National Development Strategies, the 2020 Strategy for an Efficient State, the 2020 Human Capital Development Strategy, the 2020 Social Capital Development Strategy, the National Programme for Socio-Economic Development and the Operational Programme Knowledge-Education-Development (OPKED) 2014–2020. All of these strategy documents are concerned with citizens' ability to participate in governance and public policy,[148] which implies raising the level of civic education,[149] for example by complementing the curriculum with "practical aspects of civic education"[150] and recognizing the need for a model based on solidarity and equal opportunities.[151] None of the strategies include a rights-based perspective alongside the socio-economic considerations regarding education.[152] HRE is non-existent, and civic education is framed in terms of "social projects."[153] In fact, the most detailed strategy on civic education is the 2020 Social Capital Development Strategy.

146 Council of Ministers of the Republic of Poland, *National Reform Programme Europe 2020*, April 2011, 49. It is worth noting that most educational measures appear in the sub-section regarding unemployment targets.

147 Council of Ministers of the Republic of Poland, *National Development Strategy 2020: Active Society, Competitive Economy, Efficient State*, September 25, 2012, 43.

148 Ibid. Ministry of Administration and Digitalization of the Republic of Poland, *Efficient State Strategy*, December 20, 2012; Ministry of Labour and Social Policy of the Republic of Poland, *2020 Human Capital Development Strategy*, June 18, 2013.

149 Ministry of Administration and Digitalization of the Republic of Poland, *Efficient State Strategy*, December 20, 2012, 63; Ministry of Administration and Digitalization of the Republic of Poland, *Long-Term National Development Strategy 2030*.

150 Council of Ministers of the Republic of Poland, *National Development Strategy 2020: Active Society, Competitive Economy, Efficient State*, September 25, 2012, 43.

151 Ministry of Administration and Digitalization of the Republic of Poland, *Long-Term National Development Strategy 2030*.

152 For instance, OPKED, despite drawing a general link between social inclusion, combating poverty and improving Roma education, on the one hand, and discriminations, human rights and the education system, on the other, has as its ultimate objective the increase of employment opportunities for persons at risk of social exclusion. Ministry of Infrastructures and Development of the Republic of Poland, *Operational Programme Knowledge Education Development (OPKED) 2014–2020*, December 17, 2014, 83.

153 Ibid., 124. Government of Poland, *2020 Social Capital Development Strategy*, 2016. In addition, the National Development Strategy 2020 and the National Programme for Socio-Economic Development suggest starting education for social entrepreneurship in schools. The latter argues in favour of developing pupils' competences and information

The Slovak NRP is mainly concerned with the inclusion of marginalized groups in mainstream classes, in particular Roma children, but also wants to provide textbooks in Romani and textbooks for students with visual impairments, reflecting efforts to improve both the accessibility and the adaptability of the right to education.[154] However, inclusive education is understood in terms of an improved diagnosis and a clearer distinction between children with disabilities and socially disadvantaged children, a concept that further contributes to the segregation of children with disabilities and the negation of their equal right to education. In its 2016–2020 Manifesto, the Slovak government also expresses its wish to strengthen civic education in order to prevent and counter "expressions of racism, xenophobia, antisemitism, extremism and other forms of intolerance."[155] The development of value-based education has two objectives: to eliminate risky and violent behaviour by students and to reinforce "students' respect for the ideals of freedom, humanity and conscious citizenship."[156] Overall, the Slovak government also embraces a socio-economic approach to education that has the twofold objective of ensuring that students will "successfully [join] the labour market and becom[e] economically active citizens" while attaining their personal goals and "creating a prosperous and tolerant country together."[157]

3 *HRE Strategies*

Not all countries have adopted or are currently implementing an HRE strategy, although the UN Decade for HRE encouraged states to adopt national action plans in this area. Often, HRE-related issues are addressed in the framework of education strategies or human rights strategies. The present section thus examines each country's recent attempts to define and conceptualize HRE *per se* or within a broader policy framework.

A Czech Republic

In 2001, the Czech government adopted a National Programme for the Development of Education (also known as the White Paper). A binding document, it

on "democratic enterprise management" and notes that knowledge and skills acquired within this framework may be used by pupils for the implementation of their civic education projects. Ministry of Culture and National Heritage of the Republic of Poland, *National Programme for Socio-Economic Development*, March 26, 2013, 63.

154 Ministry of Finance of the Slovak Republic, *National Reform Programme of the Slovak Republic 2015*, April 2015, 16. See also Ministry of Finance of the Slovak Republic, *National Reform Programme of the Slovak Republic 2016*, April 2016, 25.

155 Government of the Slovak Republic, *2016–2020 Manifesto*, 36.

156 Ibid., 32.

157 Ibid.

served both as a strategic framework for specific programmes and projects of the Ministry of Education and as an intellectual reflection on the situation and goals of education in light of the societal challenges faced by the country at the turn of the millennium. It reaffirmed education as a basic human right and "an inalienable and universal human value"[158] enshrined in international treaties and the Czech constitution, and it contextualized Czech educational policies against the backdrop of the UN Decade for HRE. A central commitment of the Ministry of Education was to improve teacher education in HRE. In this context, the White Paper described multicultural and anti-racist education as an "essential part of the initial education of teachers and other educational staff"[159] that should also include elements of Holocaust education. It also mentioned education for democratic citizenship for all levels of education several times, including in its recommendations. Without providing a definition, the White Paper described the core elements of "education in human rights and multiculturalism,"[160] which were meant to focus on education *about* minorities, most particularly the history and culture of the Roma, Jewish and German communities, with the aim of promoting "understanding and solidarity."[161] In this respect, the White Paper strove to make education acceptable, in addition to ensuring its accessibility for marginalized groups, by mitigating the effects "of social and cultural background, as well as all disadvantages caused by health, ethnic or specific regional conditions, and by supporting tolerant and democratic attitudes towards all members of society without distinction."[162] The White Paper also devoted specific attention to education *through* rights: mutual respect in teacher-pupil relations, the school environment as "a democratic community of equal partners" and the education system as a space "with balanced ... responsibilities ... and open to the involvement of all partners."[163] Finally, the White Paper endorsed value-based education.[164]

A true milestone in the development of HRE in the Czech Republic, this policy document was replaced in 2014 by a new strategy that takes a different direction, in line with the EU approach that subsumes education under labour market needs. Leaving behind HRE and explicit references to human rights, the strategy uses the concept of "active citizenship," which it describes as a

158 Ministry of Education, Youth and Sport, *National Programme for the Development of Education in the Czech Republic – White Paper*, 2001, 14.

159 Ibid., 47.

160 Ibid., 15.

161 Ibid.

162 Ibid., 14–15.

163 Ibid.

164 Ibid., 14–16.

"prerequisite for democratic governance and preparation for employment."[165] Yet the objective to pursue active citizenship in order to develop a "society based on solidarity, sustainable development and democratic governance"[166] is not backed up by concrete measures based on human rights values and HRE. For instance, the priority on teacher training and professional development does not reiterate the commitments of the White Paper regarding multicultural and Holocaust education or indeed those relating to teacher-pupil relations and the school environment. Likewise, the priority on responsible and efficient governance aims to improve management structures and processes within the education system but does not challenge its *raison d'être*. Thus, the only priority that is based on the right to education (in particular its availability and accessibility) – although this is not explicitly stated – relates to the reduction of inequality in education and the systematic promotion of the "inclusiveness of the education system."[167] In addition to formal equity, the strategy focuses on "the capacity of the education system to create conditions and offer effective ways to prevent and offset individuals' physical, social, cultural and other personal disadvantages."[168] Interventions to support disadvantaged students are not enough according to the strategy, which emphasizes the need to systematically promote inclusive education. However, the strategy does not offer any definition of inclusive education, nor does it outline its characteristics, principles and measures.[169] According to the latest National Action Plan for Inclusive Education for 2016–2018, inclusive education targets not only the educational conditions of pupils with special educational needs but those of all participants.[170] However, its background and current approach are clearly focused on children with disabilities and, to a lesser extent, Roma children. The Plan claims that the concepts of diversity and democracy are increasingly important in inclusive education but fails to demonstrate how and makes no explicit reference to human rights or HRE concepts. Overall, the Czech Republic has distanced itself from a rights-based approach to education and from a complex multidisciplinary HRE framework. Instead, it currently favours a

165 Ministry of Education, Youth and Sport, *Strategy for Education Policy of the Czech Republic until 2020*, 2014, 13.

166 Ibid.

167 Ibid., 14.

168 Ibid., 13.

169 Moreover, the strategy's main goal for pupils from disadvantaged backgrounds is limited to the reduction of the amount of such children not reaching "the basic level of expected learning outcomes." *Strategy for Education Policy*, 13.

170 Ministry of Education, Youth and Sport of the Czech Republic, *Akční plán inkluzivního vzdělávání na období 2016–2018*, 2015.

narrow focus on inequalities in access to education and the acquisition of basic skills by all pupils.

However, a 2016 study by the Ministry of Education on the situation of civic education criticizes the education system for focusing mainly on the needs of the labour market and draws attention to the fact that pupils are citizens who should be actively prepared for this aspect of their lives.[171] The report recalls the UN definition of HRE and laments the lack of consensus on the definition of civic education in the Czech Republic. It therefore recommends a slightly amended version of the UN definition, describing HRE as education about, through and for human rights and democracy.[172] The report presents additional recommendations for improving the curriculum based on the United Nations' and Council of Europe's approach to education: HRE should be a cross-curricular topic rather than an isolated one; the participatory and cultural dimensions of human rights and democracy should also be taught; pupils' participation in the democratic experience should be encouraged through the establishment of self-government in schools;[173] the school climate should be improved; and a "whole school" approach involving the larger community should be considered.

B Hungary

Hungary does not currently have a strategic document on HRE, something that is addressed in the National Core Curriculum (NCC). In 2009, the Hungarian Institute for Educational Research and Development published a series of recommendations for a strategy on responsible and active citizenship education,[174] but these recommendations did not lead to the adoption of a strategy, action plan or any other policy document addressing HRE. The NCC is the core document that regulates public education, setting out the educational

171 European Commission Electronic Platform for Adult Learning in Europe, "Situační zpráva v oblasti občanského vzdělávání," accessed February 28, 2017: https://ec.europa.eu/epale/cs/resource-centre/content/situacni-zprava-v-oblasti-obcanskeho-vzdelavani.

172 In the original UN definition, the element of "democracy" is absent.

173 For more details, see Metodický portál RVP.CZ, "Miroslav Kudyvejs, Žákovská samospráva," accessed February 28, 2017, http://clanky.rvp.cz/clanek/c/G/636/ZAKOVSKA-SAMOSPRAVA.html. In this article, schools are described as a "workshop for democracy" and their functioning is assimilated to a "small state" where cooperation between pupils and pedagogical staff is key. An example of an ideal structure would include a students' council, a school parliament and classroom groups or assemblies. This description clearly recalls the citizenship education approach adopted by the Czech Republic.

174 Katalin Falus, Rita Galambos, Zsuzsa Szelényi, Ottó Mihály and János Setényi, *Ajánlások az aktív és felelős allampolgárságra nevelés stratégiájához* (Budapest: Oktatáskutató és Fejlesztő Intézet, 2009).

goals, tasks and values of the education system, as well as the content of subject areas. In line with EU recommendations, the NCC seeks to improve social and civic competences and states that "positive attitudes are based on full respect for human rights, including respect for equality, democracy and religious and ethnic diversity."[175] The NCC recalls that "education must always fall in line with Hungary's Fundamental Law, the rule of law, the principle of respect for life and human dignity, freedom of conscience and religion and international agreements on the protection of the Earth, mankind, nature and culture."[176] Furthermore, the NCC stresses the importance of Hungarian national tradition and the development of a sense of national identity, thus "prioriti[zing] knowledge about Hungary and its wider region (the Carpathian Basin) – especially about the life of Hungarians living in neighbouring countries."[177] Thus, patriotic education is one of the twelve "development fields and educational goals"[178] of the NCC. National minorities in Hungary are also encouraged to cultivate their identity, and Hungary's links to Europe and the global context in general are also addressed in the NCC, but these elements do not appear as development fields and educational goals *per se*. Education for democratic citizenship is also one of the twelve educational goals. In this framework, respect for human dignity and human rights is listed as one of the characteristics of the active participation of citizens, along with "observance of the law, compliance with the rules of societal co-existence, ...non-violence and fairness."[179] In school, pupils have the "opportunity ... to learn about their main rights and obligations as citizens."[180] Active participation of citizens – and learning about it by students – is also crucial because it enhances the awareness of national belonging. Hungary's general education and HRE policy strategies remain underdeveloped, whereas the main guidelines of the NCC reveal a rather patriotic, Hungarian-centred, citizenship-biased approach to education.

175 Government Decree No. 110/2012 (VI.4.) on the Issue, Introduction and Implementation of the National Core Curriculum, Annex: National Core Curriculum, Part II: Competence Development, the Dissemination of General Knowledge, Knowledge Acquisition, Section II.1 Key competences, subsection: Social and civic competences. Available in English at http://regi.ofi.hu/download.php?docID=5846 and in Hungarian at http://www.budapest-edu.hu/data/cms149320/MK_12_66_NAT.pdf.

176 Ibid., Part I: Content Regulation and Levels of Regulation of Educational Activity at Schools, Section I.1 The Tasks and Values of Public Education.

177 Ibid.

178 Ibid., Section I.1.1 Development areas – educational goals.

179 Ibid.

180 Ibid. The sentence adds: "within this framework, it offers defence education."

C Poland

Poland chiefly addresses HRE in its 2020 Social Capital Development Strategy. Based on a study showing a low level of active citizenship in Poland, this strategy sees civic education as an essential tool for strengthening the process of democratization. Indicators used in the study include membership and participation of Polish citizens and students in NGOs, clubs, religious movements and school-related groups such as student councils. The strategy emphasizes that citizenship in adulthood is mainly about practice, highlighting the importance of pupils' personal experience. For this reason, civic education teaching methods have their own specific nature. This goes back to Osler's argument for a truly learner-centred education that takes as its starting point the child and his or her own life story in order to critically examine human rights treaties.[181] The strategy therefore promotes using the everyday experiences of pupils, events occurring in society and public life and situations from the learners' local environment. One aim is to enable students to identify and solve local issues through the implementation of social projects. In this respect, the strategy moves away from a rights-based approach, and it is unclear what kind of social projects it is referring to. According to the strategy, the acquisition of social skills and attitudes, which should be one of the education system's transversal principles, depends on the complete implementation of the curriculum in the fields of civic, cultural and media education.[182] The strategy also acknowledges the fact that deeper changes are needed, for example in teacher training, education policy, school management and the professional training of school leaders and social educators. Thus, one priority focuses on the development of a democratic culture in schools and the use of teaching methods conducive to cooperation, creativity and communication.[183] The strategy also stresses the need for students' participation in organized forms of group learning and work at the earliest possible stage. In addition to listing several attitudes that students should acquire,[184] the strategy also states that it is important for societal development to foster a civic attitude and respect for the culture and traditions of one's own nation as well as those of others. Education through rights is also present in the strategy in its focus on school functioning, in particular the right of students to self-organize. The traditional school environment is described as being safe and predictable, with pupils merely listening to, and repeating, what teachers say, as in the case of the "banking" education system described

181 Osler, *Human Rights and Schooling*, 46–61 and 104–118.

182 Government of Poland, *2020 Social capital development strategy*, 2016, 31.

183 Ibid., 39.

184 Ibid., 40. For instance, responsibility, self-esteem, respect for others, willingness to participate in culture, teamwork and so forth.

by Freire. The strategy therefore seeks to foster true teamwork and initiatives through a more individualized approach and the more systematic inclusion of non-formal education methods. Non-formal learning is said to enable students to adapt faster to changes in society and the economy.[185] Overall, Poland currently takes a rather pragmatic approach to social and civic education that ultimately aims to turn pupils into active economic players and citizens and improve the economic efficiency of the state and society.

D Slovakia

Within the framework of the UN World Programme for HRE, Slovakia implemented a National Action Plan for HRE between 2005 and 2014. The plan is a short but comprehensive document that was elaborated by the Ministry of Education in cooperation with a wide range of HRE actors. It outlines the strategy, concepts, legislative and policy framework, objectives and contents of HRE, including sections on textbooks, extra-curricular activities and non-formal education, and also focuses on teacher training and the participation of students, migrants and national minorities. Last but not least, it proposes an implementation plan with a list of relevant actors and a financial plan with timeframes. The action plan emphasizes the importance of learning from the experience of other countries and civil society organizations rather than re-inventing HRE. Acknowledging that human rights philosophy derives partly from the need for human emancipation from the state, the plan recognizes the power and legitimacy of civil society organizations, which may have more credibility to guarantee the promotion and protection of human rights than state institutions.[186] The plan further underlines the need for a deeper change in the education system and the application of human rights principles to the management of schools, arguing that it is crucial to avoid contradictions between human rights legislation and instruments, on the one hand, and everyday practice, on the other. Indeed, the learning environment should not be at loggerheads with the content of human rights teaching, otherwise human rights will be perceived by pupils merely as an abstraction that does not apply in practice. Clearly, education *through* rights and *for* rights is a core element of this policy framework. To this end, the action plan recommends that civil society organizations registered with the UN Human Rights Council should conduct an in-depth analysis of the situation.[187]

---

185 Ibid.

186 Ministry of Education of the Slovak Republic, *Národný plán výchovy k ľudským právam na roky 2005–2014*, 2005, 4.

187 Ibid., 5.

The action plan, which rejects an authoritarian, impersonal and mechanical approach to education, argues that the aim of HRE in schools is to acquire knowledge, skills and attitudes that are essential for enhancing human dignity and informed and independent participation in the development of a democratic society, in accordance with human rights values, equality, pluralism and justice. In line with its support for a learning environment that is conducive to the respect and application of human rights, the action plan addresses the teaching process and methodological issues, which should be primarily interactive, participatory and experience-based. It reiterates the principles of dignity and inviolability of the individual, which should form a basis for students to construct their opinions and social relations. It is clear from the action plan that education *about* rights cannot happen without education *for* and *through* rights: merely memorizing facts that have little concrete connection to the school environment is not a successful form of HRE. In all four Visegrád countries, this aspect regularly emerges as a major challenge for HRE practitioners, who fear that the introduction of HRE in a generally undemocratic school environment may lead to confusion, disinterest and even a backlash. The action plan reiterates the critical role of democratic schools as a prerequisite for the further development of democracy at regional, national and global level.[188] In September 2015, the Ministry of Education published a comprehensive analysis of the current state of education and training for human rights in public schools following the implementation of the 2005–2014 HRE action plan. This report is quite critical of the level of implementation of HRE, pointing to the formality and rigidity of the schools, the lack of qualifications and commitment of the teachers, the discrepancy between subjects taught and pupils' everyday experiences of bullying, human rights violations and the lack of inclusion in the learning environment. At the same time, the report found that most pupils considered HRE important and were usually able to identify a few human rights.[189]

Paradoxically, at the time of the review of the implementation of the HRE action plan, a very general and much weaker National Strategy for the Protection and Promotion of Human Rights was adopted. The strategy chiefly recalls the human rights policy framework in Slovakia, listing some measures and initiatives taken since 2011 and a few general tasks foreseen under seven priorities. One of these priorities is Human Rights Education, Professional Training

188 Ibid., 6.

189 Ministry of Education, Youth and Sport of the Slovak Republic, *Analýza súčasného stavu výchovy a vzdelávania k ľudským právam v regionálnom školstve po realizácii plánu výchovy k ľudským právam v rezorte školstva na roky 2005–2014*, 2015, 17.

and Research, and the Ministry of Education has been charged with the task of supervising the establishment of a National Commission for Education and Awareness of Human Rights and Democratic Citizenship and the preparation of a relevant national plan for 2015–2020. However, no reference has been made to the previous HRE action plan, and despite the urgency of the task[190] no new plan has been adopted and no commission has been set up. The strategy devotes less than a page to education, although it should "be seen as a key tool for developing a culture of tolerance, inclusiveness and openness," while human rights should become "a natural component of any area and any level of the process of education and schooling."[191] No link has been made between the priority of implementing HRE and the priority of adopting systematic and comprehensive measures against any form of intolerance. Overall, it is not clear from the strategy what the purpose and objectives of HRE are.

E Insights into Curricula[192]

So far, none of the four Visegrád countries have an HRE curriculum *per se*. There are several reasons for this. In some cases, governments tend to use a different term, such as citizenship, civic or global education, which often reflects a different approach to the issues taught.[193] In other cases, several education traditions are combined. Most often, however, HRE is incorporated into a broader subject area for the study of society. Thus, for example, the Czech curriculum situates citizenship education within the subject area of "People and Society," which focuses on civic and political rights as well as key concepts such as democracy and the rule of law. Human rights and children's rights are addressed under the heading of "Citizens and the State," which covers relevant

190 Committee on Research, Education and Training in Human Rights and Development Education, *Celoštátna stratégia ochrany a podpory ľudských práv v Slovenskej republike*, 25.

191 Ibid., 9.

192 Government of the Republic of Hungary, Decree No. 110/2012 (VI.4.) on the Issue, Introduction and Implementation of the National Core Curriculum; Ministry of National Education of the Republic of Poland, *Podstawa programowa kształcenia ogólnego dla gimnazjów i szkół ponadgimnazjalnych, których ukończenie umożliwia uzyskanie świadectwa dojrzałości po zdaniu egzaminu maturalnego*, August, 27, 2012; Ministry of Education, Youth and Sport of the Slovak Republic, *Rámcové učebné plány a vzdelávacie štandardy vzdelávania na získanie nižšieho stredného vzdelania*, December 30, 2015; Výzkumný ústav pedagogický v Praze, *Rámcový vzdělávací program pro gymnázia*, 2007; Výzkumný ústav pedagogický v Praze, *Rámcový vzdělávací program pro základní vzdělávání*, 2007.

193 For instance, "global education" is concerned with North-South relations and the development of the global South, and so human rights are approached in the context of the Sustainable Development Goals. Usually, global education is supported by national aid agencies that work with ministries of foreign affairs or ministries of cooperation and development.

human rights instruments, the violation and protection of human rights and the role of the ombudsman in the Czech Republic. The same subject area also covers a wide range of social issues, yet without explicit reference to human rights. Overall, the Czech approach subsumes a selection of HRE topics under a citizenship education model that focuses on the pupils' future as active citizens but fails to provide a comprehensive understanding of human rights values and the current human rights regime.

In Hungary, citizenship and civil and political rights are addressed within the broad subject area of "Man and Society,"[194] which covers history and ethics at all levels, homeland and people, society, citizenship, economy (from lower secondary school) and philosophy (from upper secondary school). Children's rights, fundamental rights and the rights and obligations of citizens, including EU citizens, are explicitly included as topics and are considered part of the pupils' knowledge of "social rules" and "citizenship." However, it is unclear whether – and if so how – the complexity and the various facets of human rights are tackled, as the NCC is silent on this issue. In Poland, human rights topics are covered under the heading of "History and Society" at primary school level and "Knowledge about Society" at secondary school level. In primary education, the curriculum approaches human rights through the functioning of the state, society and the school. Topics covered include elections, Polish institutions, civil liberties, citizens' rights and duties, rights of the child, student's rights and responsibilities, participation and, last but not least, social issues in Poland and the world, including poverty and aid. At high school level, the curriculum focuses more deeply and broadly on global citizenship and human rights. Human rights are taught in all their complexity (e.g. their history, characteristics, development, violation, protection and codification in international human rights instruments) as well as on an individual basis (e.g. the right to education, the right of privacy and data protection, and women's rights). Teaching aimed at understanding and addressing racism, antisemitism, chauvinism and xenophobia is also part of the curriculum. Finally, schools are required to teach about the role of national and international institutions and organizations, including civil society organizations, in the protection of human rights.

In Slovakia, HRE topics are covered in civic education, mainly in the context of the functioning of the state and the EU but also under the heading of the Convention on the Rights of the Child, multiculturalism and antidiscrimination. On top of this, all countries cover various HRE topics, concepts

194 The Hungarian original "Ember és a társadalom" refers to mankind or human beings.

and methods throughout the curriculum, namely as cross-curricular themes and transversal skills. In the Czech Republic, for instance, cross-curricular subjects include multiculturalism, global and environmental issues, humanitarian aid and the EU, albeit with little reference to human or children's rights. HRE topics are mostly taught in subject areas covering societal issues and history. Alternatively, they are mainstreamed in a variety of subjects or through project work and other non-formal educational initiatives. Social issues are also widely covered, including inequality, poverty and equal opportunities, yet they are not explicitly linked to human rights. In Slovakia, human rights are also addressed in history lessons through Holocaust education. The Hungarian NCC also offers scope for addressing human rights-related issues in history, literature, geography or biology lessons, leaving the details to the discretion of local school curricula. Finally, education *for* and *through* rights may also be addressed in schools through structural mechanisms such as pupils' self-government.[195]

Overall, it is quite common for curricula to separate human rights, which are understood mostly as civil and political rights, from issues of social justice, which are not addressed through a rights-based approach nor linked to the broader human rights framework. Much attention is devoted to national institutions, but it is unclear whether this topic is framed within the broader European and international context of human rights issues in a way that would encourage a more complex and cosmopolitan understanding of citizenship.[196] Furthermore, with education aiming to shape students' personality and foster their self-development, all curricula pay attention to the development of personal and moral personality traits, such as the respect for others, empathy, self-esteem, willingness to participate and so forth. However, this usually happens within ethics classes,[197] and it therefore remains unclear how the objective of individual emancipation is connected to the objective of collective emancipation.

195 Such is the case in Poland, for instance, where pupils' self-government is established by all pupils in a given school and constitutes the only body representing them. It can propose motions to the school council, the pedagogical council and the school head concerning school matters, in particular those related to the fulfilment of the basic rights of pupils, such as the right to open and justified assessment of learning and conduct, the right to publish a school newspaper and the right to organize cultural, educational and sports events according to pupils' needs.

196 Osler, *Human Rights and Schooling*, 119–129.

197 The exception is the Czech Republic, which lists ethics within cross-curricular subjects but does not offer specific classes.

IV Conclusion

This study has sought to understand how governmental actors and public institutions in the Visegrád countries envision, plan and implement HRE through an analysis of national educational policies contextualized within a European framework. It has found that human rights are not firmly embedded in education and that the right to education is mostly understood *stricto sensu*. Thus, only a few basic elements of HRE are promoted and realized, while more complex aspects, such as rights in education and education for rights, receive little attention. As a result, the conditions for meaningful and coherent policies in the field of HRE are not met, and civil society may currently be the only actor capable of supporting and advancing it. Because civil society actors operate largely within formal educational settings, monitor the work of policy-makers and encourage governments to mainstream HRE in schools, it is crucial for them to maintain good working relationships with state institutions. In light of the numerous obstacles they face, however, their expectations concerning governmental actors are generally low.

In 2008, a report by Global Education Network Europe on the state of global education in the Czech Republic warned against the existing "tension between a model of educational response to globalisation [that] focuses on education as preparation for the needs of the marketplace, and a model [that] emphasises citizenship, participation, democracy and global justice."[198] This tension exists in all four Visegrád countries – as well as at European level. While the Council of Europe has been a major contributor to HRE, educational policies encouraged by the European Union offer little scope in this area. More worryingly, some aspects of HRE, such as participation and active citizenship, are promoted on the basis of a neoliberal approach to education that is driven by the needs of the labour market. As a result, HRE is not only distorted as a tool for growth and competitiveness but also loses its entire substance and meaning. This concern clearly echoes the broader discussion on the aims, ambitions and achievements of the contemporary human rights movement and regime in the struggle for social justice in a context of "market fundamentalism."[199]

198 Global Education Network Europe, *Global Education in the Czech Republic* (Amsterdam: GENE, 2008), 32–33.

199 Samuel Moyn, "Human Rights and the Age of Inequality," in *Can Human Rights Bring Social Justice? Twelve Essays*, ed. Doutje Lettinga and Lars van Troost (Amnesty International Netherlands, 2015), 16.

Printed in the United States
By Bookmasters